Making Gluten-Free Living Easy!

Cecelia's Marketplace
Kalamazoo, Michigan

www.CeceliasMarketplace.com

Gluten-Free

GROCERY SHOPPING GUIDE

2012/2013 EDITION

Dr. Mara Matison
Dainis Matison

khP
Kal-Haven Publishing

Cecelia's Marketplace
Gluten-Free Grocery Shopping Guide

by Dr. Mara Matison & Dainis Matison

khP

Kal-Haven Publishing
P.O. Box 20383
Kalamazoo, MI 49019 U.S.A.

ISBN 978-0-9831659-2-7

2012 / 2013 Edition

Printed in the United States of America
Cover illustration: Lilita Austrins

CONTENTS

Acknowledgments

There are many people that have contributed to the creation of this book. The support from our family and friends has made this journey more enjoyable. Lilita A. for editing, cover illustration, and all the gluten-free meals that kept us going; Mik for editing, critiquing and successful business strategies; Ray for the reference materials and guidance to becoming successful entrepreneurs; Ligita for supporting us and all the delicious gluten-free recipes along the way; Caroline for packaging & shipping; Lija for marketing & advertising; Lilita M. for showing us 'The Secret'; Liana, Velta, Ilga, Ryan, Matiss, Lukas, Tom, Tim and Stella for believing in us; Our meticulous data collection and editing team of Annette Hensley, Caroline Aasen, Jessica Rector, Jessica Schmidt, Lauma Matison, Leah Gorske, and Lija Austrins-Tyree; Jonnie Bryant for all the publishing advice and knowledge; Dr. Heidi Gjersoe for the diagnosis and support; Tracy Clupper for data entry & document styling; Natural Health Center for the wonderful gluten-free book signing events; Dr. Arnis Pone, Kal-Haven Publishing, McNaughton & Gunn, and all our fellow "celiacs" for all the support.

Disclaimer

This book has been prepared for the gluten-free consumer in order to make gluten-free grocery shopping easier.

This book should be used as an aid to guide the gluten-free consumer in the right direction when trying to find gluten-free products. The content of this book is not medical advice. The authors, Cecelia's Marketplace, and Kal-Haven Publishing shall have neither liability, nor responsibility to any person or entity with respect to gluten ingestion or any health consequence.

Every effort has been made to make this gluten-free product guide as complete and accurate as possible. However, there may be errors, both typographical and in content. Therefore this text should be used only as a general guide, not as the ultimate source for gluten-free information. Food companies and manufacturers indicate that product ingredients may change periodically; therefore, the consumer needs to always check the ingredients on the manufacturers' labels before consuming their products. For specific questions or further information on celiac disease, please consult your physician.

If you do not wish to be bound by the above, you may return this book to the publisher within 30 days of purchase for a full refund (minus any shipping fees).

About the Authors

The co-author of this book, Dr. Mara Matison, received her Doctor of Dental Surgery degree from University of Detroit Mercy, and her Bachelor of Arts degree in Psychology from Villanova University. Her husband and co-author, Dainis Matison, received his Master of Science degree in Information Technology and Bachelor of Arts degree in Finance from Ball State University. They are both members of Celiac Disease Foundation, Celiac Sprue Association, Gluten Intolerance Group, and supporters of National Foundation For Celiac Awareness, Talk About Curing Autism and Generation Rescue. These are nationwide organizations that support people with celiac disease, gluten intolerance, gluten sensitivity and autism.

Cecelia's Marketplace was established by both Mara and Dainis in 2006, soon after Mara was diagnosed with celiac disease. The couple struggled with Mara's huge lifestyle change, which included adhering to a strict gluten-free diet. Shopping trips to the grocery store were very frustrating. Spending time calling food manufacturers to find out if products were gluten-free seemed like a daily routine. They knew there had to be an easier way, so they decided to compile a gluten-free grocery shopping guide. Since then, Mara has also been diagnosed with a casein and soy intolerance, which brought about the need for the *Gluten/Casein Free Grocery Shopping Guide* and the *Gluten/Casein/Soy Free Grocery Shopping Guide*. In addition to the guides, she has recently published an *Easy 30 Day Gluten-Free Diet* book and a *Gluten-Free Mexican Cookbook*.

Thanks to all of Cecelia's Marketplace gluten-free resources, gluten-free living has now become easier not only for the authors, but also their families, friends and thousands of celiacs nationwide.

Preface - Note to the Reader

Cecelia's Marketplace Gluten-Free Grocery Shopping Guide has been written to help people that are in search of gluten-free products. Whether you are on a gluten-free diet, prepare gluten-free meals for yourself or others, or just enjoy eating gluten-free foods, this book is for you. It will help guide you to easy grocery shopping and eliminate the frustration and headaches that you've experienced trying to find gluten-free products. This guide is also great for restaurant owners, chefs, dieticians, family members, friends, and others that shop for or prepare gluten-free foods. For those that are not familiar with gluten-free cooking, we have included two special sections in the front of the book: *What is Gluten?* and *Gluten-Free Kitchen Tips*.

We have alphabetized our *Gluten-Free Grocery Shopping Guide* to help you quickly find brand names of the products you are looking for. The guide is easy to use: just pick a product, look it up, and you'll have gluten-free brands at your fingertips. The book is small enough so that it can be carried with you to the grocery store when searching for products. Use it anytime, anywhere. In addition to the *Gluten-Free Grocery Shopping Guide*, there is a section in the back of the book that lists gluten-free over the counter (OTC) pharmacy products. Gluten-free shopping has never been easier. Treasure this book and enjoy all the gluten-free products that are available!

Due to periodic changes in ingredients and new products, *Cecelia's Marketplace Gluten-Free Grocery Shopping Guide* is updated annually. Product alerts & updates are posted on our website throughout the year at www.CeceliasMarketplace.com.

A percentage of our proceeds are donated to nationwide nonprofit organizations that support people with celiac disease, gluten intolerance and other gluten sensitivities.

Dr. Mara Matison & Dainis Matison

Our Data Collection

The product information in this book was collected between February 2012 - April 2012. The information was received directly from product manufacturers and major supermarkets via internet, e-mail, phone, mail or product labels.

The Food and Drug Administration (FDA) has proposed to define the term "gluten-free" as containing less than 20 parts per million (ppm) gluten. A final rule on this proposal will be issued no later than four years after the law's enactment date of August 2008. For further information on this regulation please visit www.fda.gov.

Some food manufacturers test their products for the presence of gluten. Those products that have not passed this test have been excluded from this book. Currently, not all companies test their products, therefore, we cannot guarantee that all the products listed in our book are less than 20 ppm gluten.

Those products that have been manufactured in the same facility or on shared equipment with gluten, but follow strict cross-contamination control guidelines, have been included and marked with symbols. We have tried our best not to include products from manufacturers that do not take measures to prevent cross-contamination.

Product alerts & updates are posted on our website throughout the year. www.CeceliasMarketplace.com.

Symbols

There are some companies that manufacture their products in a dedicated gluten-free facility or environment. Some products also go through strict guidelines and vigorous testing by either the Celiac Sprue Association (CSA) Recognition Seal Program or the Gluten Intolerance Group (GIG) Gluten-Free Certification Organization (GFCO) to be verified as gluten-free. Some companies choose to do private testing for <20ppm gluten, however are not certified by CSA or GFCO. In this guide we have marked these manufacturers and products with the following symbols:

▲ - manufactured in a dedicated gluten-free facility or environment
● - verified, tested, or certified gluten-free by either the CSA Recognition Seal Program or the GIG Gluten-Free Certification Organization
★ - private testing for <20 ppm gluten (includes Elisa testing)

Celiac Spruce Association®

Certified **GF**™ Gluten-Free

There are also some manufacturers that label their gluten-free products as being manufactured in the same facility or on the same equipment with gluten. In this guide we have labeled those products with the following symbols:

! - manufactured in the same facility as other products containing gluten

!! - manufactured on the same equipment as other products containing gluten

What is Gluten?

Gluten is a protein that is most commonly found in wheat, rye, and barley. It is found in most cereals, breads, pastas, soups and pizza crusts. It may also be hidden in foods such as seasonings, salad dressings, sauces, additives, fillers and natural flavors. People that have celiac disease, gluten intolerance or gluten sensitivity may suffer from a wide array of adverse symptoms after ingesting gluten.

What is Gluten Intolerance?

Gluten intolerance, or sometimes referred to as gluten sensitivity, is when an individual develops adverse health symptoms when ingesting gluten. Though some of these symptoms may be similar to celiac disease, this condition has not advanced to the severity of intestinal lining damage. Gluten intolerance can be effectively managed with a gluten-free diet. Some experts believe that gluten intolerance may be as common as 1 in every 20 Americans.

What is Celiac Disease?

Celiac disease is an inherited autoimmune disorder. When people with celiac disease consume foods containing gluten, an immune reaction occurs, and the villi (the small hair-like projections) of the small intestine become damaged. Without healthy villi the body is unable to absorb nutrients and becomes malnourished. There is no cure for celiac disease, however, it can be managed effectively with a gluten-free diet. Studies show that approximately 1 in 133 Americans have celiac disease[1].

1. University of Maryland Medical Center, Dr. Alessio Fasano, 2003 Archives of Internal Medicine

Possible Symptoms

Maintaining a strict gluten-free diet may help alleviate most symptoms of gluten intolerance and celiac disease. After gluten is completely eliminated from the diet, symptoms usually start to disappear within a few weeks.

Symptoms of gluten intolerance and celiac disease vary from person to person. Below is a list of possible symptoms that may be related to gluten ingestion.

Abdominal Pain
Acid Reflux
Anemia
Bloáting
Bone Loss
Bone Pain
Constipation
Delayed Growth In Children
Dental Enamel Defects
Depression
Diarrhea
Fatigue/Loss Of Energy
Hair Loss
Heart Palpitations
Infertility

Irritability
Joint Pain
Malnutrition
Migraine Headaches
Muscle Cramps
Painful Itchy Bumps On The Skin
Panic Attacks/Anxiety
Recurrent Miscarriage
Restless Legs
Seizures
Skin Rashes
Tingling Of Hands Or Feet
Unexplained Weight Loss/Gain
Vitamin & Mineral Deficiencies

Testing Options

Here are a few testing options for celiac disease and gluten intolerance.

- **AT HOME:**
  At-Home Celiac Genetic Saliva Test:
  Prometheus Laboratories: www.myceliacid.com

  At-Home Food Intolerance Stool Sample Test:
  EnteroLab: www.enterolab.com

- **AT THE DOCTOR'S OFFICE:**
  Celiac Genetic Blood Test:
  Celiac Genetic Assessment HLA DQ2/DQ8

  Celiac Disease Serology Blood Test:
  Anti-human tissue transglutaminase (Hu-tTG) IgA recombinant antigen, Anti-endomysial IgA, Total serum IgA, Anti-gliadin IgA, Anti-gliadin IgG

  Endoscopy Procedure:
  A biopsy of the small intestinal lining is performed by a gastroenterologist to confirm damaged intestinal villi, signifying celiac disease.

- **RESEARCH CENTERS:**
  Columbia University - Celiac Disease Center
  University of Chicago - Celiac Disease Center
  University of Maryland - Center for Celiac Research

Safe vs. Unsafe Foods

GLUTEN-FREE	POSSIBLE HIDDEN GLUTEN	CONTAINS GLUTEN
Amaranth	Bouillon Cubes	Barley
Arrowroot	Broth	Barley Malt
Beans	Caramel Color	Batter
Buckwheat	Caramel Flavoring	Beer
Carob	Dextrins	Bran
Coconut	Emulsifiers	Breading
Corn	Flavoring	Bulgur
Cornstarch	Food Starch	Couscous
Distilled Alcohol	Gravy	Hydrolyzed Wheat Protein
Distilled Vinegar	Hydrolyzed Protein	
Eggs	Hydrolyzed Vegetable Protein	Hydrolyzed Wheat Starch
Flax		
Fresh Fruits & Vegetables	Maltodextrin	Kamut
	Miso	Malt
Fresh Meat	Modified Food Starch	Malt Vinegar
Fresh Poultry		Oats*
Fresh Seafood	Natural Flavoring	Orzo
Lentils	Salad Dressings	Rye
Milk	Sauces	Semolina
Millet	Soups	Spelt
Nuts	Soy Sauce	Triticale
Oil (Canola, Olive, Vegetable)	Spice Blends	Triticum Vulgaris
	Stabilizers	Wheat
Potatoes	Teriyaki Sauce	Wheat Flour
Pure Herbs & Spices		Wheat Germ Oil
Quinoa		Wheat Gluten
Rice		
Sorghum		* Certified Gluten-Free Oats Are Safe
Soy		
Tapioca		
Teff		

Gluten-Free Kitchen Tips

It is very important prior to preparing a gluten-free meal to clean the cooking area, including: kitchen surfaces, pots, pans, utensils and any other items being used. Bread crumbs, flour particles and other gluten-containing foods left in the cooking area can potentially contaminate a gluten-free meal.

Here are some tips to help prevent gluten contamination:

- Use an uncontaminated or new sponge to wash all working surfaces with soap and water.

- Clean and inspect pots, pans, utensils, cutting boards and other kitchenware for gluten residue.

- Use clean kitchen hand towels.

- If grilling, place aluminum foil over the grilling surface.

- Avoid using wooden utensils. Gluten residue can stay embedded in wooden utensils and cutting boards.

- Use a separate toaster for gluten-free bread, rice cakes, etc.. If a separate toaster is not available, toast your bread on a warm frying pan.

- Do not deep fry foods in contaminated oil (e.g. from breaded chicken wings, breaded chicken tenders, mozzarella sticks).

- Use squeeze bottle mayonnaise, mustard, ketchup, peanut butter, jelly/jam, butter/margarine and other condiments to prevent cross-contamination.

Other Products Available
by Cecelia's Marketplace

Grocery Shopping Guides:
Gluten/Casein Free
Gluten/Casein/Soy Free

Gluten-Free Diet Book:
Easy 30 Day Gluten-Free Diet

Cookbook:
Gluten-Free Mexican

Other Products:
Gluten-Free Dining Out Cards
Gluten-Free Safety Labels

FREE Email Newsletter:
Gluten-Free Product of the Day

For more information about our products please visit us online:

www.CeceliasMarketplace.com

Scan me with your smartphone

This book is dedicated to:

All those in search of gluten-free products.

Gluten-Free
Grocery Shopping Guide (A-Z)

A A

Alfredo Sauce
 Bertolli - Garlic Alfredo, Mushroom, Regular
 Classico - All Varieties
 Full Flavor Foods ▲ - Alfredo Sauce Mix ●
 Mayacamas - Chicken Fettuccine ★, Regular ★
 Newman's Own - Alfredo, Roasted Garlic Alfredo
 Ragu - Cheesy (Classic Alfredo, Light Parmesan Alfredo)
 Riega ▲ - Alfredo Sauce Mix ★
 Road's End Organics - Organic GF Alfredo Chreese Mix
 Safeway Select - Regular, Roasted Garlic
 Simply Organic - Alfredo Sauce Mix ●
 Walden Farms
Almond Beverages...see Nut Beverages
Almonds...see Nuts
Amaranth
 Arrowhead Mills - Whole Grain
 Bob's Red Mill ▲ - Organic (Flour ★, Organic Grain ★)
 Nu-World Foods ▲ - Flour, Pre Gel Powder, Puffed, Seed,
    Toasted Bran Flour
Anchovies
 Amore - Anchovy Paste
 Crown Prince - Flat In Olive Oil, Natural (Anchovy Paste, Fillets Of
    Anchovies In Olive Oil), Rolled w/Capers In Olive Oil
 Star - Fillets Of Anchovies
Animal Crackers...see Cookies
Apple Butter
 Apple Time - Regular
 Eden Organic - Apple, Apple Cherry, Cherry
 Fischer & Wieser - Pecan
 Lucky Leaf
 Manischewitz
 Musselman's
Apple Cider...see Cider/Cider Mix

A

Apple Rings
   Lucky Leaf - Spiced
   Musselman's - Spiced

Apples
   ... *All Fresh Fruits & Vegetables Are Gluten-Free
   Annie's - Organic Orchard Real Fruit Bites Apple **! !**
   Augason Farms ▲ - Gluten Free Freeze Dried Apple Dices ●
   Country Crock - Cinnamon
   Dole - All Fruits Bowls *(Except Fruit Crisps)*, Apples & Creme Fruit Parfait
   Earthbound Farm - Organic Sliced
   Lucky Leaf - Fried, Sliced
   Mariani - Dried Berries & Apples **! !**, Sliced Dried **! !**
   Musselman's - Sliced
   Nuts.com - Dried Apples (Cinnamon Wedges ●, Diced Fuji ●, Dried ●, Infused Dried Wedges ●, Organic (Chips ●, Dried ●, Simply ●))
   Trader Joe's - Chunky Spiced Apples
   Woodstock Farms - Apple Rings Unsulphured, Organic Apple Rings

Applesauce
   Apple Time - Regular
   Beech-Nut - Applesauce (Stage 1 Fruits, Stage 2 Fruits)
   Eden Organic - Organic Apple (Cherry, Cinnamon, Regular, Strawberry)
   Food Club Brand - Applesauce (Chunky, Cinnamon, Natural, Original, Strawberry)
   Full Circle - Organic (No Sugar Added, Sweetened)
   Great Value Brand (Wal-Mart) - Applesauce Jar (Cinnamon, Regular, Unsweetened No Sugar Added), Applesauce Plastic Cups (All Natural No Sugar Added, Cinnamon, Light, Natural, Original, Strawberry)
   Hy-Vee - Applesauce, Cinnamon, Light (w/Mixed Berry, w/Strawberry), Natural
   Lowes Foods Brand - Chunky, Cinnamon, Regular, Unsweetened
   Lucky Leaf - Cherry Fruit 'N Sauce, Cinnamon, Natural, Regular, Strawberry Fruit 'N Sauce

A

Meijer Brand - Chunky, Cinnamon, Mixed Berry, Natural, Organic (Cinnamon, Sweetened, Unsweetened), Original, Regular, Strawberry

Midwest Country Fare - Home Style, Natural w/ (Cinnamon, Peaches, Raspberries, Strawberries)

Momma's Old-Fashioned Applesauce - No Sugar Added, Original Flavor

Mott's - Chunky, Cinnamon, Homestyle, Natural w/No Sugar Added, Original

Musselman's - Chunky, Cinnamon (Lite, Regular), Golden Delicious, Granny Smith, Healthy Picks (Blueberry Pomegranate, Cupucacu Key Lime, Raspberry Acai), Homestyle (Cinnamon, Regular), Lite Fruit 'N Sauce (Cherry, Grape, Orange Mango, Peach, Raspberry, Strawberry), McIntosh Apple, Organic (Regular, Unsweetened), Regular, Totally Fruit (Apple, Mixed Berry, Peach, Strawberry), Unsweetened

O Organics - Berry, Cinnamon, Organic, Unsweetened

Pastor Chuck Orchards - Organic (Sweetened ●, Unsweetened ●)

Publix - Chunky, Cinnamon, Old Fashioned, Unsweetened

Publix GreenWise Market - Organic Unsweetened

Safeway Brand - Cups (Natural, Organic), Natural, Original, Sweetened, Unsweetened

Santa Cruz ▲ - Fruit Sauces (All Varieties)

Spartan Brand - Cinnamon, Natural, Original, Peach, Raspberry, Strawberry

Sweet Perry Orchards - Unsweetened

Tree Top - Cinnamon, Naturally Sweetened, No Sugar Added Natural, Organic, Raspberry, Strawberry

Wegmans Brand - Chunky, Cinnamon, FYFGA Natural (Chunky, No Sugar Added), McIntosh, Mixed Berry, Peach Mango, Regular

Winn Dixie - Cinnamon, Sweetened, Unsweetened

Apricots

A

... *All Fresh Fruits & Vegetables Are Gluten-Free*

Del Monte - Canned/Jarred Fruit (All Flavors), Fruit Snack Cups Plastic

Gordon Food Service - Halves Unpeeled (In Juice, Lite Syrup)

Hy-Vee - Lite Unpeeled Halves Sweetened w/Splenda, Unpeeled Halves

Mariani - Dried (California ‼, Mediterranean ‼, Ultimate ‼)

Meijer Brand - Canned Halves Unpeeled In Pear Juice

Nuts.com - Dried Fruit (California ●, Diced ●, Dried ●, Organic California ●, Organic Turkish ●, Pluots ●)

Oskri Organics - Dried Apricots

Publix - Canned Halves Unpeeled In Heavy Syrup

S&W - All Canned/Jarred Fruits

Wegmans Brand - Canned FYFGA Halved Unpeeled

Winn Dixie - Unpeeled Halves In Heavy Syrup

Woodstock Farms - Organic Turkish Apricots

Artichokes

... *All Fresh Fruits & Vegetables Are Gluten-Free*

Birds Eye - All Plain Frozen Vegetables

C & W - All Plain Frozen Vegetables ‼

Cara Mia - In Water, Marinated, Salad

Kirkland Signature - Jarred Hearts

Meijer Brand - Frozen Artichoke Quarters

Mezzetta ▲ - Grilled, Marinated Hearts

Native Forest - Artichoke Hearts (Marinated, Quartered, Whole)

Reese - Marinated, Regular

Safeway Select - Marinated Artichoke

Spartan Brand - Quarters

Trader Joe's - Artichoke Antipasto, Artichoke Hearts In Water, Artichoke Red Pepper Tapenade ‼, Frozen Artichoke Hearts

Wegmans Brand - Artichoke Hearts (Halves & Quarters, In Brine, Marinated Quartered), Marinated Long Stemmed

Asparagus

... *All Fresh Fruits & Vegetables Are Gluten-Free*

Birds Eye - All Plain Frozen Vegetables

A
B

Cara Mia - Marinated Green
Del Monte - All Canned Varieties
Food Club Brand - Canned Cuts & Tips
Great Value Brand (Wal-Mart) - Canned (Cut Spears & Tips, Extra
   Long All Green)
Green Giant - Canned Cut Spears, Canned Spears
Hannaford Brand - Cuts & Tips, Whole Tall
Hy-Vee - Cut Spears
Meijer Brand - Canned Cuts & Tips, Frozen Green Spears
Native Forest - Green (Cuts & Tips, Spears)
Nuts.com - Simply Asparagus Freeze Dried Vegetables ●
S&W - All Canned Vegetables
Safeway Brand - Canned Cut
Spartan Brand - Spears Cuts w/Tips
Trader Joe's - Frozen Asparagus Spears (Grilled, Regular)
Wegmans Brand - Cut Green Spears & Tips
Woodstock Farms - Organic Frozen Whole Baby Asparagus

Avocado
   *... *All Fresh Fruits & Vegetables Are Gluten-Free*
   Wholly - 100% Avocado

B

Baby Food

Baby Mum-Mum ▲ - Rice Rusks (Banana, Organic Original,
   Original, Vegetable)
Beech-Nut -
   Cereals (Rice, Rice & Chiquita Bananas)
   Stage 1 Fruits (Applesauce, Chiquita Bananas, Peaches, Pears)
   Stage 1 Meats (Beef & Beef Broth, Chicken & Chicken Broth,
     Turkey & Turkey Broth)
   Stage 1 Vegetables (Butternut Squash, Tender Golden Sweet
     Potatoes, Tender Sweet Carrots, Tender Sweet Peas, Tender
     Young Green Beans)
   Stage 2 Cereals Rice Cereal & Apples w/Cinnamon

baby food

B

Stage 2 Dinners (Apples & Chicken, Chicken & Rice, Chicken
Noodle, Ham Apples Pineapple & Rice, Hearty Vegetable Stew,
Macaroni & Beef w/Vegetables, Pineapple Glazed Ham, Sweet
Potato & Turkey, Sweet Potatoes & Chicken, Turkey Rice, Turkey
Tetrazzini, Vegetables & Chicken)

Stage 2 Fruits (Apples & Bananas, Apples & Blueberries, Apples
& Cherries, Apples Mango & Kiwi, Apples Pears & Bananas,
Applesauce, Apricots w/Pears & Apples, Banana Apple Yogurt,
Chiquita Bananas, Chiquita Bananas & Strawberries, DHA
Plus Apple Delight, DHA Plus Apples w/Pomegranate Juice,
DHA Plus Banana Supreme, Mango, Peaches, Pears, Pears &
Pineapple, Pears & Raspberries)

Stage 2 Vegetables (Corn & Sweet Potatoes, DHA Plus Squash w/
Corn, DHA Plus Sweet Potatoes, Green Giant (Garden
Vegetables, Green Beans, Mixed Vegetables, Squash, Sweet
Carrots, Sweet Peas, Sweet Potatoes), Sweet Corn Casserole,
Sweet Potatoes & Apples)

Stage 3 Cereals Rice Cereal & Pears

Stage 3 Dinners (Turkey Rice, Vegetable Medley w/Turkey,
Vegetables & Chicken)

Stage 3 Fruits (Apples & Bananas, Apples Cherries & Plums,
Chiquita Bananas, Cinnamon Raisins & Pears, Peaches Apples &
Bananas, Pears & Blueberries)

Stage 3 Vegetables (Green Beans & Potatoes, Green Beans Corn &
Rice, Sweet Corn & Rice, Sweet Potatoes)

Belle's Biscuits - Teething Biscuits (Blueberry, Maple, Vanilla)

Bright Beginnings - Pediatric Soy Vanilla Drink

Cream of Rice - Hot Cereal

Earth's Best Organic Baby Food -

1st Foods (Apples, Bananas, Carrots, Pears, Peas, Prunes, Squash,
Sweet Potatoes)

2nd Antioxidant Blend (Apple Butternut Squash, Banana Mango,
Carrot Tomato, Sweet Potato Apricot)

B

2nd Dinners (Chicken & Brown Rice Country Dinner, Rice & Lentil Dinner, Summer Vegetable Dinner, Sweet Potatoes & Chicken Dinner)

2nd Fruits (Apples, Apples & Apricots, Apples & Bananas, Apples & Blueberries, Apples & Plums, Bananas, Bananas Peaches & Raspberries, Cherry Pear Brown Rice Super Fruit, Pears, Pears & Mangos, Pears & Raspberries, Plum Banana Brown Rice Fruit & Whole Grain Combination)

2nd Gourmet Meals (Chicken Mango Risotto, Creamy Chicken Apple Compote, Sweet Pea Turkey Wild Rice)

2nd Grains Blueberry Banana Brown Rice Yogurt

2nd Seasonal Harvest (Pumpkin Apple, Sweet Potato Cinnamon),

2nd Vegetables (Carrots, Corn & Butternut Squash, Garden Vegetables, Green Beans & Rice, Peas & Brown Rice, Sweet Potatoes, Winter Squash)

3rd Dinners Vegetable Beef Pilaf

3rd Fruits (Banana & Strawberries, Chunky Orchard Fruit)

3rd Vegetable Medleys (Sweet Corn & Carrot, Sweet Peas & Creamed Spinach)

Infant Puree Pouches (Banana Blueberry, Butternut Squash Pear, First Bananas, First Pears, Orange Banana, Peach Mango, Pear Carrot Apricot, Pumpkin Cranberry Apple, Sweet Potato Apple)

Whole Grain Rice Cereal (Apples, Plain)

Ella's Kitchen -

Smoothie Fruits (The Green One, The Purple One, The Red One, The Yellow One)

Stage I Baby Food (Apples & Bananas, Baby Brekkie (Banana, Blueberry & Pear, Mango, Raisin & Prune), Broccoli Pears & Peas, Butternut Squash Carrots Apples & Prunes, Carrots Apples & Parsnips, Carrots Peas & Pears, First Tastes (Apples Apples Apples, Bananas Bananas Bananas, Mangoes Mangoes Mangoes, Pears Pears Pears), Fruit & Rice (Bananas Apricots & Baby Rice, Carrots Apples & Baby Rice, Peaches Pears & Baby Rice, Pears Apples & Baby Rice), Green Beans Raisins & Apples, Peaches & Bananas, Plums Pears Parsnips & Swedes,

Spinach Apples & Swedes, Strawberries & Apples, Sweet Potatoes Broccoli & Carrots, Sweet Potatoes Pumpkin Apples & Blueberries, Sweetcorn Pumpkin & Peas)

Stage 2 Baby Food (Big Smiles Cheesy Pie w/Veggies, Chick Chick Chicken Casserole, Fabulously Filling Fish Pie w/Mash, Hugely Hearty Four Bean Feast w/Big Flavour, Lovely Lamb Roast Dinner w/All The Trimmings, Nice Rice Just For Me, Oh So Creamy Chicken & Sweetcorn Mash w/Herb Sprinkles, Punchy Pork Roast Dinner w/Apples, Really Yummy Rice Pudding w/Mangoes & Apples, The Italian One Cooking Sauce, Very Very Tasty Vegetable Bake w/Lentils, Wonderfully Warming Beef Stew w/Spuds)

Stage 3 Baby Food (Chick Chick Chicken Casserole w/Rice, Full Of Sunshine Thai Curry w/Lots of Veg, Seriously Comforting Cottage Pie w/A Pinch Of Cinnamon, Super Scrummy Salmon Risotto w/A Sprinkle Of Cheese, Totally Cook Caribbean Chicken w/Mangoes)

Gerber -

100% Juice (Apple, Apple Banana, Apple Grape, Apple Prune, Mixed Fruit, Pear, White Grape)

1st Foods Fruits & Vegetables (Nature Select (Apples, Bananas, Carrots, Green Beans, Peaches, Pears, Peas, Prunes, Squash, Sweet Potatoes), Smart Nourish (Apples, Bananas, Carrots, Pears, Prunes, Sweet Peas, Sweet Potatoes))

2nd Foods Dinners (Beef & Beef Gravy, Chicken & Chicken Gravy, Ham & Ham Gravy, Nature Select (Apples & Chicken, Chicken & Rice, Vegetable Beef, Vegetable Chicken), Turkey & Turkey Gravy)

2nd Foods Fruits & Vegetables (Apple Blueberry, Apples Mangos & Rice Cereal, Bananas, Carrots, Nature Select (Apple Blueberry, Apple Strawberry Banana, Apples, Apples & Cherries, Applesauce, Apricots w/Mixed Fruit, Banana Mixed Berry, Banana Orange Medley, Banana Plum Grape, Banana w/Apples & Pears, Bananas, Carrots, Garden Vegetables, Green Beans, Green Beans, Mixed Vegetables, Peaches, Pear Pineapple, Pears,

B

Peas, Prunes w/Apples, Squash), Pears, Peas, Smart Nourish (Apple Blackberry, Apple Strawberry, Apple Sweet Potato, Apples, Apples & Summer Peaches, Banana Mango, Bananas, Butternut Squash & Corn, Carrots, Green Beans, Pear & Wild Blueberry, Pear Raspberry, Pears, Peas, Pineapple Orange Medley, Sweet Potatoes, Sweet Potatoes & Corn), Squash, Strawberry Banana, Sweet Potatoes)

2nd Foods Meals Smart Nourish (Spring Garden Vegetables w/ Brown Rice, Vegetable Risotto w/Cheese)

2nd Foods Smoothies (Banana Yogurt, Fruit Medley, Mango, Nature Select Hawaiian Delight, Peach Cobbler)

3rd Foods Dinners Nature Select (Mixed Vegetables & Beef, Mixed Vegetables & Chicken, Mixed Vegetables & Turkey, Turkey Rice & Vegetables)

3rd Foods Fruits & Vegetables (Nature Select (Apple Banana & Peach, Apple Mango & Kiwi, Apples, Banana Strawberry, Bananas, Broccoli & Carrots w/Cheese, Green Beans w/Rice, Pears, Squash, Sweet Potatoes), Smart Nourish Apple Sweet Potato),

3rd Foods Smoothie Fruit Medley

Graduates Finger Foods (Apple Wagon Wheels, Cheesy Carrot Wagon Wheels)

Graduates For Preschoolers Healthy Meals (Mixed Vegetables Chicken & Rice In Sauce w/Carrots)

Graduates Fruit & Veggie Melts (Truly Tropical Blend, Very Berry Blend)

Graduates Fruit Splashers (Grape, Strawberry Kiwi, Tropical Fruit)

Graduates Fruit Splashers Single Serve (Apple Berry, Mixed Berry)

Graduates Fruit Twists (Apple & Strawberry, Cherry Berry, Strawberry & Grape)

Graduates Grabbers Squeezables (Apple & Sweet Potato w/ Cinnamon, Apple Mango & Strawberry, Apple Pear & Peach, Banana Blueberry, Pear & Squash)

Graduates Juice Treats (Fruit Medley, Tropical)

Graduates Lil' Crunchies (Cinnamon Maple, Garden Tomato, Mild Cheddar, Veggie Dip)

Graduates Lil' Sticks (Chicken, Meat, Turkey)

Graduates Pick Ups (Diced Apples, Diced Carrots)

Graduates Smart Sips (Plain, Strawberry, Vanilla)

Graduates Toddler Meals (Rice & Turkey In Gravy, White Turkey Stew w/Rice & Vegetables)

Graduates Yogurt Melts (Mixed Berries, Peach, Strawberry)

Harvest Juice (Apple Carrot, Mango Puree w/Pineapple & Carrot Juice Blend)

Organic Juice (Apple, Pear)

Water (Graduates Lil Water, Pure Water)

Yogurt Blend Snacks (Banana, Peach, Pear, Strawberry)

Yogurt Juice (Banana, Peach Mango)

GoGo squeeZ ▲ - Applesauce On The Go (Apple Apple, Apple Banana, Apple Cinnamon, Apple Peach, Apple Strawberry)

Happy Bellies - Organic Brown Rice Cereal w/DHA

Healthy Times - Brown Rice Cereal For Baby

Meijer Brand - DND (Chocolate, Strawberry, Vanilla), Gluco Burst (Arctic Cherry, Chocolate Diabetic Nutritional Drink, Strawberry DND, Vanilla DND), Little Fruit (Apple, Strawberry/Banana), Little Veggies Corn, PND (Bright Beginnings Vanilla Soy, Chocolate, Strawberry, Vanilla Soy, Vanilla w/Fiber), Term Formula (Regular, Soy), Vanilla Pediatric Nutritional Drink, w/DHA (Follow On, Gentle Protein, Lactose Free, Milk, Soy)

O Organics -

Stage 1 (Applesauce, Bananas, Carrots, Pears, Peas, Sweet Potatoes)

Stage 2 (Apple Apricot, Apple Banana, Apple Wild Blueberry, Applesauce, Bananas, Carrots, Mixed Vegetables, Peach Rice Banana, Pear Raspberry, Pears, Peas & Brown Rice, Prunes, Squash, Summer Vegetables, Sweet Potatoes)

Stage 3 Sweet Potato Chicken Dinner

Toddler Mum-Mum ▲ - Organic Rice Biscuits (Caramel, Original, Strawberry)

Voyaging Foods - Baby First Food Taro Flakes ●

Baby Formula

Bright Beginnings - Baby Formulas (Gentle Baby, Organic Baby, Premium, Soy)

Earth's Best - Organic Infant Formula w/DHA & ARA (Regular, Soy)

B

EleCare - For Infants ★
Enfamil - All Varieties
Gerber -
   Good Start Gentle (Concentrate, Powder, Ready To Feed)
   Good Start Protect (Concentrate, Powder, Ready To Feed)
   Good Start Soy (Concentrate, Powder, Ready To Feed)
Hy-Vee - Baby Formula (Formula 2, Gentle, Sensitivity, Soy), Pediatric
   Electrolyte (Fruit, Grape, Regular Unflavored)
Neocate - Infant (DHA & ARA, Regular), Junior (Chocolate, Tropical,
   Unflavored), Junior w/Prebiotic Vanilla, Junior w/Prebiotics
   Unflavored, Nutra
Nutramigen - All Varieties
Pregestimil - Baby Formula
Similac - All Varieties

Bacon
   Applegate - Deli Counter Prosciutto !, Natural (Canadian !,
      Pancetta !, Sunday !, Turkey !), Organic (Sunday !, Turkey !)
   Busseto - Pancetta, Prosciutto
   Butterball - Turkey Bacon (Lower Sodium, Original, Thin & Crispy)
   Coleman's Natural Foods - Uncured Hickory Smoked
   Dietz & Watson ▲ - Canadian Style ●, Deli Counter Pancetta ●,
      Gourmet Imported ●, Pre Sliced Pancetta ●
   Dorothy Lane Market - Uncured (All Varieties)
   Eating Right - Turkey Bacon
   Eckrich - Fresh Hickory Smoked Bacon
   Farmer John - Center Cut, Classic, Premium (Applewood, Low
      Sodium, Old Fashioned Maple, Thick Cut)
   Five Star Brand ▲ - Canadian
   Garrett County Farms - Beef ★, Canadian Style ★, Canadian
      Style Nugget ★, Classic Sliced (Dry Rubbed ★, Turkey ★,
      Turkey Peppered ★), Dry Rubbed Applewood Smoked ★, Fully
      Cooked Hickory Smoked ★, Sliced (Canadian Style Turkey ★,
      Dry Rubbed Applewood ★, Maple ★, Panchetta ★, Pepper Dry
      Rubbed ★, Regular ★, Turkey Peppered ★), Thick Range Sliced
      Dry Rubbed ★, Whole Panchetta ★

Gordon Food Service - Cooked (Slices, Whole Muscle), Sliced Fresh

Great Value Brand (Wal-Mart) - Hickory Smoked, Lower Sodium

Hertel's - All Varieties

Honeysuckle White - Smoked Turkey Bacon

Hormel - Black Label (Applewood, Thick Sliced), Black Label Bacon (Center Cut, Lower Sodium, Maple, Mesquite, Original), Canadian Natural Choice, Fully Cooked, Microwave, Natural Choice (Canadian, Original, Uncured), Range Brand Bacon

Hy-Vee - Double Smoked, Hickory Smoked Fully Cooked, Lower Sodium, Sweet Smoked Peppered Maple Applewood Center Cut, Turkey Bacon

Jennie-O Turkey Store - Bacon (Extra Lean Turkey, Turkey)

Jimmy Dean - Fully Cooked Slices (Hickory Smoked, Thick Sliced (Hickory Smoked, Maple))

Jones Dairy Farm - Canadian ●, Old Fashioned Slab ●, Sliced (Cherry Hardwood Smoked ●, Regular ●, Thick ●)

Kirkland Signature - Bacon (Fully Cooked, Regular)

Meijer Brand - Canadian, Center Cut, Lower Sodium, Precooked, Regular, Thick Sliced, Turkey

My Essentials - Hardwood Smoked Maple Flavored, Hickory, Lower Sodium, Turkey Bacon Fully Cooked

Old Smokehouse - Applewood, Maple Peppered, Original

Open Nature - Uncured (Applewood Smoked, Canadian)

Organic Prairie - Hardwood Smoked Turkey Bacon, Organic Hardwood Smoked Uncured, Organic Retail Hardwood Smoked Uncured (Pork, Turkey)

Oscar Mayer - Center Cut (Original, Thick Slice), Fully Cooked (Bacon, Canadian Style), Lower Sodium, Maple, Natural Smoked Uncured, Naturally Hardwood Smoked (Regular, Thick Cut), Super Thick Cut Applewood Smoked, Turkey (Lower Sodium w/Sea Salt, Smoke Cured 50% Less Fat)

Publix - All Varieties

Pure Market Express ▲ - Bac'un ●

Safeway Brand - Fully Cooked, Hickory Smoked

B

Safeway Select - 40% Less Sodium, Regular Sliced, Thick Sliced

Smithfield - Brown Sugar, Center Cut 40% Lower Fat, Cracked Peppercorn, Maple, Natural Hickory Smoked (Hometown Original, Thick Sliced), Sliced Hickory Smoked Pork Jowl

Tom & Ted's - Thick Sliced Sugar Cured

Trader Joe's - Sliced Prosciutto, Turkey, Uncured

Wellshire Farms - Beef ★, Canadian Style ★, Canadian Style Nugget ★, Classic Sliced (Dry Rubbed ★, Turkey ★, Turkey Peppered ★), Dry Rubbed Applewood Smoked ★, Fully Cooked Hickory Smoked ★, Sliced (Canadian Style Turkey ★, Dry Rubbed Applewood ★, Maple ★, Panchetta ★, Peppered Dry Rubbed ★, Regular ★, Turkey Peppered ★), Thick Range Sliced Dry Rubbed ★, Wellshire Organic (Dry Rubbed Classic, Turkey Bacon), Whole Panchetta ★

Winn Dixie - Hickory Sweet Sliced Bacon (Hardwood Smoked, Lower Sodium, Thick, Thin, Turkey)

Bacon Bits

Augason Farms ▲ - Gluten Free Vegetarian Meat Substitute ●

Badia - Imitation ●

Garrett County Farms - Salt Cured Bacon Bits ★

Gordon Food Service - Crumbles

Great Value Brand (Wal-Mart) - Imitation, Real Bacon Pieces

Hill Country Fare H-E-B - Bacon Bits

Hormel - Bacon (Bits, Crumbles, Pieces)

Kirkland Signature - Crumbled

McCormick - Imitation Bacon Flavored (Bac'n Pieces, Bac'n Pieces Flavored Chips)

Oscar Mayer - Real Bacon Bits, Real Pieces

Spartan Brand - Bacon Chips

Wellshire Farms - Salt Cured Bacon Bits ★

Bagels

Against The Grain Gourmet ▲ - Cinnamon/Raisin, Sesame, Sun Dried Tomato/Basil

Everybody Eats ▲

Gluten-Free Creations ▲ - Berry ●, Cinnamon Raisin ●, Everything ●, Jalapeno Cheese ●, Plain ●

Glutino ▲ - Premium (Cinnamon & Raisin, Multi Grain, Plain, Poppy Seed, Sesame)

Heaven Mills ▲ - Gluten & Egg Free Bagels ●

Joan's GF Great Bakes ▲ - All Flavors

Kinnikinnick ▲ - Tapioca Rice (Cinnamon Raisin, New York Style Plain, Sesame)

Mariposa Artisan-Crafted Gluten-Free ▲ - Bagel Sets (Plain, Sesame)

Molly's Gluten-Free Bakery ▲ - Everything, Plain

Rose's Bakery ▲ - Salted

The Grainless Baker ▲ - Cinnamon Raisin, Onion, Plain

Trader Joe's - Gluten Free Bagels

Udi's Gluten Free Foods ▲ - Gluten Free (Cinnamon Raisin ●, Plain ●, Whole Grain ●)

Baguettes...see Bread

Baked Apples

Lucky Leaf - Dutch

Musselman's - Dutch

Baking Bars

Baker's - Bittersweet, German's Sweet, Select (Bittersweet, Semi Sweet), Semi Sweet, Unsweetened, White

Dagoba ▲ - Semisweet ★, Unsweetened ★

SunSpire - Fair Trade Organic (100% Cacao Unsweetened, 65% Cacao Semi Sweet)

Trader Joe's - Unsweetened Belgium Baking Chocolate

Baking Chips

Andes - Creme De Menthe, Peppermint Crunch

Baker's - Chocolate Chunks

Chocolate Dream - Semi Sweet

Enjoy Life ▲ - Semi Sweet Chocolate (Mega Chunks ●, Mini Chips ●)

Food Club Brand - Baking Chips (Butterscotch, Milk Chocolate, Peanut Butter, Semi Sweet, Vanilla)

Ghirardelli - Chocolate Chips (60% Cacao Bittersweet, Milk Chocolate, Semi Sweet)

B

Gordon Food Service - Semi Sweet Chocolate

Guittard - Chips (Butterscotch, Green Mint, Real Milk Chocolate, Real Semisweet Chocolate)

Hannaford Brand - Semi Sweet Chocolate Chips

Hershey's - Chocolate Chips (Milk, Semi Sweet, Special Dark), Cinnamon Chips

Hy-Vee - Chips (Butterscotch, Milk Chocolate, Mini Semi Sweet, Peanut Butter, Semi Sweet Chocolate, Vanilla Flavored White)

Kroger Brand - Jumbo Semi Sweet

Lowes Foods Brand - Chocolate (Milk, Semi Sweet)

Manischewitz - Chocolate Morsels

Meijer Brand - Butterscotch Chips, Chocolate Chips Semi Sweet, Milk Chocolate Chips, Peanut Butter Chips, White Baking Chips

Midwest Country Fare - Chocolate Flavored Chips

Nestle - Milk Chocolate Morsels, Peanut Butter & Milk Chocolate Morsels, Premier White Morsels, Semi Sweet Chocolate (Chunks, Mini Morsels, Morsels)

NoNuttin' Foods ▲ - Dark Chocolate Chunks ●, Semi Sweet Mini Chocolate Chips ●

Publix - Morsels (Butterscotch, Milk Chocolate, Semi Sweet Chocolate)

Safeway Brand - Butterscotch, Milk Chocolate, Semi Sweet

Spartan Brand - Baking Chips (Butterscotch, Chocolate Semi Sweet, Milk Chocolate, Premium White)

SunSpire - Fair Trade Organic (42% Cacao, 65% Cacao), Grain Sweetened Dark Chocolate, Peanut Butter, Sun Drops, White Chocolate

Trader Joe's - Chocolate Chips Semi Sweet, Milk Chocolate Peanut Butter Chips, Milk Chocolate Peanut Butter, White Chocolate

Wegmans Brand - Chocolate Morsels Semi Sweet

Winn Dixie - Milk Chocolate, Semi Sweet

Woodstock Farms - Organic Dark Chocolate Chips w/Evaporated Cane Juice

baking decorations & frostings

B

Baking Cocoa

Dagoba ▲ - Organic ★

Equal Exchange - Organic

Ghirardelli - Premium Unsweetened Cocoa, Sweet Ground Chocolate & Cocoa **!!**

Hershey's - Unsweetened Baking Cocoa

Hy-Vee

Spartan Brand - Baking Cocoa

Trader Joe's - Organic Cocoa Powder

Watkins - Baking Cocoa

Baking Decorations & Frostings

Badia - All Sprinkles & Nonpareils ●

Betty Crocker - Cookie Icing (Blue, Green, Red, White), Decorating Decors (All Sugars, Chocolate Sprinkles, Nonpareils, Rainbow Mix Sprinkles, Red White & Blue Sprinkles, Stars), Decorating Gels (All Colors), Decorating Icing (All Colors), Easy Flow Icing (All Colors), Rich & Creamy Frosting (Butter Cream, Cherry, Chocolate, Coconut Pecan, Cream Cheese, Creamy White, Dark Chocolate, Lemon, Milk Chocolate, Rainbow Chip, Triple Chocolate Fudge Chip, Vanilla), Whipped Frosting (Butter Cream, Cream Cheese, Fluffy White, Milk Chocolate, Strawberry Mist, Vanilla, Whipped Cream)

Cake Mate - Decorating Gels (All Colors), Decorating Icing (All Colors), Festive Fixings Sugar Crystals (Green, Red)

Cherrybrook Kitchen - Frosting Mix (Chocolate, Vanilla), Ready To Spread Vanilla Frosting

Dagoba ▲ - All Varieties ★

Duncan Hines - Frosting (Coconut Pecan, Creamy Home Style (Buttercream, Caramel, Chocolate Buttercream, Classic Chocolate, Classic Vanilla, Cream Cheese, Dark Chocolate Fudge, Lemon Supreme, Milk Chocolate, Strawberries 'N Cream), Whipped (Chocolate, Cream Cheese, Fluffy White, Vanilla))

Earthly Treats ▲ - Sugar Sprinkles ●

B

Food-Tek Fast & Fresh - Chocolate Flavored Icing ★, Vanilla Icing ★
Let's Do...Sprinkelz - Carnival, Chocolatey, Confetti
Lowes Foods Brand - Vanilla Frosting
Namaste Foods ▲ - Frosting Mix (Chocolate Fudge, Toffee Vanilla)
Nuts.com - Butterscotch Crunch ●, Filling (Chocolate ●, Poppy Seed ●),
Macaroon Crunch ●, Marzipan ●, Paste (Hazelnut Praline ●, Pistachio
Nut ●), Prune Butter ●
Pamela's Products ▲ - Frosting Mix (Dark Chocolate, Vanilla)
Whole Foods Market Gluten Free Bakehouse ▲ - Frosting
(Chocolate, Vanilla)

Baking Mix...see Bread Mix
Baking Powder
Argo - Double Acting Aluminum Free
Barkat
Bob's Red Mill ▲ ★
Clabber Girl - All Sizes *(Except 22 oz. size)*
Davis
Durkee
El Peto ▲ - Aluminum Free (Corn Free, Regular)
Ener-G ▲ - Regular
Hain Pure Foods - Gluten Free ★
Hannaford Brand
Hearth Club
Hy-Vee - Double Acting
KC
Nuts.com - Double Active ●
Really Great Food Company ▲ - Baking Powder Aluminum Free/
Double Acting
Royal
Rumford
Spartan Brand
Spice Islands
Tones
Watkins
Wegmans Brand - Double Acting

B

Baking Soda
   Arm & Hammer
   Bob's Red Mill ▲ ★
   Durkee
   El Peto ▲
   Ener-G ▲ - Regular
   Food Club Brand
   Gordon Food Service
   Hannaford Brand
   Lowes Foods Brand
   Meijer Brand
   Nuts.com - Arm & Hammer Baking Soda ●
   Spartan Brand
   Spice Islands
   Tones
Bamboo Shoots
   Native Forest - Organic Sliced
Banana Chips
   Brothers All Natural ▲ - Crisps (Banana, Strawberry Banana)
   Nuts.com - Dried Fruit (Chips ●, Organic Chips ●)
   Woodstock Farms - Organic, Sweetened
Bananas
   *... *All Fresh Fruits & Vegetables Are Gluten-Free*
   Chiquita
   Dole
   Mariani - Chips **!!**
   Nuts.com - Dried Fruit (Organic Simply ●, Simply ●)
   Woodstock Farms - Organic Frozen Bananas
Barbeque Sauce
   A & W - Rich 'N Hearty
   Ah So - Original Chinese BBQ For Pork/Chicken & Barbecue,
      Smokey Chinese BBQ
   Annie's Naturals - Organic (Hot Chipotle **!!**, Original **!!**, Smokey
      Maple **!!**, Sweet & Spicy **!!**)

B

Bone Suckin' Sauce - Hot, Original, Thicker Style

Bull's-Eye - Original, Regional Flavors (Carolina Style, Kansas City Style, Memphis Style, Texas Style)

Cattlemen's - Kansas City Classic, Memphis Sweet, Mississippi Honey BBQ

Daddy Sam's - Bar B Que Sawce (Medium Ginger Jalapeno, Original)

Dorothy Lane Market - Original

Dr. Pepper - Sweet & Kickin'

Emeril's - BAM BQ (KickedUp, Sweet Original, Sweet N Easy Molasses)

Fischer & Wieser - Plum Chipotle Grilling Sauce, Texas Pit

Follow Your Heart - Balsamic Barbeque (Mild !, Spicy !)

Food Club Brand - BBQ Sauce (Hickory, Honey, Regular)

Frank's RedHot - Kickin' BBQ

Frontera - Original Sweet & Smoky, Roasted Chipotle Pineapple, Texas Black Pepper

Gordon Food Service - Barbeque Sauce (Pit Style, Sweet, Traditional)

H-E-B - Specialty Series (Carolina, Kansas City, Memphis, South Texas)

Hannaford Brand - Honey, Kansas City Style, Original, Sweet & Zesty

Heinz - Chicken & Rib, Garlic, Honey Garlic, Original

Hunt's - All Flavors

Hy-Vee - Hickory, Honey Smoke, Original

Isaly's - All Varieties

Jack Daniel's - Hickory Brown Sugar, Honey Smokehouse, Original No. 7 Recipe, Spicy Original

Jim Beam - Original, Spicy Bourbon

Kraft - Brown Sugar, Char Grill, Hickory Smoke, Honey (Hickory Smoke, Mustard, Original, Roasted Garlic, Spicy), Hot, Light Original, Mesquite Smoke, Original

Kurtz - Hickory, Honey, KC Style, Original

Lowes Foods Brand - Hickory, Honey, Regular

Midwest Country Fare - Hickory, Honey, Original

Mother's Mountain - Aunt Ruby's Red, Honey Hickory

Mr. Spice Organic - Honey BBQ ★

Mrs. Renfro's - Barbecue Sauce

Naturally Delicious - Regular

NOH - Hawaiian Barbecue (Regular, Spicy)

Nomato - Nomato Barbeque Sauce

Organicville - Organic BBQ Sauce (Original ●, Tangy ●)

Pig Chaser - BBQ Sauce (Bacon, Garlic, Habanero, Original, Pineapple Mango)

Publix - Original

Royal Food Products - Garden Fresh Wagonwheel Barbeque, Gourmet Choice (Baby Back Rib, Chipotle, South Texas), Royal Deluxe (Santa Fe, Texas Style)

Safeway Brand - Hickory Smoked, Honey Smoked, Mesquite Smoke, Original

San-J - Gluten Free Asian BBQ ●

Saz's - Original, Sassy, Vidalia Onion

Spartan Brand - Hickory & Brown Sugar, Honey, Original

Steel's - Agave (Chipotle ●, Regular ●)

Stubb's - Bar B Q Sauce (Hickory Bourbon ●, Honey Pecan ●, Mild ●, Original ●, Smokey Mesquite ●, Spicy ●)

Sweet Baby Ray's - Hickory & Brown Sugar **! !**, Honey **! !**, Honey Chipotle **! !**, Original **! !**, Raspberry Chipotle **! !**, Sweet 'N Spicy **! !**, Sweet Vidalia Onion **! !**

Taste Of Inspiration - Maple Chipotle **!**, Spicy Mango **!**, Wild Maine Blueberry **!**

Trader Joe's - All Natural, Kansas City

Walden Farms - Hickory Smoked, Honey, Original, Thick & Spicy

Wegmans Brand - Brown Sugar, Memphis Style

Western Prime - All Varieties

Winn Dixie - Hickory, Honey, Original

Bars...(includes Breakfast, Energy, Fruit, Protein, etc.)

1-2-3 Gluten Free ▲ - Sweet Goodness Pan Bars ●

AllerEnergy ▲ - Nutrition Bars (Apple Cinnamon, Cherry Blossom, Chocolate Chip, Wild Blueberry)

Alpsnack - Apricots & Cranberries, Coconut/Mango & Pineapple, Fair Trade (Dark Chocolate, Espresso Chocolate), Plums & Currants

B

Apple's Bakery ▲ - Gluten Free Dessert Assortment

Attune Foods - Chocolate Probiotic Wellness Milk Chocolate Crisp ●, Probiotic Chocolate Bar (Dark Chocolate ●, Mint Chocolate ●)

Bakery On Main - Granola Bars (Cranberry Maple Nut ●, Extreme Trail Mix ●, Peanut Butter Chocolate Chip ●, Soft & Chewy (Apple Cinnamon ●, Chocolate Almond ●, Peanut Butter & Jelly ●)), Truebar (Apricot Almond Chai ●, Coconut Cashew ●, Fruit & Nut ●, Hazelnut Chocolate Cherry ●, Raspberry Chocolate Almond ●, Walnut Cappuccino ●)

Betty Lou's - Fruit Bar (Apple Cinnamon ●, Apricot ●, Blueberry ●, Cherry ●, Strawberry ●), Organic (Chocolate Dream Greens ●, Cranberry Crave ●), Organic Vegan (Cacao Acai ●, Fruit & Veggie ●, Superberry Acai ●)

Boomi Bar - Almond Protein Plus, Apricot Cashew, Cashew Almond, Cashew Protein Plus, Cranberry Apple, Fruit & Nut, Healthy Hazel, Macadamia Paradise, Maple Pecan, Perfect Pumpkin, Pineapple Ginger, Pistachio Pineapple, Walnut Date

Bora Bora - Antioxidant (Hula Cacao Hazelnut, Pacific Mango Macadamia, Paradise Walnut Pistachio, Tiki Blueberry Flax), Energy (Island Brazil Nut Almond, Tribal Cinnamon Oatmeal, Volcanic Chocolate Banana), Organic Traditional Apricot Quinoa, Superfood (Exotic Coconut Almond, Native Acai Walnut, Tropical Sesame Cranberry, Wild Pomegranate Pecan)

Breakaway Bakery ▲ - Lemon ●, Shortbread Crumble & Bar Dough ●

Bumble Bar - Bumble Bar (Amazing Almond, Awesome Apricot, Chai Almond, Cherry Chocolate, Chocolate Crisp, Chunky Cherry, Classic Cashew, Harvest Hazelnut, Lushus Lemon, Mixed Nut Medley, Original Peanut, Paradise Pineapple), Junior Bars (Amazing Almond, Chocolate Crisp, Original Peanut), Variety Pack (Basic, Fruity, Junior Bars, Nutty)

Candice Foods ▲ - Protein Bars (Blueberry Vanilla, Chocolate Cherry, Chocolate Fudge, Chocolate Mint, Chocolate Orange, Mocha Java, Raspberry Banana)

Carb Safe - Sugar Free Chocolate Bars Dark

Choices Rice Bakery ▲ - Almond Squares, Lemon Squares, Pecan Squares, Raw Bars (Cashew Coconut, Cocoa Mint, Cocoa Nut Drop, Gingersnap, Nutty Brownie), Rice Quinoa Granola Bar

Chunks Of Energy - Cacao w/Goji Berries ●, Chia Orange ●, Date Flax w/Turmeric ●, Lemon Pomegranate ●

Clif Nectar - Organic (Cherry Pomegranate, Cranberry Apricot Almond, Dark Chocolate Walnut, Lemon Vanilla Cashew)

Crispy Cat - Candy Bars (Chocolate Sundae !!, Mint Coconut !!, Toasted Almond !!)

Dagoba ▲ - All Chocolate Bars ★

Deerfields Gluten Free Bakery ▲ - The Gluten Free Bar

Eat Natural -
  100% Organic Brazils Hazelnuts & Sultans
  Almonds Apricots & Yoghurt Coating
  Blueberries Pistachios & Yoghurt Coating
  Brazils Sultanas Almonds & Hazelnuts
  Cherries Almonds & Yoghurt Coating
  Cranberries Apricots & Yoghurt Coating
  Cranberries Macadamias & Dark Chocolate
  Dark 70% Chocolate Brazils & Apricots
  Dates Walnuts & Pumpkin Seeds
  Macadamias Brazils & Apricots
  Peanuts Almonds & Hazelnuts
  Peanuts Cranberries Pistachios & Milk Chocolate

Ener-G ▲ - Chocolate Chip Snack

Enjoy Life ▲ - Boom Choco Boom (Dark Chocolate ●, Ricemilk Chocolate ●, Ricemilk Crunch ●), Chewy Bars (Caramel Apple ●, Cocoa Loco ●, Sunbutter Crunch ●, Very Berry ●)

EnviroKidz Organic - Crispy Rice Bars (Berry Blast ●, Chocolate ●, Fruity Burst ●, Peanut Butter ●, Peanut Choco Drizzle ●)

Glenny's - Peanuts & Peanut Butter Whole Peanut Bar ●, Whole Fruit & Nut Bar (Cashew & Almond ●, Classic Fruit & Nut ●, Cranberry & Almond ●)

Gluten Free Cafe - Chocolate Sesame ●, Cinnamon Sesame ●, Lemon Sesame ●

B

Glutino ▲ - Breakfast Bars (Apple, Blueberry, Cherry, Strawberry), Candy Bars Chocolate Peanut Butter, Organic Bars (Chocolate Banana, Chocolate Peanut Butter, Wildberry)

GoMacro - MacroBar (Almond Butter w/Carob, Banana Almond, Cashew Butter, Cashew Caramel, Cherries 'N Berries, Chocolate Protein, Granola w/Coconut, Peanut Butter Chocolate Chip, Peanut Protein, Tahini Date)

Gopal's - Rawma (Apple Delicious, Carob Quinoa, Pineapple Nut, Pumpkin Agave, Sesame Mango, Walnut Fig), Sprout Bar (Almond, Brazil Nut, Hazelnut, Macadamia)

Go Raw ▲ - Organic (Banana Bread Flax ●, Live Granola ●, Live Pumpkin ●, Real Live Flax ●, Spirulina Energy ●)

Gorge Delights ▲ - Acai Fruit Bars (Apple Cherry, Apple Raspberry, Pear Cranberry, Pear Strawberry), Just Fruit Bar (Apple, Apple Blueberry, Apple Cherry, Apple Raspberry, Pear, Pear Blueberry, Pear Cranberry, Pear Strawberry)

Grandma Ferdon's ▲ - Lemon ●, Pumpkin ●

JK Gourmet - Granola Bars (Nuts & Blueberry, Nuts & Cranberries, Nuts & Dates, Nuts & Raisins, Nuts & Seeds)

Jungle Grub - Berry Bamboozle ●, Chocolate Chip Cookie Dough ●, Peanut Butter Groove ●

KIND ▲ - Fruit & Nut (Almond & Apricot ★, Almond & Coconut ★, Almonds & Apricots In Yogurt ★, Apple Cinnamon & Pecan ★, Fruit & Nut Delight ★, Fruit & Nuts In Yogurt ★, Macadamia & Apricot ★, Mini (Almond & Apricot ★, Fruit & Nut Delight ★), Nut Delight ★, Sesame & Peanuts ★, Walnut & Date ★), PLUS (Almond Cashew w/Flax ★, Almond Walnut Macadamia ★, Blueberry Pecan ★, Cranberry Almond ★, Dark Chocolate Cherry Cashew ★, Mango Macadamia ★, Mini (Almond Cashew w/Flax ★, Cranberry Almond ★), Peanut Butter Dark Chocolate ★, Pomegranate Blueberry Pistachio ★)

Larabar -
Apple Pie
Banana Bread

Blueberry Muffin
Cappuccino
Carrot Cake
Cashew Cookie
Cherry Pie
Chocolate Chip (Brownie, Cherry Torte, Cookie Dough)
Chocolate Coconut Chew
Coconut Cream Pie
Ginger Snap
Jocalat (Chocolate, Chocolate Coffee, Chocolate Hazelnut, Chocolate Mint)
Key Lime Pie
Lemon Bar
Peanut Butter (& Jelly, Chocolate Chip, Cookie)
Pecan Pie
Tropical Fruit Tart
Uber (Apple Turnover, Bananas Foster, Cherry Cobbler, Roasted Nut Roll)

Lydia's Organics - Cacao Crunch, Figtastic, Lemon Ginger, Raspberry, Spirulina, Tropical Mango

Manischewitz - Raspberry Jell Bars

Mareblu Naturals ▲ - Crunch (Almond ●, Cashew ●), Trail Mix Crunch (BlueCran Pomegranate ●, Mango Pomegranate ●, Pistachio ●, Strawberry Pomegranate ●)

Mariani - HoneyBar (Cranberry !!, Sesame !!, Trail Mix !!)

Marion's Smart Delights ▲ - Lemon Bar Baking Mix ●

Mariposa Artisan-Crafted Gluten-Free ▲ - Coconut Lemon Squares

Meijer Brand - Xtreme Snack Bars

Mixes From The Heartland ▲ - Coffee Bars Mix (Apple Cinnamon●, Cranberry ●, Tropical ●)

Molly's Gluten-Free Bakery ▲ - Squares (Lemon, Pumpkin)

Mrs. May's Naturals - Trio (Blueberry ●, Cranberry ●, Strawberry ●, Tropical ●)

B

Nature Crops - Quinoa (& Prunes, & Strawberry, Almonds & Sesame Seeds)

Nature Valley - Roasted Nut Crunch (Almond, Peanut)

Necco - Clark Bar, Skybar

NoNuttin' Foods ▲ - Granola Bars (Apple Cinnamon ●, Chocolate Chip ●, Double Chocolate Chunk ●, Raisin ●)

NuGO Free - Gluten Free Bars (Carrot Cake ●, Dark Chocolate Crunch ●, Dark Chocolate Trail Mix ●)

Nutiva - Organic Hemp (Flax & Raisin, Hemp Chocolate, Hempseed Original)

Omega Smart Bars ▲ -

Banana Chocolate Chip ●

Organic (Apricot & Almond ●, Chocolate Nut ●, Cinnamon Apple ●, Raisin Spice ●)

Pomegranate Strawberry Colada ●

Pumpkin Spice ●

Youth In A Bar (Organic Almond Macaroon ●, Organic Wild Blueberry w/Orange Essence ●, Yummy Cherry Berry ●)

Orchard Bar - Blueberry Pomegranate & Almond, Pineapple Coconut & Macadamia, Strawberry Raspberry & Walnut

Organic Food Bar -

Organic Food Bar (Active Greens, Active Greens Chocolate, Chocolate Chip, Cranberry, Omega 3 Flax, Original, Protein, Vegan, Wild Blueberry)

Organic Food Bar Kids Keerunch Chocolate Brownie Crunch

Raw Organic Food Bar (Chocolate Coconut, Chocolatey Chocolate Chip, Cinnamon Raisin, Fiber Chocolate Delite)

Oskri Organics -

Apricot

Apricot Almond

Coconut Bar (Almond, Cherry, Dark Chocolate, Mango, Milk Chocolate, Original, Pineapple, Strawberry)

Date Walnut Bar

Fiber Bar (Almonds, Cashews, Milk Chocolate, Pecans & Raisins)

Fruit Bar (Date, Fig)

Honey Bar (Almond, Cashew, Desert Date, Flax Seed, Granola, Mixed Nuts, Muesli)

Mini Bars

    Coconut (Original w/Dark Chocolate, Original w/Milk Chocolate)

    Fig

    Honey Cashew

Nut Free Granola (w/Milk Chocolate, Raisin w/Dark Chocolate)

Protein Bar (Almond & Cranberry, Cashew & Cranberry)

Quinoa

Sesame Bar (Black Sesame, Chewy, Chewy Black Sesame, Date Syrup & Fennel, Molasses, Molasses & Black Cumin, Molasses & Fennel, w/Date Syrup, w/Date Syrup & Black Cumin)

Pamela's Products ▲ - Whenever Bars (Oat Blueberry Lemon, Oat Chocolate Chip Coconut, Oat Cranberry Almond, Oat Raisin Walnut Spice)

Probar - Fruition Chocolate Orange **!!**

PURE Bar - Naturals (Chocolate Almond ●, Peanut Raisin Crunch ●, Superfruit Nutty Crunch ●), Organic (Apple Cinnamon ●, Cherry Cashew ●, Chocolate Brownie ●, Cranberry Orange ●, Dark Chocolate Berry ●, Wild Blueberry ●)

Pure Market Express ▲ - Cherry Honey Crunch ●

PureFit - Chocolate Brownie, Crunch (Almond, Berry Almond, Granola, Peanut Butter)

Quejos ▲ - Cranberry Raisin

Quest Bar - Peanut Butter Supreme, Vanilla Almond Crunch

Raw Revolution ▲ - Apple Cinnamon, Cashews & Agave, Chocolate & Cashews, Chocolate & Coconut, Coconut & Agave, Hazelnut & Chocolate, Lemon Dew, Raspberry & Chocolate, Spiruluna & Cashew, Tropical Mango

Resveratrol - Wine Time Chocolate (Dark, Raspberry)

B

Rise -
- Breakfast Crunchy (Cashew Almond, Cranberry Apple, Honey Walnut, Macadamia Pineapple, Perfect Pumpkin)
- Energy+ (Apricot Goji, Blueberry Coconut, Cherry Almond, Coconut Acai, Raspberry Pomegranate)
- Protein+ (Almond Honey, Crunchy Carob Chip)

Ruth's HempPower - Cranberry Almond HempPower, Cranberry Trail HempPower, CranNut Flax Power, VeryBerry Flax Power, Vote Hemp

Salba - Whole Food Bars (Cranberry Nut ●, Mixed Berry ●, Tropical Fruit●)

Schar ▲ - Chocolate Hazelnut Bars

Seitenbacher - Banana Cranberry, Choco Apricot, Energy, Fitness, High Protein, High Protein Strawberry, Natural (Energizer, Sports), Sweet Romance, Xtra Fiber

Shakti Bar - Organic (Blueberry Chia, Goldenberry Goji, Mango Maca)

Simple Squares - Nut & Honey (Coconut !, Rosemary !, Sage !)

Soy Joy - Apple, Banana, Berry, Blueberry, Mango Coconut, Pineapple, Strawberry

SunRype - FruitSource (Blueberry Pomegranate, Mango Strawberry, Strawberry)

Taste Of Nature -
- Exotics (Canadian Maple Forest, Caribbean Ginger Island, Himalayan Goji Summit, Mediterranean Pistachio Passion, Persian Pomegranate Garden)
- Regular (Argentina Peanut Plains, Brazilian Nut Fiesta, California Almond Valley, Nova Scotia Blueberry Fields, Quebec Cranberry Carnival)

The Good Bean - Roasted Chickpea Snacks Fruit & Seeds Trail Mix !, The Fruit & No Nut Bar (Apricot Coconut !, Chocolate Berry !)

The Grain Exchange - Oatmeal Caramel Delight

thinkThin -
- Blueberry & Mixed Nuts
- Brownie Crunch
- Caramel Fudge
- Cherry & Mixed Nuts

Chocolate (Covered Strawberries, Espresso, Fudge)
Cookies & Creme
Cranberry Apple & Mixed Nuts
Crunch Bars (Caramel Chocolate Dipped, Chocolate Dipped, Mixed Nuts, White Chocolate Dipped)
Dark Chocolate
Lemon Cream Pie
Peanut Butter (Chunky, Creamy)
Tangerine Creamsicle
White Chocolate
Tiger's Milk -
Peanut Butter **!**
Peanut Butter & Honey **!**
Protein Rich **!**
Timtana Gluten Free ▲ - PrOatina Lemon Bar Mix ●
Two Moms In The Raw -
Granola Bars (Blueberry ●, Cranberry ●, Goji Berry ●, Raisin ●)
Nut Bar (Blueberry ●, Cranberry ●, Goji Berry ●)
Voyaging Foods - Vegan Energy Bars ●
Wegmans Brand - FYFGA Fruit Flats (Cherry, Grape, Raspberry, Strawberry)

Basmati Rice...see Rice
Beans
*... *All Fresh Fruits & Vegetables Are Gluten-Free*
Amy's -
Organic Light In Sodium (Black Refried ★, Traditional Refried ★)
Organic Refried Beans (Black ★, Traditional ★, w/Green Chiles ★)
Organic Vegetarian Baked ★
Arrowhead Mills - Adzuki, Anasazi, Chickpeas/Garbanzo, Green Split Peas, Lentils (Green, Red), Pinto, Soybeans
Augason Farms ▲ - Pinto ● *(Pail Size Only)*
B&M Baked Beans - All Varieties
Birds Eye - All Plain Frozen Vegetables

B

Bush's Best -
  Baked Beans (Bold & Spicy, Boston Recipe, Country Style,
    Homestyle, Honey, Maple Cured Bacon, Onion, Original,
    Vegetarian)
  Black
  Butter (Baby, Large, Speckled)
  Cannellini
  Chili Beans *(Must Be NEW Recipe)* (Hot, Medium, Mild)
  Chili Magic Chili Starter *(Must Be NEW Recipe)* (Texas Recipe,
    Traditional Recipe)
  Garbanzo
  Great Northern
  Grillin' Beans (Black Bean Fiesta, Bourbon & Brown Sugar,
    Smokehouse Tradition, Southern Pit Barbecue, Steakhouse
    Recipe, Texas Ranchero)
  Kidney (Dark Red, Light Red)
  Microwaveable Cup Original
  Navy
  Pinto (Regular, w/Pork)
  Red
  Refried Beans Traditional
C & W - All Plain Frozen Vegetables **! !**
Del Monte - All Canned Vegetables
Eden Organic -
  Curried Rice & Lentils
  Mexican Rice & Black Beans
  Moroccan Rice & Garbanzo Beans
  Organic (Aduki, Baked w/Sorghum & Mustard, Black, Black
    Eyed Peas, Black Soybeans, Butter, Cannellini, Caribbean Black,
    Garbanzo, Great Northern, Kidney, Navy, Pinto, Rice & Cajun
    Small Red, Rice & Caribbean Black, Rice & Garbanzo, Rice &
    Kidney, Rice & Lentils, Rice & Pinto, Small Red)
  Organic Bulk Dried (Aduki, Black, Black Soybeans, Garbanzo,
    Green (Lentils, Split Peas), Kidney, Navy, Pinto, Small Red)

Refried (Black, Black Soy & Black, Kidney, Pinto, Spicy Black, Spicy Pinto)

Spanish Rice & Pinto Beans

Fantastic World Foods - Hummus Original, Instant (Black, Refried)

Food Club Brand -

Canned

Baked (Homestyle, Maple Cured, Original, Vegetarian, w/Onion)

French Style Green No Salt Added

Great Northern Regular

Green Beans (Cut, Cut No Salt, French Style, French Style No Salt, Wax Cut, Whole)

Kidney (Dark Red, Light Red)

Navy

Pinto

Pork & Beans

Dried Beans (Blackeyed Pea, Great Northern, Lima Large, Navy, Pinto, Red Kidney)

Frozen (Green Cut, Green Whole, Lima Beans, Steamin' Easy (French Cut Green Beans, Green Beans Cut))

Refried Beans (Authentic, Fat Free)

Freshlike - Frozen Plain Beans

Friend's - All Varieties

Full Circle - Canned Organic (Baked Beans (Maple & Onion, Original), Black, Garbanzo, Green Cut, Red Kidney, Refried (Black, Green Chile & Lime, Vegetarian)), Dried (Kidney, Lentil, Lima, Navy, Pinto)

Grand Selections - Frozen (Fancy Green, Petite Green, Whole Green)

Great Value Brand (Wal-Mart) - Canned (Cut Green, No Salt Added Cut Green), Dried (Baby Lima, Black, Garbanzo, Great Northern, Large Lima, Light Red Kidney, Pinto, Small Red), Dried Peas (Blackeyed, Chick, Green Split)

B **Green Giant -**
  Canned
    Cut Green (50% Less Sodium, Regular)
    French Style Green
    Kitchen Sliced Green
    Three Bean Salad
  Frozen (Baby Lima & Butter Sauce, Simply Steam (Baby Lima,
    Green Beans & Almonds)
  Valley Fresh Steamers (Cut Green Beans, Roasted Red Potatoes
    Green Beans & Rosemary Butter Sauce, Select Whole Green
    Beans)
Hannaford Brand - All Dried, Baked, Black, Cut Green, Cut Wax,
  Dark Red Kidney, French Green, Great Northern, Light Red
  Kidney, No Salt Green (Cut, French), Pinto, Refried (Fat Free,
  Traditional), Whole Green
Heinz - Vegetarian Beans
Hill Country Fare H-E-B - Baked (Homestyle, Original, w/Onions),
  Pork & Beans, Refried (Regular, w/Jalapenos), Texas Style
Hy-Vee -
  Butter
  Chili (Beans, Style In Chili Gravy)
  Country Style Baked
  Cut Green
  Dark Red Kidney
  Dried (Baby Lima, Black, Large Lima, Lentils, Mixed Soup, Navy)
  Fat Free Refried
  French Style Green
  Frozen (Cut Green, French Cut Green)
  Garbanzo Beans Chick Peas
  Great Northern (Dried, Regular)
  Home Style Baked
  Large Lima
  Lentils
  Light Red Kidney
  Maple Cured Bacon Baked

Navy
Onion Baked
Original Baked
Pinto (Dried, Regular)
Pork & Beans
Red (Dried, Kidney, Regular)
Refried Black
Spicy Refried
Steam In A Bag Frozen Beans
Vegetarian Refried
Whole Green

Joan Of Arc - Black, Butter, Dark Red Kidney, Garbanzo, Great Northern, Light Red Kidney, Pinto, Red

Kid's Kitchen - Beans & Wieners

Kirkland Signature - Canned Cut Green Beans

Kroger Brand - Baked (Country Style, Homestyle, Original), Canned Green Beans Cut

Las Palmas - Refried, Vegetarian Chili

Lowes Foods Brand -
Canned (Baked Brown Sugar & Bacon, Black, Chili, Cut Green No Salt, French, Garbanzo, Great Northern, Green (Cut, French Style, Whole), Lima, Pinto (Regular, w/Pork), Pork & Beans, Red Kidney Beans (Dark, Light), Refried (Fat Free, Mexican Style), Whole Green), Dry (Baby Lima, Black Eyed Peas, Great Northern, Lentil, Lima, Mixed, Navy, Pinto)
Frozen (Deluxe Whole Green, Green (Cut, French Cut, Regular), Lima (Baby, Deluxe Tiny, Regular), Speckled Butter)

Meijer Brand -
Baked Beans Organic
Canned Beans (Black (Organic, Regular), Butter, Garbanzo (Organic, Regular), Great Northern, Lima, Mexican Style, Pinto (Organic, Regular), Red Kidney (Dark, Dark Organic, Light, Regular), Refried (Fat Free, Regular, Vegetarian), Refried Organic (Black Bean, Black Bean Jalapeno, Roasted Chili Lime, Traditional), Wax Cut)

B

Canned Green Beans Cut (Blue Lake, French Style (Blue Lake, No Salt, Organic, Veri Green), No Salt, Organic, Regular, Veri Green)

Canned Green Beans (Cut French Style Regular, Whole)

Dry Beans (Black, Blackeye, Great Northern, Green Split Beans & Peas, Lentil, Lima Large, Navy, Pinto, Red Kidney)

Frozen Edamame Soybeans

Frozen Green Beans (Cut (Organic, Original), French Cut, Italian Cut, Steamer)

Frozen Lima Beans (Baby (Organic, Regular), Fordhook), Pork & Beans

Midwest Country Fare - Chili Style, Cut Green, French Style Green, Pork & Beans

Nielsen-Massey - Madagascar Bourbon Pure Vanilla Bean Paste ●, Whole Vanilla Beans ●

Nuts.com -

Ceci Fava Mix ●

Chickpeas (Roasted Golden (Salted ●, Unsalted ●), Roasted White (Salted ●, Unsalted ●)

Cranberry Beans ●

Dry Roasted Edamame (Salted ●, Unsalted ●)

Giant Fava Beans ●

Organic Cannellini Beans ●

Organic Dry Roasted Soybeans (Salted Whole ●, Unsalted Whole ●)

Simply Green Beans Freeze Dried Vegetables ●

Soy Beans (Dry Roasted Halves ●, Hickory Smoked ●, Spicy BBQ ●)

Wasabi Beans ●

O Organics - Canned (Black, Cut Green, Garbanzo, Kidney, Pinto), Chili Beans In Sauce, Frozen Whole Green

Old El Paso - Refried Beans (Fat Free, Spicy Fat Free, Traditional, Vegetarian, w/Green Chiles)

Ortega - Refried (Fat Free, Regular)

Pictsweet - All Plain Frozen Vegetables, Cracked Pepper Seasoned Green, Roasted Garlic Seasoned Baby Whole Green, Seasoned Corn & Black Beans

beans

Private Selection - Frozen Green Beans, Organic Green Beans
   Canned

Publix -
   Canned (Green (Lima, Original, Veggi Green), Kidney
      (Dark, Light), Pork & Beans)
   Dry (Baby Lima, Black, Blackeye Peas, Garbanzo, Great Northern,
      Green Split Peas, Large Lima, Lentils, Light Red Kidney, Navy,
      Pinto, Small Red)
   Frozen (Green (Cut, French Cut), Lima (Baby, Fordhook),
      Speckled Butter Beans)

Publix GreenWise Market - Organic Canned (Black, Dark Red
   Kidney, Garbanzo, Green, Pinto, Soy)

Rodelle - Madagascar Bourbon Vanilla Beans

S&W - All Canned Vegetables

Safeway Brand -
   Baked (Homestyle, Original, Vegetarian)
   Canned (Black (Eyed, Regular), Butter, Chili Beans Mexican Style,
      Dark Kidney, Garbanzo, Green (Cut, Cut No Salt, French Style,
      Whole), Light Kidney, Lima, Pinto)
   Dried (Black (Eyed, Regular), Great Northern, Green Split, Large
      Lima, Lentils, Light Red Kidney, Navy, Pink, Pinto, Small (Red,
      White))
   Frozen (Baby Lima, Cut Green, Fordbook Lima, French Style,
      Whole)
   Refried Beans (Traditional, Vegetarian)

Spartan Brand -
   Canned (Baked (Homestyle, Maple Cured Bacon, Original,
      w/Onions), Black, Butter, Chili Beans, Dark Red Kidney,
      Garbanzo, Great Northern, Green (Cut, French Style, Whole),
      Light Red Kidney, Lima, Pinto, Pork & Beans, Red, Wax Cut)
   Dried (Black, Black Eyed, Great Northern, Kidney, Lentil,
      Lima (Baby, Large), Navy, Pinto)
   Frozen (Baby Lima, Green (Cut, French Cut, Whole))

St. Dalfour - Gourmet On The Go Three Beans w/Sweetcorn

B

Taco Bell - Refried Beans (Fat Free, Vegetarian Blend)

Trader Joe's - All Canned Plain **!!**, All Plain Dried Varieties, Frozen
Haricot Vert Extra Fine Green Beans **!!**

Wegmans Brand -
Canned (Black, Butter, Dark Red Kidney (No Salt Added, Regular),
FYFGA (Black, Great Northern, Lima, Wax Cut), Light Red
Kidney, Light Red Kidney, Pinto, Pork & Beans In Tomato Sauce,
Seasoned Chili)
Canned Baked Beans (FYFGA Vegetarian, Original, w/Brown
Sugar & Bacon)
Canned FYFGA (Cut Green Beans (No Salt, Regular), French Style
Green Beans (No Salt, Regular))
Canned Italian Classics (Cannellini Beans, Garbanzo Beans),
Frozen (FYFGA Baby Lima, Lima)
Frozen Green FYFGA (Cut, French Style, Italian Cut, Whole)

Westbrae -
Green Beans (Cut, French Cut)
Organic (Black, Chili, Garbanzo, Great Northern, Kidney, Lentils,
Pinto, Red, Salad, Soy)

Winn Dixie -
All Dried
Canned Beans (Baby White Lima, Baked Brown Sugar w/Onion,
Baked Brown Sugar & Bacon, Chili Mexican Style, Dark Red
Kidney, Garbanzo, Great Northern, Green & White Lima, Green
Cut, Green French Style Sliced, Green Lima, Green No Salt
Added, Green Whole, Light Red Kidney, Navy)
Frozen Green Beans (Butter Speckled, Cut, French Style Sliced,
Italian, Organic Cut, Whole)
Frozen Lima Beans (Baby, Fordhook, Petite, Speckled)
Pork & Beans
Refried (Fat Free, Traditional)
Soy
Steamable Green Beans Cut

B

Woodstock Farms - Dried Green Beans, Organic Frozen (Baby French Beans, Cut Green Beans, Lima)

Beef...see also Deli Meat

... *All Fresh Meat Is Gluten-Free (Non-Marinated, Unseasoned)

Always Tender - Flavored Fresh Beef Peppercorn

Applegate -
Deli Counter (Peppered Eye **!**, Regular Roast **!**)
Deli Meat Natural Roast Beef **!**
Organic (Frozen Beef Burger **!**, Roast Beef **!**)

Armour - Deli (Corned Beef, Pastrami, Roast Beef (Italian Style, Regular))

Augason Farms ▲ - Gluten Free Freeze Dried Chunks ●

Boar's Head - All Varieties

Buddig - Deli Cuts Roast Beef, Original Beef

Castle Wood Reserve - Deli Meat (Angus Corned Beef, Angus Roast Beef)

Coleman's Natural Foods - All Natural Uncured Hot Dog

Di Lusso - Deli Counter (Roast Beef (Rare, Seasoned Italian Style), Seasoned, Seasoned Cajun Style)

Dietz & Watson ▲ -
Classic Top Round Dried Beef ●
Corned Beef (Brisket ●, California Style ●, Cap Off Top Round ●)
Deli Counter Roast Beef (Choice Top Round ●, Italian ●, London Broil ●, Oven Roasted (Medium ●, Rare ●), Pre Sliced (London Broil ●, Premium Homestyle ●), Premium Angus ●, Top Round (Medium ●, Rare ●), USDA Choice Eye Round ●, USDA Pepper Choice ●)
Top Round Dried ●

Eating Right - Deli Sliced Roast Beef

Eckrich - Deli Meat (Choice Top Roast Beef, Cooked Corned Beef, Lite Roast Beef, Seasoned Roast Beef)

Five Star Brand ▲ - Corned Beef, Jumbo Beef Wieners, Roast Beef, Synthetic Casing Beef Wieners

Garrett County Farms - Roast Beef Sliced ★

B

Giant Eagle Brand - Shredded w/BBQ Sauce

Gordon Food Service - Taco Filling

Great Value Brand (Wal-Mart) - Frozen 100% Pure Beef Patties

H-E-B - Premium Pork & Beef Sausage Ring, Premium Sausage
(Link, Original Pork & Beef Value Pack), Roast Beef (All Natural
Lunchmeat, Cajun, Mesquite Smoked (Pre Sliced, Regular),
Seasoned (Pre Sliced, Regular), Tub)

Hill Country Fare H-E-B - Cajun Roast, Smoked Sausage (Cocktail,
Regular, Skinless Beef)

Hillshire Farms - Deli Select Thin Sliced (Corned Beef, Roast Beef),
Deli Select Ultra Thin Roast Beef

Hormel - Always Tender Non Flavored Fresh Beef, Deli Meat Natural
Choice Roast Beef, Dried Beef, Fully Cooked Entrees (Beef Roast
Au Jus, Italian Style Beef Roast), Mary Kitchens (Corned Beef Hash,
Reduced Fat Corned Beef Hash), Natural Choice Deli Meat Roast

Hy-Vee - Deli Thin Sliced Roast Beef, Thin Sliced (Corned Beef,
Regular)

Isaly's - All Deli Meat

John Soules Foods - Angus Carne Asada Fully Cooked Grilled Diced
Beef, Fully Cooked Angus Beef Steak, Fully Cooked Fajitas (Angus
Beef, Beef), Ready To Cook Beef For Fajitas

Jones Dairy Farm - Golden Brown All Natural Fully Cooked Beef
Sausage Links ●

Kayem - Deli Roast Beef (Seasoned Garlic **!!**, Seasoned Original **!!**),
Roast Beef Classic **!!**

Kirkland Signature - Fresh (Brisket, NY Strip, Organic Ground Beef,
Ribeye, Ribs, Roast, Steaks, Top Round), Frozen Ground Beef Patties
(Organic, Regular), Roast Beef (Canned In Beef Broth, Cooked
Sliced Top Round)

Kroger Brand - Smoked All Beef Sausage

Lloyd's - Center Cut Beef Ribs w/Original BBQ Sauce, Shredded Beef
In Original BBQ Sauce

Meijer Brand - Ground Beef (Chuck Fine, Fine)

Organic Prairie -
  Frozen Organic Retail (Beef Liver, Ground Beef Patties, Ground
    Chub, New York Strip Steak, Ribeye Steak)
  Organic (Beef Liver Steak, Brisket, Cubed, Flank Steak, Grass
    Fed Ground, Grass Fed Prime Rib Roast, Ground Beef, Pot
    Roast, Premium (Filet Mignon, Flat Iron Steak, New York Strip
    Steak, Ribeye Steak, Sirloin Steak, Steak Burger Patties), Short
    Ribs, Tri Tip Roast)
  Organic Retail Ground Beef (85% Lean, 90% Lean, Grass Fed
    85% Lean)
Oscar Mayer - Carving Board Deli Meat Roast Beef, Deli Fresh
  (French Dip Roast Beef, Slow Roasted Cured Roast Beef, Slow
  Roasted Roast Beef)
Private Selection - Deli Meat (Corned Beef, Roast Beef)
Publix - Premium Certified Beef
Publix GreenWise Market -
  Beef (Cubed Steak, For Stew)
  Beef Back Ribs
  Bottom Round (Regular, Steak)
  Brisket Flat
  Chuck (Eye Steak, Roast Boneless, Short Rib Boneless, Short Ribs,
    Steak Boneless)
  Eye Round (Regular, Steak)
  Flank Steak
  Flap Meat
  Flat Iron Steak
  Ground (Chuck, Chuck For Chili, Chuck Patties, Round,
    Round Patties)
  Porterhouse Steak
  Rib Eye (Roast Boneless, Steak Bone In, Steak Boneless)
  Rib Roast
  Round Cubes
  Rump Roast
  Shoulder (Roast Boneless, Steak)

B

    Sirloin (Flap Meat, For Kabobs, For Stir Fry, Tip Roast, Tip Side
        Steak, Tip Steak)

    Skirt Steak (Inside, Outside)

    Strip Steak Boneless

    T Bone Steak

    Tenderloin (Roast, Steak)

    Top Blade (Roast Boneless, Steak)

    Top Round (For Stir Fry, London Broil, Regular, Steak,
        Steak Thin Sliced)

    Top Sirloin (Filet Steak, Steak Boneless)

    Tri Tip (Roast, Steak)

Safeway - Deli Meat (All Thin Sliced & Regular)

Sara Lee - Deli Meat Slices Roast Beef

Spartan Brand - Corned Beef Hash

Sweet Bay - All Fresh Beef, All Fresh Veal

Thumann's - All Varieties ●

Trader Joe's - Fresh All Natural, Fully Cooked & Seasoned Beef Prime
    Rib, Shepherds Pie Beef

Wellshire Farms - Roast Beef Sliced ★

Beef Jerky...see Jerky/Beef Sticks

Beef Sticks...see Jerky/Beef Sticks

Beer

    Alchemist - Celia Saison

    Anheuser-Busch - Redbridge Beer

    Bard's - The Original Sorghum Malt Beer

    Bi-Aglut (Italy) - Birra 76 Lager

    Bosk - Gluten Free Homebrew Kit

    Brauerei Grieskirchen AG (Austria) - Beer Up Glutenfrei Pale Ale

    Carlsberg Brewery (Finland) - Saxon Premium Lager

    Fine Ale Club (England) - Against The Grain

    Fox Tail - Gluten Free Ale

    Glutaner (Belgium) - Glutenfrei Pils

    Green's (England) - Bottle Fermented (Blonde Ale, Brown Ale,
        Dark Ale), Discovery Amber Ale, Endeavor Dubbel Ale, Premium
        Golden Apple, Premium Pils, Quest Tripel Ale, Trailblazer

Hambleton Ales (England) - GFA, GFL

Harvester Brewing - Dark Ale, Experiment Ale, Pale Ale

Joseph James Brewing Co - Fox Tail Gluten Free Ale

Lakefront Brewery - New Grist Beer

Les Bieres de la Nouvelle France (Canada) - Messagere ★, Messagere Millet ★, Messagere Red Ale ★

New Planet - 3R Raspberry Ale ★, Off Grid Pale Ale ★, Tread Lightly Ale ★

O'Brien (Australia) - Brown Ale, Natural Light, Pale Ale, Premium Lager

Ramapo Valley Brewery ▲ - Passover Honey Lager

Schnitzer Brau (Germany) - German Hirse Premium, Hirse Lemon

Sprecher - Shakparo

St. Peter's Brewery (England) - G Free

Beets

*... *All Fresh Fruits & Vegetables Are Gluten-Free*

Del Monte - Sliced

Earthbound Farm - Organic Whole

Food Club Brand - Canned (Pickled, Sliced, Whole)

Hannaford Brand - Cut, Sliced, Whole

Hy-Vee - Fancy (Diced, Sliced)

Lowes Foods Brand - Canned (Cut, Whole)

Meijer Brand - Harvard Sweet Sour, Sliced (No Salt, Pickled, Regular), Whole (Medium, Pickled)

Publix - Canned

S&W - All Canned Vegetables, Pickled

Safeway Brand - Canned (Sliced, Whole), Pickled

Spartan Brand - Diced, Sliced, Whole

Trader Joe's - Steamed

Wegmans Brand - Canned FYFGA (Sliced (No Salt Added, Regular), Whole Regular), Harvard, Jarred (Sliced Pickled, Whole Pickled)

Berries

*... *All Fresh Fruits & Vegetables Are Gluten-Free*

Del Monte - Canned & Jarred Fruit (All Varieties), Fruit Snack Cups Plastic

B

Great Value Brand (Wal-Mart) - Frozen Berry Medley

Mariani - Dried (Berries & Apples ‼, Berries & Cherries ‼),
Enhanced Wellness (Berry Defense ‼, Berry Thrive ‼)

Meijer Brand - Frozen Berry Medley, Frozen Triple Berry Blend

Navitas Naturals ▲ - Goji (Berries, Powder), Goldenberries, Maqui
Powder, Mulberries, Powdered Acai

Nuts.com - Dried Fruit (Goji Berries ●, Mulberries ●, Simply
Boysenberries ●, Simply Elderberries ●)

Organic Nectars - Goji Berries

Publix - Frozen Mixed Berries

Spartan Brand - Frozen Berry Medley

Wegmans Brand - Frozen Berry Medley

Woodstock Farms - Organic (Frozen Mixed Berries, Goji)

Beverages...see Drinks/Juice

Biscotti

Choices Rice Bakery ▲ - Cranberry Almond Spice

Eena Kadeena ▲ - Mandel Cookie Mix

Ener-G ▲ - Chocolate, Chocolate Chip, Cranberry, Raisin

Foods By George - Currant Nut & Seed

Ginny Bakes ▲ - Tuscan Sunshine Mix ●, Tuscan Sunshine ●

JK Gourmet - Almond Raisin, Dried Peach & Pistachio, Lemon Poppy
Seed, Orange Cranberry

Mariposa Artisan-Crafted Gluten-Free ▲ - Almond, Cinnamon
Toast, Ginger Spice

My Dad's Gluten Free Bakery ▲ - Chocolate Chip ●

Orgran ▲ - Amaretti, Classic Chocolate

Pamela's Products ▲ - Almond Anise, Chocolate Walnut, Lemon
Almond

PatsyPie - Almond Raisin, Chocolate Chip, Cranberry Orange, Pecan

Really Great Food Company ▲ - Anise, Lemon Poppy

Shabtai ▲ - Chocolate Chip

Silly Yak Bakery - GF Almond Biscotti ●

Sorella ▲ - Biscottines (Chocolate Almond, Chocolate Chip,
Cinnamon Swirl, Hazelnut, Vanilla)

biscuits/biscuit mix

B

The Grain Exchange - Chocolate Chip
Trenipoti - Gluten Free ●
West Meadow Farm Bakery - Almond Coconut (Biscotti ●, Biscotti Bites ●), Almond Joyful ●, Classic Almond (Biscotti ●, Biscotti Bites ●), Vermont Maple Walnut (Biscotti ●, Biscotti Bites ●)

Biscuits/Biscuit Mix

1-2-3 Gluten Free ▲ - Southern Glory Biscuits ●
Abundant Life Foods ▲ - Biscuit Mix
Andrea's Gluten Free ▲ - Biscuit Dough
Augason Farms ▲ - Gluten Free Buttermilk Biscuit Mix ●
Better Batter - Pancake & Biscuit Mix ●
Bi-Aglut - Biscottino, Biscuits, Gocce, Granulated Biscuits, Ruote, Rustici
Bisquick ▲ - Gluten Free Pancake & Baking Mix
Bob's Red Mill ▲ - Gluten Free Biscuit & Baking Mix ★
Cause You're Special ▲ - Hearty Biscuit Mix
Choices Rice Bakery ▲ - Buttermilk, Cornbread
Food-Tek Quick-Bake - Homestyle Biscuit Mix ★
Gifts Of Nature ▲ - Buttermilk Biscuit & Baking Mix ●
Grandma Ferdon's ▲ - Baking Powder Biscuit Mix ●, Biscuits (Baking Powder ●, Cinnamon Raisin ●)
Kneaded Specialties ▲ - Honey Butter ●
Mixes From The Heartland ▲ - Biscuit Mix (Country ●, Garlic Roasted Pepper ●, Gluten Free Sun Dried Tomato Biscuit Mix ●)
Namaste Foods ▲ - Biscuits Piecrust & More Mix
Nuts.com - Gluten Free Biscuit Mix ●
Really Great Food Company ▲ - Biscuit Loaf Mix, Old Time Biscuit Mix, Spinach & Cheese Biscuit Mix Sugar Free
Silly Yak Bakery - GF Bites (Cheddar Bites ●, Pepperoni Bites ●)
Voyaging Foods - Taro Cakes ●
Whole Foods Market Gluten Free Bakehouse ▲ - Cheddar Biscuits, Cream Biscuits
ZeroGrano - Chocolate ZeroGrano Plus

B **Blackberries**
  ... *All Fresh Fruits & Vegetables Are Gluten-Free*
  Food Club Brand - Frozen
  Great Value Brand (Wal-Mart) - Frozen
  Lowes Foods Brand - Frozen
  Meijer Brand - Frozen
  Nuts.com - Dried Blackberries (Dried ●, Simply ●)
  Publix - Frozen
  Safeway Brand - Frozen
  Spartan Brand - Frozen
  Wegmans Brand - Frozen
  Winn Dixie - Frozen
  Woodstock Farms - Organic Frozen Blackberries

Blueberries
  ... *All Fresh Fruits & Vegetables Are Gluten-Free*
  Augason Farms ▲ - Gluten Free Freeze Dried Whole ●
  C & W - Frozen ‼
  Food Club Brand - Frozen
  Great Value Brand (Wal-Mart) - Frozen
  Hy-Vee - Frozen
  Lowes Foods Brand - Frozen
  Mariani - Dried Wild ‼
  Meijer Brand - Frozen (Organic, Regular)
  Nuts.com - Dried Blueberries (Dried ●, Natural Dried ●, Natural
    Dried Juice Infused ●, Organic Wild ●, Simply ●)
  O Organics - Frozen
  Oskri Organics - Dried Blueberries
  Publix - Frozen
  Safeway Brand - Frozen
  Spartan Brand - Frozen
  Trader Joe's - Frozen (Fresh Blueberries, Organic Wild Blueberries,
    Wild Boreal)
  Wegmans Brand - Frozen
  Winn Dixie - Frozen
  Woodstock Farms - Dried, Organic Frozen Wild Blueberries

Bok Choy

   ... *All Fresh Fruits & Vegetables Are Gluten-Free*

Bologna

   Applegate - Deli Counter Uncured Turkey **!**, Organic Uncured Turkey **!**, Turkey Bologna **!**

   Armour - Deli (Beef Bologna, Turkey Pork Chicken Beef Bologna)

   Boar's Head - All Varieties

   Di Lusso - Beef

   Dietz & Watson ▲ - Beef ●, Black Forest German ●, Gourmet Lite ●, Natural Casing Classic Ring ●, Original ●, Pre Sliced (Beef ●, Regular ●)

   Eckrich - Deli Meat (Beef, Fried, Garlic, Low Sodium, Meat), Lunch Meat Bologna (Beef, Lite, Regular, Ring)

   Empire Kosher - Turkey Bologna Slices

   Five Star Brand ▲ - Beef, Leona, Natural Casing, Pork & Beef

   Garrett County Farms - Sliced Beef Bologna ★

   Hebrew National - Beef, Lean Beef

   Hill Country Fare H-E-B - Bologna (Beef, Meat)

   Honeysuckle White - Turkey

   Hy-Vee - Garlic, German Brand, Regular, Thick, Thin, Turkey

   Kayem - Beef **!!**, German Style **!!**, Large **!!**, Original **!!**

   Old Wisconsin - Ring Bologna

   Oscar Mayer - Deli Meat Variety Pack Bologna/Chopped Ham/White Smoked Turkey

   Publix - Deli Pre Pack Sliced Lunch Meat German Bologna

   Publix GreenWise Market - Beef

   Wellshire Farms - Sliced Beef Bologna ★

Bouillon/Bouillon Cubes

   Better Than Bouillon - Au Jus, Beef, Chicken, Chili, Clam, Fish, Ham, Kosher Passover (Chicken, Vegetable), Lobster, Organic (Beef, Chicken, Mushroom, Turkey, Vegetable), Reduced Sodium Chicken, Turkey, Vegetarian (No Beef, No Chicken)

   Celifibr ▲ - Bouillon Cubes (Vegetable Medley, Vegetarian Beef, Vegetarian Chicken)

B

Edward & Sons - Garden Veggie, Low Sodium Veggie, Not Beef, Not Chick'n

El Peto ▲ - Soup Concentrate (Beef, Chicken, Onion, Tomato, Tomato Vegetable, Vegetable)

Food Club Brand - Beef Cubes

Herb-Ox - Instant Powder (Beef, Chicken), Packets/Cubes (Beef, Chicken), Sodium Free (Granulated (Beef, Chicken), Packets (Beef, Chicken))

Hy-Vee - Bouillon Cubes (Beef, Chicken), Instant Bouillon (Beef, Chicken)

Kum Chun - Chicken Bouillon Powder

Lee Kum Kee - Chicken Bouillon Powder

Luda H - Bouillon Mix (Beef, Chicken, Vegetable)

Marigold - Organic (Swiss Vegetable (Reduced Salt ★, Regular ★), Vegetable (Reduced Salt ★, Regular ★, Yeast Free ★)), Swiss Vegetable (Reduced Salt ★, Regular ★)

Massel - Ultracubes (Beef Style, Chicken Style, Vegetable)

Spartan Brand - Soup Bouillon Cube (Beef, Chicken), Soup Bouillon Granules (Beef, Chicken)

Bourbon

... *All Distilled Alcohol Is Gluten-Free*

Bowls

Amy's - Broccoli & Cheddar Bake ★, Brown Rice & Vegetable Bowl (Light In Sodium ★, Regular ★), Brown Rice Black Eyed Peas & Veggies Bowl ★, Cream Of Rice Hot Cereal ★, Light & Lean Soft Taco Fiesta ★, Mexican Casserole (Light In Sodium ★, Regular ★), Non Dairy Rice Pasta Baked Ziti Bowl ★, Santa Fe Enchilada ★, Teriyaki ★, Tortilla Casserole & Black Beans ★

Chi-Chi's - Fiesta Plates (Creamy Chipotle Chicken, Salsa Chicken, Savory Garlic Chicken)

Helen's Kitchen - Burrito Bowls (Baja Pinto Bean Bowl, Fiesta Black Bean Bowl, Veggie Fajita Bowl), Homestyle Black Eyed Peas Bowl

Lundberg ▲ - Organic Brown Rice Bowls (Country Wild, Long Grain, Short Grain)

B

Organic Bistro - Asian Style Coconut Lemongrass w/Chicken, Sesame Ginger Wild Salmon, Thai Style Red Curry w/Beef, Thai Style Yellow Curry w/Chicken

Simply Asia - Rice Noodle Soup Bowl (Garlic Sesame, Sesame Chicken, Spring Vegetable)

Tabatchnick - Microwavable Bowl (Balsamic Tomato & Rice, Southwest Bean, Split Pea, Vegetarian Chili)

Thai Kitchen - Rice Noodle Soup Bowl (Lemongrass & Chili, Roasted Garlic, Spring Onion, Thai Ginger & Vegetables)

Bratwurst...see Sausage

Bread

Against The Grain Gourmet ▲ - Baguette (Fresh Rosemary, Original)

Aleia's ▲ - Cinnamon Raisin ●, Farmhouse White ●

Amy's - Sandwich Rounds ★

Andrea's Gluten Free ▲ - Loaf Multigrain, Pumpkin Mini Loaf

Apple's Bakery ▲ - Gluten Free Loaf (Banana Walnut, Olive Oil, Poppyseed, Pumpkin Raisin, Tea Bread Combination, White Sandwich)

Bi-Aglut - Baguette, Home Style, Rustic Style Bread, Sesame Breadsticks, Toasted Bread, White Sliced

Bodhi's Bakehouse - Chia Linseed, Gluten & Yeast Free

Canyon Bakehouse ▲ - Cinnamon Raisin, Colorado Caraway, Mountain White, Rosemary & Thyme Focaccia, San Juan 7 Grain

Celiac Specialties ▲ - Bread (Apple Cinnamon, Cheddar Herb, Cinnamon Raisin, Flat, Flaxseed, Light White, Multigrain, Navy Bean, White), Garlic Bread, Multigrain Sandwich

Choices Rice Bakery ▲ - Brown Rice (Cinnamon Raisin, Foccacia, Regular), Flaxseed, Multiseed, Quinoa Multigrain, Soda (Cinnamon Raisin, Regular), Sourdough, Sweet Loaves (Banana, Blueberry, Chocolate, Gingerbread, Lemon Poppy, No Egg (Banana, Chocolate), Pumpkin, Pumpkin Cranberry)

Deerfields Gluten Free Bakery ▲ - Gluten Free (Multi Grain, White), Gluten Free Mini Baguette

B

El Peto ▲ - Cheese, Gourmet, Italian Style, Millet, Potato, Raisin, Supreme Italian Style, Tapioca, White, White Rice, Whole Grain (Brown, Flax Seed, Multi Grain), Whole Grain Brown Sandwich, Yeast Free (Flax Seed, Potato, Whole Grain Brown)

Ener-G ▲ - Sliced Breads (Brown Rice, Corn, Egg Free Raisin, High Fiber, Light (Brown Rice, Tapioca, White Rice, White Rice Flax), Papas, Rice Starch, Seattle Brown, Tapioca Loaf (Regular Sliced, Thin Sliced), White Rice (Flax, Regular), Yeast Free (Brown Rice, Flax Meal, White Rice)), Specialty Bread Focaccia Crust, Specialty Breads (Bread Crumbs, Communion Wafers, Plain Croutons)

Everybody Eats ▲ - Baguette, Banana Bread, Egg Challah, Multigrain High Fiber Loaf, White Bread

Food For Life - Brown Rice, Raisin Pecan, Wheat & Gluten Free (Bhutanese Red Rice, Millet, Rice Almond, Rice Pecan, White Rice, Yeast Free (Brown Rice, Multi Seed Rice))

French Meadow Bakery - Gluten Free (Cinnamon Raisin Bread ●, Multigrain Bread ●, Sandwich Bread ●)

Gillian's Foods ▲ - Cinnamon Raisin Loaf ●, Crostini ●, French Loaf ●, Rye No Rye Loaf ●, Sandwich Loaf ●

Glutano - Dreikornbrot, Mehrkornbrot, Mehrkornbrötchen, Weissbrot

Gluten Free Life ▲ - Country Brown Pure, Multi Grain Pure, Pumpernickel

Gluten-Free Creations ▲ - Awelicious Bread ●, Awelicious Nutty Whole Grain Bread ●, Cheddar Cheese ●, Fruit & Nut ●, Herb Baguettes ●, Herb Loaf Bread ●, Honey Oat ●, Mock Rye Bread w/ Caraway Seeds ●, Pumpkin ●, Sandwich ●, Seeded Multigrain ●, White ●

GlutenOut - Pantondi ★

Glutino ▲ - English Muffins, Genius (Multigrain Sandwich, White Sandwich), Premium (Cinnamon & Raisin, Fiber, Flaxseed, Harvest Corn)

Grandma Ferdon's ▲ - Bread Sticks ●, Buttermilk ●, Cinnamon Raisin ●, Cocktail Pumpernickel ●, Egg ●, Pumpernickel ●

bread

Heaven Mills ▲ - Challa (Gluten & Egg Free ●, Gluten & Sugar Free ●, Gluten Egg & Sugar Free ●, Gluten Free ●), Croissants (Apricot ●, Raspberry ●, Vanilla ●), Gluten Free Vunder Bread (Herb ●, Plain ●), Mezonos Bread ●, Oat Bread (Gluten & Egg Free ●, Gluten & Sugar Free ●, Gluten Egg & Sugar Free ●, Gluten Free ●), Pita Bread ●

Jensen's Bread And Bakeries ▲ - Golden Sandwich Bread ●, Multi Grain & Seed Bread ●, Perfect Sandwich Bread ●

Joan's GF Great Bakes ▲ - Italian

Katz Gluten Free ▲ - Bread (White ●, Whole Grain ●), Challah (Large Braided ●, Sliced ●), Chocolate Strip ●, Cinnamon Strip ●, Honey Loaf ●, Kishka Kugel ●, Wholesome ●

Kinnikinnick ▲ - Brown Sandwich, Festive, Many Wonder Multigrain Rice, Robins Honey Brown Rice, Soft (Multigrain, White), Sunflower Flax Rice, Tapioca Rice (Cheese, Italian White, Raisin, Regular), White Sandwich, Yeast Free (Candadi Multigrain Rice, Tapioca)

Kneaded Specialties ▲ - Deluxe Sandwich ●, French Bread Loaf ●, Vegan (Deluxe ●, White ●), White Sandwich ●

Lakewood Matzoh ▲ - Oat Matzoh (Hand Made ●, Machine Made ●)

Lydia's Organics - Sunflower Seed

Mariposa Artisan-Crafted Gluten-Free ▲ - Crostini, Foccaccia, Loaves (Multi Grain, Sandwich Bread), Rustic Baguettes

Molly's Gluten-Free Bakery ▲ - Cocktail Mock Rye, Loaves (Ancient Grains, French (Jumbo, Regular, Rustic, Sandwich, Small), Italian Herb, Mock Rye (Regular, Rustic), White), Pita

Nu-World Foods ▲ - Flatbread Amaranth (Buckwheat, Garbanzo, Sorghum)

O'Doughs Bakery ▲ - Loaf (Flax ●, White ●)

PaneRiso ▲ - Brown Rice ●, Flax Seed ●, No Rye Rye ●, Raisin & Cinnamon Bread ●, White Rice ●

Pure Knead ▲ - Baguette ●, Boule (Harvest Grain ●, Kalamata Olive ●, Sun Dried Tomato ●), Pita ●, Table Loaves ●

Pure Market Express ▲ - Garlic ●, Onion ●

Quejos ▲ - Non Dairy (Banana Bread, Banana Loaf)

B

Rose's Bakery ▲ - Banana, French Bread (Loaf, Rolls), Millet, Orange Cranberry Tea, Pita, Sandwich Bread, Seeded Sandwich Bread, Teff

Rudi's Gluten-Free Bakery - Cinnamon Raisin ●, Multigrain ●, Original ●

Russo's Gluten Free Gourmet ▲ - Italian

Sandwich Petals - Flatbread (Agave Grain, Chimayo Red Chile, Spinach Garlic)

Schar ▲ - Baguette, Bread (Classic White, Deli Style, Hearty Grain, Hearty White, Multigrain)

Silly Yak Bakery -

CFGF (Brown Rice (Honey ●, Honey Swirl ●), Cinnamon Apple Swirl ●, Cinnamon Raisin ●, Cinnamon Swirl ●, Cranberry Orange Sweet ●, Cranberry Orange Yeast ●, Garlic Chive ●, Multi Seed ●, Onion Dill ●, Raisin Walnut ●, Rice ●, Tomato Basil ●)

GF (Amaranth ●, Bavarian ●, Buckwheat ●, Caraway ●, Cheddar Onion ●, Cinnamon Apple Swirl ●, Cinnamon Raisin Swirl ●, Cinnamon Swirl ●, Classic Rice ●, Cottage Dill ●, Cranberry Orange Toasting ●, Cranberry Wild Rice ●, Garlic Cheddar ●, Holiday ●, Holly's Health ●, Honey Brown Rice ●, Honey Oat ●, Honey Raisin Brown Rice ●, Irish Soda ●, Jalapeño Cheddar ●, Multi Seed Montina ●, Onion Dill Montina ●, Quinoa Poppy Seed ●, Raisin Walnut Montina ●, Rosemary Red Onion ●, Sesame Sunflower Millet ●, Sourdough ●, Spinach Feta ●, Sweet Bread (Banana ●, Blueberry ●, Blueberry Peach ●, Cherry Almond ●, Cranberry Almond ●, Cranberry Orange Sweet ●, Lemon Blueberry ●, Lemon Poppy Seed ●, Peach Rice ●, Pumpkin ●, Raspberry ●), Teff & Pumpkin Seed ●, Tomato Basil Feta ●, Tomato Parmesan Spinach ●, Wild Rice & Chives ●)

Sweet Christine's Bakery - Baguette ●, Raisin ●, Sandwich ●

Three Bakers ▲ - 7 Ancient Grain, Whole Grain Rye Style, Whole Grain White

Toovaloo - Flatbread (Artisan, Gluten Free)

Trader Joe's - Ryeless "Rye"

Udi's Gluten Free Foods ▲ - Gluten Free (Cinnamon Raisin ●, Millet Chia ●, Omega Flax & Fiber ●, White Sandwich ●, Whole Grain ●)

Venice Bakery - Gluten Free (Flatbread ●, Focaccia Bread ●)

Voyaging Foods - Vegan Pumpkin Taro Mini Loaves ●

West Meadow Farm Bakery - Cinnamon Raisin ●, Lynne's Mocking Rye ●, Oatrageous Oatmeal ●, Super Seeded ●, West Meadow White ●

Whole Foods Market Gluten Free Bakehouse ▲ - Bread (Banana, Cinnamon Raisin, Honey Oat, Light White Sandwich, Prairie, Sandwich, Sundried Tomato & Garlic)

Bread Mix

1-2-3 Gluten Free ▲ - Aaron's Favorite Rolls ●, Meredith's Marvelous Muffin/Quickbread Mix ●, Olivia's Outstanding Multi Purpose Fortified Flour Mix ●

Abundant Life Foods ▲ - White Bread Mix

AgVantage Naturals ▲ - Master Blend Baking Mix ●, Multi Grain Bread Mix ●, Sandwich Bread Mix ●

Arnel's Originals - Bread Mix

Arrowhead Mills - Gluten Free All Purpose Baking Mix

Augason Farms ▲ - Gluten Free French Bread Mix ●

Authentic Foods ▲ - Pancake & Baking Mix ●, White Bread Mix ●, Wholesome Bread Mix ●

Bi-Aglut - Regular

Bloomfield Farms ▲ - Gluten Free Loaf ●

Bob's Red Mill ▲ - Gluten Free Biscuit & Baking Mix ★, Gluten Free Bread Mix (Cinnamon Raisin ★, Hearty Whole Grain ★, Homemade Wonderful ★)

Breads From Anna ▲ - Bread Mix (Banana, Classic Herb, Gluten Free, Gluten Free & Yeast Free All Purpose, Original Gluten Free, Pumpkin)

Bready - Cha Cha Cheddar ●, Cherish My Chocolate Cake Mix ●, Gluten Free Bread Mix (Apple Of My Eye ●, Heavenly White ●, Nearly Dearly Rye ●, Tuscan Love Affair ●), Go Bananas ●, Nuts About You ●, Squeeze My Buns Gluten Free Hamburger Bun Mix ●, That's Amore Gluten Free Pizza Dough ●

B

C4C - Gluten Free Flour

Cause You're Special ▲ - Bread Mix (Homestyle White, Traditional French)

Chebe ▲ - Bread Mix (All Purpose ●, Cinnamon Rolls ●, Focaccia Mix ●, Original Cheese ●, Pizza Crust ●), Frozen Dough (Bread Sticks ●, Ciabatta Rolls ●, Original Cheese ●, Pizza Crust ●, Tomato Basil Bread Sticks ●), Garlic Onion Breadsticks Mix ●

El Peto ▲ - Breadmaker (Brown, Italian, Potato, White)

Ener-G ▲ - Mix (Corn, Potato, Rice)

Fearn - Baking Mix (Brown Rice **!!**, Rice **!!**)

Food-Tek Fast & Fresh - White Bread Mix ★

Gifts Of Nature ▲ - Sandwich White Bread & Roll Mix ●

Gillian's Foods ▲ - All Purpose Baking Mix ●, French Bread Mix ●

Gluten Free Pantry ▲ - Favorite Sandwich Bread Mix, French Bread & Pizza Mix, Yankee Cornbread Mix

Gluten-Free Creations ▲ - Bread Mix Cinnamon Raisin ●

Grandma Ferdon's ▲ - Banana Bread Muffin Mix ●, Buttermilk Bread Mix ●, Frozen Buttermilk Bread Dough ●

Hodgson Mill ▲ - Gluten Free (Bread Mix, Multi Purpose Baking Mix)

Jules Gluten Free ▲ - Bread Mix ●

King Arthur Flour ▲ - Gluten Free Bread Mix ●

Kinnikinnick ▲ - Candadi Yeast Free Rice, Cornbread & Muffin Mix, Kinni Kwik Bread & Bun Mix

Lakewood Matzoh ▲ - Matzoh Meal ●

Laurel's Sweet Treats ▲ - Banzo Bread, Dinner Rolls

Maninis ▲ - Classic Peasant ●, Country Oat ●, Multi Purpose Flour Mix ●, Rustic Multigrain ●

Mixes From The Heartland ▲ - Sweet Bread Mix (Banana ●, Banana Flax Seed ●, Blueberry ●, Cranberry ●, Hawaiian ●)

Montana Gluten Free ▲ - Toasted Oat ●

Mrs. Crimble's - Bread Mix

Namaste Foods ▲ - Bread Mix

Nuts.com - Gluten Free (Bread Mix (Cinnamon Raisin ●, Hearty Whole Grain ●, Homemade ●), Cornbread Mix ●)

B

Orgran ▲ - Bread Mix (Alternative Grain Wholemeal, Easy Bake)

Pamela's Products ▲ - Baking & Pancake Mix, Bread Mix & Flour Blend, Gluten Free Bread Mix

PaneRiso ▲ - Rice Bread & Baking Mix

Really Great Food Company ▲ - Bread Mix (Brown Rice, Dark European, French/Country Farm, Home Style Cornbread, Old Fashioned Cinnamon, Original White, Rye Style), Irish Soda

Sanavi - Harifen Low Protein

Sanavi Harisin - Bread & Pastry Mix

Schar ▲ - Classic White Bread Mix

Silly Yak Bakery - GF Classic Rice Bread Mix ●

Simply Organic ▲ - Gluten Free Banana Bread Mix ●

Sof'ella - Gluten Free All Purpose Baking Mix ★

Something Good ▲ - Classic ★, Super Grain ★

The Cravings Place ▲ - Create Your Own

The Pure Pantry ▲ - Pancake & Baking Mix (Organic Buckwheat Flax ●, Organic Old Fashioned ●)

Timtana Gluten Free ▲ - Bread Mix (Gluten Free Timtana Dark ●, Gluten Free Timtana Lite Brown ●), PrOatina Pumpkin Pastry Mix ●

Breadcrumbs...see Coating

Breadsticks

Bi-Aglut

Chebe ▲ - Garlic & Onion Breadsticks Mix ●, Tomato Basil Frozen Dough ●

Farmer - Grissini

Pure Knead ▲ - Breadsticks ●

Sanavi Harisin - Bastoncitos

Schar ▲ - Italian Breadsticks

Sweet Christine's Bakery - Cinnamon Sticks ●

Breakfast

Amy's - Gluten Free Tofu Scramble Breakfast Wrap ★, Mexican Tofu Scramble ★

Cedarlane - Egg White Omelette (Green Chile Cheese & Ranchero Sauce, Spinach & Mushroom, Uncured Turkey Bacon Vegetable & Cheese)

B

Celiac Specialties ▲ - Breakfast Rolls (Apple, Blueberry), Breakfast Sandwiches

Farmer John - Pork Roll Sausage (Mild, Spicy), Pork Sausage Links (Chorizo Style, Classic, Old Fashioned Maple, Original Lower Fat), Pork Sausage Patties (Mild, Original Lower Fat, Spicy)

Great Value Brand (Wal-Mart) - Sausage (Fully Cooked (Beef Breakfast Patties, Original Pork Patties, Pork Links, Turkey Breakfast Patties), Maple Pork Patties, Spicy Pork Patties)

Honeysuckle White - Breakfast Sausage (Links, Patties, Roll)

Ian's - Wheat Free Gluten Free Recipe French Toast Sticks, Wheat Free Gluten Free Wafflewiches (Egg & Maple Cheddar, Maple Sausage & Egg)

Isernio's - Sausage (Chicken Apple Link ●, Chicken Breakfast Link ●, Pork Breakfast Link ●), Sausage Roll (Chicken Breakfast Sausage ●, Spicy Chicken Breakfast Sausage ●)

Jennie-O Turkey Store - Breakfast Lover's Turkey Sausage, Fresh Breakfast Sausage (Maple Links, Mild Links, Mild Patties)

Jimmy Dean -

Breakfast Bowls (Bacon Eggs Potatoes & Cheddar Cheese, Delights (Ham, Turkey Sausage), Ham Eggs Potatoes & Cheddar Cheese, Sausage Eggs Potatoes & Cheddar Cheese)

Breakfast Skillets (Bacon, Ham, Sausage)

Fresh Sausage (Maple Links, Original Links, Original Patties)

Fully Cooked Hearty Sausage Crumbles (Hot, Original, Turkey)

Fully Cooked Sausage Links (Maple, Original, Turkey)

Fully Cooked Sausage Patties (Hot, Maple, Original, Turkey)

Heat 'N Serve (Sausage Links (Hot, Maple, Original, Turkey), Sausage Patties (Original, Turkey)

Omelets (Ham & Cheese, Sausage & Cheese, Three Cheese)

Pork Roll Sausage (All Natural Regular, Country Mild, Hot, Italian, Maple, Reduced Fat, Regular, Sage)

Johnsonville - Sausage Links (Brown Sugar & Honey, Original, Vermont Maple Syrup, Wisconsin Cheddar Cheese), Sausage Patties (Original, Vermont Maple Syrup)

Jones Dairy Farm -
   All Natural (Pork Sausage (Original Roll ●, Patties ●), Pork Sausage
      Links (& Rice ●, Hearty ●, Little ●, Little Maple ●)),
   Golden Brown All Natural Fully Cooked (Sausage & Rice Links
      (Light ●, Regular ●), Sausage Links (Beef ●, Maple ●, Mild ●, Pork
      & Uncured Bacon ●, Spicy Pork ●, Turkey ●), Sausage Patties
      (Maple ●, Mild ●))

Medifast - Original Style Eggs ●

Van's Natural Foods - Wheat & Gluten Free Cinnamon French Toast
   Sticks ★

Broccoli
   ... *All Fresh Fruits & Vegetables Are Gluten-Free

Birds Eye - All Plain Frozen Vegetables

C & W - All Plain Frozen Vegetables ‼

Dr. Praeger's - Broccoli Littles !

Earthbound Farm - Organic Whole

Food Club Brand - Frozen (Chopped, Cut, Spears, Steamin' Easy
   Broccoli Cuts)

Freshlike - Frozen Plain Broccoli

Green Giant - Frozen (Broccoli & Cheese Sauce, Broccoli
   Cauliflower Carrots & Cheese Sauce), Valley Fresh Steamers
   (Broccoli Cuts, Chopped Broccoli, Select Broccoli Florets)

Hy-Vee - Frozen (Chopped, Cuts, Florets)

Lowes Foods Brand - Frozen (Chopped, Cut, Deluxe Baby Florets,
   Deluxe Florets, Spears)

Meijer Brand - Frozen (Chopped, Cuts (Original, Steamer), Florets
   (California, Organic), Spears)

Mezzetta ▲ - Broccoli Flowerettes

Midwest Country Fare - Frozen (Chopped, Cuts)

Nuts.com - Simply Broccoli Freeze Dried Vegetables ●

Pictsweet - All Plain Frozen Vegetables

Private Selection - Frozen Broccoli Florets

Publix - Frozen (Chopped, Cuts, Spears)

Safeway Brand - Frozen (Cuts, Florets, Steam In Bag)

Spartan Brand - Frozen (Cuts, Florets)

B

    Trader Joe's - Frozen Broccoli Florets, Frozen Organic Broccoli Florets

    Wegmans Brand - Broccoli (Chopped, Cuts), Broccoli Cuts & Cauliflower Florets (& Carrots, Regular), Spears

    Winn Dixie - Frozen (Chopped, Cuts, Florets, Spears), Steamable Broccoli Cut

    Woodstock Farms - Organic Frozen Broccoli Florets

Broth

    Baxters - Chicken

    Bowman & Landes - Chicken, Turkey

    Central Market H-E-B - Organics (Beef, Free Range Chicken, Low Sodium Chicken, Vegetable)

    College Inn Broth - Beef (Organic, Tender Bold), Chicken (Fat Free Low Sodium, No MSG Light), Garden Vegetable, White Wine & Herb Culinary

    Food Club Brand - Beef, Chicken *(Box Only)* Regular

    Full Circle - Beef !, Chicken !, Vegetable !

    H-E-B - Beef (Reduced Sodium, Regular), Chicken (Reduced Sodium, Regular)

    Hannaford Brand - Chicken *(Only In Resealable Box)*, Chicken & Beef (Boxed, Canned Reduced Sodium)

    Hill Country Fare H-E-B - Reduced Sodium Chicken

    Hy-Vee - Chicken (Box, Can, Fat Free), Vegetable Stock

    Imagine - Low Sodium (Beef, Free Range Chicken, Vegetable), No Chicken, Regular (Beef, Free Range Chicken, Vegetable)

    Kroger Brand - Beef, Chicken (Fat Free, Regular)

    Lowes Foods Brand - Beef, Chicken (Low Sodium, Regular)

    Meijer Brand - Chicken (Aseptic, First Line, Original)

    Midwest Country Fare - Chicken

    Nature's Basket - Organic (Chicken Low Sodium, Vegetable Fat Free)

    Nature's Place - Boxed Broth (Chicken, Vegetable)

    O Organics - Chicken, Low Sodium Chicken, Vegetable

    Pacific Natural Foods - Natural (Beef, Free Range Chicken), Organic (Beef, Free Range Chicken, Low Sodium (Beef, Chicken, Vegetable), Mushroom, Vegetable)

    Progresso - Beef Flavored, Chicken (Reduced Sodium, Regular)

B

Safeway Brand - Beef Box, Canned Beef, Chicken (Box, Canned (Fat Free Reduced Sodium, Regular))

Savory Choice - Concentrate (Beef, Chicken, Turkey, Vegetable)

Shelton's - Chicken (Fat Free Low Sodium, Regular), Organic (Chicken, Chicken Fat Free Low Sodium)

Spartan Brand - Beef, Chicken

Swanson - Chicken Broth (Canned, Carton), Natural Goodness Chicken Broth (Canned, Carton), Vegetable Broth Canned

Tabatchnick - Chicken, Gourmet Beef, Organic Chicken, Passover Chicken, Vegetable

Trader Joe's - Organic (Hearty Vegetable ‼, Low Sodium Chicken ‼), Savory Broth Concentrate Reduced Sodium ‼

Winn Dixie - Canned (Clear Beef, Clear Chicken)

Wolfgang Puck - Organic (Free Range Chicken, Vegetable)

Brown Sugar...see Sugar

Brownies/Brownie Mix

1-2-3 Gluten Free ▲ - Devilishly Decadent Brownies Mix ●, Divinely Decadent Brownies Mix ●

3 Fellers Bakery ▲ - Chocolate Brownies (Mint ●, Peanut Butter ●, Raspberry ●, Regular ●)

Abundant Life Foods ▲ - Brownie Mix (Fudge, Gluten Free Blonde, Mocha)

Andrea's Gluten Free ▲ - Red Velvet Cheesecake Brownies

Arrowhead Mills - Gluten Free Brownie Mix

Augason Farms ▲ - Gluten Free Chocolate Chip Brownie Mix ●

Authentic Foods ▲ - Double Chocolate Brownie Mix ●

Better Batter - Fudge Brownie Mix ●

Betty Crocker ▲ - Gluten Free Chocolate Brownie Mix

Bloomfield Farms ▲ - Gluten Free Brownie Mix ●

Bob's Red Mill ▲ - Gluten Free Brownie Mix ★

Breads From Anna ▲ - Black Bean Brownie Mix

Breakaway Bakery ▲ - Brownies ●

Cause You're Special ▲ - Chocolate Fudge

Celiac Specialties ▲ - Brownie Mix, Brownies (Plain, Round, Tray)

B

Cherrybrook Kitchen - Gluten Free Fudge Brownie Mix *(Box Must Say Gluten Free)* ★

Choices Rice Bakery ▲ - Bite Sized, Brownies, Cheesecake Brownies

Cookies For Me - Brownie Bites, Brownies

Crave Bakery ▲ - Brownies (Dark Chocolate, Toasted Pecan)

Deerfields Gluten Free Bakery ▲ - Triple Chocolate Gluten Free Brownie

Dowd & Rogers ▲ - Brownie Mix Dark Chocolate

El Peto ▲ - Brownie Mix, Corn Free, Pure Bliss Mini Brownies

Ener-G ▲ - Brownies

Everybody Eats ▲ - Brownies Fudge

Food-Tek Fast & Fresh - Gooey Brownie Decadence Mix ★

Foods By George ▲ - Brownies

Frankly Natural Bakers - Gluten Free Brownies (Cherry Berry, Java Jive, Misty Mint, Wacky Walnut)

French Meadow Bakery - Gluten Free Fudge Brownies ●

Gifts Of Nature ▲ - Chocolate Fudge Brownie Mix ●

Gillian's Foods ▲ - Brownie Mix ●, Brownies ●

Ginny Bakes ▲ - Lovely Brownie Bliss ●

Gluten Free Life ▲ - Brownie Mix, Brownies, The Ultimate Gluten Free Cake Muffin & Brownie Mix

Gluten Free Pantry ▲ - Chocolate Truffle Brownie Mix

Gluten-Free Creations ▲ - Rich Brownie Mix ●, Rich Brownies ●

Gluten-Free Naturals - Brownie Mix

Gopal's - Raw Brownie (Cherry, Original)

Grandma Ferdon's ▲ - Brownies ●

Hodgson Mill ▲ - Gluten Free Brownie Mix

Hol Grain ▲ - Chocolate Brownie Mix ●

King Arthur Flour ▲ - Gluten Free Brownie Mix ●

Kinnikinnick ▲ - JB Brownie Squares

Kneaded Specialties ▲ - Cherry Bites ●, Ooey Gooey Fudge ●

Laurel's Sweet Treats ▲ - Chocolate Dream Brownie Mix

Mariposa Artisan-Crafted Gluten-Free ▲ - Truffle Brownies (Triple Chocolate, Walnut)

Medifast - Brownie ●

Mixes From The Heartland ▲ - Brownie Mix (Microwave ●, Pumpkin ●, Sweet Potato ●)

Molly's Gluten-Free Bakery ▲ - Brownies (Fudge, Mint Chocolate)

Moondance - All Flavors

Mrs. Crimble's - Double Chocolate Brownies

Namaste Foods ▲ - Blondie Mix, Brownie Mix

Nuts.com - Gluten Free Brownie Mix ●

Pamela's Products ▲ - Chocolate Brownie Mix

PatsyPie - Double Chocolate Minis

Pure Knead ▲ - Dark Chocolate Brownies ●

Quejos ▲ - Non Dairy (Chocolate, Dark Chocolate)

Really Great Food Company ▲ - Aunt Tootsie's Brownie Mix

Rose's Bakery ▲ - Brownies

Shabtai ▲ - Brownie Bites, Super Moist Brownie

Silly Yak Bakery - GF Brownies ●

Simply Organic ▲ - Gluten Free Cocoa Brownie Mix ●

Simply Shari's Gluten Free & Fabulous ▲ - Fudge Brownies ●

Solterra - Happy Body Brownie Mix

Sweet Christine's Bakery - Brownies ●

The Cravings Place ▲ - Ooey Gooey Chocolatey Chewy Brownie Mix

The Grain Exchange - Brownie Domes, Brownies

The Naked Cookie - Gluten Free Chocolate Brownie Batter (Dark, Milk, Standard, White)

Three Senses Gourmet ▲ - Brownie Bites ●, Brownie Pops ●, Chocolate Smothers ●

Trader Joe's - Gluten Free Brownie Mix

Udi's Gluten Free Foods ▲ - Gluten Free Dark Chocolate Brownie Bites ●

West Meadow Farm Bakery - Gluten Free Bodacious Brownies ●

WOW Baking Company ▲ - Chocolate Brownie ●

Bruschetta

Classico - All Varieties

Santa Barbara

B

Tassos - Mediterranean, Olivara
Trader Joe's - Bruschetta Sauce
Brussels Sprouts
... *All Fresh Fruits & Vegetables Are Gluten-Free*
Birds Eye - All Plain Frozen Vegetables
C & W - All Plain Frozen Vegetables **! !**
Food Club Brand - Frozen
Hy-Vee - Frozen
Lowes Foods Brand - Frozen (Brussels Sprouts, Deluxe Baby)
Meijer Brand - Frozen
Mezzetta ▲ - Dilled Brussels Sprouts
Midwest Country Fare - Frozen
Pictsweet - All Plain Frozen Vegetables
Private Selection - Frozen
Publix - Frozen
Safeway Select - Frozen Petite
Spartan Brand - Frozen
Trader Joe's - All Plain Frozen
Wegmans Brand - Frozen (In Butter Sauce, Regular)
Winn Dixie - Frozen
Buckwheat
Arrowhead Mills
Arzu - Chai ●, Original ●, Southwest ●
Bob's Red Mill ▲ - Organic Kasha ★, Organic Buckwheat Groats ★
Pocono - Buckwheat Flour Light, Whole
Buckwheat Groats
Arrowhead Mills
Wolff's - Whole
Buffalo Wing Sauce...see Wing Sauce
Buffalo Wings...see Wings
Buns
Andrea's Gluten Free ▲ - Hamburger, Multigrain, White Hamburger
Canyon Bakehouse ▲ - Hamburger
Celiac Specialties ▲ - Buns (Hamburger, Hot Dog, Sub)

Choices Rice Bakery ▲ - Brown Rice (Cheddar & Herb, Hamburger, Hot Dog), Flaxseed, Multiseed, Quinoa Multigrain, Sourdough

El Peto ▲ - Dinner Rolls Fruit, Gourmet Mini Subs, Hamburger Buns (Brown Rice, Italian, Multigrain, Potato), Hot Cross, Hot Dog Buns (Italian, Potato), Yeast Free (Brown Rice Hamburger, Potato Hamburger, Potato Hotdog)

Ener-G ▲ - Hamburger Buns (Brown Rice, Seattle, Tapioca, White Rice), Hot Dog Buns (Seattle, Tapioca)

Food-Tek Fast & Fresh - Hamburger Bun Mix ★

Gluten-Free Creations ▲ - Hamburger Buns (Awelicious ●, Regular ●, White ●), Hot Dog Buns ●, Skinny Buns ●

Grandma Ferdon's ▲ - Hamburger ●, Hot Dog ●

Heaven Mills ▲ - Frankfurter Buns ●

Jensen's Bread And Bakeries ▲ - Better Buns ●, Better Hot Dog Buns ●

Joan's GF Great Bakes ▲ - Bialys

Katz Gluten Free ▲ - Hamburger ●, Hot Dog ●

Kinnikinnick ▲ - Soft (Hamburger Buns, Hot Dog), Tapioca Rice Buns (Cinnamon, Hot Cross, Tray)

Kneaded Specialties ▲ - Hamburger Buns w/Sesame Seeds ●, Hamburger ●, Hot Dog ●, Vegan (Hamburger ●, Hot Dog ●)

Laurel's Sweet Treats ▲ - Freshly Baked Cheese

Molly's Gluten-Free Bakery ▲ - French (Brat, Hamburger), Mock Rye Hamburger

O'Doughs Bakery ▲ - Apple Cranberry Breakfast ●, Flax ●, White ●

Pure Knead ▲ - Burger ●, Hot Dog (Original ●, Poppy Seed ●), Multigrain Hamburger ●

Quejos ▲ - Cheese (Black Olives, Extra Cheese, Flaxseed & Almond, Fresh Garlic, Fresh Jalapeno, Fresh Spinach & Onion, Sundried Tomato & Basil), Cocktail Balls, Non Dairy (Flaxseed & Almond, Fresh Spinach & Onion, Tropical Treat), Soya (Fresh Jalapeno, Plain, Sundried Tomato & Basil)

Rose's Bakery ▲ - Hamburger, Hot Dog

Rudi's Gluten-Free Bakery - Multigrain (Hamburger ●, Hot Dog Rolls ●)

B

Silly Yak Bakery -
    CFGF (Garlic Chive ●, Multi Seed ●, Onion Dill ●, Raisin Walnut ●,
      Rice Millet ●, Tomato Basil Buns ●)
    GF (Amaranth ●, Bavarian ●, Buckwheat ●, Caraway ●, Cheddar
      Onion ●, Classic Rice ●, Cottage Dill ●, Cranberry Orange
      Toasting ●, Cranberry Wild Rice ●, Dill Montina ●, Garlic
      Cheddar ●, Holiday ●, Holly's Health ●, Honey Brown Rice●,
      Honey Oat ●, Jalapeño Cheddar ●, Multi Seed Montina ●,
      Onion Dill Montina ●, Quinoa Poppy Seed ●, Raisin Walnut
      Montina ●, Rosemary Red Onion ●, Sesame Sunflower Millet ●,
      Sourdough●, Spinach Feta ●, Teff and Pumpkin Seed ●, Tomato
      Basil Feta ●, Tomato Parmesan Spinach ●, Wild Rice & Chives ●)
Sweet Escapes Pastries ▲ - Gourmet Burger ●, Hoagie Sub ●
Three Bakers ▲ - Whole Grain (Hamburger, Hoagie, Hot Dog)
Udi's Gluten Free Foods ▲ - Gluten Free Classic Hot Dog Buns ●,
    Gluten Free Hamburger Buns (Classic ●, Whole Grain ●)
Whole Foods Market Gluten Free Bakehouse ▲ - Hamburger Buns

Burgers

*... *All Fresh Ground Meat Is Gluten-Free (Non-Marinated, Unseasoned)*

Amy's - Bistro ★, Sonoma Veggie ★
Amylu - Sweet Caramelized Onion Chicken
Applegate - Organic (Beef !, Turkey !)
Asherah's Gourmet - Vegan Burgers (Chipotle ●, Original ●)
Bell & Evans - Chicken !
Butterball - Turkey Burgers (Fresh (All Natural, Seasoned), Frozen
    Seasoned)
De Canto's - BestBurger (Garlic, Original, Quinoa)
Don Lee Farms - Gluten Free Veggie Patties
Dr. Praeger's - California Veggie Burger !
Franklin Farms - Fresh Veggiburger (Chili Bean, Original Recipe,
    Portabella)
Garrett County Farms - All Natural Frozen (Beef Hamburgers ★,
    Turkey Burgers ★)
Great Value Brand (Wal-Mart) - 100% Frozen Beef Patties

Helen's Kitchen - Chik'n GardenSteak, The Original GardenSteak

Henry & Lisa's - Salmon Burgers Wild Alaskan (Regular, Teriyaki)

Hillary's Eat Well - Spicy Adzuki Bean Burger, The World's Best Veggie Burger

Homestead Creek - Gourmet Roasted Garlic & Herb Chicken

Honeysuckle White - Fresh Ground Turkey Patties

Jennie-O Turkey Store - Fresh Lean Turkey Patties, Frozen Turkey Burgers

Kirkland Signature - Frozen (Beef Ground Sirloin & Loin of Beef Patties, Lean Ground Beef Patties, Premium Extra Lean All Natural Turkey Burgers)

Old World Kitchen - Caramelized Onion & Swiss Chicken Burgers

Perdue - Ground Burgers (Chicken, Turkey)

Shelton's - Turkey

Sol Cuisine - Mushroom Rice !, Organic Falafel !, Original !, Spicy Black Bean !, Sweet Curry Vegetable !, Veggie Breakfast Patties !

Sunshine Burgers - Organic (Barbecue ★, Breakfast ★, Falafel ★, Garden Herb ★, Original ★, South West ★)

Trader Joe's - Chili Lime Chicken, Premium Salmon Patties, Salmon, Tofu Veggie !

Trident Seafood Corporation - Salmon Burgers ●

Wellshire Farms - All Natural Frozen (Beef Hamburgers ★, Turkey Burgers ★)

Wildwood - Organic Tofu Veggie Burger (Original, Reduced Fat Original, Shiitake, Southwest)

Winn Dixie - Frozen Angus Beef Patties (Original, w/Grill Seasoning, w/Sweet Onion)

Burritos

Amy's - Gluten Free Cheddar Cheese Burrito ★, Gluten Free Non Dairy Burrito ★

GlutenFreeda ▲ - Beef & Potato, Chicken & Cheese, Vegetarian (Bean & Cheese, Dairy Free)

Butter...see also Spread

Blue Bonnet - All Spreads

Cabot - 83, Salted, Unsalted

B

Country Crock - All Spreadable Butters

Earth Balance - Natural Buttery Spread (Olive Oil, Original, Soy Free, Soy Garden), Natural Shortening, Organic Buttery Spread Original Whipped, Vegan Buttery Sticks

Eden Organic - Apple, Apple Cherry, Cherry

Garelick Farms - Salted Sweet Cream Butter

Gordon Food Service - Margarine Whipped

Great Value Brand (Wal-Mart) - Buttery Spread, Cardio Choice, I Totally Thought It Was Butter, Light Cardio Choice, Margarine, Salted Sweet Cream Butter, Unsalted Sweet Cream Butter

H-E-B - You'd Think It's Butter

Hannaford Brand - Salted, Tastes Like Butter (Light 40% Vegetable Oil, Regular 58% Vegetable Oil), Unsalted

Horizon Organic - All Varieties

Hy-Vee - Best Thing Since Butter, Sweet Cream Butter (Quarters & Solid, Unsalted, Whipped), Unsalted Sweet Quarters

I Can't Believe It's Not Butter - All Varieties

Kirkland Signature - Organic Salted, Sweet Cream (Salted, Unsalted)

Land-O-Lakes - Butter w/Olive Oil, Fresh Buttery Taste, Garlic Butter, Honey Butter, Margarine, Salted Butter, Spreadable Butter w/Canola Oil, Unsalted Butter, Whipped Salted Butter, Whipped Unsalted Butter

Lowes Foods Brand - Margarine (Patties, Quarters, Soft 1 lb., Squeeze), Sweet Cream (Salted, Unsalted)

Lucerne - Butter (Salted, Unsalted), Whipped

Manischewitz - Apple Butter

Meijer Brand - Butter (AA CTN Quarters, Organic (Quarters Salted, Quarters Unsalted, Whipped), Quarters Unsalted)

Move Over Butter - All Spreads

Navitas Naturals ▲ - Cacao

Nuts.com - Organic Cacao Butter ●

Odell's - Clarified Butter, Original Popcorn Butter, Seafood Butter

Olivio - Butter Spread (Light, Original), Buttery Spray, Spreadable (Light Butter, Regular)

B

C

Organic Valley - Cultured Unsalted, European Style Cultured, Pasture Cultured, Salted, Whipped Salted

Parkay - All Spreads

Pastor Chuck Orchards - Apple Butter ●

Phildesco - Coconut Butter

Prairie Farms - Salted, Unsalted

Private Selection - Organic Unsalted Butter

Publix - Salted, Sweet Cream, Unsalted, Whipped (Salted, Unsalted)

Publix GreenWise Market - Organic (Salted, Unsalted)

Purity Farms - Organic Ghee Clarified Butter

Smart Balance - Buttery Blend Spray, Buttery Spread (Extra Virgin Olive Oil, Light (Extra Virgin Olive Oil, Heart Right, Omega 3, Original, Original w/Flax), Omega 3, Organic Certified, Original, Original w/Flax, w/Calcium, Whipped Low Sodium Lightly Salted), Sticks (Omega 3, w/Extra Virgin Olive Oil)

Spartan Brand - 48% Vegetable Spread, 70% Quarters Spread, Is It Butter 70% Spread, Soft Tub Margarine, Sweet Cream Salted, Unsalted

Spectrum - Spread

Tillamook - All Varieties **!**

Trader Joe's - All Varieties

Wegmans Brand - Club Pack Salted Sweet Cream Butter Sticks, Finishing Butter (Bearnaise, Chipotle Lime, Garlic Cheese, Lemon Dill), Solid Butter, Sweet Cream Butter Sticks (Salted, Unsalted), Whipped Tub (Salted, Unsalted)

Winn Dixie - Salted, Unsalted, Whipped

Woodstock Farms - Organic Butter (Salted, Unsalted)

Buttermilk...see Milk

C

Cabbage

   ... *All Fresh Fruits & Vegetables Are Gluten-Free

Cake

3 Fellers Bakery ▲ - Cake Pops (Chocolate ●, Chocolate Coconut ●, Chocolate Peanut Butter ●), Tea Cakes (Chocolate ●, Chocolate

C

Peanut Butter ●, Chocolate Raspberry ●, Coconut ●, Tropical Carrot Cake ●)

Amy's - Gluten Free Non Dairy Organic Chocolate Cake ★, Pound Cake ★

Andrea's Gluten Free ▲ -
Cake (Angel Food, Red Velvet)
Casein Free Decorated Cake (Chocolate Chunk, Yellow)
Chocolate Cake w/Chocolate Icing
Cinnamon Streusel Coffee Cake
Decorated Cake (Chocolate, Chocolate Chip Cookie Cake, Yellow)
Gooey Butter
Yellow Cake w/White Icing

Apple's Bakery ▲ - GF White Layer Cake Kit, Gluten Free Cake (Buttermilk Pecan Coffee, Lemon Poundcake)

Bi-Aglut - Apricot Plumcake, Chocolate Plum Cake, Plum Cake, Yoghurt Plumcake

Bridge City Baking ▲ - Decaf Cappuccino Cheesecake ●, Gluten Free Coffee Cake (Marionberry ●, Original ●)

Cause You're Special ▲ - Golden Poundcake

Celiac Specialties ▲ - Angel Food Cake, Angel Wings, Coffee Cake, Mini Boston Creme Pie, Pumpkin Cake

Choices Rice Bakery ▲ - Tiramisu

Crave Bakery ▲ - 6" Decorated Chocolate, 8" Sugar Free Cheesecake, Mama Z's Chocolate Cake

Deerfields Gluten Free Bakery ▲ - Cheesecake, Coffeecake (Blueberry Cream Cheese, Pecan Sour Cream)

Eena Kadeena ▲ - Tea Loaf (Chocolate Lovers', Coconut, Vanilla)

Ener-G ▲ - Poundcake

Everybody Eats - Made To Order (Chocolate, Yellow)

Fabe's Bakery - 6" Gluten Free Cake (Chocolate Fudge ●, Homestyle Carrot ●)

Foods By George ▲ - Crumb Cake, Poundcake

Glutano - Marmorkuchen Marble Cake

C

Gluten-Free Creations ▲ - Cinnamon Coffee Cake ●, Whoopie Pie (Chocolate ●, Yellow ●), Winkies ●

GlutenFreeda ▲ - Cheesecake (Chocolate Truffle, New York Style, Strawberry Swirl)

GlutenOut - Profiterol ★, Tiramisu ★, Torta Al Chocolato Cake ★

Grandma Ferdon's ▲ - Carrot Cake ●, Coffee Cake ●

Heaven Mills ▲ - Cake (Brownie ●, Carrot ●, Chocolate Strip ●, Cinnamon Strip ●, Marble ●)

Jennies ▲ - Pound Cake Minis (Classic ●, Marble ●, Raisin ●)

Joan's GF Great Bakes ▲ - Crumb Cake

Katz Gluten Free ▲ - Cake (Coffee Bundt ●, Marble ●)

Kneaded Specialties ▲ - Square (Carrot ●, Chocolate ●, Coffee Cake●, Luscious Lemonade Cake ●, Vegan Orange Dream ●, White ●)

Lean On Me - Carrotcake

Mariposa Artisan-Crafted Gluten-Free ▲ - Sour Cream Coffeecake

Molly's Gluten-Free Bakery ▲ - Chocolate Cake (w/Chocolate Icing, w/Vanilla Icing), Specialty Cakes (Creme, Raspberry), Spice Cake (w/Chocolate Icing, w/Vanilla Icing), Yellow Cake (w/Chocolate Icing, w/Vanilla Icing)

Mrs. Crimble's - Bakewell Cake Slices

O'Doughs Bakery ▲ - Cake (Banana ●, Carrot ●, Chocolate ●)

Pamela's Products ▲ - Cake (Chocolate Fudge Cake, Coffee Cake), Cheesecake (Hazelnut w/Chocolate Crust, New York, New York Agave Sweetened, White Chocolate Raspberry, Zesty Lemon)

Pure Knead ▲ - Carrot Cake ●

Pure Market Express ▲ - Boston Cream Pie, Cheesecake (Chocolate ●, Key Lime ●), Chocolate Raspberry Ganache Layer Cake ●, Strawberry Shortcake ●

Really Great Food Company ▲ - Coffee Crumb Cake

Russo's Gluten Free Gourmet ▲ - Tiramisu

Shabtai ▲ - Cake (7 Inch Occasion Layer, Honey Cake Loaf, Marble, Seven Layer (Devils Food, White), Sponge Cake Loaf), Rolls (Apricot, Devils Stix Baby Swiss, Raspberry, Swiss Chocolate)

C

Silly Yak Bakery -
CFGF Classic Rice Cake ●
GF (Majestic Valley Sour Cream Coffee Cake (Raspberry ●, Almond ●, Apple Walnut ●, Blueberry ●, Pumpkin Pecan ●, Regular●), Marble Rice Cake ●, Rice Cake (Chocolate ●, Classic ●, Frosted Chocolate ●, Frosted Vanilla ●))

Skye Foods - Heart Cake ●, Spice Cake ●

Sweet Christine's Bakery - Chocolate Lava Cake ●

The Grain Exchange - Cakes (Bavarian Torte Cake, Birthday, Chocolate Chip Cookie, Coffee Cake, Pineapple Upside Down Cake, Small Wedding, Specialty)

The Lite-Ful Cheesecake ▲ - Cheesecake (Amaretto Almond ●, Blueberry ●, Chocolate Bliss ●, Chocolate Swirl ●, Cinnamon ●, Grand Marnier ●, Kahlua ●, Lemon ●, Mandarin ●, Mocha ●, Peanut Butter ●, Plain Vanilla ●, Pumpkin ●, Strawberry ●)

Three Senses Gourmet ▲ - Souffle (Caramel ●, Chocolate ●)

Tia's Bakery ▲ - German Chocolate ●, Grandma's Chocolate ●, Strawberry Shortcake ●, Tropical Banana ●

Trader Joe's - Flourless Chocolate Cake ‼

Voyaging Foods - Vegan Fudgie Cakes ●, Whoopee Cake ●

Whole Foods Market Gluten Free Bakehouse ▲ - Carrot Cake, Chocolate Cake, Yellow Cake

Cake Mix

1-2-3 Gluten Free ▲ - Delightfully Gratifying Bundt Poundcake Mix ●, Devil's Food Cake Mix ●, Peri's Perfect Chocolate Bundt Poundcake Mix ●, Yummy Yellow Cake Mix ●

Abundant Life Foods ▲ - Cake Mix (Banana, Carrot, Chocolate, Ginger, Golden, Lemon, Spice)

AgVantage Naturals ▲ - Angel Food Cake Mix ●

Arrowhead Mills - Bake With Me Gluten Free Cupcake Mix (Chocolate, Vanilla), Gluten Free Vanilla Cake Mix

Augason Farms ▲ - Gluten Free Cake Mix (Angel Food ●, Chocolate ●, Yellow ●)

Authentic Foods ▲ - Cake Mix (Chocolate ●, Devil's Food Chocolate ●, Lemon ●, Vanilla Bean ●)

cake mix

C

Better Batter - Chocolate ●, Yellow ●

Betty Crocker ▲ - Gluten Free Cake Mix (Devil's Food, Yellow)

Bloomfield Farms ▲ - Gluten Free Cake Mix ●

Bob's Red Mill ▲ - Gluten Free Cake Mix (Chocolate ★, Vanilla ★)

Bready - Cherish My Chocolate Cake Mix ●

Cause You're Special ▲ - Moist (Lemon, Yellow), Rich Chocolate

Cherrybrook Kitchen - Gluten Free Chocolate Cake Mix ★ *(Box Must Say Gluten Free)*, Gluten Free Yellow Cake Mix ★ *(Box Must Say Gluten Free)*

Dowd & Rogers ▲ - Cake Mix (Dark Vanilla, Dutch Chocolate, Golden Lemon)

Easy Cake - Microwaveable Cake (Chocolate w/Dark Chocolate, Mocha, Vanilla w/White Confection)

Eena Kadeena ▲ - Cupcake Mix Snickerdoodle

El Peto ▲ - Cake Mix (Chocolate, Lemon, White), Corn Free (Chocolate Cake Mix, Lemon Cake Mix, White Cake Mix)

El Torito - Sweet Corn Cake Mix

Food-Tek Fast & Fresh - Cake Mix (Chocolate ★, Cinnamon Coffee ★, Double Chocolate ★, White ★, Yellow ★)

Full Circle - Gluten Free Spice Cake Mix

Gifts Of Nature ▲ - Yellow Cake Mix ●

Gluten Free Life ▲ - The Ultimate Gluten Free Cake Muffin & Brownie Mix

Gluten Free Pantry ▲ - Chocolate Chip Cookie & Cake Mix, Decadent Chocolate Cake Mix, Old Fashioned Cake & Cookie Mix

Gluten-Free Creations ▲ - Cake Mix Angel Food ●

Gluten-Free Naturals - Yellow Cake Mix

Grandma Ferdon's ▲ - Angel Food Cake Mix ●

Happy Kitchen ▲ - Cake Mix (Butter, Chocolate)

Hodgson Mill ▲ - Gluten Free (Chocolate Cake Mix, Yellow Cake Mix)

King Arthur Flour ▲ - Gluten Free Cake Mix (Chocolate ●, Yellow ●)

Kinnikinnick ▲ - Cake Mix (Angel Food, Chocolate, White)

Laurel's Sweet Treats ▲ - Cake Mix (Cinnamon Spice, Mom's Chocolate, Vanilla)

C

Manischewitz - Chocolate, Vanilla

Mixes From The Heartland ▲ - Cake Mix (Cheesecake ●, Chocolate Angel Food ●, Chocolate Poundcake ●, Cinnamon Orange ●, Lime Angel Food ●, Lime Poundcake ●, Orange Angel Food ●, Pineapple Poundcake ●, Raspberry Poundcake ●, Strawberry Angel Food ●, Strawberry Poundcake ●, Vanilla Angel Food ●, Vanilla Poundcake ●)

Namaste Foods ▲ - Cake Mix (Chocolate, Spice, Vanilla)

Nuts.com - Gluten Free Cake Mix (Chocolate ●, Vanilla ●)

Orgran ▲ - Cake Mix (Chocolate, Vanilla)

Pamela's Products ▲ - Cake Mix (Chocolate, Classic Vanilla)

PaneRiso ▲ - Rice Cake & Cookie Mix

Really Great Food Company ▲ - Cake Mix (Angel Food, Banana Bread, Chocolate, Chocolate Cupcake, Colonial Spice, Devil's Food, Gingerbread, Golden, Lemon Poppy, Orange, Pineapple, Pound, Pumpkin Bread, Pumpkin Spice, White, Yellow)

Simply Organic ▲ - Gluten Free (Carrot Cake Mix ●, Cocoa Cayenne Cupcake Mix ●, Devil's Food Cake Mix ●, Golden Vanilla Cake Mix ●)

Sof'ella - Gluten Free Chocolate Cake Mix & Frosting Mix ★

Solterra - French Vanilla Mini Chip Cake Mix, Key Lime Cake Mix

Something Good ▲ - Chocolate Mud Cake Mix ★, Cupcake Mix ★

Sylvan Border Farm - Chocolate, Lemon

The Cravings Place ▲ - Cinnamon Crumble Coffeecake Mix, Create Your Own, Dutch Chocolate Cake Mix, Raisin Spice

The Pure Pantry ▲ - Wholegrain Dark Chocolate Cake Mix ●

WOW Baking Company ▲ - Gourmet Cake Mix (Chocolate ●, Yellow ●)

Candy/Candy Bars

Amanda's Own - All Varieties

Andes - Creme De Menthe Sugar Free, Thins (Cherry Jubilee, Creme De Menthe, Mint Parfait, Toffee Crunch)

Baby Ruth - Baby Ruth Bar

Bequet - Handmade Caramels ●

Brown & Haley - Milk Chocolate Roca Crunch ‼, Mountain Bar (Cherry ‼, Peanut Butter ‼, Vanilla ‼), Roca Buttercrunch (Almond‼, , Candy Cane ‼, Cashew ‼, Macadamia ‼,

C

Mocha **!!**, Toffee Thins (Dark **!!**, Milk **!!**), Truffle (Caramel Thins **!!**, Dark Thins **!!**, Double Dark **!!**))

Candy Tree - Licorice (Cherry (Bites, Laces, Twists), Gluten Free Black Licorice (Lariats, Twists), Raspberry (Bites, Laces, Twists), Strawberry (Bites, Laces, Twists)), Lollipops (Lemon, Organic Red, Strawberry)

Caramel Apple Pops

Carb Safe - Sugar Free Chocolate Bars Dark

Caribou - Valentine's Marshmallows

Caring Candies - All Natural Sugar Free Bon Bons, Sugar Free Lollipops

Cella's - Chocolate Covered Cherries (Dark, Milk)

Charleston Chew - Chocolate, Mini Vanilla, Strawberry, Vanilla

Charms - Blow Pops (Bubblegum, Minis, Regular), Flat Pops, Fluffy Stuff (Regular, Tear Jerkers), Sweet Pops

Chase - Coconut Bon Bons

ChocAlive ▲ - Truffles (Almond, Chocolate Chip Mint, Coconut, Dark Chocolate, Dark Chocolate Crunch, Pistachio)

Choices Rice Bakery ▲ - Rumballs

Coffee Rio's - All Flavors Coffee Caramels

Crispy Cat - Candy Bars (Chocolate Sundae **!!**, Mint Coconut **!!**, Toasted Almond **!!**)

Cry Baby - Extra Sour (Bubble Gum, Candy), Gumballs, Tears, Twist Gum

Dots - Crows, Fruit Flavor, Tropical Flavor, Yoghurt Flavor

Dubble Bubble - Bonz

Frooties - Fruit Flavored Chewy Candy

Gimbal's Fine Candies ▲ - All Varieties

Glee Gum - Make Your Own (Chocolate, Gummies)

Glutino - Chocolate Peanut Butter Candy Bar

Goelitz - Candy Corn

Goody Good Stuff - Gummies (Cheery Cherries, Cola Breeze, Gummy Bears, Strawberry Cream, Summer Peach, Tropical Fruit), Sours (Fruit Salad, Mix & Match)

Great Value Brand (Wal-Mart) - Cinnamon Discs, Fruit Slices, Gummy Bears, Orange Slices, Spearmint Starlight Mints, Spice Drops, Starlight Mints

C

Hannaford Brand - Chocolate (Covered Raisins !, Non Pareils !),
Circus Peanuts, Gummi (Bears, Sour Neon Worms, Worms),
Jelly Beans, Jelly Rings, Licorice Bears, Spice Drops, Sugar Free
(Cinnamon Buttons, Peppermint Starlights, Rootbeer Barrels)

Haribo - Alphabet Letters, Centipedes, Clown Fish, Fizzy Cola, Frogs,
Fruit Salad, Fruity Frutti, Gold Bear Minis, Gold Bears, Grapefruit,
Gummi Apples, Happy Cola, Mini Rainbow Fish, Mini Rainbow
Frogs, Peaches, Pink Grapefruit, Raspberries, Rattle Snakes,
Roulettes (Mega, Regular), Sour Cherries, Strawberries, Strawberries
& Cream, Super Cola, Techno Bears, Tropi Frutti, Twin Cherries

Hershey's -
Heath Bar
Jolly Ranchers (Gummies, Hard Candy)
Kisses Milk Chocolate (Meltaway, Original, w/Almonds, w/Caramel,
w/Cherry Cordial Creme)
Kisses Special Dark
Milk Chocolate Bar (Original, w/Almonds)
Mr. Goodbar
PayDay
Reese's Peanut Butter Cups (Original)
Skor
York Peppermint Patty

Hubba Bubba - Squeeze Pop All Flavors

Hy-Vee -
Butterscotch Buttons !
Chocolate (Covered Raisins !, Peanut Clusters !, Stars !)
Cinnamon Imperials !
Circus Peanuts !
Double Dipped Chocolate Covered Peanuts !
Dubble Bubble Gum !
Gum Drops !
Gummi (Bears !, Peach Rings !, Sour Worms !, Worms !)
Lemon Drops !
Orange Slices !
Smarties !

C

Spice Drops **!**
Starlight Mints
Wax Bottles

Indie Candy ▲ - Dark Chocolate Drizzled Fresh Marshmallows, Dark Chocolate Lollipop Shapes, Lollipop Bouquet, Lollipop Flowers, Make Your Own Gummies Kit, Zoo Animals Gummis, Zoo Animals Lollipops

Jelly Belly - Jelly Beans (All Varieties)

Junior Mints - Deluxe, Inside Outs, Junior (Caramels, Mints), Minis

Justin's - Candy Bar (Dark Chocolate Peanut ●, Milk Chocolate Almond ●, Milk Chocolate Peanut ●), Peanut Butter Cups (Dark Chocolate ●, Milk Chocolate ●)

KatySweet ▲ -
  Chewy Nut Clusters ●
  Chewy Pralines (Almond ●, Coconut Pecan ●, Maple Walnut ●, Peanut Pie ●, Pecan ●)
  Creamy Fudge Pralines (Pecan ●, Pecan Holiday (Star ●, Tree ●), State Shaped ●)
  Creamy Original Pralines (Almond ●, Pecan ●, Pecan Holiday (Star ●, Tree ●), Pecan State Shapes ●, Walnut ●)
  Creamy Pralines (German Chocolate ●, Maple Walnut ●)
  Katy's Toffee ●
  Lil' Tex Praline ●
  No Sugar Added Chewy Pralines (Almond ●, Mixed Nut ●, Pecan ●, Sweet Rewards ●, Walnut ●)
  Organic Chewy Pralines (Fudge Pecan ●, Maple Walnut ●, Original (Pecan ●, Walnut ●), Pecan ●)
  Organic Pecan Krunch ●
  Organic Pecan Rewards Pralines ●
  Pecan (Krunch ●, Rewards Pralines ●)
  Raspberry Lemon Almond Bark ●

Let's Do...Organic - Gummy Bears (All Varieties)

C

Lifesavers - Fruit Tarts (Orange, Purple), Gummies (5 Flavors, Assorted Sours, Island Fruits, Wild Berries, Wild Berries Sours), Hard Candy (5 Flavors, Butter Rum, Cherry Lemonade, Cryst O Mint, Orange Mint, Pep O Mint, Spear O Mint, Strawberry Apple, Wild Berries, Wild Cherry, Wint O Green), Sugar Free Hard Candy (5 Flavors, Pep O Mint, Wint O Green)

Lowes Foods Brand - Candy Corn, Chocolate (Peanuts, Raisins), Cinnamon Imperials, Dubble Bubble Gum, Gummi (Bears, Worms, Worms Sour), Kiddie Mix, Laffy Taffy, Orange Slices, Rainbow Dinner Mints, Starlight Mints, Sweet Twists

Lucky Leaf - Cherries Jubilee

M & M's - *(Packaging labels differ. Please double check ingredient label for allergens.)* Dark Chocolate, Milk Chocolate, Peanut, Peanut Butter

Manischewitz - Chocolate Frolic Bears, Hazelnut Truffles, Mallo Cups, Max's Magic Lollycones, Patties (Peppermint, Tender Coconut), Raspberry Gel Bars, Swiss Chocolate Mints

Maple Grove Farms Of Vermont - Blended Maple, Pure Maple

Mars - *(Packaging labels differ. Please double check ingredient label for allergens)*
Dove Chocolates (All Varieties)
M & M's (Dark Chocolate, Milk Chocolate, Peanut, Peanut Butter)
Milky Way (Midnight, Simply Caramel)
Munch Bar
Snickers (Dark Bar, Original Bar)

Milky Way - *(Packaging labels differ. Please double check ingredient label for allergens)* Midnight, Simply Caramel

Munch Bar - *(Packaging labels differ. Please double check ingredient label for allergens)*

Necco - Banana Split Chews, Canada Mint & Wintergreen Lozenges, Candy Eggs Easter, Candy Stix, Clark Bar, Haviland Chocolate Thin Mints, Mary Janes (Peanut Butter Kisses, Regular), Mint Julep Chews, Skybar, Squirrel Nut (Caramels, Zippers), Sweethearts

Conversation Hearts (Valentines Only), Talking Pumpkins Halloween, Wafers

Nestle - Baby Ruth, Bit O Honey, Butterfinger *(Except Crisp & Stixx)*, Goobers, Milk Chocolate, Nips (Regular, Sugar Free), Oh Henry, Raisinets, Sno Caps, Spree **!!**

Newman's Own Organics - All Chocolate (Bars **!!**, Cups **!!**)

Nik-L-Nip - Wax Bottles

Nuts.com - Turkish Delight (Almond ●, Mixed Nut ●, Pistachio ●)

Organic Nectars - All Varieties Of Raw Cacao

Orgran ▲ - Molasses Licorice

Peeps - Pink Bunnies, Yellow Chicks (Chocolate Dipped, Regular *(Except Easter Rainbow Pops On A Stick)*, Sugar Free)

Publix - Brittle (Chocolate, Peanut), Double Dipped Chocolate Peanuts, Gummi (Sour Worms **!!**, Worms), Party Time Mix **!!**, Smarties Candy **!**, Starlight Mints (Spearmint **!!**, Original **!!**)

Pure Market Express ▲ - Bliss Balls ●

Razzles - Gum (Regular, Sour, Tropical)

Safeway Brand - Gummi Bears, Gummi Worms, Jelly Beans

Schar ▲ - Chocolate Hazelnut Bars

Seitenbacher - Roses For You, Sunhats (Black Currant, Cherry, Cherry Dolphins, Passion Fruit, Smooch Lions, Strawberry, Strawberry Alligators), Vampires Lunch

Shabtai ▲ - Bon Bons

Sipahh - Milk Flavoring Straws

Skittles - All Varieties

Smarties - All Varieties

Snickers - *(Packaging labels differ. Please double check ingredient label for allergens)* Dark, Snickers Original

Sour Patch Kids - All Varieties

Spangler ▲ - Candy Canes, Cane Classics, Dum Dum (Canes, Chewy Pops, Pops), Marshmallow Circus Peanuts, Saf T Pops, Swirl Saf T Pops

St. Claire's Organics ▲ - All (Candy, Mints, Sweets, Tarts)

Starburst - All Varieties (Fruit Chews, GummiBursts, Jelly Beans)

C

Sugar Babies - Sugar Babies (Caramel Apple, Chocolate Covered, Original)

Sugar Daddy - Caramel Pops

Sugar Mama - Caramels

SunSpire - Chocolate Cups (Almond Butter, Peanut Butter), Coconut, Coconut Almond, Dark Chocolate Covered (Almonds, Cranberries), Peppermint Pattie, SunDrops (Milk Chocolate, Peanut)

Surf Sweets - Gummi (Bears, Sour Berry Bears, Swirls, Worms)

Swedish Fish - Aqualife, Assorted, Red

Taffy Tree ▲ - All Varieties

The Ginger People - Crystallized Ginger Candy !, Gin Gins !, Gin Gins Boost !, Ginger Chews (Hot Coffee !, Original !, Peanut !, Spicy Apple !)

The Naked Cookie - Nut Brittle (Almond, Cashew, Macadamia, Peanut, Pecan, Pistachio)

Tootsie Roll - Child's Play Assortment of Favorites, Tootsie Fruit Rolls, Tootsie Pops (Bunch Pops, Miniatures, Original, Pop Drops), Tootsie Roll (Mini Chews, Regular, Sugar Free)

Trader Joe's - Almond Clusters, Brown Rice Marshmallow Treats, English Toffee, Green Tea Mints, Organic Pops, Pecans Praline !, Yogurt Raisins

Tubi's - Gluten Free Soft Black Licorice

Wack-O-Wax - Wax Fangs, Wax Lips

Weight Watchers - Whitman's Candies (Coconut !!, Mint Patties !!)

Wonka - Bottlecaps !, Gobstoppers (Chewy !, Everlasting !), Laffy Taffy, Laffy Taffy Rope, Lik M Aid Fun Dip !, Mix Ups !, Nerds (Chewy !!, Regular !, Rope !), Original Spree !, Pixy Stix !, Runts (Chewy !, Original !), SweeTarts (Chewy !, Roll !)

Woodstock Farms - Vegetarian Organic Gummy Cubs

YumEarth - Gummy Bears, Sour Beans

Yummy Earth - Lollipops

Zip-A-Dee - Mini Pops

Canned Chicken

Bumble Bee - Premium In Water (Breast, White)

Great Value Brand (Wal-Mart) - Chunk Chicken Breast

Hormel - Chicken, Chunk Meats Breast Of Chicken
Meijer Brand - Chicken Chunk White
Member's Mark - Premium Chunk Chicken Breast In Water
Spartan Brand - Chunk Chicken Breast

Canned Ham
Great Value Brand (Wal-Mart) - Luncheon Meat
Hormel - Black Label, Chunk Meats Ham
SPAM - Classic, Hickory Smoke Flavored, Hot & Spicy, Less Sodium, Lite, w/Bacon, w/Cheese
Underwood - Deviled Ham Spread

Canned Salmon...see Fish

Canned Tuna...see Tuna

Canned Turkey
Hormel - Chunk Meats Turkey
Member's Mark - Premium Chunk Turkey Breast In Water
SPAM - Oven Roasted Turkey

Cannoli
Russo's Gluten Free Gourmet ▲ - Cannoli Shells

Canola Oil...see Oil

Cantaloupe
*... *All Fresh Fruits & Vegetables Are Gluten-Free*
Nuts.com - Dried Fruit (Chunks ●, Dried ●)

Capers
B&G - Capote, Nonpareil
Mezzetta ▲ - Capote Capers, Non Pareil (Capers, Capers In Balsamic Vinegar)
Safeway Select - Nonpareil
Star - Imported Nonpareil Capers
Trader Joe's - Nonpareil
Wegmans Brand - Italian Classics (Capote, Nonpareil)

Capuccino...see Coffee

Caramel...see Candy/Candy Bars and/or Dip/Dip Mix

Carbonated Beverages...see Soda Pop/Carbonated Beverages

C Carrots

... *All Fresh Fruits & Vegetables Are Gluten-Free

Augason Farms ▲ - Gluten Free Dehydrated Diced ●

Birds Eye - All Plain Frozen Vegetables

Bolthouse Farms - Baby Cut, Premium

C & W - All Plain Frozen Vegetables **! !**

Del Monte - Canned Sliced

Earthbound Farm - Bunched & Cello, Dippin' Doubles, Mini Peeled

Embasa - Sliced

Food Club Brand - Canned (Peas & Sliced Carrots, Sliced, Sliced No Salt), Frozen (Crinkle Cut, Whole Baby)

Freshlike - Frozen Plain Carrots

Great Value Brand (Wal-Mart) - Canned Sliced Carrots

Hannaford Brand - All Frozen, Sliced, Whole Baby

Hy-Vee - Classic Cut & Peeled Baby, Frozen Crinkle Cut, Sliced

Lowes Foods Brand - Canned Sliced, Frozen (Deluxe Whole Baby, Peas & Carrots, Sliced)

Meijer Brand - Canned Sliced (No Salt, Regular), Frozen Carrots (Crinkle Cut, Whole Baby)

Mezzetta ▲ - Gourmet Baby

Midwest Country Fare - Sliced Carrots

Nuts.com - Simply Carrots Freeze Dried Vegetables ●

Pictsweet - All Plain Frozen Vegetables

Publix - Canned Carrots, Frozen (Crinkle Cut, Whole Baby)

Publix GreenWise Market - Organic (Baby, Carrots, Chips, Juicing, Shredds, Snack)

S&W - All Canned Vegetables

Safeway Brand - Carrots Canned Sliced

Spartan Brand - Canned (Peas & Sliced Carrots, Sliced), Frozen (Crinkle Cut, Peas & Carrots, Whole Baby)

Wegmans Brand - Canned (Sliced Carrots (No Salt Added, Regular), Whole Style), Frozen (Baby, Broccoli Cuts/Cauliflower Florets & Carrots, FYFGA (Carrots/Potatoes/Celery & Onions, Crinkle Cut))

Winn Dixie - Frozen (Crinkle Cut, Whole Baby)

Cashews...see Nuts

Cassava

 Badia - Canned ●

Cauliflower

 *... *All Fresh Fruits & Vegetables Are Gluten-Free*

 Birds Eye - All Plain Frozen Vegetables

 C & W - All Plain Frozen Vegetables **!!**

 Earthbound Farm - Organic Whole

 Food Club Brand - Frozen Florets

 Freshlike - Frozen Plain Cauliflower

 Green Giant - Frozen Cauliflower & Cheese Sauce

 Hy-Vee - Frozen Cauliflower Florets

 Lowes Foods Brand - Frozen Cauliflower

 Meijer Brand - Frozen Cauliflower Florets

 Mezzetta ▲ - Dilled, Hot

 Midwest Country Fare - Frozen Cauliflower

 Pictsweet - All Plain Frozen Vegetables

 Publix - Frozen

 Safeway Brand - Frozen

 Spartan Brand - Frozen Florets

 Trader Joe's - All Plain Frozen

 Wegmans Brand - Florets

 Winn Dixie - Frozen

 Woodstock Farms - Organic Frozen (Cauliflower & Broccoli Mix, Cauliflower Blend w/Broccoli & Carrots, Cauliflower Florets)

Caviar

 Romanoff - Black Lumpfish, Red Salmon, Vodka Lumpfish, Whitefish

Celery

 *... *All Fresh Fruits & Vegetables Are Gluten-Free*

 Augason Farms ▲ - Gluten Free Dehydrated Cross Cut ●

Cereal

 Aimee's Livin' Magic - Oh Happy Day

 Amy's - Cream Of Rice Hot Cereal Bowl ★

 Ancient Harvest Quinoa - Quinoa Flakes

C

Arrowhead Mills - Hot (Rice & Shine, Yellow Corn Grits), Maple Buckwheat Flakes, Sweetened Rice Flakes

Bakery On Main - Granola (Apple Raisin Walnut ●, Cranberry Orange Cashew ●, Extreme Fruit & Nut ●, Nutty Cranberry Maple ●, Rainforest ●)

Barbara's Bakery - Honey Rice Puffins, Multigrain Puffins, Organic Brown Rice Crisps

Better Balance - Apple Cinnamon ●, French Vanilla ●, Honey Almond ●

Bob's Red Mill ▲ - Creamy Rice Hot Cereal (Organic ★, Regular ★), Gluten Free Mighty Tasty Hot ★, Organic Creamy Buckwheat ★

Cerealvit - Benevit Multigrain ★, Choco Stars ★, Coffee Flakes ★, Corn Flakes ★

Chex ▲ - Chocolate, Cinnamon, Corn, Honey Nut, Rice

Cocoa Pebbles

Cream of Rice - Hot Cereal

Earth's Best Organic Baby Food - Whole Grain Rice Cereal (Apples, Plain)

Eco-Planet ▲ - 7 Whole Grains Hot Cereal (Apples & Cinnamon ●, Maple & Brown Sugar ●, Original ●)

El Peto ▲ - Balls (Coco, Vanilla Corn), Coco Rice Puffs, Corn Flakes (No Refined Sugar, Sweet Iced, Whole Grain), Cream Of Rice (w/Apple & Cinnamon, White, Whole Grain Brown), Instant Quinoa Flakes

Ener-G ▲ - Cinnamon Crackers Pieces, Rice Bran

Enjoy Life ▲ - Granola Crunch (Cinnamon Raisin ●, Double Chocolate●, Very Berry ●), Perky's (Crunchy Flax ●, Crunchy Rice ●)

EnviroKidz Organic - Amazon Frosted Flakes ●, Gorilla Munch ●, Koala Crisp ●, Leapin Lemurs ●, Peanut Butter Panda Puffs ●

Erewhon - Corn Flakes ●, Crispy Brown Rice (Cocoa ●, Gluten Free Regular ●, w/Mixed Berries ●), Rice Twice ●, Strawberry Crisp ●

Fruity Pebbles

General Mills ▲ - Chex (Chocolate, Cinnamon, Corn, Honey Nut, Rice)

Gerber - DHA & Probiotic Rice, Single Grain (Organic Smart Nourish Brown Rice, Rice Cereal)

Glutano ▲ - Cornflakes

Gluten Free Sensations ▲ - Cream Of Brown Rice, Granola (Apple Crisp, Blueberry Pecan, Cherry Vanilla Almond, Chocolate Bliss, Cranberry Pecan, French Vanilla Almond)

Glutino ▲ - Apple & Cinnamon, Honey Nut, Sensible Beginnings (Berry, Frosted, Original)

H·E·B - Rice Squares

Hodgson Mill ▲ - Gluten Free Creamy Buckwheat w/Milled Flax

Kay's Naturals - Protein Cereal (Apple Cinnamon ●, French Vanilla ●, Honey Almond ●), Protein Puffs (Almond Delight ●, Tomato Basil ●, Veggie Pizza ●)

Kellogg's - Gluten Free Rice Krispies *(Box Must Say Gluten Free)*

Kinnikinnick ▲ - KinniKrisp Rice Cereal

Les Moissonneries Du Pays ▲ - Buckwheat Porridge

Lydia's Organics - Apricot Sun, Berry Good, Grainless Apple, Sprouted Cinnamon, Vanilla

Marshmallow Pebbles

Meijer Brand - Grits (Buttered Flavored Instant, Quick)

Montana Monster Munchies - Whole Grain Oat Bran ●

Nabisco - Cream Of Rice Hot Cereal

Nature's Path - Corn Puffs !, EnviroKidz Organic (Amazon Frosted Flakes ●, Gorilla Munch ●, Koala Crisp ●, Leapin Lemurs ●, Peanut Butter Panda Puffs ●), Millet Puffs !, Organic (Corn Flakes ●, Crispy Rice ●, Crunchy Maple Sunrise ●, Crunchy Vanilla Sunrise ●, Honey'd Corn Flakes ●, Mesa Sunrise ●, Whole O's ●), Rice Puffs !

New Morning - Cocoa Crispy Rice

Nu·World Foods ▲ - Puffed Amaranth Cereal

Nuts.com - Organic Hot Cereal (Amaranth ●, Buckwheat Toasted ●, Raw White Buckwheat ●), Superfood Cereal (Acai Blueberry ●, Cacao Crunch ●, Chia Ginger ●, Hemp & Greens ●), Teff Whole Grain Hot Cereal ●

Orgran ▲ - Kids Itsy Bitsy Cocoa O's, Multigrain O's w/Quinoa, Puffed Amaranth Breakfast Cereal, Rice O's Wild Berry Flavor

Paskesz - Chocorios, Fruitos, Honey Crunchios

Pocono - Cream Of Buckwheat

C

Post - Cocoa Pebbles, Fruity Pebbles, Marshmallow Pebbles

Pure Market Express ▲ - Count Rawcula ●, Strawberry Crunch ●

Purely Elizabeth ▲ - Ancient Grain Granola Cereal (Cranberry Pecan ●, Original ●, Pumpkin Fig ●)

Rice Krispies - Gluten Free Rice Krispies *(Box Must Say Gluten Free)*

Ruth's Hemp Power - Chia Goodness (Apple Almond Cinnamon, Chocolate, Cranberry Ginger, Original)

Seitenbacher - Musli #7, Whole Grain Cornflakes

Shiloh Farms - Organic Soybean Flakes **!!**

Trader Joe's - Gluten Free Granola, Golden Roasted (Flaxseed w/ Blueberries, Whole Flaxseed)

Wegmans Brand - Rice Squares

Chamomile Tea...see Tea

Champagne

... *All Champagne/Sparkling Wine Made In The USA Is Gluten-Free*

Cheese

Alouette -

Baby Brie (Double Creme, Garlic & Herbs, Wedge (Double Creme, Garlic & Herbs, Smoked))

Creme De Brie (Garlic & Herbs, Original)

Crumbled Cheese (Blue, Feta, Feta Garlic & Herbs, Feta Mediterranean, Goat, Gorgonzola, Provencal Goat)

Double Creme Brie Log

Extra Creamy Brie

Gourmet Spreadable Cheese (Garlic & Herbs, Sundried Tomatoes)

Soft Spreadable Cheese (Flavored (Bacon Cheddar, Sharp Cheddar), Garlic & Herbs, Light (Garlic & Herbs, Spinach Artichoke), Pepper Medley, Savory Vegetable, Spinach Artichoke, Sundried Tomato & Basil)

American Burger Classics - American, Cheddar, Swiss

Andrew & Everett - All Varieties

Applegate - Deli Counter (American **!**, Cheddar **!**, Emmentaler Swiss **!**, Provolone **!**), Natural (American **!**, Cheddar **!**, Emmentaler Swiss **!**, Extra Sharp Aged Cheddar **!**, Havarti **!**, Monterey Jack w/Jalapeno

Peppers **!**, Muenster **!**, Provolone **!**), Organic (American **!**, Mild Cheddar **!**, Monterey Jack **!**, Muenster **!**, Provolone **!**), Probiotic Yogurt Cheese **!**

Athenos - Blue Crumbled, Feta (Basil & Tomato, Black Peppercorn, Garlic & Herb, Mild, Reduced Fat Tomato & Basil, Reduced Fat Traditional, Roasted Bell Pepper & Garlic, Traditional), Gorgonzola Crumbled

Bakers & Chefs - Cheddar Cheese Sauce, Nacho Cheese Sauce

Belgioioso ▲ - American Grana, Asiago, Auribella, Burrata, Crescenza Stracchino, Fontina, Fresh Mozzarella, Gorgonzola, Italico, Kasseri, Mascarpone, Mozzarella Prosciutto & Basil Roll, Parmesan, Pepato, Peperoncino, Provolone, Ricotta Con Latte, Ricotta Salata, Romano, Unwrap & Roll Mozzarella, Vegetarian Parmesan

Boar's Head - All Varieties

Borden - All Varieties *(Except Applewood Bacon Cheddar)*

Cabot -

Aged Cheddars (Extra Sharp, Mild, New York Extra Sharp, Seriously Sharp, Sharp)

Flavored Cheddars (Chipotle, Garlic & Herb, Horseradish, Hot Buffalo Wing, Hot Habanero, Smoky Bacon, Tomato Basil, Tuscan)

Other Cheeses (All Natural Swiss Slices, American Slices, Colby Jack, Monterey Jack, Muenster, Pepper Jack)

Reduced Fat Cheddars (50% Jalapeno, 50% Pepper Jack, 50% Sharp, 75% Sharp)

Seriously Snacking Bars 75% Reduced Fat Habanero Cheddar

Shredded Cheeses (Fancy Blend, Mozzarella)

Specialty Cheddars (3 Year, Classic Vermont Sharp, Clothbound Wheel, Private Stock, Reserve, Vintage Choice)

Spreadable Tub (Extra Sharp Cheddar, Habanero Cheddar, Horseradish Cheddar)

Castle Wood Reserve - Slices (Baby Swiss, Medium Cheddar, Mild Cheddar, Muenster, Pepper Jack, Provolone, Reduced Fat (Light Swiss, Medium Cheddar), Sharp Provolone, Smoked Gouda)

C

Cheez Whiz - Cheese Dip Original
Copper Cowbell - Asiago Spread
Cracker Barrel -
    Cheddar (2% Extra Sharp, Extra Sharp, Extra Sharp White, Reduced
      Fat (2% Sharp, Extra Sharp White, Sharp White), Sharp, Shredded
      (2% Extra Sharp Reduced Fat, Sharp), Vermont (2% Sharp White,
      Sharp White))
    Cheddar Cheese Sticks (Extra Sharp 2%, Natural Extra Sharp
      White, Natural Sharp)
    Swiss Baby
Daiya - Shreds (Cheddar Style ●, Mozzarella Style ●, Pepperjack Style ●)
Di Lusso - American (White, Yellow), Cheddar (Medium, Wisconsin
    Sharp), Colby (Jack, Mini Horn), Havarti, Muenster, Pepper Jack
    Natural, Provolone, Swiss (Baby, Regular), Whole Milk Mozzarella
Dietz & Watson ▲ -
    Aalsbruk (Aged Gouda ●, Edam ●, Gouda ●, Smoked Gouda ●)
    Aged Cheddar w/Habanero & Jalapeno ●
    Baby Swiss ●
    Danish (Blue ●, Fontina ●, Havarti ●)
    Deli Counter
      American White ●
      Baby Swiss ●
      Cheddar (Buffalo Wing Hot Sauce ●, Horseradish ●, Jalapeno &
        Cayenne Pepper ●, Roasted Garlic ●, Sharp Red Wax ●, Sharp
        White ●, Sharp Yellow ●)
      Colby (Jack ●, Jalapeno ●, Regular ●)
      Havarti w/Dill ●
      Hot Pepper Jack ●
      Lacy Swiss ●
      Monterey Jack ●
      Muenster ●
      Peppadew ●
      Pepperoni Cheddar ●
      Provolone ●

Smoked Gouda ●
Swiss ●
Feta ●
Gorgonzola ●
Habanero & Jalapeno Wheel ●
Havarti w/Dill ●
Horseradish Wheel ●
Hot Pepper Buffalo Wing Cheddar ●
Jarlsberg ●
Monterey Jack ●
Mozzarella ●
Muenster ●
New York State (Aged Cheddar (Xtra Sharp ●, XXXtra Sharp ●),
    Cheddar (Buffalo Wing Wheel ●, Champagne ●, Champagne
    Wheel ●, Double Cream ●, Peppadew ●, Sharp Yellow ●,
    w/Horseradish ●, w/Horseradish & Smokey Bacon ●, w/Jalapeno
    & Cayenne Peppers ●, w/Roasted Garlic ●, w/Toasted Onion ●,
    White ●))
Pepper Jack ●
Port Wine Cheddar ●
Sharp Italian Table Cheese (w/Picante Olives ●, w/Tomato & Basil ●)
Slices (American (White ●, Yellow ●), Cheddar (Horseradish ●,
    Jalapeno & Cayenne Pepper ●, Roasted Garlic ●), Muenster ●,
    Provolone ●, Swiss ●)
Smoked Cheddar ●
Smoked Gouda Wheel ●
Swiss Gruyere ●
Triple Cream Bergenost ●
Dorothy Lane Market - Mozzarella (All Varieties)
Finlandia -
Club Store Products (Deli Slices (Monterey Jack/Colby Jack,
    Muenster), Imported Deli Slices (Light Swiss, Swiss, Thin Sliced
    Swiss))

C

Deli Slices Imported (Double Gloucester, Gouda, Havarti, Light Swiss, Muenster, Swiss, Thin Sliced Swiss)

Deli Sticks Imported (Gouda, Havarti, Light Swiss, Muenster, Swiss)

Sliced To Order (Finlandia Lappi, Finlandia Swiss, Imported Light Swiss, Imported Muenster, Lacey Swiss)

Specialty Cheeses (Oltermanni Baby Muenster, Viola)

Follow Your Heart - Vegan Gourmet (Cheddar !, Monterey Jack !, Mozzarella !, Nacho !)

Food Club Brand -

Cheddar Cheese Sauce

Cheese Bar (Cheddar (All Varieties), Colby Jack, Monterey Jack, Mozzarella)

Chunk (Cheddar (Medium, Mild, Sharp), Colby Jack, Monterey Jack, Mozzarella, Pepper Jack, Swiss)

Shredded (Cheddar, Colby Jack, Italian Blend, Mexican Blend, Mild Cheddar, Mozzarella, Parmesan, Pizza Blend, Sharp Cheddar, Swiss)

Sliced (American, Sharp Cheddar, Swiss)

Spray Aerosol (American, Cheddar, Sharp Cheddar)

Friendship - All Natural Farmer Cheese

Full Flavor Foods ▲ - Cheese Sauce Mix ●

Galaxy Nutritional Foods - All Varieties (Rice, Rice Vegan, Vegan, Veggie, Veggy, Wholesome Valley Organic)

Giant Eagle Brand -

Chunk (Cheddar (Extra Sharp, Mild, New York Extra Sharp, New York Sharp, New York White, Sharp), Colby Jack, Monterey Jack, Mozzarella, Pepper Jack, Swiss)

Easy Melt

Fancy Shredded (Cheddar (Mild, Sharp), Colby Jack, Parmesan, Swiss, Taco Blend)

Mozzarella Ball

Shredded (4 Cheese Italian, Cheddar (Mild, Sharp), Four Cheese Mexican, Mexican Blend, Mozzarella, Whole Milk Mozzarella)

Sliced (Colby Jack, Deluxe American, Muenster, Pepper Jack, Provolone, Sharp Cheddar, Swiss)

Gopal's - Rawmesan, Rawmesan Herbs N' Spice

Gordon Food Service -
Chunk (Colby, Colby Jack, Mild Cheddar, Monterey Jack, Monterey Jack w/Jalapeno Peppers, Mozzarella)
Mozzarella Loaf (Part Skim, Whole Milk)
Shredded Cheddar
Sliced (3% Mozzarella, Colby Jack, Mild Cheddar, Monterey Jack, Monterey Jack w/Jalapeno Peppers, Provolone, Swiss)
String

Great Value Brand (Wal-Mart) - All Deli Style Slices, All Shredded, American Slices (Deluxe, Fat Free), American Slices Reduced Fat, Chunk Cheese (All Flavors), Easy Melt, Parmesan, Reduced Fat Parmesan Style Grated Topping

H-E-B - Crumbled Blue, Fresh Mozzarella (Bocconcini, Ciliegine), Goat Cheese Crumbled, Goat Cheese Log (Cranberry Cinnamon, Garlic & Herb, Honey, Peppadew, Plain), Havarti w/Peppers, Horseradish Cheddar

Hannaford Brand - All (Blocks, Shredded, Sliced), Cheese Spread, Parmesan Grated, Parmesan Romano, Ricotta

Hill Country Fare H-E-B - Cracklin Curls (Hot & Spicy, Original), Muenster, Part Skim Mozzarella, Quesadilla Cheese w/Peppers, Swiss

Horizon Organic - All Varieties

Hormel - Pepperoni Stix & Cheese

Hy-Vee -
American (Fat Free Singles, Singles, Singles 2% Milk)
Cheddar (Extra Sharp, Fancy Shredded Jack, Fancy Shredded Mild 2%, Finely Shredded Mild, Lil' Hunk Mild, Medium, Medium Longhorn, Mild, Mild Cubes, Mild Hunk, Mild Shredded, Mild Slices, Sharp, Sharp Hunk, Sharp Longhorn, Sharp Shredded)
Colby (1 lb., Half Moon Longhorn, Hunk, Longhorn, Slice Singles)
Colby Jack (1 lb., Cubes, Fancy Shredded, Finely Shredded, Half Moon Longhorn, Hunk, Lil' Hunk, Shredded, Slices)

C

  Hot Pepper
  Monterey Jack (1 lb, Hunk)
  Mozzarella (1 lb, Fancy Shredded, Fancy Shredded 2% Milk, Hunk,
   Shredded, Sliced Low Moisture Part Skim)
  Muenster (1 lb, Slices)
  Nacho Cheese Shredded
  Parmesan (Grated, Shredded)
  Pepper Jack Cheese (1 lb, Cubes, Hunk, Singles, Slices)
  Provolone Cheese (1 lb, Slices)
  Ricotta Cheese (Low Fat, Part Skim)
  Shredded Blends (Fancy 4 Italian, Mexican Blend, Pizza, Taco)
  Swiss (1 lb, Fat Free Slices, Singles, Slices)

Isaly's - All Original Cheeses

Kirkland Signature - American Slices, Block (Colby Jack, Creamy
 American Blue, Mild Cheddar, Parmigiano Reggiano, Pecorino
 Romano, Sharp Cheddar), Shredded (4 Cheese Mexican Style,
 Cheddar Jack, Mild Cheddar, Mozzarella, Parmigiano Reggiano)

Kraft -

 Block (Cheddar & Monterey Jack, Colby, Colby & Monterey
  Jack, Colby Longhorn, Extra Sharp Cheddar, Medium Cheddar,
  Mild Cheddar, Monterey Jack, Mozzarella Low Moisture, Sharp
  Cheddar)
 Cracker Cuts Natural Baby Swiss
 Crumbles Sharp Cheddar Aged Wisconsin
 Deli Fresh Slices (Colby Jack 2% Milk, Mild Cheddar, Pepper Jack
  2% Milk)
 Easy Cheese (American, Cheddar, Cheddar 'N Bacon,
  Sharp Cheddar)
 Grated (100% Parmesan, 100% Parmesan & Romano, 100%
  Romano, Original Parmesan, Parmesan Reduced Fat)
 Natural Cheese Sticks (Extra Sharp Cheddar, Mild Cheddar, Sharp
  Cheddar 2% Milk)
 Natural Shredded
  2% Milk w/Added Calcium (Colby & Monterey Jack, Sharp
   Cheddar)

Cheddar (Mild, Mild Cheddar & Monterey Jack)
Colby & Monterey Jack (Finely Shredded, Regular)
Fat Free (Cheddar, Mozzarella)
Italian Classic Fine Shred
Italian Style Five Cheese
Mexican Cheddar Pepperjack Finely Shredded
Mexican Four Cheese
Mild Cheddar Fine Shred
Monterey Jack
Mozzarella
Pizza Four Cheese
Pizza Mozzarella & Cheddar
Sharp Cheddar Aged Wisconsin
w/2% Milk (Italian Three Cheese, Mexican Style Four Cheese, Mexican Style Taco)
w/2% Milk & Added Calcium (Finely Shredded Cheddar, Mild Cheddar Finely Shredded, Mozzarella, Mozzarella Low Moisture Part Skim)
w/A Touch Of Philadelphia (Italian Five Cheese, Mexican Style Four Cheese, Mexican Style Queso Quesadilla, Mozzarella, Pepper Jack, Three Cheese, Triple Cheddar)
Natural Slices (Big Slices (2% Swiss, Aged Swiss, Colby Jack, Jalapeno White Cheddar, Sharp Cheddar 2% Milk), Havarti, w/A Touch Of Philadelphia (Colby Jack, Monterey Jack))
Parmesan Seasoning Blends (Cracked Black Pepper & Toasted Onion, Hearty Tuscan Herbs, Rosemary & Garlic)
Parmesan Tubs (Grated, Shaved)
Polly O String Ums (Mozzarella, Twist Ums Mozzarella & Cheddar)
Shredded (Parmesan, Parmesan Romano & Asiago)
Singles (2% Milk (American, Pepperjack, Sharp Cheddar, Swiss, White American), Deli Deluxe (2% American, American, Swiss Slices, White American), Fat Free (American, Sharp Cheddar, Swiss, White American), Regular (American, Sharp Cheddar), White American)

C

String Cheese (Mozzarella & Cheddar Super Long Twist Ums, Tomato & Basil)

Krinos - Feta (All Varieties)

Land-O-Lakes -

Chunk (American (30% Less Sodium w/Sea Salt, Naturally Slender 25% Less Fat, New Yorker, New Yorker Hot Pepper, White, Yellow), Cheddar (Extra Sharp, Medium, Mild, Sharp), Cheddarella, Colby, Monterey Jack, Mozzarella, New Yorker Provolone w/Smoke Flavor)

Deli Counter Alpine Lace (American, Muenster, Smoked Provolone, Swiss)

Deli Slices (American, Baby Swiss, Co Jack, Colby, Havarti, Mozzarella, Muenster, Pepper Jack, Provolone, Swiss)

Singles Process American

Snack 'N Cheese To Go (Cheddarella, Co Jack (Reduced Fat, Regular), Medium Cheddar, Mild Cheddar (Reduced Fat, Regular))

Laughing Cow - All Varieties (Mini Babybel, Wedges)

Lifetime - All Varieties

Lifeway ▲ - All Varieties

Lisanatti ▲ - Almond Cheese (Cheddar, Garlic & Herb, Jalapeño Jack, Mozzarella), Rice Cheeze (Cheddar, Pepper Jack), RiceCheeze Snack Sticks (American, Mozzarella), SoySation (Chunk (Cheddar, Mozzarella), Shreds (3 Cheese Blend, Cheddar, Mozzarella, Parmesan), Slices (Cheddar, Swiss))

Litehouse - Heart Of Bleu Cheese, Idaho Bleu Cheese Crumbles, Monarch Mountain Gorgonzola Crumbles

Lowes Foods Brand - Cheddar (Extra Sharp Bar, Fancy Shredded Mild, Fancy Shredded Sharp, Medium Bar, Medium Chunk, Mild Bar, Mild Chunk, Mild Shredded, NY Sharp Chunk, Sharp Bar, Sharp Chunk, Sharp Slices, Shredded, Shredded Sharp), Cheddar Jack Shredded, Colby Chunk, Colby Jack (Bar, Chunk, Shredded), Hot Pepper Jack Chunk, Monterey Jack Chunk, Mozzarella (Bar, Chunk, Fancy Shredded, Shredded, Sliced), Muenster Chunk, Parmesan Shredded, Pepper Jack (Bar, Slices), Provolone Sliced, Shredded Blends (Fancy

Italian, Fancy Mexican, Fancy Pizza w/Mozzarella & Cheddar, Nacho/Taco Blend), Swiss (Chunk, Sliced)

Lucerne - Cheese Slices (All Varieties), Ricotta, String

Meijer Brand -

Aerosol Cheese (American, Cheddar, Sharp Cheddar)

American Processed Slices

Cheddar (Fancy Mild Shredded, Fancy Sharp Shredded, Fancy Shredded, Medium Bar, Midget Horn, Mild Bar, Mild Chunk, Sharp Bar, Sharp Chunk, Sharp Shredded, Sharp Shredded Zipper Pouch, Shredded, Shredded Zipper Pouch, Sliced Longhorn Half Moon, X Sharp Bar)

Cheddar Marble C&W Cheddar

Cheddar/Monterey Jack (Bar, Fancy Shred Zip Pouch)

Cheese Food Individually Wrapped (2% American, 2% Sharp, Fat Free Sharp, Sliced Pepper, Swiss)

Cheezy Does It (Jalapeño, Spread Loaf)

Colby (Bar, Chunk, Fancy Shredded, Midget Horn)

Colby Jack (Bar, Fancy Shredded, Longhorn Half Moon, Sliced Single)

Colby Longhorn (Full Moon, Half Moon, Half Moon Sliced)

Hot Pepper Jack Chunk

Italian Blend Fancy Shredded

Mexican Blend (Fancy Shredded, Shredded)

Monterey Jack Chunk

Mozzarella (Fancy Shredded, Shredded, Sliced Single)

Mozzarella Low Moisture Part Skim (Bar, Chunk, Shredded, Sliced Chunk, Square, String Cheese)

Muenster Sliced Single

Parmesan (1/3 Less Fat, & Romano Grated, Grated)

Pepperjack (Bar, Sliced Stack Pack)

Pizza Blend Shredded

Provolone Stacked Slice

String Cheese

Swiss (Chunk, Sliced Sandwich Cut, Sliced Single)

Taco/Nacho Fancy Shredded

C

Midwest Country Fare - American Sandwich Slices, Shredded Cheese (Cheddar, Mozzarella)

Organic Valley - Baby Swiss, Cheddar (Mild (Regular, Shredded), Raw (Mild, Sharp), Reduced Fat & Sodium, Sharp, Vermont (Extra Sharp, Medium, Sharp)), Colby, Feta, Italian Blend Shredded, Mexican Blend Shredded, Monterey Jack (Reduced Fat, Regular), Mozzarella (Low Moisture Part Skim Shredded, Regular), Muenster, Parmesan (Grated, Shredded), Pepper Jack, Provolone, Ricotta, Stringles (Cheddar, Colby Jack, Mozzarella), Wisconsin Raw Milk Jack Style

Ortega - Nacho Cheese Sauce Pouch

Polly-O - Fresh Style Ball Mozzarella (Cherry Sized, Fat Free, Part Skim, Whole Milk), Parmesan (& Romano Grated, Grated), Ricotta (Fat Free, Lite, Original, Part Skim), Shredded Mozzarella (Fat Free, Finely Shredded, Lite, Part Skim, w/Provolone Romano & Parmesan, Whole Milk)

Primo Taglio - Cheddar (American, Imported Aged White, Medium, Mild), Jack Hot Pepper, Lacy Swiss, Muenster, Provolone, Smoked Fontina, Swiss

Publix -

Natural (Cheddar (Extra Sharp, Medium, Mild, Sharp), Colby, Colby Jack, Monterey Jack (& Cheddar Shredded, Regular, w/ Jalapeno Peppers), Mozzarella, Muenster, Provolone, Ricotta, Shredded (Italian 6 Cheese Blend, Mexican 4 Cheese Blend), Swiss)

Processed (American Cheese Food Pasteurized Processed Singles (Regular, Thick Slice), Cheese Spread, Deluxe American Slices, Swiss Cheese Pasteurized Processed Singles)

Specialty (Asiago Wedge, Blue Crumbled, Crumbled Goat, Feta (Chunk, Crumbled, Crumbled Reduced Fat, Reduced Fat Chunk), Gorgonzola Crumbled, Parmesan (Grated, Shredded, Wedge))

Pure Market Express ▲ - Artisanal (Cheddar Spread ●, Cilantro Jalapeno Cheese ●, Creamy Herb Cheese ●, Good As Gouda ●, Mexi Cheese ●, Pepper Jack Cheese ●, Simply Basil ●, Spicy Peppercorn ●, Sundried Tomato Basil Cheese ●, Wasabi Chive ●)

Ragu - Cheesy Double Cheddar Sauce

Redwood Hill Farm - Bucheret, California Crottin, Camellia, Goat Milk Cheddar, Raw Milk Feta, Smoked Goat Cheddar

Rice Shreds (Galaxy Nutritional Foods) - All Varieties (Rice, Rice Vegan, Vegan, Veggie, Veggy, Wholesome Valley Organic)

Riega ▲ - Sauce Mix (Alfredo ★, Pepper Jack ★, White Cheddar ★, Yellow ★)

Road's End Organics - Organic (GF Alfredo Chreese Mix, GF Cheddar Chreese Mix)

Safeway Brand - Grated Parmesan

Safeway Select - Parmesan Shredded

Sara Lee - Slices (American, Baby Swiss, Colby & Jack, Mild Cheddar, Mozzarella, Muenster, Smoked Provolone)

Sargento -

Artisan Blends (Authentic Mexican, Double Cheddar, Mozzarella & Provolone, Parmesan, Parmesan & Romano, Swiss, Whole Milk Mozzarella, Wisconsin Sharp White Cheddar)

Bistro Blends (Italian Pasta Cheese, Mozzarella & Asiago w/ Roasted Garlic, Nacho & Taco, Taco)

Classic Fancy (4 Cheese Mexican, 6 Cheese Italian, Cheddar Jack, Colby Jack, Mild Cheddar, Monterey Jack, Mozzarella, Pizza Double, Sharp Cheddar)

Classic Old Style (Extra Sharp Cheddar, Mild Cheddar, Mozzarella, Pepper Jack)

Deli Style (Aged Swiss, Baby Swiss, Chipotle Cheddar, Colby, Colby Jack, Duo Pack (Medium Cheddar & Colby Jack, Provolone & Mild Cheddar, Swiss & Baby Swiss), Extra Sharp Cheddar, Gouda, Havarti, Jarlsberg, Medium Cheddar, Mild Cheddar, Monterey Jack, Mozzarella, Muenster, Natural Blends (Cheddar Mozzarella, Colby Pepper Jack, Double Cheddar), Pepper Jack, Provolone, Reduced Fat (Colby Jack, Medium Cheddar, Pepper Jack, Provolone, Swiss), Sharp Cheddar, Sharp Provolone, Swiss, Ultra Thin (Colby Jack, Mild Cheddar, Provolone, Swiss), Vermont Sharp White Cheddar)

C

Fine Cheese (Grated Parmesan, Grated Parmesan & Romano)

Fine Cheeses (Fat Free Ricotta, Hard Grating Parmesan, Light Ricotta, Part Skim Ricotta, Whole Milk Ricotta)

Natural (Colby Jack (Cubes, Sticks), Light String Cheese, Mild Cheddar (Cubes, Sticks), String)

Reduced Fat (Cheddar Jack, Deli Style (Colby Jack, Medium Cheddar, Pepper Jack), Shredded (4 Cheese Italian, 4 Cheese Mexican, Colby Jack, Mild Cheddar, Mozzarella, Sharp Cheddar))

Reduced Sodium (Deli Style (Colby Jack, Pepper Jack, Provolone), Shredded (Mild Cheddar, Mozzarella))

Snacks (Colby Jack Sticks (Reduced Fat, Reduced Sodium, Regular), Double Cheddar Sticks, Mild Cheddar Bars, Monterey Jack Sticks, Natural Blends (Cheddar Mozzarella, Provolone Mozzarella), Pepper Jack Sticks, Reduced Fat Sharp Cheddar Sticks, Reduced Sodium Mild Cheddar Sticks, Sharp Cheddar Sticks, String Cheese (Light, Reduced Sodium, Regular), Vermont Sharp White Cheddar Sticks)

Sister River Foods - Parma Vegan Parmesan (Chipotle Cayenne, Garlicky Green, Original)

Soy Kaas - Lactose Free Cheese All Flavors *(Except Vegan Varieties)*

Spartan Brand - American Singles (2% Milk, Fat Free), Cheddar Chunk Cheese (Extra Sharp, Medium, Milk, Sharp), Colby Cheese Chunks, Colby Jack Cheese (Chunks, Shredded, Sliced), Finely Shredded Cheese (Colby Jack, Italian 4 Cheese, Mexican Style 4 Cheese, Mild Cheddar, Mozzarella, Parmesan, Sharp Cheddar, Taco), Mild Cheddar Cheese (Shredded, Sliced), Monterey Jack Cheese (Chunks, Shredded), Mozzarella Cheese (Chunks, Round, Shredded, Sliced), Pizza Blend Shredded, Processed American (Deluxe Sliced, Sliced), Sharp Cheddar Shredded, String Cheese (Light, Regular), Swiss Cheese (Chunks, Sliced), Taco Spice Shredded

Tasty Bite - Paneer Makhani **!**

The Vegetarian Express - Parma Zaan Sprinkles **!**

Tillamook - All Varieties **!**

Trader Joe's - Blocks *(Except Dubliner Irish Stout Cheese)*,
Parmesan & Romano Cheese Blend, Shredded, Soy Cheese Slices,
Wedges *(Except Dubliner Irish Stout Cheese)*

Velveeta - Chunk (2%, Mexican Mild, Pepperjack, Regular), Slices
(Extra Thick, Regular)

Wayfare - We Can't Say It's Cheese (Cheddar Sauce ●, Cheddar
Spread ●, Hickory Cheddar ●, Mexi Cheddar ●)

Wegmans Brand -
American Cheese Slices (Fat Free (White, Yellow), Reduced Fat
2% Milk (White, Yellow), White, Yellow)
Colby Jack (2% Shredded, Block, Shredded, Sliced, Thin Sliced),
Deluxe American Slices (White, Yellow)
Extra Sharp Cheddar (White, Yellow)
Fancy Shredded (2% Milk Mexican Blend, 2% Milk Mild Cheddar,
Mexican, Mild Cheddar, Pizza, Taco)
Longhorn Style Colby
Mild Cheddar (Shredded, White, White Shredded, Yellow)
Monterey Jack
Mozzarella Cheese (2% Milk Low Moisture Part Skim Shredded,
Low Moisture Part Skim Shredded, Low Moisture Part Skim Thin
Sliced, Whole Milk Shredded)
Muenster (Block, Thin Sliced)
Parmesan Cheese (Finely Shredded, Grated, Grated w/Romano)
Pepper Jack (Block, Reduced Fat 2% Milk Slices)
Provolone Thin Sliced
Romano Grated
Sharp Cheddar (2% Milk Shredded, Extra Sharp White, Extra Sharp
Yellow, Fat Free Yellow Slices, Reduced Fat 2% Milk Slices,
Shredded, Thin Sliced, Vermont White)
Swiss (Block, Fat Free White Slices, Heart O' Swiss Sliced, Reduced
Fat 2% Milk Slices, Thin Sliced)

Weight Watchers - Reduced Fat (Cream Cheese Spread, Singles)

Winn Dixie - American Pasteurized Process Cheese (American,
Deluxe, Reduced Fat), Blue Cheese, Cheddar (Extra Sharp, Jack,
Medium, Mild, NY Extra Sharp, NY Sharp), Colby (Jack, Regular),

C

Feta, Gorgonzola, Italian Blend Shredded, Mexican Blend, Monterey Jack (Regular, w/Jalapeno Peppers), Mozzarella, Muenster, Parmesan (& Romano, Grated), Pasteurized Process Swiss Cheese Product, Pimento Cheese (Chunky, Regular, w/Jalapenos), Provolone, Ricotta (All Types), String Cheese, Swiss, White Cheddar

Cheese Puffs...see Snacks

Cheese Spread...see Cheese and/or Spread

Cheesecake...see also Cake

    Chuckanut Bay Foods - Gluten Free Cheesecakes (Chocolate Truffle ●, New York ●, Pumpkin ●, Strawberry ●, Tuxedo ●)

    Lean On Me - Blueberry, Chocolate Dipped, Marble, Original

    Moondance - All Flavors

    Pamela's Products ▲ - Cheesecake (Hazelnut w/Chocolate Crust, New York, New York Agave Sweetened, White Chocolate Raspberry, Zesty Lemon)

    The Grain Exchange

Cherries

    ... *All Fresh Fruits & Vegetables Are Gluten-Free

    Annie's - Organic Orchard Real Fruit Bites Cherry **!!**

    Cella's - Chocolate Covered Cherries (Dark, Milk)

    Food Club Brand - Frozen Dark Sweet Cherries, Maraschino (Green, Red, Red w/Stems), Pitted Red Tart

    Gordon Food Service - Maraschino

    Great Value Brand (Wal-Mart) - Maraschino

    Hy-Vee - Frozen Cherry Berry Blend, Red Maraschino Cherries (Regular, w/Stems)

    Lowes Foods Brand - Frozen, Maraschino (Red, Red w/Stems)

    Lucky Leaf - Red Tart Pitted Cherries

    Mariani - Dried (Berries & Cherries **!!**, Flavor Sensations Cherry Pie Flavored **!!**, Regular **!!**)

    Meijer Brand - Frozen (Dark Sweet, Tart), Maraschino Cherry (Red, Red w/Stems)

    Mezzetta ▲ - Maraschino Cherries (w/o Stems, w/Stems)

    Midwest Country Fare - Maraschino Cherries

    Musselman's - Red Tart Pitted Cherries

Nuts.com - Dried Fruit (Bing ●, Organic Bing ●, Rainier ●, Simply ●, Sour Tart ●)

Oskri Organics - Dried Cherries

Publix - Frozen Dark Sweet Cherries, Maraschino

S&W - All Canned/Jarred Fruits

Safeway Brand - Frozen Dark Sweet, Maraschino Cherries

Santa Barbara Olive Co. - Maraschino Red

Spartan Brand - Frozen Dark Sweet Cherries, Maraschino Cherries Red (Regular, w/Stems)

Star - Maraschino w/Stems

Trader Joe's - Dark Chocolate Covered Cherries, Frozen Very Cherry Berry Blend

Wegmans Brand - Canned Triple Cherry Fruit Mix In Light Syrup, FYFGA Frozen Dark Sweet, Jarred Maraschino (Jumbo w/o Stems, w/o Stems, w/Stems)

Winn Dixie - Dark Sweet Cherries, Maraschino Cherries

Woodstock Farms - Dried Cherries Unsulphured, Organic Frozen Dark Sweet Cherries

Chewing Gum

5 - All Varieties

B Fresh

Between - Dental Gum

Big League Chew - All Varieties

Big Red

Bubblicious - All Varieties

Charms - Blow Pops (Minis, Regular, Super)

Cry Baby - Extra Sour Bubble Gum, Gumballs

Dentyne - Fire (All Varieties), Ice (All Varieties)

Doublemint

Dubble Bubble - Gumballs, Twist Gum

Eclipse - All Flavors

Extra - All Varieties

Freedent - All Varieties

Glee Gum - All Varieties, Make Your Own Chewing Gum Kit

Hubba Bubba - All Varieties **!!** *(Except Tape)*

C

Indie Candy - Make Your Own Chewing Gum Kit
Juicy Fruit - All Varieties
Lowes Foods Brand - Double Bubble Gum
Meijer Brand - Nicotine Gum (Mint, Regular)
Nicorette
Orbit - All Varieties
Orbit White
Spearmint
Stride - All Varieties
Trident - All Varieties
Winterfresh

Chick Peas...see Beans

Chicken...see also Deli Meat

... *All Fresh Chicken Is Gluten-Free (Non-Marinated, Unseasoned)*

Al Fresco -
Breakfast Sausages (Apple Maple, Country Style, Wild Blueberry)
Chicken Meatballs (Teriyaki Ginger, Tomato & Basil)
Dinner Sausage Fully Cooked (Buffalo Style, Roasted Garlic, Roasted
    Pepper & Asiago, Spicy Jalapeno, Spinach & Feta, Sundried Tomato,
    Sweet Apple, Sweet Italian Style)
Fresh Dinner Sausages (Buffalo Style, Hot Italian, Roasted Garlic &
    Herb, Spicy Chipotle, Sweet Apple, Sweet Italian Style)

AllergyFree - Breaded (Boneless Breast ★, Nuggets ★, Tenderloins ★,
    Tenders ★, Wings ★)

Applegate - Deli Counter (Chipotle !, Natural Barbecue !, Oven Roasted
    Breast !, Smoked !), Deli Meat Organic Smoked Chicken Breast !,
    Gluten Free Chicken Breast Tenders ●, Natural Gluten Free Chicken
    Nuggets ●, Natural Grilled Breast Strips (Grilled !, Southwest Style !),
    Organic Roasted Chicken Breast !

Augason Farms ▲ - Gluten Free (Freeze Dried Chicken Breast Chunks ●,
    Vegetarian Meat Substitute ●)

Bell & Evans - Chicken Burgers !, Gluten Free (Breaded Chicken Breast !,
    Breaded Chicken Patties !, Chicken Breast Tenders !, Chicken
    Nuggets !), Grilled Breasts !, Pulled BBQ !

Blue Ribbon Restaurants - Naked Nuggets

Boar's Head - All Varieties

Buddig - Deli Cut Rotisserie Chicken, Fix Quix Grilled Chicken Breast Cubes, Original Deli Meat

Bumble Bee - Premium In Water (Breast, White)

Butterball - Chicken Breast Strips (Grilled, Oven Roasted, Southwestern Style), Deli Meat Thin Sliced Oven Roasted Chicken Breast

Casual Gourmet - Chicken Sausage Roasted Red Pepper & Spinach

Chi-Chi's - Fiesta Plates (Creamy Chipotle, Salsa, Savory Garlic)

Coleman's Natural Foods -

Bone In Skin On Thigh

Boneless Skinless (Breast, Fresh For The Freezer Breasts, Thigh)

Chicken Sausage (Mild Italian, Spicy Andouille, Spicy Chipotle, Spicy Cilantro, Spicy Italian, Spinach & Feta Cheese, Sun Dried Tomato & Basil)

Drummettes

Drumsticks

Gluten Free Nuggets ●

Gourmet Meatballs (Italian Parmesan, Pesto Parmesan, Spinach Fontina Cheese & Roasted Garlic, Sun Dried Tomato Basil Provolone)

Organic (Bone In Skin On Thigh, Buffalo Style Wings, Chicken Sausage (Mild Italian, Spinach & Feta, Sun Dried Tomato & Basil, Sweet Apple), Drummettes, Drumsticks, Fresh For The Freezer Breasts, Split Breast, Whole Chicken, Wings)

Split Breast

Whole Chicken

Wings

Di Lusso - Deli Counter (Mesquite, Oven Roasted)

Dietz & Watson ▲ -

Deli Counter (Buffalo Style ●, Gourmet Breast ●, Honey Barbecue ●, Momma Dietz (Parmigiana ●, Roast ●), Rotisserie Breast ●, Southern Fried ●)

Pre Sliced (Buffalo Style ●, Southern Style ●)

C

Dinty Moore - Compleats Microwave Meals Rice & Chicken

Eating Right - Deli Sliced Oven Roasted

Eckrich - Deli Meat Fried Chicken Breast

Empire Kosher - 8 Piece Cut Up, Boneless Skinless Breasts, Chicken Bologna Slices, Chicken Franks, Drumsticks, Frozen (Boneless Skinless Breasts, Drumsticks, Leg Quarters, Rock Cornish Broiler, Split Breasts, Thighs, Wing Drumettes), Fully Cooked BBQ, Leg Quarters, Organic (Boneless Skinless Breasts, Drumsticks, Whole Broiler), Quarter Broiler, Ready To Roast Garlic & Herb, Split Breasts, Thighs, Whole Broiler

Food Club Brand - Chunk White Chicken

Garrett County Farms - Chicken Franks ★

GF Naturals - Breaded (Boneless Breast Filets ●, Boneless Chicken Wings ●, Boneless Nugget ●, Breast Tenderloins ●)

Giant Eagle Brand - Shredded Breast w/BBQ Sauce, Wrapped Breasts

Golden Platter - All Natural Gluten Free (Nuggets, Patties, Tenders)

Great Value Brand (Wal-Mart) -
    Canned Chunk Chicken Breast
    Frozen (Boneless Skinless Breast, Drumsticks, Thighs, Wing Sections)

H-E-B - All Natural Chicken Breast Oven Roasted Lunchmeat, Chicken (Canned, Premium Breast), Chicken Sausage (Andouille, Fajita, Poblano & Cheddar), Rotisserie Chicken Tub, Rotisserie Flavor Chicken Breast, Seasoned Chicken Breast (Cilantro Lime, Italian Style, Lemon Herb, Southwest Style, Sweet Chile)

Hannaford Brand - Chicken Breast Chunk In Water

Hillshire Farms - Deli Select Oven Roasted Chicken Breast, Deli Select Ultra Thin Chicken Breast Rotisserie Seasoned, Grilled Essentials Chicken Breast (Garlic & Herb, Grilled, Italian Style, Lemon Pepper)

Homestead Creek - Chicken Nuggets

Honeysuckle White -
    Chicken Breast Deli Meat (BBQ, Buffalo Style, Oil Browned)
    Wings (Barbecue Glazed, Buffalo Style, Oven Roasted)

C

Hormel - Carved Chicken Breast (Grilled, Oven Roasted), Chunk Meats (Breast of Chicken, Chicken), Natural Choice (Grilled Strips, Oven Roasted Chicken Strips, Rotisserie Style Deli Meat)

Hy-Vee -
100% Natural Fresh (Boneless Skinless, Boneless Skinless Breasts, Breast Tenderloins, Drumsticks, For Roasting w/Neck & Giblets, Gizzards, Leg Quarters, Split Breasts, Split Breasts w/Ribs, Thighs, Whole Cut Up w/Neck & Giblets, Wing Drummettes, Wings, Young w/Neck & Giblets)
Canned 98% Fat Free Breast of Chicken
Thin Sliced Chicken

Ian's - Wheat Free Gluten Free Recipe (Chicken Nuggets, Chicken Nuggets Kids Meal, Chicken Patties, Chicken Tenders, Space Nuggets)

Isernio's - Ground Chicken ●

John Soules Foods -
Fully Cooked Chicken Breast Strips (Grilled, Italian Style, Rotisserie Style)
Fully Cooked Fajitas Chicken
Pollo Asado Fully Cooked Diced Chicken Breast
Ready To Cook For Fajitas (Thigh, Breast)
Rotisserie Style Fully Cooked Chicken Breast Fillets

Kayem - Deli Meat Rotisserie Style **! !**

Kirkland Signature -
Canned Chicken Breast
Frozen (Breasts, Tenderloin, Wings)

Lloyd's - Shredded Chicken In Original BBQ Sauce, Woodfire Shredded

Meijer Brand - Canned Chicken Chunk White, Lunch Meat Sliced Chipped Meat

Member's Mark - Canned Premium Chunk Chicken Breast In Water

Nature's Place - Fresh Chicken

O Organics - Fresh Chicken Breast (Regular, Tenders)

C

Organic Prairie - Frozen Organic Retail (Breasts (Halves, Whole), Ground Chub, Whole Young), Organic (Boneless Skinless Chicken Breasts, Chicken Italian Sausage, Ground Chicken, Whole Chicken), Pre Sliced Deli Meat Roast Slices

Oscar Mayer - Carving Board Deli Meat Rotisserie, Deli Fresh (BBQ, Cajun Seasoned Chicken Breast, Honey Roasted, Oven Roasted, Oven Roasted Chicken Breast 98% Fat Free, Rotisserie Style Chicken Breast, Shaved Oven Roasted Breast), Deli Meat (Oven Roasted Breast, Oven Roasted Homestyle White)

Perdue - Ground Chicken (Breast of Chicken, Burgers), Individually Frozen Chicken (Breasts, Tenderloins, Wings), Perfect Portions Boneless Skinless Chicken Breast (All Natural, Italian Style), Short Cuts Carved Chicken Breast (Grilled Southwestern, Honey Roasted, Original Roasted)

Publix - All Natural Fresh, Deli Rotisserie Chicken (Barbecue Flavored w/Barbecue Seasoning **!!**, Lemon Pepper Flavored w/Lemon & Herb Seasoning **!!**, Original Roasted **!!**), Frozen (Boneless Skinless Chicken (Breasts, Cutlets), Chicken Breast Tenderloins, Chicken Wingettes)

Publix GreenWise Market - Boneless Breast, Boneless Thighs, Cutlet, Drummettes, Drumsticks, Fillet, Ground Chicken, Skinless Drumstick, Skinless Thighs, Split Breast, Tenderloin, Thighs, Whole, Wings

Rocky Jr. - Bone In Skin On Thigh, Boneless Skinless (Breast, Thigh), Breast Tenders, Drummettes, Drumsticks, Rocky Dogs Uncured Hot Dog, Split Breast, The Range Chicken, Whole Chicken, Wings

Rosie - Organic (Bone In Skin On Thigh, Boneless Skinless (Breast, Thigh), Breast Tenders, Drummettes, Drumsticks, Split Breast, Whole Chicken, Wings)

S'Better Farms ▲ - Chicken (Ballontine, Fingers, Party Wings, Siciliano, Szechwan)

Safeway - Deli Meat All Thin Sliced & Regular

Safeway Brand - Canned Chunk White Breast

Sara Lee - Deli Meat Slices Oven Roasted Chicken Breast

Saz's - Barbecue Chicken Meat Tub

Shelton's - Capon, Free Range (Breasts, Thighs, Whole), Organic (Boneless Breast, Boneless/Skinless Breast, Breast, Cut Up, Whole Chicken, Whole Legs)

Signature Cafe - Roasted Chicken Homestyle

Smart Chicken - All Varieties

Smart Ones - Frozen Entrees Lemon Herb Chicken Piccata

Spartan Brand - Canned Chicken Breast Chunk, Frozen Boneless Skinless (Breasts, Tenders)

Sweet Bay - All Fresh Chicken

The Original Brat Hans - Chicken Burger (Florentine w/Spinach & Fontina Cheese, Jalapeno & Sharp Cheddar, Pesto Parmesan, Uncured Bacon & Cheddar), Chicken Sausage (Mild Italian, Organic (Apple, Bratwurst, Breakfast Links, Spinach & Feta, Sweet Italian), Skinless Breakfast Links, Spicy Andouille, Spicy Chipotle, Spicy Cilantro, Spicy Italian, Spinach & Feta, Sun Dried Tomato & Basil, Sweet Apple), Gourmet Chicken Meatballs (Aged Parmesan & Fennel, Buffalo Style, Chipotle Pepper & Cheddar, Pesto Parmesan, Pineapple Teriyaki, Spinach/Fontina & Roasted Garlic)

Thumann's - All Varieties ●

Trader Joe's - Chicken Salad Wine Country w/Cranberries, Fresh All Natural, Frozen Chicken (Gorgonzola, Pomodoro), Frozen Chicken Wings, Fully Cooked & Seasoned Roasted Chicken **!!**, Grilled Chicken Breast Strips (Balsamic & Rosemary **!!**, Chili Lime **!!**, Lemon Pepper **!!**, Plain **!!**), Handcrafted Chicken & Cheese Tamales, Just Chicken Plain, Pulled Chicken Breast In Smoky BBQ Sauce

Tropical Traditions - Pastured Whole Chicken, Whole Chicken Cut Into Parts

Tyson - All Natural Fresh (All Varieties)

Valley Fresh - All Varieties

Wellshire Farms - Chicken Franks ★, Kids Dino Shaped Chicken Bites Refrigerated ●

Winn Dixie - Canned Breast, Frozen (Breasts, Tenderloins)

C Chicken Broth...see Broth

Chicken Nuggets...see Chicken

Chicken Wings...see Wings

Chiles

    Chi-Chi's - Green Chiles

    Food Club Brand - Green Mild

    La Victoria - Fire Roasted Green (Diced, Whole)

    Las Palmas - Green (Diced, Strips, Whole)

    Meijer Brand - Diced Mild Mexican Style

    Old El Paso - Green (Chopped, Whole)

    Ortega - Green (Diced, Fire Roasted Diced Hot, Whole)

    Safeway Brand - Diced Green

    Spartan Brand - Green Chiles

Chili

    Amy's - Organic Chili (Medium ★, Medium Black Bean ★, Medium Light In Sodium ★, Medium w/Vegetables ★, Southwestern Black Bean ★, Spicy ★, Spicy Light In Sodium ★)

    Augason Farms ▲ - Gluten Free Southwest Mix ●

    Cookwell & Company - Chili Two Step Mix

    Food Club Brand - Chili w/Beans

    Frontera - Chili Starter Chipotle Black Bean, Chipotle & Black Bean Chili Mix, New Mexican Three Bean Chili

    Frontier Soups - Chili Mix (California Gold Rush White Bean ★, Michigan Ski Country ★, Midwest Weekend Cincinnati ★)

    Hormel - Chili Master (Chipotle Chicken w/Beans, White Chicken Chili w/Beans), Chili w/Beans (Chunky, Hot, Less Sodium, Regular)

    Hy-Vee - Hot Chili w/Beans, Mild w/Beans

    Kettle Cuisine - Angus Beef Steak Chili w/Beans ●, Chicken Chili w/White Beans ●, Three Bean ●

    Meijer Brand - Chili (No Beans Regular, w/Beans Regular), Hot Dog Chili Sauce

    Mimi's Gourmet - Black Bean & Corn, Spicy White Bean & Jalapeno, Three Bean w/Rice

Shelton's - Mild (Chicken, Turkey), Spicy (Chicken, Turkey)

Spartan Brand - w/Beans

Stagg - Chunkero, Classic, Dynamite Hot, Ranch House Chicken, Silverado Beef, Steak House, Vegetable Garden, White Chicken

StoreHouse Foods - Classic Vegetarian Chili

Tabatchnick - Frozen Vegetarian Chili, Vegetarian Chili Microwavable Bowl

Trader Joe's - Beef Chili w/Beans, Chicken Chili w/Beans, Organic Vegetarian **!!**, Vegetarian Three Bean Chili

Wegmans Brand - Spicy Red Lentil Chili

Winn Dixie - w/Beans

Chili Powder

Chugwater Chili

Durkee - Dark

McCormick - Gourmet Collection, Hot Mexican Style, Regular

Meijer Brand

Spartan Brand

Spice Islands

Tones

Chili Sauce

A Taste Of Thai - Garlic Chili Pepper Sauce, Sweet Red Chili Sauce

Food Club Brand

Frank's RedHot - Chile 'N Lime

Great Value Brand (Wal-Mart) - Regular

Hannaford Brand

Heinz

La Victoria - Red

Las Palmas - Red Chile Sauce

Lee Kum Kee - Sriracha Chili Sauce

Meijer Brand - Regular

Organicville - Organic ●

Safeway Brand

Spartan Brand

Texas Pete ▲ - No Beans, Original

C

Thai Kitchen - Roasted Red Chili Paste, Spicy Thai, Sweet Red

Trader Joe's - Chili Pepper !!, Sweet !!

Chips

Arico - Casava Chips (Barbeque Bliss, Original, Sea Salt Mist, Thai Ginger)

Baked Lay's - Original ★, Parmesan & Tuscan Herb ★, Sour Cream & Onion ★, Southwestern Ranch ★

Baked Ruffles - Cheddar & Sour Cream ★, Original ★

Baked Tostitos - Scoops Tortilla Chips ★

Beanitos - Black Bean ★, Cheddar Cheese ★, Chipotle BBQ ★, Pinto Bean and Flax ★

Better Balance - Protein Chips (Chili Nacho Cheese ●, Crispy Parmesan ●, Lemon Herb ●)

Better Made Snack Foods - All Varieties (Flavored Potato Chips, Potato Sticks), Regular Potato Plain Unseasoned

Blue Diamond ▲ - Baked Nut Chips (Nacho ●, Sea Salt ●, Sour Cream & Chive ●)

Boulder Canyon Natural Foods -

Canyon Cut Potato Chips (Honey Barbeque ★, Sour Cream & Chives ★, Totally Natural ★)

Kettle Cooked Potato Chips (60% Reduced Sodium ★, Balsamic Vinegar & Rosemary ★, Compostable Packaging (Hickory Barbeque ★, Parmesan & Garlic ★, Sea Salt & Cracked Pepper ★, Totally Natural ★), Hickory Barbeque ★, Jalapeno Cheddar ★, Olive Oil ★, Parmesan & Garlic ★, Red Wine Vinegar ★, Sea Salt & Cracked Pepper ★, Spinach & Artichoke ★, Totally Natural ★)

Lightly Salted Hummus Chips (Regular ★, w/Sesame ★)

Tortilla Chips w/Hummus Lightly Salted & Sesame ★

Brothers All Natural ▲ - Potato Crisps (Black Pepper w/Sea Salt, Onion & Garlic, Original w/Sea Salt, Szechuan Pepper & Fresh Chives)

Cape Cod - Chef's Recipe Roasted Garlic & Red Pepper, Potato (40% Less Fat (Aged Cheddar & Sour Cream, Original, Sea Salt &

Vinegar, Sweet Mesquite Barbeque), Chef's Recipe Feta & Rosemary, Original (Harvest Gold, Kettle Cooked, Parmesan & Roasted Garlic, Sea Salt & Cracked Pepper, Sea Salt & Vinegar, Sour Cream & Green Onion, Sweet & Spicy Jalapeno, Sweet Mesquite Barbeque), Waffle Cut (Sea Salt, Seasoned Pepper))

Central Market H-E-B - Organic Tortilla (Thin Salted, Ultra Thin Unsalted, White Corn)

Chi-Chi's - Fiesta All Natural Tortilla Chips (Authentic, Rounds)

Covered Bridge Potato Chips ▲ - Old Fashioned Kettle Style (Creamy Dill ●, Homestyle Ketchup ●, Montreal Steak Spice ●, Sea Salt (& Cracked Pepper ●, & Vinegar ●, Extra Thick Cut ●, Regular ●), Smokin' Sweet BBQ ●, Sweet Potato (w/Cinnamon & Brown Sugar ●, w/Sea Salt ●)), Tortilla Chips (Chipotle ●, Lime ●, Sea Salt ●)

Danielle - Crispy Fruit Chips (Honey Banana, Roasted Coconut, Sweet Mango), Crispy Veggie Chips (Crunchy Pumpkin, Spicy Carrot)

Deep River Snacks - Asian Sweet & Spicy ●, Cracked Pepper & Sea Salt●, Lightly Salted ●, Mesquite BBQ ●, Original Salted ●, Rosemary & Olive Oil ●, Salt & Vinegar ●, Sweet Maui Onion ●, Zesty Jalapeno ●

Doritos - Late Night All Nighter Cheeseburger !!, Reduced Fat Tortilla Chips (Cool Ranch !!, Nacho Cheese !!, Spicy Nacho !!), Tortilla Chips (Baked Nacho Cheese !!, Blazin' Buffalo & Ranch !!, Cool Ranch !!, Fiery Fusion Sizzlin' Cayenne & Cheese !!, Flamas !!, Four Cheese !!, Pizza Supreme !!, Salsa Rio !!, Salsa Verde !!, Sour Cream & Onion !!, Spicy Nacho !!, Taco !!, Tangy Buffalo Wing !!, Tapatio !!, Toasted Corn ★)

Dorothy Lane Market - Kettle Cooked Potato Chips, Organic Tortilla Chips

Dutch Crunch ▲ - Kettle Chips (Hot Buffalo Wing w/Creamy Bleu Cheese, Jalapeno & Cheddar, Mesquite BBQ, Original, Parmesan & Garlic, RipL Low Sodium)

Dutch Gourmet ▲ - Thick Cut Potato Chips (Honey Dijon Vinaigrette, Sea Salt, Slow Cooked Ribs, Szechwan)

Eat Smart - Naturals (Garden Veggie (Crisps ●, Stix), MultiGrain Tortilla●, Potato Crisps (Mesquite BBQ, Original, Sea Salt & Vinegar))

C

Enjoy Life ▲ - Plentils (Dill & Sour Cream ●, Garlic & Parmesan ●, Light Sea Salt ●, Margherita Pizza ●)

Flamous Brands - Falafel Chips (Original ●, Spicy ●)

Food Club Brand - Potato Chips (BBQ, Original), Tortilla Chips Bite Size White Mini Rounds

Food Should Taste Good -

Dipping Chips (Blue Corn ●, White Corn ●)

Sweet Potato Chips (Barbeque ●, Original ●, Salt & Pepper ●, Salt & Vinegar ●)

Tortilla Chips (Blue Corn ●, Cantina ●, Cheddar ●, Chocolate ●, Hatch Chile ●, Hemp ●, Jalapeno w/Cheddar ●, Kettle Corn ●, Lime ●, Multigrain ●, Olive ●, Sweet Potato ●, The Works ●, Toasted Sesame ●, White Cheddar ●)

Fritos - Corn Chips (Lightly Salted ★, Original ★, Scoops ★, Tapatio **!!**), Honey BBQ Flavor Twists **!!**

Frontera - Tortilla Chips (Blue Corn, Lime w/Sea Salt, Thick & Crunchy, Thin & Crispy)

Full Circle - All Natural (BBQ, Natural Potato), Kettle Cooked (Lightly Salted, Salt & Vinegar)

Garden Of Eatin' - Mini Tortilla (Rounds (White, Yellow), White Strips), Tortilla (Baked Blue Chips, Baked Yellow Chips, Black Bean, Black Bean Chili, Blue Chips (No Salt Added, Regular), Chili & Lime, Focaccia, Guac A Mole, Key Lime Jalapeno, Little Soy Blues, Maui Onion, Nacho Cheese, Pico De Gallo, Popped Blues, Red Chips, Red Hot Blues, Sesame Blues, Sunny Blues, Tamari, Three Pepper, White Chips, Yellow Chips), Veggie Chips (Beet & Garlic, Vegetable Medley)

Glenny's - Spud Delites Natural Potato Crisps (Sea Salt ●, Sour Cream & Onion ●, Texas BBQ ●)

Glutino ▲ - Bagel Chips (Original, Parmesan Garlic)

Good Health Natural Foods ▲ - Potato Chips (Avocado Oil (Barcelona Barbeque, Chilean Lime, Regular), Glories Sweet, Olive Oil (Cracked Pepper & Sea Salt, Garlic, Rosemary, Sea Salt))

Go Raw ▲ - Super Chips (Pumpkin ●, Spirulina ●)

Gordon Food Service - Corn Tortilla (Restaurant Style, Seasoned

C

Round), Potato (Original, Rippled (Regular, Sour Cream & Onion, Sweet Barbeque))

Grandma Ferdon's ▲ - Taco Seasoned Tortilla Chips ●, Tortilla Chips ●

Green Mountain Gringo ▲ - Tortilla Strips (Blue Corn ●, Original ●, White Corn ●)

H-E-B - Rice & Adzuki Bean (Chipotle Cheese Flavored, Salted)

Hannaford Brand - Potato (Classic, Ripple, Sour Cream & Onion, Wavey), Tortilla (Bite Size, Restaurant Style, Yellow)

Herr's - BBQ Flavor Corn Chips, Potato Chips (Cheddar & Sour Cream, Crisp 'N Tasty, Heinz Ketchup, Honey BBQ, Kettle (Jalapeno, Original, Russet), Lightly Salted, No Salt, Old Bay, Old Fashioned, Red Hot, Ripple, Salt & Pepper, Salt & Vinegar), Tortilla Chips (Bite Size Dippers, Nacho Cheese, Restaurant Style)

Hill Country Fare H-E-B - Corn Chips

Hippie Chips - Ancient Grains ●, Multi Seed ●, Three Bean ●, Tuscan Tomato ●

Hy-Vee - Kettle Cooked (BBQ, Jalapeno & Cheddar, Original, Parmesan & Garlic, Salt & Pepper), Tortilla (Blue Corn, Cantina Style, Margarita)

Kettle Brand -

40% Reduced Fat (Salt & Fresh Ground Pepper, Sea Salt, Sea Salt & Vinegar)

Baked Potato Chips (Aged White Cheddar, Hickory Honey Barbeque, Salt & Fresh Ground Pepper, Sea Salt, Sea Salt & Vinegar)

Krinkle Cut Potato Chips (Buffalo Bleu, Cheddar & Sour Cream, Classic Barbeque, Salt & Fresh Ground Pepper, Sea Salt, Zesty Ranch)

Organic Potato Chips (Chipotle Chili Barbeque, Country Style Barbeque, Lightly Salted, Salt & Fresh Ground Pepper, Sea Salt)

Potato Chips (Backyard Barbeque, Fully Loaded Baked Potato, Honey Dijon, Jalapeno, New York Cheddar, Sea Salt, Sea Salt & Vinegar, Sour Cream & Onion, Spicy Thai, Sweet Onion, Unsalted, Yogurt & Green Onion)

C

Kirkland Signature - Organic Tortilla Chips !, Tortilla Strips

Kiwa - Vegetable Chip Mix

Kroger Brand - Tortilla (Bite Size, Spicy Salsa, Traditional, Yellow Traditional), Tortilla Chips (Nacho Cheese, Ranch, Thin Restaurant Style)

Late July - Dude Ranch ●, Mild Green Mojo ●, Sea Salt By The Seashore ●, Summertime Blues ●, Sweet Potato ●

Laurel Hill - Potato Chips (40% Reduced Fat (Barbeque ●, Cracked Black Pepper ●, Sea Salt ●), Jalapeno ●, Sea Salt & Vinegar ●, Sea Salt ●), Tortilla Chips (Multigrain ●, Olive & Caper ●, Pumpkin Seed ●, Sea Salt & Lime ●)

Lay's -

Baked (Original ★, Parmesan & Tuscan Herb ★, Sour Cream & Onion ★, Southwestern Ranch ★)

Potato Chips

Balsamic Sweet Onion !!

Cajun Herb & Spice !!

Cheddar & Sour Cream !!

Chile Limon !!

Chipotle Ranch !!

Classic ★

Creamy Garden Ranch !!

Deli Style ★

Dill Pickle !!

Garden Tomato & Basil !!

Honey BBQ !!

Honey Mustard !!

Hot & Spicy Barbecue !!

Kettle Cooked (Creamy Mediterranean Herb !!, Crinkle Cut Spice Rubbed BBQ !!, Harvest Ranch !!, Jalapeno !!, Maui Onion !!, Original !!, Reduced Fat Original !!, Sea Salt & Cracked Pepper !!, Sea Salt & Vinegar !!, Sharp Cheddar !!, Spicy Cayenne & Cheese !!)

Light Original !!

Lightly Salted ★
Limon ‼
Natural Sea Salt Thick Cut ★
Salt & Vinegar ‼
Sour Cream & Onion ‼
Southwest Cheese & Chiles ‼
Sweet Southern Heat BBQ ‼
Tangy Carolina BBQ ‼
Wavy (Au Gratin ‼, Hickory BBQ ‼, Original ★, Ranch ‼)
Stax
Cheddar ★
Hot 'N Spicy BBQ ‼
Mesquite Barbecue ★
Original ★
Pizza ‼
Salt & Vinegar ★
Sour Cream & Onion ★
Lowes Foods Brand - Corn Chips, Potato Chips (Original, Ripple, Sour Cream & Onion), Tortilla Chips (Restaurant Style, White Round)
Lundberg ▲ - Rice Chips (Fiesta Lime, Honey Dijon, Organic (Cracked Black Pepper, Spicy Black Bean), Pico De Gallo, Santa Fe Barbecue, Sea Salt, Sesame & Seaweed, Wasabi)
Majans - Monsoon Chips (Hot & Spicy, Vinegar & Salt)
Manischewitz - Potato Chips (All Varieties)
Maui Style - Potato Chips (Maui Onion ‼, Regular ‼, Salt & Vinegar ‼)
Mediterranean Snacks - Baked Lentil (Cracked Pepper, Cucumber Dill, Parmesan Garlic, Roasted Pepper, Rosemary, Sea Salt), Veggie Medley !
Michael Season's - Kettle Cooked Potato Chips (Honey BBQ ★, Jalapeno ★, Lightly Salted ★, Sea Salt & Balsamic Vinegar ★, Unsalted ★), Popped Black Bean Chips (Nacho ★, Roasted Red Pepper ★, Sea Salt ★), Thin & Crispy (Honey Barbecue ★, Lightly Salted ★, Mediterranean ★, Ripple Lightly Salted ★, Salt & Pepper ★, Unsalted ★)

C

Miguel's - Organic Tortilla Dippers (Everything ●, Three Pepper ●, Vegetable & Seed ●), Plantain Strips (Honey, Salted), Tortilla Chips (Blue Corn ●, White Corn ●)

Miss Vickie's - Kettle Cooked Potato Chips (Jalapeno ‼, Sea Salt & Cracked Pepper ‼, Sea Salt & Vinegar ‼, Simply Sea Salt ‼)

Mission - Corn Tortillas Super Thin Tortilla Chips❗

Mr. Krispers -

Baked Nut Chips Toasted Almond ●

Baked Rice Krisps (Barbecue ●, Nacho ●, Sea Salt & Pepper ●, Sour Cream & Onion ●, Sun Dried Tomato & Basil ●, White Cheddar & Herbs ●)

Multi Seed Chips Original ●

Tasty Snack Crackers Original Sesame ●

Nuts.com - Carrot Chips ●, Fruit Chips ●, Green Bean Chips ●, Sweet Potato Chips ●, Taro Chips ●, Veggie Chips (No Salt Added ●, Regular ●)

Old Dutch -

Potato Chips (Baked (Cheddar & Sour Cream, Original), Bar B Q, Dill Pickle, Onion & Garlic, Original, RipL, RipL Cheddar & Sour Cream, RipL Low Sodium, Sour Cream & Onion)

Restaurante Style Tortilla Chips (Bite Size Original, Original, Strips)

Ripples Potato Chips (Cheddar & Sour Cream, Creamy Dill, French Onion, Loaded Spud, Mesquite Bar B Que, Original)

On The Border - Tortilla Chips (Blue Corn, Cafe Style, Cantina Thins, Premium Rounds, Southwest Thins)

Ortega - Round Tortilla Chips

Pan De Oro - Tortilla Chips (Blue ●, Red White & Blue ●, Regular ●)

Peppadew ▲ - Potato Chips

Pinnacle Gold - Natural Baked (Potato Chips Original, Veggie Chips)

Popchips - Potato (Barbecue ●, Cheddar ●, Chili Lime ●, Jalapeno ●, Original ●, Parmesan Garlic ●, Salt & Pepper ●, Sea Salt & Vinegar ●, Sour Cream & Onion ●, Sweet Potato ●)

Popcorn Indiana - Chip'ins (Hot Buffalo Wing, Jalapeno Ranch, Sea Salt, White Cheddar)

Popcorners - Popped Corn Chips (Butter, Caramel, Cheesy Jalapeno, Kettle, Sea Salt, White Cheddar)

Potato Flyers - Baked Potato Chips (Homestyle Barbeque, Sour Cream & Onion, The Original)

Pringles - Fat Free (Original, Sour Cream & Onion)

Publix - Potato Chips (Dip Style, Original Thins, Salt & Vinegar), Tortilla Chips (White Corn Restaurant Style, Yellow Corn Round Style)

Publix GreenWise Market - Tortilla Chips (Blue !!, Yellow !!)

Pure Market Express ▲ - BBQ Thins ●, Chili Lime Chips ●, Corn Chips ●, Mexi Chips ●

Que Pasa - Hand Cut Organic Corn !, Organic Corn Tortilla Chips (Blue !, Red !, White !, Yellow !), Snack Chips (Fritas Del Sol !, Queso Picante !)

RiceWorks - Rice Crisps (Parmesan & Sun Dried Tomato, Salsa Fresca, Sea Salt, Sweet Chili, Tangy BBQ)

Ruffles -
    Baked (Cheddar & Sour Cream Potato Crisps !!, Original Potato Crisps ★)
    Potato Chips (Authentic Barbecue !!, Cheddar & Sour Cream !!, Loaded Chili & Cheese !!, Molten Hot Wings !!, Natural Reduced Fat Sea Salted ★, Original (Light !!, Reduced Fat ★, Regular ★), Queso !!, Queso Jalapeno !!, Smokehouse Style BBQ !!, Sour Cream & Onion !!, Tapatio Limon !!)

RW Garcia - Flax ●, MixtBag Tortilla Chips (Red & Yellow Corn ●, Yellow & Blue Corn ●, Yellow & White Corn ●), Spice ●, Thai ●, Tortilla Chips (Classic (Blue ●, Gold ●), Organic Blue ●, Stone Ground ●), Veggie Tortilla Chips ●

Santitas - Tortilla Chips (White Corn Triangles ★, Yellow Corn Rounds ★, Yellow Corn Strips ★, Yellow Corn Triangles ★)

Skeete & Ike's - Organic Sea Salt Corn !!

Snikiddy - Eat Your Vegetables (Italian Herb & Olive Oil, Jalapeno Ranch, Sea Salt, Sour Cream & Onion)

Snyder's Of Hanover - Eat Smart Naturals (Garden Veggie Crisps ●, Whole Grain Tortilla Chips ●)

C

Spartan Brand - Corn Big Dipper, Kettle Cooked (Jalapeno, Mesquite BBQ, Original), Potato (Regular, Ripple), Sour Cream & Onion

Terra Chips -

Classic Potato Chips (Au Naturel Unsalted, Hickory BBQ Unsalted, Kettles (Arrabiatta, General Tso, Pesto & Smoked Mozzarella, Sea Salt, Sea Salt & Pepper, Sea Salt & Vinegar), Lemon Pepper Unsalted), Exotic Potato Chips (Blue (Crinkles Jalapeno Chili, Original Blues), Red Bliss (Crinkles Bloody Mary, Made w/Olive Oil, Olive Oil & Fine Herbs), Yukon Gold (Crinkles Garlic Mashed, Original, Salt & Pepper))

Exotic Vegetable Chips (Exotic Harvest (Sea Salt, Sweet Onion), Mediterranean, Original Chips, Original Taro, Stripes & Blues Sea Salt, Terra Stix, Thai Basil Curry, Zesty Tomato)

Sweet Potato Chips (Crinkles Candied, Krinkle Cut (Sea Salt, Sweets & Beets, Sweets & Carrots), Plain, Spiced)

The Better Chip - Tortilla Chips (Fresh Corn, Jalapeno, Red Pepper, Sweet Onion)

Tostitos - Tortilla Chips (Bite Size Rounds ★, Crispy Rounds ★, Extra Thin ★, Restaurant Style (Hint of Lime ‼, Hint of Pepper Jack ‼, Natural Blue Corn ★, Natural Yellow Corn ★, Original ★), Salsa Verde ‼, Scoops (Baked! ★, Hint Of Jalapeno ‼, Multigrain ‼, Original ★), Thick & Hearty Rounds ★)

Trader Joe's - Organic Chips (Baked Tortilla (Blue Corn, Nacho), Corn Dippers ‼, Corn Tortilla (Blue ‼, White ‼, Yellow ‼), Restaurant Style White Corn Tortilla Chips, Tortilla Longboard), Regular Chips (BBQ Potato, Blue Corn Tortilla, Corn Tortilla Strips White ‼, Red Bliss Potato, Round Popped Potato (Barbecue ‼, Salted ‼), Salsa Tortilla, Salt 'N Vinegar Potato, Salted Potato ‼, Sea Salt & Pepper Rice Crisps ‼, Soy & Flaxseed Tortilla (Regular, Spicy), Vegetable Root ‼, Veggie (& Flaxseed Tortilla, Regular ‼), Yellow Corn Tortilla Chips), Ridge Cut Potato Chips (Lightly Salted ‼, Salt 'N Pepper ‼), Roasted Plantain, Tortilla Chips (Reduced Guilt Tortilla Strips ‼, Sweet Potato)

UTZ -
> All Natural Kettle Cooked (Dark Russet, Lightly Salted, Reduced Fat, Salt & Cracked Pepper, Sea Salt & Vinegar)
> Grandma UTZ Kettle Cooked (BBQ, Regular)
> Kettle Classics (Dark Russet, Jalapeno, Maui BBQ, Original, Reduced Fat, Smokin' Sweet Potato (Reduced Fat, Regular), Sweet Potato)
> Mystic Kettle Cooked Chips (Dark Russet, Plain, Reduced Fat, Sea Salt & Vinegar)
> Potato Chips (Barbeque, Carolina BBQ, Cheddar & Sour Cream, Crab, Honey BBQ, No Salt (BBQ, Regular), Onion & Garlic, Plain (Original, Ripple, Wavy Cut), Red Hot, Salt & Pepper, Salt & Vinegar, Sour Cream & Onion)
> Tortilla Chips (Baked, Multigrain)

Way Better Snacks - Tortilla Chips (Black Bean ●, Multi Grain ●, No Salt Naked Blues ●, Simply Sweeet Potato ●, Sweet Chili ●, Unbeatable Blues ●)

Wegmans Brand - Chips Corn Original, FYFGA Tortilla Chips Made w/Organic Corn (Blue, White, Yellow), Tortilla 100% White Corn (Bite Size Round, Crisp Round, Lime Flavored, Restaurant Style)

Wild Riceworks - Sea Salt & Black Sesame

Winn Dixie - Cheddar & Sour Cream, Classic, Natural (Original, Reduced Fat), Pork Rinds, Puffed Cheese Curls, Sour Cream & Onion, Wavy, Wavy Ranch

Wise -
> Corn Chips (Bar B Q Flavor, Dipsy Doodles Wavy Corn Chips (Bar B Q, Original), Nacho Twisters, Original Flavor)
> Potato Chips (All Natural, Baked (Barbecue, Original), Lightly Salted, New York Deli Kettle Cooked (All Natural, Buffalo Wing, Jalapeno), Onion & Garlic, Ridgies (All Natural, Cheddar & Sour Cream, Sour Cream & Onion), Salt & Vinegar, Unsalted, Wise Wavy)
> Tortilla Chips Bravos (Crispy Rounds, Nacho Cheese, Ranch, Restaurant Style, Sweet & Spicy)

C Chocolate

Aimee's Livin' Magic - All Chocolates

Alter Eco - Dark Bars (Almond **!**, Blackout 85% **!**, Cacao 73% **!**, Mint **!**, Quinoa **!**, Twist **!**, Velvet **!**)

Andes - Creme De Menthe Sugar Free, Thins (Cherry Jubilee, Creme De Menthe, Mint Parfait, Toffee Crunch)

Baby Ruth - Baby Ruth Bar

Baker's - Bittersweet, German's Sweet, Select (Bittersweet, Semi Sweet), Semi Sweet, Unsweetened, White

Carb Safe - Sugar Free Chocolate Bars Dark

Cella's - Chocolate Covered Cherries (Dark, Milk)

Chocolate Dream - Creamy Sweet, Dark (Almond, Pure, Raspberry, Rice Crunch)

Coco Polo - 70% Cocoa Dark (Cocoa Nibs, Elderberry, Plain, Tart Montmorency Cherries, w/Ginger, Whole Almonds)

Dagoba ▲ - All Chocolate ★, Chocodrops ★, Chocolate Covered Espresso Beans ★, Organic Cacao Nibs ★

Dove - *(Packaging labels differ. Please double check ingredient label for allergens)* Dove Chocolates (All Varieties)

Eli's Earth ▲ - Bars (Celebrate, Dream Big, Treasure)

Endangered Species ▲ -

All Natural Chocolate Bars (Dark Chocolate (Extreme ●, Supreme●), Dark Chocolate w/ (Blueberries ●, Cacao Nibs ●, Cranberries & Almonds ●, Espresso Beans ●, Hazelnut Toffee ●, Mint ●, Raspberries ●), Milk Chocolate (Regular ●, w/Almonds ●, w/Cherries ●))

All Natural Chocolate Squares (Dark Chocolate (Extreme ●, Supreme ●, w/Cranberries & Almonds ●, w/Mint ●), Smooth Milk ●), Bulk Chocolate Treats (Dark Chocolate (Extreme ●, Halloween ●, Supreme ●, w/Cranberries & Almonds ●, w/Mint ●), Milk Chocolate (Halloween ●, Smooth ●))

Organic Bites (Bug Bites (Dark ●, Milk ●), Chimp Mints ●)

Organic Chocolate Bars 1.4 oz (Dark Chocolate (& Cherry ●, & Orange●), Milk Chocolate (& Peanut Butter ●, Smooth ●))

Organic Chocolate Bars 3oz Dark Chocolate w/Goji Berry Pecans & Maca ●

chocolate

C

Organic Chocolate Bars 3oz (Dark Chocolate w/ (Cacao Nibs Yacon & Acai ●, Golden Berry & Lucuma ●, w/Goji Berry Pecans & Maca ●) Milk Chocolate ●)

Enjoy Life ▲ - Boom Choco Boom Gluten Free Bar (Dark Chocolate ●, Ricemilk Chocolate ●, Ricemilk Crunch ●), Semi Sweet Chocolate (Mega Chunks ●, Mini Chips ●)

Fruit Advantage - Chocolate Covered Dried Fruit (All Varieties)

Ghirardelli -

Baking Bars (100% Cocoa Unsweetened, 60% Bittersweet, Semi Sweet, White)

Filled Chocolate (Dark w/Mint **!!**, Dark w/Raspberry **!!**, Milk w/Caramel **!!**)

Intense Dark (Evening Dream 60% Cacao **!!**, Midnight Reverie 86% Cacao **!!**, Sea Salt Soiree **!!**, Twilight Delight 72% Cacao **!!**)

Luxe Milk Milk **!!**

Solid Chocolate Sublime White w/Vanilla Dream **!!**

Glee Gum - Make Your Own Chocolate Kit

Hershey's -

Heath Bar

Jolly Ranchers (Gummies, Hard Candy)

Kisses Milk Chocolate (Meltaway, Original, w/Almonds, w/ Caramel, w/Cherry Cordial Creme)

Kisses Special Dark

Milk Chocolate Bar (Original, w/Almonds)

Mr. Goodbar

PayDay

Reese's Peanut Butter Cups Original

Skor

York Peppermint Patty

Ian's - Chocolate Covered Wafer Bites

Indie Candy - Dark Chocolate Covered "Oreos", Dark Chocolate Lollipop Shapes

KatySweet ▲ - Chocolate Dipped Strawberries ●

C

M & M's - *(Packaging labels differ. Please double check ingredient label for allergens)* Dark Chocolate, Milk Chocolate, Peanut, Peanut Butter

Manischewitz - Chocolate Frolic Bears, Chocolate Morsels, Hazelnut Truffles, Mallo Cups, Patties (Peppermint, Tender Coconut), Swiss Chocolate Mints

Mars - *(Packaging labels differ. Please double check ingredient label for allergens)*
Dove Chocolates (All Varieties)
M & M's (Dark Chocolate, Milk Chocolate, Peanut, Peanut Butter)
Milky Way (Midnight, Simply Caramel)
Munch Bar
Snickers (Dark Bar, Original Bar)

Milka Chocolate - Alpine Milk Chocolate Confection Bar

Milky Way - *(Packaging labels differ. Please double check ingredient label for allergens)* Midnight, Simply Caramel

Munch Bar - *(Packaging labels differ. Please double check ingredient label for allergens)*

Navitas Naturals ▲ - Organic Superfood Chocolate Kit (Cacao Nib, Goji Berries, Goldenberry)

Necco - Candy Eggs Easter, Clark Bar, Haviland Thin Mints, Skybar, Squirel Nut (Caramels, Zippers), Talking Pumpkins Halloween

Nestle -
Baby Ruth
Bit O Honey
Butterfinger *(Except Crisp & Stixx)*
Goobers
Milk Chocolate
Nips (Regular, Sugar Free)
Oh Henry
Raisinets
Sno Caps

Newman's Own Organics - All Chocolate Bars **!!**, All Chocolate Cups **!!**

Nuts.com - Chocolate Covered (Sunflower Seeds ●, Toasted Corn ●), Organic Cacao Paste ●, Organic Chocolate Covered Cacao Nibs ●, Organic Sugar Cacao Nibs ●, Raisins Organic (Dark Chocolate

Covered ●, Milk Chocolate Covered ●), Raw Cacao Almonds & Raisins ●, Raw Organic Cacao Nibs ●, White Chocolate Chip Almonds Cashews & Cacao Nibs ●

Organic Nectars - All Varieties Of Raw Cacao

Oskri Organics - Honey Mint Patties

Pure Market Express - Almond Bliss

Righteously Raw ▲ - Bar (Acai ●, Caramel ●, Goji ●, Maca ●, Rose ●), Bite Size (Divine Mint ●, Pure Dark ●, Synergy Spice ●), Raw Coconut Macaroons ●

Safeway Select - Creamy Milk Chocolate, Dark w/Lemon & Pepper, Extra Dark, Extra Dark w/Almond & Blueberry, Extra Dark w/ Cranberry & Orange, Milk Chocolate w/Hazelnuts, White Chocolate w/Blueberries

Shabtai ▲ - Bon Bons

Sjaak's ▲ -
  Bunny (Almond Butter, Milk Chocolate)
  Eggs (Dark Chocolate, Milk Chocolate)
  Organic Chocolate (Bars (Chocolate, Dark Chocolate, Dark Chocolate Almond, Dark Chocolate w/Creamy Caramel, Dark Chocolate w/Raspberry, Extra Dark 70%, Milk Chocolate, Milk Chocolate w/Almond Butter, Milk Chocolate w/Almonds, Milk Chocolate w/Creamy Caramel, Milk Chocolate w/Peanut Butter), Bite Sized Chocolates (Almond Butter Bites, Caramel Small Bites, Chocolate Caramel, Chocolate Covered Almonds, Chocolate Covered Hazelnuts, Dark Chocolate Covered Almonds, Dark Chocolate Covered Hazelnuts, Dark Chocolate Hearts, Dark Chocolate Lavender Truffles, Extra Dark Bites, Hazelnut Butter Bites, Hearts of Cherry, Milk Chocolate Hearts, Mint Mills, Orange Bites, Peanut Butter Bites, Raspberry Bites, Vegan Mint Bites, Winter Wonderfuls))
  Peanut Butter Crunch Egg
  Vegan Dark Chocolate Bunny

Suncups - Caramel, Dark Chocolate, Milk Chocolate, Mint

Terry's - Chocolate Orange (Dark, Milk, Pure Milk)

C

Toblerone - Dark, Fruit & Nut, Milk Chocolate, Minis Milk Chocolate, White

Trader Joe's -
  Chocolate (Almond Clusters, Sunflower Seed Drops)
  Chocolate Covered (Blueberries, Orange & Raspberry Sticks)
  Dark Chocolate (Almonds Sea Salt & Sugar, Mint Creams)
  Dark Chocolate Covered (Almonds !!, Caramels !, Cherries !!, Power Berries !, Raisins !!, Toffee)
  Milk & Dark Chocolate Covered Almonds !!
  Milk Chocolate (Covered Raisins !!, Peanut Butter Cups)
  Mini Milk Chocolate Peanut Butter Cups !
  Unsweetened Belgian Baking Chocolate

Two Moms In The Raw - Almond Butter Cacao Truffle ●

Woodstock Farms -
  Chocolate Ginger w/Evaporated Cane Juice
  Dark Chocolate w/Evaporated Cane Juice Almonds
  Organic Dark Chocolate w/Evaporated Cane Juice (Chips, Raisins)
  Organic Milk Chocolate w/Evaporated Cane Juice Raisins

YC Chocolate - All Bars

Chocolate Bars...see Candy/Candy Bars and/or Baking Bars

Chocolate Chips...see Baking Chips

Chocolate Dip
  Baker's - Real Milk Chocolate, Real Dark Semi Sweet
  Marzetti - Chocolate Fruit Dip
  Walden Farms - Chocolate Fruit Dip

Chocolate Milk...see Milk

Chocolate Sauce
  Emmy's Organics ▲ - Original Dark
  Wegmans Brand - Chocolate (Milk, Raspberry, Triple Chocolate)

Chocolate Syrup...see Syrup

Chutney
  Baxters - Albert's Victorian, Cranberry & Caramelized Red Onion, Spiced Fruit, Tomato
  Garner's - Organic Apple & Onion Sweet
  Patak's Original - Hot Mango, Major Grey, Sweet Mango

Sharwood's - Green Label (Mango, Mango Chili)

Trader Joe's - Mango Ginger **!!**

Wild Thymes - Apricot Cranberry Walnut, Caribbean Peach Lime, Mango Papaya, Plum Currant Ginger

Cider/Cider Mix

Crispin - *(Alcoholic)*

All Limited Release Flavors

Artisanal Reserves (Cho Tokkyu, Honey Crisp, Lansdowne, The Saint)

Browns Lane

Natural Hard Apple Cider (Brut, Draught, Light, Original)

Doc's Draft - Apple, Pear, Raspberry *(Alcoholic)*

Lucky Leaf - Apple Cider, Sparkling Apple Cider

Magners - Cider *(Alcoholic)*

Musselman's - Cider, Fresh Pressed, Sparkling Cider

Pure Market Express ▲ - Mulled Apple Cider, Mulled Apple Cider ●

Safeway Brand - Apple Cider

Sonoma Sparkler - Natural (Blood Orange, Peach, Pear, Raspberry), Organic (Apple, Lemonade)

Strongbow - *(Alcoholic)*

Woodchuck ▲ - Hard Cider (All Varieties) *(Alcoholic)* ★

Woodpecker ▲ - Premium Cider *(Alcoholic)* ★

Wyder's ▲ - Hard Cider (All Varieties) *(Alcoholic)* ★

Cinnamon

Durkee - Ground

McCormick - Gourmet Collection (Roasted Saigon, Saigon, Stick), Ground, Sticks

Meijer Brand

Simply Organic - Cinnamon (Ground, Sticks)

Spice Islands

The Spice Hunter - 100% Organic Cinnamon, Cinnamon Ground, Cinnamon Sticks

Tones

Watkins - Purest Ground

C Cinnamon Rolls

    Apple's Bakery ▲ - Gluten Free Frosted

    Celiac Specialties ▲ - Cinnamon Rolls

    Chebe ▲ - Cinnamon Roll Mix ●

    Choices Rice Bakery ▲ - Cinnamon Buns

    Grandma Ferdon's ▲ - Regular ●

    Heaven Mills ▲ - Chocolate Buns ●, Cinnamon Buns ●

    Mariposa Artisan-Crafted Gluten-Free ▲

    Molly's Gluten-Free Bakery ▲ - Cinnamon Rolls

    Pure Market Express ▲ - Cinnamon Rolls ●

    Silly Yak Bakery - CFGF Cinnamon Roll ●, GF Cinnamon Roll ●

    The Grainless Baker ▲ - Cinnamon Buns

    Udi's Gluten Free Foods ▲ - Gluten Free Cinnamon Rolls ●

Clams

    ... **All Fresh Seafood Is Gluten-Free (Non-Marinated, Unseasoned)*

    Bumble Bee - Chopped, Fancy Whole Baby, Minced, Smoked

    Chicken Of The Sea - Minced, Premium Whole Baby Clams, Whole
        Baby Clams

    Crown Prince -

        Baby Boiled, Baby Clams Smoked In Oil

        Natural (Boiled Baby Clams In Water, Clam Juice, Smoked Baby
          Clams In Olive Oil)

    Ocean Prince - Chopped

Club Soda...see Soda Pop/Carbonated Beverages

Coating

    A Taste Of Thai - Spicy Peanut Bake

    Aleia's ▲ - Breadcrumbs (Plain ●, Savory ●)

    Andrea's Gluten Free ▲ - Seasoned Bread Crumbs

    Bi-Aglut - Bread Crumb Coating

    Bloomfield Farms ▲ - Gluten Free Seasoned Flour ●

    Bodhi's Bakehouse - Wheat Free Gluten Free

    Celiac Specialties ▲ - Seasoned Bread Crumbs

    Choice Batter ▲ - Original Recipe w/Spices ●, Unspiced ●

    Dakota Lakes ▲ - Gourmet Coating ●

C

El Peto ▲ - Bread Crumbs

Ener-G ▲ - Breadcrumbs

Gillian's Foods ▲ - Bread Crumbs (Cajun Style ●, Italian Style ●, Plain ●)

Glutino ▲ - Bread Crumbs

Grandma Ferdon's ▲ - Bread Crumbs ●, Fish Batter Mix ●

Hodgson Mill - Gluten Free Seasoned Mix

Hol Grain ▲ - Batter Mix (Onion Ring ●, Tempura ●), Brown Rice Bread Crumbs ●, Crispy Chicken Coating Mix ●

Katz Gluten Free ▲ - Bread Crumbs ●

Kinnikinnick ▲ - Bread Cubes, Chocolate Cookie Crumbs, Graham Style Crumbs, Panko Style Bread Crumbs

Laurel's Sweet Treats ▲ - All Purpose Batter Mix

Mamma Mia! - Beer Batter Fry Mix

Mary's Gone Crackers ▲ - Just The Crumbs (Caraway ●, Original ●, Savory ●)

Molino Nicoli - Bread Crumbs

Namaste Foods ▲ - Seasoned Coating Mix (Barbecue, Homestyle, Hot 'N Spicy, Italian Herb)

Nicole's - Nikki's New Gluten Free Cracker Crumbs ●

Orgran ▲ - All Purpose Rice Crumbs, Buckwheat Crumbs, Corn Crispy Crumbs, Multigrain Crumbs w/Quinoa

Oven Fry - Seasoned Fish Fry For Fish

Paskesz - Original Bake Or Fry, Pesach Crumbs

Pure Knead ▲ - Bread Crumbs ●

Russo's Gluten Free Gourmet ▲ - Bread Crumbs

Schar ▲ - Bread Crumbs

Shabtai ▲ - Pread Crumbs

Southern Homestyle - Corn Flake Crumbs, Tortilla Crumbs

Still Riding Pizza - Breadcrumbs

West Meadow Farm Bakery - Gluten Free Breadcrumbs (Seasoned ●, Unseasoned ●)

Cocktail Mix

Bacardi Mixers - Frozen (Fuzzy Navel, Margarita, Mojito, Peach Daiquiri, Pina Colada, Rum Runner, Strawberry Daiquiri)

C

Big Bucket - Blue Hawaiian, Margarita, Margarita Lite, Mojito, Strawberry Margarita/Daiquiri

Margaritaville - Margarita Mix (Lime, Mango)

Master Of Mixes -

Lite (Margarita, Strawberry Daquiri, Strawberry Daquiri/Margarita, Sweet 'N Sour)

Regular (Cocktail Martini, Mai Tai, Mango Daquiri/Margarita, Manhattan, Margarita, Mojito, Old Fashioned, Pina Colada, Sour Apple Martini, Strawberry Colada, Strawberry Daquiri, Sweet 'N Sour, Tom Collins, Whiskey Sour)

Mr. & Mrs. T's - Bloody Mary (Bold & Spicy *(Not Premium Blend)*, Original *(Not Premium Blend)*), Mai Tai, Manhattan, Margarita, Old Fashioned, Pina Colada, Strawberry Daiquiri/Margarita, Sweet & Sour, Tom Collins, Whiskey Sour

On The Border - Bottles Margarita Lite, Buckets (Frozen Margarita, Mojito, Strawberry Mango)

Rose's - Grenadine, Infusions (Blue Raspberry, Cosmopolitan, Pomegranate Twist, Sour Apple), Infusions Light Mix Cosmopolitan, Mojito Cocktail Mix (Mango, Passion Fruit, Traditional), Sweetened Lime Juice

Scorned Woman - Cocktail Magic

Cocktail Sauce...see also Seafood Sauce

Food Club Brand

Hannaford Brand

Heinz - Regular, Zesty

Hill Country Fare H-E-B - Regular

Hy-Vee - Cocktail Sauce For Seafood

Ken's Steak House - Refrigerated, Shelf Stable

Legal - Seafood Cocktail

Lou's Famous - Cocktail Sauce

Lowes Foods Brand - Regular

McCormick - Extra Hot, Golden Dipt, Original Cocktail Sauce, Seafood Sauce (Cajun Style, Lemon Butter Dill (Fat Free, Regular), Lemon Herb, Mediterranean, Santa Fe Style, Scampi)

C

Old Bay

Royal Food Products - Garden Fresh, Royal Deluxe

Safeway Brand

Spartan Brand

Steel's - Agave ●

Trader Joe's - Seafood Cocktail Sauce ‼

Cocoa Mix/Powder

Caribou - All Natural Gourmet Drinking Chocolate (Dark, Milk, White)

Dagoba ▲ - Drinking Chocolate (Authentic ★, Chai ★, Unsweetened ★, Xocolatl Hot Chocolate ★), Professional Cocoa Powder ★

Food Club Brand - Hot Cocoa (Mini Marshmallows, No Sugar Added, Regular)

Ghirardelli - Drinking Chocolate (Chocolate Hazelnut ‼, Chocolate Mocha ‼, Double Chocolate ‼, White Mocha ‼)

Gloria Jean's - All Hot Chocolate Varieties

Gordon Food Service - Hot Cocoa Mix (Bulk, No Sugar Added, Packet)

Hannaford Brand - No Sugar Added, w/Marshmallows

Hershey's -
Chocolate Syrup (Lite, Regular, Special Dark)
Cocoa Special Dark

Hy-Vee - Instant Chocolate Flavored Drink Mix, Instant Hot Cocoa (No Sugar Added, Regular), Rich Chocolate, w/Marshmallows

Kroger Brand - Dutch Cocoa (Regular, w/Mini Marshmallows)

Land-O-Lakes - Cocoa Classics (All Flavors)

Lowes Foods Brand - Hot Cocoa Mix (Regular, w/Marshmallows)

Meijer Brand - Instant Marshmallow, No Sugar Added, Organic Regular, Regular, Sugar Free, w/Marshmallows

Midwest Country Fare - Hot Cocoa Mix, Instant Chocolate Flavored Drink Mix, Regular

Navitas Naturals ▲ - Cacao (Beans, Nibs, Raw Powder, Sweet Nibs)

Nestle - Cocoa

Nuts.com - Organic Cacao Powder (Raw ●, Regular ●)

O Organics - Hot Cocoa Mix

Publix - Hot Cocoa Mix (Mini Marshmallow, No Sugar Added, Original)

C

    Righteously Raw ▲ - Rawcholatl Cacao Spice Drink ●
    Safeway Brand - Hot Cocoa Mix (Fat Free, w/Marshmallows), Regular
    Safeway Select - European Café Style (Regular, White Chocolate)
    Shiloh Farms - Organic Cocoa Powder ‼
    Spartan Brand - Hot Cocoa Mix (Lite, Regular, w/Marshmallows)
    St. Claire's Organics ▲ - Hot Cocoa (All Cocoa Varieties)
    Swiss Miss - All Flavors ★
    Trader Joe's - Conacado Organic Cocoa, Sipping Chocolate
    Winn Dixie - Cocoa Mix (Classic, Marshmallow, No Sugar Added)

Coconut
    Baker's - Angel Flake Sweetened In Bag
    Great Value Brand (Wal-Mart) - Sweetened Flaked
    Hannaford Brand - Fancy Sweetened
    Hy-Vee - Regular, Sweetened Flake
    Let's Do...Organic - Organic (Creamed, Flakes, Shredded (Reduced Fat, Regular))
    Lowes Foods Brand - Flakes
    Nutiva - Coconut Manna
    Nuts.com - Diced ●, Organic Unsweetened Chips ●, Shredded Organic ●, Unsweetened Chips ●
    Peter Paul - Toasted Coconut Chips
    Phildesco - Desiccated, Sweetened, Toasted
    Publix - Flakes
    Safeway Brand - Sweetened (Flaked, Shredded)
    Shiloh Farms - Shredded Organic Coconut ‼
    Spartan Brand - Flakes
    Tropical Traditions - Chips, Flakes, Shredded
    Wegmans Brand - Sweetened Flaked
    Winn Dixie
    Woodstock Farms - Organic Medium Shred

Coconut Milk
    A Taste Of Thai - Lite, Regular
    Blue Diamond - Almond Breeze Almond Coconut Milk (Original, Unsweetened, Vanilla, Vanilla Unsweetened)

Coconut Dream - Original
Ka-Me - Lite **!**, Regular **!**
Native Forest - Organic (Classic, Light)
NOH
Peter Paul - Coconut Cream, Regular
Phildesco - Regular
Silk - Pure Coconut (Original, Vanilla)
So Delicious -
  Coconut Milk (Chocolate ●, Original ●, Unsweetened ●, Vanilla ●)
  Sugar Free Coconut Milk (Original ●, Vanilla ●)
Thai Kitchen - Lite, Organic (Lite, Regular), Regular
Trader Joe's - Light

Cod...see Fish
  ... *All Fresh Fish Is Gluten-Free (Non-Marinated, Unseasoned)*

Coffee
Adina -
  Barista Brews (Double XXPresso, Mocha Madness)
  Organic Coffees (Ethiopian Espresso, Indian Chai Latte, Mayan
    Mocha, Sumatran Vanilla Latte)
Brown Gold - All Varieties
Caribou - All (Coffee Beans, Ground Coffee, Iced Coffee)
Food Club Brand - Ground Coffee (Breakfast Blend, Classic Roast,
  Colombian, Decaf, Evening Blend, French Roast, House Blend, Lite),
  Instant Coffee (Decaf, Regular)
Gloria Jean's - All Brewed Coffee
Great Value Brand (Wal-Mart) - Ground Coffee In Can (100% Arabica
  Premium, 100% Colombian, Classic Decaf, Classic Roast, Dark
  Roast), Instant Coffee (Decaf Premium, Premium 100% Arabica)
Green Mountain Coffee - All Coffee Bean Varieties *(Not K-Cups)*
Hannaford Brand - All Varieties
Higgins & Burke - All Varieties
Hy-Vee - 100% Colombian, Breakfast Blend, Classic Blend, Classic
  Decaf, Coffee Instant Regular, Decaf Instant Regular, French Roast

C illy issimo - Caffe (No Sugar, Regular), Cappuccino, Latte Macchiato, Mochaccino

Kirkland Signature - Ground Coffee World Blend Medium Roast, In A Tin Fine Grind (100% Colombian, Decaffeinated), Instant Coffee Drink Mix Cafe Cappuccino, Whole Bean (100% Columbian Supremo, Fair Trade Certified (Decaffeinated Whole Bean, House Blend Medium Roast), Rwandan)

Lowes Foods Brand - Bag (100% Colombian (Decaf, Regular), French Roast, Signature Blend), Brick (100% Colombian, Decaf, French Roast, Lite, Regular), Instant (Decaf, Regular), Singles Microwaveable

Maxwell House -
Coffee Bags (Decaf, Master Blend, Regular)
Filter Packs & Singles (Decaf, Original)
Ground (All Varieties)
Instant (Decaf, Original)
International Cafe (Cafe Francais, Cafe Vienna, Cappuccino (Original, Toasted Hazelnut), French Vanilla (Regular, Sugar Free, Sugar Free & Decaffeinated), Hazelnut, Latte (Chai, Mocha, Vanilla Bean, Vanilla Caramel), Suisse Mocha (Regular, Sugar Free, Sugar Free & Decaffeinated))
Pods (All Flavors)

Medifast - Cappuccino ●

Meijer Brand - Decaf, French Roast, Ground (Colombian, French Roast, Lite 50%, Lite 50% Decaf), Regular

Midwest Country Fare - Classic Blend

Mother Parkers - All Varieties

Nescafe - Classic Instant, Taster's Choice Instant (Flavored, Non Flavored, Singles (All Varieties))

O Organics - All Whole Beans

Publix - All Varieties

Pura Vida - All Varieties

Safeway Brand - Classic Roast (Decaf, Half Caff, Regular), Espresso Coffee Beans, French Roast

Safeway Select - Whole Bean (All Flavored)

Sanka - Decaf Coffee

Spartan Brand - French Roast, Ground (Classic Roast, Colombian, Decaf Roast, Half Caff), Instant (Decaf, Regular)

Taster's Choice - All Varieties

Trader Joe's - All Coffee

Tully's - All Varieties

Wegmans Brand - Ground (100% Colombian (Medium Roast, Regular), Decaf, French Roast, Lite Caffeine, Traditional (Light Roast, Regular)), Instant, Traditional Coffee Singles, Whole Bean 100% Colombian Decaf, Whole Bean Coffee (100% Colombian Medium Roast, Espresso Dark Roast, Espresso Dark Roast Decaf)

Winn Dixie - All Varieties

Yuban - Ground (100% Arabica, 100% Colombian, Breakfast Blend, Dark Roast, Decaf, Hazelnut, Original), Instant Regular, Organic (Latin American, Medium Roast)

Coffee Creamer...see Creamer

Coffee Flavorings

Flavour Creations - Flavoring Tablets (Almond Amaretto, Dutch Chocolate, French Vanilla, Hazelnut, Irish Creme)

Torani -

Sugar Free Syrup

Almond (Regular, Roca)

Brown Sugar Cinnamon

Caramel (Regular) *(NOT Classic Caramel Or Sugar Free Classic Caramel)*

Chocolate (Chip Cookie Dough, Macadamia Nut, Regular, White)

Coconut

Coffee

English Toffee

Gingerbread

Hazelnut (Classic, Regular)

Irish Cream

Peppermint

Pumpkin Pie

C

    Salted Caramel
    Sweetener
    Vanilla (Bean, Regular)
  Syrup
    Almond (Regular, Roca)
    Amaretto
    Bananas Foster
    Brown Sugar Cinnamon
    Butter (Pecan, Rum)
    Butterscotch
    Cane Sugar Sweetener
    Caramel Salted
    Caramel (Regular) *(NOT Classic Caramel Or Sugar Free Classic Caramel)*
    Chai Tea Spice
    Chocolate (Bianco, Chip Cookie Dough, Macadamia Nut, Milano, Mint)
    Cinnamon (Regular, Vanilla)
    Coconut
    Coffee
    Creme (Caramel, De Banana, De Cacao, De Menthe)
    English Toffee
    Ginger
    Hazelnut (Classic, Regular)
    Irish Cream
    Peppermint
    Pumpkin (Pie, Spice)
    Shortbread
    Tiramisu
    Vanilla (Bean, French *(NOT Sugar Free French Vanilla)* Honey, Regular)
Cold Cuts...see Deli Meat
Cole Slaw Dressing...see Salad Dressing

Collards...see Greens

Communion Wafers

    Ener-G ▲ - Communion Wafers

Concentrate...see Drinks/Juice

Cones

    Barkat - Ice Cream Cones, Waffle Cones

    Cerrone Cone - Waffle Cones

    Goldbaum's ▲ - Gluten Free Ice Cream Cones (Cocoa Sugar, Jumbo, Regular, Sugar)

    Joy - Gluten Free Ice Cream Cones (Cake ★, Sugar ★)

    Let's Do...Sprinkelz - Gluten Free (Ice Cream Cones, Sugar Cones)

    PaneRiso ▲ - Ice Cream Cups

Cookie Dough

    3 Fellers Bakery ▲ - Chocolate Chip ●, Sugar ●

    Andrea's Gluten Free ▲ - Allergen Free Chocolate Chip Dough, Chocolate Chip, Oatmeal

    Di Manufacturing - Gluten Free Cookie Dough (Chocolate Chip ●, M&M's ●, White Chocolate Macadamia Nut ●)

    EatPastry - Gluten Free Cookie Dough (Chocolate Chip ●, Snickerdoodle ●, Sugar Mama ●)

    El Peto ▲ - Gingerbread Cookie Dough

    French Meadow Bakery - Gluten Free Chocolate Chip ●

    Grandma Ferdon's ▲ - Chocolate Grande ●, Cut Out ●, Gingersnap●

    InclusiLife ▲ - Chocolate Chip ●, Fudge Brownie ●, Sugar ●

    Mim's Kitchen - Ready To Bake Cookies (Chocolate Chip ●, Chocolate Chocolate Chip ●, Ginger ●, Peanut Butter Chocolate Chip ●, Sugar ●, White Chocolate Macadamia Nut ●)

    The Naked Cookie - Gluten Free (Chocolate, Macaroon, Naked, Peanut Butter, Sugar)

    Trenipoti - Gluten Free Pre Portioned ●

Cookie Mix

    1-2-3 Gluten Free ▲ - Chewy Chipless Scrumdelicious Cookie Mix●, Lindsay's Lipsmackin' Roll Out & Cut Sugar Cookies ●, Sweet Goodness Pan Bars ●

C

Abundant Life Foods ▲ - Gluten Free Cookie Mix (Butterscotch Chip, Chocolate Chip, Cinnamon Butter, Ginger, Lemon, Oatmeal Old Fashion, Sugar Drop)

AgVantage Naturals ▲ - Basic Cookie Mix ●

Arrowhead Mills - Gluten Free Chocolate Chip Mix

Augason Farms ▲ - Gluten Free (Basic ●, Chocolate Chip ●)

Authentic Foods ▲ - Chocolate Chunk Cookie Mix ●

Betty Crocker ▲ - Gluten Free Chocolate Chip Cookie Mix

Bloomfield Farms ▲ - Gluten Free ●

Bob's Red Mill ▲ - Gluten Free Chocolate Chip Cookie Mix ★

Cause You're Special ▲ - Chocolate Chip, Classic Sugar

Cherrybrook Kitchen -
   Gluten Free Chocolate Chip Cookie Mix ★ *(Box Must Say Gluten Free)*
   Gluten Free Sugar Cookie Mix ★ *(Box Must Say Gluten Free)*

Earthly Treats ▲ - Sugar Cookie Mix ●

El Peto ▲ - Sugar Cookie

Food-Tek Quick-Bake - Cookie Mix (Chocolate Chip ★, Double Chocolate Chip ★, Sugar ★)

Full Circle - Gluten Free Cookie Mix

Gifts Of Nature ▲ - Short Bread/Sugar Cookie Mix ●

Ginny Bakes ▲ - Chocolate Chip Love ●, Coconut Oatmeal Bliss ●, Naked Love Vegan ●

Gluten Free Life ▲ - Chocolate Chip, Snicker Doodle, The Ultimate Gluten Free Cookie Mix

Gluten Free Mama ▲ - Mama's Cookie Mix ●

Gluten Free Pantry ▲ - Cookie & Cake Mix (Chocolate Chip, Old Fashioned)

Gluten Free Sensations ▲ - Chocolate Chip Cookie Mix, Sugar Cookie Cutout Mix

Gluten-Free Naturals - Cookie Blend

Grandma Ferdon's ▲ - Pumpkin Bar Mix ●

Hodgson Mill ▲ - Gluten Free Cookie Mix

Hol Grain ▲ - Chocolate Chip ●

Jules Gluten Free ▲ - Cookie Mix ●, Graham Cracker/Gingersnap Mix ●

C

King Arthur Flour ▲ - Gluten Free Cookie Mix ●
Kinnikinnick ▲ - Gingerbread, Sugar Cookie Mix
Laurel's Sweet Treats ▲ - Chocolate Chip, Gourmet Chocolate Cookie w/White Milk Chocolate Chips, Roll 'Em Out Sugar
Marion's Smart Delights ▲ - Cookie & Muffin Mix ●, Lemon Bar Baking Mix ●
Montana Gluten Free ▲ - Italian Pizzelle Mix ●
Namaste Foods ▲ - Cookie Mix
Nuts.com - Gluten Free Chocolate Chip ●, Gluten Free Shortbread ●
Only Oats ▲ - Grandma's Oatmeal Cookie Mix ●
Pamela's Products ▲ - Chocolate Chunk
PaneRiso ▲ - Rice Cake & Cookie Mix
PrOatina ▲ - Italian Pizzelle Mix ●
Pure Living - Cookie Mix (European Chocolate Truffle w/Tart Cherry Slivers ●, Julienne Cranberries Zante Currants & Essence Of Raspberry Orange Blossom ●, Saigon Cinnamon Oat Zante Currants & Essence Of Chai Tea ●)
Purely Elizabeth ▲ - Chocolate Chip ●, Oatmeal Cherry Chocolate Chip ●, Oatmeal Cinnamon Raisin ●
Really Great Food Company ▲ - Butter, Chocolate Crinkle, Versatile
Silly Yak Bakery - GF (Holiday Cut Out Cookie Dough Mix ●, Snickerdoodle Cookie Mix ●)
Simply Organic ▲ - Gluten Free Spice Cookie Mix ●
Sweet Christine's Bakery - Chocolate Chip ●
The Cravings Place ▲ - Chocolate Chunk (Double, Regular), Create Your Own, Peanut Butter, Raisin Spice
The Grain Exchange - Cookie Mix In A Jar (Chocolate Chip, Oatmeal Raisin)
The Pure Pantry ▲ - Old Fashioned Chocolate Chip ●, Organic Sugar ●, Wholegrain Oatmeal Spice ●
Timtana Gluten Free ▲ - Italian Pizzelle Mix ●
WOW Baking Company ▲ - Cookie Dough (Chocolate Chip ●, Ginger Molasses ●, Peanut Butter ●, Sugar ●)

C Cookies

A Taste Of Thai - Toasted Coconut Fortune Cookies

Aleia's ▲ - Almond Horn ●, Chocolate Chip ●, Chocolate Coconut Macaroon ●, Coconut Macaroon ●, Ginger Snap ●, Peanut Butter ●, Pignoli Nut ●, Snickerdoodle ●

Amy's - Almond Shortbread ★, Chocolate Chip Shortbread ★, Classic Shortbread ★

Andean Dream ▲ - Chocolate Chip, Cocoa Orange, Coconut, Orange Essence, Raisins & Spice

Andrea's Gluten Free ▲ - Chocolate Chip, Decorated Chocolate Chip Cookie Cake, Gooey Butter, Gooey Truffle, Iced Sugar, Oatmeal

Annie's - Gluten Free Bunny Cookies (Cocoa & Vanilla ‼, Ginger Snap ‼, Snickerdoodle ‼)

Apple's Bakery ▲ - Gluten Free (Chocolate Chip No Nut, Coconut Meltaway, Dried Cranberry White Chocolate, Fudge Ranch, Lemon Drop, Molasses, Ranger Chip, Snickerdoodle, Thumbprint, Vegan Oatmeal)

Aunt Gussie's ▲ - Gluten Free Chocolate Chip ●, Chocolate Spritz ●, Mini Chocolate Chip ●, Sugar Free Chocolate Chip w/Almonds ●, Sugar Free Vanilla Spritz ●, Vanilla Swirl ●

Barkat - Cream Filled Wafers (Chocolate, Lemon, Vanilla)

Bella Lucia - Pizzelles ★

Bi-Aglut - Chocolate Covered Waferbars, Chocolate Filled, Cioco Stelle, Riso Ciock, Snack w/Cream Filling, Snack w/Hazelnut Filling, Sugar Free Frollini, Wafers w/Chocolate Filling

Biscottea - Gluten Free Tea Shortbreads (Blueberry, Chai, Earl Grey)

Bodhi's Bakehouse - Chocolate Latte, Chocolate Macadamia, Chocolate Orange Jaffa, Lemon Shortbread

Bonnievilles ▲ - Power Cookies (Cinnamon Ginger ●, Cocoa Cocoa ●, Coconut Almond ●, P B & J ●, Salty Peanut ●)

Boundless Nutrition - Perfect Fit Protein Cookies (Chocolate Chip, Peanut Butter, White Chocolate Macadamia Nut)

C

Breakaway Bakery ▲ - Chocolate Chip ●, Cookies (Molasses ●, Snickerdoodle ●)

Bridge City Baking ▲ - Rugelach (Apricot ●, Chocolate Chip Raisin ●, Cinnamon Raisin ●, Raspberry ●)

Caveman Cookies ▲ - Alpine ●, Original ●, Rainforest ●, Tropical ●

Cherrybrook Kitchen -
  Mini Cookies (Gluten Free Chocolate Chip ★*(Box Must Say Gluten Free)*, Gluten Free Vanilla Graham ★*(Box Must Say Gluten Free))*

Choices Rice Bakery ▲ - Almond Stars & Moons, Butter Shortbread, Cookies (Bird's Nest, Chocolate Chip, Ginger, Mediterranean Macaroons, Mexican Wedding, Raisin Sunflower), Double Chocolate Fudge, Fruit & Nut Powder, Lady Fingers

Cookie Momsters ▲ - Chocolate Chip, Double Chocolate Chip, Soy Free (Chocolate Chip, Double Chocolate), Sugar

Cookies For Me - Chocolate Chip, Dairy Free (Decorated Sugar, Ginger Spice, Lemon Iced Sugar), Mini, Snicker Doodle

Crave Bakery ▲ - Monster Cookie

Deb's Farmhouse Kitchen - Chocolate Chip ●, Oatmeal Raisin ●

Deerfields Gluten Free Bakery ▲ - Day Dreams, Lemon Buttons, Triple Chips

Delicious Delights ▲ - Chewy Gingerbread Cookies

Dolcetti - Artisan Italian Cookies (Almond, Hazelnut Chocolate, Macadamia Coconut, Peanut Chocolate, Pistachio)

Eena Kadeena ▲ - Chocolate Chew, Coconut Macaroons

El Peto ▲ - Almond Shortbread, Carob Chip, Chocolate (Chip, Coconut Macaroons, Hazelnut), Cinnamon Hazelnut, Coconut Macaroons, Gingerbread, Hazelnut Raspberry, Old Fashioned Anise Cookies

Emmy's Organics ▲ - Macaroons (Chai Spice, Choco Chili, Choco Orange, Coconut Vanilla, Dark Cacao, Lemon Ginger, Mint Chip)

Ener-G ▲ - Chocolate Chip Snack Bars, Cookies (Chocolate Chip Potato, Cinnamon, Ginger, Sunflower, Vanilla)

C

Enjoy Life ▲ -
> Crunchy Cookies (Chocolate Chip ●, Double Chocolate ●, Sugar Crisp ●, Vanilla Honey Graham ●)
> Soft Baked Cookies (Chewy Chocolate Chip ●, Double Chocolate Brownie ●, Gingerbread Spice ●, Happy Apple ●, Lively Lemon ●, No Oats Oatmeal ●, Snickerdoodle ●)

Everybody Eats ▲ - Chocolate Chip Cookies

Fabe's Bakery - Gluten Free Mini Cookies (Cranberry Orange ●, Dark Chocolate ●, Ginger Snap ●, Organic Macaroons ●)

Gillian's Foods ▲ - Choco Chip Cookie Dough ●

Ginny Bakes ▲ - Fresh Baked Box (Chocolate Chip Love ●, Coconut Oatmeal Bliss ●, Double Chocolate Happiness ●, Naked Love ●)

Glenny's - Gluten Free Oatmeal Cookies (Oatmeal Chocolate Chip ●, Oatmeal Raisin ●)

Glow Gluten Free ▲ - Chocolate Chip ●, Double Chocolate Chip ●, Gingersnap ●, Snickerdoodle ●

Glutano ▲ - Butterkeks, Choco Chip Keks, Chocolate O's, Custard Creams, Hoops, Kakaowaffeln, Landtaler, Luxury, Nussy, Zitronenwaffeln

Gluten Free Life ▲ - Deluxe Cookie (Chocolate Chip, Flax Shortbread, Snicker Doodle, Sugar, w/Gluten Free Oats (Chocolate Chip Oatmeal, Oatmeal Mocha, Oatmeal Raisin))

Gluten-Free Creations ▲ - Chocolate Chip ●, Oatmeal Raisin ●, Peanut Butter ●, Simply Pumpkin Chocolate Chip ●, Snickerdoodle ●

Glutino ▲ - Chocolate Vanilla Creme, Cookies Chocolate Chip, Vanilla Creme, Wafers (Chocolate, Lemon, Vanilla)

Gopal's - Nature's Gift Cookies (Almond Raisin, Goldenberry Brazil, Hazelnut Cherry, Macadamia Goji)

Go Raw ▲ - Super Cookies (Carrot Cake ●, Chocolate ●, Ginger Snaps●, Lemon ●, Masala Chai ●, Original ●)

Grandma Ferdon's ▲ - Cookies (Chocolate Grande ●, Gingersnap ●, Peanut Butter ●), Lemon Bars ●, Pumpkin Bars ●

Hail Merry ▲ - Macaroons (Blonde ●, Choco ●)

Heaven Mills ▲ -
Cookies (Apricot Sandwich ●, Black & White ●, Chocolate Chip
Jumbo ●, Chocolate Chip ●, Chocolate Dipped ●, Coffee●,
Gluten & Egg Free Oatmeal ●, Gluten Sugar & Egg Free
(Chocolate Chip ●, Vanilla Chocolate Chip ●), Honey ●, Poppy
Seed Lemon ●, Raisin ●, Raspberry Sandwich ●, Sugar Free
(Chocolate Chip ●, Vanilla Chocolate Chip ●), Vanilla Chocolate
Chip Jumbo ●, Vanilla Chocolate Chip ●, Vanilla Drop ●, Vanilla
Rainbow ●, Vanilla ●)
Hamantaschen/Tarts Raspberry ●
Rugelach (Chocolate ●, Cinnamon ●, Gluten & Sugar Free
(Chocolate ●, Cinnamon ●, Vanilla ●), Raspberry ●, Vanilla ●)

Homefree - Gluten Free (Mini Chocolate Chip ●, Mini Chocolate
Chocolate Chip ●, Mini Vanilla ●, Oatmeal ●)

Ian's - Animal Cookies, Wheat Free Gluten Free Cookie Buttons
(Chocolate Chip ★, Crunchy Cinnamon ★)

Indie Candy - Dark Chocolate Covered "Oreos"

Jennies ▲ - Omega 3 Macaroons (Almond Flavored, Chocolate,
Coconut), Zero Carb Macaroons (Carob, Chocolate, Coconut)

Jo-Sef ▲ - Animal Vanilla ●, Animal Cookies Chocolate ●, Sandwich
(Chocolate O's ●, Cinnamon O's ●, Vanilla O's ●), Square
(Chocolate ●, Cinnamon ●, Vanilla ●)

Jovial - Chocolate Cream Filled ●, Fig Fruit Filled ●, Vanilla Cream
Filled ●

Katz Gluten Free ▲ - Apricot Tart ●, Chocolate Chip ●, Chocolate
Dipped ●, Colored Sprinkled ●, Hamantaschen (Apricot ●,
Raspberry ●), Rugelech (Chocolate ●, Cinnamon ●, Vanilla ●), Snack
Poppers (Regular ●, Sugared ●), Vanilla ●

Kay's Naturals - Cookie Bites (Cinnamon Almond ●, Honey
Almond ●)

Kinnikinnick ▲ - Chocolate Cookie Crumbs, Cookies (Montana's
Chocolate Chip, Ginger Snap, KinniKritters Animal Cookies
(Chocolate, Graham Style, Regular), KinniToos Sandwich Cookies
(Chocolate Vanilla, Fudge Creme, Vanilla Creme))

C

Kneaded Specialties ▲ - Chocolate Cherries Jubilee ●, Chocolate Chip●, Double Chocolate Chip ●, Holiday Sugar ●, Lemon Creme ●, Lemon Sugar ●, Orange Creme ●, Snickerdoodle ●, Vegan (Chocolate Cookie Dreams ●, "Cinn" Full Dream ●)

Kookie Karma -

Holistic (Choclate Chip ●, Choco Lot ●)

Raw (Banana Bread ●, Carob Truffle ●, Cherry Cashew ●, Granola Bar ●, Lemon Fig ●)

Le Veneziane - Chocolate Hazelnut, Coconut, Mixed Berries

Liz Lovely - Gluten Free (Chocolate Chip ★, Chocolate Fudge ★, Coconut Lemon ★, German Chocolate Cake ★, Ginger Molasses ★, Oatmeal Raisin ★, Peanut Butter w/Dark Chocolate ★, Snickerdoodle ★, Triple Chocolate Mint ★)

Lucy's ▲ - Chocolate ●, Chocolate Chip ●, Cinnamon Thin ●, Ginger Snap ●, Maple Bliss ●, Oatmeal ●, Sugar ●

Manischewitz - Caramel Cashew Patties, Chocolate Frolic Bears

Mary's Gone Crackers ▲ - Chocolate Chip ●, Double Chocolate ●, Ginger Snaps ●, N'Oatmeal Raisin ●

Mi-Del - *(Package Must Say Gluten Free)* Arrowroot Animal ★, Chocolate Caramel ★, Chocolate Chip ★, Cinnamon Snaps ★, Ginger Snaps ★, Pecan ★, Sandwich (Chocolate ★, Royal Vanilla ★), S'mores ★

Molly's Gluten-Free Bakery ▲ - Chocolate Chip, Ginger Snap, Iced Cut Outs, Mexican Wedding, Sugar

Montana Monster Munchies - Legacy Valley Original Cookie ●

Moondance - All Flavors

Mrs. Crimble's - Macaroons (Chocolate, Coconut, Jam Coconut Rings), Peanut Cookies

My Dad's Gluten Free Bakery ▲ - Black & White ●, Chocolano ●, Chocolate Chip ●, Chocolate Dipped Vanilla Graham Cookie ●, Chocolate Fancy ●, Chocolate Sandwich ●, Cranergy ●, Ginger Spice ●, Italian Chocolate & Raspberry ●, Raspberry Linzer ●

Nana's -

Gluten Free Cookie Bites (Fudge ●, Ginger ●, Lemon ●)

No Gluten Cookie (Chocolate ●, Chocolate Crunch ●, Ginger ●, Lemon ●)

No Gluten Cookie Bars (Berry Vanilla ●, Chocolate Munch ●, Nana Banana ●)

Nicole's - Vegan & Gluten Free Cookies (Chocolate Chip ●, Chocolate Raspberry ●, Mint Chocolate ●, Yuzu Lemon ●)

Orgran ▲ -

Essential Fibre Rotondo Biscuits

Kids (Dinosaur Wholefruit Cookies Wildberry Flavor, Face Biscuits Vanilla, Itsy Bitsy Bears (Choc Berry Flavored Bits, Choc Flavored Bits), Mini Outback Animals (Chocolate, Vanilla), Outback Animals (Chocolate, Vanilla))

Shortbread Hearts

Shortbread Thistle Biscuits

Wild Raspberry Fruit Flavored Biscuits

Pamela's Products ▲ -

Butter Shortbread

Chocolate Chip (Chunky, Walnut)

Ginger w/Sliced Almonds

Lemon Shortbread

Organic (Chocolate Chunk Pecan Shortbread, Dark Chocolate/ Chocolate Chunk, Espresso Chocolate Chunk, Old Fashioned Raisin Walnut, Peanut Butter Chocolate Chip, Spicy Ginger w/ Crystallized Ginger)

Peanut Butter

Pecan Shortbread

Shortbread Swirl

Simplebites Mini Cookies (Chocolate Chip, Extreme Chocolate, Ginger Snapz)

PaneRiso ▲ - Chocolate Chip ●, Cinnamon ●, Coconut ●, Double Chocolate Delite ●, Ginger Snap ●, Maple ●, Orange ●, Soft Chocolate Chip ●

PatsyPie - Chocolate Chip, Lemon Shortbread, Peanut Butter, Raisin, Snappy Ginger

C

Pure Knead ▲ - Brown Sugar Chocolate Chip ●, Lemon Currant ●, Oatmeal Raisin ●

Pure Market Express ▲ - Caramel Macaroons ●, Chocolate Chip Cookies ●, Chocolate Chocolate Chip Cookies ●, Chocolate Macaroons ●, Macaroon Trio ●, No Bake Cookies ●, Vanilla Macaroons ●

Quejos ▲ - Butter Shortbread, Non Dairy (Chocolate Chip, Dark Chocolate Chip, Hemp Heart, Hemp Heart Raisin)

Rose's Bakery ▲ - Chocolate Chip, Gingersnap, Macaroons, Mudslide, Oatmeal, Oatmeal Cranberry Chocolate Chip, Sugar Free (Double Chocolate, Lemon Ginger)

Russo's Gluten Free Gourmet ▲ - Ladyfingers

Sanavi Harisin - Bizcochos Vanilla, Celi Chip Chocolate Chip, Cubanitos, Mantecados Cinnamon Almond, Negritos, Pastas De Almendra Almond, RosCeli Vanilla Rings, Roscos De Cacao Cocoa Rings

Schar ▲ -
Chocolate Dipped Cookies
Chocolate O's
Chocolate Sandwich Cremes
Cocoa
Ladyfingers
Shortbread
Vanilla Sandwich Cremes
Wafers (Hazelnut, Vanilla)

Shabtai ▲ - Chocolate Chip, Florentine Lace, Lady Fingers, Mini Black & White, Pecan Meltaway, Rainbow Cookie Square

Silly Yak Bakery -
CFGF (Cranberry Almond ●, Gingerbread ●, Snickerdoodle ●)
GF (Chocolate Chip ●, Chocolate Pecan ●, Cranberry Almond ●, Cranberry Oatmeal Walnut ●, M&M ●, Oatmeal ●, Oatmeal Chocolate Chip ●, Oatmeal Raisin ●, Peanut Butter ●, Peanut Butter Chocolate Chip ●, Raisin Pecan ●, Snickerdoodle ●, Sugar ●)

Simply Shari's Gluten Free & Fabulous ▲ - Chocolate Chip Cookies ●, Shortbread (Almond ●, Lemon ●, Plain ●)

Skye Foods - Chocolate Chip ●, White Chocolate Macadamia Nut ●

St. Julien Macaroons - Macaroons (All Flavors)

Sunstart - Crunch (Caramel & Chocolate Delights, Chocolate Chip, Golden (Chocolate Wrapped, Ginger, Raspberry, Supreme), Rocky Road)

Sweet Christine's Bakery - Chocolate Chip ●, Oatmeal Raisin ●, Sugar ●

Sweet Escapes Pastries ▲ - Big Chocolate Chip Cookie ●

The Grain Exchange - Chocolate Chip, Chocolate Chip Cookie Cake, Chocolate Chocolate Chunk, Chocolate Mint, Gingersnap, Hamantashen, Oatmeal Raisin, Pumpkin Chocolate Chip, Rocky Road, Snickerdoodle, Sugar, White Chocolate Chip & CranRaisin

The Naked Cookie - Gluten Free (Cafe Con Leche, Chocolate Mint, Death By Chocolate Macaroons, Fiesta Sugar, Triple Chocolate Chunk)

Tia's Bakery ▲ - Chocolate Chip ●, Oatmeal Raisin ●

Trader Joe's - Gluten Free Ginger Snaps, Meringues (All Varieties **! !**)

Trenipoti - Gluten Free Pizzelles ●

Udi's Gluten Free Foods ▲ - Gluten Free (Chocolate Chip ●, Oatmeal Raisin ●, Snickerdoodle ●)

West Meadow Farm Bakery - Gluten Free (Chocolate Chip ●, Gingersnaps ●, Oatmeal Chocolate Chip ●, Oatmeal Raisin ●, Peanut Butter ●)

Whole Foods Market Gluten Free Bakehouse ▲ - Almond, Chocolate Chip Walnut, Molasses Ginger, Nutmeal Raisin, Peanut Butter

WOW Baking Company ▲ - Chocolate Chip ●, Ginger Molasses ●, Lemon Burst ●, Oregon Oatmeal ●, Peanut Butter ●, Snickerdoodle ●

ZeroGrano - Chocolate Wafers, Frollini

Cooking Spray

Emeril's - Buttery, Original Canola Oil

Filippo Berio ▲ - Extra Virgin Olive Oil

Food Club Brand - Butter, Canola Oil, Olive Oil

Hannaford Brand - Butter Flavored, Olive Oil

Hy-Vee - Butter, Canola Oil, Olive Oil, Vegetable Oil

Lowes Foods Brand - Butter, Regular

C

Manischewitz - Butter Flavored Olive Oil, Garlic Flavored Olive Oil, Olive Oil

Mazola - No Stick (Butter, Original)

Meijer Brand - Butter, Olive Oil Extra Virgin, Vegetable Oil

Mishpacha - Canola Oil

Mother's Choice - Olive Oil

O Organics - Canola Oil, Olive Oil

Pam's - All Varieties *(Except 'Baking' Flavor)*

Publix - Butter Flavored, Grill, Olive Oil, Original Canola

Safeway Brand - Canola Oil Blend, Grill, Olive Oil, Vegetable Oil

Smart Balance - Non Stick Omega

Spartan Brand - Butter Flavored, Extra Virgin Olive Oil, Regular

Trader Joe's - All Canola Oil Sprays

Wegmans Brand - Canola Oil, Corn Oil, Natural Butter Flavor Canola Oil, Olive Oil

Winn Dixie - Butter, Canola Oil, Corn, Grill, Olive Oil

Cooking Wine

Eden Organic - Mirin Rice

Holland House - All Varieties

Regina - All Varieties

Corn

... *All Fresh Fruits & Vegetables Are Gluten-Free*

Augason Farms ▲ - Dent Corn *(Pail Size Only)* ●, Gluten Free Freeze Dried Sweet ●

Birds Eye - All Plain Frozen Vegetables

C & W - All Plain Frozen Vegetables **!!**

Del Monte - All Canned Vegetables

Food Club Brand -
Canned (Cream Style, Crisp & Sweet, Gold & White, Golden, White, Whole Kernel (Golden No Salt, Regular))
Frozen (Corn On Cob (Mini Ear, Regular), Whole Kernel, Whole Kernel Golden)

Freshlike - Frozen Plain Corn

Full Circle - Organic Gold Corn

C

Great Value Brand (Wal-Mart) - Canned (Cream Style Corn, Golden Sweet Whole Kernel Corn, No Salt Added Golden Sweet Whole Kernel Corn)

Green Giant -
Canned
Cream Style Sweet Corn
Mexicorn
Niblets (Extra Sweet, No Salt Added, Whole Kernel Sweet Corn, Whole Kernel Sweet Corn 50% Less Sodium)
Southwestern Style
Super Sweet Yellow & White Corn
White Shoepeg
Frozen
Nibblers Mini Ears (Extra Sweet, Regular)
Shoepeg White Corn & Butter Sauce
Valley Fresh Steamers (Extra Sweet Niblets, Niblets Corn, Select White Shoepeg Corn)

Hannaford Brand - Cream Style, Crisp & Sweet, Whole Kernel

Hill Country Fare H-E-B - Cream

Hy-Vee - Corn On The Cob, Cream Style Golden Corn, Frozen Steam In A Bag Corn, Frozen Cut Golden Corn, Whole Kernel (Corn, Golden Corn, White Sweet Corn)

Kirkland Signature - Canned Golden Sweet

Kroger Brand - Canned Whole Kernel Corn

Lowes Foods Brand - Canned White, Frozen (Corn Cob Full Ear, Corn Cob Mini Ear, Whole Kernel)

Meijer Brand -
Canned (Cream Style, Golden Sweet Organic, Whole Kernel (Crisp & Sweet, Golden, Golden No Salt, White))
Frozen (Corn Cob Mini Ear, Corn On The Cob, Fire Roasted Corn, Sweet Corn Steamer, White Sweet Corn Organic, Whole Kernel, Whole Kernel Golden)

Mezzetta ▲ - Gourmet Baby

Midwest Country Fare - Cream Style, Frozen Cut, Whole Kernel

Native Forest - Organic Baby Corn

C

Nuts.com - Simply Sweet Corn Freeze Dried Vegetables ●
O Organics - Canned Whole Kernel, Frozen Golden Cut
Pictsweet - All Plain Frozen Vegetables, Seasoned Corn & Black
Beans
Private Selection - Organic Whole Corn Canned
Publix -
Canned (Cream Style Golden, Golden Sweet, Whole Kernel)
Frozen (Corn On The Cob, Cut)
Publix GreenWise Market - Organic Canned Whole Kernel
S&W - All Canned Vegetables
Safeway Brand - Cream Style, Frozen Corn On The Cob, Steam
In Bag (Petite, White), Whole Kernel (No Salt, Regular)
Spartan Brand -
Canned Golden (Sweet Corn Cream Style, Whole Kernel)
Frozen (Baby Corn Blend, Corn On The Cob, Mini Ear Corn On
The Cob, White Super Sweet, Whole Kernel)
Trader Joe's - Frozen (Cut White Corn, Organic Super Sweet Cut
Corn, Pacific Northwest Cut White Corn, Roasted Corn)
Wegmans Brand -
Canned FYFGA (Cream Style, Whole Kernel (Bread & Butter,
Crisp 'N Sweet, No Salt, Regular))
Frozen On The Cob
Frozen Whole Kernel (FYFGA Bread & Butter Sweet, In Butter
Sauce, Regular)
Westbrae - Whole Kernel (Golden, White)
Winn Dixie -
Canned (Creamed Style, White Whole Kernel, Yellow Whole
Kernel, Yellow Whole Kernel No Salt)
Frozen (On The Cob (Mini, Regular), Organic Yellow Cut,
Steamable Yellow Cut, White Cut, Yellow Cut)
Woodstock Farms - Organic Frozen Cut Corn Supersweet (Regular,
White), Toasted Corn
Corn Dogs
Applegate - Natural Wheat Free Beef !

Ian's - Wheat Free Gluten Free Recipe Popcorn Turkey Corn

S'Better Farms ▲ - Beef Corn Dogs

Corn Syrup...see Syrup

Cornbread/Cornbread Mix

1-2-3 Gluten Free ▲ - Micah's Mouthwatering Cornbread Mix ●

Abundant Life Foods ▲ - Corn Muffin Mix

Bloomfield Farms ▲ - Gluten Free Cornbread & Muffin Mix ●

Bob's Red Mill ▲ - Gluten Free Cornbread Mix ★

Celiac Specialties ▲ - Corn Bread Mix

Chi-Chi's - Fiesta Sweet Corn Cake Mix

Choices Rice Bakery ▲ - Biscuits, Jalapeno Cornbread

El Torito - Sweet Corn Cake Mix

Food-Tek Fast & Fresh - Corn Bread Mix ★

Gifts Of Nature ▲ - Buttermilk Cornbread Mix ●

Gluten Free Pantry ▲ - Yankee Cornbread

Gluten-Free Naturals - Cornbread & Corn Muffin Mix

Grandma Ferdon's ▲ - Cornbread Mix ●

Hill Country Fare H-E-B - Corn Masa Mix

Joan's GF Great Bakes ▲ - Corn Bread

Laurel's Sweet Treats ▲ - Good Ol' Cornbread

Mixes From The Heartland ▲ - Corn Bread Mix ●

Orgran ▲ - Cornbread & Muffin Mix

Pamela's Products ▲ - Cornbread & Muffin Mix

Really Great Food Company ▲ - Home Style Cornbread Mix

Sof'ella - Gluten Free Cornbread Mix ★

The Cravings Place ▲ - Grandma's Unsweetened Cornbread Mix

The Grain Exchange - Cornbread

Whole Foods Market Gluten Free Bakehouse ▲ - Cornbread

Corned Beef...see also Beef

Armour - Corned Beef Hash

Buddig - Original Regular

Castle Wood Reserve - Deli Meat Angus Corned Beef

Di Lusso - Deli Counter

Food Club Brand - Hash

C

Garrett County Farms - Brisket (Half ★, Whole ★), Round ★, Whole ★

Great Value Brand (Wal-Mart) - Corned Beef Hash

Hormel - Mary Kitchens (Corned Beef Hash, Reduced Fat Hash)

Kayem - Extra Lean !!

Meijer Brand - Hash, Lunch Meat Sliced Chipped Meat

Safeway Brand - Corned Beef Hash

Smithfield - Cooked Round

Spartan Brand - Hash

Wellshire Farms - Brisket (Half ★, Whole ★), Round ★, Whole ★

Winn Dixie - Corned Beef Hash

Cornflake Crumbs...see Coating

Cornish Hens

... *All Fresh Poultry Is Gluten-Free (Non-Marinated, Unseasoned)*

Shelton's - Game Hens

Cornmeal

Arrowhead Mills - Organic (Blue, Yellow)

Bob's Red Mill ▲ - Gluten Free Cornmeal ★

Cause You're Special ▲ - Fine Ground Cornmeal

El Peto ▲

Gifts Of Nature ▲ - Yellow Cornmeal ●

Hodgson Mill - Sweet Yellow

Publix - Plain Yellow

Really Great Food Company ▲

Safeway Brand - Yellow Corn Meal

Shiloh Farms - Polenta (Coarse Corn Meal) !!

Cottage Cheese

Breakstone's -

Cottage Doubles (Peach, Pineapple, Strawberry)

Large Curd (2% Milk Fat, 4% Milk Fat)

Small Curd (2% Milk Fat, 2% Milk Fat w/Pineapple, 4% Milk Fat, Fat Free)

Cabot - No Fat, Regular

Daisy Brand - All Varieties

Food Club Brand - 1% Low Fat, Large Curd, Small Curd

Friendship - All Varieties

Gordon Food Service - Large Curd, Small Curd
Hannaford Brand - All Varieties
Hood - All Varieties
Horizon Organic - All Varieties
Hy-Vee - 1% Low Fat Small Curd, 4% Large Curd, 4% Small Curd
Kemps - All Varieties
Knudsen - All Varieties
Lactaid - All Varieties
Light 'N Lively - Fat Free, Lowfat
Lowes Foods Brand - 4%, Non Fat, Small Curd
Lucerne - Cottage Cheese *(Except Fruit Added)*
Michigan Brand - All Varieties
Midwest Country Fare - 1% Small Curd, 4% Small Curd
Nancy's - All Cultured Dairy & Soy Products
Prairie Farms - Dry Curd, Fat Free, Large Curd, Low Fat, Small Curd
Publix - Fat Free, Large Curd 4% Milk Fat, Low Fat, Low Fat w/ Pineapple, Small Curd 4% Milk Fat
Shamrock Farms - Fat Free, Low Fat, Traditional
Spartan Brand - Large Curd 4% Milk Fat, Low Fat 1%, Small Curd (Non Fat, Regular)
Wegmans Brand - 1% Large Curd, Fat Free Pineapple, Non Fat, Small Curd (1%, 4%)
Winn Dixie - 4% Large Curd, 4% Small Curd, Fat Free, Low Fat

Couscous
Lundberg ▲ - Brown Rice (Mediterranean Curry, Plain Original, Roasted Garlic & Olive Oil, Savory Herb)

Crab Cakes
Star Of The Sea Seafood - Gluten Free Crab Cakes ●

Crabmeat
... *All Fresh Seafood Is Gluten-Free (Non-Marinated, Unseasoned)*
Blue Horizon - New England Crab Bites
Bumble Bee - Lump, Pink, White
Chicken Of The Sea - All Crab Products
Crown Prince - Fancy Pink, Fancy White, Lump White, Natural Fancy White Lump

C

Great Value Brand (Wal-Mart) - Crab Meat

Ocean Prince - Pink

Star Of The Sea - Crab Cakes

Trader Joe's - Crabmeat

Crackers

Aimee's Livin' Magic - All Crackers

Andre's - Crackerbread (Cheddar Cheese, Country Onion, Old World Rye, Original, Roasted Garlic, Sweet Cinnamon, Tangy Parmesan, Toasted Sesame, Zesty Italian)

Back To Nature - Rice Thins (Multi Seed, Sesame Seed, White Cheddar)

Barkat - Matzo

Bi-Aglut - Original

Blue Diamond ▲ - Nut Thins (Almond ●, Cheddar Cheese ●, Country Ranch ●, Hazelnut ●, Hint Of Sea Salt ●, Pecan ●, Pepper Jack Cheese●, Smokehouse ●)

Casabi Organics ▲ - Cinnamon, Garlic, Onion, Original

Crunchmaster -

　7 Ancient Grains (Cracked Pepper & Herb ●, Hint Of Sea Salt ●)

　Healthy Gatherings ●

　Multi Grain (Roasted Vegetable ●, Sea Salt ●, White Cheddar ●)

　Multi Seed (Original ●, Roasted Garlic ●, Rosemary & Olive Oil ●, Toasted Onion ●)

　Multi Seed Grain Club Pack (Five Seed Multi Grain ●, Five Seed Multi Seed ●, Multi Grain ●)

　Rice Crackers (Artisan Four Cheese ●, Toasted Sesame ●)

Eden Organic - Brown Rice, Nori Maki Rice

Edward & Sons -

　Brown Rice Snaps (Black Sesame, Cheddar, Onion Garlic, Tamari (Seaweed, Sesame), Toasted Onion, Unsalted Plain, Unsalted Sesame, Vegetable)

　Exotic Rice Toast (Brown Jasmine Rice & Spring Onion, Purple Rice & Black Sesame, Thai Red Rice & Flaxseeds)

Ener-G ▲ - Cinnamon, Cinnamon Crackers Pieces, Flax, Gourmet, Seattle

Food Should Taste Good - Brown Rice ●

Foods Alive - Organic Flax Crackers (BBQ, Hemp, Italian Zest, Maple & Cinnamon, Mexican Harvest, Mustard, Onion Garlic, Original)

Garden Fields - Garlic, Original, Pizza

Glutano - Kric Kroc, Snackers

Glutino ▲ - Gluten Free Crackers (Cheddar, Multigrain, Original, Table, Vegetable)

H-E-B - Cheesy (American, Cheddar)

Hol Grain ▲ - Brown Rice (Lightly Salted ●, No Salt ●, Onion & Garlic ●, w/Sesame Seeds Lightly Salted ●)

Ka-Me - Gluten Free Rice Crackers (Black Sesame & Soy Sauce, Cheese, Mini, Original, Seaweed, Sesame, Wasabi *(Package Must Say Gluten Free)*)

Kookie Karma - All Varieties ●

Lydia's Organics - Fiesta, Ginger Nori, Green, Italian, Luna Nori

Mary's Gone Crackers ▲ - Black Pepper ●, Caraway ●, Herb ●, Onion ●, Original ●

Mediterranean Snacks ▲ - Lentil Crackers (Cracked Pepper, Rosemary Herb, Sea Salt)

Mr. Krispers - Tasty Snack Crackers Original Sesame ●

Mrs. Crimble's - Original Cheese, Rosemary & Onion, Sun Dried Tomato & Pesto

Mum-Mum Snax ▲ - Rice Crackers (Apple Cinnamon, White Cheddar)

Nicole's - Divine Crackers (Be Sure To Flax Me ●, Dilly Dillingham ●, My Dreams Come True ●, Tomato Tomahto ●)

Orgran ▲ - Deli Multigrain w/Poppyseed

Pure Knead ▲ - Crackers (Spicy Firecrackers ●, Spring Onion ●, Sun Dried Tomato ●)

Pure Market Express ▲ - Italian Flax Crackers ●

Real Foods ▲ - Corn Thins (BBQ, Multigrain, Original, Sesame, Sour Cream & Chives, Soy & Linseed, Tasty Cheese), Rice Thins

Roland - Feng Shui Rice Crackers (Hot Wasabi, Nori Seaweed, Original)

RW Garcia - 5 Seed (Onion & Chive ●, Rosemary & Garlic ●, Tellicherry Cracked Pepper ●)

C

Sakata - Traditional Rice (Cheddar Cheese, Original, Seaweed)

San-J - Brown Rice Crackers (Tamari ●, Tamari Black Sesame ●, Tamari Brown Sesame ●, Teriyaki Sesame ●)

Schar ▲ - Crispbread, Snack, Table Crackers

Sharwood's - Spiced Thai Crackers !!

The Grainless Baker ▲ - Cheddar Snackers

The Kitchen Table Bakers - Gourmet Wafer Crisps (Aged Parmesan ●, Everything ●, Flax Seed ●, Garlic ●, Italian Herb ●, Jalapeno ●, Rosemary ●, Sesame ●)

Trader Joe's - Savory Thins (Edamame !!, Minis !!, Original !!)

Two Moms In The Raw - Sea Crackers (Garden Herb ●, Pesto ●, Tomato Basil ●)

Wellaby's ▲ -
Cheese Ups (Classic, Parmesan, Smoked)
Mini (Grated Parmesan, Original Cheese, Red Cheddar)
Regular (Classic Cheese, Feta Oregano & Olive Oil, Parmesan & Sun Dried Tomato, Rosemary & Onion)

ZeroGrano - Crackers

Cranberries...see also Dried Fruit

*... *All Fresh Fruits & Vegetables Are Gluten-Free*

Mariani - Dried (Flavor Sensations Concord Grape Juice Flavored !!, Sweetened !!)

Nuts.com - Dried Fruit (Natural Juice Infused ●, Organic ●, Simply ●, Sliced ●, Whole ●)

Ocean Spray - Craisins (Blueberry, Cherry, Original, Pomegranate)

Oskri Organics - Dried Cranberries

Trader Joe's - Frozen Sliced Sweetened Cranberries

Woodstock Farms - Organic Sweetened, Sweetened

Cranberry Sauce

Baxters

Great Value Brand (Wal-Mart) - Jellied, Whole Berry

Hannaford Brand

Hy-Vee - Jellied, Whole Berry

Lowes Foods Brand

Ocean Spray - Jellied, Whole Berry

cream cheese

C

    Pacific Natural Foods - Organic (Jellied, Whole Berry)
    Publix - Whole
    S&W - All Canned/Jarred Fruits
    Safeway Brand - Jellied, Whole
    Spartan Brand - Jellied, Whole
    Wegmans Brand - Jellied, Whole Berry
    Wild Thymes - Cranberry Apple Walnut, Cranberry Fig, Cranberry
        Raspberry, Original
    Winn Dixie - Jellied
Cream...see Milk and/or Creamer
Cream Cheese
    Breakstone's - TempTee Whipped Cream Cheese
    Cabot - Neufchatel, Regular
    Follow Your Heart - Vegan Gourmet **!**
    Galaxy Nutritional Foods - Cream Cheese Alternative (Chive &
        Garlic, Classic Plain)
    Great Value Brand (Wal-Mart) - Chive & Onion, Light, Regular, Salsa,
        Strawberry, Whipped
    Hannaford Brand - 1/3 Less Fat, Fat Free, Neufchatel, Regular
    Horizon Organic - All Varieties
    Hy-Vee - 1/3 Less Fat, Blueberry, Fat Free (Regular, Soft, Strawberry),
        Garden Vegetable, Onion & Chives, Regular, Soft (Light, Regular),
        Strawberry, Whipped
    Lowes Foods Brand - Bar, Neufchatel Bar Less Fat, Soft (Light, Regular)
    Lucerne - Soft (Garden Vegetable, Neufchatel, Onion & Chive,
        Strawberry, Whipped Spread), Soft Bars (Fat Free, Light)
    Nancy's - All Cultured Dairy & Soy Products
    Organic Valley - Neufchatel, Regular
    Philadelphia -
        Block (Fat Free, Light, Neufchatel 1/3 Less Fat, Original)
        Tubs
            1/3 Less Fat
            Blueberry
            Cheesecake
            Chive & Onion (1/3 Less Fat, Regular)

C

    Fat Free
    Garden Vegetable (1/3 Less Fat, Regular)
    Honey Nut
    Light
    Pineapple
    Regular
    Salmon
    Strawberry (1/3 Less Fat, Fat Free, Regular)
  Whipped (Cinnamon 'N Brown Sugar, Garlic 'N Herb, Mixed Berry, Ranch, Regular, w/Chives)
Publix - Fat Free (All Flavors), Light (All Flavors), Neufchatel, Regular (All Flavors), Soft (All Flavors)
Spartan Brand - Bar, Tubs (Lite, Neufchatel, Original, Strawberry, Whipped)
Trader Joe's - All Varieties
Winn Dixie - Lite, Regular, Soft
Cream Of Tartar
  Cause You're Special
Creamer
  Borden - Cremora Non Dairy Creamer (Lite & Creamy, Original)
  Coffee-Mate - All Varieties (Liquid, Powder)
  Cremora - Non Dairy Creamer (Lite & Creamy, Original)
  Food Club Brand - French Vanilla, Hazelnut, Non Dairy Coffee Creamer (Fat Free French Vanilla, Fat Free Hazelnut, Original), Powdered Fat Free
  Garelick Farms - Fresh (Half & Half, Light Cream), Ultra Pasteurized (Fat Free Half & Half, Half & Half, Heavy Cream, Light Cream)
  Giant Eagle Brand - Coffee Cream Light, Half & Half (Fat Free, Regular), Non Dairy Creamer
  Good Karma - Coffee Creamer (French Vanilla, Hazelnut, Original)
  Gordon Food Service - Half & Half, Nondairy Liquid
  Great Value Brand (Wal-Mart) - Powdered (Extra Rich, Fat Free, French Vanilla, Hazelnut, Regular), Refrigerated Liquid Ultra Pasteurized
  H-E-B - Creamer (French Vanilla, Hazelnut, Plain)

creamer

C

Hannaford Brand - Non Dairy Coffee Creamer, Refrigerated

Hood - Country Creamer (Fat Free, Regular)

Horizon Organic - All Varieties

Hy-Vee -

Coffee Creamer (Creamy Chocolate, Dry Original, Dry Vanilla Caramel, Fat Free Original, French Vanilla, Hazelnut)

Refrigerated (French Vanilla, Hazelnut, Original, Vanilla Caramel)

Refrigerated Fat Free (French Vanilla, Hazelnut)

International Delight - All Varieties

Kemps - All Varieties

Kroger Brand - Creme Brulee, Sugar Free Hazelnut, Vanilla Caramel

Laura Lynn - Non Dairy Creamer (Amaretto, French Vanilla, Hazelnut, Irish Creme, Lite, Original, Sugar Free (French Vanilla, Hazelnut))

Lowes Foods Brand - Non Dairy (Fat Free French Vanilla, French Vanilla, Hazelnut, Original, Sucralose No Calorie)

Lucerne - Coffee Creamer (French Vanilla (Fat Free, Regular), Original, Powdered Original), Half & Half, Liquid Creamer (Creme Brule, Hazelnut), Vanilla Caramel

Meijer Brand - Creamer (French Vanilla, Hazelnut, Organic), Ultra Pasteurized Non Dairy Creamer

MimicCreme -

Almond & Cashew Cream (Sugar Free Sweetened, Sweetened, Unsweetened)

Almond & Cashew Cream For Coffee (French Vanilla, Hazelnut Biscotti, Unsweetened Original)

Nestle - Coffee Mate All Varieties (Liquid, Powder)

Organic Valley - Half & Half (French Vanilla, Hazelnut, Regular)

Prairie Farms - Half & Half (Fat Free, Heavy Whipping, Regular, Ultra Pasteurized, Ultra Pasteurized Heavy Whipping Cream, Whipped Cream Aerosol)

Publix - Liquid (Coffee Creamer, Fat Free Non Dairy Creamer, Half & Half (Fat Free, Regular)), Powder Non Dairy Creamer (French Vanilla, Lite, Regular)

Publix GreenWise Market - Half & Half

C

Shamrock Farms - Fat Free Half & Half (French Vanilla, Regular), Half & Half, Heavy Cream

Silk Soymilk - French Vanilla, Hazelnut, Original

Simply Smart - Half & Half Fat Free

So Delicious - Coconut Milk (French Vanilla ●, Hazelnut ●, Original ●)

Spartan Brand - Coffee Creamer Powdered Non Dairy (French Vanilla, Hazelnut, Lite, Regular, Vanilla Caramel)

Wildwood - Soymilk Creamer Original

Winn Dixie - Half & Half (Fat Free, Regular), Non Dairy Coffee Creamer (Fat Free, Original), Whipping (Heavy, Regular)

Crepes

Kinnikinnick ▲ - Crepe Mix

Crispbread

Bi-Aglut - Fette Tostate (Mediterranean, Original)

Le Pain Des Fleurs ▲ - Chestnut, Quinoa

Mauk Family Farms - Raw (Breakfast Crusts ●, Mineral Rich Crusts ●, Wheat Free Crusts ●)

Natural Nectar - Cracklebread (Multigrain, Original, Sun Dried Tomato & Oregano)

Orgran ▲ - Crispibread (Buckwheat, Corn, Essential Fibre, Multigrain w/Quinoa, Rice)

Schar ▲ - Crispbread

Crisps

Baked Lay's - Potato Crisps (Original ★, Parmesan & Tuscan Herb ★, Sour Cream & Onion ★, Southwestern Ranch ★)

Baked Ruffles - Potato Crisps (Cheddar & Sour Cream ★, Original ★)

Boulder Canyon Natural Foods - Vegetable Crisps (Hearty Cheddar ★, Red Ripe Tomato ★, Sour Cream & Chive ★)

Brothers All Natural ▲ -
Fruit Crisps (Apple Cinnamon, Asian Pear, Banana, Fuji Apple, Mandarin Orange, Mixed Berry, Organic Strawberry, Peach, Pineapple, Strawberry, Strawberry Banana)
Potato Crisps (Black Pepper w/Sea Salt, Onion & Garlic, Original w/Sea Salt, Szechuan Pepper & Fresh Chives)

Crunchmaster - Multi Grain ●

Full Circle - Soy (Barbecue, Ranch, Sea Salt)

Glenny's - Soy Crisps (Apple Cinnamon ●, Barbeque ●, Caramel ●, Cheddar ●, Creamy Ranch ●, Lightly Salted ●, No Salt Added ●, Olive Oil Garlic & Feta Cheese ●, Onion & Garlic ●, Organic (Barbeque ●, Creamy Ranch ●, Sea Salt ●, White Cheddar ●), Salt & Pepper ●, White Cheddar ●)

Grace Island Specialty Foods ▲ - All Varieties

Ka-Me - Gluten Free Brown Rice Crisps (Korean Barbecue, Original, Szechuan, Teriyaki)

Mauk Family Farms - Raw Flax Seed (Garlic & Parsley ●, Hickory & Paprika ●, Jalapeno ●, Onion & Cumin ●)

Michael Season's - Baked Potato Crisps (Cheddar & Sour Cream ★, Original ★, Sweet Barbecue ★)

Mr. Krispers -
  Baked Nut Chips Toasted Almond ●
  Baked Rice Krisps (Barbecue ●, Nacho ●, Sea Salt & Pepper ●, Sour Cream & Onion ●, Sun Dried Tomato & Basil ●, White Cheddar & Herbs ●)
  Multi Seed Chips Original ●
  Tasty Snack Crackers Original Sesame ●

Munchos - Regular Potato Crisps ‼

Polenta Crisps ▲ - Caramelized Red Onion & Balsamic Vinegar, Parmesan Cheese, Rosemary & Garlic

The Kitchen Table Bakers - Parmesan Gourmet Wafer Crisps (All Flavors ●)

Trader Joe's - Sea Salt & Pepper Rice Crisps ‼

UTZ - Rice Crisps (Garden Salsa, Sea Salt, Sweet Chili, Sweet Potato)

Croutons

  Aleia's ▲ - Classic ●, Parmesan ●
  Gillian's Foods ▲ - Garlic Croutons ●
  Pure Knead ▲ - Original Recipe ●
  Rose's Bakery ▲ - Seasoned
  West Meadow Farm Bakery - Gluten Free ●

C Cucumbers
   ... *All Fresh Fruits & Vegetables Are Gluten-Free

Cupcakes
3 Fellers Bakery ▲ - Chocolate ●, Chocolate Peanut Butter ●, Coconut ●, Tropical Carrot Cake ●, Vanilla ●

Andrea's Gluten Free ▲ - Apple Cinnamon, Carrot w/Cream Cheese Frosting, Lemon Raspberry, Orange Zinger

Breakaway Bakery ▲ - Chocolate ●, Chocolate Chip ●, Lemon Cinnamon ●

Crave Bakery ▲ - Chocolate, Confetti, Vanilla

Gluten-Free Creations ▲ - Chocolate ●, Cinnamon Roll ●, Vanilla Bean ●

Heaven Mills ▲ - Sprinkled ●

Katz Gluten Free ▲ - Chocolate ●, Chocolate Frosted ●, Vanilla ●

Kneaded Specialties ▲ - Cupcakes (Carrot ●, Chocolate ●, Lemon Berry ●, Vegan (Chocolate Creme ●, Orange Creme ●, Vanilla Creme ●), White ●)

Mariposa Artisan-Crafted Gluten-Free ▲ - Filled Cupcakes (Penguin, Polar Bear)

Molly's Gluten-Free Bakery ▲ - Chocolate (w/Chocolate Icing, w/ Vanilla Icing), Spice (w/Chocolate Icing, w/Vanilla Icing), Yellow (w/ Chocolate Icing, w/Vanilla Icing)

Pure Knead ▲ - Chocolate ●, Lemon ●, Mexican Latte ●, Strawberry ●, Vanilla Cardamom ●, Vanilla ●

Shabtai ▲ - Ring Ting

Silly Yak Bakery -
   CFGF (Frosted Chocolate Cupcake ●, Frosted Vanilla Cupcake ●)
   GF (Frosted Chocolate Cupcake ●, Frosted Vanilla Cupcake ●)

Sweet Christine's Bakery - Chocolate w/Vanilla Icing ●, Vanilla w/ Vanilla Icing ●

The Grain Exchange - Jar Full Of Cupcakes (Chocolate, Pumpkin, Red Velvet, Vanilla), Strawberry Shortcake Cupcakes

Udi's Gluten Free Foods ▲ - Vanilla ●

Whole Foods Market Gluten Free Bakehouse ▲ - Cupcakes (Chocolate, Vanilla)

Curry Paste
    A Taste Of Thai - Curry Paste (Green, Panang, Red, Yellow)
    Patak's Original - Biryani, Hot, Korma, Madras, Mild, Rogan Josh,
        Tikka Masala, Vindaloo
    Sharwood's - Green
    Thai Kitchen - Curry Paste (Green, Red, Roasted Red Chili)
Curry Powder...see also Seasonings
    Durkee
    McCormick - Gourmet Collection (100% Organic, Regular)
    Tones
Curry Sauce
    Sharwood's - Thai (Green, Red)
Custard
    Orgran ▲ - Custard Mix

D

Dates
    Mariani - Chopped **!!**, Pitted **!!**
    Nuts.com - Dried Fruit (Jumbo Medjool ●, Organic Medjool ●,
        Organic Pitted ●, Pitted ●)
    Oskri Organics - Dried Dates
    Woodstock Farms - Deglet w/Pit, Organic California Medjool
        Dates w/Pit
Deli Meat
    Applegate -
        Deli Counter (Bologna Uncured Turkey **!**, Chicken (Chipotle **!**,
            Oven Roasted Breast **!**, Smoked Breast **!**), Ham (Black
            Forest **!**, Hand Tied Maple **!**, Slow Cooked **!**, Virginia Brand
            !), Pastrami **!**, Pepperoni (Sliced **!**, Whole **!**), Prosciutto **!**,
            Roast Beef (Peppered Eye **!**, Regular **!**), Salametti **!**, Salami
            (Genoa **!**, Herb **!**, Pepper **!**, Turkey **!**), Soppressata **!**, Turkey
            (Herb Breast **!**, Honey Maple **!**, No Salt **!**, Oven Roasted Breast
            Layout **!**, Peppered **!**, Smoked **!**, Southwestern **!**))
        Natural (Barbecue Chicken **!**, Black Forest Ham **!**, Coppa **!**,

D

Genoa Salami !, Herb Turkey !, Honey & Maple Turkey Breast !, Honey Ham !, Hot Soppressata !, Pancetta !, Prosciutto !, Roast Beef !, Roasted Chicken Breast !, Roasted Turkey !, Slow Cooked Ham !, Smoked Turkey Breast !, Soppressata !, Turkey Bologna !, Turkey Salami !, Uncured Cooked Capricola Ham !, Uncured Pepperoni !)

Organic (Genoa Salami !, Herb Turkey Breast !, Roast Beef !, Roasted Chicken !, Roasted Turkey Breast !, Smoked Chicken !, Smoked Turkey Breast !, Uncured Ham !, Uncured Turkey Bologna !)

Armour -
Beef (Corned Beef, Italian Style Roast Beef, Pastrami, Roast Beef)
Bologna (Beef, Turkey Pork Chicken Beef)
Ham (Cooked, Cooked Ham & Water Product, Honey Cured, Lite, Spiced Luncheon Meat, Virginia Brand)
Sandwich Style Pepperoni
Turkey (Oven Roasted, Oven Roasted w/Broth, Smoked)

Boar's Head - All Varieties

Buddig -
Deli Cuts (Baked Honey Ham, Brown Sugar Baked Ham, Honey Roasted Turkey, Oven Roasted Turkey, Pastrami, Roast Beef, Rotisserie Chicken, Smoked Ham, Smoked Turkey)
Original (Beef, Brown Sugar Ham, Chicken, Corned Beef, Ham, Honey Ham, Honey Roasted Turkey, Mesquite Turkey, Oven Roasted Turkey, Pastrami, Turkey)

Busseto - Bresaola, Coppa (Dry, Hot Dry), Dry Salami (Black Pepper, Italian, Rosette De Lyon), Herbs De Provence, Pancetta, Pepper Coated Salami, Premium Genoa Salami, Prosciutto

Butterball -
Extra Thin Sliced Deep Fried Turkey Breast (Buttery Herb, Cajun Style, Original, Thanksgiving Style)
Extra Thin Sliced Turkey Breast (Honey Roasted, Oven Roasted, Rotisserie Seasoned, Smoked)

Lean Family Size (Honey Roasted Turkey Breast, Oven Roasted
Turkey Breast, Smoked Turkey Breast, Turkey Bologna,
Turkey Ham)

Thick Sliced Deep Fried Turkey Breast (Cajun Style, Original,
Thanksgiving Style)

Thick Sliced Turkey Breast (Honey Roasted, Oven Roasted, Smoked)

Thin Sliced Oven Roasted Chicken Breast

Thin Sliced Turkey Breast (Honey Roasted, Oven Roasted, Rotisserie
Seasoned, Smoked)

Castle Wood Reserve - Angus Corned Beef, Angus Roast Beef, Black
Forest Ham, Ham Deluxe Cooked, Hard Salami, Herb Roasted Turkey,
Hickory Smoked Turkey, Honey Ham, Oven Roasted Turkey, Turkey
Pastrami, Virginia Brand Smoked Ham

Columbus Salame -

Beef (Corned, Italian Roast, Roast)

Chicken Breast (Buffalo Style, Oven Roasted)

Ham (Applewood Smoked, Black Forest, Holiday Carving, Maple
Syrup Honey Cured, Reduced Sodium Honey)

Pastrami

Roasted Pork Loin

Turkey Breast (Cracked Pepper, Cured Maple Syrup Honey Coated,
Herb, Holiday Carving, Pan Roasted, Reduced Sodium, Smoked,
Southwestern)

Di Lusso -

Chicken (Mesquite, Oven Roasted)

Corned Beef

Ham (Black Forest, Brown Sugar, Deluxe Deli, Double Smoked,
Honey Maple, Prosciutto, Smoked Honey Roasted)

Pastrami

Pepperoni

Roast Beef (Seasoned, Seasoned Cajun Style, Seasoned Italian Style,
Seasoned Rare)

Salami (Genoa !, Hard, Italian Dry, Natural Casing Genoa, Sopressata)

Turkey (Cajun Style, Cracked Pepper, Golden Brown, Honey, Honey
Mesquite, Reduced Sodium, Smoked, Sun Dried Tomato)

D Dietz & Watson ▲ -
   Deli Counter
      Black Forest (Beerwurst ●, Braunschweiger Liverwurst ●,
         Braunschweiger Liverwurst Natural Casing ●)
      Blutwurst ●
      Bologna (Beef ●, Black Forest German ●, Gourmet Lite ●, Regular ●)
      Capocollo (Ham ●, Hot ●, Sweet ●)
      Classic Loaf (Deluxe ●, Peppered ●)
      Lunch Roll ●
      Mortadella (Regular ●, w/Pistachios ●)
      Olive Loaf ●
      Pancetta ●
      Pickle & Pimiento Loaf ●
      Prosciutto (American Style ●, Classico ●)
      Salami (Beef Cooked ●, Cooked ●, Genoa ●, Hard ●)
      Sausage (Head Cheese ●, Honey Roll ●, Krakow ●)
      Slicing Pepperoni ●
      Sopressata (Hot ●, Sweet ●)
      Souse Roll ●
      Spiced Luncheon Meat ●
   Pre Sliced
      Black Forest Smoked Turkey ●
      Bologna (Beef ●, Regular ●)
      Capocollo (Hot ●, Sweet ●)
      Chicken (Buffalo Style ●, Southern Style ●)
      Ham (Black Forest Smoked ●, Capocolla ●, Cooked ●, Gourmet Lite
         Cooked ●, Smoked Maple ●, Tavern ●, Virginia Brand ●)
      Mortadella ●
      P&P Loaf ●
      Pancetta ●
      Prosciutto (Regular ●, Shelf Stable ●)
      Roast Beef (London Broil ●, Premium Homestyle ●)
      Salami (Cooked ●, Genoa ●)
      Sopressata ●

     Spiced Beef Pastrami ●

     Salami Natural Casing Genoa ●

Eating Right - Deli Sliced (Honey Ham, Oven Roasted Chicken, Oven Roasted Turkey, Pastrami, Roast Beef, Smoked Turkey)

Eckrich -

  Deli Counter

    Bologna (Beef, Fried, Garlic, Low Sodium, Meat)

    Chicken Fried Chicken Breast

    Corned Beef Cooked

    Ham (Black Forest Brand Nugget, Brown Sugar Nugget, Canadian Maple, Chopped, Ham Steak, Honey Cured, Honey Maple, Imported, Off The Bone, Smoked Pitt, Spiced Luncheon Meat, Spiral Sliced Holiday, Virginia Brand)

    Loaf (Braunschweiger, Head Cheese, Honey, Jalapeno, Minced Luncheon, Old Fashioned, Olive, Peppered, Pickle & Pimento, Souse)

    Pastrami Peppered

    Pepperoni Regular

    Regular Summer Sausage

    Roast Beef (Choice Top, Lite, Seasoned)

    Salami (Cotto, Genoa, Hard, Lo Fat Hard)

    Turkey (Fried Skinless, Mesquite Smoked, Oven Roasted, Smoked)

  Lunch Meat

    Bologna (Beef, Lite, Meat, Ring Bologna)

    Ham (Chopped, Virginia Brand Thin Sliced)

    Loaf (Ham & Cheese, Honey, Old Fashioned, Olive, Pickle)

    Pepperoni Regular

    Salami (Cotto Salami, Hard Salami)

Farmer John - Lunch Meats (Brown Sugar & Honey Sliced Ham, Lower Sodium Sliced Ham, Sliced Ham, Sliced Turkey), No Preservatives (Ham (Honey, Smoked), Roast Beef, Turkey Breast (Roasted, Smoked))

Gordon Food Service - Turkey Sliced Breast (Regular, Smoked)

D   **Great Value Brand (Wal-Mart)** -
    97% Fat Free Ham Water Added (Baked, Cooked, Honey)
    Deli Sliced (Mesquite Smoked Turkey Breast, Oven Roasted
       Turkey Breast, Roast Beef, Smoked Ham, Smoked Honey Ham)
    Fat Free (Smoked Turkey Breast, Turkey Breast)
  H-E-B - Artisan Mozzarollo (Capicola & Pepperoncini, Prosciutto &
    Basil, Wine Salami)
  Hebrew National - Beef Bologna, Beef Salami, Lean Beef (Bologna,
    Salami)
  Hillshire Farms -
    Deli Select (Baked Ham, Corned Beef, Honey Ham, Smoked
      (Chicken Breast, Turkey Breast))
    Deli Select Premium Hearty Slices (Honey (Ham, Roasted Turkey),
      Oven Roasted Turkey Breast)
    Deli Select Thin Sliced (Brown Sugar Baked Ham, Honey Roasted
      Turkey Breast, Pastrami, Roast Beef, Smoked Ham)
    Deli Select Ultra Thin (Brown Sugar Baked Ham, Baked Ham,
      Cracked Black Pepper Turkey Breast, Hard Salami, Hickory
      Smoked Chicken Breast, Honey Roasted Turkey Breast, Honey
      Ham, Honey Roasted Turkey, Lower Sodium (Honey Ham,
      Honey Roasted Turkey, Oven Roasted Turkey Breast, Smoked
      Ham), Mesquite Smoked Turkey Breast, Oven Roasted Turkey
      Breast Regular, Pastrami, Roast Beef, Rotisserie Seasoned
      Chicken Breast, Smoked Ham)
  Honeysuckle White -
    Chicken Breast (BBQ, Buffalo Style, Oil Browned)
    Lunch Meats Deli Sliced (Hickory Smoked Turkey Breast (Honey,
      Regular), Oven Roasted Turkey Breast, Turkey Pastrami)
    Turkey Bologna
    Turkey Breast Deli Meats (Cajun Style Hickory Smoked, Golden
      Roasted, Hickory Smoked (Original, Pastrami, Peppered),
      Honey Mesquite Smoked, Oil Browned, Original Rotisserie,
      Oven Prepared)

Turkey Breast Estate Recipe (Buffalo Style, Canadian Brand Maple, Dry Roasted, Hickory Smoked (Honey Pepper, Original, Sun Dried Tomato), Honey Smoked, Mesquite Smoked)

Turkey Ham

Hormel -

Natural Choice

Chicken (Oven Roasted, Rotisserie)

Deli Counter (Cooked Ham, Oven Roasted Turkey Breast, Smoked Ham)

Ham (Brown Sugar, Cooked Deli, Honey Deli, Smoked Deli)

Hard Salami

Pepperoni

Roast Beef

Turkey (Honey Deli, Mesquite, Oven Roasted Deli, Smoked Deli)

Hy-Vee - Loaf (Pickle, Spiced Luncheon)

Jennie-O Turkey Store - Grand Champion Turkey Breast (Hickory Smoked, Honey Cured, Oven Roasted)

Jones Dairy Farm - Deli Style Ham Slices (Honey & Brown Sugar Cured●, Old Fashioned ●)

Kayem -

Bologna (Beef **!!**, German Style **!!**, Large **!!**, Original **!!**)

Chicken Rotisserie Style **!!**

Extra Lean Corned Beef **!!**

Ham (Amber Honey Cured **!!**, Black Forest **!!**, Carving **!!**, Honeycrust **!!**, Old English Tavern **!!**, Peppercrust **!!**)

Old World Liverwurst **!!**

Olive Loaf **!!**

Pastrami (Extra Lean Black **!!**, New England Red **!!**, New York Style Black **!!**)

Peppercrust Loaf **!!**

Pickle & Pepper Loaf **!!**

Roast Beef (Classic **!!**, Seasoned Garlic Oven Roasted **!!**, Seasoned Original Oven Roasted **!!**)

Turkey (Buffalo Style Breast **!!**, Homestyle Breast **!!**, Homestyle Breast w/Skin On **!!**)

D

Kirkland Signature -
> Ham (Extra Lean, Smoked Honey)
> Oven Roasted Turkey Breast
> Turkey Breast (Honey Roasted Sliced, Oven Roasted Browned In Vegetable Oil)

Meijer Brand -
> Deli Meat (Double Smoked Ham, Hickory Smoked Turkey Breast, Honey Roasted Ham, Honey Roasted Turkey Breast)
> Lunch Meat
>> 97% Fat Free (Cooked Ham, Honey Ham, Turkey Breast)
>> Sliced Chipped Meat (Beef, Chicken, Corned Beef, Ham, Pastrami, Turkey)

My Essentials -
> Sliced (Cooked Ham, Danish Brand Ham, Honey Ham, Oven Roasted Turkey)
> Thin Sliced (Black Forest Turkey Breast, Honey Cured Turkey Breast, Honey Ham, Oven Roasted Turkey, Roast Beef)

Norwestern Deli Turkey - Hickory Smoked, Oven Roasted

Open Nature - Honey Ham, Turkey (Oven Roasted, Smoked)

Organic Prairie - Chicken Roast Slices, Ham Hardwood Smoked Uncured, Roast Beef, Turkey (Roast Slices, Smoked Slices)

Oscar Mayer -
> Bologna (All Varieties)
> Carving Board (Oven Roasted Turkey, Roast Beef, Rotisserie Chicken, Slow Cooked Ham)
> Chicken Oven Roasted Homestyle White
> Combos (Honey Ham & Roast Beef, Honey Smoked Turkey & Honey Ham, Oven Roasted Turkey & Smoked Ham)
> Cotto Salami w/Oven Roasted & White Chicken
> Deli Fresh (BBQ Chicken, Beef Salami, Black Forest Ham, Brown Sugar Ham, Cajun Seasoned Chicken Breast, Cracked Black Peppered Turkey Breast, French Dip Roast Beef, Honey Ham, Honey Smoked Turkey Breast, Mesquite Turkey Breast, Oven Roasted (98% Fat Free Turkey, Chicken Breast, Turkey Breast),

Oven Roasted Turkey Breast, Rotisserie Style Chicken Breast, Slow Roasted Cured Roast Beef, Slow Roasted Roast Beef, Smoked Ham, Smoked Turkey Breast, Virginia Brand Ham)

Ham (Baked Cooked, Boiled, Chopped, Honey, Lower Sodium, Smoked)

Loaf (Chicken & Pork Olive, Ham & Cheese, Liver Cheese, Pickle & Pimento)

Natural (Oven Roasted Turkey Breast, Smoked Ham)

Oven Roasted White Turkey

Roast Beef Slow Roasted

Sausage (Braunschweiger, Hard Salami, Pepperoni Slices)

Smoked White Turkey

Sub Kit (Ham & Beef Salami, Ham & Turkey Breast)

Turkey (Breast & White Honey Smoked, Mesquite Smoked White, Oven Roasted, Oven Roasted w/Cheese, Premium Smoked, Smoked, Smoked & White, Turkey Ham w/Smoke Flavor, White Honey Smoked)

Turkey Ham

Variety Pack (Bologna/Chopped Ham/White Smoked Turkey, Bologna/Turkey/Ham, Cotto Salami/Bologna/Chopped Ham, Ham & Turkey Breast, Ham/Turkey Breast/Canadian Bacon, Turkey)

Perdue -

Deli Dark Turkey Pastrami Hickory Smoked

Deli Pick Ups Sliced Turkey (Golden Browned, Honey Smoked, Mesquite Smoked, Oven Roasted, Smoked)

Deli Pick Ups Sliced Turkey Ham Honey Smoked

Deli Turkey (Bologna, Breast Oil Browned, Ham Hickory Smoked, Salami)

Sliced Chicken Breast Oil Fried

Primo Taglio -

Black Forest Ham w/Natural Juices Coated w/Caramel Color

Chicken Breast Oven Roasted Browned

Cooked Hot Capocolla

D

Genoa Salami
Italia Dry Salami
Maple Ham Old Fashioned w/Natural Juices
Mortadella Black Pepper Added
Pancetta
Prosciutto Dry Cured Ham
Sopressata
Turkey Breast w/Natural Smoke Flavoring

Private Selection - Corned Beef, Ham (Hickory Smoked, Honey), Roast Beef, Turkey (Honey Smoked, Oven Roasted)

Publix - Deli Pre Pack Sliced Lunch Meat (Beef Bottom Round Roast, Cooked Ham, Extra Thin Sliced (Honey Ham, Oven Roasted Turkey Breast, Smoked Turkey Breast), German Bologna, Hard Salami Reduced Fat, Smoked Turkey, Sweet Ham, Tavern Ham, Turkey Breast)

Publix GreenWise Market - Deli Pre Pack Sliced Lunch Meat (Beef Bologna, Virginia Brand Ham)

Safeway - All Thin Sliced & Regular, Hard Salami

San Remo - Genoa Salami

Sara Lee -
Slices
Brown Sugar Ham
Cracked Pepper Turkey Breast
Hardwood Smoked Turkey Breast
Honey Ham
Honey Roasted Turkey Breast
Oven Roasted Chicken Breast
Oven Roasted Turkey Breast
Roast Beef
Virginia Brand Baked Ham

Smithfield - Ham (Black Forest, Brown Sugar, Chopped, Cooked, Turkey, Virginia Brand), Turkey Breast (Mesquite, Oven Roasted, Smoked)

Thumann's - All Varieties ●

Trader Joe's - Oven Roasted Turkey Breast, Sliced Prosciutto, Smoked Turkey Breast

Wegmans Brand - Thin Sliced Turkey Breast (Oven Roasted, Smoked, Smoked Honey)

Winn Dixie - Thin Sliced (All Varieties)

Dill Pickles...see Pickles

Dinner Meals...see Meals

Dip/Dip Mix

   Cabot - Bac 'N Horseradish, French Onion, Garden Veggie, Ranch, Salsa Grande

   Cedarlane - 5 Layer Mexican Dip

   Cheez Whiz - Cheese Dip Original

   Dean's - All Flavors

   Emeril's - Party Dip Mix (Guacamole, Veggie Ranch)

   Flamous Brands - Dip (All Varieties)

   Fritos - Bean Dip !!, Chili Cheese Dip !!, Hot Bean Dip !!, Jalapeno & Cheddar Cheese Dip !!, Mild Cheddar Cheese Dip !!, Southwest Enchilada Black Bean Dip !!

   Frontera - Guacamole Mix (Jar, Mild, Spicy)

   Great Value Brand (Wal-Mart) - Dip (French Onion, Ranch), White Salsa Con Queso

   H-E-B - Bean & Cheese Dip, Bean Dip (Hot Jalapeno, Regular), Chipotle Con Queso, Salsa Con Queso

   Herr's - Jalapeno Cheddar, Mild Cheddar

   Hill Country Fare H-E-B - Bean, Bean & Cheese, Jalapeno Bean (Hot, Regular), Nacho Cheese, Ranch Dry Dip Mix, Salsa Con Queso

   Hy-Vee - Black Bean

   Kemps - French Onion, Ranch Style

   Kraft - Cheez Whiz Original, Dip (Bacon & Cheddar, Creamy Ranch, French Onion, Green Onion)

   Lay's - Dip Creations Dry Dip Mix (Country Ranch !!, Garden Onion !!), French Onion Dip !!, Smooth Ranch Dip !!

   Litehouse - Avocado, Caramel (Cinnamon, Low Fat, Original), Chocolate (Caramel, Regular), Cream Cheese, Dilly Dip (Lite,

D

Regular), French Onion, Ranch (Garden, Homestyle, Mild
Jalapeno, Southwest, Veggie Dippers), Spinach Parmesan, Yogurt
Fruit (Creamy Vanilla, Strawberry)

Lowes Foods Brand - French Onion, Ranch

Marzetti -

Blue Cheese

Caramel Apple (Cinnamon Caramel, Fat Free, Light, Old
Fashioned, Peanut Butter, Sweet & Salty)

Chocolate Fruit

Cream Cheese Fruit (Regular, Strawberry)

Dill (Fat Free, Light, Regular)

French Onion (Light, Regular)

French Vanilla Yogurt Fruit Light

Guacamole

Otria Greek Yoghurt (Caramelized Onion, Chipotle Cheese,
Cucumber Dill Feta, Garden Herb Ranch, Roasted Red Pepper,
Salsa Cilantro, Spinach Artichoke)

Ranch (Fat Free, Light, Organic Veggie, Regular)

Spinach

McCormick - Dip Mix Ranch

Mixes From The Heartland ▲ -

Dessert Dip Mix (Black Raspberry ●, Cantaloupe ●, Key Lime ●,
Lemon ●, Orange ●, Pumpkin Pie ●, Raspberry ●, Strawberry ●),
Snack Dip Mix (Cucumber ●, Cucumber Dill ●, Dilly ●, Fiesta ●,
Garlic Roasted Pepper ●, Garlic Sun Dried Tomato ●, Green
Chili Veggie ●, Italian Veggie ●, Spinach & Chives ●, Veggie ●)

On The Border - Bean Dip, Monterey Jack Queso, Salsa Con Queso

Pace - Salsa Dip (Medium, Mild)

Prairie Farms - Bacon Cheddar, French Onion, Jalapeno Fiesta Dip,
Ranch

Publix - French Onion, Guacamole

Sabra - Babaganoush, Caponata, Greek Style Veggie Dip (Onion
& Fresh Herbs, Roasted Garlic, Spinach & Artichoke, Sun Dried
Tomato)

Salpica - Cowgirl White Bean, Dip (Chipotle Black Bean, Cowboy Red Bean, Jalapeno Jack Queso, Salsa Con Queso)

Santa Barbara - Five Layer Dip

Sharwood's - Green Label Mango Chutney Chilli

Signature Cafe - Bacon Cheddar Ranch, Guacamole (Hot, Mild)

Simply Organic - Dip Mix (Chipotle Black Bean ●, Creamy Dill ●, French Onion ●, Fruit ●, Guacamole ●, Ranch ●, Spinach ●)

Spartan Brand - Dip (French Onion, Ranch)

Taco Bell - Black Bean Con Queso, Chili Con Queso w/Beef, Salsa Con Queso (Medium, Mild)

Tostitos -
  Creamy Southwestern Ranch Dip !!
  Creamy Spinach Dip !!
  Dip Creations Freshly Made Dry Dip Mix !!
  Monterey Jack Queso !!
  Salsa Con Queso Dip !!
  Smooth & Cheesy Dip !!
  Spicy Nacho Dip !!
  Zesty Bean & Cheese Dip !!

Trader Joe's - Cilantro & Chive Yogurt, Fat Free Spicy Black Bean, Guacamole (Avocado's Number, w/Spicy Pico De Gallo !!), Queso Cheese Dip !, Spinach & Sour Cream

UTZ - Cheddar & Jalapeno, Mild Cheddar Cheese

Walden Farms -
  Fruit Dip (Caramel, Chocolate, Marshmallow)
  Veggie & Chip Dip (Bacon, Blue Cheese, French Onion, Ranch)

Wegmans Brand - Salsa Con Queso Cheddar Cheese Dip

Wildwood - Emerald Valley Organic 3 Bean Dip

Wise - Dip (French Onion, Ranch, Salsa Con Queso), Dip Mix (Green Onion, Guacamole, Ranch)

Donuts/Doughnuts

Bi-Aglut - Chocolate, Regular

Celiac Specialties ▲ -
  Donut Holes (Cinnamon Sugar, Glazed, Plain, Powder Sugar)

D

Donuts (Chocolate, Cinnamon Sugar, Coconut, Glazed, Plain, Powder Sugar)

Mini Donuts (Cinnamon Sugar, Plain, Powder Sugar)

Ener-G ▲ - Plain Doughnut (Holes, Regular)

Gluten-Free Creations ▲ - Donuts4U (Chocolate ●, Cinnamon & Sugar ●, Insane Chocolate ●, Plain Jane ●)

Glutino ▲ - Glazed (Chocolate, Original)

Grandma Ferdon's ▲ - Donut Holes ●, Plain Donuts ●

Heaven Mills ▲ - Danish (Chocolate ●, Cinnamon ●, Round Cherry ●, Round Chocolate ●, Round Custard ●, Vanilla ●)

JD's Best Gluten Free Pizza ▲ - Donut Holes ●

Kinnikinnick ▲ - Chocolate Dipped, Cinnamon Sugar, Maple Glazed, Pumpkin Spice, Vanilla Glazed

Kneaded Specialties ▲ - Orange Danish ●

Molly's Gluten-Free Bakery ▲ - Danish Rolls

Pure Market Express ▲ - Donut Holes ●

Silly Yak Bakery - GF Doughnuts (Chocolate Doughnut w/Glaze●, Chocolate Doughnut w/Sprinkles ●, Spice Doughnut ●, Vanilla Doughnut w/Sprinkles ●)

Sweet Christine's Bakery - Baked ●

Dressing...see Salad Dressing and/or Stuffing

Dried Fruit

Bare Fruit - Cherries, Cinnamon Apple, Fuji Apple, Granny Smith Apple, Mangos, Pears

Brothers All Natural ▲ - Fruit Crisps (Apple Cinnamon, Asian Pear, Banana, Fuji Apple, Mandarin Orange, Mixed Berry, Organic Strawberry, Peach, Pineapple, Strawberry, Strawberry Banana)

Daily Chef - Dried Mediterranean Apricots

Earthbound Farm - Cranberries, Dates, Mangos, Plums, Premium Jumbo Seedless Raisins (Flame, Thompson), Thompson Seedless Raisin Packs (Mini, Snack)

Eden Organic - Cranberries, Montmorency Dried Tart Cherries, Wild Blueberries

Fruit Advantage - All Varieties (Chocolate Covered Dried Fruit, Dried Super Fruits)

Great Value Brand (Wal-Mart) - All Natural California Raisins, Pitted Prunes

Hy-Vee - Apples **!**, Banana Chips **!**, Blueberries **!**, Cherries **!**, Cranberries **!**, Mixed (Berries **!**, Fruit **!**), Pineapple **!**, Prunes & Apricots **!**

Kirkland Signature - Dried Cherries **!!**, Whole Dried Blueberries **!!**

Mariani -

Apricots (California **!!**, Mediterranean **!!**, Ultimate **!!**)

Banana Chips **!!**

Cherries **!!**

Cranberries Sweetened **!!**

Dates (Chopped **!!**, Pitted **!!**)

Enhanced Wellness (Berry Defense **!!**, Berry Thrive **!!**, Plum Support **!!**)

Flavor Sensations (Cherry Pie Flavored Cherries **!!**, Concord Grape Juice Flavored Cranberries **!!**)

Island Fruits **!!**

Mangoes (Philippine **!!**, Regular **!!**)

Mixed Fruit **!!**

Pineapple (Tango **!!**, Tropical **!!**)

Pitted Dried Plums (Bite Size **!!**, Plus **!!**, Regular **!!**)

Sliced Dried Apples **!!**

Strawberries **!!**

Tropical Medley **!!**

Wild Blueberries **!!**

Mrs. May's Naturals - All Varieties ●

Nuts.com -

Apples (Cinnamon Wedges ●, Diced Fuji ●, Dried ●, Infused Dried Wedges ●, Organic Chips ●, Organic Dried ●, Simply Organic ●)

Apricots (California ●, Diced ●, Dried ●, Organic California ●, Organic Turkish ●)

Bananas (Chips ●, Organic Chips ●, Organic Simply ●, Simply ●)

Blackberries ●

Blueberries (Dried ●, Natural Dried ●, Natural Dried Juice Infused●, Organic Wild ●, Simply ●)

D

Cantaloupe (Dried ●, Dried Chunks ●)

Cherries (Bing ●, Organic Bing ●, Rainier ●, Simply ●, Sour Tart ●)

Cranberries (Natural Juice Infused ●, Organic ●, Simply ●, Sliced ●, Whole Dried ●)

Currants ●

Dates (Jumbo Medjool ●, Organic Medjool ●, Organic Pitted ●, Pitted ●)

Diced Fruit Medley ●

Figs (California ●, Diced ●, Mission ●, Organic California ●, Organic Calimyrna ●, Organic Mission ●, Organic Turkish ●, Turkish ●)

Fruit Chips ●

Ginger (Crystallized ●, Organic Crystallized ●)

Goji Berries ●

Guava ●

Kiwi ●

Lemons ●

Mango (Dried (Diced ●, Less Sugar Added ●, Organic ●, Regular ●), Simply ●)

Mulberries ●

Nectarines (Dried ●, Organic ●, White ●)

Organic Dried Oranges ●

Organic Goji Berries ●

Organic Lucuma Slices ●

Papaya (Chunks ●, Diced ●, Natural ●, Organic ●, Regular ●),

Peaches (Diced ●, Dried ●, Organic ●, Simply ●, White ●)

Pears (Diced ●, Dried ●, Organic ●, Simply ●)

Persimmons (Dried ●, Organic ●)

Pineapple (Dried (Chunks ●, Diced ●, Regular ●), Natural ●, Organic Chunks ●, Organic ●, Simply ●)

Plums (Angelino ●, Jumbo Prunes ●, No Pit ●, October Sun ●, Organic (Angelino ●, No Pit ●))

Pluots ●

Raisins (Crimson ●, Dark ●, Jumbo (Flame ●, Golden ●, Golden Flame ●, Thompson Seedless ●), Midget ●, Organic (Dark Chocolate Covered ●, Milk Chocolate Covered ●), Organic ●)

dried fruit

Raspberries (Dried Red ●, Simply ●)

Simply (Black Currants ●, Blackberries ●, Boysenberries ●, Elderberries ●, Fruit Cocktail ●, Grapes ●, Pomegranates ●)

Strawberries (Dried ●, Natural Dried Juice Infused ●, Organic ●, Organic Simply ●, Simply ●, Simply Whole ●)

Strawberry Rhubarb ●

Tomatoes (Julienne ●, Sun Dried (Organic ●, Regular ●, w/Olive Oil ●)

Ocean Spray - Craisins (Blueberry, Cherry, Original, Pomegranate)

Oskri Organics - 3.5oz. bag (Apricots, Blueberries, Cherries, Cranberries, Dates, Figs, Golden Raisins, Prunes, Strawberries)

Safeway Brand - Berries & Cherries, Cranberries, Philippine Mango, Raisins

Sensible Foods - Cherry Berry, Orchard Blend, Organic Apple Harvest, Tropical Blend

Shiloh Farms -
Cranberries **!!**
Himalayan Goji Berries **!!**
Organic (Black Mission Figs **!!**, Calimyrna Figs **!!**, Pitted Prunes **!!**, Sundried Pear Slices **!!**, Thompson Seedless Raisins **!!**, Turkish Figs**!!**)
Pitted (Deglet Organic Dates **!!**, Prunes **!!**, Sour Red Cherries **!!**, Sun Dried Bing Cherries **!!**)
Turkish Apricots **!!**
Wild Blueberries **!!**

Spartan Brand - Cranberries, Pitted Prunes, Raisins

St. Dalfour - All Flavors

Sun-Maid - Raisins (Baking, Golden, Natural California, Regular), Zante Currants

thinkFruit - Dried Fruit Snacks (Blueberries, Cherry, Cinnamon Apple, Cranberries, Peaches, Pineapple Tidbits)

Trader Joe's - All Varieties, Roasted Plantain Chips

Wegmans Brand - Dried (Apricots, FYFGA Sweetened (Cherries, Cranberries), Pitted Prunes, Sweetened Philippine Mango, Tropical Pineapple, Wild Blueberries), FYFGA Seedless Raisins

D

Woodstock Farms -
    Apple Rings (Organic, Unsulphured)
    Banana Chips (Organic, Sweetened)
    Blueberries
    Cherries Unsulphured
    Cranberries Sweetened (Organic, Regular)
    Dates (Deglet w/Pit, Organic California Medjool w/Pit)
    Figs (Calmyrna, Organic Black Mission)
    Ginger (Organic Crystallized w/Raw Sugar, Slices Unsulphured)
    Goji Berries
    Mango (Organic Slices, Slices Unsulphured)
    Organic Pitted Prunes
    Organic Turkish Apricots
    Papaya Spears Lo Sugar Unsulphured
    Pineapple Slices Unsulphured
    Raisins (Flame !, Organic (Jumbo Thompson, Select Thompson,
        Thompson), Thompson)
Drink Mix
    Augason Farms ▲ - Gluten Free Delight (Apple ●, Orange ●, Peach ●)
    Caffe D'Vita - Spiced Enchanted Chai
    Cera - CeraLyte (50 ●, 70 ●, 90 ●), CeraSport (All Varieties ●),
        CeraSport EXI (All Varieties ●)
    Country Time - All Flavors
    Crystal Light -
        Appletini
        Decaf Iced Tea (Lemon, Regular)
        Enhanced (Energy Peach Mango, Energy Wild Strawberry,
            Hunger Satisfaction Strawberry Banana, Metabolism Green Tea
            Peach Mango, Natural Wild Cherry Pomegranate (Antioxidant,
            Immunity))
        Fusion Fruit Punch
        Iced Tea (Green Tea Honey Lemon, Green Tea Raspberry, Natural
            Lemon, Peach, Sugar Free (Lemon, Peach, Peach Blossom,
            Raspberry))

Lemonade (Pink, Pure, Raspberry, Strawberry Orange Banana, Sugar Free (Pink, Raspberry, Regular))

Margarita

Mojito

Pure (Fitness Lemon Lime, Grape, Mixed Berry, Strawberry Kiwi, Tropical Blend)

Pure Fitness Lemon Lime

Raspberry Ice

Skin Essentials (Pomegranate Lemonade, White Peach Tea)

Sugar Free (Antioxidant Raspberry Green Tea, Fruit Punch, Raspberry Ice, Strawberry Kiwi)

Sunrise Classic Orange

Flavor Aid - Powdered Soft Drinks

Food Club Brand - Drink Mixes (Cherry, Grape, Lemonade, Orange, Punch), Drink Stix (Iced Tea w/Lemon, Lemonade, Peach Tea, Raspberry Ice), Iced Tea Mix

Guayaki - Bottled Yerba Mate All Flavors

Hannaford Brand - Sugar Free (Fruit Punch, Iced Tea, Lemon Lime, Lemonade, Raspberry Lemonade)

Hawaiian Punch - All Varieties

Hy-Vee - Simply Light (Fruit Punch, Iced Tea (Lemon, Peach, Raspberry), Lemonade, Pink Lemonade, Raspberry Ice & Lemonade), Splash Drink Mix (Cherry, Grape, Lemonade, Orange, Raspberry, Strawberry, Tropical, Tropical Fruit Punch)

Kool-Aid -

All Varieties

Fun Fizz

Soft Drink Mix (Sugar Free, Sugar Sweetened, Unsweetened)

Meijer Brand - Breakfast Orange, Cherry, Chocolate Flavor, Grape, Ice Tea, Lemon Sugar Free, Lemonade, Lemonade Stix, Orange (Free & Lite, Regular), Pink Lemonade (Regular, Sugar Free), Punch, Raspberry Stix, Raspberry Sugar Free, Strawberry (Flavor, Regular), Strawberry/Orange/Banana

My Essentials - Regular (Cherry, Fruit Punch, Lemonade, Orange, Strawberry)

D

Pacific Chai - Vanilla Chai Latte

Safeway Brand - Fruit Punch, Peach (Light Iced Tea, Regular), Pink
Lemonade (Light, Regular), Raspberry (Light, Regular), Spiced
Apple Cider, Sugar Free Raspberry & Lemonade

Spartan Brand - Fruit Punch, Natural Lemonade, Pink Lemonade,
Raspberry Lemonade

Wegmans Brand - Powdered Drink Mix (Lemonade, Pink Lemonade)

Winn Dixie -

Regular (Cherry, Fruit Punch, Grape, Lemonade, Orange, Pink
Lemonade, Raspberry, Strawberry Kiwi)

Sugar Free (Fruit Punch, Lemon Iced Tea, Lemonade, Peach Iced
Tea, Pink Lemonade)

Wyler's - Powdered Soft Drinks (Light, Light Sugar Free, Regular)

Drinks/Juice

Adina -

Barista Brews (Double XXPresso, Mocha Madness)

Holistics (Blackberry Hibiscus w/Rooibos ●, Coconut Guava w/
Lychee ●, Cranberry Grapefruit w/Goji ●, Jade Green Tea w/
Tulsi ●, Mango Orange w/Chamomile ●, Passion Peach w/
Amalaki ●, Pomegranate Acai w/Yumberry ●)

Holistics Zero (Mandarin Melon Berry ●, Wild Black Cherry ●)

Organic Coffees (Ethiopian Espresso, Indian Chai Latte, Mayan
Mocha, Sumatran Vanilla Latte)

Alo -

Aloe Vera (Allure, Appeal, Elated, Enliven, Enrich, Escape, Exposed)

Coco Exposed (Goji Berry & Lychee, Mangosteen & Mango,
Passion Fruit & Pineapple)

Apple & Eve - All Drinks/Juice

Bigelow Tea - Coconut Water w/Green Tea Mix (Mango,
Pomegranate Acai, Regular)

Bolthouse Farms -

Fruit Smoothie (Amazing Mango, Berry Boost, Blue Goodness,
C Boost, Green Goodness, Strawberry Banana)

Juice (100% Carrot, 100% Pomegranate, 50/50 Berry, 50/50
Tropical, Passion Orange Guava)

Mango Lemonade
Perfectly Protein (Mocha Cappuccino, Vanilla Chai Tea)
Protein Plus (Chocolate, Mango)
Bossa Nova -
Acai (The Original, w/Blueberry, w/Mango, w/Passionfruit, w/
Raspberry)
Acerola (w/Mango, w/Red Peach)
Goji Berry w/Tart Cherry
Mangosteen (w/Dragonfruit, w/Passionfruit)
Bragg - Organic Apple Cider Vinegar Drink (Apple Cinnamon,
Concord Grape Acai, Ginger Spice, Limeaid, Sweet Stevia, Vinegar
& Honey)
Bright & Early - Apple, Grape, Orange
Brisk - Fruit Punch, Lemonade, Tea Lemonade
Calistoga - Sparkling Juice Beverages (All Flavors)
Campbell's - Tomato Juice Original
Capri Sun - All Flavors
Ceres - All Varieties
Country Time - Lemonade
Dei Fratelli - Juice (Tomato (Regular, Tasty Tom Spicy), Vegetable)
Dole - All Fruit Juice
Earth's Best Organic Baby Food - Apple Juice, Pear Juice
Eating Right - Juice (All Varieties), Juice Boxes (All Flavors)
Eden Organic - Apple Juice, Cherry Concentrate, Concord Grape,
Montmorency Tart Cherry Juice
Five Alive - Citrus
Food Club Brand -
Frozen Juice Concentrate (100% Grape, Apple, Fruit Punch,
Grapefruit, Lemonade, Orange Juice (High Pulp, Original, Pulp
Free, w/Calcium), Pink Lemonade)
Juice (Apple, Cranberry (Apple, Blend, Cocktail, Light, Raspberry,
White Cocktail, White Peach, White Strawberry), Cranberry
Grape (Light, Regular), Fruit Punch, Grape, Grapefruit, Lemon,
Lime, Pineapple, Pomegranate, Pomegranate Blueberry, Prune,

D

Ruby Red Grapefruit, Tangerine & Ruby Red, Tomato Regular, Vegetable, White Grape)

Lemonade

Refrigerated Orange Juice (From Concentrate, Original, Premium, w/ Calcium)

Refrigerated Juice Orange Juice Pulp Added

Thirst Quenchers (Berry Rain Type, Fruit Punch, Lemon Lime, Orange)

Fruit Advantage - All Varieties Juice Concentrates

Fruit2O ▲ - All Varieties

Full Circle - Organic (Blueberry Juice, Cranberry Cocktail, Cranberry Red Raspberry, Tomato Juice)

Function - All Varieties

Fuze - Banana Colada, Mixed Berry, Orange Mango, Slenderize (Blueberry Raspberry, Cranberry Raspberry, Pomegranate Acai Berry, Strawberry Melon, Tropical Punch), Strawberry Guava

Garelick Farms -

Chug (Apple Juice, Fruit Punch, Lemonade, Orange Juice From Concentrate, Orange Juice Not From Concentrate)

Orange Juice (Calcium Rich, From Concentrate)

Gold Peak - Black Tea Raspberry, Green Tea (Lemonade, Regular), Iced Tea (Diet, Lemon, Sweet, Unsweetened)

Great Value Brand (Wal-Mart) -

From Concentrate (100% Apple Juice No Sugar Added, Apple Punch, Cranberry, Cranberry & Concord Grape, Cranberry Apple, Cranberry Black Cherry, Cranberry Juice Blend, Grape, Natural Strength Lemon Juice, Ruby Red Grapefruit, Unsweetened White Grapefruit Juice, Vegetable Juice, White Grape, White Grape Peach)

Frozen Juice Concentrate (Apple, Country Style Orange Juice, Florida Grapefruit Juice Pure Unsweetened, Fruit Punch, Grape, Grape Juice Cocktail, Lemonade, Limeade, Orange Juice w/Calcium, Pink Lemonade)

Prune Juice

Refrigerated 100% Orange Juice (Country Style, Regular, w/Calcium)

Refrigerated Orange Juice (High Pulp, Pulp Free Regular, Pulp Free w/Calcium)

D

Vegetable Juice Blends (Light Pomegranate Blueberry, Light Strawberry Banana)

Hannaford Brand - All (Frozen, Refrigerated, Shelf Stable)

Hansen's - All Varieties

Harvest Valley - Juice (Apple, Cranberry Cocktail (10%, 30%, Raspberry), Grape, Grapefruit Unsweetened, Lemon, Orange, Pineapple, Prune, Tomato, White Grape), Juice Drink Fruit Punch

Hawaiian Punch - All Varieties

Hi-C - Blazin' Blueberry, Boppin' Strawberry, Flashin' Fruit Punch, Grabbin' Grape, Kiwi Kraze, Orange Lavaburst, Poppin' Lemonade, Smashin' Wild Berry, Torrential Tropical Punch, Wild Cherry

Hollywood - Organic Carrot Juice

Honest -

Ade (Cranberry Lemonade, Limeade, Orange Mango w/Mangosteen, Pomegranate Blue, Super Fruit Punch, Zero Calorie Classic Lemonade)

CocoaNova (Cherry Cacao, Mint Cacao, Mocha Cacao)

Kids (Apply Ever After, Berry Berry Good Lemonade, Goodness Grapeness, Super Fruit Punch, Tropical Tango Punch)

Sublime Mate

Hood - All Juices

Hy-Vee -

100% Juice Blend (Blueberry Pomegranate, Cranberry)

Apple

Frozen Concentrate (Apple Light Regular, Fruit Punch, Grape Juice Cocktail, Lemonade, Limeade, Orange (Regular, w/Calcium), Pink Lemonade)

Juice Cocktail From Concentrate (Cranberry, Cranberry Apple, Cranberry Grape, Cranberry Raspberry, Grapefruit, Lemon, Light (Apple Kiwi Strawberry, Apple Raspberry, Cranberry Raspberry), Ruby Red Grapefruit)

Juice From Concentrate (100% Apple, 100% Unsweetened Prune, 100% White Grape, Apple, Country Style Orange, Lemonade, Light Apple Raspberry, Orange Juice, Orange Juice w/Calcium, Pineapple, Prune Juice, Tomato, Vegetable)

D

No Concentrate (Country Style Orange, Orange, Orange w/
Calcium, Ruby Red Grapefruit)

Izze - All Varieties

Juicy Juice - All Flavors (100% Juice, Sparkling Fruit Juice)

Kemps - All Varieties (Yo J Nonfat Yogurt & Fruit Juice)

Kirkland Signature -
Frozen Orange Juice Concentrate
Juice (Apple, Cranberry Raspberry)

Kool-Aid -
Bursts (Berry Blue, Cherry, Grape, Lime, Tropical Punch)
Juice Jammers (All Varieties)

Lakewood - All 100% Pure Fruit & Vegetable

Langers Juices - All Flavors

Lincoln - Apple Juice

Litehouse - Apple Cider All Varieties

Lowes Foods Brand - Juice (Apple (Natural, Regular), Cranberry
Apple, Cranberry Cocktail (Light, Regular), Cranberry Grape
(Light, Regular), Cranberry Raspberry, Grape, Grape Cocktail
Light, Grove Select Orange, Lemon (Regular, Squeeze), Orange
(Original, Premium), Orange Plus Calcium, Original w/Calcium,
Premium Cranberry Blend 100% Juice, Prune, Vegetable Juice,
White Grape)

Lucky Leaf - Apple (Cider, Juice, Premium Juice, Sparkling Cider)

Manischewitz - Grape Juice

Medifast - Fruit Drinks (Cranberry Mango ●, Tropical Punch ●)

Meijer Brand -
100% Juice (Berry, Cherry, Cranberry/Raspberry, Grape, Punch)
Apple Juice Not From Concentrate
Cranberry Juice Drink (Grape, Raspberry, Strawberry)
Drink Thirst Quencher (Fruit Punch, Lemon Lime, Orange)
Frozen Concentrate Juice (Apple, Fruit Punch, Grape, Grapefruit,
Lemonade, Limeade, Orange, Pink Lemonade, White Grape
Cocktail)

D

Frozen Concentrate Orange Juice (High Pulp, Pulp Free, w/Calcium)

Fruit Punch (Genuine, Light, Regular)

Juice (Apple, Apple Natural, Cherry, Fruit Mix, Grape, Grapefruit, Lemon, Lime, Orange, Orange Peach Mango, Orange Strawberry Banana, Pineapple, Pineapple Orange, Pineapple Orange Banana, Pink Grapefruit, Prune, Ruby Red Grapefruit, Tangerine, Tangerine & Ruby Red, White Grape, White Grapefruit)

Juice Blend (Acai & Blueberry, Acai & Grape, Pomegranate & Blueberry, Pomegranate & Cranberry, White Cranberry, White Grape & Peach, White Grape & Raspberry)

Juice Carafe (Apple, Grapefruit, Lemonade, Limeade, Orange Juice (Valencia, Valencia w/Calcium, Valencia w/Pulp), Raspberry Lemonade)

Juice Cocktail (Cranapple, Cranberry (Light, Regular), Cranberry Grape (Light, Regular), Cranberry Raspberry (Light, Regular), Cranberry Strawberry, Cranberry White Peach, Light Grape w/Splenda, Ruby Red Grapefruit (Light, Light 22%, Regular), White Cranberry, White Cranberry Peach, White Cranberry Strawberry, White Grapefruit)

Juice From Concentrate (Apple, Grape, White Grape)

Juice Refrigerated Orange (Original, Reconstituted)

Juice Refrigerated Orange Premium (Calcium Carafe, Carafe, Hi Pulp Carafe, Original, w/Calcium)

Lemon Juice Squeeze Bottle

Orange Juice (Premium Omega 3, Refrigerated (Organic, Plastic, w/Calcium), Shelf Stable Premium (Lite, w/Pulp))

Orange Reconstituted (Original, Pulp, w/Calcium)

Organic Juice (Apple, Concord Grape, Cranberry, Lemonade)

Splash (Berry Blend, Strawberry/Kiwi, Tropical Blend)

Midwest Country Fare - 100% Concentrated Orange Juice

D **Minute Maid -**

Apple Juice (Regular, Strawberry, w/Vitamin C, w/Vitamin C
Calcium & Potassium, White Grape w/Vitamin C Calcium &
Potassium)

Berry Punch

Citrus Punch

Coolers (Berry Punch, Clear Cherry, Fruit Punch, Orange
Strawberry, Pink Lemonade, Tropical Punch)

Cranberry (Apple, Apple Raspberry w/Vitamin C, Grape
w/Vitamin C)

Fruit Falls (Berry, Tropical)

Fruit Punch (Just 10, Regular, w/Vitamin C Calcium & Potassium)

Grape (w/Vitamin C & Calcium, w/Vitamin C & E & Potassium)

Grape Punch

Kids + MINIS (Apple Juice, Fruit Punch, Grape)

Lemonade (Light, Pink, Pomegranate, Raspberry, Regular,
w/Vitamin C & Calcium)

Light Raspberry Passion

Limeade (Cherry, Light, Light Cherry, Regular)

Mixed Berry (w/Vitamin C & Calcium, w/Vitamin C & E &
Potassium)

Orange Juice (Country Style, Heart Wise, Home Squeezed Style
w/Calcium & Vitamin D, Kids +, Light, Light Tangerine, Low
Acid, No Pulp (Regular, w/Calcium & Vitamin D), Original, Pulp
Free, Pure Squeezed (Calcium, Light, Original, Some Pulp),
w/Calcium & Vitamin D, w/Vitamin C)

Orangeade (Light, Regular)

Pineapple Orange w/Vitamin C

Pomegranate Blueberry

Ruby Red Grapefruit

Strawberry Kiwi

Tropical Punch

Watermelon

Mio - Liquid Water Enhancer (Berry Pomegranate, Fruit Punch,

Mango Peach, Orange Tangerine, Peach Tea, Strawberry Watermelon, Sweet Tea)

Mondo - Fruit Squeezers (Chillin' Cherry, Global Grape, Kiwi Strawberry Splash, Legendary Berry, Outstanding Orange, Primo Punch)

Mott's - All Varieties

Mountain Sun - Bottled (Blueberry Green Tea, Grape & Acai, Pomegranate & Black Cherry, Pomegranate Rooibos Tea, Pure Cranberry)

Musselman's - Apple (Cider, Fresh Pressed Cider, Juice, Premium Juice, Sparkling Cider)

Naked -
  Juice (O J, Orange Mango, Pomegranate Acai, Pomegranate Blueberry)
  Juice Smoothie (Berry Blast, Berry Veggie, Mighty Mango, Orange Carrot, Protein Zone, Protein Zone Double Berry, Protein Zone Mango, Reduced Calorie (Citrus Lemongrass, Lychee, Peach Guava, Tropical), Strawberry Banana)

Nantucket Nectars - All Varieties

Nature Factor - Organic Young Coconut Water

Nature's Place - Apple Juice

Nestea -
  Brews (Berry Oolong, Classic, Mango)
  Diet White Tea Berry Honey
  Green Tea Citrus (Diet, Regular)
  Half & Half
  Iced Tea (Lemon (Diet, Sweetened), Raspberry)
  Instant Tea Mix (All Varieties)
  Red Tea
  Tropical Mango
  Unsweetened

Newman's Own -
  Gorilla Grape
  Lemonade (Diet All Natural Virgin, Lightly Sweetened, Old Fashioned Roadside Virgin, Organic, Pink Virgin, Pomegranate)

D

Orange Mango Tango

Virgin Lemon Aided Iced Tea

Virgin Limeade

O Organics -

Bottle Juices (Apple, Berry Blend, Blueberry Blend, Cranberry Cocktail, Grape, Lemonade, Unfiltered Apple)

Orange Juice (All Refrigerated Varieties)

Refrigerated Orange

Ocean Spray - All Varieties

OneSource -

Chocolate (1% Formula ●, 2% Formula ●)

Coffee 2% Formula ●

Strawberry (1% Formula ●, 2% Formula ●)

Vanilla 1% Formula ●

Open Nature - All Juice Varieties

Organic B.R.A.T. - Feel Better Drink (Original, Vanilla)

Organic Valley - Orange Juice (Calcium Added, w/o Pulp, w/Pulp)

Phildesco - Coconut Water

Powerade -

Ion 4 (Fruit Punch, Grape, Lemon Lime, Mountain Berry Blast, Orange, Sour Melon, Strawberry Lemonade, White Cherry)

Zero (Fruit Punch, Grape, Lemon Lime, Mixed Berry, Orange, Strawberry)

Prairie Farms -

Flavored Drinks (Blue Raspberry, Fruit Punch, Grape, Lemon, Lemonade, Orange, Pink Lemonade)

Orange Juice (Light Pulp Premium, No Pulp, Plus Calcium, Regular)

Publix -

From Concentrate (Orange Juice (Regular, w/Calcium), Ruby Red Grapefruit Juice)

Frozen Concentrated Orange

Refrigerated (Premium Orange Juice (Calcium Plus, Grove Pure, Old Fashioned, Original), Premium Ruby Red Grapefruit Juice)

D

Shelf Stable (Apple, Cranberry (Apple Juice Cocktail, Juice Cocktail, Reduced Calorie Cocktail), Grape, Grape Cranberry Juice Cocktail, Lemonade Deli Old Fashion, Pineapple, Raspberry Cranberry Juice Cocktail, Ruby Red Grapefruit Regular, Tomato, White Grape)

Publix GreenWise Market - Organic (100% Apple, Cranberry, Grape, Lemonade, Tomato)

Pure Market Express ▲ -
  Cacao Bean ●
  Carrot (Cucumber ●, Orange ●)
  Carrot Juice Straight Up ●
  Drop Of Sunshine Juice ●
  Green Sweet Tart Juice ●
  Master Cleanse Lemonade ●
  Watermelon Juice ●

ReaLemon - 100% Lemon Juice

ReaLime - 100% Lime Juice

Refreshe - Juice (Cranberry (Light Raspberry, Raspberry), Grape, Grapefruit (Regular, Ruby Red Cocktail), Lemon, Orange, Prune, Tomato, Vegetable, White Grape)

Safeway - Orange Juice (All Refrigerated Varieties)

Safeway Brand -
  Frozen (Apple, Berry Punch, Cranberry, Grape, Lemonade, Limeade, Orange, Orange Country Style, Orange w/Calcium, Pink Lemonade, Raspberry Lemonade)
  Juice (Apple (Cider, Light, Regular), Cranberry (Apple, Cocktail, Light Cocktail)

Safeway Select - Orange Juice (All Refrigerated Varieties)

Sambazon - Acai Juice

Santa Cruz ▲ - All Varieties (100% Citrus, Bottled Juice, Champagne Style Sparkling Juice, Juice Boxes, Super Fruits)

Siggi's ▲ - Probiotic Drinkable Non Fat Yogurt (Blueberry ●, Plain ●, Strawberry ●)

Silk - Fruit & Protein (Mango Peach, Mixed Berry, Strawberry Banana)

D

Simply - Apple, Grapefruit, Lemonade (Original, w/Raspberry),
Limeade, Orange (Calcium & Vitamin D, Country Stand Calcium,
Grove Made, Original, w/Mango, w/Pineapple)

Snapple -
100% Juiced (Fruit Punch, Grape, Green Apple, Orange Mango)
Can (Grape Berry Punch, Mango Punch, Verry Cherry Punch)
Cranberry Raspberry
Diet (Cranberry Raspberry, Half N Half, Noni Berry)
Fruit Punch
Go Bananas
Grapeade
Half N Half
Kiwi Strawberry
Lemonade
Mango Madness
Orangeade
Peach Mangosteen
Pink Lemonade
Pomegranate Raspberry
Raspberry Peach
Snapple Apple
Summer Peach
Watermelon Punch

SoBe -
Energize (Citrus Energy, Green Tea, Mango Melon, Power Fruit Punch)
Lean Diet (Fuji Apple Cranberry, Honey Green Tea, Raspberry
Lemonade)
Smooth (Orange Cream, Pina Colada, Strawberry Banana,
Strawberry Daiquiri)
Vita Boom (Cranberry Grapefruit, Orange Carrot)

Sonoma Sparkler - Natural (Blood Orange, Peach, Pear, Raspberry),
Organic (Apple, Lemonade)

Spartan Brand -
Apple Juice (Apple Cherry Lite, Regular)
Cranberry Juice Cocktail (Light, Lite, Regular)

D

Cranberry Juice Drink (Apple, Pomegranate, Raspberry)

Frozen Concentrate (Fruit Punch, Grape Juice Cocktail, Lemonade, Orange Juice (Country Style, Pulp Free, Regular, w/Calcium & Vitamin D), Pink Lemonade)

Grape Juice (Regular, White)

Lemon Juice

Pineapple

Premium Orange Juice (Homestyle, No Pulp, w/Calcium & Vitamin D)

Reconstituted Orange Juice (Country Style Pulp, w/Calcium & Vitamin D)

Ruby Red Grapefruit Juice

Tomato Juice

Vegetable Juice Cocktail

Sunny D - All Varieties

Sweet Leaf - Bottled Original Lemonade

Swiss Premium - Naturally Flavored Lemonade

Tampico ▲ - All Beverages

The Ginger People - Ginger Beer !, Ginger EnerGizer !, Ginger Juice !, Ginger Soother !, Lemon Ginger Beer !

Tipton Grove - 100% Apple Juice

Trader Joe's - Concentrate (Lemon, Orange), French Market Sparkling Beverages (All Flavors), Juices (All Varieties), Organic Mango Lemonade, Organic Sparkling Beverages (All Flavors), Sparkling Juice Beverages (All Flavors)

Tropicana - All 100% Juices

V8 -

Diet Splash (Berry Blend, Tropical Blend)

Splash (Berry Blend, Fruit Medley, Mango Peach, Strawberry Kiwi Blend, Tropical Blend)

Splash Smoothies (Strawberry Banana, Tropical Colada)

V Fusion (Acai Mixed Berry, Concord Grape Raspberry, Cranberry Blackberry, Goji Raspberry, Peach Mango, Pomegranate Blueberry, Strawberry Banana)

D

V Fusion + Tea (Pineapple Mango Green Tea, Pomegranate Green Tea, Raspberry Green Tea)

V Fusion Light (Acai Mixed Berry, Cranberry Blackberry, Peach Mango, Pomegranate Blueberry, Strawberry Banana)

V Fusion Smoothie (Mango, Strawberry Banana, Wild Berry)

Vegetable Juice (100% Vegetable Juice, Essential Antioxidants, High Fiber, Low Sodium, Low Sodium Spicy Hot, Spicy Hot)

Vita Coco - Coconut Water (Acai & Pomegranate, Original, Pineapple, Tangerine)

Vitaminwater (Glaceau) - All Varieties

Vruit - Apple Carrot, Berry Veggie, Orange Veggie, Tropical

Walnut Acres - Juice (Apple, Apricot, Blueberry, Cherry, Concord Grape, Cranberry, Cranberry Blueberry, Cranberry Raspberry, Incredible Vegetable, Mango Nectar, Orange Carrot, Peach, Pineapple, Raspberry)

Wegmans Brand -

Drink Mix (Lemonade Flavor, Pink Lemonade Flavor)

Frozen Juice Concentrate (Fruit Punch, Grape, Lemonade, Limeade, Pink Lemonade)

FYFGA Frozen Juice Concentrate (Apple (Regular, w/Calcium), Orange (Country Style, Pulp Free, Regular, w/Calcium))

FYFGA Sparkling Juice (Alcohol Free Cranberry Juice Blend, Alcohol Free Grape (Pink, Red, White))

Organic FYFGA Juice From Concentrate (Apple, Cranberry, Orange)

Refrigerated FYFGA Juice From Concentrate (Orange Juice (Calcium Enriched, Regular), Orange Peach Mango Flavor Juice Blend, Pineapple Orange)

Refrigerated FYFGA Premium 100% Juice Not From Concentrate (Orange (Extra Pulp, No Pulp, Some Pulp, w/Calcium, w/Calcium & Vitamins), Ruby Red Grapefruit)

Refrigerated Juice From Concentrate (Lemonade, Limeade)

Shelf Stable FYFGA Juice (Apple (Natural Style, Regular, w/Calcium), Flavor Juice Blend (Berry, Cherry, Cranberry,

Cranberry Apple, Cranberry Concord Grape, Cranberry Peach, Cranberry Raspberry, Fruit Punch, White Grape Cranberry, White Grape Raspberry), Grape, Grapefruit, Orange, Prune, Ruby Red Grapefruit, White Grape Peach)

Shelf Stable FYFGA Juice From Concentrate (100% Juice (Tomato, Vegetable No Salt Added, Vegetable Regular), Blueberry Flavor Juice Blend, Pomegranate Flavor Juice Blend)

Shelf Stable Juice From Concentrate (Cranberry (Cocktail, Grape Light, Light, Raspberry Cocktail, Raspberry Light), Lemon, White Grape)

Welch's ▲ - All Varieties

Winn & Lovett - Juice (Black Cherry, Cranberry, Pomegranate)

Winn Dixie -

All Frozen Juice Varieties

Juice (Cranberry, Cranberry Apple, Cranberry Raspberry, Light Cranberry, Light Cranberry Grape, Light Grape, Pomegranate Blend, Pomegranate Blueberry Blend, Pomegranate Cranberry Blend, Premium Apple, Reconstituted Lemon, Ruby Red Grapefruit, Ruby Red Grapefruit Cocktail, Vegetable)

Juice From Concentrate (Apple, Apple Cider, Grape, Grapefruit, Prune, Prune w/Pulp, White Grape)

Nectar Drinks (Guava, Mango, Mango Pineapple Guava, Peach, Pear)

Orange Juice (From Concentrate, From Concentrate w/Calcium, Premium Not From Concentrate)

Organic Juice (Apple, Cranberry, Grape, Lemonade, Mango Acai Berry Blend, Orange Mango Blend, Tomato)

Yo-J - All Varieties

Yoo-Hoo - All Varieties

Zola - Acai (Original, w/Blueberry, w/Pomegranate)

Duck

... *All Fresh Poultry Is Gluten-Free (Non-Marinated, Unseasoned)*

Bell & Evans - Duck Breast Fillets **!**

Shelton's - Duckling

D

Duck Sauce

> **Ah So** - Duck Sauce

E

> **Ka-Me** - Duck !

Dumplings

> **Eena Kadeena** ▲ - Mock Za Ball Mix
>
> **Feel Good Foods** - Chicken, Chicken & Vegetable, Pork, Shrimp, Vegetable
>
> **Grandma Ferdon's** ▲ - Frozen Parsley Dumplings ●
>
> **Mixes From The Heartland** ▲ - Country Dumpling Mix ●
>
> **Philadelphia Gluten Free Ravioli Pasta Company** - Mix (Potato & Spinach Gnocci ●, Potato Gnocci ●), Potato & Spinach Gnocci ●, Potato Gnocci ●
>
> **Skye Foods** - Hungarian Egg Dumplings ●
>
> **Star Ravioli** - Gluten Free (Gnocchi, Spinach Gnocchi)

E

Edamame

> **Birds Eye** - All Plain Frozen Vegetables
>
> **C & W** - All Plain Frozen Vegetables ! !
>
> **Franklin Farms** - Shelled Soybeans, Soybeans In Pods
>
> **Meijer Brand** - Edamame Soybeans In Shell
>
> **Melissa's** - In Shell
>
> **Nuts.com** - Dry Roasted Edamame (Salted ●, Unsalted ●), Organic Dry Roasted Soybeans (Salted Whole ●, Unsalted Whole ●), Soy Beans (Dry Roasted Halves ●, Hickory Smoked ●, Spicy BBQ ●), Wasabi Beans ●
>
> **Roland** - Roasted & Salted
>
> **Safeway** - Frozen
>
> **Safeway Brand** - Shelled Boiled Edamame
>
> **Seapoint Farms** - Dry Roasted (Goji Blend, Lightly Salted, Wasabi), Frozen (Pods, Ready To Eat, Shelled), Organic (Dora The Explorer, Pods, Shelled, SpongeBob), Veggie Blends (Garden, Organic Eat Your Greens, Oriental)
>
> **Sunrich Naturals** - Fiesta Blend, In The Shell, Organic, Shelled

Trader Joe's - Frozen (Fully Cooked, Shelled Soybeans, Soybeans In Pod, Soycutash)

Woodstock Farms - Organic Frozen Edamame (Shelled, Whole Pods)

Egg Replacer/Substitute

All Whites - All Varieties

Better'n Eggs - All Varieties

Deb El - Just Whites

Egg Beaters - All Flavors ★

El Peto ▲ - Egg White Powder

Ener-G ▲ - Egg Replacer

Food Club Brand - Refrigerated Egg Substitute

Great Value Brand (Wal-Mart) - Liquid Egg Whites, Liquid Eggs

Hannaford Brand - Egg Mates, Egg Whites

Horizon Organic - All Varieties

Lowes Foods Brand - Refrigerated Egg Substitute

Lucerne - Liquid Eggs All Whites

Meijer Brand - Refrigerated Egg Substitute

NuLaid - ReddiEgg Real Egg Product

Orgran ▲ - No Egg Egg Replacer

Oskaloosa Food Products - All Dried, Liquid & Frozen Egg Products

PaneRiso ▲ - Egg Replacer Mix

Publix - Egg Stirs

Spartan Brand - Eggmates

Wegmans Brand - Egg Busters (FYFGA, Regular)

Egg Rolls

Feel Good Foods - Shrimp & Vegetable, Vegetable

Eggnog

Earth Balance - Organic Soy Nog

Hood - Cinnamon, Gingerbread, Golden, Light, Pumpkin, Sugar Cookie, Vanilla

Horizon Organic

Lactaid

Organic Valley - Eggnog,

Prairie Farms - Regular

Pure Market Express ▲ - Pecan Nog ●

E

    Shamrock Farms - Low Fat, Regular

    Trader Joe's

    Vitasoy ▲ - Holly Nog

Eggplant

    ... *All Fresh Fruits & Vegetables Are Gluten-Free*

    Sabra - Grilled Eggplant, Spanish Eggplant

    Tasty Bite - Punjab Eggplant !

    Trader Joe's - Frozen Misto Alla Grigio !, Garlic Spread

Eggs

    ... *All Fresh Eggs Are Gluten-Free*

Emulsifier

    Augason Farms ▲ - Gluten Free (Lecithin Granules ●, Lecithin
       Powder ●)

Enchilada Sauce

    Frontera - Chipotle Garlic, Green Chile, Red Chile

    Hill Country Fare H-E-B - Hot, Medium, Mild

    La Victoria - Green Mild, Red (Hot, Mild), Red Chili

    Las Palmas - Red

    McCormick - Enchilada Sauce Mix

    Safeway Brand - Green, Red

    Simply Organic - Seasoning Mix ●

Enchiladas

    Amy's -

       Black Bean Vegetable (Light In Sodium ★, Regular ★)

       Cheese ★

       Light & Lean Black Bean & Cheese Enchilada ★

       Santa Fe Enchilada Bowl ★

       Whole Meals (Cheese Enchilada ★, Verde Spinach & Cheese ★,
          w/Spanish Rice & Beans ★)

    Cedarlane - Low Fat Garden Vegetable, Three Layer Enchilada Pie

    Trader Joe's - Chicken Enchiladas In Salsa Verde Frozen, Organic
       Black Bean & Corn

Energy Bars...see Bars

Energy Drinks

AMP Energy - Active (Lemonade, Lemonade Sugar Free), Boost (Cherry, Grape, Original, Original Sugar Free), Focus Mixed Berry

Blue Sky - Blue (Natural !, Shot !, Zero Calorie !), Cafe (Mountain Mocha !, Vanilla Sky !), Juiced Energy !

CalNaturale Svelte ▲ - Sustained Energy Protein Drink (Cappuccino ●, Chocolate ●, French Vanilla ●, Spiced Chai ●)

Celestial Seasonings - Kombucha Energy Shots (Berry, Citrus, Pomegranate Xtreme)

Full Throttle - Blue Agave, Citrus, Coffee (Caramel, Mocha), Red Berry

Guayaki - All Organic Energy Shots

Hansen's - All Varieties

Hi-Ball - Sparkling Energy Water (Orange, Wild Berry)

Inko's White Tea - White Tea Energy

Mio Energy - Liquid Water Enhancer (Black Cherry, Green Thunder)

Monster -

Absolutely Zero

Assault

Black Ice

DUB Edition

Energy + Juice (Khaos, M 80)

Hammer X Presso

Import (Light, Regular)

Java Monster (Irish Blend, Kona Blend, Loco Moca, Mean Bean, Toffee, Vanilla Light)

Lo Carb

M 3

Midnite X Presso

Nitrous (Anti Gravity, Killer B, Super Dry)

Regular

Rehab

NOS - All Varieties

Red Bull - Cola, Energy Shots, Regular, Sugar Free

Red Rain - Diet, Regular

Relentless - Fire, Original

E

Rock Star -
  2X Energy
  Coconut Water
  Energy Cola
  Iced
  Juiced (Mango Orange Passion Fruit, Tropical Guava)
  Original
  Punched
  Recovery (Grape, Lemonade, Orange)
  Relax
  Roasted (Latte, Light Vanilla, Mocha)
  Sugar Free
  Xdurance
  Zero Carb
Sambazon - Amazon Energy (Acai Berry (Low Calorie, Regular),
  Passion Fruit Berry)
Steaz - Berry, Diet Berry, Orange
English Muffins
  Celiac Specialties ▲ - English Muffins
  El Peto ▲ - Regular
  Ener-G ▲ - Regular
  Food For Life - Wheat & Gluten Free (Brown Rice, Multi Seed)
  Foods By George ▲ - English Muffins (Cinnamon Currant, No Rye
    Rye, Plain)
  Gillian's Foods ▲ - English Muffins ●
  Gluten-Free Creations ▲ - English Muffins ●
  Glutino ▲ - Premium English Muffins
  Grandma Ferdon's ▲ - Regular ●
  Joan's GF Great Bakes ▲ - Multi Grain, Plain
  Kinnikinnick ▲- Tapioca Rice English Muffins
  Molly's Gluten-Free Bakery ▲ - White
  Sweet Escapes Pastries ▲ - English Muffins ●
Espresso...see Coffee

Extract

Badia - All Flavors ●

Durkee - All Liquid Extracts, Vanilla (Imitation, Pure)

Flavorganics - Almond, Anise, Chocolate, Coconut, Hazelnut, Lemon, Orange, Peppermint, Rum, Vanilla

Food Club Brand -
Imitation Flavoring Vanilla
Pure Extract (Almond, Lemon, Vanilla)

Gordon Food Service - Pure Lemon, Pure Vanilla

Great Value Brand (Wal-Mart) - Pure Vanilla Extract

Hannaford Brand -
Imitation (Almond, Vanilla)
Pure (Lemon, Vanilla)

Hill Country Fare H-E-B - Imitation Vanilla

Hy-Vee - Vanilla (Imitation, Pure)

McCormick -
Cinnamon
Gourmet Collection 100% Organic Pure Madagascar Vanilla
Imitation (Almond, Banana, Butter Flavor, Cherry, Clear Vanilla, Coconut, Maple, Rum, Strawberry, Vanilla Butter & Nut)
Premium Vanilla
Pure (Almond, Anise, Coffee, Lemon, Mint, Orange, Peppermint, Vanilla)
Raspberry
Root Beer

Meijer Brand - Imitation Vanilla, Vanilla

Midwest Country Fare - Imitation Vanilla Flavor

Nielsen-Massey - Orange Blossom Water ●, Pure (Almond ●, Chocolate ●, Coffee ●, Lemon ●, Madagascar Bourbon Vanilla●, Mexican Vanilla ●, Orange ●, Organic Vanilla ●, Peppermint ●, Tahitian Vanilla ●, Vanilla Extract Blend ●), Rose Water ●

Publix - Almond, Lemon, Vanilla

Rodelle - Extract (Almond, Chocolate, Lemon, Vanilla (Alcohol Free, Gourmet, Organic, Pure)), Vanilla Paste

Safeway Brand - All Varieties

E

F

Simply Organic - Almond, Lemon Flavor, Orange Flavor, Peppermint Flavor, Ugandan Vanilla, Vanilla

Spartan Brand - Vanilla (Imitation, Pure)

Spice Islands - All Liquid Extracts, Vanilla (Imitation, Pure)

The Spice Hunter - Pure Almond, Pure Lemon, Pure Vanilla

Tones - All Liquid Extracts, Vanilla (Imitation, Pure)

Trader Joe's - Vanilla

Watkins - Pure (Almond, Lemon, Orange, Peppermint, Vanilla)

Wegmans Brand - Vanilla Extract

F

Fajita Seasoning Mix...see also Seasonings

McCormick - Fajita Seasoning Packet

Old El Paso - Seasoning Mix

Safeway Brand

Simply Organic - Fajita Seasoning Mix ●

Falafel

Falafapita - Uncooked Frozen Falafel Balls

Falafel Republic - Roasted Garlic ●, Traditional ●

Falafel Mix

Authentic Foods ▲ - Falafel Mix ●

Orgran ▲

Feta Cheese...see Cheese

Fettuccini...see Pasta

Figs

Nuts.com - Dried Fruit (California ●, Diced ●, Mission ●, Organic (California ●, Calimyrna ●, Mission ●, Turkish ●), Turkish ●)

Oskri Organics - Dried Figs

Woodstock Farms - Calmyrna, Organic Black Mission

Fish

... *All Fresh Fish Is Gluten-Free (Non-Marinated, Unseasoned)*

A&B Famous - Kosher For Passover (Homestyle Gefilte Fish (Carb Free w/Splenda ●, Less Sugar ●, Pike & White ●, Salmon ●, Sugar Free ●, Sweet ●), Old Fashion Sweet Gefilte Fish (Family Pack ●,

Roll ●, Twin Pack ●), Pike & White Gefilte Fish ●)

Beacon Light - Steam Series (Garlic & Herb Mahi Mahi, Lemon & Dill
Atlantic Salmon, Lemon & Herb Haddock, Mediterranean Cod,
Tomato & Basil Tilapia)

Blue Horizon - English Style Fish & Chip Bites, Wild Alaskan Salmon
Bites

Crown Prince - Kipper Snacks, Natural Kipper Snacks

Dr. Praeger's - All Natural Potato Crusted (Fish Fillets **!**, Fish Sticks **!**,
Fishies **!**)

Great Value Brand (Wal-Mart) - Canned Alaskan Pink Salmon

Henry & Lisa's -
4 oz. Wild Alaskan (Cod, Salmon)
Wild Alaskan Fish Nuggets *(Box Must Say Gluten Free)*
Wild South American Mahi Mahi

Hy-Vee - Canned Alaskan Pink Salmon, Frozen (Salmon, Tilapia)

Ian's - Wheat Free Gluten Free Recipe Fish Sticks

Kirkland Signature - Fresh (Catfish, Steelhead, Tilapia), Frozen
(Steelhead Trout, Tilapia Loins)

Morey's -
Fish Creations (Garden Pesto Tilapia, Lemon Pepper Tilapia,
Mediterranean Cod, Pineapple Mango Mahi Mahi, Seasoned
Grill Tilapia, Sweet Mango Tilapia)
Marinated Tilapia (Lemon Pepper, Seasoned Grill, Sweet Mango)
Smoked (Lake Trout, Smoked Whiting Goldies, Whitefish)

Ocean Prince - Imitation Abalone

Star Of The Sea - Stuffed Flounder

Star Of The Sea Seafood - Gluten Free Stuffed Flounder ●

Starfish - Crispy Battered Wild Caught Fish (Cod ●, Haddock ●,
Halibut ●)

Sweet Bay - All Frozen Fillets

Trader Joe's - Marinated Ahi Tuna Steaks, Premium Salmon Patties **! !**,
Salmon Burger, Seasoned Mahi Mahi Fillets, Skinless Boneless Pink
Salmon, Skinless Boneless Sardines In Olive Oil

F

Wegmans Brand - Atlantic Salmon Fillets Farm Raised, FYFGA (Alaskan Halibut, Chilean Sea Bass, Lobster Tails, Mahi Mahi, Pacific Cod, Sockeye Salmon, Swordfish, Yellowfin Tuna), Tilapia Fillets

Whole Catch - Frozen Fillet (Cod, Mahi Mahi, Sockeye Salmon)

Winn Dixie - Frozen (Cod, Grouper, Tilapia, Whiting)

Fish Sauce
  A Taste Of Thai - Regular
  Ka-Me - Fish !
  Thai Kitchen - Premium Fish Sauce

Fish Steaks
  Crown Prince - Fish Steaks In Lousiana Hot Sauce
  Ocean Prince - Fish Steaks (In Lousiana Hot Sauce, In Oil, w/Green Chilies)

Fish Sticks
  Dr. Praeger's - All Natural Potato Crusted (Fish Sticks !, Fishies !)
  Henry & Lisa's - Fish Nuggets Wild Alaskan *(Box Must Say Gluten Free)*
  Ian's - Wheat Free Gluten Free Recipe Fish Sticks

Flan
  Kozy Shack - All Varieties
  Royal - Caramel Custard

Flax Seed
  Arrowhead Mills - Flax Seed, Flax Seed Meal, Flax Seeds Organic Golden
  Bob's Red Mill ▲ - Flaxseed Meal (Golden ★, Organic ★, Original ★)
  Flax USA - Organic Golden Flax
  Hodgson Mill ▲ - Milled, Organic Golden Milled, Travel Flax All Natural Milled, Travel Flax Organic Golden Milled, Whole Grain Brown
  Nature's Path - Organic FlaxPlus Meal !
  Navitas Naturals ▲ - Flax Powder
  Puravida - Sprout Revolution Sprouted Ground Flax (Ground, w/Blueberries, w/Goji & Cranberry)
  Shiloh Farms - Organic (Brown Flax !!, Golden Flax !!)
  Spectrum - Organic (Ground, Ground w/Mixed Berries, Roasted, Whole)

Trader Joe's - Golden Roasted (Flax Seed w/Blueberries, Whole)
Woodstock Farms - Organic Flax Seed
Flax Seed Oil...see Oil
Flour
1-2-3 Gluten Free ▲ - Olivia's Outstanding Multi Purpose Fortified Flour Mix ●
Abundant Life Foods ▲ - All Purpose Mix
AgVantage Naturals ▲ - Master Blend ●, Millet Flour ●, Premium Fine Milled Sorghum Flour ●, Quinoa Flour ●, Rice Flour ●
Andrea's Gluten Free ▲ - Gluten Free Flour Blend, Super Fine Grind Rice Brown
Arrowhead Mills - All Purpose Baking Mix, Brown Rice, Organic (Buckwheat, Millet, Soy, White Rice)
Augason Farms ▲ - Gluten Free (Featherlite ●, Tapioca Flour ●, Whole Grain Brown Rice ●)
Avec Baking - Gluten Free Flour Mix ●
Bay State Milling - Gluten Free All Purpose Flour ●
Better Batter - Gluten Free All Purpose Flour ●, Seasoned Flour ●
Bi-Aglut - For Bread, Regular
Bisquick ▲ - Gluten Free Pancake & Baking Mix
Bloomfield Farms ▲ - Gluten Free All Purpose Blend ●
Bob's Red Mill ▲ -
  Almond Meal/Flour ★
  Black Bean ★
  Brown Rice ★
  Fava Bean ★
  Garbanzo Bean ★
  Gluten Free (All Purpose Baking ★, Corn ★, Garbanzo & Fava ★, Masa Harina ★, Masa Harina Golden Corn Flour ★, Oat ★, Sorghum ★)
  Green Pea ★
  Hazelnut Meal/Flour ★
  Millet ★
  Organic (Amaranth ★, Brown Rice ★, Coconut ★, Quinoa ★, White Rice ★)

F

Potato ★
Sweet White Rice ★
Tapioca ★
Teff ★
White (Bean ★, Rice ★)

C4C - Gluten Free Flour

Cargill - Prolia Soy Flour

Cause You're Special ▲ - All Purpose, White Rice

Celiac Specialties ▲ - Celiac Specialties Flour Blend

Chateau Cream Hill Estates - Lara's Whole Grain Oat Flour ●

ConAgra Mills - Amaranth ●, Millet ●, Multigrain 5 Grain ●, Quinoa ●, Sorghum ●, Teff ●

Deerfields Gluten Free Bakery ▲ - Quick Mix For Sugar Buttons

Domata - Gluten Free All Purpose Flour ●, Seasoned ●

Dowd & Rogers ▲ - California Almond, Italian Chestnut

Eagle Mills - Gluten Free All Purpose Multigrain Blend ●

El Peto ▲ - All Purpose Flour Mix, Bean, Corn, Corn Free All Purpose Mix, Garfava Bean Mix, Millet, Organic Amaranth, Potato, Quinoa, Sorghum, Sweet Rice, Tapioca Starch, White Rice, Whole Grain Brown Rice, Whole Grain Flax Seed

Ener-G ▲ - Brown Rice, Potato, Sweet Rice, Tapioca, White Rice

Expandex ▲ - Modified Tapioca Starch ●

Gifts Of Nature ▲ - All Purpose Blend ●, Baby Lima Bean ●, Brown Rice ●, Sweet Rice ●, Tapioca ●, White Rice ●

Gillian's Foods ▲ - All Purpose Baking Mix ●, Brown Rice ●, Imported Tapioca ●, Rice ●

Glutano ▲ - Flour Mix It

Gluten Free Mama ▲ - Gluten Free Flour Mix (Mama's Coconut Blend ●, Mama's Almond Blend ●)

Gluten Free Oats ▲ - Whole Grain Gluten Free Oat Flour (Organic ●, Regular ●)

Gluten Free Pantry ▲ - All Purpose Gluten Free Baking Flour

Gluten-Free Creations ▲ - Baking Flours (Basic ●, Enriched ●, Sweet ●)

flour

F

Gluten-Free Naturals - All Purpose Blend, Bread Flour (Multi Grain, Sandwich)

Grandma Ferdon's ▲ - Grandma Ferdon's Flour Mix ●, Potato ●, Rice (Sweet ●, White ●)

Gulf Pacific ▲ - Long Grain White Rice Flour

Heaven Mills ▲ - Oat Flour ●

Hodgson Mill ▲ - Gluten Free All Purpose Baking Flour

JK Gourmet - Almond Flour

Jules Gluten Free ▲ - All Purpose Flour ●

King Arthur Flour ▲ - Gluten Free Multi Purpose Flour ●

Kinnikinnick ▲ - All Purpose

Laurel's Sweet Treats ▲ - Baking Flour Mix

Les Moissonneries Du Pavs ▲ - Organic Green Buckwheat Flour

Let's Do...Organic - Organic Coconut Flour

Lundberg ▲ - Brown Rice Flour (California Nutra Farmed, Organic)

Mamma Mia - Easy Mix & Bake

Maninis ▲ - Multi Purpose Flour Mix ●

Maple Grove Farms Of Vermont - Gluten Free All Purpose Baking Mix

Meister's Gluten Free Mixtures ▲ - All Purpose Gluten Free Flour ●

Minn-Dak Growers - Fancy Buckwheat Flour

Mixes From The Heartland ▲ - Gluten Free ●, Mix (Brown Rice ●, Tapioca Flour Starch ●, White Rice ●), Potato ●

Montana Gluten Free ▲ - Toasted Oat ●

Montana Monster Munchies - Whole Grain Oat Flour ●

Namaste Foods ▲ - Perfect Flour Blend

Nu-World Foods ▲ - Amaranth (Flour, Pre Gel Powder, Toasted Bran Flour)

Nuchia - 100% Chia Seed ●, Original Chia Seed ●

Nuts.com - Arrowroot Powder ●, Flour (Almond ●, Cashew ●, Chestnut ●, Chia ●, Chickpea ●, Gluten Free (All Purpose Baking ●, Black Bean ●, Corn ●, Fava Bean ●, Garbanzo Fava ●, Green Pea ●, Masa Harina Corn ●, Organic Coconut ●, Sweet White Rice ●, Sweet White Sorghum ●, White Bean ●), Hazelnut ●, Millet ●, Natural

F

    Almond ●, Organic (Almond ●, Amaranth ●, Brown Rice ●, Quinoa ●, White Rice ●), Peanut ●, Pistachio ●, Potato ●, Sprouted Super ●, Tapioca ●, Teff ●, White Chia ●)

Only Oats ▲ - Pure Whole Grain Oat Flour ●

Orgran ▲ - All Purpose Pastry Mix, All Purpose Plain, Gluten Substitute, Self Raising

Peter Paul - Coconut Flour

Phildesco - Coconut Flour

Pocono - Buckwheat Flour

PrOatina ▲ - Gluten Free Toasted Oat Flour ●

Really Great Food Company ▲ - All Purpose Rice, Brown Rice, Flour Potato Starch, Sweet Rice, Tapioca, White Rice

Shiloh Farms - Almond ‼, Brown Rice ‼, Mesquite ‼, Potato ‼, Quinoa ‼, Tapioca ‼, Teff ‼

Silly Yak Bakery - GF Flour Mix (Brown Rice ●, Regular ●)

Stashu's ▲ - All Purpose Blend ●

Sylvan Border Farm - General Purpose Flour

The Grain Exchange - Buckwheat Mix

The Grainless Baker ▲ - All Purpose Flour

The Pure Pantry ▲ - Organic All Purpose Baking Mix ●

Timtana Gluten Free ▲ - Timtana Gluten Free All Purpose Flour ★ ●

Tom Sawyer ▲ - All Purpose Gluten Free

Tropical Traditions - Organic Coconut Flour

Twin Valley Mills - Sorghum Flour

Voyaging Foods - Hawaiian Ali'i Taro Flour ●

West Meadow Farm Bakery - Pastry Blend ●

Food Coloring

    Badia - All Colors ●

    Durkee - All Varieties

    Hy-Vee - Assorted

    McCormick - All Varieties

    Safeway Brand - Assorted

    Spice Islands - All Colors

    Tones - All Varieties

Frankfurters...see Sausage

French Fries

  Alexia Foods -

    Crispy Potatoes w/Seasoned Salt Waffle Fries **!**

    Julienne Fries (Spicy Sweet Potato **!**, Sweet Potato **!**, w/Sea Salt Yukon Gold **!**)

    Olive Oil & Sea Salt Oven Fries **!**

    Olive Oil Parmesan & Roasted Garlic Oven Reds **!**

    Olive Oil Rosemary & Garlic Oven Fries **!**

    Organic (Classic Oven Crinkles **!**, Oven Crinkles Onion & Garlic **!**, Oven Crinkles Salt & Pepper **!**, Yukon Gold Julienne Fries w/Sea Salt **!**)

  Chester's - Chili Cheese Flavored Fries **! !**, Flamin' Hot Fries **! !**

  Gordon Food Service - 1/2" Oven, Extra Long (1/2" Crinkle Cut, 5/16" w/Skin, Coated (1/4", 3/8", 5/16"), Steak), Long (1/2", 3/8", 5/16"), Wedge Cut w/Skin

  Hannaford Brand - Frozen (Crinkle Cut, Shoestring, Steak Style, Straight Cut)

  Ian's - Alphatots, Sweet Potato Fries

  Lowes Foods Brand - Crinkle Cut, Shoestring, Steak Cut

  Meijer Brand - Crinkle Cut, Original, Shoestring, Steak Cut

  Open Nature - Crinkle Cut Sweet Potato

  Ore-Ida -

    Country Style Steak Fries

    Crispers

    Crunch Time Classics Straight Cut

    Easy Fries Golden Crinkles

    Extra Crispy (Fast Food Fries, Golden Crinkles)

    Golden (Crinkles, Fries)

    Golden Twirls

    Shoestrings

    Steak Fries

    Sweet Potato Fries

    Waffle Fries

F

    Publix - Frozen (Crinkle Cut, Steak Fries)

    Safeway Brand - Frozen (French Fries Classic, Shoestring, Steak Cut)

    Spartan Brand - Frozen (Crinkle Cut, Extra Crispy Fast, French Fried, Steak)

    Winn Dixie - Frozen (Crinkle Cut, French, Matchstick, Shoestring, Steak Cut)

    Woodstock Farms - Organic Frozen (Crinkle Cut Oven Fries, Shredded Hash Browns, Tastee Taters)

French Toast

    Ian's - Wheat Free Gluten Free Recipe French Toast Sticks

    Van's Natural Foods - Wheat & Gluten Free Cinnamon French Toast Sticks ★

Frosting...see Baking Decorations & Frostings

Frozen Desserts...see Ice Cream and/or Popsicles and/or Sorbet

Frozen Dinners...see Meals

Frozen Vegetables...see Mixed Vegetables

Frozen Yogurt...see Ice Cream

Fruit Bars...see Bars and/or Popsicles

Fruit Cocktail

    Del Monte - Canned/Jarred Fruit (All Varieties), Fruit Snack Cups Plastic

    Food Club Brand - In Heavy Syrup, In Juice

    Great Value Brand (Wal-Mart) - In Heavy Syrup

    Hannaford Brand - All Varieties

    Hy-Vee - Regular

    Lowes Foods Brand - In Heavy Syrup, In Juice

    Meijer Brand - Heavy Syrup, In Juice, In Pear Juice Lite

    Midwest Country Fare

    Safeway Brand - Canned (Lite, Regular)

    Spartan Brand - Heavy Syrup, Light Juice

    Wegmans Brand - FYFGA (In Pear Juice, Regular), In Heavy Syrup, Triple Cherry Fruit Mix Cherry Flavored In Light Syrup, Tropical Fruit Salad

    Winn Dixie - Fruit Cocktail (Heavy Syrup, Light Syrup)

Fruit Drinks...see Drinks/Juice

Fruit Leather...sea also Fruit Snacks

    Matt's Munchies - Apple Licious ●, Apple Pie ●, Banana ●, Chili Chocolate ●, Choco Nana ●, Ginger Spice ●, Island Mango ●, Mango ●, Raspberry Delight ●

    Stretch Island Fruit Co. - All Varieties

    Trader Joe's - All Varieties

Fruit Salad

    Meijer Brand - Canned Tropical

    Native Forest - Canned Organic Tropical

    Safeway Brand - Canned Tropical Fruit

Fruit Snacks...see also Snacks

    Annie's - Organic Bunny Fruit Snacks (Berry Patch !!, Pink Lemonade !!, Summer Strawberry !!, Sunny Citrus !!, Tropical Treat !!), Organic Grapes Galore !!, Organic Orchard Real Fruit Bites (Apple !!, Cherry !!, Grape !!, Strawberry !!)

    Brothers All Natural ▲ - Fruit Crisps (Apple Cinnamon, Asian Pear, Banana, Fuji Apple, Mandarin Orange, Mixed Berry, Organic Strawberry, Peach, Pineapple, Strawberry, Strawberry Banana)

    Food Club Brand - Fruit Snacks (Curious George, Dinosaurs, Sharks, Variety Pack)

    Fruit By The Foot - Berry Blast, Berry Tie Dye, Boo Berry, Color By The Foot, Strawberry

    Fruit Gushers - Double Dare Berry, Flavor Shock, Fruit Punch, Punch Berry, Rockin' Blue Raspberry, Strawberry Splash, Strawberry/ Watermelon/Tropical Variety Pack, Triple Berry Shock, Tropical, Watermelon Blast

    Fruit Roll-Ups - Blastin' Berry Hot Colors, Boo Berry Razzle Boo Blitz, Flavor Wave Berry Berry Cool, Franken Berry Strawberry Scream, Scoops Fruity Ice Cream Flavors, Simply Fruit Rolls Wildberry, Stickerz (Stars Mixed Berry, Twisters Tropical Berry), Strawberry, Tropical Tie Dye, Variety Pack (Stickerz Mixed Berry/Tropical Berry, Tropical/Strawberry/Berry Orange)

F

Fruit Shapes - Batman, Create A Bug, Easter, My Little Pony, Mystery Variety Pack, Ni Hao Kai Lan, Oceanspray Assorted Fruit, Oceanspray Berries & Cherries, Organic Go Diego Go, Scooby Doo, Shark Bites, Spiderman, Sponge Bob, Sunkist Mixed Fruit, The Penguins Of Madagascar, Thomas & Friends, Tom & Jerry, Transformers

Great Value Brand (Wal-Mart) - Fruit Smiles

Meijer Brand -

Fruit Rolls (Justice League Galactic Berry, Rescue Heroes, Strawberry (Garfield, Regular), Wildberry Rush)

Fruit Snacks (African Safari, Curious George, Dinosaurs, Jungle Adventure, Justice League (Big Box, Regular), Mixed Fruit, Peanuts, Rescue Heroes Big Box, Sharks, Underwater World, Variety Pack (Big Boy, Regular), Veggie Tales)

Niagara Natural - Tropical Fruit Bites

Safeway Brand - Creatures

Sharkies ▲ -

Kids Omega 3 Smart Twists (Berry Surf, Tropical Wave)

Kids Organic Fruit Chews (Berry Bites, Fruit Splash)

Kids Sports Chews (Berry Blasters, Tropical Splash)

Organic Sports Chews (Berry Blast, Citrus Squeeze, Fruit Splash, Watermelon Scream)

Spartan Brand - Curious George, Dinosaurs, Star Wars, Variety Pack

Stretch Island Fruit Co. - FruitaBu Smooshed Rolls (Apple, Grape, Strawberry)

SunRype -

100% Fruit Strip (Strawberry, Strawberry Banana, Wildberry)

FruitSource 100% Fruit Mini Bites (Mixed Berry, Strawberry)

Squiggles 100% Fruit & Veggie Twist (Strawberry, Wildberry Plus Veggie)

Tasty - Organic Gluten Free Mixed Fruit

thinkFruit - Dried (Blueberries, Cherry, Cinnamon Apple, Cranberries, Peaches, Pineapple Tidbits)

Welch's ▲ - All Varieties *(Except Filled Licorice)*

F

Fruit Spread...see Jam/Jelly and/or Spread

Fudge

    Emmy's Organics ▲ - Super Fudge (Chocolate, Goji Berry, Mocha, Peppermint)

    KatySweet ▲ - Creamy Fudge Pralines (Pecan ●, Pecan Holiday (Star ●, Tree ●), State Shaped ●), Creamy Fudge Walnut ●, Organic Pecan ●, Organic Walnut ●, Pecan ●, Plain (Organic ●, Regular ●), Walnut ●

G

Gai Lan

    ... *All Fresh Fruits & Vegetables Are Gluten-Free*

Garbanzo Beans...see Beans

Garlic...see also Seasonings

    ... *All Fresh Garlic Is Gluten-Free*

    Amore - Garlic Paste

    Earthbound Farm - Organic Garlic

    Hill Country Fare H-E-B - Minced In Oil

    Kirkland Signature - Minced California

    Lee Kum Kee - Minced

    Mezzetta ▲ - Crushed Garlic, Spicy Pickled Garlic

    The Spice Hunter - 100% Organic Garlic, Fresh At Hand Garlic, Garlic (California, Roasted)

    Trader Joe's - Crushed (Frozen, Regular)

Garlic Powder...see Seasonings

Garlic Salt...see Seasonings

Gelatin

    Food Club Brand - All (Regular, Sugar Free)

    Gifts Of Nature ▲ - Unflavored Beef Gelatin ●

    Gordon Food Service - Gelatin Mix (Assorted (Citrus, Red), Cherry, Lemon, Lime, Orange, Raspberry, Strawberry)

    Great Value Brand (Wal-Mart) - Regular (Lemon, Lime, Orange, Peach, Strawberry), Sugar Free (Cherry, Lime, Orange, Raspberry, Strawberry, Strawberry Banana)

G **Hannaford Brand** - Sugar Free (Cherry, Lime, Orange, Raspberry)

Hy-Vee -

Gelatin (Berry Blue, Cherry, Cranberry, Lemon, Lime, Orange, Raspberry, Strawberry, Strawberry Banana)

Sugar Free (Berry Blue, Cherry, Cranberry, Lime, Orange, Raspberry, Strawberry)

Jell-O -

Gel Cups (Sugar Free Low Cal Strawberry/Raspberry/Orange, X Treme Cherry & Blue Raspberry, X Treme Watermelon & Green Apple)

Regular Instant (Apricot, Berry Blue, Black Cherry, Blackberry Fusion, Cherry, Cranberry, Grape, Island Pineapple, Lemon, Lime, Margarita, Melon Fusion, Orange, Peach, Pina Colada, Raspberry, Strawberry (Banana, Kiwi, Regular), Tropical Fusion, Watermelon)

Snack Cups (Chunks Of Pineapple In Tropical Fusion Sugar Free Gel, Pear Chunks In Cherry Pomegranate Gel, Strawberry, Strawberry/Orange, Strawberry/Raspberry)

Sugar Free Low Calorie Instant (Black Cherry, Cherry, Cranberry, Lemon, Lime, Orange, Peach, Raspberry, Strawberry (Banana, Regular))

Sugar Free Snack Cups (Cherry/Black Cherry, Lemon Lime/ Orange, Peach/Watermelon, Raspberry/Orange, Strawberry, Strawberry Kiwi/Tropical Berry)

Kool-Aid - Gels (All Varieties)

Kozy Shack - All Varieties SmartGels

Meijer Brand -

Gelatin Dessert (Berry Blue, Cherry, Cranberry, Grape, Lime, Orange, Raspberry, Strawberry, Unflavored, Wild Strawberry)

Sugar Free Gelatin Dessert (Cherry, Cranberry, Lime, Orange, Raspberry, Strawberry)

Royal - All Varieties

Spartan Brand - Berry Blue, Cherry (Regular, Sugar Free), Lime (Regular, Sugar Free), Orange (Regular, Sugar Free), Raspberry (Regular, Sugar Free), Strawberry (Regular, Sugar Free)

Wegmans Brand - Original Strawberry, Sugar Free (Black Cherry & Cherry, Grape & Fruit Punch, Raspberry & Orange, Strawberry)

Zen - Juice Gels (Orange, Strawberry)

Gin

... *All Distilled Alcohol Is Gluten-Free*

Ginger

Lee Kum Kee - Minced

Nuts.com - Dried Fruit (Crystallized ●, Organic Crystallized ●)

The Ginger People - Organic Grated !, Organic Minced !, Organic Natural Pickled Sushi !, Organic Syrup !

The Spice Hunter - 100% Organic Ginger, Fresh At Hand Ginger, Ginger (Australian Crystallized Chopped, Chinese Ground)

Wel-Pac - Pickled Ginger (Benzi, Kizami), Sushi Ginger

Woodstock Farms - Organic Crystallized w/Raw Sugar, Slices Unsulphured

Ginger Ale...see Soda Pop/Carbonated Beverages

Glaze

Ah So - Ham Glaze

Daddy Sam's - Salmon Glaze

Litehouse - Dessert Glaze (Peach, Strawberry, Sugar Free Strawberry)

Marzetti - Glaze For (Blueberries, Peaches, Strawberries, Sugar Free Strawberries)

Graham Crackers

Celiac Specialties ▲ - Graham Cracker Crumbs

Jules Gluten Free ▲ - Graham Cracker/Gingersnap Mix ●

Kinnikinnick ▲ - Graham Style Cracker Crumbs, S'moreables Graham Style Crackers

Laurel's Sweet Treats ▲ - Honey Grahamless Crackers

The Grainless Baker ▲ - Crumbs, Regular

Grains

Arrowhead Mills - Amaranth, Hulled Millet, Quinoa

Augason Farms ▲ - Organic Quinoa Grain ●

Bob's Red Mill ▲ - Organic Amaranth ★, Rice Bran ★, Teff Whole ★

Eden Organic - Buckwheat, Millet, Quinoa, Red Quinoa, Wild Rice

G El Peto ▲ - Black Chia Grain, Rice Bran

Nuts.com - Gluten Free (Corn Grits Polenta ●, Corn Meal ●, Millet Grits ●, Organic Brown Rice Farina ●, Rice Bran ●, Sweet White Sorghum Grain ●), Millet ●, Organic (Amaranth ●, Millet ●, Purple Corn Kernels ●, Quinoa ●, Raw White Buckwheat ●, Toasted Buckwheat ●), Simply Sweet Corn ●, Teff Whole Grain ●, Yellow Corn Meal ●

Shiloh Farms - Hulled Millet **!!**, Whole Sorghum **!!**

Woodstock Farms - Organic White Quinoa

Granola

Bakery On Main -

Apple Raisin Walnut ●

Cranberry Orange Cashew ●

Extreme Fruit & Nut ●

Fiber Power (Cinnamon Raisin ●, Triple Berry ●)

Nutty Cranberry Maple ●

Rainforest ●

Chappaqua Crunch - Gluten Free Granola (w/Fruit & Flax ★, w/Vanilla & Flax ★)

Deb's Farmhouse Kitchen - Cherry Almond ●, Espresso ●, Pistachio ●

Deerfields Gluten Free Bakery ▲ - Almond Cherry, Chocolate Chip, Vanilla Maple

Emmy's Organics ▲ - Apricot Flax, Original, Peanut Butter Banana, Walnut Ginger Fig

Enjoy Life ▲ - Crunch (Cinnamon Raisin ●, Double Chocolate ●, Very Berry ●)

Gluten Free Oats ▲ - Oatmeal Cookie Crisp Granola ●

Gluten Free Sensations ▲ - Apple Crisp, Blueberry Pecan, Cherry Vanilla Almond, Chocolate Bliss, Cranberry Pecan, French Vanilla Almond

GlutenFreeda ▲ - Apple Almond Honey, Cranberry Cashew Honey, Raisin Almond Honey

Go Raw ▲ - Apple Cinnamon ●, Chocolate ●, Original ●, Simple ●

Hail Merry ▲ - Grawnola (Cherry Almond Hemp ●, Lemon Blue Agave ●, Orange Cranberry ●)

grape leaves

G

Jessica's Natural Foods - Gluten Free Granola (Almond Cherry, Chocolate Chip, Vanilla Maple)

JK Gourmet - Grain Free (Apple Spice & Raisin, Cranberry & Cashew, Hazelnut & Date, Mission Fig & Apricot, Nuts & Raisins Original)

Kaia Foods ▲ - Buckwheat Granola (Cherry Pie ●, Cocoa Bliss ●, Dates & Spices ●, Raisin Cinnamon ●)

KIND ▲ - Clusters (Cinnamon Oat ★, Dark Chocolate & Cranberry ★, Maple Walnut ★, Oats & Honey ★, Peanut Butter Whole Grain ★, Vanilla Blueberry ★)

Kookie Karma - All Varieties ●

Love Grown Foods ▲ - Apple Walnut Delight ●, Cocoa Goodness ●, Raisin Almond Crunch ●, Simply Oats ●, Sweet Cranberry Pecan ●

Michaelene's - Gluten Free Granola (Amazing Almond Vanilla, Berry Best)

Montana Monster Munchies - Bridger Blueberry ●, Chinook Chocolate ●, Cut Bank Cranberry ●, Mariah's Gold Peanut ●, Red Lodge Raisin ●

NoNuttin' Foods ▲ - Blueberry Maple ●, Cranberry Apple ●, Vanilla Caramel ●, Vanilla Cinnamon ●

Oskri Organics - Almond, Cashew, Peach, Raisin

Purely Elizabeth ▲ - Ancient Grain Granola Cereal (Cranberry Pecan ●, Original ●, Pumpkin Fig ●)

Rose's Bakery ▲

Silly Yak Bakery - GF Granola w/Fruit ●

Thoughtful Food ▲ - Giddy Up & Go Granola (Notoriously Nutty ●, Seriously Seedy ●)

Trader Joe's - Gluten Free Granola

Udi's Gluten Free Foods ▲ - Gluten Free (Au Naturel ●, Cranberry ●, Original ●, Vanilla ●)

West Meadow Farm Bakery - Feelin Groovy ●

Whole Foods Market Gluten Free Bakehouse ▲ - Fruit & Nut Granola

Grape Leaves

Krinos - Imported

Mezzetta ▲ - California

Peloponnese - Dolmas

G Grapefruit
  ... *All Fresh Fruits & Vegetables Are Gluten-Free
  Del Monte - Canned/Jarred Fruit (All Varieties), Fruit Snack Cups Plastic Regular
  Meijer Brand - Sections (In Juice, In Syrup)
  Winn Dixie - Canned Regular

Grapes
  ... *All Fresh Fruits & Vegetables Are Gluten-Free
  Annie's - Organic Orchard Real Fruit Bites Grape **‼**

Gravy/Gravy Mix
  Cuisine Sante ▲ - Au Jus Clear Gravy Mix ●
  Full Flavor Foods ▲ - Gravy (Beef ●, Chicken ●, Pork ●, Turkey ●)
  Imagine - Organic Gravy (Roasted Turkey Flavored, Savory Beef Flavored)
  Leahey Gardens - Gravy (Creamy, Golden, Mushroom, No Beef Brown, No Beef Mexican Style)
  Luda H - Instant Gravy (Beef, Poultry)
  Massel - Chicken Style Gravy Mix, Supreme Gravy Mix
  Maxwell's Kitchen - Gravy Mix (Brown, Chicken, Pork, Turkey)
  Mayacamas - Gravy Mix (Brown ★, Chicken ★, Savory Herb ★, Turkey ★)
  Orgran ▲ - Gravy Mix
  Road's End Organics - Organic Gluten Free Gravy Mixes (All Varieties)
  Simply Organic - Gravy Mix (Brown ●, Roasted Chicken ●, Roasted Turkey ●, Vegetarian Brown ●)
  Trader Joe's - All Natural Turkey Gravy

Green Beans...see Beans
Green Olives...see Olives
Green Peppers
  ... *All Fresh Fruits & Vegetables Are Gluten-Free
Green Tea...see Tea
Greens
  ... *All Fresh Fruits & Vegetables Are Gluten-Free
  Birds Eye - All Plain Frozen Vegetables
  C & W - All Plain Frozen Vegetables **‼**

Food Club Brand -
　Canned (Mustard Greens, Turnip Greens)
　Frozen (Chopped Collards, Mustard Greens Chopped, Turnip Chopped)
Lowes Foods Brand - Frozen (Chopped Collard, Turnip Greens)
Meijer Brand -
　Canned Chopped (Kale, Mustard, Turnip)
　Frozen Chopped (Collards, Kale, Mustard, Turnip)
Pictsweet - All Plain Frozen Vegetables
Publix - Frozen (Collard Chopped, Turnip Chopped, Turnip w/Diced Turnips)
Publix GreenWise Market - Mixed Baby Spinach Blend
Spartan Brand - Chopped (Collard, Mustard, Turnip)
Winn Dixie -
　Canned (Collard No Salt, Mustard, Turnip)
　Frozen (Collard Greens Chopped, Mustard Greens, Steamable Mixed Vegetables)

Grits
Bob's Red Mill ▲ - Gluten Free Corn Grits ★, Millet ★, Soy Grits ★
Food Club Brand - Instant Grits Butter Flavored, Quick Grits
Meijer Brand - Butter Flavored Instant, Quick
San Gennaro Foods - Frozen Sharp Cheddar Cheese Grits, Southern Style

Groats
Arrowhead Mills - Buckwheat
Bob's Red Mill ▲ - Organic Buckwheat ★
Chateau Cream Hill Estates - Lara's Oat Groats ●
Montana Monster Munchies - Raw & Sproutable Oat Groats ●
Pocono - Kasha Whole Buckwheat

Ground Beef...see Beef
　... *All Fresh Meat Is Gluten-Free (Non-Marinated, Unseasoned)

Ground Turkey...see Turkey
　... *All Fresh Meat Is Gluten-Free (Non-Marinated, Unseasoned)

G Guacamole...see also Dip/Dip Mix

H

> **Calavo** - Authentic Recipe, Caliente Recipe, Pico De Gallo Recipe
> **Emeril's** - Guacamole Party Dip Mlx
> **Fischer & Wieser** - Guacamole Starter
> **Frontera** - Guacamole Mix (Jar, Mild Pouch, Spicy Pouch)
> **Marzetti** - Regular
> **Ortega** - Guacamole Mix
> **Sabra** - Classic, Spicy
> **Santa Barbara** - Regular
> **Signature Cafe** - Hot, Mild
> **Tostitos** - Dip Creations Freshly Made Dry Dip Mix **!!**
> **Trader Joe's** - Avocado's Number, w/Spicy Pico De Gallo **!!**
> **Wholly** - Classic, Guaca Salsa, Organic, Pico De Gallo, Spicy

Guar Gum

> **AgVantage Naturals** ▲ - Guar Gum ●
> **Bob's Red Mill** ▲ - Guar Gum ★
> **El Peto** ▲ - Guar Gum
> **Gillian's Foods** ▲ - Guar Gum●
> **Grandma Ferdon's** ▲ - Guar Gum ●
> **Nuts.com** - Guar Gum ●
> **Polypro** - Guar Gum

Gum...see Chewing Gum

H

Half & Half...see Milk

Halibut...see Fish

Ham...see also Deli Meat

> Applegate -
>> Deli Counter (Black Forest **!**, Hand Tied Maple **!**, Slow Cooked **!**, Virginia Brand **!**)
>> Deli Meat (Natural (Black Forest **!**, Honey **!**, Slow Cooked **!**), Organic Uncured **!**)
>> Natural Uncured Cooked Capicola **!**

Armour - 1877 (Canadian Maple, Honey Cured, Virginia Brand), Deli (Cooked, Cooked Ham & Water Product, Honey Cured, Lite, Spiced Luncheon Meat, Virginia Brand)

Bar S - Classic Chopped, Deli Shaved (Black Forest, Honey, Smoked), Deli Style (Honey, Smoked), Deli Thin Cut (Honey, Smoked), Extra Lean Cooked, Premium Deli (Honey, Smoked), Steaks (Honey, Smoked)

Boar's Head - All Varieties

Buddig -
Deli Cuts Ham (Baked Honey, Brown Sugar Baked, Smoked)
Fix Quix Smoked Ham Cubes
Original (Brown Sugar Ham, Deli Meat Ham, Honey Ham)

Castle Wood Reserve - Deli Meat (Black Forest Ham, Deluxe Cooked, Honey Ham, Virginia Brand Smoked Ham)

Celebrity - Boneless Cooked

Di Lusso - Deli Counter (Black Forest, Brown Sugar, Deluxe Deli, Double Smoked, Honey Maple, Prosciutto, Smoked Honey Roasted), Spiced

Dietz & Watson ▲ -
Black Forest (Cooked ●, Cured Honey ●, Deep Smoked ●, Smoked ●)
Branded Cooked ●
Breakfast Ham Fillets ●
Brown Sugar & Molasses ●
Cajun ●
Chef Carved Hickory Smoked ●
Chopped ●
Classic Dinner ●
Classic ●
Cooked Round ●
Cubes ●
Deli Counter (Capocolla ●, Prosciutto (American Style ●, Classico ●, Regular ●))
Gourmet Lite (Cooked ●, Cooked ●, Virginia Brand ●, Virginia Ham Decorated ●, Virginia Low Salt ●)

H

Honey Cured (Dinner ●, Tavern ●)
Imported Cooked ●
Maple Glazed ●
Pepper ●
Pre Sliced (Black Forest Smoked ●, Capocolla ●, Cooked ●,
    Gourmet Lite Cooked ●, Imported Tavern ●, Prosciutto (Regular ●,
    Shelf Stable ●), Smoked Maple ●)
Rosemary ●
Semi Boneless Smoked ●
Square Red Pepper ●
Steak (Brown Sugar & Molasses ●, Honey Cured ●, Maple Cured ●,
    Traditional ●)
Tiffany ●
Tomato & Basil ●
Virginia Baked ●
Eating Right - Deli Sliced Honey Ham
Eckrich -
    Deli Meat (Black Forest Brand Nugget, Brown Sugar Nugget,
        Canadian Maple, Chopped, Ham Steak, Honey Cured, Honey
        Maple, Imported, Off The Bone, Smoked Pitt, Spiced Luncheon
        Meat, Spiral Sliced Holiday, Virginia Baked)
    Lunch Meat (Chopped, Virginia Brand Thin Sliced)
Farmer John -
    Gold Wrapped Whole Hams,
    Ham Half (Regular, Spiral Sliced)
    Ham Steaks (Clove, Maple, Original, Pineapple & Mango)
Five Star Brand ▲ - Bavarian, Cottage Ham, Golden Hickory, Honey
    Cured, Lower Sodium Virginia, Spiced Cello
Garrett County Farms - Black Forest (Boneless Nugget ★, Deli ★,
    Sliced ★), Old Fashioned Boneless (Half ★, Whole ★), Semi Boneless
    (Half ★, Whole ★), Sliced Tavern ★, Smoked Ham Shanks ★, Sunday
    Breakfast ★, Turkey Half Ham ★, Virginia Brand (Boneless Steak ★,
    Honey Nugget ★, Sliced Deli ★)

Giant Eagle Brand - Boneless (Half, Quarter, Whole), Ground, Semi Boneless (Half, Whole)

Great Value Brand (Wal-Mart) -
   Canned Ham Luncheon Meat
   Deli Meat (97% Fat Free (Baked Ham Water Added, Cooked Ham Water Added, Honey Ham Water Added), Thinly Sliced Smoked (Ham, Honey Ham))

H-E-B - 45% Lower Sodium Honey, All Natural Chicken Breast Honey Ham Lunchmeat, Applewood Smoked, Black Forest, Bourbon Glazed, Brown Sugar, Ham Tub (Black Forest, Brown Sugar, Honey, Mesquite Smoked, Refill (Honey, Mesquite Smoked)), Honey Mesquite, Old Fashioned Ham Off The Bone, Premium Sliced w/ Natural Juices

Habbersett - Dainty Ham, Ham Slices, Ham Steak

Hill Country Fare H-E-B - Ham (Chopped, Cooked)

Hillshire Farms -
   Deli Select Thin Sliced (Honey Ham, Smoked Ham)
   Deli Select Ultra Thin (Brown Sugar Baked Ham, Honey Ham, Lower Sodium (Honey Ham, Smoked Ham), Smoked Ham)
   Whole/Half (All Flavors)

Hormel -
   Black Label (Canned, Chopped)
   Chunk Meats Ham
   Cure 81 (Brown Sugar Sliced, Sliced, Spiral Sliced, Unsliced Whole)
   Diced
   Ham Patties
   Julienne
   Natural Choice Deli Meat (Brown Sugar, Cooked Deli, Honey Deli, Smoked Deli)

Hy-Vee - 96% Fat Free (Cubed Cooked, Diced Cooked), Cooked Ham, Deli Thin Slices (Honey, Smoked), Thin Sliced (Ham w/ Natural Juices, Honey Ham w/Natural Juices)

Isaly's - All Deli Meat

H

Jones Dairy Farm -
   Deli Style Ham Slices (Honey & Brown Sugar Cured ●, Old Fashioned ●)
   Naturally Hickory Smoked (Dainty Ham ●, Half Family ●, Slices ●,
      Steaks ●, Whole Family ●)
   Whole Hickory Smoked (Country Club ●, Natural Juices ●, Old
      Fashioned Cure ●)
Kayem - Deli Meat (Amber Honey Cured ‼, Black Forest ‼, Carving ‼,
   Honeycrust Baked ‼, Old English Tavern ‼, Peppercrust ‼)
Kirkland Signature -
   Deli Meat (Extra Lean, Smoked Honey)
   Smoked (Applewood Cured Spiral Whole, Hickory Boneless Steak,
      Spiral Sliced Hickory)
Meijer Brand -
   Deli Meat (Double Smoked, Honey Roasted)
   Lunch Meat (Honey Ham 97% Fat Free, Sliced Chipped Meat, Sliced
      Cooked Ham 97% Fat Free)
Open Nature - Deli Honey Ham
Organic Prairie - Frozen Organic Retail Hardwood Smoked Boneless
   Quarter, Organic (Hardwood Smoked Boneless, Hardwood Smoked
   Spiral), Organic Fresh Retail Bone In Spiral Sliced Smoked Half, Pre
   Sliced Deli Meat Hardwood Smoked Uncured
Oscar Mayer -
   Carving Board Deli Meat Slow Cooked
   Deli Fresh (Black Forest, Honey Ham, Smoked Ham)
   Deli Meat (Baked Cooked, Boiled, Chopped, Deli Fresh Smoked Ham,
      Honey, Lower Sodium, Natural Smoked, Smoked, Sub Kit (Ham &
      Beef Salami, Ham & Turkey Breast), Variety Pack Bologna/Chopped
      Ham/White Smoked Turkey)
Primo Taglio - Black Forest Ham w/Natural Juices, Prosciutto Dry Cured
   Ham, Smoked Ham Old Fashioned
Private Selection - Deli Meat Ham (Hickory Smoked, Honey)
Publix - Deli Pre Pack Lunch Meat (Cooked Ham, Extra Thin Sliced Honey
   Ham, Sweet Ham, Tavern Ham), Hickory Smoked Ham Semi Boneless,
   Fully Cooked, Honey Cured Ham w/Brown Sugar Glaze (Bone In Ham,
   Boneless Ham)

Publix GreenWise Market - Deli Pre Pack Sliced Lunch Meat Virginia Brand

Russer - Reduced Sodium Cooked, Smoked Virginia

Safeway - Deli Meat (All Thin Sliced & Regular)

Safeway Brand - Boneless Honey

Safeway Select - 2 lb. Half Boneless

Sara Lee - Deli Meat Slices (Brown Sugar Ham, Honey Ham, Virginia Brand Baked Ham)

Smithfield - All Unflavored Spiral & Glazed Hams *(Except HEB Private Label)*, Country Biscuit Ham Slices, Ham Steak (Boneless, Center Cut, Center Cut, Hickory Smoked), Hickory Smoked Boneless Ham, Hickory Smoked Spiral Sliced, Quarter Ham, Smoked Ham Half Picnic

SPAM - Classic, Hickory Smoke Flavored, Hot & Spicy, Less Sodium, Lite, w/Bacon, w/Cheese

Spartan Brand - Frozen Ham Loaf, Whole Boneless

Taste Of Inspiration - Regular

Underwood - Deviled Ham Spread

Wegmans Brand - Thin Sliced w/Natural Juices (Cooked, Smoked, Smoked Honey)

Wellshire Farms - Black Forest (Boneless Nugget ★, Deli ★, Sliced ★), Old Fashioned Boneless (Half ★, Whole ★), Semi Boneless (Half ★, Whole ★), Sliced Tavern ★, Smoked Ham Shanks ★, Sunday Breakfast ★, Turkey Half Ham ★, Virginia Brand (Boneless Steak ★, Honey Nugget ★, Sliced Deli ★)

Hamburger Buns...see Buns

Hamburgers...see Burgers

*... *All Fresh Meat Is Gluten-Free (Non-Marinated, Unseasoned)*

Hash Browns...see Potatoes

Hearts Of Palm

*... *All Fresh Fruits & Vegetables Are Gluten-Free*

Badia - Canned ●

Native Forest - Organic Hearts Of Palm

Trader Joe's - All Varieties

H Herbal Tea...see Tea

Herbs
  ... *All Fresh Herbs Are Gluten-Free

Hoisin Sauce
  Premier Japan - Wheat Free
  Wok Mei - All Natural Hoisin

Hollandaise Sauce
  Mayacamas - Gourmet Sauce ★
  Simply Organic - Hollandaise Sauce Mix ●

Hominy
  Bush's Best - Golden, White
  Food Club Brand - Canned White
  Hy-Vee - Golden, White
  Lowes Foods Brand - White
  Meijer Brand - White
  Safeway Brand - Golden, White
  Spartan Brand - Golden, White
  Winn Dixie - Golden, White

Honey
  Food Club Brand - Honey
  Gordon Food Service - Pure Honey
  Great Value Brand (Wal-Mart) - Clover Honey
  Hannaford Brand - All Varieties
  Hy-Vee - Honey, Honey Squeeze Bear
  Kirkland Signature - Clover
  Lowes Foods Brand - Squeeze Bear
  Meijer Brand - Honey, Honey Squeeze Bear
  Publix - Clover, Orange Blossom, Wildflower
  Publix GreenWise Market - Organic Honey
  Safeway Select - Clover Honey
  Shiloh Farms - Raw Alfalfa
  Spartan Brand - Regular
  Trader Joe's - All Varieties
  Tropical Traditions - Canadian Raw Honey

Virginia Brand - 100% All Natural

Wegmans Brand - Clover, Orange Blossom, Squeezeable Bear

Winn Dixie

Honey Mustard Sauce...see Mustard

Horseradish Sauce

Baxters

Beaver - Cream Style ●, Deli ●, Extra Hot ●, Kosher (Beet ●, Hot ●),
Regular ●, Wasabi ●, Whipped ●

Di Lusso - Regular

Dietz & Watson ▲ - Cranberry ●, Hot & Chunky ●, Red ●, Smoky ●

Follow Your Heart - Horseradish Sauce !

Heinz - Horseradish Sauce

Inglehoffer - Cream Style ●, Extra Hot ●, Wasabi ●

Lou's Famous - Horseradish Organic

Manischewitz - All Varieties

Melissa's - Cream Style

Mezzetta ▲ - Cream Style Horseradish

Royal Food Products - Royal Deluxe (w/Real Horseradish, Zesty)

Simply Delicious - Organic Creamed Horseradish

Wegmans Brand - Horseradish Cream, Prepared Horseradish

Woeber's - Sandwich Pal Horseradish Sauce

Hot Chocolate Mix...see Cocoa Mix/Powder

Hot Dog Buns...see Buns

Hot Dogs...see Sausage

Hot Sauce

Amore - Hot Pepper Paste

Badia - Caribbean Heat (Chili Pepper ●, Habanero Pepper ●),
Louisiana Cajun ●

Bone Suckin' Sauce - Habanero Sauce

Dave's Gourmet - Adjustable Heat, Cool Cayenne Pepper, Crazy
Caribbean, Ginger Peach, Hot Sauce & Garden Spray, Hurtin'
Habanero, Hurtin' Jalapeño, Insanity Sauce, Jammin' Jerk Sauce &
Marinade, Jump Up & Kiss Me (Chipotle, Original, Passion Fruit),

H

Roasted Garlic, Roasted Red Pepper & Chipotle, Scotch Bonnet,
Temporary Insanity, Total Insanity, Ultimate Insanity

Emeril's - Kick It Up Green Sauce

Food Club Brand - Louisiana

Frank's RedHot - Chile 'N Lime, Original, Sweet Chili, Thick, Xtra Hot

Frontera - Hot Sauce (Chipotle, Habanero, Jalapeno, Red Pepper)

Hannaford Brand

Jim Beam - Original

Ka-Me - Sriracha !, Sweet Chili !

La Victoria - Chunky Jalapeno, Salsa Brava

Mezzetta - California Habanero, California Hot Sauce

Mr. Spice Organic - Tangy Bang ★

Mrs. Renfro's - Mexican Hot Sauce, Mexican Mild Sauce

Organicville - Sriracha Sauce ●

Peppadew ▲ - Splash On

Sauza - Fiery Tequila

Scorned Woman - Chipotle & Garlic Pepper, Original

Texas Pete - Chipotle, Garlic, Hotter Hot, Original

The Wizard's - Hot Stuff

Trader Joe's - Jalapeno

Trappey's - Bull Brand Louisiana Hot Sauce, Chef Magic Jalapeno
Sauce, Indi Pep Pepper Sauce, Louisiana Hot Sauce, Mexi Pep Hot
Sauce, Pepper Sauce, Red Devil Cayenne Pepper Sauce

Winn Dixie - Louisiana Hot

Hummus

Athenos - Hummus (Artichoke & Garlic, Black Olive, Cucumber Dill,
Greek Style, Original, Pesto, Roasted (Eggplant, Garlic, Red Pepper),
Scallion, Spicy Three Pepper)

Casbah - Hummus

Cedar's - Hommus (Garden Vegetable, Garlic Lovers, Horseradish,
Organic (Garlic Lovers, Original, Red Pepper), Original Tahini,
Roasted Red Chili Pepper, Roasted Red Pepper, Sundried Tomato &
Basil, Zesty Lemon)

Eating Right - Garlic, Roasted Red Pepper, Traditional

Fantastic World Foods - Original Hummus

Flamous Brands - Hummus Dressing & Dip (All Varieties)

H-E-B - Four Pepper, Mediterranean Olive, Roasted (Garlic, Red Pepper), Traditional

Marzetti - Southwest Chipotle

Melissa's - Roasted Red Pepper, Traditional

Private Selection - Garlic Chive, Regular, Roasted Red Pepper

Pure Market Express ▲ - Hummus & Onion Bread ●

Sabra - Hummus (Basil & Pesto, Buffalo Style, Chipotle, Classic, Greek Olive, Jalapeno, Luscious Lemon, Roasted Garlic, Roasted Pine Nut, Roasted Red Pepper, Spinach & Artichoke, Sun Dried Tomato, Supremely Spicy, Tahini)

Salpica - Chipotle Hummus Dip

Trader Joe's - Chipotle Pepper **!**, Edamame **!**, Garlic **!**, Kalamata Olive **!!**, Mediterranean **!!**, Organic **!**, Original **!**, Roasted Garlic**!**, Smooth & Creamy (Cilantro & Jalapeno, Classic Rice Bread Mix, Roasted Red Pepper, Spicy), Three Layer **!!**, Tomato & Basil **!!**, w/Freshly Ground Horseradish **!!**

Tribe ▲ -
Organic (Classic, Roasted Garlic, Sweet Roasted Red Peppers)
Original Blended (Classic, Cracked Chili Peppers, Forty Spices, Horseradish, Jalapeno, Kalamata Olive, Roasted Eggplant, Roasted Garlic, Spicy Chipotle, Sundried Tomato & Basil, Sweet Roasted Red Peppers, Zesty Lemon)
With Toppings (Cilantro Chimichurri, Mediterranean Style, Olive Tapenade, Roasted Vegetable, Savory Mushroom, Spicy Red Pepper, Zesty Spice & Garlic)

Wild Garden - Black Olive, Fire Roasted Red Pepper, Jalapeno, Roasted Garlic, Sun Dried Tomato, Traditional

Wildwood - Organic Emerald Valley (Greek Olive & Garlic, Roasted Red Pepper, Smoked Jalapeno & Garlic, Traditional)

I

Ice Cream...see also Popsicles and/or Sorbet

Breyer's -

All Natural (Butter Almond, Butter Pecan, Caramel Praline Crunch, Chocolate (Black Raspberry, Crackle, Extra Creamy, Regular, Triple), Chocolate Chip, Coffee, Dulche De Leche, Lactose Free Vanilla, Mint Chocolate Chip, Peach, Rocky Road, Strawberry, Vanilla (Caramel, Cherry, Chocolate, Chocolate Strawberry, Extra Creamy, French, Fudge Twirl, Homemade, Regular))

Blasts (Heath Toffee Bar, Reese's Peanut Butter Cups, Snickers Caramel Swirl Chunk)

Carb Smart (Bar (Fudge, Vanilla, Vanilla & Almond), Chocolate,Vanilla)

No Sugar Added (Butter Pecan, Vanilla, Vanilla Chocolate Strawberry)

Smooth & Dreamy Bars Chocolate (Covered Strawberry, Triple Chip)

Smooth & Dreamy Fat Free (Creamy Vanilla, French Chocolate, Strawberry)

Smooth & Dreamy Half Fat (Butter Pecan, Chocolate (Chocolate Chip, Creamy, Dark Velvet), Mint Chocolate Chip, Rocky Road, Strawberry Cheesecake, Vanilla (Bean, Chocolate Strawberry, Creamy))

Chapman's - *(All Flavors Must Say 'Sans Gluten Free')* Blueberry Cheesecake, Butterscotch Ripple, Chocolate (& Vanilla, Caramel, Ripple), Cookies & Cream, Dutch Chocolate, Maple Twist, Mint Chip, Neapolitan, Orange Pineapple, Peppermint Stick, Raspberry Ripple, Rum & Raisin, Strawberry (Banana, Regular), Swiss Mocca, Tiger Tail, Vanilla (Canadian Eh, Cherry, Chip, French, Regular)

ChocAlive ▲ - Ice Cream All Flavors

Clemmy's -

Novelties (Bars (Cherry Vanilla !, Chocolate Fudge !, Orange Creme !, Strawberries 'N Creme !), Ice Cream O's)

Pint (Butter Pecan, Chocolate, Chocolate Chip, Coffee, Orange Creme, Peanut Butter Chocolate Chip, Toasted Almond, Vanilla Bean)

Double Rainbow - Coffee Blast **!!**, Dulce De Leche **!!**, French Vanilla **!!**, It's A Goody **!!**, Mint Chocolate Chip **!!**, Perfectly Pumpkin **!!**, Soy Cream (Blueberry **!!**, Cinnamon Caramel **!!**, Mint Chocolate Chip **!!**, Vanilla Bean **!!**, Very Cherry Chip **!!**), Strawberry **!!**, Ultra Chocolate **!!**

Dove -

All Pints *(Except Chocolate & Brownie Affair)*

Dark Chocolate Ice Cream Bar w/(Almonds, Chocolate Ice Cream, Vanilla Ice Cream)

Milk Chocolate Ice Cream Bar w/Vanilla Ice Cream

Miniature Ice Cream Bars

Dreyer's -

Fruit Bars Orange & Cream

Fun Flavors (Butter Pecan, Chocolate Peanut Butter Cup, Dulce De Leche, Mocha Almond Fudge, Spumoni)

Grand (Chocolate (Chip, Regular), Coffee, Double Vanilla, French Vanilla, Mint Chocolate Chip, Neapolitan, Real Strawberry, Rocky Road, Vanilla (Bean, Chocolate, Regular))

Sherbet (Berry Rainbow, Orange Cream, Tropical Rainbow)

Slow Churned Rich & Creamy (Butter Pecan, Caramel Delight, Chocolate (Chip, Regular), Coffee, French Vanilla, Fudge Tracks, Mint Chocolate Chip, Neapolitan, No Sugar Added (Butter Pecan, Coffee, French Vanilla, Fudge Tracks, Mint Chocolate Chip, Neapolitan, Triple Chocolate, Vanilla, Vanilla Bean), Peanut Butter Cup, Rocky Road, Shakes (Chocolate, Strawberry, Vanilla), Smoothies (Mixed Berry, Strawberry Banana, Sunrise Blend, Tropical), Strawberry, Vanilla, Vanilla Bean Regular)

Yogurt Blends (Black Cherry Vanilla Swirl, Cappucino Chip, Caramel Praline Crunch, Chocolate Vanilla Swirl, Key Lime, Peach, Vanilla (Fat Free, Original))

Edy's -

Fun Flavors (Butter Pecan, Chocolate Peanut Butter Cup, Dulce De Leche, Espresso Chip, Mocha Almond Fudge, Spumoni)

Grand (Chocolate, Chocolate Chip, Coffee, Double Vanilla,
French Vanilla, Mint Chocolate Chip, Neapolitan, Real
Strawberry, Rocky Road, Vanilla, Vanilla Bean, Vanilla Chocolate)

Sherbet (Berry Rainbow, Orange Cream, Tropical Rainbow)

Slow Churned Rich & Creamy (Butter Pecan, Caramel Delight,
Chocolate, Chocolate Chip, Coffee, French Vanilla, Fudge
Tracks, Mint Chocolate Chip, Mocha Almond Fudge,
Neapolitan, No Sugar Added (Butter Pecan, French Vanilla,
Fudge Tracks, Mint Chocolate Chip, Neapolitan, Triple
Chocolate, Vanilla, Vanilla Bean), Peanut Butter Cup, Rocky
Road, Strawberry, Vanilla, Vanilla Bean, Yogurt Blends (Black
Cherry Vanilla Swirl, Cappucino Chip, Caramel Praline Crunch,
Fat Free Vanilla, Peach, Vanilla))

Food Club Brand -

Ice Cream (Butter Pecan, Chocolate, Neapolitan, Peppermint,
Strawberry, Vanilla)

Novelties (Fudge Bar, Ice Cream Bar)

Sherbet (Cherry, Lime, Orange, Pineapple, Rainbow, Raspberry)

Gaga - Sherbetter (Chocolate, Key Lime, Lemon, Orange, Rainbow,
Raspberry, Toasted Coconut)

GlutenFreeda ▲ - Julie's Organic Ice Cream & Glutenfreeda's Ice
Cream Cookie Sandwiches

GlutenOut - Coni Gelato (Fiordilatte ★, Vaniglia/Nocciola ★)

Good Karma -

Chocolate Covered Bars (Chocolate Chocolate, Very Vanilla)

Organic Rice Divine (Banana Fudge, Carrot Cake, Chocolate
Chip, Chocolate Peanut Butter Fudge, Coconut Mango, Key
Lime Pie, Mint Chocolate Swirl, Mudd Pie, Very Cherry, Very
Vanilla)

Haagen-Dazs -

Bars (Chocolate Dark Chocolate, Coffee Almond Crunch Snack
Size, Vanilla Dark Chocolate, Vanilla Milk Chocolate, Vanilla
Milk Chocolate Almonds)

Five (Caramel, Coffee, Lemon, Milk Chocolate, Mint, Strawberry,
Vanilla Bean)

Frozen Yogurt (Coffee, Vanilla, Vanilla Raspberry Swirl)
Ice Cream (Banana Split, Butter Pecan, Cherry Vanilla, Chocolate,
  Chocolate Chocolate Chip, Chocolate Peanut Butter, Coffee,
  Creme Brulée, Dark Chocolate, Dulce De Leche, Green Tea,
  Java Chip, Mango, Mint Chip, Pineapple Coconut, Pistachio,
  Rocky Road, Rum Raisin, Strawberry, Vanilla, Vanilla Bean,
  Vanilla Chocolate Chip, Vanilla Swiss Almond)

Hannaford Brand -
Bars (Artic, Fudge, Ice Cream, Orange Cream)
Black Cherry
Butter Pecan
Chocolate
Chocolate Chip
Churn Style Light (Black Raspberry, Butter Pecan, Chocolate,
  Vanilla)
Frozen Yogurt (Black Cherry, Peach, Vanilla)
Fudge Sticks (No Sugar Added, Regular)
Heavenly Hash
Maple Walnut
No Sugar (Butter Pecan, Vanilla)
Strawberry
Strawberry Cheesecake
Three Flavors (Neapolitan)
Tin Roof
Vanilla (Chocolate, French, Fudge, Regular)

Hood -
Frozen Novelty Items (Hoodsie (Cups, Sundae Cups), Ice Cream
  Bar, Karnival Stix, Orange Cream Bar)
Frozen Yogurt Fat Free (Chocolate, Mane Blueberry & Sweet
  Cream, Mocha Fudge, Strawberry, Strawberry Banana, Vanilla)
New England Creamery (Boston Vanilla Bean, Colonial Chocolate
  Almond, Homemade Vanilla, Light (Chocolate Chip, Coffee,
  Martha's Vineyard Black Raspberry, Vanilla), Maine Blueberry &
  Sweet Cream, Martha's Vineyard Black Raspberry, Rhode Island

Lighthouse Coffee, Sherbet (Black Raspberry, Orange, Rainbow, Wildberry), Vermont Maple Nut, White Gold (Limited Edition))

Red Sox Grand Slam Vanilla

Regular (Butter Pecan, Chocolate, Chocolate Chip, Classic Trio, Creamy Coffee, Fudge Twister, Golden Vanilla, Maple Walnut, Natural Vanilla Bean, Patchwork, Strawberry)

Horizon Organic - All Varieties

Hy-Vee -

Ice Cream (Fudge Bars (Fat Free, No Sugar Added), Galaxy Reduced Fat (Orange, Regular), Pop (Cherry, Grape, Orange, Root Beer), Sundae Cups (Chocolate & Strawberry, Sherbet, Vanilla))

Ice Cream Cup Single Serve Chocolate Chip

Regular (Butter Crunch, Cherry Nut (Light, Regular), Chocolate (Chip (Light, Regular), Marshmallow, Regular, Vanilla Flavored), Dutch Chocolate Light, Fudge Marble, Lime Sherbet, Mint Chip, Neapolitan (Light, Regular), New York Vanilla, Orange Sherbet, Root Beer Float, Sherbet (Lime, Orange, Pineapple, Rainbow, Raspberry), Star Tracks, Strawberry, Vanilla (Light, Regular))

It's Soy Delicious - Fruit Sweetened Non Dairy Frozen Dessert (Almond Pecan ●, Awesome Chocolate ●, Chocolate Almond ●, Chocolate Peanut Butter ●, Green Tea ●, Raspberry ●, Vanilla ●)

IttiBitz - Banana Split, Cotton Candy, Mint Chip, Neapolitan

Jamba - Novelty Bars (Coconut Pineapple Passion Smashin' !, Peach Blackberry Smash !, Strawberry Lemonade Swirl !, Vanilla Blueberry Pomegranate Perfection !, Vanilla Strawberry Jubilation !)

Jell-O - X Treme Chocolate Pudding Sticks

Kemps -

Bear Creek Caramel

Black (Jack Cherry, Raspberry Swirl)

Caramel Cow Tracks

Caribou Coffee (Java Chunk, Light Java Chunk)

Cherry Fudge Chunk

Chocolate (Almond Cluster, Chip, Monster, Regular)

Cotton Candy

Family Size (Chocolate, Chocolate & Vanilla, Chocolate Chip, Chocolate Marshmallow, Chocolate Swirl, Mint Chocolate Chip, Neapolitan, New York Vanilla, Strawberry Swirl, Tin Roof Sundae, Vanilla)

Frozen Novelties (Float Bars, Fudge Jr.'s, Moo Jr.'s, Orange Cream Bars, Sugar Free Pop Jr.'s)

Frozen Yogurt (Chocolate Chip, Dark Chocolate Almond, Fat Free (Black Raspberry Swirl, Blueberries & Cream, Caramel Praline Crunch, Chocolate, Peach, Strawberry, Strawberry Banana, Vanilla), Low Fat (Black Jack Cherry, Chocolate, Mint Chocolate Chip, Strawberry, Vanilla), Moose Tracks, No Sugar Added Fat Free Vanilla)

FroZing Frozen Yogurt (Mango Peach, Pomegranate Blueberry, Raspberry Vanilla, Vanilla)

Fudge Bars

Gone Fishin'

Homemade Vanilla

Light (French Silk Chocolate, Mint Chocolate Chip, Vanilla)

Maple Nut

Mint (Chocolate Chip, Cow Tracks, Fudge)

Moose Tracks

Neapolitan

New York Vanilla

Old Fashioned (All Natural Vanilla, Blueberries 'N Sweet Cream, Butter Pecan, Chocolate, Chocolate Chip, French Vanilla, Homemade Vanilla, Neapolitan, New York Vanilla, Peppermint Bon Bon, Strawberries 'N Cream, Toasted Almond Fudge, Vanilla, Vanilla Custard)

Orange Cream Dream

Pecan Turtle Trail

Pink Peppermint

Raspberry Cow Tracks

Rocky Road

Sherbet (Lemon, Lime, Orange, Pineapple, Rainbow, Raspberry, Wild Strawberry)

Singles (Cherry Fudge Chunk, Cow Tracks Caramel, Frozen Yogurt
Parfait (Strawberries 'N Cream, White Chocolate Raspberry, Wild
Blueberry, Wildberry), Gone Fishing, Java Chunk, Pecan Turtle Trail)

Strawberry

Tin Roof Sundae

Turtle Tracks

Under the Stars

Vanilla (Bean, Regular)

Kirkland Signature - Vanilla !

Lactaid - Butter Pecan, Chocolate, Strawberry & Cream, Vanilla

Larry & Luna's Coconut Bliss -

Bars (Dark Chocolate Bars, Naked Coconut Bars)

Ice Cream (Cappuccino, Cherry Amaretto, Chocolate
Hazelnut Fudge, Chocolate Peanut Butter, Chocolate Walnut
Brownie, Dark Chocolate, Ginger Cookie Caramel, Lunaberry
Swirl, Mint Galactica, Mocha Maca Crunch, Naked Almond Fudge,
Naked Coconut, Pineapple Coconut, Vanilla Island)

Lifeway - Frozen Kefir

Living Harvest - Tempt Frozen Desserts (All Varieties)

Lowes Foods Brand -

Bars (Fudge, Ice Cream, Orange Cream)

Cups (Swirls, Vanilla)

Lite (Chocolate, Neapolitan, Vanilla)

Premium (Butter Pecan (Light, Regular), Mint Chocolate Chip,
Moose Tracks, Peach, Peanut Butter Cup, Rocky Road Light)

Regular (Butter Pecan, Chocolate, Fudge Swirl, Mint Chocolate
Chip, Neopolitan, Vanilla (Bean, Cherry, French, Regular))

Sherbet (Lime, Orange, Rainbow, Raspberry)

Lucerne -

Bars (Creamy Orange, Fudge, Krunch, Root Beer Float, Sundae)

Creamery Fresh (Black and White, Butter Pecan Light, Dutch
Chocolate, Light Vanilla, Mint Chocolate Chip, Mint Chocolate
Chip Light, Ranch Pecan, Rocky Road, Vanilla)

Regular (Chocolate, Chocolate Chip, French Vanilla, Mint Chip, Neopolitan, Rocky Road, Strawberry, Vanilla Low Fat)

Medifast - Soft Serve (Chocolate Mint ●, Coffee ●, Mango ●, Peanut Butter ●)

Meijer Brand -

Black Cherry

Brr Bar

Butter Pecan (Gold Georgian Bay, Lite No Sugar Added w/Splenda, Original)

Candy Bar Swirl

Carmel Pecan Crunch Fat Free No Sugar Added

Chocolate (Bordeaux Cherry, Carb Conquest, Chip, Mint (Chip, Original), Original, Peanut Butter Fudge, Thunder)

Combo Cream (Birthday Cake, Cotton Candy (Confetti, Original), Dream Bars, Dulce De Leche, Fudge Bars (No Sugar Added, Original), Fudge Swirl, Gold (Caramel Toffee Swirl, Double Nut Chocolate, Peanut Butter Fudge Swirl, Peanut Butter Fudge Tracks, Thunder Bay Cherry), Heavenly Hash)

Ice Cream Bars

Mackinaw Fudge

Mint Moosetrack

Neapolitan (Lite, Original)

Novelties (Gold Bar, Toffee Bar)

Peanut Butter Fudge

Peppermint

Praline Pecan

Scooperman

Sherbet (Cherry, Lemonberry Twist, Lime, Orange, Pineapple, Rainbow, Raspberry)

Tin Roof

Toffee Bars

Vanilla (Carb Conquest, Fat Free No Sugar Added w/Splenda, Gold Victorian, Golden, Lite No Sugar Added w/Splenda, Original)

Strawberry (Awesome, Totally Awesome)

Midwest Country Fare - Chocolate (Chip, Regular), Neapolitan, New York Vanilla, Vanilla (Lite, Regular)

My Essentials - Sundae Cups

NadaMoo - Creamy Coconut ●, Gotta Do Chocolate ●, Java Crunch●, Lotta Mint Chip ●, Mmm Maple Pecan ●, Vanilla Ahhh ●

Nature's Place - All Varieties

North Star -
  Bars (Banana Creams **!!**, Fat Free Fudge **!!**, Fudge **!!**, Health Wise Fat Free No Sugar Added Fudge Bar **!!**, Ice Cream **!!**, Orange Dream **!!**, Premium English Toffee **!!**, Premium Old Recipe **!!**, Star Lite Reduced Fat **!!**)
  Lotta Pops Fudge **!!**
  Popsicles Lotta **!!**
  Specialty (King Size Root Beer Float **!!**, Vanilla Slice **!!**)
  Sundae Ice Cream Cups (Chocolate **!!**, Chocolate Strawberry **!!**, Strawberry **!!**, Vanilla **!!**)

Open Nature - Cherry Vanilla, Milk Chocolate Caramel, Mint Chip, Strawberry, Vanilla Bean

Organic Nectars - All Flavors Of Cashew Gelato

Organicville - Organic Low Fat Ice Cream (Caramel Swirl ●, Chocolate ●, Dark Chocolate ●, Mint Chocolate Chip ●, Strawberry ●, Strawberry Banana ●, Vanilla ●, Vanilla Bean ●)

Prairie Farms -
  Classic (Chocolate, Chocolate Chip, French Vanilla, Mint Chip, Vanilla)
  Frozen Yogurt (Chocolate, Strawberry, Vanilla)
  Ice Cream Vanilla Orange
  Old Recipe (Belgian Chocolate, French Vanilla, Vanilla Regular)
  Sherbet (All Flavors)

Prestige - Chocolate, Chocolate Almond, Vanilla

Publix -
  Ice Cream (Chocolate (Marshmallow, Regular), Fudge Royal, Neapolitan, Vanilla)
  Low Fat Frozen Yogurt (Black Jack Cherry, Butter Pecan, Chocolate, Peach, Peanut Butter Cup, Strawberry, Vanilla)

Low Fat Ice Cream (Chocolate, Fudge Royal, Neapolitan, Vanilla)

Novelties (Fudge (Bar, Sundae Cups), Ice Cream Bar, Ice Cream Squares Regular, No Sugar Added Ice Cream Bars, Vanilla Cups)

Premium (Banana Split, Bear Claw, Black Jack Cherry, Butter Pecan, Cherry Nut, Chocolate (Almond, Cherish Passion, Chip, Regular), Coffee Almond Fudge, Dulce De Leche, French Vanilla, Heavenly Hash, Homemade Vanilla, Mint Chocolate Chip, Neapolitan, Otter Paws Peanut Butter Goo Goo, Strawberry, Vanilla)

Premium Light (Butter Pecan, Chocolate, Coffee Almond Fudge, Neapolitan, Strawberry, Vanilla)

Premium Limited Editon (Peppermint Stick, Rum Raisin)

Sherbet (Cool Lime, Exotic Fruit Medley, Peach Mango Passion, Rainbow Dream, Raspberry Blush, Sunny Orange (No Sugar Added, Regular), Tropic Pineapple)

Pure Market Express ▲ - Ice Cream (Cherry Chocolate Chip●, Chocolate ●, Chocolate Fudge Brownie ●, Coffee ●, Cookie Dough●, French Vanilla ●, Maple ●, Maple Nut ●, Mocha ●, Peanut Butter Cup ●, Strawberry ●)

Purely Decadent -

Coconut Milk Ice Cream (Chocolate ●, Mint Chip ●, Passionate Mango ●, Vanilla Bean ●)

Dairy Free Ice Cream (Belgian Chocolate ●, Cherry Nirvana ●, Chocolate Obsession ●, Cookie Dough ●, Dulce De Leche ●, Mint Chip ●, Mocha Almond Fudge ●, Peanut Butter Zig Zag●, Pomegranate Chip ●, Praline Pecan ●, Purely Vanilla ●, Turtle Trails ●)

Rice Dream - Non Dairy Frozen Desserts (Carob Almond, Cocoa Marble Fudge, Neapolitan, Orange Vanilla Swirl, Strawberry, Vanilla)

Safeway Select -

Churned Moose Tracks

Churned Light (Butter Pecan, Caramel Caribou, Chocolate Moose Tracks, Mint Chocolate Chip, Rocky Road, Strawberry, Vanilla, Vanilla Bean)

Premium (Black Cherry, Black Walnut, Butter Pecan, Chocolate, Coconut Pineapple, Dolce De Leche, French Vanilla, Neapolitan, Rocky Road, Vanilla)

Regular Moose Tracks Chocolate

Sherbet (Berry Patch, Key Lime, Mandarin Orange, Orange Chocolate Chip, Pineapple Raspberry Orange, Strawberry Kiwi)

So Delicious -

Coconut Milk Ice Cream (Chocolate Peanut Butter Swirl ●, Coconut ●, Coconut Almond Chip ●, Cookie Dough ●, German Chocolate ●, Green Tea ●, Pomegranate Chip ●, Swiss Almond ●, Turtle Trails ●)

Coconut Water Sorbet (Hibiscus ●, Lemonade ●, Mango ●, Raspberry●)

Creamy Orange Dairy Free Bars ●

Minis Bar (Dairy Free Fruit Bars Strawberry ●, Made w/Coconut Milk (Coconut Almond ●, Fudge ●, Vanilla ●))

No Sugar Added Bar (Fudge, Vanilla)

No Sugar Added Dairy Free Ice Cream (Butter Pecan ●, Chocolate ●, Mint Chip ●, Toasted Almond Chip ●, Vanilla Bean ●)

Organic Dairy Free Ice Cream (Butter Pecan ●, Chocolate Peanut Butter ●, Chocolate Velvet ●, Creamy Vanilla ●, Dulce De Leche ●, Mint Marble Fudge ●, Mocha Fudge ●, Neapolitan ●, Strawberry ●)

Soy Dream - Non Dairy Frozen Desserts (Butter Pecan !, French Vanilla !, Green Tea !, Mocha Fudge !, Vanilla (Fudge !, Regular !))

Spartan Brand - All American Cherry, Black Cherry, Butter Pecan, Golden Vanilla, Light Churn (Butter Pecan, Chocolate, Moose Tracks, Vanilla), Moose Tracks (Chocolate, Regular), Vanilla

Sweet Nothings - Non Dairy Bars (Fudge ●, Mango Raspberry ●)

The Skinny Cow -

Bars (Caramel Truffle ●, Chocolate Truffle ●, French Vanilla Truffle ●, Fudge ●, Mini Fudge Pops ●, White Mint Truffle ●)

Cups (Dulce De Leche ●, Strawberry Cheesecake ●)

Tillamook - Old Fashioned Vanilla !!, Peppermint Candy !!

Trader Joe's -
> Ice Cream Bars (Mango Vanilla, Raspberry Vanilla)
> Soy Creamy (Cherry Chocolate Chip, Organic Vanilla)
> Super Premium Ice Cream (French Vanilla, Golden Caramel Swirl, Mint Chocolate, Peanut Butter, Ultra Chocolate)

Wegmans Brand -
> Black Raspberry
> Chocolate (Chip, Marshmallow, Regular, Vanilla)
> Creme De Menthe
> Egg Nog Flavored
> French Vanilla
> Hazelnut Chip Coffee
> Heavenly Hash
> Ice Cream Bars (Cherry w/Dark Chocolate, Fudge (No Sugar Added, Regular), Vanilla & Dark Chocolate Premium)
> Ice Cream Cups (Peanut Butter Candy, Peanut Butter Cup)
> Low Fat (Cappuccino Chip, Mint Chip, Praline Pecan, Raspberry Truffle, Vanilla)
> Maple Walnut
> Neapolitan (All Natural, Regular)
> Peak Of Perfection (Black Cherry, Mango)
> Peanut Butter (Cup, Sundae, Swirl)
> Premium (Butter Pecan, Cherry Armagnac, Chocolate, Chocolate Caramel, Coconut Mango, Coffee Explosion, Creamy Caramel, Creme Brulee, Dark Chocolate, French Roast, French Vanilla, Hazelnut Chip, Jamocha Almond Fudge, Mint Chocolate Chip, Peanut Butter & Jelly, Peanut Butter Cup, Pistachio, Rum Raisin, Strawberry, Vanilla, Vanilla Fudge)
> Raspberry Cashew Swirl
> Strawberry
> Tin Roof
> Vanilla (Pistachio Swirl, Raspberry Sorbet, Regular, w/Orange Sherbet)

Weight Watchers -
  Bars (Chocolate Dipped Strawberry, Dark Chocolate Raspberry,
    Dark Chocolate Raspberry Cheesecake, Snack Size Chocolate
    Fudge, Strawberry Smoothie)
  Giant Bars (Chocolate Fudge, Latte, Wildberry & Orange Sorbet
    And Ice Cream)
  Mint Chocolate Chip Cups
WholeSoy & Co. - All Frozen Yogurts **! !**
Winn Dixie - Banana Pops, Classic (Chocolate, Neapolitan, Strawberry,
  Vanilla), Fudge Bars, Ice Cream Bars, Orange Cream Bars
Ice Cream Cones...see Cones
Ice Cream Toppings...see also Syrup
  A & W - Root Beer Float Dessert Topper
  Dr. Pepper - Cherry Dessert Topper
  Eating Right -
    Frozen Yogurt (Black Cherry Chocolate Chip, Chocolate, Vanilla)
    Vanilla No Sugar Lite
  Gordon Food Service - Butterscotch, Caramel, Mallow, Pineapple,
    Strawberry, Wild Cherry
  Hershey's - Chocolate Syrup (Lite, Regular, Special Dark)
  Jelly Belly - Toasted Marshmallow Dessert Topper, Very Cherry Dessert
    Topper
  KatySweet ▲ -
    Caramel ●
    Crumbles (Praline ●, Toffee ●)
    Organic Crumbles (Praline ●, Toffee ●)
    Saucy Stuff (Organic Caramel ●, Organic Pralines w/Pecans ●,
      Pralines w/Pecans ●)
  Melissa's - Dessert Sauces (Caramel, Chocolate, Kiwi Lime, Mango,
    Raspberry, White Chocolate)
  Mr. Sprinkles - Rainbow
  Mrs. May's Naturals - Fruit & Nut Toppers (Blueberry Almond ●,
    Cranberry Almond ●, Raspberry Almond ●, Strawberry Almond ●)
  Orange Crush - Orange & Vanilla Cream Dessert Topper

I

J

Smucker's ▲ -
- Black Cherry
- Magic Shell (Caramel, Chocolate, Chocolate Fudge, Cupcake, Orange Creme)
- Microwaveable (Hot Caramel, Hot Fudge)
- Plate Scrapers Dessert Topping (Caramel, Chocolate, Chocolate Fudge, Lime, Raspberry, Strawberry, Vanilla)
- Special Recipe (Butterscotch, Dark Chocolate, Hot Fudge, Milk Chocolate, Triple Berry)
- Sugar Free (Caramel, Hot Fudge, Strawberry)
- Sugar Free Sundae Syrup (Caramel, Chocolate)
- Sundae Syrups (Butterscotch, Caramel, Chocolate, Strawberry)
- Toppings (Apple Cinnamon, Blueberry, Butterscotch, Chocolate Fudge, Hot Caramel, Hot Fudge, Marshmallow, Pecans In Syrup, Pineapple, Strawberry, Walnuts In Syrup)

Stuckey's - Pecan Log Roll Dessert Topper

Iced Tea/Iced Tea Mix...see Tea

Icing...see Baking Decorations & Frostings

Instant Coffee...see Coffee

J

Jalapenos

... *All Fresh Fruits & Vegetables Are Gluten-Free

Chi-Chi's -   Green Jalapenos (Wheels, Whole), Red

Dietz & Watson ▲ - Sliced ●, Spread ●

Embasa - Nacho Sliced, Sliced, Whole

Food Club Brand - Sliced

Great Value Brand (Wal-Mart) - Sliced Jalapenos En Rajas, Whole Jalapenos

Las Palmas - Sliced, Whole

Mezzetta ▲ - Deli Sliced (Hot Jalapeno Peppers, Tamed Jalapeno Peppers), Gourmet Deli (Sweet & Hot Jalapeno Pepper Rings, Tamed Diced Jalapeno Peppers, Tamed Fire Roasted w/Chipotle Peppers)

J

Mt. Olive ▲ - Diced Jalapeno Peppers, Jalapeno Slices
Old El Paso - Pickled Slices
Ortega - Diced, Sliced
Safeway Brand - Sliced Regular
Trappey's - Sliced, Whole
Winn Dixie - Regular

Jalfrezi Sauce
  Seeds Of Change - Jalfrezi Sauce **! !**
  Sharwood's - Jalfrezi Sauce

Jam/Jelly
  Baxters -
    Conserve (Country Berry, Raspberry, Rhubarb & Ginger, Strawberry)
    Jelly (Cranberry, Mint, Red Currant)
    Marmalade (Lemon, Orange Lemon & Grapefruit, Seville Orange)
  Bonne Maman -
    Jelly (Blackberry, Blackcurrant, Grape, Redcurrant)
    Preserves (Apricot, Apricot Raspberry, Blackberry, Cherry, Fig, Four
      Points, Mandarin, Mixed Berries, Orange Marmalade, Peach, Plum,
      Raspberry, Strawberry, Wild Blueberry)
  Central Market H-E-B - Organic Preserve (Apricot, Blueberry, Morello
    Cherry, Raspberry, Strawberry)
  Eden Organic - Butter (Apple, Apple Cherry, Cherry)
  Fischer & Wieser -
    Apple Pecan Butter
    Jam (Almond Cherry Jubilee, Original Roasted Raspberry Chipotle)
    Jelly (Mild Green Jalapeno, Red Hot Jalapeno)
    Marmalade (Apricot Orange, Whole Lemon Fig)
    Peach Pecan Butter
    Preserves (Amaretto Peach Pecan, Jalapeno Peach, Old Fashioned
      Peach, Southern Style, Strawberry Rhubarb)
    Pumpkin Pie Butter
  Food Club Brand - Grape Jam, Grape Jelly, Jelly Apple, Preserves
    (Apricot, Blackberry Seedless, Marmalade, Peach, Red Raspberry,
    Strawberry)

Full Circle - Apricot, Strawberry

Gordon Food Service - Assorted (Reduced Calorie, Regular), Jelly (Grape, Mixed Fruit), Strawberry Jam

H-E-B - More Fruit Spread (Apricot, Blackberry, Cherry/Blueberry, Four Berry, Grape, Peach, Peach Mango, Pineapple, Red Plum, Red Raspberry, Strawberry), Sabor Traditional Cajeta

Hannaford Brand - Jelly (Apple, Currant, Grape, Strawberry), Orange Marmalade, Preserves (Apricot, Blueberry, Concord Grape, Red Raspberry)

Hill Country Fare H-E-B - Jam (Grape, Red Plum, Strawberry), Jelly (Apple, Grape), Preserves (Apricot, Peach, Pineapple, Red Raspberry, Strawberry)

Hy-Vee -
  Jelly (Apple, Blackberry, Cherry, Grape, Plum, Red Raspberry, Strawberry)
  Orange Marmalade
  Preserves (Apricot, Cherry, Concord Grape, Peach, Red Raspberry, Strawberry)

Lowes Foods Brand - Jam Grape, Jelly (Apple, Grape), Preserves Strawberry

Meijer Brand -
  Apple Jelly
  Fruit Spread (Apricot, Blackberry Seedless, Red Raspberry, Strawberry)
  Grape Jam
  Grape Jelly
  Preserves (Apricot, Blackberry Seedless, Marmalade Orange, Peach, Red Raspberry, Red Raspberry w/Seeds, Strawberry)

Midwest Country Fare - Jelly Concord Grape

O Organics - Preserves (Apricot, Blackberry, Blueberry, Raspberry, Strawberry)

Oskri Organics - Spread (Date, Fig, Sesame)

Polaner ▲ - All (All Fruit w/Fiber, Jam, Jellies, Preserves)

J

Publix - All (Jam, Jellies, Preserves)
Safeway Brand - All (Jams, Jellies, Preserves)
Safeway Select - All (Jellies, Preserves)
Santa Cruz ▲ - Fruit Spread (All Varieties)
Shiloh Farms - Apple Butter
Smucker's ▲ - All (Fruit Butter, Jams, Jellies, Low Sugar, Marmalades,
    Orchard's Finest Preserves, Organic, Preserves, Simply Fruit,
    Squeeze, Sugar Free w/NutraSweet, Sugar Free w/Splenda)
Spartan Brand -
    Grape Jam
    Jelly (Apple, Currant, Grape, Strawberry)
    Orange Marmalade
    Preserves (Apricot, Blackberry, Cherry, Peach, Red Raspberry,
        Strawberry)
St. Dalfour - All Flavors
Taste of Inspiration - All Flavors **!**
Trader Joe's -
    Organic Fruit Spread (Blueberry, Strawberry, Superfruit)
    Organic Preserves Reduced Sugar (Blackberry **!!**, Blueberry **!!**,
        Raspberry **!!**, Strawberry **!!**), Preserves (Apricot **!!**,
        Blackberry **!!**, Blueberry **!!**, Boysenberry **!!**, Raspberry **!!**)
Walden Farms - Spread (Apple Butter, Apricot, Blueberry, Grape,
    Orange, Raspberry, Strawberry)
Wegmans Brand -
    Fruit Spread (Apricot/Peach/Passion Fruit, Blueberry/Cherry/
        Raspberry, Raspberry/Strawberry/Blackberry, Strawberry/
        Plum/Raspberry)
    Jelly (Apple, Cherry, Grape, Red Currant, Red Raspberry,
        Strawberry)
    Organic FYFGA Fruit Spread (Jammin' Red Raspberry, Jammin'
        Strawberry)
    Preserves (Apricot, Cherry, Concord Grape, Orange Marmalade,
        Peach, Pineapple, Red Raspberry, Seedless Blackberry,
        Strawberry)

Sugar Free Fruit Spread (Apricot/Peach/Passion Fruit, Raspberry/
Wild Blueberry/Blackberry, Strawberry/Plum/Raspberry)

Welch's ▲ - All (Jam, Jellies, Preserves)

Winn Dixie - All (Jams, Jellies, Preserves)

Jello...see Gelatin

Jerky/Beef Sticks

  Buffalo Guys - Buffalo Jerky (Mild, Old Style)

  Cook's Bison Ranch - Buffalo Jerky (BBQ, Original, Sweet Pepper)

  Garrett County Farms - Snack Sticks (Hot 'N Spicy ★, Matt's Beef
    Pepperoni ★, Turkey Tom Tom ★)

  Gary West -

    All Certified Angus Beef Steak Strips Varieties *(Except Teriyaki)*

    All Original Steak Strips Varieties *(Except Teriyaki)*

    Buffalo & Elk Strips

    Silver Fork Natural Steak Strips

  Hormel - Dried Beef

  Hy-Vee - Original Jerky

  Lowes Foods Brand - Beef Jerky (Honey BBQ, Original, Peppered)

  Oberto -

    All Natural BBQ Pork

    Bacon Cheddar (Bites, Stick)

    Beef Jerky (All Natural (Hickory, Original, Peppered, Spicy Sweet),
      Original (Peppered Thin, Tender Style, Thin))

    Queso Jalapeno (Bites, Stick)

  Old Wisconsin - Snack Bites (Beef, Pepp, Turkey), Snack Sticks (Beef,
    Pepp, Turkey)

  Organic Prairie - Organic Beef Jerky (Prairie Classic, Smoky
    Chipotle, Spicy Hickory)

  Shelton's - Beef Jerky, Turkey Jerky (Hot Turkey, Regular)

  Wellshire Farms - Snack Sticks (Hot 'N Spicy ★, Matt's Beef
    Pepperoni ★, Turkey Tom Tom ★)

Juice Mix...see Drink Mix

Juice...see Drinks/Juice

K K

Kale
... *All Fresh Fruits & Vegetables Are Gluten-Free*
Pictsweet - Cut Leaf

Kasha
Bob's Red Mill ▲ - Organic ★
Shiloh Farms - Organic ‼
Wolff's - Regular

Kefir
Lifeway ▲ - All Varieties, ProBugs (All Varieties)
Nancy's - All Cultured Dairy & Soy Products
Trader Joe's - Regular

Ketchup
Bakers & Chefs - Fancy Ketchup
Central Market H-E-B - Organic
Food Club Brand - Regular, Upside Down Squeeze Bottle
Full Circle - Regular
Gordon Food Service - Tomato (Bottle, Can, Packet)
Great Value Brand (Wal-Mart) - Regular
H-E-B - Regular
Heinz - Easy Squeeze Regular, Hot & Spicy, No Salt, Organic, Reduced Sugar, Regular, Simply Heinz
Hill Country Fare H-E-B - Regular
Hunt's - All Flavors
Hy-Vee - Regular, Squeezable Thick & Rich Tomato, Thick & Rich Tomato
Jim Beam - Original
Kroger Brand - Tomato Ketchup Inverted Bottle
Kurtz - No Salt, Regular
Lowes Foods Brand - Regular
Meijer Brand - Regular, Squeeze, Tomato Organic
Midwest Country Fare - Regular
Mother's Mountain - Catsup
My Essentials - Regular

Nature's Basket - Organic
Nomato - Nomato Ketchup
O Organics - Regular
Organicville - Organic ●
Publix - Regular
Publix GreenWise Market - Organic
Safeway Brand - Regular
Spartan Brand - Regular
Trader Joe's - Organic
Walden Farms - Regular
Wegmans Brand - Organic FYFGA, Regular
Westbrae - Unsweetened Un Ketchup
Winn Dixie - Regular
Woodstock Farms - Organic Tomato

Kielbasa...see Sausage

Kipper Snacks
Ocean Prince - In Mustard, Naturally Smoked

Kiwi
... *All Fresh Fruits & Vegetables Are Gluten-Free*

Kohlrabi
... *All Fresh Fruits & Vegetables Are Gluten-Free*

Korma
Amy's - Indian Vegetable ★
Seeds Of Change - Korma Sauce ❗❗
Sharwood's - Korma
Tasty Bite - Vegetable Korma ❗

L

Lamb
... *All Fresh Meat Is Gluten-Free (Non-Marinated, Unseasoned)*
Kirkland Signature - Boneless Leg, Frenched Rack, Fresh Rib Roast
Sweet Bay - All Fresh Lamb
Trader Joe's - Fresh All Natural

L

Lasagna/Lasagne

    Amy's - Gluten Free Dairy Free Vegetable ★, Gluten Free Garden
       Vegetable ★

    Caesar's - Gluten Free & Wheat Free Lasagna (Cheese Entree !!,
       Vegetable Entree !!)

    Conte's ▲ - Cheese Lasagna Microwave Meal ●

    Foods By George - Cheese

Lasagna Noodles...see Pasta

Leeks

    ... *All Fresh Fruits & Vegetables Are Gluten-Free*

Lemonade...see Drinks/Juice

Lemons

    ... *All Fresh Fruits & Vegetables Are Gluten-Free*

    Nuts.com - Dried ●

    Sunkist

Lentils...see also Beans

    Tasty Bite - Bengal !, Jodphur !, Lentil Magic !, Madras !, Snappy Soya !

    Trader Joe's - Curried Lentils w/Basmati Rice, Steamed

Lettuce

    ... *All Fresh Fruits & Vegetables Are Gluten-Free*

Licorice...see Candy/Candy Bars

Limes

    ... *All Fresh Fruits & Vegetables Are Gluten-Free*

Liquid Aminos

    Bragg - Liquid Aminos

    Marigold - Liquid Aminos ★

Liverwurst

    Five Star Brand ▲ - Natural Casing Braunschweiger (Chubs, Regular)

    Garrett County Farms - ★

    Jones Dairy Farm -

       Braunschweiger (Sandwich Slices ●, Sliced ●)

       Chub Braunschweiger Liverwurst (Light ●, Mild & Creamy ●, Original●,
        w/Onion ●)

       Chunk Braunschweiger (Light ●, Original ●)

Old Wisconsin - Spreadable Pate (Black Pepper, Onion & Parsley, Original)

Wellshire Farms - Liverwurst ★

Lobster

... *All Fresh Seafood Is Gluten-Free (Non-Marinated, Unseasoned)*

Lunch Meat...see Deli Meat

M

Macaroni & Cheese

Amy's - Rice Mac & Cheese ★, Rice Macaroni w/Non Dairy Cheeze ★

Annie's - Gluten Free (Deluxe Rice Pasta & Cheddar !!, Microwaveable !!, Rice Pasta & Cheddar !!, Rice Shells w/Creamy White Cheddar !!)

DeBoles - Elbow Style Pasta & Cheese ●, Shells & Cheese ●

Ian's - Wheat Free Gluten Free Mac & No Cheese

Mrs. Leeper's - Mac & Cheese Dinner

Namaste Foods ▲ - Say Cheez

Orgran ▲ - Buontempo Mac & Cheese (Farm Animals, Regular)

Pastariso ▲ - Bunny Rice Macaroni & Yellow Cheese ●, Dolphin Rice Macaroni & Yellow Cheese ●, Elephant Rice Macaroni & White Cheese ●, Gorilla Rice Mini Shells & White Cheese ●, Rhino Rice Mini Shells & Yellow Cheese ●

Pastato ▲ - Potato (Bobcat Mini Shells & Yellow Cheddar Cheese ●, Orangutan Mac & White Cheddar Cheese ●, Panda Mac & Yellow Cheddar Cheese ●, Tiger Mini Shells & White Cheddar Cheese ●)

Road's End Organics - Dairy Free (Organic Mac & Chreese Alfredo Style, Organic Penne & Chreese Cheddar Style)

Simply Shari's Gluten Free & Fabulous ▲ - Macaroni & Cheese ●

Trader Joe's - Rice Pasta & Cheddar

Macaroons...see Cookies

Mackerel...see also Fish

... *All Fresh Fish Is Gluten-Free (Non-Marinated, Unseasoned)*

Bumble Bee - Jack Mackerel

Chicken Of The Sea - All Mackerel Products

Crown Prince - Jack Mackerel In Water

M Mahi Mahi
... *All Fresh Fish Is Gluten-Free (Non-Marinated, Unseasoned)*

Mandarin Oranges
... *All Fresh Fruits & Vegetables Are Gluten-Free*

Del Monte - Canned/Jarred Fruit (All Varieties), Fruit Snack Cups Plastic

Dole - Bowls *(Except Fruit Crisps)*, Canned, Jars

Food Club Brand - In Lite Syrup

Great Value Brand (Wal-Mart) - Canned In Light Syrup, Plastic Cups In Light Syrup

Hy-Vee - Fruit Cups (Light Syrup, Orange Gel), Light Syrup, Mandarin Oranges

Kroger Brand - Cups

Lowes Foods Brand - In Lite Syrup

Meijer Brand - Light Syrup

Publix - In Gel, In Light Syrup

Spartan Brand - Canned, Fruit Cups

Trader Joe's - In Light Syrup

Wegmans Brand - Regular, Whole Segment

Winn Dixie - Regular

Mangos
... *All Fresh Fruits & Vegetables Are Gluten-Free*

C & W - All Plain Frozen Fruits **!!**

Del Monte - Canned/Jarred Fruit All Varieties, Fruit Snack Cups Plastic

Mariani - Mangoes Regular **!!**, Philippine **!!**

Meijer Brand - Frozen (Chunks, Sliced)

Native Forest - Organic Mango Chunks

Nuts.com - Dried Mango (Diced ●, Less Sugar Added ●, Organic ●, Regular ●, Simply ●)

O Organics - Frozen

Trader Joe's - Frozen (Mango Chunks, Sweet Mango Halves), Mangolicious Fruit Blend

Winn Dixie - Frozen Mango Chunks

Woodstock Farms - Organic Frozen Mangos, Organic Slices, Slices Unsulphured

Maple Syrup...see Syrup

Maraschino Cherries...see Cherries

Margarine...see Butter and/or Spread

Marinades

7up - Citrus

A.1. - Chicago Steakhouse, Classic, Jamaican Jerk, New Orleans Cajun, New York Steakhouse

Adolph's - Marinade In Minutes (Meat **!!**, Meat Sodium Free **!!**)

Allegro - Game Tame, Hickory Smoke, Hot & Spicy, Original, Teriyaki

Badia - Mojo ●

Biltmore - Apple Rosemary

Cains - Franklin Italian

Central Market H-E-B - All Natural (Island Habanero, Remoulade)

Cookwell & Company - Fin & Feather Citrus, Italian Herb & Olive Oil

Dave's Gourmet - Jammin' Jerk Sauce & Marinade

Devya - Tandoori Chicken

Dr. Pepper - More Than Mesquite

Drew's - Quick Marinade (Buttermilk Ranch, Classic Italian, Greek Olive, Honey Dijon, Organic (Aged Balsamic, Peppercorn Ranch), Poppy Seed, Raspberry, Roasted Garlic & Peppercorn, Romano Caesar, Rosemary Balsamic, Smoked Tomato)

Food Club Brand - 30 Minute Marinades Lemon Pepper

Hill Country Fare H-E-B - Herb & Garlic, Lemon Pepper, Mesquite Lime

Hy-Vee - Citrus Grill, Herb & Garlic, Lemon Pepper, Mesquite

Jack Daniel's EZ Marinader - Honey Teriyaki, Slow Roasted Garlic & Herb

Ken's Steak House - Buffalo Wing Sauce, Herb & Garlic

Lawry's - Baja Chipotle **!!**, Balsamic Herb **!!**, Buffalo BBQ **!!**, Caribbean Jerk **!!**, Havana Garlic & Lime **!!**, Herb & Garlic**!!**, Lemon Pepper **!!**, Louisiana Red Pepper **!!**, Mesquite **!!**, Signature Steakhouse **!!**, Tuscan Sun Dried Tomato **!!**

Lea & Perrins - White Wine

M

McCormick - Grill Mates (Marinade Packets (25% Less Sodium Montreal Steak, Baja Citrus, Carolina Country, Chipotle Pepper, Garlic Herb & Wine, Mesquite, Mojito Lime, Montreal Steak, Peppercorn & Garlic, Southwest, Spiced Brandy & Herb, Tomato Garlic & Basil), Mexican Fiesta)

Meijer Brand - Garlic & Herb, Lemon Pepper, Mesquite

Moore's Marinade - Original ★, Teriyaki ★

Mother's Mountain - Maine (Atlantic, Cajun, Dijon Dill, Original)

Mr. Spice Organic - Sauce & Marinade (Garlic Steak ★, Ginger Stir Fry ★, Honey BBQ ★, Honey Mustard ★, Hot Wing ★, Indian Curry ★, Sweet & Sour ★, Thai Peanut ★)

Newman's Own - Herb & Roasted Garlic, Lemon Pepper, Mesquite w/Lime

Patak's Original - Tandoori

Safeway - Herb & Garlic, Lemon Pepper

Safeway Select - Buffalo Wing, Caribbean Jerk, Roasted Garlic & Honey Mustard, Sweet & Sour, Sweet & Spicy Chili, Sweet Citrus Herb

San-J - Gluten Free (Sweet & Tangy ●, Szechuan ●, Teriyaki ●, Thai Peanut ●)

Simply Organic - Grilling Seasons Mixes (Garlic & Herb, Lemon Pepper, Steak)

Stubb's - Bar B Q Baste Moppin' Sauce ●, Marinade (Beef ●, Chicken ●, Pork ●, Texas Steakhouse ●)

Sweet Baby Ray's - Buffalo Wing Sauce !!, Steakhouse !!

Taste Of Inspiration - Roasted Garlic !, Steak House !, Texas Tumbler !

Weber Grill Creations - Marinade Mix (Black Peppercorn, Chipotle, Italian Herb, Tequila Lime, White Wine & Herb)

Wegmans Brand - Chicken BBQ, Citrus Dill, Fajita, Greek, Honey Mustard, Lemon & Garlic, Mojo, Rosemary Balsamic, Santa Fe, Spiedie, Steakhouse Peppercorn, Tangy, Zesty (Savory, Thai)

Wild Thymes - Chili Ginger Honey, New Orleans Creole, Tropical Mango Lime

Winn Dixie - Mojo

Wright's - Liquid Smoke (Hickory Seasoning, Mesquite)

Marmalade...see Jam/Jelly

Marshmallow Dip

    Walden Farms - Calorie Free Marshmallow Dip

Marshmallows

    AllerEnergy ▲ - Marshmallow Creme, Regular

    Elyon - Natural Vanilla (Mini, Regular)

    Food Club Brand - Mini, Regular

    Gordon Food Service - Mini, Regular

    Great Value Brand (Wal-Mart) - Marshmallows (Flavored, Miniature, Regular)

    Hannaford Brand - Miniature, Regular

    Hy-Vee - Colored Marshmallows, Miniatures, Regular

    Jet-Puffed - Chocomallows, FunMallows, Mini Variety, Miniatures, Regular, StarMallows Vanilla, StrawberryMallows, SwirlMallows Vanilla, Toasted Coconut

    Kroger Brand - Big, Miniature

    Lowes Foods Brand - Mini, Regular

    Manischewitz - Regular

    Marshmallow Fluff ▲ - Original, Raspberry, Strawberry

    Meijer Brand - Mini, Mini Flavored, Regular

    Publix - Regular

    Safeway Brand - Large, Mini

    Spartan Brand - Miniature, Regular

    Winn Dixie - Miniature, Regular

Masala

    A Taste Of India - Masala Rice & Lentils

    Ethnic Gourmet - Chicken Tikka

    Loyd Grossman - Tikka Masala

    Saffron Road - Chicken Tikka Masala ●, Tikka Masala Simmer Sauce●

    Seeds Of Change - Tikka Masala Sauce **! !**

    Sharwood's - Black Pepper, Saag, Spicy Tikka, Tikka

    Tasty Bite - Channa **!**

    Trader Joe's - Channa, Masala Simmer Sauce

M Mashed Potatoes

Alexia Foods - Red Potatoes w/Garlic & Parmesan **!**
Country Crock - Bacon Ranch, Garlic, Homestyle, Loaded, Sweet
Edward & Sons - Organic (Chreesy, Home Style, Roasted Garlic)
Food Club Brand - Instant Mashed Potatoes
Giant Eagle Brand - Side Dishes (Garlic, Homestyle, Loaded, Sweet, White Cheddar)
Honest Earth - All Natural Creamy
Hy-Vee - Four Cheese, Real Russet, Roasted Garlic, Sour Cream & Chive
Idahoan - Instant (Baby Reds (Original, Roasted Garlic & Parmesan), Butter & Herb, Buttery Homestyle, Four Cheese, Italian Romano White Cheese, Original, Real Premium, Roasted Garlic, Southwest Flavors), Instant Cups (Buttery Homestyle, Four Cheese, Roasted Garlic)
Meijer Brand - Instant
Ore-Ida - Steam 'N Mash (Cut Russet Potatoes, Cut Sweet Potatoes, Garlic Seasoned Potatoes, Red Skin)
Potato Buds ▲ - Gluten Free 100% Real Potatoes
Safeway Brand - Instant Plain
Signature Cafe - Mash 'N Cheese
Spartan Brand - Bag (Buttery Homestyle, Four Cheese, Fully Loaded), Box (Butter & Herb, Creamy Butter, Instant, Roasted Garlic, Sour Cream & Chives)

Mayonnaise

Bakers & Chefs - Extra Heavy
Best Foods - All (Light, Low Fat, Real), Canola, w/Lime Juice
Big Y - Mayonnaise
Cains - All Natural, Fat Free, Kitchen Recipe, Light
Dietz & Watson ▲ - Mixed Pepper ●, Sandwich Spread ●, Smoky Chipotle ●, Sweet Red Pepper ●
Earth Balance - Mindful Mayo (Made w/Olive Oil, Organic, Original)
Follow Your Heart - Vegenaise (Grapeseed Oil **!**, High Omega 3 Expeller Pressed **!**, Organic **!**, Original **!**, Reduced Fat **!**)

mayonnaise

M

Food Club Brand - Light, Regular, Salad Dressing (Light Whipped, Regular)

Good - Hemp Seed Mayonnaise (Classic, Garlic)

Gordon Food Service - Heavy Duty

Hellmann's -
Canola Cholesterol Free
Light
Low Fat Mayo Dressing
Mediterranean Roasted Garlic & Herb
Real
Reduced Fat w/Olive Oil
Sandwich Spread

Hill Country Fare H-E-B - Regular

Hollywood - Canola, Safflower

Hy-Vee - Light, Regular

Kirkland Signature - Real Mayonnaise

Kraft -
Mayo (Fat Free, Light, Real, w/Olive Oil)
Sandwich Shop (Chipotle, Garlic & Herb, Horseradish Dijon, Hot & Spicy)

Kroger Brand - Sandwich Spread

Lowes Foods Brand - Regular, Southern Style, Squeeze Bottle, Whipped Salad Dressing

Mayo Gourmet - All Flavors

Meijer Brand - Lite, Regular

Miracle Whip - Free, Light, Regular

My Essentials - Lite, Regular, Squeeze

Nasoya ▲ - Nayonaise (Dijon Style, Fat Free, Original)

Naturally Delicious - Regular

Olde Cape Cod - Regular

Royal Food Products - Garden Fresh (Heavy Duty, Regular), Gourmet Choice EGGceptional Old Fashioned, Royal Deluxe Extra Heavy Duty

Safeway - Sandwich Spread

Safeway Brand - Light, Regular, w/Olive Oil

Safeway Select - Whipped Dressing

Simply Delicious - Organic Mayonnaise (Garlic, Original)

Smart Balance - Omega Plus Light

Spartan Brand - Jar, Regular Squeeze

Spectrum -
  Artisan Organic (Olive Oil, Wasabi)
  Canola (Light Eggless Vegan, Regular)
  Organic (Omega 3 w/Flax Oil, Regular)
  Squeeze Bottle (Canola (Light Eggless Vegan, Regular), Organic)

Tiger Tiger - May O (Plain !, w/Garlic !, w/Sweet Chili !, w/Tikka !, w/Wasabi !)

Trader Joe's - Real !, Reduced Fat, Wasabi Mayo !

Walden Farms - Miracle Mayo

Wegmans Brand - Classic, Light

Winn Dixie - Light, Regular

Woodstock Farms - Organic Mayo

Meals
  A Taste Of China - Szechuan Noodles
  A Taste Of India - Quick Meals (Masala Rice & Lentils, Spiced Rice w/ Raisins)
  A Taste Of Thai - Quick Meals (Coconut Ginger Noodles, Pad Thai Noodles, Peanut Noodles, Red Curry Noodles, Yellow Curry Noodles)
  Adolph's - Meal Maker Beef Stew !!
  Amy's - Asian Noodle Stir Fry ★, Kids Meals Baked Ziti ★, Light & Lean (Roasted Polenta ★, Sweet & Sour Asian Noodle ★), Thai Stir Fry ★
  Augason Farms ▲ - Gluten Free Complete Meal Pack ●
  Caesar's - Gluten Free & Wheat Free (Lasagna (Cheese !!, Vegetable !!), Manicotti !!, Stuffed Shells !!)
  Cedarlane - Low Fat Garden Vegetable Enchiladas
  Celiac Specialties ▲ - Frozen Meals (Butter Noodles, Chicken Parmesan, Lasagna, Lasagna Wraps, Mac & Cheese, Spaghetti & Meatballs)
  Chi-Chi's - Fiesta Plates (Creamy Chipotle Chicken, Salsa Chicken, Savory Garlic Chicken)

Conte's ▲ - Microwave Meal (Cheese Lasagna ●, Cheese Ravioli w/Marinara Sauce ●, Gnocchi w/Marinara Sauce ●)

CookSimple - Asian Burgers w/Stir Fried Brown Rice, Cowboy Chili w/Quinoa & Cinnamon, New Orleans Jambalaya w/Brown Rice & Peppers, Punjabi Curry w/Coconut & Brown Rice, Tamale Pie Black Bean Chili w/Cornbread Topping, Tibetan Dal Lentil Stew w/Tomatoes Cilantro & Cumin

Country Crock - Cheddar Broccoli Rice

Delimex - Bowls (Chipotle Beef Rice, Santa Fe Style Chicken Rice)

Devya - Organic Channa

Dinty Moore - Microwave Meals (Beef Stew, Rice & Chicken, Scalloped Potatoes & Ham)

Ethnic Gourmet - Chicken Biryani, Chicken Korma, Chicken Tandoori w/Spinach, Chicken Tikka Masala, Eggplant Bhartha, Lemon Grass & Basil Chicken, Malay Chicken Curry, Palak Paneer, Shahi Paneer, Vegetable Korma

Free Choice Foods ▲ - Chickpea & Potato Curry w/Roasted Peanuts ●, Creole Red Bean Jambalaya Rice & Bean Mix ●, Cuban Style Black Beans & Rice ●, Middle Eastern Lentil Pilaf ●, Quinoa Lentil Pilaf w/Almonds & Raisins ●, Quinoa Vegetable Pilaf ●, Red Quinoa & Black Bean Salad Starter ●, Taboule Style Quinoa Salad Starter ●, Tuscan Style White Beans & Rice Mix ●, Wild Rice Pilaf Mix w/Roasted Pecans ●

Garden Lites - Souffle (Broccoli, Butternut Squash, Cauliflower, Roasted Vegetable, Spinach, Zucchini), Zucchini Marinara, Zucchini Portabella

Garden of Eatin' - Blue Corn Taco Dinner Kit, Yellow Corn Taco Dinner Kit

Giant Eagle Brand - Broccoli Rice & Cheese Casserole

Gluten Free Cafe - Asian Noodles ●, Fettuccini Alfredo ●, Homestyle Chicken & Vegetables ●, Lemon Basil Chicken ●, Pasta Primavera●, Savory Chicken Pilaf ●

Glutino ▲ - Frozen Meals (Chicken Penne Alfredo, Macaroni 'N Cheese, Pad Thai w/Chicken, Penne Alfredo)

GoPicnic - Hummus & Crackers **!!**, Salmon & Crackers **!!**, Sunbutter & Crackers **!!**, Tuna & Crackers **!!**, Turkey Pepperoni & Cheese **!!**, Turkey Stick & Crunch **!!**

Helen's Kitchen - Bay Island Plantain, Cheese Enchiladas, Indian Curry, Thai Green Curry, Thai Red Curry, Thai Yellow Curry, Vegetarian Enchilada

Hormel - Compleats Chicken & Rice, Refrigerated Entrees Turkey Breast Roast

Ian's - Wheat Free Gluten Free Mac & No Cheese

Kid's Kitchen - Beans & Wieners

Lucini - Chickpea Farinata Mix Tuscan Street Food (Savory Rosemary, Traditional, Tuscan Fiery Chili)

Mayacamas - Skillet Toss (Black Olive Pesto ★, Dried Tomato ★, Garden Style Recipe ★, Green Olive Pesto ★, Mushroom Sauce ★, Seafood Pasta Recipe ★, Spicy Pasta Recipe ★)

Mixes From The Heartland ▲ - Meal Mix (Baked Chicken Salad ●, BBQ Beef & Pasta ●, Beef Skillet ●, Cheeseburger Pie ●, Garden Meat Loaf ●, Green Chili ●, Mexican Chicken N' Rice ●, Mexican Rice Bake ●, Mexican Style Casserole ●, Noodle Casserole ●, Sausage Casserole ●, Southwest Potato Casserole ●, Sweet Corn Casserole ●, Taco Rice Skillet ●, Tex Mex Meat Loaf ●, Texas Bean Bake ●, Texas Goulash ●, Tuna Casserole ●)

Mrs. Leeper's -
Beef (Lasagna Dinner, Stroganoff Dinner)
Cheeseburger Mac Dinner
Chicken Alfredo Dinner
Creamy Tuna Dinner
Mac & Cheese Dinner

My Own Meal - Beef Stew, Chicken & Black Bean, Chicken Mediterranean, My Kind Of Chicken, Old World Stew

Namaste Foods ▲ - Pasta Meals (Pasta Pisavera, Say Cheez, Taco)

Old El Paso - Stand 'N Stuff Taco Dinner Kit, Taco Dinner Kit

Organic Bistro -
Bakes (Cheddar Beef Bake, Chicken Parmesan Bake, Turkey

Cheddar Bake, Wild Alaskan Salmon Bake, Wild Albacore Tuna Bake)

Entrees (Alaskan Salmon Cake, Chicken Citron, Ginger Chicken, Grass Fed Beef w/Mushroom Sauce, Savory Turkey, Southwest Style Grass Fed Beef, Spiced Chicken Morocco, Wild Salmon, Wild Salmon w/Pesto)

Ortega - Hard Shell Taco Dinner Kit (12 Count, 18 Count, Whole Grain Corn)

Patak's Original - Butter Chicken w/Rice, Chickpea Curry w/Rice, Potato & Spinach Curry w/Rice, Vegetable Korma Curry w/Rice

Pure Market Express ▲ - Baked Macaroni & Cheese ●, Creamy Garlic Dill Pasta ●, Garlic Alfredo Pasta ●, Lasagna ●, Pad Thai ●, Pad Thai Kit●, Pasta Meal Kits (Creamy Garlic Dill ●, Garlic Alfredo ●), Ravioli●, Salmon & Hollandaise ●, Stir Fry Less Sauce ●, Turkey Salad Wrap ●, Walnut Pesto Pasta w/Shrimp Bites Kit ●

Saffron Road - Chicken Biryani ●, Chicken Nuggets ●, Chicken Tikka Masala ●, Lamb Koftis ●, Lamb Saag ●, Lamb Vindaloo ●, Lemon Grass Basil Chicken ●

Sharwood's - Vegetable Curry

Simply Shari's Gluten Free & Fabulous ▲ - Pasta Quinoa & Marinara●

Smart Ones - Frozen Entrees (Broccoli & Cheddar Roasted Potatoes, Chicken Santa Fe, Cranberry Turkey Medallions, Lemon Herb Chicken Piccata, Santa Fe Rice & Beans)

Spaa - Tasty Thai (Pad Thai Noodles, Peanut Satay)

StoreHouse Foods - Classic Vegetarian Chili, French Quarter Chicken Gumbo, Santa Fe Black Beans & Rice, Southwestern BBQ Chicken w/Rice & Beans

Tambobamba - Mojo Bowls (Brazilian Rice & Beans, Caribbean Rice & Beans, Peruvian Rice & Beans)

Tasty Bite - Agra Peas & Greens !, Aloo Palak !, Bangkok Beans!, Bombay Potatoes !, Channa Masala !, Chunky Chickpeas !, Jaipur Vegetables !, Kashmir Spinach !, Kerala Vegetables !, Madras Lentils !, Malaysian Lodeh !, Mushroom Takatak !, Paneer Makhani!, Punjab Eggplant !, Spinach Channa !, Tofu Corn Masala!, Zesty Lentils and Peas !

Thai Kitchen -
- Microwave Rice Noodles & Sauce (Ginger & Sweet Chili, Original Pad Thai, Thai Basil & Chili)
- Noodle Carts (Pad Thai, Thai Peanut)
- Stir Fry Rice Noodles (Lemongrass & Chili, Original Pad Thai, Thai Peanut)

Trader Joe's - All Indian Fare Meals, Chicken Tikka Masala, Peruvian Style Chimichurri Rice w/Vegetables **!!**, Shrimp Stir Fry

Meatballs

Aidells - Spicy Mango Jalapeno/Caramelized Onion Twin Pack, Zesty Italian

Al Fresco - Teriyaki Ginger Chicken Meatballs, Tomato & Basil Chicken Meatballs

Andrea's Gluten Free ▲ - Meatballs

Franklin Farms - Portabella Veggiballs

Open Nature - Chicken Basil & Parmesan, Chicken Italian

Tre Bella Foods - Gluten Free Turkey Mini Meatballs

Wildwood - Meatless Meatballs Original

Melon

... *All Fresh Fruits & Vegetables Are Gluten-Free

Milk

Augason Farms ▲ - Morning Moos Low Fat Milk Alternative (Chocolate ●, Regular ●)

Borden Eagle Brand - Condensed Milk (Fat Free, Low Fat, Sweetened)

Carnation - Evaporated (Fat Free, Low Fat, Regular, Regular w/ Vitamin D), Instant Non Fat Dry, Sweetened Condensed Milk

Central Market H-E-B - Organics Original Ancient Grains

Dairy Ease - Lactose Free Milk

Dari Free - Non Dairy Milk Alternative (Chocolate, Original)

Food Club Brand - 1%, 1% Chocolate, 2%, Buttermilk (Fat Free, Whole), Chocolate, Condensed Milk, Evaporated Fat Free, Evaporated Milk Regular, Half And Half (Fat Free, Regular), Instant (Pouches, Regular), Lactose Free (2%, No Fat, Whole), Skim, Whole Chocolate

M

Friendship - Light Cultured Buttermilk

Garelick Farms -
Chug (1% Low Fat Milk, TruMoo Chocolate, TruMoo Coffee Low Fat, TruMoo Low Fat Chocolate, TruMoo Strawberry, Whole Milk)
Cultured Low Fat Buttermilk
Flavored (Over the Moon Chocolate, TruMoo Chocolate, TruMoo Coffee, TruMoo Strawberry)
Fresh (Half & Half, Light Cream)
Ultra Pasteurized (Fat Free Half & Half, Half & Half, Heavy Cream, Light Cream)
White (1% Low Fat, 2% Reduced Fat, Fat Free, Over the Moon 1% Low Fat, Over the Moon Fat Free, Skim & More, Whole)

Giant Eagle Brand - Heavy Cream

Good Karma - Flax Milk (Original, Unsweetened, Vanilla)

Great Value Brand (Wal-Mart) - Evaporated Milk, Evaporated Skimmed, Fat Free Half & Half, Fat Free Sweetened Condensed, Half & Half, Lactose Free (Fat Free, Reduced Fat, Vitamin D), Organic (Fat Free, Reduced Fat, Vitamin D), Sweetened Condensed

H-E-B - Half & Half (Fat Free Ranch, Regular)

Hannaford Brand - Half & Half, Instant

Hood - All Creams, All Flavored (Full Fat, Low Fat), All Fluid Milk (All Fat Levels), Buttermilk, Calorie Countdown (All Varieties)

Horizon Organic - All Varieties

Hy-Vee - ½%, 1% Low Fat, 2% Reduced Fat, Enriched (Original Rice, Vanilla Rice), Evaporated, Fat Free (Evaporated, Skim), Instant Non Fat Dry, Original Soy, Refrigerated Soy (Chocolate, Original, Vanilla), Skim, Sweetened Condensed, Vanilla Soy, Vitamin D

Kemps - All Varieties (Cream, Milk)

Kirkland Signature - 2%, Fat Free, Low Fat (Organic, Regular)

Lactaid - All Varieties

Living Harvest - Tempt Hempmilk (All Varieties)

Lowes Foods Brand - Half & Half, Half & Half Fat Free, Whipping Cream (Heavy, Light, Regular)

M

Lucerne - Buttermilk Low Fat, Chocolate, Fat Free, Half & Half, Lactose Free (All Varieties, Fat Free, Whole), Whole

Meijer Brand - ½% Low Fat, 1% Low Fat, 2% Reduced Fat, Chocolate (1% Low Fat, Regular), Evaporated (Lite Skimmed, Small, Tall), Fat Free, Instant, Lactose Free Milk (2% w/Calcium, Fat Free w/Calcium), Milk Sweetened Condensed, Strawberry Milk, Ultra Pasteurized Heavy Half & Half, Vitamin D

My Essentials - All Regular, Condensed, Evaporated

Nesquik - Ready To Drink (All Flavors)

O Organics - Fat Free, Whole

Organic Valley - Buttermilk, Chocolate 2%, Fat Free/Non Fat/Skim, Half & Half, Heavy Whipping Cream, Lactose Free, Low Fat 1%, Omega 3, Powder (Buttermilk Blend, Non Fat Dry Milk), Reduced Fat 2%, Shelf Stable Liters (Chocolate 2%, Half & Half, Whole), Shelf Stable Single Serves (Chocolate, Low Fat, Strawberry, Vanilla), Whole

Pacific Natural Foods - Hemp Milk (Original, Vanilla)

Pet - Evaporated, Fat Free Evaporated Milk

Prairie Farms - Flavored Milk (1% Chocolate, 1% Strawberry, 1% Vanilla, 2% Chocolate, Chocolate), Half & Half (Fat Free, Heavy Whipping, Regular, Ultra Pasteurized, Ultra Pasteurized Heavy Whipping Cream) White Milk (1% Low Fat, 2% Low Fat, 2% Reduced Fat, Fat Free)

Publix - Chocolate, Fat Free Regular, Instant Non Fat Dry, Low Fat (Chocolate, Regular), Reduced Fat, Whole

Publix GreenWise Market - Organic Milk (Fat Free, Whole)

Safeway - Condensed, Evaporated, Instant Dry

Shamrock Farms - Buttermilk 1% Low Fat, Flavored Mmmmilk (Cafe Mocha, Chocolate, Dulce De Leche, No Sugar Added Low Fat 1% Chocolate, Strawberry, Vanilla, Whole Chocolate), Organic (1% Low Fat, 2% Reduced Fat, Fat Free, Whole), Regular (Low Fat 1% Chocolate, Whole), Regular Mmmmilk (1% Low Fat, 2% Reduced Fat, Fat Free, Fat Free Plus Calcium, Whole), Rockin' Refuel (Chocolate, Strawberry, Vanilla), Shamrockers (Chocolate, White)

Simply Smart - Chocolate Fat Free, Half & Half Fat Free, Milk (Fat Free, Low Fat)

Smart Balance - Fat Free (Calcium, Heart Right, Lactose Free (Calcium, Omega 3), Omega 3), Low Fat & Omega 3

Spartan Brand - 1% Chocolate, 1% Low Fat, 2% Reduced Fat, Half & Half (Fat Free, Ultra Pasteurized), Instant Nonfat Dry, Skim, Sweetened Condensed

Wegmans Brand - 1% Regular, 2% Regular, Evaporated (Fat Free, Regular), Fat Free Skim (Regular, Rich Calcium Fortified), Half & Half (Fresh, Ultra), Homogenized, Low Fat Chocolate, Sweetened Condensed, Ultra Heavy Cream

Winn Dixie - Evaporated, Fat Free, Instant Non Fat Dry, Low Fat (1%, 2%), Organic (1% Low Fat, 2% Low Fat, Fat Free, Whole), Soy (Chocolate, Plain, Unsweetened, Vanilla), Sweetened & Condensed, Whole

Woodstock Farms - Organic Milk (1% Low Fat, 2% Reduced Fat, Fat Free Skim, Whole)

Yoo-Hoo - All Varieties

Millet

Arrowhead Mills - Hulled Millet, Organic Millet Flour

Bob's Red Mill ▲ - Flour ★, Grits ★, Hulled Millet ★

Mints

Altoids -

Curiously Strong Mints Large Tin (Cinnamon, Cool Honey, Creme De Menthe, Ginger, Liquorice, Peppermint, Spearmint, Wintergreen)

Sugar Free Smalls (Cinnamon, Simply Mint, Wintergreen)

Dentyne - Pure (All Varieties)

Eclipse - All Flavors

Lifesavers -

Hard Candy (Cryst O Mint, Orange Mint, Pep O Mint, Spear O Mint, Wint O Green)

Sugar Free Hard Candy (Pep O Mint, Wint O Green)

Lowes Foods Brand - Starlight Mints

St. Claire's Organics ▲ - All Mints

M **Vermints** ▲ - Cafe Express ●, Chai ●, Cinnamint ●, Gingermint ●, Peppermint ●, Wintermint ●

Miso

    Eden Organic - Organic Miso (Genmai, Shiro)

    Edward & Sons - Miso Cup Savory Soup w/Seaweed

    South River - Azuki Bean **!!**, Chick Pea **!!**, Dandelion Leek **!!**, Garlic Red Pepper **!!**, Golden Millet **!!**, Hearty Brown Rice **!!**, Sweet Tasting Brown Rice **!!**, Sweet White **!!**, Tamari **!!**

    Westbrae - Brown Rice Bag, Paste (Mellow Brown Rice, Mellow Red, Mellow White)

Mixed Fruit

    *... *All Fresh Fruits & Vegetables Are Gluten-Free*

    Augason Farms ▲ - Gluten Free Freeze Dried Fruit & Vegetable Pack●

    C & W - All Plain Frozen Fruits & Medleys **!!**

    Del Monte - Canned/Jarred Fruit All Varieties, Fruit Snack Plastic Cups

    Dole - All Frozen Mixed Fruit, Bowls *(Except Fruit Crisps)*, Canned Tropical Fruit, Mixed Fruit In 100% Fruit Juice Jars

    Great Value Brand (Wal-Mart) -

        Canned (Fruit Cocktail In Heavy Syrup, No Sugar Added Fruit Cocktail, Triple Cherry Fruit Mix In Natural Flavored Cherry, Tropical Fruit Salad In Light Syrup & Fruit Juices)

        Frozen Berry Medley

        Plastic Cups (Cherry Mixed Fruit, Mixed Fruit, No Sugar Added Mixed, Tropical)

    Hannaford Brand - All (Canned, Frozen)

    Hy-Vee - Frozen, Fruit Cups (Mixed, Tropical), Mixed Fruit (Lite Chunk, Regular)

    Lowes Foods Brand - Canned Fruit Cocktail (In Heavy Syrup, In Juice), Frozen (Berry Medley, Mixed Fruit, Tropical Blend)

    Meijer Brand - Frozen Tropical Fruit Blend, Mixed Fruit (Individually Quick Frozen, Regular)

    Publix - Canned (Chunky Mixed Fruit In Heavy Syrup, Fruit Cocktail In Heavy Syrup, Lite Chunky Mixed Fruit In Pear Juice, Lite Fruit Cocktail In Pear Juice), Frozen

    S&W - All Canned/Jarred Fruits

mixed vegetables

M

Spartan Brand - Cherry Fruit Cups, Frozen (Berry Medley, Mixed Fruit), Fruit Cocktail In Lite Syrup

Trader Joe's - Frozen (Berry Medley, Fancy Berry Medley)

Wegmans Brand - Fruit Cocktail (In Pear Juice, Regular)

Winn Dixie - Canned Chunky Mixed Fruit (Heavy Syrup, Light Syrup), Frozen (Berry Medley, Mixed Fruit), Fruit Cocktail (Heavy Syrup, Light Syrup)

Woodstock Farms - Organic Tropical Blend, Tropical Fruit Mix

Mixed Vegetables

... *All Fresh Fruits & Vegetables Are Gluten-Free

Augason Farms ▲ - Gluten Free Freeze Dried Fruit & Vegetable Pack●

Birds Eye - All Plain Frozen Vegetables

C & W - All Plain Frozen Vegetables **!!**

Del Monte - Canned

Food Club Brand - Canned Mixed Vegetables, Frozen (California Style, Fiesta, Florentine Style, Mixed Vegetables, Peas & Carrots, Stir Fry)

Freshlike - Frozen Plain Mixed Vegetables

Full Circle - Frozen Organic Mixed Vegetables

Green Giant - Valley Fresh Steamers Mixed Vegetables

Hannaford Brand - All Frozen

Hy-Vee - Canned Mixed Vegetables, Frozen (California Mix, Country Trio, Fiesta Blend, Italian Blend, Mixed Vegetables, Oriental Vegetables, Stew Vegetables, Winter Mix)

Ka-Me - Stir Fry Vegetables **!**

Kirkland Signature - Frozen (Normandy Style Vegetable Blend, Stir Fry Vegetable Blend)

Kroger Brand - Canned

Lowes Foods Brand - Frozen (California Blend, Fajita Blend, Italian Blend, Mixed Vegetables, Peking Stir Fry, Vegetables For Soup)

Meijer Brand - Canned Mixed, Frozen (California Style, Fiesta, Fire Roasted (Mukimame Blend, Southwestern Blend), Florentine Style, Italian, Mexican, Mixed Vegetables (Organic, Regular), Oriental, Parisian Style, Steamer (California Blend, Mixed Vegetables, Oriental Blend, Winter Blend), Stew Mix, Stir Fry, Tuscan Blend)

M

Mezzetta ▲ - California Hot Mix, Chicago Style Italian Sandwich Mix (Hot Giardiniera, Mild Giardiniera), Italian Mix Giardiniera, Mexi Mix Hot N' Spicy

Midwest Country Fare - Canned, Frozen (California Blend, Mixed Vegetables, Winter Mix)

Nature's Place - Frozen Organic

Nuts.com - Simply Organic Mixed Veggies Freeze Dried ●

O Organics - Frozen Mixed Vegetable Blend

Pictsweet - All Plain Frozen Vegetables, Baby California, Baby Mixed Vegetables, Cracked Pepper Seasoned (Okra & Squash, Seasoned Summer Vegetables), Ground Peppercorn Seasoned Garden Vegetables, Seasoned Corn & Black Beans, Seasoning Blend, Spring Vegetables

Private Selection - Frozen Vegetable Medley

Publix - Canned, Frozen Blends (Alpine, California, Del Oro, Gumbo, Italian, Japanese, Mixed Vegetable, Peas & Carrots, Roma, Soup Mix w/Tomatoes, Succotash)

S&W - All Canned Vegetables

Safeway Brand - Frozen Blends (Asian Style, California Style, Stew Vegetables, Stir Fry, Tuscan Style Vegetables, Winter Blend), Mixed Vegetables (Canned, Frozen)

Seapoint Farms - Veggie Blends (Garden, Organic Eat Your Greens, Oriental)

Spartan Brand - Canned Mixed Vegetables, Frozen (Baby Corn Blend, Baby Pea Blend, California Blend, Fiesta Blend, Italian Blend, Mixed Vegetables, Pepper Stir Fry, Stewed Vegetables, Vegetable Gumbo, Vegetables For Soup, Winter Blend)

Tasty Bite - Jaipur Vegetables !, Kerala Vegetables !, Vegetable Korma !

Trader Joe's - Frozen (Harvest Hodgepodge !!, Organic Foursome)

Wegmans Brand - Canned FYFGA Mixed Vegetables, Frozen (Santa Fe Mix, Southern Blend), Frozen FYFGA (Mixed Vegetables, Spring Blend)

M

Winn Dixie - Canned No Salt Added, Frozen Mixed Vegetables (Organic, Regular)

Woodstock Farms - Organic Frozen Mixed Vegetables

Mochi

Grainaissance - Cashew Date, Chocolate Brownie, Original, Pizza, Raisin Cinnamon, Sesame Garlic, Super Seed

Molasses

Brer Rabbit - Molasses (Blackstrap, Full Flavor, Mild)

Grandma's - Original, Robust

Oskri Organics - Molasses

Mousse

ChocAlive ▲ - Chocolate

Jell-O - Sugar Free Mousse Temptations (Caramel Creme, Chocolate Indulgence, Dark Chocolate Decadence)

Lean On Me - Chocolate

Orgran ▲ - Chocolate Mousse Mix

Muffins/Muffin Mix

1-2-3 Gluten Free ▲ - Meredith's Marvelous Muffin/Quickbread Mix●

Abundant Life Foods ▲ - Muffin Mix (Basic Vanilla, Blueberry, Cinnamon Apple, Lemon Poppy, Orange)

Andrea's Gluten Free ▲ - Muffins (Banana, Chocolate Chunk, Pumpkin Mini, Pumpkin Regular)

Apple's Bakery ▲ - Gluten Free Muffins (Assortment, Lowfat Blueberry, Red Rasperry Streusel, Vegan Pumpkin Streusel, White Chocolate Cranberry)

Augason Farms ▲ - Gluten Free Muffin Mix (Almond Poppy Seed ●, Blueberry ●, Raspberry ●, Western Scone ●)

Authentic Foods ▲ - Blueberry Muffin Mix ●, Chocolate Chip Muffin Mix ●

Bi-Aglut - Chocolate Muffins w/Apricot Filling, Cocoa Muffin w/Cream Filling, Margherita Muffin, Muffins w/Hazelnut Cream Filling, Sugar Free Apricot, Yoghurt Raisin

Bloomfield Farms ▲ - Gluten Free ●

Breads From Anna ▲ - Pancake & Muffin Mix (Apple, Cranberry, Maple)

Breakaway Bakery ▲ - Muffins (Banana ●, Coffee Cake ●, Lemon Blueberry ●, Pumpkin ●)

Canyon Bakehouse ▲ - Cranberry Crunch Muffins

Cause You're Special ▲ - Classic Muffin & Quickbread Mix, Lemon Poppy Seed Muffin Mix, Sweet Corn Muffin Mix

Celiac Specialties ▲ - Mini Lemon Poppy Muffins, Mini Pumpkin Chocolate Muffins, Pumpkin Muffins

Choices Rice Bakery ▲ - Muffins (Banana, Banana Chocolate Chip, Blueberry Lemon, Bran, Cranberry Orange, Date & Walnut, Double Chocolate, Honey Carrot, Pumpkin Cranberry)

Delicious Delights ▲ - Chocolate Mini Muffins

El Peto ▲ - Corn Free Muffin Mix, Muffins (Apple & Spice, Blueberry, Chocolate Chip, Cranberry, Lemon Poppy Seed, Tropical Delight, Whole Grain Banana, Whole Grain Carrot, Whole Grain Raisin Bran), Sugar Free (Banana, Blueberry, Carrot)

Flax4Life ▲ - Flax Muffins (Chunky Chocolate Chip ●, Faithful Carrot Raisin ●, Hawaiian Pineapple Coconut ●, Tantalizing Cranberry & Orange ●, Wild Blueberry ●)

Foods By George ▲ - Muffins (Blueberry, Corn)

Gifts Of Nature ▲ - Mix (Basic ●, Cinnamon Spice ●, Vanilla Poppy Seed ●)

Ginny Bakes ▲ - Muffin Mix Peace Love & Crumble ●

Gluten Free Life ▲ - Muffin (Apple Pie, Blueberry, Carrot Cake, Chocolate Chip), The Ultimate Gluten Free Cake Muffin & Brownie Mix

Gluten Free Pantry ▲ - Muffin & Scone Mix

Gluten-Free Creations ▲ - Muffins (Chocolate Zucchini ●, Cranberry Orange Pecan ●, Lemon Poppyseed ●)

Grandma Ferdon's ▲ -
Banana Bread Muffin Mix ●
Muffins (Banana ●, Corn ●, Pumpkin ●)

Heaven Mills ▲ - Muffins (Blueberry ●, Carrot ●, Chocolate Chip ●, Cinnamon ●)

muffins/muffin mix

M

Hodgson Mill ▲ - Gluten Free Apple Cinnamon Muffin Mix

Joan's GF Great Bakes ▲ - Corn Toaster Muffins

Katz Gluten Free ▲ - Honey Muffins ●

King Arthur Flour ▲ - Gluten Free Muffin Mix ●

Kinnikinnick ▲ -
Jumbo Muffins (Chocolate Lovers, Harvest Crunch, Lemon Poppy Seed)
Regular Muffins (Blueberry, Carrot, Chocolate Chip)

Kneaded Specialties ▲ - Banana ●, Blueberry Streusel ●, Double Chocolate Chip Banana ●, Lemon Poppy Seed ●, Raspberry Swirl●, Vegan (Pumpkin ●, Very Berry ●)

Longevity Bean Muffins ▲ - Muffins (Almond, Banana, Blueberry, Cherry, Cinnamon, Cranberry, Original)

Maple Grove Farms Of Vermont - Orange Cranberry Muffin Mix

Marion's Smart Delights ▲ - Cookie & Muffin Mix ●

Midge's Muffins - Banana, Blueberry, Cherry Apple, Chocolate Chip, Cranberry, Pumpkin

Mixes From The Heartland ▲ - Streusel Muffin Mix (Apple Cinnamon●, Blueberry ●, Cranberry ●, Raspberry ●, Spring ●)

Molly's Gluten-Free Bakery ▲ - Muffins (Blueberry, Chocolate Chip, Lemon Poppyseed, Pumpkin)

Mrs. Crimble's - Muffin & Sponge Mix

Namaste Foods ▲ - Muffin Mix, Sugar Free

Only Oats ▲ - Muffin Mix (Cinnamon Spice ●, Decadent Chocolate ●)

Orgran ▲ - Muffin Mix Chocolate

Pamela's Products ▲ - Cornbread & Muffin Mix

PatsyPie - Morning Glory w/Flax Mini Muffins

Purely Elizabeth ▲ - Muffin Mix (Apple Spice ●, Blueberry ●, Cacao Chocolate Chip ●)

Quejos ▲ - Non Dairy Muffins (Chocolate Chip Banana, Cranberry Banana, Hemp Heart Banana)

Really Great Food Company ▲ - Muffin Mix (Apple Spice, Cornbread, English, Maple Raisin, Sweet, Vanilla)

Silly Yak Bakery -
- CFGF Muffins (Apple ●, Apple Sorghum ●, Blueberry Rice ●, Blueberry Sorghum ●, Carrot Raisin Sorghum ●, Peach Rice ●, Raspberry Rice ●)
- GF Muffins (Almond Joy ●, Almond Poppy Seed ●, Apple Rice ●, Banana ●, Blueberry Peach ●, Blueberry Rice ●, Cherry Almond●, Chocolate Caramel ●, Chocolate Cherry ●, Chocolate Mint ●, Chocolate Raspberry ●, Cinnamon Apple Rice ●, Cranberry Almond ●, Cranberry Orange ●, Lemon Blueberry ●, Lemon Poppyseed ●, Peach Rice ●, Pumpkin ●, Pumpkin w/Frosting ●, Raspberry ●, Turtle ●)

Skye Foods - Muffins (Blueberry ●, Chocolate Chunk ●)

Sweet Christine's Bakery - Muffins (Banana Chocolate Chip ●, Chocolate Chip ●, Flaxseed ●)

The Cravings Place ▲ - Chocolate Chunk Double, Create Your Own

The Grain Exchange - Muffins (Blueberry, Cinnamon)

The Grainless Baker ▲ - Blueberry, Chocolate Chip

Udi's Gluten Free Foods ▲ -
- Gluten Free Muffin Tops (Blueberry Oat ●, Chocolate Chia ●)
- Gluten Free Muffins (Blueberry ●, Double Chocolate ●, Lemon Streusel ●)

Whole Foods Market Gluten Free Bakehouse ▲ - Muffins (Blueberry, Cherry Almond Streusel, Lemon Poppyseed, Morning Glory)

Mushrooms

*... *All Fresh Fruits & Vegetables Are Gluten-Free*

Birds Eye - All Plain Frozen Vegetables

Cara Mia - Marinated

Eden Organic - Maitake Dried, Shiitake (Dried Sliced, Dried Whole)

Food Club Brand - Canned (Pieces & Stems, Sliced, Whole)

Fungus Among Us - All Dried

Great Value Brand (Wal-Mart) - Canned Mushrooms (Pieces & Stems, Sliced)

Green Giant - Canned Mushrooms (Pieces & Stems, Sliced, Whole)

M

Hy-Vee - Stems & Pieces, Whole Button

Ka-Me - Stir Fry **!**, Straw **!**

Lowes Foods Brand - Canned Sliced, Jar Sliced

Meijer Brand - Canned (Sliced, Whole), Canned Stems & Pieces (No Salt, Regular)

Midwest Country Fare - Mushrooms & Stems (No Salt Added, Regular)

My Essentials - Stems & Pieces (No Salt, Regular)

Native Forest - Organic (Crimini Sliced, Pieces & Stems, Portobello Sliced)

Nuts.com - Simply Mushrooms Freeze Dried Vegetables ●

Pennsylvania Dutchman - Chunky Style Portabella, Sliced, Stems & Pieces, Whole

Publix GreenWise Market - Portabella, Regular, Sliced Portabella

Safeway Brand - Canned (Stems & Pieces, Whole, Whole Sliced)

Spartan Brand - Canned Buttons (No Salt Added Pieces & Stems, Pieces & Stems, Sliced, Whole)

Trader Joe's - Marinated w/Garlic

Wegmans Brand - Canned Pieces & Stems

Woodstock Farms - Organic Frozen (Mixed, Shiitake)

Mustard

Annie's Naturals - Organic (Dijon **!!**, Honey **!!**, Horseradish **!!**, Yellow **!!**)

Beaver - American Picnic Yellow ●

Best Foods - Dijonnaise, Honey

Bone Suckin' Sauce - Regular, Sweet & Hot

Di Lusso - Chipotle, Cranberry Honey, Deli Style, Dijon, Honey Sweet & Hot, Jalapeno

Dietz & Watson ▲ - Champagne Dill ●, Chipotle ●, Cranberry Honey ●, Jalapeno ●, Spicy Brown ●, Stone Ground ●, Sweet & Hot●, Wasabi ●, Whole Grain Dijon ●, Yellow ●, Zesty Honey ●

Dorothy Lane Market - All Flavors

Eden Organic - Organic (Brown, Yellow)

Emeril's - Dijon, Kicked Up Horseradish, New York Deli Style, Smooth Honey, Yellow

Fischer & Wieser - Smokey Mesquite, Sweet Heat

Food Club Brand - Dijon, Honey, Horseradish, Regular, Spicy Brown

French's - Classic Yellow, Dijon, Honey, Honey Dijon, Horseradish, Spicy Brown

Frontera - Chipotle Honey Mustard Grilling Sauce

Full Circle - Organic (Spicy Brown, Yellow)

Gordon Food Service

Great Value Brand (Wal-Mart) - All Natural Yellow, Dijon, Honey, Southwest Spicy, Spicy Brown

Grey Poupon - Country Dijon, Deli, Dijon, Harvest Coarse Ground, Hearty Spicy Brown, Mild & Creamy, Savory Honey

H-E-B - Dijon Squeeze

Hannaford Brand - Dijon, Honey, Spicy Brown, Yellow

Heinz - Deli, Dijon, Honey, Spicy Brown, Yellow

Hellmann's - Deli, Dijonnaise, Honey

Hill Country Fare H-E-B - Honey, Spicy Brown, Yellow

Hy-Vee - Dijon, Honey, Regular, Spicy Brown

Jack Daniel's - Hickory Smoke, Honey Dijon, Horseradish, Old No. 7, Spicy Southwest, Stone Ground Dijon

Jim Beam - Original

Ka-Me - Hot Mustard !

Kurtz - Honey Mustard

Lou's Famous - Organic Horseradish

Lowes Foods Brand - Regular, Spicy Brown

Meijer Brand - Dijon Squeeze, Gold (Bavarian, Blueberry Honey, Champagne Dill, Cherry Honey, Zesty Whole Grain), Honey Squeeze, Horseradish Squeeze, Hot & Spicy, Organic (Dijon, Regular, Spicy Brown), Salad Squeeze, Spicy Brown Squeeze

Midwest Country Fare - Yellow

Mother's Mountain -
Honey Mustard (Classic, Zesty)
Peppercorn Dijon

Mr. Spice Organic - Honey Mustard Sauce & Marinade ★

Napa Valley - Dijon w/Garlic & Herbs ●, Whole Grained w/Chilis & Garlic ●

O Organics - Dijon

Olde Cape Cod - All Varieties

Organicville - No Added Sugar (Dijon ●, Stone Ground ●, Yellow ●)

Publix - Classic Yellow, Deli Style, Dijon, Honey, Spicy Brown

Publix GreenWise Market - Creamy Yellow, Spicy Yellow, Tangy Dijon

Rose City Delicacies - Creamy Mustard (Grand Marnier ●, Mazama Infused Pepper Vodka ●, Oregon Pinot (Gris ●, Noir ●))

Royal Food Products - Gourmet Choice Paris Style Honey Dijon, Royal Deluxe (Dijon Honey, Honey), Slender Select Fat Free Honey

Safeway Brand - Coarse Ground Dijon, Dijon, Honey Mustard, Spicy Brown, Sweet & Spicy, Yellow

Spartan Brand - Dijon, Honey, Horseradish, Southwestern Sweet & Hot, Yellow

Taste of Inspiration - Cranberry !, Honey !, Irish Stout !, Maine Maple !, Roasted Garlic !

Texas Pete ▲ - Honey Mustard

The Spice Hunter - Yellow Mustard Ground

Trader Joe's - Dijon, Organic Yellow ! !

Wegmans Brand - Dijon (Honey, Traditional, Whole Grain), Horseradish, Spicy Brown, Yellow

Wellshire Farms - Wellshire Organic Dill Mustard

Winn Dixie - Dijon, Honey, Horseradish, Spicy Brown, Yellow

Woeber's - All Flavors Are Gluten Free *(Except Sauces)*

Woodstock Farms - Organic (Dijon, Stoneground, Yellow)

N

Neufchatel...see Cream Cheese

Noodles...see also Pasta

A Taste Of Thai - Rice Noodles (Pad Thai For Two, Regular, Thin, Vermicelli, Wide)

N

Annie Chun's - Rice Noodles (Maifun, Maifun Brown, Pad Thai, Pad Thai Brown)

Grandma Ferdon's ▲ - Chow Mein ●

King Soba -

Organic (100% Brown Rice, 100% Buckwheat, Black Rice, Brown Rice & Wakame, Milled & Brown Rice, Pumpkin Ginger & Rice, Sweet Potato & Buckwheat, Thai Rice)

Organic Fair Trade (Pad Thai, Vermicelli)

Ramen (Brown Rice, Buckwheat)

Manischewitz - Passover Noodles, Shell Shaped, Spiral Shaped

Mixes From The Heartland ▲ - Noodle Mix (Pesto ●, Plain ●, Spinach ●)

Paskesz - Chow Mein, Premium Egg Medium

Seitenbacher - Gluten Free Rigatoni, Gourmet Noodles Gluten Free Golden Ribbon

Spaa - Tasty Thai (Pad Thai Noodles, Peanut Satay)

Star Lion - Rice Noodles (Nests, Stick)

Thai Kitchen -

Instant Rice Noodle Soup (Lemongrass & Chili, Roasted Garlic, Thai Ginger & Vegetables)

Rice Noodle Carts (Pad Thai, Thai Peanut)

Rice Noodles (Stir Fry Rice Noodles, Thin Rice Noodles)

Stir Fry Rice Noodle Meal Kit (Lemongrass & Chili, Original Pad Thai, Thai Peanut)

Take Out Boxes (Ginger & Sweet Chili, Original Pad Thai, Thai Basil & Chili)

Trader Joe's - Rice Noodles

Nut Beverages

Almond Dream - Almond Drink (Original, Unsweetened, Vanilla)

Blue Diamond - Almond Breeze (Chocolate, Original, Vanilla), Almond Breeze Unsweetened (Chocolate, Original, Vanilla), Refrigerated Almond Breeze (Chocolate, Original, Unsweetened Vanilla, Vanilla)

Pacific Natural Foods - Hazelnut (Chocolate, Original), Organic Almond (Chocolate, Low Fat (Original, Vanilla), Unsweetened (Original, Vanilla))

nutritional supplements

N

Central Market H-E-B - Organics Almond (Original, Vanilla)

H-E-B - Almond Milk (Chocolate, Original, Vanilla (Regular, Unsweetened))

Laura Lynn - Natural Almond Milk (Original, Unsweetened Vanilla, Vanilla)

MimicCreme - Almond & Cashew Cream (Sugar Free Sweetened, Sweetened, Unsweetened)

O Organics - Almond Milk

Pure Market Express ▲ - Brazil Nut Milk ●

Silk - Pure Almond (Dark Chocolate, Original, Unsweetened (Original, Vanilla), Vanilla)

Nut Butters...see Peanut Butter

Nutritional Supplements

Boost -

Calorie Smart (Rich Chocolate, Very Vanilla)

Glucose Control (Rich Chocolate, Very Vanilla)

High Protein (Creamy Strawberry, Rich Chocolate, Very Vanilla)

High Protein Drink Mix **! !**

Kid Essentials (Chocolate, Vanilla)

Original (Creamy Strawberry, Rich Chocolate, Very Vanilla)

PLUS (Creamy Strawberry, Rich Chocolate, Very Vanilla)

Bragg - Braggzyme Systemic Enzymes

Carnation - Breakfast Essentials All Powdered Instant Breakfast *(Except Chocolate Malt)*

Ensure - All Liquid Products, Vanilla Nutrition Powder

Fruit Advantage - All Varieties Dietary Supplements

Glucerna - All Shakes

Meijer Brand - Diet Quick Extra Thin (Chocolate, Strawberry, Vanilla), Gluco Burst (Artic Cherry, Chocolate Diabetic Nutritional Drink, Strawberry DND, Vanilla DND)

MLO - Brown Rice Protein Powder

Navitas Naturals ▲ - Maca (Powder, Raw Powder), Superfood Blend, Twister Powder

N

Pedialyte - Freezer Pops, Hospital Sized Bottles, One Liter Bottles, Powder Packs, Single Juice Boxes

Pediasure - Drinks (Banana, Berry, Chocolate, SideKicks (Chocolate, Strawberry, Vanilla), Strawberry, Vanilla, Vanilla w/Fiber)

Ruth's Hemp Power - Organic Hemp Protein Powder (E3Live & Maca, Hemp Protein Power, Hemp w/Sprouted Flax & Maca)

Safeway Brand - All Flavors Of Nutritional Shakes (Plus, Regular)

Salba - Ground Salba Seed ●, Salba Seed Oil Gelcaps ●, Salba Seed Oil ●, Whole Salba Seed ●

Worldwide Pure Protein - Shake (Banana Cream, Frosty Chocolate, Strawberry Cream, Vanilla Cream)

Nuts

Aimee's Livin' Magic - All Nuts

Back To Nature - Sea Salt Roasted California Almonds, Sea Salt Roasted Cashew Almond Pistachio Mix, Sea Salt Roasted Jumbo Cashews, Tuscan Herb Roasts, Unroasted Unsalted California Almonds, Unroasted Unsalted Walnuts

Blue Diamond -

Almonds

100 Calorie Packs (Cinnamon Brown Sugar, Dark Chocolate, Lightly Salted, Sea Salt, Whole Natural)

Bold Flavors (Blazin' Buffalo Wing, Carolina Barbeque, Habanero BBQ, Jalapeno Smokehouse, Salt N' Vinegar)

Cooking & Baking (Sliced, Slivered, Whole)

Oven Roasted (Butter Toffee, Chocolate Mint, Cinnamon Brown Sugar, Dark Chocolate, Honey, No Salt, Sea Salt)

Traditional Flavors (Honey Roasted, Lightly Salted, Roasted Salted, Smokehouse, Whole Natural)

Don Enrique - Chile Pistachio

Eden Organic - Tamari Dry Roasted Almonds

Frito-Lay - Cashews !!, Deluxe Mixed !!, Peanuts (Honey Roasted !!, Hot !!, Salted !!), Praline Pecans !!, Roasted Salted Almonds !!, Trail Mix (Nut & Chocolate !!, Nut & Fruit !!, Original !!)

Gordon Food Service - Dry Roasted Peanuts

Hail Merry ▲ - Pecans (Chimayo Chile ●, Chocolate Chile ●, Lemon Thyme ●, Orange Rosemary ●)

Just Almonds - All Varieties

KatySweet ▲ -

Organic Pecans (Glazed ●, Roasted & Salted ●, Smokin Chipotle ●, Sugar & Spice ●)

Pecans (BBQ ●, Glazed ●, Holy Mole ●, Jalapeno Glazed ●, Orange ●, Peppered ●, Roasted & Salted ●, Smokin Chipotle ●, Sugar & Spice ●, Wasabi ●)

Red Hot Almonds ●

Kirkland Signature - Pine Nuts !, Variety Snacking Nuts Almonds, Peanuts, Cashews !

Kroger Brand - Peanuts In Shell (Raw, Roasted)

Lowes Foods Brand - Cashews (Halves & Pieces, Whole), Mixed Nuts, Mixed w/Peanuts (Lightly Salted, Regular), Peanuts (Blanched Salted, Dry Roasted (Lightly Salted, Regular, Unsalted), Honey Roasted, Spanish)

Mareblu Naturals ▲ -

Crunch Bags (Almond ●, Cashew ●, Cashew Coconut ●, CranMango Cashew ●, Dark Chocolate Almond ●, Pecan Cinnamon ●, Pecan Cranberry Cinnamon ●)

Dry Roasted Nuts (Almonds ●, Cashews ●, Pistachios ●)

Glazed Whole Nuts Pecans w/Cranberry & Cinnamon ●

Trail Mix Crunch Bags (Blueberry Pomegranate ●, Cranberry Pomegranate ●, Cranblueberry ●, Cranstrawberry ●, Pecan ●, Pistachio ●)

Meijer Brand - Almonds (Blanched (Sliced, Slivered), Natural Sliced, Slivered, Whole), Cashews (Halves w/Pieces, Halves w/Pieces Lightly Salted, Whole), Mixed (Deluxe, Lightly Salted, Regular), Nut Topping, Peanuts (Blanched (Regular, Slightly Salted), Butter Toffee, Dry Roasted (Lightly Salted, Regular, Unsalted), Honey Roasted, Hot & Spicy, Regular, Spanish), Pecan (Chips, Halves), Pine, Walnuts (Black, Chips, Halves & Pieces)

N

Munchies - Lime & Chili Almonds **! !**, Peanuts (Flamin' Hot **! !**, Honey Roasted **! !**)

Navitas Naturals ▲ - Cashew

Nut Harvest - Natural Lightly Roasted Almonds **! !**, Natural Nut & Fruit Mix **! !**, Natural Sea Salted Whole Cashews **! !**

Nuts.com -

Almonds (Organic (Blanched ●, Dry Roasted Salted ●, Natural Sliced ●, Natural Slivered ●, Raw No Shell ●, Roasted Unsalted ●), Organic Dark Chocolate Covered ●, Organic Milk Chocolate Covered ●, Raw (In Shell ●, No Shell ●), Roasted (Salted ●, Unsalted ●), Sliced Natural ●, Sliced ●, Slivered ●, Sprouted ●, Tamari ●, Whole Blanched ●)

Brazil Nuts (In Shell ●, Organic Raw No Shell ●, Pieces ●, Raw No Shell ●, Roasted (Salted ●, Unsalted ●))

Cashews (Organic (Pieces Raw ●, Raw ●, Salted Dry Roasted ●, Unsalted Dry Roasted ●), Pieces ●, Raw ●, Roasted (Salted ●, Unsalted ●), Supreme Raw ●, Supreme Roasted (Salted ●, Unsalted ●), Thai Coconut Curry ●)

Cilantro Lime Pistachios & Pepitas ●

Hazelnuts (Blanched ●, Organic Raw No Shell ●)

Hazelnuts/Filberts (In Shell ●, Raw No Shell ●, Roasted (Salted ●, Unsalted ●))

Macadamia Nuts (In Shell ●, Organic Raw ●, Pieces ●, Raw ●, Roasted (Salted ●, Unsalted ●))

Mixed Nuts In Shell ●

Peanuts (Blanched ●, Cajun Roasted Salted In Shell ●, In Shell (Jumbo Raw ●, Jumbo Roasted ●), Organic Dry Roasted (Salted No Shell ●, Unsalted No Shell ●), Organic Raw (In Shell ●, No Shell ●), Organic Roasted (In Shell ●, Salted In Shell ●), Organic Wild Jungle Raw ●, Raw Redskin ●, Raw Spanish ●, Roasted Salted In Shell ●, Roasted Super Jumbo Virginia (Salted No Shell ●, Unsalted No Shell ●), Roasted Virginia (Salted No Shell ●, Unsalted No Shell ●), Super Jumbo Blanched ●)

Pecans (Georgia Raw No Shell ●, Hard Shell ●, Organic (Pieces●, Raw No Shell ●), Paper Shell ●, Pieces ●, Roasted (Salted ●, Unsalted ●))

Pine Nuts (Mediterranean Pignolias ●, Organic Raw No Shell ●, Pignolias ●, Raw In Shell ●)

Pistachios (Dry Roasted (Salted ●, Unsalted ●), Organic Raw (In Shell ●, No Shell ●), Raw (In Shell ●, No Shell ●), Red ●, Roasted (Salted In Shell ●, Salted No Shell ●, Unsalted In Shell ●, Unsalted No Shell ●), Roasted Organic (Salted In Shell ●, Unsalted In Shell●), Sweet & Spicy Chipotle ●, Turkish Siirt ●)

Raw Cacao (Almonds & Raisins ●, Brazil Nuts & Mulberries ●)

Rosemary Garlic Pistachios & Almonds ●

Sesame Teriyaki Almonds & Cashews ●

Walnuts (Black ●, English (Halves Raw No Shell ●, In Shell ●, Raw No Shell ●), Maple Mesquite Pod ●, Organic (Pieces Raw ●, Raw No Shell ●), Pieces ●, Roasted Salted ●, Roasted Unsalted ●)

White Chocolate Chip Almonds Cashews & Cacao Nibs ●

Planters -

Almonds (Pumpkin Spice, Smoked, Tailgate Honey Smoked)

Cashews (Chocolate Lovers Milk Chocolate, Deluxe Jumbo w/Sea Salt, Deluxe Whole, Deluxe Whole w/Sea Salt, Dry Roasted, Halves & Pieces, Halves & Pieces w/Pure Sea Salt, Jumbo 100% Natural Harvest, Whole (Deluxe Honey Roasted, Lightly Salted, Regular))

Chocolate Covered (Cashews, Peanuts)

Chopped Hazelnuts

Go Nuts (Lightly Salted Almonds, Lightly Salted Heart Healthy Mix, Peanuts Heat)

Macadamias (Chopped, w/Sea Salt)

Mixed (Dark Chocolate Forest Blend **!!**, Deluxe (Cashews Almonds Brazils Hazelnuts & Pecans, Lightly Salted, Macadamia Cashew, Unsalted, w/Sea Salt), Honey Roasted, Lightly Salted, Pecan Lovers, Pistachio Lovers, Pistachio Mix w/Peanuts &

N

Almonds, Regular, Salt & Pepper, Select (Cashews Almonds & Pecans w/Sea Salt, Macadamia Cashew & Almonds), Unsalted, Winter Spiced)

Nut Rition (Almonds, Heart Healthy, Omega 3 **! !**)

Peanuts (Cocktail (Holiday Collection Honey Roasted/Sweet & Crunchy/Cocktail, Honey Roasted, Lightly Salted, Lightly Salted w/Pure Sea Salt, Raging Buffalo Wings, Redskin Spanish, Regular, Smoky Bacon, Unsalted, w/Sea Salt, White Hot Wasabi), Dry Roasted (Honey Roasted, Lightly Salted w/Sea Salt, Regular, Unsalted), Roasted Salted In Shell, Salted, Sweet & Crunchy, Wicked Hot Chipotle)

Pine Nuts

Pistachios Dry Roasted

Recipe Ready (Almond (Slices, Slivers, Whole), Pecan (Chips, Halves, Pieces), Walnut (Black, Pieces), Walnuts Regular)

Publix - Virginia Peanuts

Roland - Feng Shui Roasted Chestnuts

Safeway Brand - Baking (Almonds, Pecans, Walnuts)

Sahale - Glazed Nuts (Almonds w/Cranberries Honey & Sea Salt●, Cashews w/Pomegranate & Vanilla ●), Nut Blends (Ksar●, Soledad●, Valdosta ●), Seasoned Nuts (Almonds (Barbeque ●, Tuscan ●), Southwest Cashew ●)

Shiloh Farms - Organic (American Native Pecans **! !**, Brazil **! !**, Hazelnuts **! !**, Pine Nuts **! !**, Premium Walnut Pieces **! !**, Raw (Macadamia **! !**, Pistachio Splits **! !**, Pistachios Shelled **! !**, Whole Almonds **! !**, Whole Cashews **! !**), Sweet Apricot Kernels **! !**, Walnut Pieces & Halves **! !**), Pecan Halves **! !**, Pistachios Roasted & Salted **! !**, Raw Whole Cashews **! !**, Sliced Almonds **! !**, Whole Almonds **! !**

Sjaak's ▲ - Christmas Nuts & Chews Box, Reindeer Nuts & Chews Box

Spartan Brand - Cashews (Halves w/Pieces, Whole), Mixed w/Peanuts, Peanuts (Butter Toffee, Dry Roasted (Lightly Salted, No Salt, Regular), Honey Roasted, Roasted Salted Blanched)

Sunkist - Pistachios (Dry Roasted, Kernels)

Trader Joe's - All Raw & Roasted Nuts, Cinnamon Almonds, Marcona Almonds

True North - Crunch (Almond Pecan, Cashew, Peanut)

Wegmans Brand -

Cashews (Salted, Unsalted)

Dry Roasted Macadamias Salted

Honey Roasted Whole Cashews

Italian Classics Pine Nuts

Natural Whole Almonds

Party Peanuts (Roasted Lightly Salted, Salted)

Peanuts (Butter Toffee, FYFGA Unsalted In Shell, Honey Roasted, Salted In Shell)

Peanuts Dry Roasted (Lightly Salted, Seasoned, Unsalted)

Roasted (Almonds Salted, Cashews Halves & Pieces Salted, Deluxe Mixed Nuts w/Macadamias Salted, FYFGA Virginia Peanuts Salted, Jumbo (Cashew Mix w/Almonds Pecans & Brazils, Cashews), Marcona Almonds Salted, Mixed Nuts w/Peanuts Lightly Salted, Party Mixed Nuts w/Peanuts Salted, Party Peanuts (Lightly Salted, Salted), Spanish Peanuts Salted, Whole Cashews (Salted, Unsalted))

Virginia Peanuts Chocolate Covered

Winn & Lovett - Pecan Praline **!!**

Woodstock Farms -

Almonds (Chocolate w/Evaporated Cane Juice, Cocoa Dusted Dark Chocolate, Natural Thick Slice, Non Pareil, Roasted & Salted, Roasted No Salt, Tamari, Yogurt w/Evaporated Cane Juice)

Brazil

Cashew Large Whole (Regular, Roasted No Salt)

Deluxe Mixed Nuts Roasted & Salted

Extra Fancy Mixed Nuts Roasted & Salted

Hazelnuts Filberts

Honey Roasted Peanuts

N

O

Organic Brazil

Organic Nuts (Almonds (Dark Chocolate w/Evaporated Cane Juice, Regular), Brazil, Cashews (Large Whole, Large Whole Roasted & Salted, Pieces), Pecan Halves, Pine, Pistachios (Dry Roasted & Salted, Dry Roasted No Salt), Soy Nuts (Dry Roasted & Salted, Dry Roasted No Salt), Walnuts Halves & Pieces)

Pecan Halves

Pine

Soynuts Dry Roasted (No Salt, Salted)

Walnuts Halves & Pieces

O

Oatmeal

Bakery On Main - Instant Oatmeal (Apple Pie ●, Maple Multigrain Muffin ●, Strawberry Shortcake ●)

Brothers All Natural ▲ - Fruit & Oats (Apple Cinnamon, Apple Raspberry, Mixed Berry, Strawberry Banana)

Eco-Planet ▲ - Gluten Free Instant Hot Cereal (All Flavors ●)

GlutenFreeda ▲ - Instant Oatmeal (Apple Cinnamon w/Flax, Banana Maple w/Flax, Maple Raisin w/Flax, Natural, Variety Pack)

Pure Market Express ▲ - French Toast Oatmeal ●

Simpli ▲ - Gluten Free Instant (Apricot ●, Plain ●, Raspberry ●)

Oats

Augason Farms ▲ - Gluten Free Regular Rolled Oats ●

Bob's Red Mill ▲ - Gluten Free (Quick Cooking ★, Rolled ★, Steel Cut ★)

Celiac Specialties ▲ - Oats

Chateau Cream Hill Estates - Lara's Rolled Oats ●

Gifts Of Nature ▲ - Old Fashioned Rolled Oats ●, Whole Oat Groats●

Gluten Free Oats ▲ - Oat Groats ●, Old Fashioned Rolled Oats (Organic ●, Regular ●)

Montana Monster Munchies - Whole Grain (Quick Oats ●, Rolled Oats ●)

Only Oats ▲ - Pure Whole Grain (Quick Oat Flakes ●, Rolled Oats ●, Steel Cut Oats ●)

PrOatina ▲ - Gluten Free (Oat Bran ●, Old Fashioned Oatmeal ●)

Simpli ▲ - Gluten Free Premium Oats ●

Tom Sawyer ▲ - Gluten Free

Oil

Badia - Extra Virgin Olive ●

Bakers & Chefs - 100% Pure Clear Frying Oil, 100% Pure Peanut Oil, 100% Pure Vegetable Oil, 100% Soybean Salad Oil, Soybean Oil

Bertolli - All Olive Oils

Bionaturae ▲ - Organic Extra Virgin Olive Oil

Bragg - All Varieties

Carapelli - Olive Oil (Extra Light In Taste, Extra Virgin (Il Numerato, Organic, Premium 100% Italian))

Dr. Bronner's - Coconut Oil (Virgin, Whole)

Eden Organic - Olive Oil Spanish Extra Virgin, Organic (Hot Pepper Sesame Oil, Safflower Oil, Sesame Oil Extra Virgin, Soybean Oil), Toasted Sesame Oil

Filippo Berio ▲ - Olive (Extra Light, Extra Virgin (Organic, Regular, Special Selection), Regular)

Food Club Brand - Canola, Canola & Vegetable Blend, Corn, Olive, Peanut, Vegetable

Foods Alive - Organic Gourmet (Hemp, High Lignan Golden Flax Oil)

Full Circle - Canola, Organic Extra Virgin Olive Oil

Gordon Food Service - Pure Olive Oil

Grand Selections - 100% Pure & Natural Olive Oil

Great Value Brand (Wal-Mart) - Canola Oil Blend, Olive Oil (Extra Light, Extra Virgin, Pure), Pure Oil (Canola, Corn, Vegetable)

Hannaford Brand - Canola Oil, Corn Oil, Olive (Extra Virgin, Extra Virgin Imported, Light Pure), Vegetable Oil

Hollywood - Enriched (Canola, Expeller Pressing Safflower, Gold Peanut)

House Of Tsang - Oil (Hot Chili Sesame, Mongolian Fire, Sesame, Wok)

Hy-Vee - 100% Pure Oil (Canola, Corn, Vegetable), Natural Blend Oil

Ka-Me - Pure Sesame **!**

Kernel Season's - Movie Theater Butter Popping & Topping Oil ●

Kirkland Signature - Block Goat, Extra Virgin Olive Oil, Pure Olive, Soybean

Krinos - Olive Oil (All Varieties)

Lee Kum Kee - Oil (Blended Sesame, Chili, Pure Sesame)

Living Harvest - Hemp Oil

Lowes Foods Brand - Canola, Corn, Extra Virgin, Olive 100% Pure, Peanut, Vegetable

Lucini - Extra Virgin Olive Oil (Delicate Lemon, Estate Select, Fiery Chili, Premium Select, Robust Garlic, Tuscan Basil)

Manischewitz - Vegetable

Manitoba Harvest - Hemp Seed Oil (Organic, Regular)

Mazola - Canola Oil, Corn Oil, Corn Oil Plus, Olive Oil (Extra Virgin, Pure), Vegetable Plus

Meijer Brand - Blended Canola/Vegetable, Canola, Corn, Oil Olive Infused (Garlic & Basil Italian, Roasted Garlic Italian, Spicy Red Pepper Italian), Olive (100% Pure Italian Classic, Extra Virgin (Italian Classic, Regular), Italian Select Premium Extra Virgin, Milder Tasting, Regular), Peanut, Sunflower, Vegetable

Mezzetta ▲ - Extra Virgin Olive Oil

Midwest Country Fare - 100% Pure Vegetable Oil

Montana Gluten Free ▲ - Omega Montana Virgin Camelina Oil ●

Navitas Naturals ▲ - Coconut Oil

Newman's Own Organics - Extra Virgin Olive Oil !!

Nutiva - Organic (Extra Virgin Coconut Oil, Hemp Oil)

Nuts.com - Organic Hemp Oil ●

O Organics - Extra Virgin Olive

Odell's - Popcorn Popping Oil

OmegaMontana - Virgin Camelina Oil ●

Oskri Organics - Extra Virgin Olive Oil, Flax Seed Cooking Oil, Grapeseed Cooking Oil, Omega 3 Extra Virgin Olive Oil, Sesame Oil

Peter Paul - Virgin Coconut

Phildesco - Virgin Coconut

Publix - Canola, Corn, Olive, Peanut, Vegetable

O

Ruth's Hemp Power - Hemp
Safeway Brand - Canola, Corn, Peanut, Vegetable, Vegetable Blend
Safeway Select - Olive Oil (Extra Light, Extra Virgin, Regular)
Santa Barbara Olive Co. - Olive Oil (Extra Virgin, Geno's Garlic Nectar)
Smart Balance - Cooking
Spartan Brand - Blended, Canola, Corn, Olive (Extra Virgin, Pure), Vegetable
Star - California Extra Virgin, Extra Light Olive, Extra Virgin Olive, Family Reserve Infused Olive Oil (Fresh Basil, Fresh Rosemary, Lemon Peel, Roasted Garlic), Grapeseed, Original Garlic Olive, Original Olive, Special Reserve Olive
Tassos - Olive Oil (Extra Virgin, Fine, Organic Extra Virgin, Peza Crete Extra)
Trader Joe's - All Oils
Tropical Traditions - Organic Virgin (Coconut, Palm Oil)
Wegmans Brand - 100% Pure Olive, Basting w/Garlic & Herbs, Canola, Corn, Extra Virgin (Campania Style, FYFGA (Black Truffle, Sicilian Lemon), Novello Unfiltered, Olive, Sicilian Style, Tuscany Style), FYFGA Grapeseed, Mild Olive, Organic FYFGA Sunflower Oil, Organic High Oleic Sunflower Oil, Peanut, Pumpkin Seed, Submarine Sandwich, Vegetable
Wesson Oil - All Flavors
Winn & Lovett - Olive Oil (Balsamic, Extra Virgin, Garlic, Mediterranean, Roasted Garlic, Zesty Italian)
Winn Dixie - Canola, Corn, Olive, Peanut, Vegetable

Okra

... *All Fresh Fruits & Vegetables Are Gluten-Free
Food Club Brand - Frozen (Cut, Whole)
Meijer Brand - Frozen (Chopped, Whole)
Mezzetta ▲ - Hors D'Oeuvres Gourmet, Marinated Hot
Mt. Olive ▲ - Mild Okra
Pictsweet - All Plain Frozen Vegetables, Cracked Pepper Seasoned Okra & Squash
Publix - Frozen (Cut, Whole Baby)

O
    Safeway Brand - Frozen
    Spartan Brand - Frozen (Cut, Whole)
    Trappey's - Cocktail Okra
    Winn Dixie - Frozen (Cut, Diced, Whole)

Olive Oil...see Oil

Olives

B&G - Black, Green

Di Lusso - Green Ionian, Mediterranean Mixed, Pitted Kalamata

Food Club Brand - Manzanilla Stuffed, Pitted, Queen Stuffed, Salad
    Sliced, Sliced

Great Value Brand (Wal-Mart) - California Chopped Ripe, California
    Medium Pitted Ripe, California Sliced Ripe, Jumbo Pitted Ripe,
    Large Pitted Ripe, Minced Pimento Stuffed Manzanilla, Sliced
    Salad

Hannaford Brand - Pitted Ripe (Extra Large, Large, Medium, Small),
    Sliced Ripe, Sliced Salad, Stuffed (Manzanilla, Queen)

Hy-Vee - Chopped Ripe, Manzanilla Olives, Medium Ripe Black,
    Ripe Black Large

Krinos - Imported (Alfonso, Black, Gaeta, Green Cracked, Green
    Olives (Plain/Not Marinated), Italian Style Oil Cured, Kalamata
    Olives (Plain/Not Marinated), Marinated Green Olives, Marinated
    Kalamata Olives, Olive Medley, Sicilian Style)

Kurtz - Salad Olives, Small Pitted Black Olives

Lowes Foods Brand - Chopped Ripe, Manzanilla Stuffed, Pitted
    (Jumbo, Large, Medium, Small), Queen (Plain, Stuffed), Salad
    Sliced, Sliced (Buffet Ripe, Ripe)

Meijer Brand - Manzanilla Stuffed (Placed, Thrown, Tree), Queen
    (Stuffed Placed, Whole Thrown), Ripe (Large, Medium, Pitted
    Jumbo, Pitted Small, Sliced), Salad, Salad Sliced

Mezzetta ▲ -
    Calamata Greek
    Castelvetrano Whole Green
    Colossal Spiced Sicilian
    Fancy Colossal Green

Garlic

Garlic Queen

Home Style Cured Pitted

Jalapeno Garlic (Queen w/Minced Pimento, Regular)

Marinated Cracked Deli

Mediterranean Nicoise Style

Napa Valley Bistro (Applewood Smoked Olives, Garlic Stuffed Olives, Italian Olive Antipasto, Jalapeno Stuffed Olives, Olive Medley, Pitted Kalamata Olives, Roasted Garlic Stuffed Olives)

Organics (Pitted Kalamata, Whole Kalamata)

Pitted Calamata

Salad

Sliced Calamata

Spanish Colossal Queen w/Minced Pimento

Spanish Manzanilla w/Minced Pimento

Spanish Queen Martini In Dry Vermouth

Stuffed Olives (Anchovy, Bleu Cheese, Garlic, Greek Style Feta Cheese, Jalapeno)

Midwest Country Fare - Large Ripe Black, Sliced Ripe Black

Peloponnese - Antipasto Party, Country Gourmet Mixed, Cracked Gourmet Green, Halved Kalamata Gourmet Black, Ionian Gourmet Green, Kalamata Olive Spread, Pitted Kalamata Gourmet Black

Publix - Colossal, Green, Large, Ripe, Small

Safeway Brand - All Varieties

Santa Barbara Olive Co. - Bleu Cheese Stuffed, Canned (Green, Jumbo, Large, Medium), Sun Dried (Black, Organic California, Pitted Black)

Spartan Brand - Manzanilla, Queen, Ripe Pitted Olives (Jumbo, Large, Medium, Sliced, Small), Sliced Spanish Salad

Star - Cannonballs, Farmer's Market Olive Pouch (Medium Pitted, Pitted, Seasoned w/Basil, Seasoned w/Provencal Herbs, Stuffed w/Minced Pimento), Manzanilla Green Olives Whole, Spanish Olives (Manzanillas, Queen, Salad)

O

Tassos -
> In Red Wine Vinegar & Tassos Extra Virgin Olive Oil Natural Black
> In Sea Salt Brine (Almond Stuffed, Halkidikis Olives)
> In Tassos Extra Virgin Olive Oil & Red Wine Vinegar Mediterranean Medley
> Kalamata (Organic In Tassos Organic Extra Virgin Olive Oil & Organic Red Wine Vinegar, Pitted In Tassos Extra Virgin Olive Oil & Red Wine Vinegar, Regular)
> Stuffed (Almond, Blue Cheese, Chili Pepper, Feta Cheese, Garlic, Garlic & Jalapeno, Jalapeno, Pimiento)

Trader Joe's - Colossal Olives Stuffed w/(Garlic Cloves, Jalapeño Peppers), Stuffed Queen Sevillano

Wegmans Brand - Greek Mix, Kalamata (Pitted, Whole), Pitted Ripe (Colossal, Extra Large, Medium), Sliced Ripe, Spanish (Manzanilla, Queen, Salad), Stuffed w/(Almonds, Garlic, Red Peppers)

Winn Dixie - All Varieties (Green, Ripe)

Onions
> ... *All Fresh Fruits & Vegetables Are Gluten-Free*

Augason Farms ▲ - Gluten Free Dehydrated Chopped ●

Birds Eye - All Plain Frozen Vegetables

C & W - All Plain Frozen Vegetables **! !**

Dietz & Watson ▲ - Sweet Vidalia In Sauce ●

Food Club Brand - Frozen Diced

Ian's - Gluten Free Golden Battered Onion Rings

Lowes Foods Brand - Frozen Diced

Meijer Brand - Frozen (Chopped, Diced)

Mezzetta ▲ - Hors D'Oeuvres Onions, Imported Cocktail Onions

Ore-Ida - Chopped Onions

Publix - Frozen Diced

Star - Imported Onions

Trader Joe's - Frozen Peeled & Ready To Use Pearl Onions

Wegmans Brand - FYFGA Jarred Whole Onions In Brine

Winn Dixie - Frozen Pearl Onions

Orange Juice...see Drinks/Juice

END THE BATTLE BETWEEN
GOOD & EVIL
SNACKING.

- ▶ WHOLE GRAIN BROWN RICE
- ▶ ALL-NATURAL
- ▶ WHEAT- & GLUTEN-FREE
- ▶ NO PRESERVATIVES
- ▶ NO ARTIFICIAL FLAVORS

- ▶ NO TRANS FAT
- ▶ NO CHOLESTEROL
- ▶ VEGAN- & CELIAC-FRIENDLY
- ▶ 100% CRUNCHY!

Try All Our Delicious Flavors

Sweet Chili   Salsa Fresca   Sea Salt
Parmesan Tomato   Tangy BBQ   Sea Salt & Black Sesame

riceworks®
TASTES EVIL, BUT ISN'T.

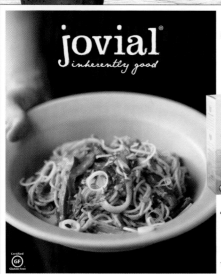

Sayonara, Gluten.
Hello, Genuine
Asian Flavors.

Let lucky kitty introduce you to San-J Tamari Gluten Free Soy Sauces made with 100% soy, Asian Cooking Sauces, and Salad Dressings all made with no wheat. They may be certified gluten-free, but they are also rich and delicious. It starts with our traditional brewing process, and ends with the most mouthwatering creations imaginable. Bring home San-J today, and make everyone at your dinner table feel lucky.

Authentic Taste. Naturally Gluten-Free.

Visit us at www.san-j.com for gluten-free recipe ideas, coupons and much more!

FREE!

Not Just Gluten-Free…
Also <u>Free</u> of the 8 Most Common Allergens.

At Enjoy Life, our mission is producing great-tasting foods
that are safe for the whole family to enjoy. That's why all of our foods
are specially made to be gluten-free and free of the 8 most common allergens.

Gluten-free you can Trust…Taste you will *Love!*

Gluten-Free Resources

1-2-3 Gluten Free
These award-winning, great-tasting baking mixes, made in a dedicated gluten-free and allergen-free U.S. facility (certified gluten-free, kosher) are versatile, make large amounts and are available at stores nationwide and www.123glutenfree.com

Amy's Kitchen
Amy's offers delicious, nourishing meals for health-conscious people. Using natural and organic ingredients, we prepare them with the same careful attention as you would in your home. We Love to Cook for You! www.amys.com

Bakery On Main
Bakery On Main started in the bakery of our natural foods market in Glastonbury, Connecticut. Founder Michael Smulders listened to his Celiac customers complain about the taste of many gluten free foods. He made it his mission to create products that were good for them but taste like they aren't. www.bakeryonmain.com

Bard's Tale Beer
Bard's Beer is America's first gluten-free sorghum beer and the only beer brewed with 100% malted sorghum to provide traditional beer flavor and aroma. Visit www.bardsbeer.com or call 877-440-2337.

Breads From Anna

All Breads From Anna® mixes are gluten, soy, rice and nut free, several are also corn, dairy and yeast free. Unique - because of a smooth, non-grainy texture, high in protein and fiber and an outstanding taste! www.breadsfromanna.com

Buddig / Old Wisconsin

Buddig Deli Cuts and Original Meats are all produced gluten free to be enjoyed for lunch, dinner and snack occasions. Visit us at www.buddig.com and www.oldwisconsin.com

Conrad Rice Mill

Conrad Rice Mill, Inc. a 100 year old rice milling operation produces Certified Gluten Free, Non-GMO , Kosher products under the KONRIKO and Hol Grain brands. Our newest products are Rice Starch - a gravy thickener, Gluten Free Chili and Gluten Free Fajitas mix. Look for our products at your favorite natural store or supermarket or on our website www.conradricemill.com

Crunchmaster

Crunchmaster® is the #1 brand of gluten free crackers in North America. With great multi-grain taste, they are all natural, cholesterol free, low in saturated fat & certified gluten free. www.crunchmaster.com

Delight Gluten-Free Magazine

Delight Gluten-Free Magazine is a quarterly food & lifestyle publication for people living with food allergies and sensitivities. Filled with enlightening articles, glossy photographs and gourmet recipes, Delight Gluten-Free Magazine is on par with other popular mainstream food magazines on newsstands today. www.delightglutenfree.com

Ener-G Foods

Since 1962 Ener-G Foods has met the challenging requirements for diet restricted consumers. We offer over 150 wheat-free, gluten-free, dairy-free, nut-free, kosher certified baked goods, flours, and mixes. www.ener-g.com

Enjoy Life Foods

Our whole business is making smile-good foods that keep people's insides happy. That's why our foods are Gluten-Free and free of the 8 most common allergens, so everyone can EAT FREELY! www.enjoylifefoods.com

Gluten-Free Living Magazine

Gluten-Free Living is the only magazine necessary for a gluten-free lifestyle, bringing you the latest on gluten-free ingredients, labeling, recipes, nutrition, new products and more. www.glutenfreeliving.com

Jones Dairy Farm

From all natural sausage and Canadian bacon to hams, bacon and braunschweiger, Jones Dairy Farm has a 120-year heritage of producing a wide variety of delicious gluten-free products. Visit www.jonesdairyfarm.com

Jovial Foods

Jovial™ gluten free products were developed out of a heartfelt compassion for all of us who have had a food intolerance affect personal health and wellness. We believe eating gluten free should be pleasurable and not feel like a sacrifice. We utilize traditional Italian methods to create traditional, wholesome foods. Try our award winning pasta and our delicious cookies, our products are gluten free, but you would never know.
www.jovialfoods.com

Kettle Cuisine

Experience Kettle Cuisine's all natural, gluten free soups, chilis and chowders. These chef inspired varieties deliver restaurant quality taste without anything artificial. Look for Kettle Cuisine in the natural food freezer. www.kettlecuisine.com

Riceworks

It isn't just what we put into our whole grain brown rice crisps that make them perfect for snacking. It's what we leave out. Like artificial flavors, preservatives and gluten. So the gourmet flavor of Sweet Chili, Salsa Fresca or Sea Salt comes through in every crispy crunch. 6 great flavors.
www.riceworks.com

Rudi's Gluten-Free Bakery

From its founding in 1976, Rudi's has been passionate about baking better breads for families. At the heart of it all, we believe good health leads to happiness. The launch of Rudi's Gluten Free Bakery is a natural extension of our commitment to baking on the bright side by creating healthy and wholesome breads for the whole family. We hope to give families that suffer from celiac disease and gluten intolerances a healthy, brighter outlook by letting them truly enjoy bread again. To learn more about our products and to find a store near you, visit us online. www.rudisglutenfree.com

San-J

Pour on the flavor with San-J! Our delectable and all-natural Asian cooking sauces, salad dressings and Organic Wheat Free Tamari are certified gluten free by the Gluten Free Certification Organization. www.san-j.com

Schär

Schar - Europe's #1 gluten-free food brand. Over 30 dedicated gluten-free items in the US make Schar your gluten-free solution for bread, pasta, cookies, snacks, crackers & pizza. www.schar.com

Simply Organic

Simply Organic offers 12 irresistible baking mixes and over 50 seasoning mixes which are certified gluten-free. Available at Natural Food and Grocery outlets. www.simplyorganic.com. www.simplyorganicfoods.com

Udi's Gluten Free Foods

Udi's is a new approach to gluten-free. No more bland, crumbly, and tasteless food. Udi's sources natural ingredients, making delicious products that fill your stomach and warm your soul.

www.udisglutenfree.com

Venice Bakery

Tested and certified by the Celiac Sprue Association, Venice Baking Company offers a wide variety of delicious, health conscious products. Special attention to ingredients and processes set our Gluten-Free Vegan products apart from others. Like us on Facebook for special offers!

www.venicebakery.com

Woodchuck Cider

Woodchuck Hard Cider is handcrafted in small batches at our cidery nestled within the Green Mountains of Vermont. Made with a unique combination of nature's best ingredients, Woodchuck is easy to drink with a variety of styles from sweet to dry. www.woodchuck.com

Nationwide Support Groups

CDF – Celiac Disease Foundation
Celiac Disease Foundation is a non-profit, public benefit corporation dedicated to providing services and support regarding Celiac Disease and Dermatitis Herpetiformis, through programs of awareness, education, advocacy and research. www.celiac.org

CSA – Celiac Sprue Association
The Celiac Sprue Association® remains the largest non-profit celiac support group in America, with over 125 chapters and resource units across the country and over 9,000 members worldwide. www.csaceliacs.info

GIG – Gluten Intolerance Group
The mission of the Gluten Intolerance Group of North America is to provide support to persons with gluten intolerances, including celiac disease, dermatitis herpetiformis, and other gluten sensitivities, in order to live healthy lives. www.gluten.net

NFCA - National Foundation for Celiac Awareness
NFCA is a not-for-profit organization to raise awareness of celiac disease among the general public and the healthcare community, and to facilitate research to better understand the causes, mechanisms, and treatment of celiac disease. www.celiaccentral.org

Celiac Disease Reserach Centers

Columbia University – Celiac Disease Center
was established within the Department of Medicine at Columbia University in 2001. Its mission: to redefine the future of celiac disease and treatment on an ongoing basis, through continuing advances in research, patient care, and physician and public education.

University of Chicago – Celiac Disease Center
is an international center of excellence providing comprehensive patient and professional education, expert diagnosis and treatment for both children and adults, groundbreaking bench and clinical research, and active leadership in advocacy efforts. The Celiac Disease Center is part of the University of Chicago, a nonprofit organization.

Univ. of Maryland – Center for Celiac Research
is dedicated to improving the quality of life for Celiac Disease patients, while learning the cause of the disease and finding a cure. Located in downtown Baltimore, the Center for Celiac Research provides comprehensive clinical care and long-term support for adults and children who suffer from this genetically based-autoimmune disease, which affects 1 out of every 133 people in the United States.

Gluten-Free Dining Out Tips

- Choose a restaurant with a gluten-free menu. For a list of these restaurants please see below.

- If you are dining out at a restaurant that does not have a gluten-free menu, explain your dietary needs to your wait staff. Ask to speak with the chef to see if there are any naturally gluten-free foods that can be prepared for you.

- Go to restaurants at times when they are not very busy, to prevent cross contamination of your meal.

- Use Cecelia's Marketplace 'GF Dining Out Card' when dining out. This helps to educate your wait staff and chef about which foods you can and cannot have.

Nationwide restaurant chains offering gluten-free menus:

Austin Grill
Bertucci's Italian Restaurant
Biaggi's Ristorante Italiano
BJ's Restaurant & Brewhouse
Bonefish Grill
Bugaboo Creek Steak House
Burtons Grill

Carino's Italian
Carrabba's Italian Grill
Charlie Brown's Steakhouse
Cheeseburger In Paradise Bar & Grill
Claim Jumper Restaurants
Daily Grill
Fleming's Prime Steakhouse
Garlic Jim's Famous Gourmet Pizza
Glory Days Grill
Lee Roy Selmon's
Legal Sea Foods Restaurant
Mama Fu's Asian House
Mitchell's Fish Market
Ninety Nine 99
Not Your Average Joe's
Old Spaghetti Factory
Outback Steakhouse
P.F. Chang's China Bistro
Pei Wei Asian Diner
Pizza Fusion
Rockfish Seafood Grill
Sam & Louie's
The Melting Pot
Village Tavern
Weber Grill Restaurant
Wildfire Steaks, Chops & Seafood
Z' Tejas Southwestern Grill

Gluten-Free Tips

Fresh papaya and pineapple have natural digestive enzymes to help promote healthy digestion.

• • •

Wheat-Free does not mean Gluten-Free.

• • •

If you have been diagnosed with celiac disease or a gluten intolerance, have other family members tested.

• • •

Children's gluten-free camps are available throughout the United States.

• • •

If you can not find gluten-free specialty products in your local area, most are available for purchase online.

• • •

Attend gluten-free food fairs in your local area for free tastings of gluten-free food products such as bread, donuts, cookies and gravies.

• • •

Consider taking probiotics to help promote a healthy stomach/intestinal lining.

Walt Disney World is very accommodating to families with food allergies or intolerances.

• • •

Make sure to eat a well-balanced diet, rotating foods, to avoid developing other food intolerances.

• • •

Use gluten-free hand and body lotions. Some contain wheat germ oil or other gluten ingredients.

• • •

Make sure to use oats that are certified gluten-free. Oats are generally cross contaminated in the mills with wheat, rye or barley.

• • •

Medical professionals should avoid using powdered latex/rubber gloves. These may contain gluten.

• • •

Use a separate colander for draining gluten-free pasta.

• • •

Do not deep fry foods in contaminated oil (i.e. from breaded chicken wings, breaded chicken tenders, mozzarella sticks).

• • •

Make sure your toothpaste and mouthwash are gluten-free.

Double check to make sure your shampoo and conditioner are gluten-free. Using ones that contain gluten can cause irritation of the skin, scalp, eyes, as well as may be ingested by accident.

• • •

Make sure your pet food is gluten-free. Most dog and cat food contains wheat flour. Pets can easily pass on gluten to their owner through close contact.

• • •

Always make sure cosmetics, such as lipstick, eye shadow, and blush, are gluten-free.

• • •

Speak with you pharmacist to make sure your prescription medication is gluten-free.

• • •

Never lick envelopes when closing letters. The sticky residue on the envelopes may contain gluten.

• • •

Make sure your dentist and hygienist are aware of your sensitivity to gluten.

• • •

Use squeeze bottle condiments, such as mayonnaise, mustard, ketchup, peanut butter, jelly/jam, butter/margarine, to prevent cross contamination.

FAN GLUTENFREE TASTIC

Why are we calling attention to the fact that Jones All Natural Sausage contains no gluten and none of the ingredients hidden in other brands? Because we thought you'd like to know. It's just pork, salt and spices—has been for over 120 years. Plus our sausage is frozen so it's always fresh. Always fantastic.

Visit **jonesdairyfarm.com/glutenfree** for great recipes and special savings.

No nitrites

No MSG

No artificial flavors

Find us on Facebook!

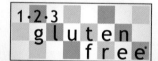

Delight Gluten-Free Magazine

Recipes

Every issue of Delight features more than **60 fully tested gluten-free recipes.** Each recipe has a photo.

Cooking Tips

Our expert chefs will teach you everything you need to know about gluten-free cooking. Learn cooking techniques and watch interactive videos.

Ask-the-Doc

Questions about the medical stuff? No worries. Our medical advisory board answers your questions in every issue!

City Maps

Are you a g-free globetrotter? Use our city maps to navigate your gluten-free way through cities around the world.

TO TRY IT IS TO LOVE IT

Bakery On Main Premium Gluten Free Granola

Delightfully Addictive • Certified Gluten Free Kosher OU Parve • All Natural
Non GMO • Free from Wheat, Gluten, Dairy, Casein, Trans Fat & Cholesterol
Low in Sodium & Saturated fat

SAVE $1.50 when you join the club at www.bakeryonmain.com & LOVE IT MORE

Follow us on:

www.Facebook.com/CeceliasMarketplace

@GlutenFreeGuide

O

P

Oranges

... *All Fresh Fruits & Vegetables Are Gluten-Free

Nuts.com - Organic Dried Oranges ●

Sunkist

Oyster Sauce

Panda Brand - Lo Mein Oyster Flavored Sauce, Oyster Flavored Sauce *(Green Label Only)*

Wok Mei - All Natural Oyster Flavored

Oysters

... *All Fresh Seafood Is Gluten-Free (Non-Marinated, Unseasoned)

Bumble Bee - Fancy Smoked, Fancy Whole

Chicken Of The Sea - Smoked In Oil, Whole

Crown Prince - Fancy Whole Smoked In Cottonseed Oil, Natural (Boiled Whole In Water, Smoked Oysters In Olive Oil)

Great Value Brand (Wal-Mart) - Smoked Oysters

Ocean Prince - Smoked In Cottonseed Oil (Cocktail, Fancy Whole), Whole Boiled

Trader Joe's - Whole Smoked Oysters In Olive Oil

P

Pancakes/Pancake Mix

1-2-3 Gluten Free ▲ - Allie's Awesome Buckwheat Pancake Mix ●

Abundant Life Foods ▲ - Pancake Mix (Blueberry, Buttermilk)

Arnel's Originals - Pancake Mix

Arrowhead Mills - Gluten Free Pancake & Waffle Mix

Authentic Foods ▲ - Pancake & Baking Mix ●

Better Batter - Pancake & Biscuit Mix ●

Bisquick ▲ - Gluten Free Pancake & Baking Mix

Bloomfield Farms ▲ - Gluten Free Pancake & Waffle Mix ●

Bob's Red Mill ▲ - Gluten Free Pancake Mix ★

Bodhi's Bakehouse - Fibre Rich Pancake Mix

Breads From Anna ▲ - Pancake & Muffin Mix (Apple, Cranberry, Maple)

Cause You're Special ▲ - Hearty Pancake & Waffle Mix

Celiac Specialties ▲ - Pancake Mix (Buttermilk, Flaxseed, Plain)

P

Cherrybrook Kitchen - Gluten Free Chocolate Chip Pancake Mix ★ *(Box Must Say Gluten Free)* , Gluten Free Pancake Mix ★ *(Box Must Say Gluten Free)*

Eena Kadeena ▲ - Chai Pancake Mix

El Peto ▲ - Corn Free Pancake Mix, Pancake Mix

Gifts Of Nature ▲ - Pancake & Waffle Mix ●

Gluten Free Mama ▲ - Mama's Pancake Mix ●

Gluten Free Pantry ▲ - Brown Rice Pancake Mix

Gluten Free Sensations ▲ - Pancake & Waffle Mix

Gluten-Free Creations ▲ - Buckwheat Pancake Mix ●, Mighty Mesquite Pancake Mix ●

Gluten-Free Naturals - Pancake Mix

Grandma Ferdon's ▲ - Pancake/Waffle Mix ●

Hodgson Mill ▲ - Gluten Free Pancake & Waffle Mix w/Flaxseed

Hol Grain ▲ - Pancake & Waffle Mix ●

Julian's Recipe - Gluten Free Pancakes (Buttermilk ●, w/Belgian Chocolate ●, Wild Blueberry ●)

King Arthur Flour ▲ - Gluten Free Pancake Mix ●

Kinnikinnick ▲ - Pancake & Waffle Mix

Larrowe's - Instant Buckwheat Pancake Mix

Laurel's Sweet Treats ▲ - Bulk Pancake Mix, Pancake & Waffle Mix

Linda's Gourmet Latkes - Potato Pancake Latkes !

Mamma Mia - Pancake Mix

Maple Grove Farms Of Vermont - Gluten Free Pancake Mix

Mixes From The Heartland ▲ - Pancake Mix (Apple Cinnamon ●, Blueberry ●, Country ●, Cranberry ●)

Mrs. Crimble's - Pancake Mix

Namaste Foods ▲ - Waffle & Pancake Mix

Nuts.com - Gluten Free Pancake Mix ●

Only Oats ▲ - Whole Oat Pancake Mix ●

Orgran ▲ - Apple & Cinnamon Pancake Mix, Buckwheat Pancake Mix

Pamela's Products ▲ - Baking & Pancake Mix

Pure Market Express ▲ - Banana Chocolate Chip Pancakes ●

Purely Elizabeth ▲ - Perfect Pancake Mix ●

Really Great Food Company ▲ - Pancake Mix (Brown Rice, Classic, Jumbo Classic)

Silly Yak Bakery - GF Flap Jack Mix ●

Simply Organic ▲ - Gluten Free Pancake & Waffle Mix ●

Sylvan Border Farm - Pancake & Waffle Mix

The Cravings Place ▲ - All Purpose

The Pure Pantry ▲ - Pancake & Baking Mix (Organic Buckwheat Flax ●, Organic Old Fashioned ●)

Trader Joe's - Gluten Free Homestyle Pancakes, Gluten Free Pancake & Waffle Mix

Voyaging Foods - Taro Cakes ●

Paneer

Amy's - Indian Mattar Paneer (Light In Sodium ★, Regular ★), Indian Palak Paneer ★, Indian Paneer Tikka ★

Tasty Bite - Paneer Makhani !, Peas Paneer !

Trader Joe's - Paneer Tikka Masala !!

Papaya

... *All Fresh Fruits & Vegetables Are Gluten-Free*

Native Forest - Organic Papaya Chunks

Nuts.com - Dried Papaya (Chunks ●, Diced ●, Dried ●, Natural ●, Organic ●)

Woodstock Farms - Organic Frozen Papaya Chunks, Spears Lo Sugar Unsulphured

Paprika...see Seasonings

Parmesan Cheese...see Cheese

Pasta

Allegaroo - Chili Mac, Spaghetti, Spyglass Noodles

Ancient Harvest Quinoa - Elbows, Garden Pagodas, Linguine, Rotelle, Shells, Spaghetti, Veggie Curls

Andean Dream ▲ - Quinoa (Fusilli, Macaroni, Shells, Spaghetti)

Annie Chun's - Rice Noodles (Maifun, Maifun Brown, Pad Thai, Pad Thai Brown)

Aproten - Bucatini, Fettuccine, Linguine, Spaghetti, Tagliatelle

P

Barkat - Gluten Free (Alphabet Shapes, Animal Shapes, Macaroni, Spaghetti, Spirals)

Bi-Aglut -
Corn PastaMia (Fusilli, Penne, Spaghetti)
Egg PastaMia (Lasagne, Sedani, Tagliatelle)
PastaMia (Bucatini, Ditalini, Fusilli, Gemmini, Linguini, Maccheroncini, Micron, Penne, Penne Lisce, Pipe, Rigatoni, Sedani, Spaghetti, Stelline)

Bionaturae ▲ - Organic Gluten Free (Elbow ●, Fusilli ●, Penne ●, Spaghetti ●)

Caesar's - Gluten Free Vegan Gnocchi (Potato ‼, Spinach ‼)

China Sun - Vermicelli (Brown Rice, White Rice)

Conte's Pasta ▲ - Cheese Stuffed Shells ●, Gnocchi ●, Pierogies (Potato Cheese Onion ●, Potato Onion ●), Ravioli (Cheese ●, Cheese Spinach ●)

Cornito - Elbow Macaroni, Mystic Flames Noodles, Rainbow Rotini, Rigatoni Penne, Rotini, Sea Waves Mini Lasagna, Spaghetti Nests

DeBoles -
Gluten Free Corn Pasta (Elbow Style ●, Spaghetti Style ●)
Gluten Free Multi Grain (Penne ●, Spaghetti Style ●)
Gluten Free Rice Pasta (Angel Hair ●, Angel Hair & Golden Flax●, Elbow Style Pasta & Cheese ●, Fettucini ●, Lasagna ●, Penne ●, Shells & Cheddar ●, Spaghetti Style ●, Spirals ●, Spirals & Golden Flax ●)

Eden Organic - Bifun, Kuzu, Mung Bean

Ener-G ▲ - White Rice (Lasagna, Macaroni, Small Shells, Spaghetti, Vermicelli)

Farmo - Corn & Rice

Gillian's Foods ▲ - Fettuccini ●, Fusilli ●, Penne ●, Spaghetti ●

Glutano ▲ - Fusilli, Penne, Spaghetti

GlutenOut - Gnocchi ★, Ravioli ★, Tagliatelle ★, Trofie ★

Goldbaum's ▲ - All Natural Brown Rice (Fettuccine, Penne, Shells, Spaghetti, Spirals)

Grandma Ferdon's ▲ - Brown Rice (Chow Mein Noodles ●, Elbows ●, Fettuccini ●, Lasagna ●, Spaghetti ●)

H-E-B - Gluten Free (Fusilli, Penne, Spaghetti)

Hodgson Mill ▲ - Gluten Free Brown Rice w/Golden Milled Flax Seed (Angel Hair, Elbow, Lasagna, Linguine, Penne, Spaghetti)

Jovial ▲ - Brown Rice (Capellini ●, Caserecce ●, Fusilli ●, Penne Rigate ●, Spaghetti ●)

Katz Gluten Free ▲ - Farfel ●

Le Asolane - Corn (Penne, Spaghetti, Tagliatelle)

Le Veneziane - Anellini, Ditalini, Eliche, Fettucce, Penne, Pipe Rigate, Rigatoni, Spaghetti

Lundberg ▲ - Organic Brown Rice Pasta (Elbow, Penne, Rotini, Spaghetti)

Maninis ▲ - Lasagna Sheets ●, Lemon Thyme Linguini ●, Pasta Mix ●, Roasted Garlic Fettuccini ●, Spaghetti ●, Tre Colore Rigatoni ●

Manischewitz - Noodles (Shell Shaped, Spiral Shaped), Passover Noodles

Mixes From The Heartland ▲ -
  Creamy Italian Noodles ●
  Pasta Mix (Penne ●, Shells ●, Spaghetti ●)
  Pasta Salad (Corn 'N ●, Cucumber Dill ●, Dilled ●)

Molino Nicoli - Cous Cous

Mrs. Leeper's -
  Corn Pasta (Elbows, Rotelli, Spaghetti, Vegetable Radiatore)
  Dinners (Beef Lasagna, Beef Stroganoff, Cheeseburger Mac, Chicken Alfredo, Creamy Tuna, Mac & Cheese)
  Rice Pasta (Alphabets, Elbows, Kids Shapes, Penne, Spaghetti, Vegetable Twists)

Namaste Foods ▲ - Pasta Meals (Pasta Pisavera, Say Cheez, Taco)

Nasoya ▲ - Pasta Zero Plus (Shirataki Fettuccine, Shirataki Spaghetti)

Notta Pasta - Fettuccine, Linguine, Spaghetti, Vermicelli

Nuovo - Gluten Free Potato Gnocchi (Basil Potato ●, Classic ●, Roasted Sweet ●)

Nuts.com - Gluten Free (Fusili ●, Penne ●, Rigatoni ●)

P

Orgran ▲ -
Buckwheat Spirals
Buontempo Rice Pasta (Penne, Shells, Spirals)
Canned (Alternative Grain Spaghetti, Spaghetti In Tomato Sauce)
Chilli Pasta Spirals
Corn & Vegetable (Shells, Spirals)
Corn Pasta Spirals
Essential Fibre (Lasagnette, Penne, Spirals)
Garlic & Parsley Rice Pasta Curls
Italian Style Spaghetti
Kids (Itsy Bitsy Vegetable Shells, Outback Animals Vegetable
    Shapes, Rice & Corn Vegetable Farm Animals)
Rice & Corn (Lasagne Mini Sheets, Macaroni, Penne, Spaghetti
    (Noodles, Pasta), Spirals, Tortelli)
Rice & Millet Spirals
Rice Pasta Spirals
Super Grains Multigrain Pasta (w/Amaranth, w/Quinoa)
Vegetable Rice (Penne, Spirals)

Pastariso ▲ -
All Natural Rice (Brown Rice Elbows ●, Brown Rice Penne ●, Brown
    Rice Rotini ●, Brown Rice Spaghetti ●)
Organic Brown Rice (Angel Hair ●, Elbows ●, Fettuccine ●,
    Lasagna●, Linguine ●, Penne ●, Rotini ●, Spaghetti ●, Spinach
    Spaghetti ●, Vegetable Rotini ●, Vermicelli ●)

Pastato ▲ - Fortified Potato Pasta (Elbows ●, Penne ●, Spaghetti ●)

Pure Market Express ▲ - Pasta Meal Kits (Creamy Garlic Dill ●,
    Garlic Alfredo ●)

Rizopia ▲ -
Brown Rice (Elbows ●, Fettuccine ●, Fusilli ●, Lasagne ●, Penne●,
    Shells ●, Spaghetti ●, Spinach Spaghetti ●, Spirals ●, Vegetable
    Fusilli●)
Organic Brown Rice (Elbows ●, Fantasia ●, Fettuccine ●, Fusilli ●,
    Penne ●, Spaghetti ●)
Organic Wild Rice (Elbows ●, Fusilli ●, Penne ●, Radiatore ●, Shells ●,
    Spaghetti ●)

White Rice Spaghetti ●

Rustichella - Gluten Free Pasta (Corn Fusillotti, Corn Spaghetti, Rice Penne, Rice Spaghetti)

Sam Mills ▲ - Corn Pasta (Cornetti Rigati, Fusilli, Lasagne Corte, Pasta For Kids (Alphabet, Ducks), Rigatoni, Spaghetti)

Sanavi - Harifen Low Protein (Macaroni Penne, Orzo, Spaghetti)

Schar ▲ - Anellini, Fusilli, Multigrain Penne Rigate, Penne, Spaghetti, Tagliatelle

Seitenbacher - Gluten Free Rigatoni, Gourmet Noodles Gluten Free Golden Ribbon

Simply Shari's Gluten Free & Fabulous ▲ - Quinoa & Marinara ●

Solterra - Feather Lite Fettuccine, Gnocchi (Potato, Roasted Red Pepper, Spinach, Tre Color), Spaghettini

Still Riding Pizza - Penne, Spaghetti

Tinkyada ▲ -
Brown Rice (Elbows, Fettuccini, Fusilli, Grand Shells, Lasagne, Little Dreams, Penne, Shells, Spaghetti, Spinach Spaghetti, Spirals, Vegetable Spirals)
Organic Brown Rice (Elbows, Lasagne, Penne, Spaghetti, Spirals)
White Rice Spaghetti

Trader Joe's - All Organic Brown Rice Pasta, Rice Pasta & Cheddar, Rice Sticks Rice Pasta

Trenipoti - Gluten Free ●

Westbrae - Corn Angel Hair Pasta

Wildwood - Pasta Slim (Spaghetti, Spinach Fettuccini, Tomato & Herbs Angel Hair)

Pasta Sauce...see Sauces

Pastrami
Boar's Head - All Varieties
Buddig - Deli Cuts, Original
Castle Wood Reserve - Deli Meat Turkey Pastrami
Di Lusso - Deli Counter
Dietz & Watson ▲ - Pastrami (Bottom Round ●, New York Brisket ●), Spiced Beef Pastrami ●
Eating Right - Deli Sliced

P

    Eckrich - Deli Meat Peppered Pastrami
    Garrett County Farms - Sliced Beef ★
    Hy-Vee - Thin Sliced
    Kayem - Extra Lean Black ‼, New England Red ‼, New York Style Black ‼
    Meijer Brand - Lunch Meat Sliced Chipped Meat
    Perdue - Deli Dark Turkey Pastrami Hickory Smoked
    Wellshire Farms - Sliced Beef ★

Pastry Mix
    Mrs. Crimble's - Pastry Mix
    Orgran ▲ - All Purpose
    Sanavi Harisin - Bread & Pastry Mix

Pate
    Kootenay Kitchen - Vege Pate (Curry, Herb, Jalapeno)
    Old Wisconsin - Spreadable Pate (Black Pepper, Onion & Parsley, Original)
    Tartex - Champignon, Chardonnay Cote D'Or, Cremisso (Horseradish Apple, Peppers Chili, Tomato Basil, Zucchini Curry), Delicacy, Exquisite, Green Pepper, Herbs, Hungarian, Mediterrana, Mexicana, Olivera, Organic Pate In Tubes (Chilli, Classic, Green Olive, Herb, Herb & Garlic, Mushroom, Roasted Onion & Pink Peppercorn, Sundried Tomato), Pate (Chanterelle Mushroom, Grilled Aubergine, Porcini Mushrooms & Cranberry), Pate Creme (Rocket & Mustard, Sundried Tomato & VanDouvan), Pesto, Pomodoro D'Italia, Provence Herbs, Ratatouille, Shiitake, Truffle Champagne

Pea Pods
    ... *All Fresh Fruits & Vegetables Are Gluten-Free*
    Meijer Brand - Frozen Chinese

Peaches
    ... *All Fresh Fruits & Vegetables Are Gluten-Free*
    C & W - All Plain Frozen Fruits ‼
    Del Monte - Canned/Jarred Fruit (All Varieties), Plastic
    Dole - All Fruits Frozen, Bowls *(Except Fruit Crisps)*, Fruit Parfait

peaches

P

Peaches & Creme, Sliced Peaches In 100% Fruit Juice Jars

Food Club Brand - Frozen Peaches Sliced, Fruit Cups Diced Peaches, Halves In Heavy Syrup, Sliced In Heavy Syrup, Sliced In Juice

Gordon Food Service - Diced In Lite Syrup, Sliced

Great Value Brand (Wal-Mart) - Frozen, Yellow Cling Peaches (Sliced In Juice, Sliced No Sugar Added), Yellow Cling Sliced Peaches In Heavy Syrup

Hy-Vee - Diced, Diced Fruit Cups, Halves, Lite (Diced, Slices), Peaches In Strawberry Gel, Slices

Kroger Brand - Fruit Cups

Lowes Foods Brand - Sliced Frozen, Slices (In Heavy Syrup, In Juice)

Meijer Brand - Cling Halves (In Heavy Syrup, In Juice Lite, In Pear Juice Lite), Cling Sliced (In Heavy Syrup, In Juice, In Pear Juice Lite), Frozen (Organic, Sliced), Yellow Sliced In Heavy Syrup

Midwest Country Fare - Yellow Cling Slices (In Heavy Syrup, In Light Syrup)

Native Forest - Organic (Peach & Apricot Medley, Sliced Peaches)

Nuts.com - Dried Fruit (Diced ●, Dried ●, Organic ●, Simply ●, White●)

Publix - Canned (Lite Yellow Cling Peaches In Pear Juice Halves & Slices, Yellow Cling Peaches In Heavy Syrup Halves & Slices), Frozen Sliced Peaches

S&W - All Canned/Jarred Fruits

Safeway Brand - Canned Peaches (Halves, Halves Lite, Sliced, Sliced Lite), Frozen

Spartan Brand - Cling Halves (Heavy Syrup, Lite Syrup), Cling Slices (Heavy Syrup, Lite Syrup), Diced (Heavy Syrup, Lite Syrup), Frozen, Fruit Cups

Wegmans Brand - Canned (FYFGA Yellow Cling (Halved, Sliced, Sliced In Pear Juice), Yellow Cling Sliced In Heavy Syrup), Frozen FYFGA Sliced

Winn Dixie - Frozen Sliced, Yellow Cling Halves & Slices (Heavy Syrup, Light Syrup)

Woodstock Farms - Organic Frozen Peach Slices

P Peanut Butter...(includes Nut Butter)

Arrowhead Mills - Creamy Almond, Creamy Cashew, Organic Valencia (Creamy, Crunchy), Valencia (Creamy, Crunchy)

Barney Butter - Almond Butter (Crunchy ●, Smooth ●)

Bell Plantation - PB2 Powdered Peanut Butter (Chocolate ●, Original ●)

Central Market H-E-B - All Natural (Cashew Butter, Peanut (Crunchy, Smooth)), Peanut Butter w/Honey

Earth Balance - Creamy Natural Almond Butter, Natural Peanut Butter (Creamy, Crunchy)

Food Club Brand - Creamy (Reduced Fat, Regular), Crunchy

Full Circle - Organic Creamy

George's - Peanut Butter

Hill Country Fare H-E-B - Creamy, Crunchy, Smooth

Hy-Vee - Creamy, Crunchy, Reduced Fat

I.M. Healthy - Soy Nut Butter (Chocolate, Honey (Chunky, Creamy), Original (Chunky, Creamy), Unsweetened (Chunky, Creamy))

Justin's - Almond Butter (Chocolate ●, Classic ●, Honey ●, Maple ●), Chocolate Hazelnut Butter ●, Peanut Butter (Chocolate ●, Classic ●, Honey ●)

Kirkland Signature - Creamy

Kroger Brand - Creamy, Crunchy, Hazelnut Spread, Just Right, Reduced Fat Creamy, Roasted Peanuts & Honey (Creamy, Crunchy)

Lowes Foods Brand - Creamy, Crunchy

MaraNatha -

All Natural Almond Butter (Hint Of Salt (Creamy, Crunchy) No Stir (Creamy, Crunchy))

Dark Chocolate (Almond Spread, Peanut Spread)

Natural Almond Butter (Creamy & Raw, Natural Honey, No Salt Creamy & Roasted, No Salt Crunchy & Roasted)

Natural Cashew (Butter, Macadamia Butter)

Natural Macadamia Butter

Organic Almond Butter (Raw (No Salt Creamy, No Salt Crunchy), Roasted (No Salt Creamy, No Salt Crunchy))

Peanut Butter (All Varieties)

Sunflower Seed Butter

Meijer Brand - Creamy, Crunchy, Natural (Creamy, Crunchy),
  Organic (Creamy, Crunchy), Reduced Fat Creamy
Midwest Country Fare - Creamy, Crunchy
My Essentials - Creamy, Crunchy, No Salt Creamy, Reduced Fat
  Creamy
Natalie's - Hemp Seed Nut Less Butter
Nature's Basket - Organic (Creamy, Creamy w/No Salt Or Sugar,
  Crunchy)
Nature's Place - Natural (Creamy, Crunchy), Organic (Creamy,
  Crunchy)
NoNuts - Golden Peabutter
Nuts.com -
  Almond Butter (Organic (Raw Crunchy ●, Raw Smooth ●),
    Roasted Crunchy ●, Roasted Smooth ●)
  Almond Paste ●
  Hazelnut Praline Paste ●
  Organic Peanut Butter (Crunchy Unsalted ●, Smooth Unsalted ●)
  Organic Sunflower Butter ●
  Pistachio Nut Paste ●
  Roasted Smooth Organic Cashew Butter ●
O Organics - No Stir (Creamy, Crunchy), Old Fashioned (Creamy,
  Crunchy)
Once Again -
  Cashew Butter (Nut Butter, Organic)
  Natural Almond Butter (Creamy, Crunchy)
  Natural Old Fashioned Peanut Butter (Creamy (No Salt, w/Salt),
    Crunchy (No Salt, w/Salt))
  Organic Almond Butter (Creamy, Omega 3 Creamy, Raw Creamy,
    Raw Crunchy)
  Organic Peanut Butter (American Classic (Creamy, Crunchy),
    Creamy (No Salt, Omega 3, w/Salt), Crunchy (No Salt, w/Salt))
  Organic Raw Peanut Butter (Creamy, Crunchy)
  Organic Sunflower Seed Butter (Regular, Salt & Sugar Free)
  Tahini (Natural, Organic)

P

Peanut Butter & Co. - Cinnamon Raisin Swirl, Crunch Time, Dark Chocolate Dreams, Mighty Maple, Old Fashioned Crunchy, Old Fashioned Smooth, Smooth Operator, The Bee's Knees, The Heat Is On, White Chocolate Wonderful

Peanut Delight - Creamy, Crunchy

Peter Pan - All Flavors

Planters - Creamy, Crunchy, Natural Creamy

Safeway Brand - Creamy, Crunchy, Reduced Fat (Creamy, Crunchy)

Santa Cruz ▲ - All Varieties

Skippy - Creamy, Extra Crunchy Super Chunk, Natural (Creamy, Super Chunk), Reduced Fat (Creamy, Super Chunk), Roasted Honey Nut (Creamy, Super Chunk)

Smart Balance - Rich Roast (Chunky, Creamy)

Smucker's - Goober (Chocolate, Grape, Strawberry), Natural (Chunky, Creamy, Honey, No Salt Added Creamy, Reduced Fat Creamy), Organic (Chunky, Creamy)

Spartan Brand - Crunchy, Peanut Spread, Smooth

Sprouted Almonds - Original Sprouted Almond Butter

Sunbutter - Sunflower Seed Spread (Creamy (Natural No Stir, Regular), Natural (Crunchy, Omega 3, Regular), Organic)

Sunland -

Natural (Creamy (Banana **!**, Caramel **!**, Chocolate **!**, Raspberry**!**, Roasted Almond **!**, Salt Free Valencia **!**, Valencia **!**), Crunchy Valencia **!**, Tahini Creamy Roasted Sesame **!**)

Organic Peanut Butter (Creamy (Cherry Vanilla **!**, Dark Chocolate**!**, Thai Ginger & Red Pepper **!**, Valencia **!**), Crunchy (Chipotle Chile **!**, Valencia **!**))

Trader Joe's - Almond Butter (Creamy w/Salt, Crunchy Unsalted, Raw Crunchy Unsalted), Organic Creamy, Organic Crunchy**!**, Salted (Creamy, Crunchy), Sunflower Seed Butter, Unsalted (Creamy, Organic Crunchy)

Tropical Traditions - Coconut Peanut Butter

Walden Farms - Creamy Peanut Spread Sugar Free

Wegmans Brand - Creamy, Crunchy, Natural Peanut Butter (Creamy, Crunchy), Organic FYFGA (Creamy, Crunchy, No Stir (Creamy, Crunchy)), Reduced Fat Creamy

Winn Dixie - Creamy, Crunchy, Organic (Creamy, Crunchy)

Woodstock Farms -

All Natural (Almond Butter (Crunchy Unsalted, Smooth Unsalted), Cashew Butter Unsalted, Raw Smooth Unsalted Almond Butter, Sesame Tahini Unsalted)

Organic Nut Butters (Almond Butter (Crunchy Unsalted, Raw Smooth Unsalted), Classic Peanut Butter (Crunchy Salted, Smooth Salted), Easy Spread Peanut Butter (Crunchy Salted, Crunchy Unsalted, Smooth Salted, Smooth Unsalted), Peanut Butter (Crunchy Salted, Crunchy Unsalted, Smooth Salted, Smooth Unsalted), Raw Almond, Sesame Tahini Unsalted)

Peanut Sauce

A Taste Of Thai - Peanut Satay Sauce, Peanut Sauce Mix

Lee Kum Kee - Satay Sauce

Mr. Spice Organic - Thai Peanut Sauce & Marinade ★

San-J - Gluten Free Thai Peanut Sauce ●

Thai Kitchen - Peanut Satay

Peanuts...see Nuts

Pears

... *All Fresh Fruits & Vegetables Are Gluten-Free

Del Monte - Canned/Jarred Fruit (All Varieties), Fruit Snack Cups (All Varieties)

Dole - Bowls *(Except Fruit Crisps)*

Food Club Brand - Bartlett Canned Halves

Full Circle - Organic (Halves In Juice, Sliced In Juice)

Great Value Brand (Wal-Mart) - Bartlett Pears In Heavy Syrup (Halves, Sliced), Fruit Cocktail, Pear Halves In Juice

Hy-Vee - Bartlett Pears (Halves, Sliced), Diced Bartlett Pears Cups

Jell-O - Snack Cups Pear Chunks In Cherry Pomegranate Gel

Lowes Foods Brand - Halves (In Heavy Syrup, In Juice)

P

Meijer Brand - Halves (Heavy Syrup, In Juice, In Juice Lite, Lite), Slices (Heavy Syrup, In Juice Lite)

Midwest Country Fare - Bartlett Pear Halves In Light Syrup

Native Forest - Organic Sliced Asian Pears

Nuts.com - Dried Fruit (Diced ●, Dried ●, Organic ●, Simply ●)

Publix - Canned (Barlett Pears In Heavy Syrup (Halves, Slices), Lite Barlett Pear Halves In Pear Juice)

S&W - All Canned/Jarred Fruits

Safeway Brand - Canned Pears (Halves, Halves Lite, Sliced, Sliced Lite)

Spartan Brand - Fruit Cups, Halves (Heavy Syrup, Lite Syrup), Slices (Heavy Syrup, Lite Syrup)

Wegmans Brand - Halved (FYFGA In Pear Juice From Concentrate, In Heavy Syrup), Sliced (FYFGA In Pear Juice From Concentrate, In Heavy Syrup)

Winn Dixie - Bartlett Halves & Slices (Heavy Syrup, Light Syrup)

Peas

... *All Fresh Fruits & Vegetables Are Gluten-Free

Birds Eye - All Plain Frozen Vegetables

Bush's Best - Black Eye, Crowder, Field Peas w/Snaps, Purple Hull

C & W - All Plain Frozen Vegetables **! !**

Del Monte - All Canned Vegetables

Food Club Brand -
Canned (Black Eyed Peas, Peas & Sliced Carrots, Small, Sweet)
Frozen (Green Peas, Green Petite, Steamin' Easy Green Peas, Sugar Snap)

Freshlike - Frozen Plain Peas

Great Value Brand (Wal-Mart) - Canned (No Salt Added Sweet Peas, Sweet Peas)

Green Giant -
Canned Sweet Peas
Frozen (Baby Sweet Peas & Butter Sauce, Simply Steam (Baby Sweet Peas, Sugar Snap Peas))
Valley Fresh Steamers (Select Baby Sweet Peas, Select Sugar Snap Peas, Sweet Peas)

H-E-B - No Salt

Hannaford Brand - No Salt, Petite, Sweet

Hy-Vee - Dry Black Eyed, Dry Green Split, Frozen Sweet, Steam In A Bag Frozen Peas, Sweet

Lowes Foods Brand - Frozen (Black Eyed, Crowder, Field Peas, Green, Peas & Carrots, Tiny Peas), Peas, Split Green Peas

Meijer Brand - Canned (Blackeye, Peas & Sliced Carrots, Small, Sweet, Sweet No Salt, Sweet Organic), Frozen Peas (Green (Organic, Regular, Steamer), Green Petite (Organic, Regular))

Midwest Country Fare - Frozen Green, Sweet

Nuts.com - Fried Green Peas ●, Simply Peas Freeze Dried Vegetables ●

O Organics - Canned Sweet Peas

Pictsweet - All Plain Frozen Vegetables

Private Selection - Frozen Sugar Snap Peas, Organic Sweet Peas Canned

Publix - Canned Sweet Peas (Regular, Small), Frozen (Blackeye, Butter, Crowder, Field Peas w/Snap, Green, Peas, Petite, Purple Hull)

Publix GreenWise Market - Organic Canned Sweet Peas

S&W - All Canned Vegetables

Safeway - Canned (Black Eyed, Sweet Peas), Frozen (Green, Peas & Carrots, Petite), Steam In Bag (Petite Green, Snap)

Safeway Brand - Frozen, Steam In Bag

Spartan Brand -

Canned (Peas & Carrots, Sweet)

Dried (Blackeyed, Green Split)

Frozen (Blackeyed, Field Peas w/Snaps, Peas & Sliced Carrots, Petite, Plain, Sugar Snap)

Tasty Bite - Agra Peas & Greens **!**

Trader Joe's - Frozen (Organic Naturally Sweet, Petite Peas)

Wegmans Brand - Canned Black Eyed, Canned FYFGA Sweet (No Salt Added, Small), Frozen Petite In Butter Sauce, Frozen FYFGA (Sugar Snap, Sweet, Sweet Petite, w/Pearl Onions)

Westbrae - Sweet Peas

Winn Dixie - Canned Green Peas (Large, Medium, No Salt Added,

P

      Small, Tiny), Frozen (Field w/Snaps, Green, Organic Green, Peas &
      Carrots, Petite Green, Purple Hull)

  Woodstock Farms - Organic Frozen (Green Peas, Peas & Carrots,
     Petite Peas, Sugar Snap)

Pectin

  Certo - Premium Liquid Fruit Pectin

  MCP - Premium Fruit Pectin

  Sure Jell - Pectin No Cook Jam, Premium Fruit (100% Natural,
    Regular)

Pepperoncini...see Peppers

Pepperoni...see Sausage

Pepper Rings

  B&G - Hot

  Food Club Brand - Hot

  Meijer Brand - Banana Pepper Rings (Hot, Mild), Hot, Mild

  Mezzetta ▲ - Deli Sliced (Hot, Mild)

  Spartan Brand - Pepper Rings (Hot, Mild)

Peppers

  *... *All Fresh Fruits & Vegetables Are Gluten-Free*

  Augason Farms - Gluten Free Dehydrated Diced Red & Green Bell
    Peppers ●

  B&G -

    Giardiniera

    Hot Cherry Peppers (Red & Green, Regular)

    Hot Chopped (Jalapenos, Roasted)

    Hot Pepper Rings

    Pepperoncini

    Roasted (w/Balsamic Vinegar, w/Oregano & Garlic)

    Sandwich Toppers (Hot Chopped Peppers, Sliced Hot Jalapenos,
      Sweet Bell Bepper, Sweet Pepper Strips)

    Sweet (Cherry, Fried, Salad w/Oregano & Garlic)

  Birds Eye - All Plain Frozen Vegetables

  C & W - All Plain Frozen Vegetables ‼

  Cara Mia - Piquillo Peppers

  Di Lusso - Roasted Red

P

Dietz & Watson ▲ - Pepperoncini ●, Sliced Jalapeno ●, Sweet Roasted
   Red Pepper ●

Earthbound Farm - Organic Bell

Embasa - Chiles Gueritos, Chipotles, Sliced Nopalitos

Food Club Brand - Banana Peppers Hot Rings, Frozen Green Pepper
   Diced, Pepperoncini

Hannaford Brand - Whole Pepperoncini

Heinz - All Varieties

Hy-Vee - Diced Green Chilies, Hot Banana Peppers, Mild Banana
   Peppers, Salad Peppers, Sliced Hot Jalapenos

Krinos - Imported (Green Peppers (Hot, Mild), Hot Red Peppers,
   Pepperoncini, Roasted Peppers (All Varieties))

La Victoria - Fire Roasted (Diced Green Chiles, Diced Jalapenos, Whole
   Green Chiles), Nacho Sliced Jalapenos

Meijer Brand - Frozen Green Peppers (Chopped, Diced Bell),
   Pepperoncini

Melissa's - Fire Roasted Sweet Bell

Mezzetta ▲ -
   Deli Sliced (Hot Jalapeno Peppers, Hot Pepper Rings, Mild Pepper
      Rings, Roasted Sweet Bell Pepper Strips, Sweet Bell Pepper
      Sandwich Strips, Tamed Jalapeno Peppers)
   Deli Style (Sweet Bell Pepper Relish, Zesty Bell Pepper Relish Hot)
   Garlic & Dill Golden Peperoncini
   Golden Peperoncini
   Gourmet Deli (Mild Rosemary & Garlic Pepper Rings, Roasted
      Red Bell Pepper & Caramelized Onions, Sweet & Hot Jalapeno
      Pepper Rings, Sweet & Hot Pepper Rings, Tamed Diced Jalapeno
      Peppers, Tamed Fire Roasted Jalapeno Peppers w/Chipotle Peppers,
      Tri Color Roasted Bell Pepper Strips)
   Habanero Peppers
   Hot (Banana Wax Peppers, Cherry Peppers, Chili Peppers, Chili
      Peppers Mexican Style En Escabeche, Jalapeno Peppers En
      Escabeche, Serrano Chili Peppers)
   Italian Wax Peppers
   Organics (Fire Roasted Red Bell Peppers, Sliced Hot Jalapeno Peppers)

P

Roasted (Bell Peppers, Marinated Yellow & Red Sweet Peppers, Yellow
   & Red Sweet Peppers)
Sliced (Golden Peperoncini, Hot Cherry Peppers)
Sweet (Banana Wax Peppers, Cherry Peppers)
Tamed Jalapeno Peppers En Escabeche

Mt. Olive ▲ - Diced Jalapeno Peppers, Hot Banana Pepper Rings, Jalapeno Slices, Jalapeno Slices PepperPAK, Marinated Roasted Red Peppers, Mild Banana Pepper Rings, Pepperoncini, Roasted Red Peppers, Sliced Pepperoncini, Sweet 'N Hot Salad Peppers, Sweet Salad Peppers

Peloponnese - Florina Whole Sweet Peppers

Peppadew ▲ -
Sweet & Tangy Goldew (Diced, Whole)
Sweet Piquante (Diced, Whole Hot, Whole Mild)

Pictsweet - Chopped Green

Publix - Frozen Green Peppers Diced

Safeway Select - Fire Roasted, Frozen Pepper Strips

SanDel - All Varieties

Spartan Brand - Jalapeno

Star - Fancy Pepperoncini

Trader Joe's - Artichoke Red Pepper Tapenade **!!**, Fire Roasted Red (Regular, Sweet & Yellow), Frozen Fire Roasted Bell Peppers & Onions **!!**, Frozen Melange A Trois, Marinated Red, Red Pepper Spread w/Garlic & Eggplant

Trappey's - Banana Peppers (Sliced, Whole), Cherry Peppers, Jalapenos (Sliced, Whole), Peppers In Vinegar, Tempero Peppers, Torrido

Vlasic - All Varieties

Wegmans Brand - Roasted Red Peppers Whole

Winn Dixie - Pepperoncini, Sliced Banana Peppers

Woodstock Farms - Organic Frozen Tri Color Peppers

Pesto
   Amore - Pesto Paste

Classico - All Varieties
Fischer & Wieser - Cilantro Pepito, Sicilian Tomato
Kirkland Signature - Cibo Naturals Fresh Basil
Le Veneziane - Pesto Sauce
Mezzetta ▲ - Napa Valley Bistro Homemade Style Basil Pesto
Santa Barbara - Basil, Chipotle Basil, Spinach Cilantro, Sun Dried Tomato
Sauces 'N Love ▲ - Mint Pesto, Pesto, Pink Pesto, Sundried Tomato, Vegan Pesto
Scarpetta ▲ - Pink Pesto
Simply Organic - Sweet Basil Pesto Mix ●
Trader Joe's - Pesto Alla Genovese Basil Pesto

Picante Sauce
Chi-Chi's - Fiesta, Medium
Hill Country Fare H-E-B - Hot, Medium, Mild, Original
Hy-Vee - Hot, Medium, Mild
Pace - Extra Mild, Hot, Medium, Mild
Winn Dixie - Medium, Mild

Pickles
B&G -
Bread & Butter
Dill
Hamburger Dill
Kosher Dill (Baby Gherkins, Gherkins, Original)
NY Deli Dill
Pickle In A Pouch
Sandwich Toppers (Bread & Butter, Hamburger Dill, Kosher Dill, NY Deli, Polish Dill)
Sour
Sweet (Gherkins, Midget Gherkins, Mixed)
Tiny Treats
Zesty Dill
Boar's Head - All Varieties

P

Claussen -
Dill Sandwich Slices
Half Sour New York Deli Style Wholes
Hearty Garlic Whole Deli Style
Kosher Dill (Burger Slices, Deli Style Halves, Deli Style Spears,
Halves, Mini)
Sweet Bread 'N Butter (Pickle Chips, Sandwich Slices)
Dietz & Watson ▲ - Kosher Spear ●, New Half Sours ●, Sour Garlic ●
Food Club Brand -
Bread & Butter (Chips (Regular, Sugar Free), Sandwich Slice)
Dill (Hamburger, Kosher (Baby, Spears, Whole), Polish (Regular,
Sandwich Slice), Spears (Garlic, Polish, Zesty), Whole)
Kosher (Baby Dill, Halves, Sandwich Slice (Regular, Zesty), Whole)
Sweet (Gherkin, Midgets, Sugar Free, Whole)
Full Circle - Kosher Baby Dill, Sweet Bread & Butter
Gordon Food Service -
Dill (Kosher (Sliced, Spears, Whole), Sliced)
Sweet (Bread & Butter Chips, Gherkins)
Great Value Brand (Wal-Mart) - Bread & Butter, Dill Spears, Hamburger
Dill Chips, Kosher Baby Dill, Kosher Dill Spears, Sweet Gherkins,
Whole Dill, Whole Sweet
Hannaford Brand -
Bread & Butter (Chips, Sandwich Slices)
Kosher (Baby Dills, Dill, Dill Sandwich Slices, Dill Spears, Petite)
Polish Dill Spears
Sour Dill
Sugar Free (Bread & Butter (Chips, Spears), Sweet Gherkins)
Sweet (Gherkins, Midgets, Mixed Chips, Relish, Relish Squeeze)
Heinz - All Varieties
Hill Country Fare H-E-B - Hamburger Chips
Hy-Vee -
Bread & Butter (Sweet Chunk Pickles, Sweet Slices, Sweet Spears)
Dill (Hamburger Slices, Kosher (Baby, Spears), Pickles, Polish
(Pickles, Spears))

Refrigerated Kosher Dill (Halves, Sandwich Slices, Spears, Whole Pickles)

Special Recipe (Bread & Butter Slices, Hot & Spicy Dills, Hot & Sweet Chips, Jalapeno Baby Dills, Sweet Garden Crunch)

Sweet Gherkins

Whole (Dill, Sweet)

Zesty (Kosher Dill Spears, Sweet Chunks)

Kurtz -

Bread & Butter

Dill (Hamburger Slices, Kosher Spears, Whole, Whole Kosher)

Sweet

Laura Lynn - 16 oz. Bread & Butter Chips, Kosher Dill Spears

Lowes Foods Brand - Bread & Butter Chips, Dill (Baby Kosher, Hamburger, Kosher, Kosher Spears, Sandwich Slices), Sweet Midgets, Sweet Salad Cubes

Meijer Brand -

Bread & Butter (Chips (Regular, Sugar Free), Sandwich Slice)

Dill (Hamburger, Kosher (Baby, Spears, Whole), Polish, Sandwich Sliced Polish, Spears (No Garlic, Polish, Zesty), Whole)

Kosher (Baby Dill, Halves, Sandwich Slices (Regular, Zesty), Whole)

Sweet (Gherkin, Midgets, Sugar Free, Whole)

Mezzetta ▲ - Whole Kosher Style Dill Pickles

Midwest Country Fare - Whole Sweet

Mrs. Renfro's - Green Tomato Pickles

Mt. Olive -

Bread & Butter (Chips, Sandwich Stuffers, Spears)

Dill (Hamburger Chips, Jalapeno Flavored Baby, Jalapeno Flavored Spears, Jumbo, Kosher (Chips, Hamburger Chips, Hamburger Stuffers, Hot 'N Spicy, Hot Sauce Flavored Baby, Hot Sauce Flavored Petite Snack Crunchers, Jalapeno Flavored Spears, Kosher Baby, Petite, Petite Snack Cruncher, Polish, Zesty Garlic), Large, Polish Spears, Regular, Thin Chips)

No Sugar Added (Bread & Butter Chips, Bread & Butter Sandwich Stuffers, Bread & Butter Spears, Sweet Gherkins, Sweet Petites PicklePAK)

P

    PicklePAK (Hamburger Dill Chips, Kosher Dill Petites, Sweet Petites)
    Sour
    Sweet (Gerkins, Midgets, Mixed, Petite Snack Crunchers, Pickles)
Publix - All Varieties
Safeway Brand - All Varieties
SanDel - All Varieties
Spartan Brand -
    Bread & Butter (Chips Sweet, Slices Sandwich Chips)
    Kosher Dill (Baby, Slices (Hamburger, Sandwich), Spears, Whole)
    Polish Dill (Spears, Whole)
    Sweet (Gherkin Whole, Slices, Whole)
Trader Joe's - Organic (Kosher Sandwich Pickles **! !**, Sweet Butter Pickles)
Vlasic - All Varieties
Wegmans Brand -
    Hamburger Dill Slices
    Kosher Dill (Halves, Mini, Sandwich Slices, Spears, Whole)
    Polish Dill (Spears, Whole)
    Sweet (Bread & Butter Chips Regular, Gherkins, Midgets, Sandwich
       Slices)
Winn Dixie - Dill (All Varieties), Sweet Pickles (All Varieties), Sweet Relish
Woodstock Farms - Organic (Kosher Dill (Baby, Sliced, Whole), Sweet
    Bread & Butter)

Pie
    3 Fellers Bakery ▲ - Mini Pies (Apple ●, Coconut Cream ●, Lemon ●)
    Amy's - Mexican Tamale Pie ★, Shepherd's Pie (Light In Sodium ★,
       Regular ★)
    Andrea's Gluten Free ▲ - Cherry Oat Cobbler
    Apple's Bakery ▲ - Gluten Free (Dairy Free Pumpkin, Dutch Apple Crumb,
       Pecan)
    Bridge City Baking ▲ - Fresh Baked Hand Pies (Cherry Almond
       Chocolate●, Date Pecan ●, French Apple ●, Hood River Blueberry ●,
       Marionberry ●, Pineapple Coconut ●, Poached Pear w/Caramel ●,
       Pumpkin Mousse ●)
    Cedarlane - Three Layer Enchilada Pie

Choices Rice Bakery ▲ - Apple, Apple Cranberry, Berry Rhubarb, Cherry Blueberry, Freezer Section Egg Free (Apple, Apple Cran, Berry Rhubarb, Pumpkin), Peach Blackberry, Pumpkin

Crave Foods - Gluten Free Pies (Creamy Apple **!**, Creamy Blueberry**!**, Pecan **!**)

El Peto ▲ - Apple, Blueberry, Cherry, Peach, Strawberry Rhubarb, Walnut

Fabe's Bakery - Gluten Free Vegan Pie (Dutch Apple ●, Pumpkin ●)

Gillian's Foods ▲ - Apple ●, Blueberry ●, Pumpkin ●

Grandma Ferdon's ▲ - Apple (Crisp ●, Pie ●), Peach ●, Pumpkin ●

Katz Gluten Free ▲ - Apple ●, Blueberry ●, Cherry ●

Molly's Gluten-Free Bakery ▲ - Apple, Cherry, Pumpkin

Pure Market Express ▲ - Apple Crisp ●, Banana Cream ●, Banana Cream Pie ●, Mudslide ●, Pecan ●, Pecan Pie Truffles ●, Pumpkin Pie ●, Turtle ●

Silly Yak Bakery - GF Pie (Apple (Caramel ●, Crisp ●, Regular ●), Blackberry ●, Blueberry ●, Cherry Crisp ●, Cherry ●, Dutch Apple ●, Peach Pecan ●, Peach ●, Pecan ●, Pumpkin ●)

Skye Foods - Pie Tarts (Apple ●, Cherry ●, Pumpkin ●)

Trader Joe's - Shepherd's Pie Beef

Whole Foods Market Gluten Free Bakehouse ▲ - Apple, Cherry, Peach, Pumpkin, Southern Pecan

Pie Crust/Pie Crust Mix

Abundant Life Foods ▲ - Pie Crust Mix

Andrea's Gluten Free ▲ - Pie Crust

Arnel's Originals - Pie Crust Mix

Augason Farms ▲ - Gluten Free Pie Crust Mix ●

Authentic Foods ▲ - Pie Crust Mix ●

Breads From Anna ▲ - Piecrust Mix

Cause You're Special ▲ - Homestyle Pie Crust

Deerfields Gluten Free Bakery ▲ - Gluten Free Frozen Pie Crust

El Peto ▲ - Perfect Pie Crust Mix, Pie Crust, Pie Dough, Tart Shells (Sweetened, Unsweetened)

Fabe's Bakery - 8" Gluten Free Pie Crust

P

    Gluten Free Mama ▲ - Mama's Pie Crust Mix ●

    Gluten Free Pantry ▲ - Perfect Pie Crust

    Gluten-Free Creations ▲ - Graham Cracker Crumbs ●

    Grandma Ferdon's ▲ - Frozen Pie Crust w/Tin ●, Pie Crust Mix ●

    Heaven Mills ▲ - Pie Crust ●

    Kinnikinnick ▲ - Pie Crusts

    Mixes From The Heartland ▲ - Impossible Coconut Pie Mix ●, Pie
       Crust Mix ●

    Molly's Gluten-Free Bakery ▲ - Pie Crust

    Namaste Foods ▲ - Biscuits Pie Crusts & More

    Pure Knead ▲ - Bread Pudding Honey Tangerine ●, Flaky Tart Shell ●,
       Rustic Tart Shells ●

    Really Great Food Company ▲ - Flaky Pie Crust Mix

    Silly Yak Bakery - GF Pie Crust Mix ●

    Whole Foods Market Gluten Free Bakehouse ▲ - Pie Crust Mix

Pie Filling

    Comstock - Fruit Fillings (All Varieties)

    Fischer & Wieser - Fredericksburg Golden Peach, Harvest Apple &
       Brandy Pie, Old Fashioned Cherry

    Food Club Brand - Apple, Blueberry, Cherry, Cherry Lite, Peach

    Great Value Brand (Wal-Mart) - Apple, Blueberry, Cherry, No Sugar
       Added (Apple, Cherry)

    Hy-Vee - More Fruit Pie Filling/Topping (Apple, Blueberry, Cherry,
       Peach, Strawberry)

    Jell-O -

       Regular Cook & Serve (Banana Cream, Butterscotch, Chocolate
          (Fudge, Regular), Coconut Cream, Fat Free Tapioca, Lemon,
          Vanilla)

       Regular Instant Pudding & Pie Filling (Banana Cream,
          Butterscotch, Cheesecake, Chocolate (Fudge, Regular),
          Coconut Cream, Devil's Food Fat Free, French Vanilla, Lemon,
          Pistachio, Pumpkin Spice, Vanilla, White Chocolate Fat Free)

       Sugar Free Fat Free Cook & Serve (Chocolate, Vanilla)

Sugar Free Fat Free Instant Pudding & Pie Filling (Banana Cream, Butterscotch, Cheesecake, Chocolate, Lemon, Pistachio, Vanilla, White Chocolate)

Kroger Brand - Apple, Blueberry, Cherry (Lite, Regular), Extra Peach, Strawberry

Lowes Foods Brand - Apple, Blueberry, Cherry

Lucky Leaf - Apple, Apricot, Banana Creme, Blueberry, Cherries Jubilee, Cherry, Chocolate Creme, Coconut Creme, Dark Sweet Cherry, Key Lime Pie Creme, Lemon, Lemon Creme, Lite (Apple, Cherry), Peach, Pineapple, Premium (Apple, Blackberry, Blueberry, Cherry, Red Raspberry), Raisin, Strawberry

Meijer Brand - Apple, Blueberry, Cherry, Cherry Lite, Peach

Midwest Country Fare - Apple, Cherry

Musselman's - Apple, Apricot, Banana Creme, Blackberry, Blueberry, Cherries Jubilee, Cherry, Chocolate Creme, Coconut Creme, Dark Sweet Cherry, Key Lime Creme Pie, Lemon, Lemon Creme, Lite Apple, Lite Cherry, Peach, Pineapple, Raisin, Strawberry, Strawberry Glaze, Supreme (Blueberry & Creme, Cherries & Creme, Peaches & Creme), Vanilla Creme

My T Fine - Chocolate, Lemon, Vanilla

Nuts.com - Filling (Chocolate ●, Poppy Seed ●)

Spartan Brand - Apple, Blueberry, Cherry (Lite, Regular)

Wilderness - Fruit Fillings (All Varieties)

Winn Dixie - Apple, Blueberry, Cherry

Pilaf

Trader Joe's - Thai Style Lime, Wild & Basmati Rice

Pimentos

Meijer Brand - Pieces, Sliced

Pineapple

... *All Fresh Fruits & Vegetables Are Gluten-Free*

Augason Farms ▲ - Gluten Free Freeze Dried Chunks ●

Del Monte - Canned/Jarred Fruit (All Varieties), Fruit Snack Plastic Cups

P

Dole -
   All Canned
   All Fruits (Frozen, Pineapple Chunks In 100% Fruit Juice Jars)
   Bowls *(Except Fruit Crisps)*
   Fruit Parfait Pineapple & Creme
Food Club Brand - Chunks, Crushed, Sliced
Great Value Brand (Wal-Mart) -
   Chunks
   Pineapple In Unsweetened Pineapple Juice (Crushed, Slices)
   Tidbits
Hy-Vee - Chunk, Crushed, In Lime Gel, Sliced, Tidbit Fruit Cup
Lowes Foods Brand - Chunks In Juice, Crushed In Juice, Sliced In Juice
Mariani - Dried Tango **! !**, Tropical **! !**
Meijer Brand -
   Chunks (Heavy Syrup, In Juice)
   Crushed (Heavy Syrup, In Juice)
   Frozen Chunks
   Sliced In (Heavy Syrup, Juice)
Midwest Country Fare - Chunks, Crushed, Slices, Tidbits
Native Forest - Organic (Chunks, Crushed, Slices)
Nuts.com - Dried Fruit (Chunks ●, Diced ●, Dried ●, Natural ●, Organic ●,
   Organic Chunks ●, Simply ●)
Publix - All Varieties
Safeway Brand - Chunks, Crushed, Frozen Chunks, Sliced
Spartan Brand - Chunks, Crushed, Sliced, Tidbits
Trader Joe's - Frozen Pineapple Tidbits
Wegmans Brand - Canned FYFGA In Pineapple Juice (Chunk, Crushed,
   Sliced, Tidbits)
Winn Dixie - Chunks, Crushed, Sliced, Tidbits
Woodstock Farms - Organic Frozen Pineapple Chunks, Slices Unsulphured
Pistachio Nuts...see Nuts
Pizza
   Against The Grain Gourmet ▲ - 12" (Pesto, Three Cheese/Tomato)
   Amy's - Rice Crust Pizza (Cheese ★, Margherita ★, Non Dairy Cheeze ★,
      Non Dairy Spinach ★, Roasted Vegetable No Cheese ★)

Andrea's Gluten Free ▲ - Cheese, Pepperoni, Sausage, Spinach Artichoke

Better Bread Company - Fresh Vegetable, Margherita, Roasted Garlic & Artichoke

BOLD Organics - Deluxe, Meat Lovers, Vegan Cheese, Veggie Lovers

Celiac Specialties ▲ - 6" Casein Free Pizza, French Bread Pizza, Pizza (12" Pizza, 6" Pizza)

Choices Rice Bakery ▲ - Pizza (Pepperoni, Vegetarian, Vegetarian No Cheese)

Conte's ▲ - Margherita ●, Mushroom Florentine ●

Di Manufacturing - 10" Gluten Free Pizza (3 Cheese ●, Combo ●, Pepperoni ●, Sausage ●)

Everybody Eats ▲ - Tomato Mozzarella Pizza

Foods By George ▲ - Cheese Pizza

GlutenFreeda ▲ - Gluten Free Pizza Wraps (Italian Sausage, Pesto Chicken, Three Cheese)

GlutenOut - Pizza Alle Verdure ★, Pizza Margherita ★

Glutino ▲ - Frozen Pizza (Barbeque Chicken, Duo Cheese, Pepperoni, Spinach & Feta)

Gourmet Parlor Pizza - Gluten Free (Cheese ●, Pepperoni ●, Sausage Pepperoni ●)

Grandma Ferdon's ▲ - 6" Cheese Pizza ●

Ian's - Wheat Free Gluten Free French Bread Recipe (Soy Cheesy, Uncured Pepperoni)

JD's Best Gluten Free Pizza ▲ - Pizza (Classic GF ●, Personal Microwave/Ovenbake ●)

Joan's GF Great Bakes ▲ - Calzone, NY Ready To Bake, Sicilian

Molly's Gluten-Free Bakery ▲ - Cheese, Italian Sausage, Pepperoni

Pure Market Express ▲ - Pepperoni Pizza ●, Sausage Pizza ●

Schar ▲ - Bonta D'Italia Cheese

Simply Shari's Gluten Free & Fabulous ▲ - Cheese ●, Pepperoni ●, Pesto Margherita ●, Spinach Feta ●, Vegetable Margherita ●

Solterra - Margherita Cheese, Vegan Cheese

Stashu's ▲ - Cheese ●, Pepperoni ●

P

Three Bakers ▲ - Cheese Pizza
Udi's Gluten Free Foods ▲ - Gluten Free (Margherita ●, Pepperoni ●, Three Cheese ●)

Pizza Crust/Pizza Mix

Abundant Life Foods ▲ - Pizza Dough Mix
Against The Grain Gourmet ▲ - 12" Crust
Andrea's Gluten Free ▲ - Pizza Crust (12", 6")
Arrowhead Mills - Gluten Free Pizza Crust Mix
Augason Farms ▲ - Gluten Free Pizza & Foccacia Dough Mix ●
Authentic Foods ▲ - Pizza Crust Mix ●
Barkat - Gluten Free (Brown Rice, White Rice)
Bay State Milling - Gluten Free Pizza Crust Mix ●
Better Bread Company - Pizza Crust
Bloomfield Farms ▲ - Gluten Free Crust Mix ●
Bob's Red Mill ▲ - Gluten Free Pizza Crust Mix ★
Bodhi's Bakehouse - Wheat Free Gluten Free Bases
Breads From Anna ▲ - Pizza Crust Mix
Bready - That's Amore Gluten Free Pizza Dough ●
Cause You're Special ▲ - Famous Pizza Crust Mix
Celiac Specialties ▲ - 12" Pizza Crust, 6" Pizza Crust
Chebe ▲ - Pizza Frozen Dough ●, Pizza Mix ●
Choices Rice Bakery ▲ - Brown Rice, Sourdough
Dad's ▲ - Gluten Free Pizza Crust
Domata - Gluten Free Pizza Crust ●
El Peto ▲ - Pizza Crust (Basil, Millet, White), Yeast Free Millet, Yeast Free White Crust
Ener-G ▲ - Rice Pizza Shell (10", 6"), Yeast Free Rice Pizza Shell (10", 6")
Everybody Eats ▲ - Pizza Shells
Farmo - Pizza Mix
Food-Tek Fast & Fresh - Pizza Crust Mix ★
Foods By George ▲ - Pizza Crusts
French Meadow Bakery - Gluten Free Pizza Crust ●
Gifts Of Nature ▲ - French Bread & Pizza Crust Mix ●
Gillian's Foods ▲ - Pizza Dough Mix ●

pizza crust/pizza mix

P

Gluten Free Mama ▲ - Mama's Pizza Crust Mix ●
Gluten Free Pantry ▲ - French Bread & Pizza Mix
Gluten-Free Creations ▲ - Italian Seasoned Pizza Crust ●, Simply Pizza Crust Mix ●, Simply Pizza Crust ●
Gluten-Free Naturals - Pizza Crust Mix
GlutenOut - Base Per Pizza ★
Glutino ▲ - Premium Pizza Crust
Grandma Ferdon's ▲ - Pizza Crust Mix ●, Pizza Crust ●
Heaven Mills ▲ - Pizza Crust ●
Hodgson Mill ▲ - Gluten Free Pizza Crust Mix
Joan's GF Great Bakes ▲ - NY Pizza Crust
Katz Gluten Free ▲ - Pizza Crust ●
King Arthur Flour ▲ - Gluten Free Pizza Crust Mix ●
Kinnikinnick ▲ - Pizza Crust Personal Size (Regular, Thin Crust)
Kneaded Specialties ▲ - Vegan Pizza Crust ●
Laurel's Sweet Treats ▲ - Pizza Dough Mix
Mamma Mia! - Pizza Crust Mix
Mariposa Artisan-Crafted Gluten-Free ▲ - Pizza Crusts
Molly's Gluten-Free Bakery ▲ - Pizza Crust
Namaste Foods ▲ - Pizza Crust Mix
O'Doughs Bakery ▲ - Pizza Kit (Flax ●, White ●)
Orgran ▲ - Pizza & Pastry Multimix
PaneRiso ▲ - White Rice Pizza Crust ●
Pure Knead ▲ - Pizza Crust ●
Quejos ▲ - Cheese Thin Crust Pizza Shells, Non Dairy Thin Crust Pizza Shells
Really Great Food Company ▲ - French Bread/Pizza Crust, Pizza Crust Mix
Rose's Bakery ▲ - Pizza Crusts (14", 9", Parbaked)
Rudi's Gluten-Free Bakery - Original Pizza Crust ●
Rustic Crust ▲ - Gluten Free Napoli Herb Pizza Crust ●
Schar ▲ - Pizza Crusts
Silly Yak Bakery ▲ - CFGF 8" Pizza Crusts ●, GF (8" Pizza Crust ●, Gourmet Pizza Party ●)

P

Simply Organic ▲ - Gluten Free Pizza Crust Mix ●
Sof'ella - Gluten Free Pizza Crust Mix ★
Stashu's ▲ - Pizza Crust ●
Still Riding Pizza ▲ - Gluten Free Pizza Crust ●
Sweet Christine's Bakery - Pizza Crust ●
Sweet Escapes Pastries ▲ - Gourmet Pre Baked Pizza Crusts ●
Tasti Grain - Pizza Shells
Three Bakers ▲ - Traditional Thin Whole Grain Pizza Crust
Toovaloo - Gluten Free Pizza Crust
Udi's Gluten Free Foods ▲ - Gluten Free Pizza Crusts ●
Venice Bakery - Gluten Free Pizza Crusts (Original ●, Seasoned ●)
Whole Foods Market Gluten Free Bakehouse ▲ - Pizza Crust
Willy O's Gluten-Free Products - Pizza Crust

Pizza Sauce...see also Sauces

Classico - Traditional
Contadina - Flavored w/Pepperoni, Four Cheese, Original, Pizza Squeeze
Dei Fratelli - Canned
DelGrosso - Deluxe, New York Style, Pepperoni
Don Pepino - Regular, w/Basil
Eden Organic - Organic Pizza Pasta Sauce
Food Club Brand - Pizza Sauce
Hannaford Brand
Lowes Foods Brand
Lucini - Pizza Sauce
Meijer Brand
Ragu - Homemade Style, Pizza Quick Traditional
Rao's Specialty Foods - Homemade Pizza Sauce
Safeway Select
Sauces 'N Love ▲ - Marinara & Pizza Sauce
Sclafani - Pizza Sauce
Spartan Brand
Trader Joe's - Fat Free ‼
Wegmans Brand - FYFGA Chunky
Winn Dixie

P

Plum Sauce
  Sharwood's
  Wok Mei - All Natural Plum

Plums
  ... *All Fresh Fruits & Vegetables Are Gluten-Free*
  Mariani - Enhanced Wellness Plum Support ‼, Pitted Dried (Bite Size ‼, Plus ‼, Regular ‼)
  Safeway Brand
  Winn Dixie - Canned Whole Plums

Polenta
  Bob's Red Mill ▲ - Gluten Free Corn Grits ★
  Food Merchants Brand ▲ - Ancient Harvest (Basil & Garlic, Chili & Cilantro, Mushroom & Onion, Quinoa Heirloom Red & Black, Sun Dried Tomato & Garlic, Traditional Italian)
  Frontier Soups - Roasted Corn Polenta A La Roma ★
  Melissa's - Organic (Italian Herb, Original, Sun Dried Tomato)
  San Gennaro Foods ▲ - Basil & Garlic, Frozen Three Cheese, Sundried Tomato & Garlic, Traditional
  Trader Joe's - Organic Polenta

Pomegranate
  ... *All Fresh Fruits & Vegetables Are Gluten-Free*
  Navitas Naturals ▲ - Powder
  Trader Joe's - Frozen Pomegranate Seeds

Pop...see Soda Pop/Carbonated Beverages

Popcorn
  Act II - Microwaveable Popcorn (All Flavors)
  Angie's Artisan Treats - Kettle Corn (Caramel ●, Classic ●, Lite ●, White Cheddar ●)
  Central Market H-E-B - Organic Microwaveable (Butter, Natural)
  Chester's - Cheddar Cheese Flavored ‼
  Colby's Kettle Corn - Kettlecorn (Chili Cheese Obsession, Cinnamon Sugar Sensation, Salty Sweet Addiction, White Cheddar Passion)
  Cracker Jack - Original Caramel Coated Popcorn & Peanuts ‼

P

Deep River Snacks - Sharp White Cheddar Popcorn ●
Eden Organic - Organic Yellow Popping Kernels
Food Club Brand - Popcorn Microwave (Butter (Light, Regular),
    Butter Crazy, Natural (Lite, Regular))
Full Circle - Organic Microwave (Butter, Natural), Popcorn (Salted,
    White Cheddar)
Gordon Food Service - Butter, Cheese
Halfpops - Natural Aged White Cheddar ●, Natural Butter & Pure
    Ocean Sea Salt ●
Hannaford Brand - Microwave (Butter, Fat Free Butter, Kettle, Light
    Butter, Natural), White Cheddar Popcorn
Herr's - Light, Original, White Cheddar
Hill Country Fare H-E-B - Microwaveable (94% Fat Free, Butter
    (Flavor, Lite, Regular), Kettle, Natural, Theatre Style), Polybag
    (White, Yellow), Single Pack Popcorn (Butter, Kettle, Theater),
    Theater Style
Hy-Vee - Microwave (94% Fat Free Butter, Butter, Extra Butter (Lite,
    Regular), Kettle, Light Butter, Lightly Salted, Natural Flavor, No Salt,
    Regular, White Cheddar), Regular (White, Yellow)
Jolly Time -
    Kernel Corn (American's Best, Organic Yellow, White, Yellow)
    Microwave
        American's Best
        Better Butter
        Blast O Butter (Light, Minis, Regular)
        ButterLicious (Light, Regular)
        Crispy 'N White (Light, Regular)
        Healthy Pop (Butter Flavor, Caramel Apple, Crispy White
            Naturally Flavored, Kettle Corn, Low Sodium, Regular)
        Homemade
        KettleMania
        Low Sodium
        Mallow Magic
        The Big Cheez
        White & Buttery

Kernel Season's - All Natural (Chipotle Nacho ●, Kettle Corn ●, Real Butter ●, White Cheddar ●), Popping Corn ●

LesserEvil - Kettle Corn (Black & White **! !**, Class Kettle **! !**)

Lowes Foods Brand - Microwave (Butter, Butter 94% Fat Free, Extra Butter, Light Butter Mini Bags, Light Natural, Natural), Popcorn (Butter Flavor, White Cheddar Flavor), Yellow Bag

Meijer Brand -

  Kernels (White, Yellow)

  Microwave

    75% Fat Free Butter

    94% Fat Free

    Butter (GP, Regular)

    Extra Butter (Giant, GP, Lite, Regular)

    Hot 'N Spicy

    Kettle (Regular, Sweet & Salty)

    Mini (Butter, Extra Butter, Lite Butter)

    Natural (Butter, Double Butter, Lite Butter, Regular)

    Natural Lite

    Organic (Butter, Natural)

Mini Pops ▲ - Popped Sorghum (Baby White Cheddar ●, Cutie Caramel Clusters ●, Hot 'N Chilly Chili ●, Itsy Bitsy Chili Cheese ●, Itty Bitty Butter ●, Nano Pepper & Herb ●, Petite Plain ●, Subatomic Sea Salt ●)

Nature's Place - Butter, Natural Flavor

Newman's Own -

  Microwave (100 Calorie Natural Mini Bags, 94% Fat Free, Butter (Boom, Light, Low Sodium, Reduced Sodium, Regular), Natural, Tender White Kernels Natural)

  Regular Raw Popcorn

Newman's Own Organics - Microwave Pop's Corn (Butter Flavored **! !**, Light Butter Flavored **! !**, No Butter/No Salt 94% Fat Free **! !**)

O Organics - Microwave Popcorn (Butter Flavor, Regular)

Odell's - Movie Theatre Popcorn Kit

P

Old Dutch - Caramel Corn, Cheddar Cheese, Gourmet White, Northern Lights Fat Free Caramel Corn, White Cheddar

Orville Redenbacker - Kernels In Jars (All Flavors), Microwaveable (All Flavors)

Pop Secret -
Jumbo Popping Corn Kernels
Microwave
100 Calorie Pop (94% Fat Free Butter, 94% Fat Free Kettle Corn, Butter, Homestyle, Kettle Corn)
94% Fat Free Butter
Butter
Cheddar
Extra Butter
Homestyle
Jumbo Pop (Butter, Movie Theater Butter)
Kettle Corn
Light Butter
Magic Colors
Movie Theater Butter

Popcorn Indiana ▲ -
Kettlecorn (Bacon Ranch, Buffalo Cheddar, Cinnamon Sugar, Original, Sweet & Tangy BBQ)
Popcorn (Aged White Cheddar, Movie Theater, Touch Of Sea Salt)
Reserve (Cocoa Kettlecorn, Wasabi)

Safeway Brand - Kettle, Microwave (94% Fat Free Butter, Extra Butter, Lite Butter), White, Yellow

Skeete & Ike's - Organic (BBQ **!!**, Kettle Corn **!!**, Sea Salt **!!**, White Cheddar **!!**)

Smart Balance - Light Butter, Light Butter Mini Bags, Smart Movie Style, Smart 'N Healthy

Smartfood - Kettle Corn **!!**, Movie Theater Butter **!!**, White Cheddar Cheese Flavored (Reduced Fat **!!**, Regular **!!**)

Spartan Brand - Microwave (94% Fat Free, Butter, Extra Butter, Lite Butter, Lite Extra Butter, Natural), White, Yellow

Trader Joe's - Caramel, Gourmet White, Lite Popcorn 50% Less Salt, Microwave (94% Fat Free, Natural Butter), Organic w/Olive Oil **!**, White Cheddar, Yellow

UTZ - Popcorn (Butter, Caramel w/Peanuts, Cheese, White Cheddar)

Wegmans Brand - FYFGA Yellow Kernels, Microwave (94% Fat Free Butter Flavor, Butter Flavor, Kettle Corn, Light Butter Flavor, Movie Theater Butter)

Winn Dixie - Microwaveable (Butter, Double Butter, Light Butter, Natural), Yellow

Wise - Popcorn (Hot Cheese, Original Butter Flavored, Reduced Fat Butter Flavored, Reduced Fat White Cheddar Flavored, White Cheddar Flavored, Wise $2 Price Cheese)

Popsicles

Breyer's - Pure Fruit Bars (Berry Swirls, Pomegranate Blends, Strawberry Orange Raspberry (No Sugar Added, Regular))

ChocAlive ▲ - Italian Ice (All Flavors)

Cool Fruits - Fruit Juice Freezers (Grape & Cherry, Sour Apple & Strawberry)

Dreyer's - Fruit Bars (Acai Blueberry, Creamy Coconut, Grape, Lemonade, Lime, Mango, Pineapple, Pomegranate, Strawberry, Tangerine, Variety Pack (Grape/Cherry/Tropical, Lime/Strawberry/Wildberry), Variety Pack No Sugar Added (Black Cherry/Strawberry Kiwi/Mixed Berry, Strawberry, Strawberry/Tangerine/Raspberry))

Edy's - Fruit Bars (Acai Blueberry, Antioxidant (Acai Blueberry, Goji White Grape, Pomegranate), Cherry, Creamy Coconut, Grape, Lemonade, Lime, Lime/Strawberry/Wildberry Variety Pack, Mango, No Sugar Added (Black Cherry, Mixed Berry, Raspberry, Strawberry, Strawberry Kiwi, Tangerine), Orange & Cream, Peach, Pineapple, Pomegranate, Strawberry, Tangerine, Tropical)

Fla-Vor-Ice - Freezer Bars (Light, Regular, Tropical)

Food Club Brand - Novelties Red White Blue Pops

Frootee Ice - Freezer Pops

Hannaford Brand - Assorted Pops Citrus, Bars Real Fruit

Hawaiian Punch - Freezer Bars

P

Hood - Frozen Novelty Items (Fudge Stix, Hoodsie Pops 6 Flavor Assortment Twin Pops, Karnival Stix, Orange Cream Bar)

Hy-Vee - Assorted Twin Pops

Icee - Freezer Bars

Jelly Belly - Freezer Pops

Kemps - Fudge Jr.'s, Juice Koolers, Moo Jr.'s, Orange Cream Bars, Pop Jr.'s, All American Pops, Sugar Free Pop Jr.'s, Tropical Pops Jr's

Kool Pops - Assorted Flavors Freezer Pops

Lowes Food Brand - Orange Cream

Lowes Foods Brand - Novelties Banana Jr. Pops

Lucerne - Creamy Orange

Meijer Brand - Juice Stix, Orange Glider, Party Pops (No Sugar Added Assorted, Orange/Cherry/Grape), Red White & Blue Pops, Twin Pops

Mr. Freeze - Assorted Flavors Freezer Pops

My Essentials - Assorted Pops Regular

North Star -

Lotta Pops (Bars **!!**, Cremes **!!**, Fruita **!!**, Juice **!!**, Regular Pops **!!**, Sugar Free **!!**)

Orange Dream **!!**

Pops (Assorted Twin **!!**, Banana Twin **!!**, Blue Raspberry Twin **!!**, Cherry Twin **!!**, Health Wise Fat Free No Sugar Added Juice **!!**, King Size Root Beer Float **!!**, Melon **!!**, Patriot **!!**)

Specialty (Banana Blast, Frog Spit **!!**, Totally Tubular Orange Sherbet Push Treat **!!**)

Otter Pops - Freezer Pops (All Varieties)

Philly Swirl - Candy Push Popperz, Fudge Swirl Stix Bars, Original Italian Ice Swirls Cups, Sweet Delites Bars, Swirl Popperz, Swirl Stix Italian Ice Bars

Pop Ice - Freezer Pops (All Varieties)

Power Of Fruit - Fruit Bars (Banana Berry, Cherry Berry, Orange Tango, Original All Fruit, Tropical)

Publix - Novelties (Banana Pops, Junior Ice Pops (All Flavors), No Sugar Added Fudge Pops, Twin Pops)

Safeway - Fruit Bars (Coconut Cream, Lemonade, Mandarin Orange)

Safeway Select - Regular Fruit Bars (Lemonade, Lime, Strawberry)

Slush Puppie - Slush Bars

Smooze - Mango & Coconut, Pineapple & Coconut, Pink Guava & Coconut, Simply Coconut

So Delicious - Creamy Orange Dairy Free Bars, Minis Bar Dairy Free Fruit Bars Orange Passion Fruit ●

Soda Pops - Freezer Pops (A & W, Crush, Dr. Pepper, Variety Pack)

Trader Joe's - Gone Bananas Chocolate Dipped Bananas

WarHeads - Extreme Sour Freezer Pops

Wegmans Brand - Ice Pops Twin Stick

Weight Watchers - Bars Strawberry Fruit

Winn & Lovett - Frozen Fruit Bars (Caribbean, Mango, Raspberry, Strawberry)

Winn Dixie - Junior Pops, Orange Cream Bars

Wyler's - Italian Ices Freezer Bars

Pork

... *All Fresh Meat Is Gluten-Free (Non-Marinated, Unseasoned)

Always Tender - Flavored Fresh Pork (Apple Bourbon, Bourbon Maple, Brown Sugar Maple, Citrus, Honey Mustard, Lemon Garlic, Mediterranean & Olive Oil, Mesquite, Onion Garlic, Original, Peppercorn, Roast Flavor, Sun Dried Tomato), Non Flavored Fresh Pork

Coleman's Natural Foods - Hampshire (Chops, Loin, Ribs (Baby Back, St. Louis), Tenderloins)

Dietz & Watson ▲ - Canadian Center Cut Spare Ribs ●, Capocollo Sweet ●, Deli Counter Capocollo Hot ●, Italian Style Roast Pork ●, Our Cuban Recipe ●, Roast Sirloin Of Pork ●, Spiced Luncheon Meat ●

Farmer John -

California Natural Pork (Boneless Loin, Ground Pork, Spareribs, Tenderloins)

Seasoned Boneless Pork Chops (Citrus Jerk, Mango Roasted Green Pepper, Southwestern Chipotle)

Giant Eagle Brand - Baby Back Ribs, Pulled w/BBQ Sauce

P

H-E-B - Fully Cooked Sliced Smoked Pork Loin, Premium Pork & Beef Sausage Ring, Premium Sausage (Original Pork & Beef Value Pack, Pork & Beef Link)

Hormel - Always Tender Shoulder Rubbed w/Barbecue Seasoning, Pickled (Pigs Feet, Pork Hocks, Tidbits), Pork Roast Au Jus Fully Cooked Entrée

Isernio's - Ground Pork ●

Kirkland Signature - Swift Premium (Fresh Sirloin Tip Roast, Rack Of Pork)

Lloyd's -

Babyback Pork Ribs (w/Honey Hickory BBQ Sauce, w/Original BBQ Sauce)

Shredded Pork In Original Barbecue Sauce

Snack Rack Ribs (In Buffalo Sauce, In Honey Mustard Sauce, In Original BBQ Sauce)

St. Louis Style Spareribs w/Original BBQ Sauce

Woodfire Shredded

Organic Prairie -

Frozen Organic Retail (Chops, Ground)

Organic (Boneless Pork Loin Roast, Country Style Boneless Ribs, Ground Pork, Pork Center Cut Chops, Pork Chops Bone In, Pork Loin)

Publix - All Natural Fresh Pork

Saz's - Barbecue Pork Meat Tub, Barbecued Baby Back Ribs

Signature Cafe - Baby Back Ribs, Pulled Pork

Smithfield - All Natural & Unflavored Chops, Ground, Sirloin Chop Grillers, Sliced Fat Back, Sliced Salt, Smoked Neckbones, Sweet & Sassy Barbecue St. Louis Style Spareribs

Trader Joe's - Fresh All Natural, Refrigerated Baby Back Pork Ribs

Wegmans Brand - Canned Pork & Beans In Tomato Sauce

Potato Chips...see Chips

Potato Crisps...see Crisps

Potato Puffs...see Snacks

Potatoes

P

... **All Fresh Fruits & Vegetables Are Gluten-Free*

57th St Grille - Cheddar & Bacon Potato Skins

Alexia Foods -

Crispy Potatoes w/Seasoned Salt Waffle Fries !

Julienne Fries (Spicy Sweet Potato !, Sweet Potato !, w/Sea Salt Yukon Gold !)

Olive Oil (& Sea Salt Oven Fries !, Parmesan & Roasted Garlic Oven Reds !, Rosemary & Garlic Oven Fries !)

Organic (Classic Oven Crinkles !, Oven Crinkles Onion & Garlic !, Oven Crinkles Salt & Pepper !, Yukon Gold Julienne Fries w/Sea Salt !)

Seasoned Salt Hashed Browns !

Augason Farms ▲ - Dehydrated (Gems Complete Mashed Potatoes ●, Slices ●)

Country Crock - Au Gratin w/Bacon, Cheesy Diced

Dinty Moore - Compleats Microwave Meals Scalloped Potatoes & Ham

Dr. Praeger's - Potato Littles !

Food Club Brand -

Canned (Sliced, Whole)

Frozen Potatoes (Crinkle Cut Fries, Hashbrowns (Dried, Patties, Shredded, Southern Style), Original French Fries, Steak Fries, Tater Treats)

Gordon Food Service - Hash Browns Shredded (Regular, Supreme), Natural Cubes, Rounds

Great Value Brand (Wal-Mart) - Canned (Diced, Sliced, Whole New)

Hannaford Brand -

Canned (Diced, Whole)

Frozen (Crinkle Cut Fries, Crispy Crowns, Hash Browns (Country, Patties, Southern Style), Shoestring Fries, Steak Style Fries, Straight Cut Fries, Tasty Taters, Wedges)

Instant (Butter, Butter & Herb, Four Cheese, Regular, Roasted Garlic)

Sliced

P

Hy-Vee -
Canned (Sliced, Whole)
Frozen (Country Style Hash Brown Potatoes, Crinkle Cut Fries,
Potatoes O'Brien, Regular, Shoestring, Southern Style, Steak Fries)
Ian's - Alphatots
Idahoan - Farmhouse Fix'ins (Cheesy Hash Browns, O'Brien Hash
Browns), Loaded Baked Homestyle Casserole
Jimmy Dean - Breakfast Skillets (Bacon, Ham, Sausage)
Kroger Brand - Canned White Potatoes (Sliced, Whole), Three Cheese
Potatoes
Linda's Gourmet Latkes - Potato Pancake Latkes !
Lowes Foods Brand - Canned Sweet Potatoes Cut, Frozen (French Fries
(Crinkle Cut, Shoestring, Steak Cut), Hash Browns (Country Style,
Heat & Serve), Tater Treats), Instant Mashed
Meijer Brand -
Canned White (Sliced, Whole)
Frozen French Fries (Crinkle Cut, Original, Quickie Crinkles,
Shoestring, Steak Cut)
Frozen Hash Browns (Original, Regular, Shredded, Southern Style,
Western Style)
Frozen Tater Tots
Midwest Country Fare - Whole White Potatoes
Ore-Ida -
Country Inn Creations (Peppers & Onion Hash Browns, Savory
Seasoned Hash Browns, Sour Cream & Chives)
Country Style Steak Fries
Crispers
Extra Crispy (Fast Food Fries, Golden Crinkles, Seasoned Crinkles)
French Fries (Crunch Time Classics Straight Cut, Easy Fries Golden
Crinkles, Golden Twirls, Sweet Potato Fries)
Golden (Crinkles, Fries)
Hash Browns (Country Style, Golden Patties, Southern Style)
Potatoes O'Brien
Roasted (Garlic & Parmesan, Original)

Shoestrings

Steak Fries, Steam 'N Mash (Cut Russet Potatoes, Cut Sweet
Potatoes, Garlic Seasoned, Red Skin)

Tater Tots (ABC, Extra Crispy, Mini, Onion)

Waffle Fries

Potato Buds ▲ - Gluten Free 100% Real Potatoes

Publix - Canned White, Frozen (Crinkle Cut Fries, Southern Style
Hash Browns, Steak Fries, Tater Bites)

S&W - All Canned Vegetables

Safeway -

Canned (Sliced, Whole)

Frozen (Hash Browns Diced, Potatoes O'Brien)

Safeway Brand -

Frozen (Crinkle Cut, French Fries Classic, Mashed, Shoestring,
Steak Cut)

Regular Instant Mashed Potatoes

Sharwood's - Bombay Potatoes, Saag Aloo

Shiloh Farms - Organic Instant Potato Flakes **!!**

Signature Cafe - Side Dish (Broccoli Cheddar Au Gratin, Creamy
Mashed)

Smart Ones - Frozen Entrees Broccoli & Cheddar Roasted Potatoes

Spartan Brand -

Canned White (Sliced, Whole)

Frozen (Fries (Crinkle Cut, Extra Crispy Fast, French Fried, Steak),
Hash Browns (O'Brien, Patties, Shredded, Southern Style), Tater
Puffs)

Mashed Potatoes

Bag (Buttery Homestyle, Four Cheese, Fully Loaded)

Box (Butter & Herb, Creamy Butter, Instant, Roasted Garlic,
Sour Cream & Chives)

Tasty Bite - Aloo Palak **!**, Bombay **!**, Mushroom Takatak **!**

Trader Joe's - Frozen Mashed Potatoes, Frozen Potato Fries

Wegmans Brand -

Canned White Potatoes (Sliced, Whole Peeled)

P

Frozen (Crinkle Cut, Steak Cut, Straight Cut, Tater Puffs)

Frozen Hash Browns (Country Style, Hash Browns O'Brien, Regular)

Winn Dixie -

Canned (Diced White, No Salt Added White, Sliced White, Sweet, Whole White)

Frozen (Country Style, O'Brien, Potato Crowns, Southern Style Hashbrowns, Tater Puffs)

Instant (Regular, Roasted Garlic)

Woodstock Farms - Organic Frozen (Crinkle Cut Oven Fries, Shredded Hash Browns, Tastee Taters)

Preserves...see Jam/Jelly

Pretzels

Barkat - Pretzels (Regular, Sticks)

Better Balance - Original Pretzel Sticks ●

Dutch Country - Soft Pretzel Mix, Soft Pretzels Gluten Free

Ener-G ▲ - Bachman Gluten Free Puzzle, Regular, Sesame Pretzel Rings, Wylde Pretzels (Regular, Sesame)

Glutano ▲ - Pretzels

Glutino ▲ - Family Bag (Sticks, Twists), Pretzels (Chocolate Covered, Yogurt Covered), Sesame Ring, Snack Pack, Sticks, Twists

Kay's Naturals - Pretzel Sticks (Cinnamon Toast ●, Jalapeno Honey Mustard ●)

Mary's Gone Crackers ▲ - Sticks & Twigs (Chipotle Tomato ●, Curry ●, Sea Salt ●)

Snyder's Of Hanover - Gluten Free Pretzels (Mini ●, Sticks ●)

Tonya's Gluten Free Kitchen ▲ - Soft Pretzel Bites (Cinnamon Sugar ●, Original ●), Soft Pretzels (Cinnamon Sugar ●, Original ●)

Protein

Arbonne - Protein Shake Mix (Chocolate !, Vanilla !)

Beneprotein - Resource Beneprotein Instant Protein Powder ! !

Bob's Red Mill ▲ - Soy Protein Powder ★, TSP Textured Soy Protein ★, TVP Textured Vegetable Protein ★

CalNaturale Svelte ▲ - Sustained Energy Protein Drink (Cappuccino ●, Chocolate ●, French Vanilla ●, Spiced Chai ●)

Growing Naturals - Rice Protein Isolate Powder (Chocolate Power, Original, Vanilla Blast)

Living Harvest - Organic Hemp Protein Powder (All Varieties)

MLO - Brown Rice Protein Powder

Nutiva - Hemp Protein Powder (15g, Hi Fiber), Hemp Protein Shake (Chocolate, Super Berry, Vanilla)

Nuts.com - Organic Hemp Protein Powder ●

Ruth's Hemp Power - Powders (Regular, w/Maca & E3Live, w/Sprouted Flax & Maca)

Safeway Brand - Nutritional Shakes (Plus (All Flavors), Regular (All Flavors))

Trader Joe's - All Protein Powders **!!** *(Except Whey Quick Dissolve)*

Worldwide Pure Protein - Shake (Banana Cream, Frosty Chocolate, Strawberry Cream, Vanilla Cream)

Protein Shakes...see Protein and/or Shakes

Prunes

Great Value Brand (Wal-Mart) - Pitted Prunes

Meijer Brand - Pitted (Canister, Carton)

Nuts.com - Dried Fruit (Plums (Angelino ●, Jumbo ●, No Pit ●, October Sun ●, Organic Angelino ●, Organic No Pit ●), Pluots ●)

Oskri Organics - Dried Prunes

Spartan Brand - Prunes Pitted

Woodstock Farms - Organic Pitted

Pudding

Bi-Aglut - Apple Banana Bisconttino, Cocoa Dessert, Pear & Rice, Vanilla Dessert

Echo Farms - All Puddings

Food Club Brand -

Cook & Serve (Butterscotch, Chocolate, Vanilla)

Instant (Banana Cream, Chocolate, Coconut Cream, French Vanilla, Lemon, Pistachio, Sugar Free (Butterscotch, Chocolate, Vanilla), Vanilla)

Pudding Cups (Banana, Butterscotch, Chocolate, Fat Free Chocolate, Tapioca, Vanilla)

Refrigerated Packs (Chocolate, Chocolate Vanilla Swirl Regular)

P

Gordon Food Service - Mix (Butterscotch, Chocolate, Vanilla)

Great Value Brand (Wal-Mart) - Instant (Regular (Banana Cream, Chocolate, French Vanilla, Pistachio, Vanilla), Sugar Free (Chocolate, French Vanilla))

H-E-B - Ready To Eat (Banana Strawberry)

Handi-Snacks -

Baskin Robbins (Banana Split, Chocolate Chip, Chocolate Vanilla Sundae, Fudge Rocky Road)

Regular (Banana, Butterscotch, Chocolate, Chocolate, Rice, Vanilla)

Sugar Free Reduced Calorie (Chocolate, Creamy Caramel, Vanilla)

Hannaford Brand - All Fat Free & Sugar Free, Pudding Cook & Serve (Chocolate, Vanilla), Pudding Instant (Banana Cream, Butterscotch, Chocolate, Pistachio, Vanilla)

Hateva - Almond Pudding (Chocolate, Rice w/Cinnamon, Sugar Free (Caramel, Chocolate, Vanilla **!!**), Vanilla **!!**)

Hill Country Fare H-E-B - Ready To Eat Cup (Banana, Chocolate, Tapioca, Value Pack, Vanilla)

Hy-Vee -

Cooked Pudding (Chocolate, Vanilla)

Instant Pudding (Butterscotch, Chocolate (Fat Free/Sugar Free, Regular), Lemon, Vanilla (Fat Free/Sugar Free, Regular))

Pudding Cups (Butterscotch, Chocolate (Fat Free, Fudge, Regular), Strawberry Banana, Tapioca, Vanilla)

Jell-O -

Pudding Snacks (Cheesecake Original Strawberry, Chocolate Fudge Sundaes, Creme Savers Strawberry & Creme Swirled, Fat Free (Chocolate, Chocolate Vanilla Swirls, Devil's Food & Chocolate, Tapioca, Vanilla & Chocolate, Vanilla Caramel Sundaes), Original Chocolate, Original Chocolate Vanilla Swirls, Original Tapioca, Original Vanilla, Original w/The Taste Of Oreo Cookies, Rice Pudding (Americana Fat Free, Sugar Free Creme Brulee), Sugar Free (Chocolate, Chocolate Vanilla Swirls, Creamy Caramel, Double Chocolate, Vanilla), Sundae Toppers (Vanilla w/Caramel, Vanilla w/Chocolate))

Regular Cook & Serve (Banana Cream, Butterscotch, Chocolate (Fudge, Regular), Coconut Cream, Fat Free Tapioca, Lemon, Vanilla)

Regular Instant Pudding & Pie Filling (Banana Cream, Butterscotch, Cheesecake, Chocolate (Fudge, Regular), Coconut Cream, Devil's Food, French Vanilla, Lemon, Pistachio, Pumpkin Spice, Vanilla, White Chocolate)

Smoothie Snacks (Mixed Berry, Strawberry Banana)

Sugar Free Fat Free Cook & Serve (Chocolate, Vanilla)

Sugar Free Fat Free Instant Pudding & Pie Filling (Banana Cream, Butterscotch, Cheesecake, Chocolate, Lemon, Pistachio, Vanilla, White Chocolate)

Kozy Shack - All Varieties

Medifast - Banana ●, Chocolate ●, Vanilla ●

Meijer Brand -

Cook & Serve (Butterscotch, Chocolate, Vanilla)

Instant (Banana Cream, Butterscotch (Fat Free, Sugar Free), Chocolate (Fat Free, Regular, Sugar Free), Coconut Cream, French Vanilla, Pistachio, Vanilla (Fat Free, Regular, Sugar Free))

Premium (Chocolate Peanut Butter, French Vanilla, Orange Dream)

Snack (Banana, Butterscotch, Chocolate (Fat Free, Fudge, Regular), Multi Pack Chocolate & Vanilla, Tapioca, Vanilla)

Mixes From The Heartland ▲ - Pudding Mix (Apple Cinnamon Rice ●, Chocolate Delight ●)

Mori-Nu - Mates Pudding Mix (Chocolate ‼, Vanilla ‼)

My T Fine - Chocolate, Lemon, Vanilla

NOH - Haupia Coconut

Publix - Rice, Tapioca

Pure Knead ▲ - Bread Pudding (Apple Cinnamon ●, Chocolate Chip ●, Espresso ●, Rum Raisin ●, Tres Leches ●)

Royal - All Instant Varieties, Cook & Serve (Chocolate, Vanilla)

Safeway Brand - All Flavors Snack Cups

Snack Pack - All Flavors *(Except Tapioca)*

P

Q

Soyummi - Cherry, Dark Chocolate, Lime, Rice, Tapioca

Spartan Brand -
Cook & Serve (Chocolate, Vanilla)
Instant (Banana Cream, Butterscotch, Chocolate (Regular, Sugar Free),
Pistachio, Vanilla (French, Regular, Sugar Free))
Snack (Butterscotch, Chocolate, Tapioca)

Swiss Miss - All Flavors *(Except Tapioca)*

Trader Joe's - Puddings (Chocolate, Rice, Tapioca)

Wegmans Brand -
Chocolate (Fat Free, Regular, Sugar Free)
Chocolate Vanilla Swirl (Fat Free, Regular, Sugar Free)
FYFGA Homestyle (Chocolate, Rice, Tapioca)
Vanilla (Fat Free, Regular, Sugar Free)

ZenSoy - All Pudding Varieties, Soy Pudding (Chocolate, Vanilla, Vanilla
Chocolate Swirl)

Pumpkin

... *All Fresh Fruits & Vegetables Are Gluten-Free

Farmer's Market - Organic Pumpkin Pie Mix

Hy-Vee - Canned Pumpkin

Libby's - Canned (100% Pure Pumpkin, Easy Pumpkin Pie Mix)

Meijer Brand - Canned

Nuts.com - Pumpkin Seed Powder ●

Pacific Natural Foods - Organic Pumpkin Puree

Spartan Brand - Canned

Wegmans Brand - FYFGA Solid Pack

Puppodums

Devya - Organic (Cumin, Garlic, Plain, Spicy)

Sharwood's - Indian Puppodums (Crushed Garlic & Coriander, Plain,
Red Chilli & Cumin)

Q

Queso

Chi-Chi's - Salsa Con Queso

Cookwell & Company - Blanco Con Chile Verde, Con Salsa
Escabeche

Fischer & Wieser - Queso Starter

Great Value Brand (Wal-Mart) - White Salsa Con Queso

Lowes Foods Brand - Salsa Con Queso

Old Dutch - Restaurante Style (Monterey Jack Queso Supreme,
Salsa Con Queso)

Taco Bell -
Black Bean Con Queso
Chili Con Queso w/Beef
Salsa Con Queso (Medium, Mild)

Tostitos - Monterey Jack Queso **!!**, Salsa Con Queso **!!**

Trader Joe's - Queso Cheese Dip **!**

Winn Dixie - Salsa Con Queso

Quiche

Andrea's Gluten Free ▲ - Ham & Swiss, Spinach & Cheddar

Lean On Me - Broccoli & Cheddar, Mushroom & Swiss, Spinach &
Swiss, Tomato Basil Onion & Mozzarella Cheese

Quinoa

Alter Eco - Pearl ●, Rainbow ●, Red ●

Ancient Harvest Quinoa - Inca Red Quinoa, Quinoa Flakes, Quinoa
Flour, Traditional Quinoa Grain

Arrowhead Mills - Quinoa

Arzu - Chai ●, Original ●, Southwest ●

Minsley - Organic Cooked Quinoa Bowls

Roland - Flavored (Garden Vegetable, Mediterranean, Roasted
Garlic, Toasted Sesame Ginger)

Seeds Of Change - Amantani Whole Grain Blend Quinoa & Wild
Rice **!!**, Cuzco Whole Grain Quinoa Blend **!!**

Shiloh Farms -
Organic (Quinoa **!!**, Red Quinoa **!!**, Tri Color **!!**)
Quinoa Flakes **!!**

Trader Joe's - Organic Quinoa

Woodstock Farms - Organic White

R R

Radishes
... *All Fresh Fruits & Vegetables Are Gluten-Free

Raisins
Full Circle - Organic (Canister, Regular)
Great Value Brand (Wal-Mart) - All Natural California Raisins
Hannaford Brand - Regular
Hy-Vee - California Sun Dried Raisins Regular
Kroger Brand - Kroger Value
Lowes Foods Brand - Canister, Seedless Carton
Mariani - Raisins **! !**
Meijer Brand - Canister, Seedless Carton
Nuts.com - Crimson ●, Dark ●, Jumbo (Flame ●, Golden ●, Golden Flame ●, Thompson Seedless ●), Midget ●, Organic (Dark Chocolate Covered ●, Milk Chocolate Covered ●), Organic ●
O Organics
Oskri Organics - Golden Raisins
Publix - Raisins
Safeway
Spartan Brand
Sun-Maid - Raisins (Baking, Golden, Natural California, Regular), Zante Currants
Wegmans Brand - Seedless
Woodstock Farms - Dark Chocolate w/Evaporated Cane Juice, Flame **!**, Organic (Dark Chocolate w/Evaporated Cane Juice, Jumbo Thompson, Milk Chocolate w/Evaporated Cane Juice, Select Thompson, Thompson), Thompson, Yogurt Raisins w/Evaporated Cane Juice

Raspberries
... *All Fresh Fruits & Vegetables Are Gluten-Free
Augason Farms ▲ - Gluten Free Freeze Dried Whole ●
C & W - All Plain Frozen Fruits **! !**
Food Club Brand - Frozen Red Raspberries

Great Value Brand (Wal-Mart) - Frozen Red Raspberries
Hy-Vee - Frozen Red Raspberries
Lowes Foods Brand - Frozen
Meijer Brand - Frozen (Organic, Red Individually Quick Regular)
Nuts.com - Dried Fruit (Dried Red ●, Simply ●)
O Organics - Frozen Red Raspberries
Publix - Frozen
Safeway Brand - Frozen Red Raspberries
Spartan Brand - Frozen Red Raspberries
Trader Joe's - Frozen (Organic Raspberries, Raspberries)
Wegmans Brand - Frozen (Regular, w/Sugar)
Winn Dixie - Frozen Red Raspberries
Woodstock Farms - Organic Frozen Red Raspberries

Ravioli
  Conte's ▲ - Cheese Ravioli w/Marinara Sauce Microwave Meal ●
  Conte's Pasta ▲ - Cheese ●, Spinach & Cheese ●
  Everybody Eats ▲ - Cheese, Chicken, Spinach Ricotta
  GlutenOut - Ravioli ★
  Nuovo - Gluten Free Five Cheese ●
  Philadelphia Gluten Free Ravioli Pasta Company - Cheese &
    Spinach Mini ●, Cheese & Spinach ●, Cheese Mini ●, Cheese ●,
    Rice Breaded Cheese & Spinach ●, Rice Breaded Cheese ●
  Star Ravioli - Gluten Free Cheese Ravioli

Refried Beans...see Beans

Relish
  B&G - Dill, Emerald, Hamburger, Hot Dog, India, Sweet
  Claussen - Sweet
  Food Club Brand - All Varieties
  Gordon Food Service - Dill, Sweet
  Great Value Brand (Wal-Mart) - Sweet Pickle
  Hannaford Brand - Dill, Hot Dog
  Heinz - All Varieties
  Hill Country Fare H-E-B - Dill, Sweet
  Hy-Vee - Dill, Squeeze Sweet, Sweet

R
    Lowes Foods Brand - Regular, Sweet Pickle

    Meijer Brand - Dill Relish, Sweet Relish (Regular, Sugar Free)

    Mezzetta ▲ - Deli Style (Sweet Bell Pepper Relish, Zesty Bell Pepper Relish Hot)

    Midwest Country Fare - Sweet Pickle

    Mrs. Renfro's - Corn, Hot Chow Chow, Hot Tomato, Mild Chow Chow, Mild Tomato

    Mt. Olive ▲ - Dill Relish, Dill Salad Cubes, Hot Dog Relish, Sweet Green Salad Cubes, Sweet India Relish, Sweet Relish, Sweet Salad Cubes

    Patak's Original - Brinjal Eggplant, Chile, Garlic, Hot Lime, Hot Mango, Lime, Mango, Mixed

    SanDel - All Varieties

    Spartan Brand - Dill, Sweet

    Trader Joe's - Organic Sweet **! !**

    Vlasic - All Varieties

    Wegmans Brand - Dill, Hamburger, Hot Dog, Sweet

    Woodstock Farms - Organic (Spicy Chipotle, Sweet Relish)

Rhubarb
    ... *All Fresh Fruits & Vegetables Are Gluten-Free*

    Publix - Frozen

Ribs...see also Pork
    ... *All Fresh Meat Is Gluten-Free (Non-Marinated, Unseasoned)*

    Kirkland Signature - Fresh Spare Ribs

    Saz's - Barbecued Baby Back Ribs

    Sol Cuisine - Organic BBQ Tofu Ribs **!**

    Trader Joe's - Baby Back Pork Ribs

Rice
    A Taste Of India - Masala Rice & Lentils, Spiced Rice w/Raisins

    A Taste Of Thai - Rice (Coconut Ginger, Garlic Basil Coconut, Jasmine, Yellow Curry)

    Alter Eco - Jasmine Rice (Coral Red ●, Purple ●, Ruby Red ●, Thai White ●)

Annie Chun's - Sticky Rice (Black Pearl, Multi Grain, Sprouted Brown, White)

Arrowhead Mills - Brown Basmati, Long Grain Brown

Central Market H-E-B - Organics (Long Grain White, Short Grain Brown)

CookSimple - Cranberry Wild Rice w/Rosemary Parsley & Thyme

Country Crock - Cheddar Broccoli Rice

Dinty Moore - Compleats Microwave Meals Rice & Chicken

Eden Organic - Organic Canned (Curried Rice & Lentils, Mexican Rice & Black Beans, Moroccan Rice & Garbanzo Beans, Rice & Cajun Small Red Beans, Rice & Caribbean Black Beans, Rice & Garbanzo Beans, Rice & Kidney Beans, Rice & Lentils, Rice & Pinto Beans, Spanish Rice & Pinto Beans)

Fantastic World Foods - Arborio, Basmati, Jasmine

Food Club Brand - Instant Rice (All Plain Varieties), Long Grain

Full Circle - Organic (Basmati Brown, Basmati White, Long Grain Brown, Long Grain White)

Golden Star - Calrose Rice, Jasmine Rice, Long Grain Rice

Goose Valley ▲ -
Family Blend (Arborio & Wild Rice Risotto Fusion ●, Basmati & Wild Rice Fusion ●, Brown & Wild Rice Fusion ●, Rice & Bean Fusion ●)
Family Reserve (Certified Organic Wild Rice ●, Natural Wild Rice ●)

Gordon Food Service - Long Grain Enriched, Mexican

Great Value Brand (Wal-Mart) - Boil In Bag, Brown, Long Grain Enriched

Hannaford Brand - Frozen Steam In Bag White Rice

Hormel - Compleats Microwaveable Meals Chicken & Rice

Hy-Vee - Boil In Bag Rice, Enriched Extra Long Grain (Instant, Regular), Extra Long Grain, Instant Brown, Natural Long Grain Brown

Konriko ▲ -
Artichoke Brown Rice Mix ●
Brown Rice (Original ●, Wild Pecan ●)
Hot 'N Spicy Brown Rice Pilaf ●
Wild Pecan Rice Burlap Bag ●

R

Lotus Foods - Bhutan Red, Brown Kalijira, Forbidden, Madagascar Pink, Organic (Brown Jasmine, Brown Mekong Flower, Carnaroli, Forbidden, Jade Pearl, Jasmine, Madagascar Pink, Mekong Flower, Volcano)

Lowes Foods Brand - Boil N' Bag, Instant (Brown, White)

Lundberg ▲ - All Varieties

Meijer Brand - Brown, Instant (Boil In Bag, Brown, Regular), Long Grain, Medium Grain

Midwest Country Fare - Instant Rice

Minsley - Organic Cooked Rice Bowls (Brown, Medley, White)

Minute Rice -
  Brown
  Premium
  Ready To Serve Rice (Brown & Wild, Chicken Flavor, Spanish, White, Whole Grain Brown, Yellow)
  Steamers (Spanish, White, Whole Grain Brown)
  White

Mixes From The Heartland ▲ - Instant Rice Mix (White ●, Wild ●)

My Essentials - Enriched Long Grain, Instant

Nishiki - Sushi Rice

Nueva Cocina -
  Black Beans & Rice
  Coconut Raisin Rice
  Mexican Rice Mix
  Red Beans & Rice
  Rice Mix For (Chicken, Seafood)

O Organics - Long Grain (Brown, Thai Jasmine)

Publix - Long Grain (Brown, Enriched), Medium Grain White, Pre Cooked Instant (Boil In Bag, Brown, White), Yellow Rice Mix

Royal - Basmati Rice

Safeway Brand - Instant, Long Grain, Thai Jasmine, White

Seeds Of Change -
  Amantani Whole Grain Blend Quinoa & Wild Rice **! !**
  Cuzco Whole Grain Quinoa Blend **! !**

Havana Cuban Style Whole Grain Rice & Beans **! !**

Microwaveable (Dharamsala Aromatic Indian Rice Blend **! !**, Rishikesh Whole Grain Brown Basmati Rice **! !**, Tapovan White Basmati Rice **! !**, Uyuni Quinoa & Whole Grain Brown Rice **! !**)

Velleron French Style Herb Whole Grain Blend **! !**

Shiloh Farms - Organic (Brown Basmati Rice **! !**, California Wild Rice **! !**, Long Grain Brown Rice **! !**, Short Grain Brown Rice **! !**)

Signature Cafe - Side Dish Asparagus Risotto

Smart Ones - Frozen Entrees (Santa Fe Rice & Beans)

Spartan Brand - Instant (Boil In Bag, Brown Box, Regular Box)

Success - Boil In Bag (Basmati Rice, Jasmine Rice, White Rice, Whole Grain Brown Rice)

Tambobamba -

Mojo Bowls (Brazilian Rice & Beans, Caribbean Rice & Beans, Peruvian Rice & Beans)

Side Dishes (Cuban Black Beans & Rice, Jamaican Rice & Beans, Mexican Rice & Beans)

Tasty Bite - Basmati **!**, Brown Rice (Garlic **!**, Regular **!**), Ginger Lentil **!**, Jasmine **!**, Tandori Pilaf **!**, Tehari Herb **!**, Thai Lime Pilaf **!**

Thai Kitchen - Jasmine Rice Mixes (Green Chili & Garlic, Jasmine Rice, Lemongrass & Ginger, Roasted Garlic & Chili, Spicy Thai Chili, Sweet Chili & Onion, Thai Yellow Curry)

Trader Joe's - Biryani Curried Rice, Curried Lentils w/Basmati Rice **! !**, Frozen Peruvian Style Chimichurri w/ Vegetables, Organic All Varieties, Thai Style Lime Rice Pilaf, Wild & Basmati Rice Pilaf

Uncle Ben's -

Brown Rice (Fast & Natural Instant, Natural Whole Grain, Whole Grain Boil In Bag)

White Rice (Boil In Bag, Instant, Original)

Wegmans Brand - FYFGA (Basmati, Boil In Bag, Boxed Jasmine Rice *(Except Rice Blend)*, Enriched Long Grain White, Instant (Brown, White), Long Grain (Brown, White), Medium Grain, Medium Grain White), Italian Classics Arborio

R Rice Beverages

    Central Market H-E-B - Organics (Original, Vanilla)

    Full Circle - Organic (Original, Vanilla)

    Good Karma - Organic Ricemilk (Chocolate, Original, Unsweetened, Vanilla)

    Grainaissance - Almond Shake, Amazing Mango, Banana Appeal, Chocolate (Almond, Chimp), Cool Coconut, Go Hazelnuts, Oh So Original, Rice Nog, Tiger Chai, Vanilla (Gorilla, Pecan Pie)

    Growing Naturals - Rice Milk (Creamy Vanilla, Silky Smooth Original, Velvety Chocolate)

    Kirkland Signature - Organic Rice Milk Original

    Meijer Brand - Ricemilk (Organic, Vanilla)

    O Organics - Rice Milk

    Pacific Natural Foods - Low Fat Plain, Low Fat Vanilla

    Rice Dream - Refrigerated & Shelf Stable Rice Beverages (All Varieties)

    Trader Joe's - Rice Milk

    Wegmans Brand - Organic FYFGA (Original, Vanilla)

Rice Cakes

    Eating Right - Lightly Salted **!!**, Rice & Corn (Caramel **!!**, White Cheddar **!!**)

    Hannaford Brand - Apple Cinnamon, Caramel Corn, Lightly Salted, Multi Grain, White Cheddar

    Hy-Vee - Caramel, Lightly Salted, White Cheddar

    Lundberg ▲ -

        Eco Farmed (Apple Cinnamon, Brown Rice (Lightly Salted, Salt Free), Buttery Caramel, Honey Nut, Sesame Tamari, Toasted Sesame)

        Organic (Brown Rice (Lightly Salted, Salt Free), Caramel Corn, Cinnamon Toast, Flax w/Tamari, Koku Seaweed, Mochi Sweet Lightly Salted, Rice w/Popcorn, Sesame Tamari, Sweet Green Tea w/Lemon, Tamari w/Seaweed, Wild Rice Lightly Salted)

    Mrs. Crimble's - Apple, Caramel, Chocolate Coated, Honey, Yoghurt Coated

    Publix - Lightly Salted, Mini (Caramel **!**, Cheddar **!**, Ranch), Unsalted, White Cheddar

Quaker - Apple Cinnamon **!**, Butter Popcorn **!**, Caramel Corn **!**, Chocolate Crunch **!**, Lightly Salted **!**, Salt Free **!**, White Cheddar **!**

Spartan Brand - Caramel, Salt Free, White Cheddar

Trader Joe's - Lightly Salted Rice Cakes **! !**

Rice Noodles...see Noodles and/or Pasta

Rice Vinegar...see Vinegar

Risotto

  Lundberg ▲ -

    Eco Farmed (Butternut Squash, Creamy Parmesan, Garlic Primavera, Italian Herb)

    Organic (Alfredo Parmesan Cheese, Florentine Spinach & Mushroom, Tuscan Tomato Garlic & Onion, Wild Porcini Mushroom)

Roast Beef...see Beef and/or Deli Meat

Rolls

  3 Fellers Bakery ▲ - Dinner Rolls (Garlic ●, Onion ●, Plain ●)

  Against The Grain Gourmet ▲ - Fresh Rosemary, Original, Pumpernickel, Vermont Country

  Andrea's Gluten Free ▲ - Dinner Rolls (Herb, Multigrain, Regular)

  Better Bread Company - Sandwich

  Bi-Aglut - Breadrolls

  Celiac Specialties ▲ - Breakfast Rolls (Apple, Blueberry), Cinnamon, Multigrain, Onion Poppy

  Deerfields Gluten Free Bakery ▲ - Rice Bran Gluten Free Dinner Rolls (Plain, Poppy Seed, Sesame)

  El Peto ▲ - Dinner Rolls (Brown Rice, Cheese, Gourmet, Italian, Multigrain, Raisin)

  Ener-G ▲ - Tapioca Dinner

  Everybody Eats - Deli (Dairy Free, Multigrain, Regular)

  French Meadow Bakery - Gluten Free Italian ●

  Gillian's Foods ▲ - Carmalized Onion ●, Cinnamon Raisin ●, Everything Dinner ●, French ●, Poppy Seed ●, Sesame Seed ●

  Grandma Ferdon's ▲ - Dinner Rolls ●

R
S

Heaven Mills ▲ - Burger ●, Mini Challa Dinner Rolls (Gluten & Egg Free ●, Gluten & Sugar Free ●, Gluten Egg & Sugar Free ●, Gluten Free ●)

Katz Gluten Free ▲ - Large Challah Kaiser ●, Oat Challah ●, Small Challah Dinner Rolls ●, Whole Grain Sandwich ●

Kneaded Specialties ▲ - Cinnamon ●, Dinner ●, French Bread ●, Vegan Sourdough ●

Mariposa Artisan-Crafted Gluten-Free ▲ - Rosemary, Sandwich

Molly's Gluten-Free Bakery ▲ - Cinnamon Raisin, Dinner Rolls (Ancient Grains, French, Mock Rye, White)

Pure Knead ▲ - Dill Dinner ●, Sandwich ●

Rose's Bakery ▲ - Herbed French Bread, Wheat Free Dinner

Schar ▲ - Classic White, Multigrain Ciabatta, Parbaked Ciabatta, Sub Sandwich

Sweet Christine's Bakery - Hamburger ●, Hot Dog ●, Large Kaiser ●, Slider ●

Trader Joe's - Gluten Free French

Udi's Gluten Free Foods ▲ - Gluten Free Dinner Rolls (Classic French ●, Whole Grain Seeded ●)

Rum
... *All Distilled Alcohol Is Gluten-Free*

Rutabagas
... *All Fresh Fruits & Vegetables Are Gluten-Free*

S

Salad
... *All Fresh Fruits & Vegetables Are Gluten-Free*

Earthbound Farm - American Salad, Baby Arugula, Baby Arugula Blend, Baby Lettuces, Baby Romaine, Baby Spinach, Baby Spinach Blend, Bibb Lettuce Leaves, Butter Lettuce Leaves, Fancy Romaine Salad, Fresh Herb Salad, Fresh Spinach, Frisée, Frisée Blend, Harvest Blend, Hearts of Romaine, Heirloom Lettuce Leaves, Iceberg Lettuce, Italian Salad, Mâche, Mâche Blend, Mixed Baby Greens, Romaine Hearts, Romaine Salad, Salad Kit (Grab & Go

(Baby Spinach, Mixed Baby Greens), No Dressing (California Blend, **S**
Harvest Blend), Power Meal Blueberry Quinoa Protein Balance,
Tomatillo Black Bean Protein Energy), Spring Mix, Washed & Trimmed
Romaine Heart Leaves

Hy-Vee - American Blend, Chopped Romaine, Cole Slaw, European
Blend, Garden, Garden Supreme, Italian Blend, Riveria Blend,
Shredded Lettuce, Spring Mix

Mixes From The Heartland ▲ - Pasta Salad (Corn 'N Pasta Salad ●,
Cucumber Dill ●, Dilled ●)

Publix - Classic Blend, Cole Slaw Blend, European Blend, Italian Blend,
Romaine Lettuce Heart, Spinach

Publix GreenWise Market - Organic Salad (Baby (Arugula, Lettuce,
Mixed Greens, Romaine, Spinach), Fresh Herb, Romaine Hearts)

Pure Market Express ▲ - Salad Kit (Big Greek ●, Caesar Salad ●)

Sabra - Moroccan Matbucha, Turkish Salad

Salad Dressing

Annie's Naturals -

Natural Dressings

Artichoke Parmesan **!!**

Balsamic Vinaigrette **!!**

Cowgirl Ranch **!!**

Fat Free (Mango Vinaigrette **!!**, Raspberry Balsamic Vinaigrette **!!**)

Lemon & Chive **!!**

Lite (Goddess **!!**, Herb Balsamic **!!**, Poppy Seed **!!**)

Lite Vinaigrette (Honey Mustard **!!**, Raspberry **!!**)

Roasted Red Pepper Vinaigrette **!!**

Tuscany Italian **!!**

Organic

Buttermilk **!!**

Caesar **!!**

Cowgirl Ranch **!!**

Creamy Asiago Cheese **!!**

French **!!**

Green (Garlic **!!**, Goddess **!!**)

Oil & Vinegar **!!**

S

Papaya Poppy Seed **!!**
Thousand Island **!!**
Vinaigrette (Balsamic **!!**, Pomegranate **!!**, Red Wine & Olive
   Oil **!!**, Roasted Garlic **!!**, Sesame Ginger **!!**)

Bakers & Chefs - Ranch

Biltmore - Buttermilk Dill Ranch, Caesar, Honey Mustard, Italian
Herb Vinaigrette

Bolthouse Farms -
Olive Oil Vinaigrette (Chunky Blue Cheese, Classic Balsamic,
   Raspberry Merlot, Tropical Mango)
Yogurt Dressing (Caesar Parmigiano, Chunky Blue Cheese,
   Classic Ranch, Honey Mustard, Salsa Ranch, Thousand Island,
   Zesty French)

Bragg - Organic (Braggberry, Ginger & Sesame, Hawaiian,
Vinaigrette)

Briannas -
Classic Buttermilk Ranch
Dijon Honey Mustard
Rich (Poppy Seed, Santa Fe Blend)
The New American
True Blue Cheese
Vinaigrette (Blush Wine, Champagne Caper, Real French)
Zesty French

Cains -
Fat Free (Caesar, Honey Dijon, Italian, Peppercorn Ranch,
   Raspberry Vinaigrette, Vinaigrette Blush Wine)
Light (Caesar, French, Italian, Ranch, Vinaigrette (Blush Wine,
   Raspberry))
Regular (Blue Cheese, Creamy Caesar, French (Original, Zesty
   Tomato & Onion), Italian (Bellisimo, Cheese Trio, Country,
   Creamy, Original, Robust), Peppercorn Parmesan, Ranch
   (Chipotle, Deluxe Buttermilk, Original), Vinaigrette (Balsamic,
   Raspberry Country), White Balsamic w/Honey)

salad dressing

S

Cardini's -
   Aged Parmesan Ranch
   Caesar (Fat Free, Light, Original)
   Honey Mustard
   Italian
   Vinaigrette (Balsamic, Light Balsamic, Light Caesar, Pear, Raspberry Pomegranate)

Cookwell & Company - Vinaigrette (Cracked Pepper, Olive & Lemon, Watermelon)

Drew's -
   Buttermilk Ranch
   Classic Italian
   Greek Olive
   Honey Dijon
   Organic (Aged Balsamic, Peppercorn Ranch)
   Poppy Seed
   Quick Marinade Smoked Tomato
   Raspberry
   Roasted Garlic & Peppercorn
   Romano Caesar
   Rosemary Balsamic

Eating Right - Balsamic & Red Wine, Garlic Caesar, Honey Mustard, Italian Parmesan, Poppyseed & Caramelized Onion, Ranch, Vinaigrette (Herb & Balsamic, Roasted Sweet Pepper & Garlic), Yogurt (Blue Cheese, Ranch)

El Torito - Cilantro Pepita

Emeril's - Caesar, Vinaigrette (Balsamic, House Herb, Italian, Raspberry Balsamic)

Fischer & Wieser - Original Roasted Raspberry Chipotle Vinaigrette

Flamous Brands - Hummus Dressing & Dip (All Varieties)

Follow Your Heart -
   Low Fat Ranch **!**
   Oil Free (Citrus Poppy Seed **!**, French Dijon **!**, Tamari Miso **!**)

S

Organic (Balsamic Vinaigrette !, Caesar w/Aged Parmesan !, Chipotle Lime Ranch !, Chunky Bleu Cheese !, Creamy Caesar!, Creamy Ranch !, Italian Vinaigrette !, Miso Ginger !, Spicy Southwestern Ranch !, Thick & (Chunky Bleu Cheese !, Creamy Caesar !, Creamy Ranch !), White Balsamic Dijon Vinaigrette !)

Vegan (Caesar !, Creamy Garlic !, High Omega Ranch !, Honey Mustard !, Lemon Herb !, Sesame Dijon !, Sesame Miso !, Thousand Island !)

Food Club Brand - Blue Cheese, California French, Classic Caesar, Fat Free (California French, Italian, Ranch), Italian, Lite Ranch, Ranch, Thousand Island, Western Style

Foods Alive -

Organic Golden Flax Oil (Meg's Sweet & Sassy, Mike's Special, Sweet Mustard)

Organic Gourmet Hemp Oil Meg's Sweet & Sassy

Fosse Farms ▲ - Blackberry ●, Cranberry ●, Marionberry ●, Organic (Blackberry ●, Cranberry ●, Provencal ●, Raspberry ●), Raspberry ●

Full Circle - Organic (French, Ranch, Raspberry Vinaigrette)

Girard's -

Apple Poppyseed

Caesar

Champagne

Light (Caesar, Champagne, Raspberry)

Olde Venice Italian

Original French

Peach Mimosa

Raspberry

Romano Cheese Italian

Spinach Salad

Vinaigrette (Blue Cheese, Creamy Balsamic, Greek Feta, Lite Balsamic, White Balsamic)

Gone Native - Vinaigrette (Raspberry & Raw Honey, Strawberry & Mint)

Good - Hemp Seed Oil (Balsamic, Honey Mustard)

Good Seasons -
> Dressing Mix (Cheese Garlic, Cruet Kit Italian, Garlic & Herb, Italian, Mild Italian, Zesty Italian)
> Light Honey Mustard w/Grey Poupon Mustard
> Vinaigrette w/Extra Virgin Olive Oil (Classic Balsamic, Italian, Raspberry w/Poppy Seeds, Sun Dried Tomato)

Gordon Food Service - Packet (1000 Island, Buttermilk Ranch, French, Italian, Salad)

H-E-B - Carmelized Onion & Bacon, Light Balsamic, Light Ranch

Hannaford Brand -
> Bacon Ranch
> Balsamic Vinaigrette (Light **!!**, Regular)
> Chunky Blue Cheese
> Classic Italian
> Creamy (Dill, Italian, Ranch)
> Deluxe French
> Fat Free (California French Style, Ranch, Raspberry Vinaigrette, Sweet Herb Vinaigrette, Zesty Italian **!!**)
> Honey Dijon **!!**
> Light (Caesar, Honey Mustard **!**, Italian, Ranch)
> Old World Greek
> Peppercorn Ranch
> Robust Italian
> Thousand Island
> Vidalia Onion
> Whipped
> Zesty Italian

Hill Country Fare H-E-B - Coleslaw, Honey Mustard, Italian (Dry, Regular, XL Pourable, Zesty), Ranch (Bacon, Fat Free, Salad Dressing Mix, XL Pourable), Thousand Island

Hy-Vee -
> Dressing (Bacon Ranch, Buttermilk Ranch, French, Italian, Peppercorn Ranch, Ranch, Raspberry Vinaigrette, Thousand Island, Zesty Italian)

S

Light Salad Dressing (French, Italian, Ranch, Thousand Island),
   Squeezable Salad Dressing

Ken's Steak House -

Chef's Reserve
   Blue Cheese w/Gorgonzola
   Creamy Greek
   Farm House Ranch w/Buttermilk
   French w/Applewood Smoked Bacon
   Golden Vidalia Onion
   Honey Balsamic
   Honey Dijon
   Italian w/Garlic & Asiago Cheese
   Ranch
   Russian

Fat Free Dressings (Raspberry Pecan, Sun Dried Tomato)

Light Options
   Caesar
   Honey (Dijon, French)
   Italian w/Romano & Red Pepper
   Olive Oil & Vinegar
   Parmesan & Peppercorn
   Ranch
   Raspberry Walnut
   Vinaigrette (Balsamic, Sweet Vidalia Onion)

Lite Dressings
   Balsamic & Basil
   Caesar
   Chunky Blue Cheese
   Country French w/Orange Blossom Honey
   Creamy (Caesar, Parmesan w/Cracked Peppercorn)
   Honey Mustard
   Italian
   Northern Italian
   Ranch

salad dressing

    Raspberry Pomegranate
    Raspberry Walnut
    Sun Dried Tomato
    Sweet Vidalia Onion
    Vinaigrette (Olive Oil, Red Wine)
  Regular
    Caesar
    Chunky Blue Cheese
    Country French w/Orange Blossom Honey
    Creamy (Caesar, French, Italian)
    Greek
    Honey Mustard
    Italian (& Marinade, Three Cheese, w/Aged Romano)
    Ranch (Buttermilk, Regular)
    Red Wine Vinegar & Olive Oil
    Russian
    Sweet Vidalia Onion
    Thousand Island
    Vinaigrette Balsamic
    Zesty Italian
Kraft -
  Caesar w/Bacon
  Catalina
  Classic Caesar
  Coleslaw
  Creamy (French, Italian, Poppyseed)
  Free (Caesar Italian, Catalina, Classic Caesar, French, Honey Dijon,
    Italian, Roka Blue Cheese, Zesty Italian)
  Greek Vinaigrette
  Honey Dijon
  Light (Balsamic Vinaigrette, Balsamic Vinaigrette w/Parmesan &
    Asiago, Creamy Caesar, Creamy French Style, Raspberry
    Vinaigrette w/Extra Virgin Olive Oil, Sicilian Roasted Garlic
    Balsamic Vinaigrette, Thousand Island, Zesty Italian)

S

Light Done Right (Red Wine Vinaigrette)
Organic (Balsamic Vinaigrette, Raspberry Vinaigrette)
Ranch (Buttermilk, Cucumber, Free, Free Peppercorn, Garlic,
  Light, Light Cucumber, Light Three Cheese, Peppercorn, Regular,
  Three Cheese, w/Bacon)
Roasted Red Pepper Italian w/Parmesan
Roka Blue Cheese
Seven Seas (Green Goddess, Red Wine Vinaigrette)
Special Collection Parmesan Romano
Sweet Honey Catalina
Tangy Tomato Bacon
Thousand Island (Light, Regular, w/Bacon)
Tuscan House Italian
Vinaigrette (Balsamic, Caesar w/Parmesan, Classic Italian, Honey
  Dijon, Sun Dried Tomato, Vidalia Onion w/Roasted Red Pepper)
Zesty Italian
Kroger Brand - Coleslaw Dressing
Lily's Gourmet Dressings - Balsamic Vinaigrette, Caesar, Northern
  Italian, Poppyseed, Raspberry Walnut Vinaigrette
Litehouse -
Bleu Cheese (Bacon, Big, Chunky, Lite, Original, Yoghurt w/Kefir)
Caesar (Chunky Garlic, Classic, Parmesan, Regular, Yoghurt
  w/Kefir)
Coleslaw (Regular, w/Pineapple)
Creamy Cilantro
Honey Mustard
Lite (1000 Island, Caesar, Coleslaw, Creamy Ranch, Honey Dijon
  Vinaigrette, Jalapeno Ranch)
Organic (Balsamic Vinaigrette, Caesar, Raspberry Lime Vinaigrette)
Pear Gorgonzola
Poppyseed
Ranch (Buttermilk, Homestyle, Jalapeno, Lite, Lite Salsa, Organic,
  Regular, Yoghurt w/Kefir)
Spinach Salad

salad dressing

S

Sweet French
Thousand Island
Ultra Premium Gorgonzola
Vinaigrette (Balsamic, Bleu Cheese, Cherry, Fuji Apple, Greek,
    Harvest Cranberry, Huckleberry, Pomegranate Blueberry,
    Raspberry Walnut, Red Wine Olive Oil, Zesty Italian)
White Balsamic

Lowes Foods Brand - Chunky Blue Cheese, Creamy Caesar, French,
    Italian (Fat Free, Regular), Ranch (Lite, Regular), Thousand Island

Lucini - Artisan Vinaigrette (Bold Parmesan & Garlic, Cherry Balsamic
    & Rosemary, Delicate Cucumber & Shallot, Fig & Walnut Savory
    Balsamic, Roasted Hazelnut & Extra Virgin, Tuscan Balsamic & Extra
    Virgin)

Maple Grove Farms Of Vermont -
    Aged Parmesan & Pepper
    All Natural (Asiago & Garlic, Champagne Vinaigrette, Ginger
        Pear, Strawberry Balsamic)
    Citrus Vinaigrette
    Creamy Balsamic
    Fat Free (Cranberry Balsamic, Greek, Honey Dijon, Lime
        Basil, Poppyseed, Vidalia Onion, Vinaigrette (Balsamic,
        Raspberry), Wasabi Dijon)
    Honey Mustard (Lite, Regular)
    Lite Caesar
    Organic Vinaigrette (Balsamic w/Pure Maple Syrup, Raspberry)
    Ranch
    Sugar Free (Dijon, Vinaigrette Balsamic)
    Vermont Sweet 'N Sour

Marzetti -
    Refrigerated Dressings
        Asiago Peppercorn
        Blue Cheese (Chunky, Light Chunky, Organic, The Ultimate)
        Caesar (Light Supreme, Organic, Supreme)
        Honey Dijon (Light, Regular)

S

Honey French (Light, Regular)
Light Ancho Chipotle Ranch
Light Berry Balsamic
Organic Parmesan Ranch
Organic Raspberry Cranberry
Poppyseed
Ranch (Classic, Light Classic)
Simply Dressed (Balsamic, Blue Cheese, Caesar, Champagne,
    Coleslaw, Greek Feta, Pomegranate, Ranch, Strawberry
    Poppyseed)
Slaw (Lite, Regular)
Spinach Salad
Sweet Italian
Thousand Island
Ultimate Gorgonzola
Venice Italian
Vinaigrette (Blue Cheese Italian, Light Balsamic, Light Caesar,
    Light Raspberry Cabernet, Roasted Garlic Italian, Strawberry
    Chardonnay, White Balsamic)
Shelf Stable
  Asiago Peppercorn
  Caesar Creamy
  California French
  Country French
  Honey Dijon (Fat Free, Mustard)
  Italian (Creamy, Fat Free, House, Regular, w/Blue Cheese Crumbles)
  Poppyseed
  Potato Salad
  Ranch (Aged Parmesan, Regular)
  Slaw (Lite, Low Fat, Original)
  Sweet & Sour (Fat Free, Regular)
  Sweet Vidalia
  Thousand Island
  Vinaigrette (Balsamic, Light Balsamic, Organic Balsamic,
    Strawberry)

Midwest Country Fare - French, Italian, Ranch, Thousand Island

Miracle Whip - Free, Light, Regular

Naturally Delicious -
  Light (Blush Wine, Italian, Raspberry)
  Regular (Balsamic, Blue Cheese, Chipotle Ranch, French, Honey
    Mustard, Italian, Peppercorn Parmesan)

Nature's Basket - Organic (Balsamic, Italian, Ranch, Raspberry
  Vinaigrette, Roasted Red Pepper, Sesame Ginger)

Newman's Own -
  Lighten Up Light (Balsamic Vinaigrette, Caesar, Cranberry Walnut,
    Honey Mustard, Italian, Lime Vinaigrette, Raspberry & Walnut,
    Red Wine Vinegar & Olive Oil, Roasted Garlic Balsamic, Sun
    Dried Tomato Italian)
  Organic (Light Balsamic Vinaigrette, Tuscan Italian)
  Regular (Balsamic Vinaigrette, Caesar, Creamy Caesar, Creamy
    Balsamic, Greek Vinaigrette, Honey French, Olive Oil & Vinegar,
    Parmesan & Roasted Garlic, Poppy Seed, Ranch, Red Wine
    Vinegar & Olive Oil, Three Cheese Balsamic Vinaigrette)

Oak Hill Farms - Vidalia Onion Vinaigrette

Olde Cape Cod -
  Lite (Caesar, Chipotle Ranch, Honey French, Sundried Tomato,
    Sweet & Sour Poppyseed, Vinaigrette (Blush Wine, Raspberry))
  Regular (Balsamic (Original, w/Olive Oil), Buffalo Blue Cheese,
    Chipotle Ranch, Honey Dijon, Parmesan & Peppercorn,
    Poppyseed (Lemon, Orange), Vinaigrette (Lemon & Mint
    w/Green Tea, Zesty Mango))

Open Nature - Asian Sesame Ginger, Balsamic Vinegar, Blush Wine
  Vinegar, Poppy Seed, Raspberry Walnut

Organicville -
  Organic Dressing (French ●, Non Dairy (Caesar ●, Coleslaw ●,
    Ranch ●, Thousand Island ●))
  Organic Vinaigrette (Dijon ●, Herbs De Provence ●, Miso Ginger ●,
    Olive Oil & Balsamic ●, Orange Cranberry ●, Pomegranate ●,
    Sesame Goddess ●, Sesame Tamari ●, Sun Dried Tomato &
    Garlic ●)

S

Pfeiffer - Blue Cheese, Caesar, California French, Cole Slaw, French, Honey Dijon, Italian (Creamy, Regular, Roasted Garlic, Zesty Garlic), Ranch (Light, Regular), Sweet & Sour, Thousand Island, Vinaigrette (Balsamic, Red Wine)

Publix - Caesar, California French, Chunky Blue Cheese, Creamy Parmesan, Italian (Fat Free, Regular), Lite (Caesar, Honey Dijon, Ranch, Raspberry Walnut), Ranch, Tangy Balsamic Vinaigrette, Thousand Island (Fat Free, Regular), Zesty Italian

Pure Market Express - Caesar, Greek, Thai

Ring Bros Marketplace - All Varieties *(Except Blue Cheese)*

Royal Food Products -

Garden Fresh (Bleu Cheese (Pourable, Regular, San Francisco Style), Cole Slaw (Regular, Special), French (Red, Regular), Italian (Creamy, Golden), Ranch/Buttermilk, Thousand Island, White (Salad Dressing, Whipped))

Gourmet Choice (Balsamic Herb Vinaigrette, California Raspberry Vinaigrette, Caribbean Thousand Island, Classic Caesar, Hawaiian Honey French, Original Recipe Chunky Bleu Cheese, Paris Style Honey Dijon, Ranch/Buttermilk (Chipotle, Classic), Sweet Garden Italian, Sweet 'N Creamy Poppy Seed)

Royal Deluxe (Caesar (Creamy, Regular), Chunky Bleu Cheese, Cole Slaw (Regular, Sweet & Sour, w/Celery Seed), French (Island Honey, Red, Red Ranch, Regular), Italian (Creamy, Creamy Garlic, Golden, Oil & Vinegar, Reduced Calorie, Regular, Separating), Old Fashioned Poppy Seed, Parmesan Pepper, Ranch/Buttermilk (Ranch Style, Red Ranch, Shelf Stable), Raspberry Vinaigrette, Thousand Island, White Majestic Blend)

Slender Select (Fat Free Italian, French (Fat Free Red, Reduced Calorie Red), Ranch/Buttermilk (Fat Free, Reduced Calorie))

Safeway Brand - 1000 Island (Lite, Regular), California, Creamy Italian, Italian (Light, Regular), Ranch (Light, Regular, w/Bacon)

Safeway Select - Blue Cheese, Jalapeno Ranch, Olive Oil & Balsamic Vinaigrette, Parmesan & Herb, Tuscan Basil Herb

salad dressing

S

San-J - Gluten Free Asian Dressing (Tamari Ginger ●, Tamari Peanut ●, Tamari Sesame ●)

Seeds Of Change - Balsamic Vinaigrette ! !, French Tomato ! !, Greek Feta Vinaigrette ! !, Italian Herb Vinaigrette ! !, Roasted Red Pepper Vinaigrette ! !

Signature Cafe - Fresca Medium

Simply Organic - Dressing Mix (Classic Caesar ●, Garlic Vinaigrette ●, Italian ●, Orange Ginger Vinaigrette ●, Pineapple Cilantro Vinaigrette ●, Ranch ●)

Spartan Brand - Blue Cheese, California French Style, Italian (Lite, Regular, Zesty), Ranch (Lite, Peppercorn, Regular), Thousand Island

Teresa's Select Recipes - Asiago Pepper Creme, Blackberry Poppyseed, Light Honey Dijon, Raspberry White Balsamic, Vinaigrette (Blueberry Pomegranate, Sun Dried Tomato, Vidalia Onion)

Trader Joe's - Dressings (Balsamic Vinaigrette (Fat Free ! !, Organic ! !, Regular ! !), Organic Red Wine & Olive Oil Vinaigrette, Raspberry ! !, Romano Caesar ! !, Tuscan Italian w/Balsamic Vinegar ! !)

Virginia Brand - Vidalia Onion (Creamy Italian, Frontier Ranch, Honey Mustard, Raspberry Vinegarette, Vinegarette)

Walden Farms -
Single Serve Packets (Creamy Bacon, Honey Dijon, Italian, Ranch, Thousand Island)
Sugar Free No Carb (Asian, Bacon Ranch, Balsamic Vinaigrette, Blue Cheese, Caesar, Chipotle Ranch, Coleslaw, Creamy (Bacon, Italian), French, Honey Dijon, Italian (Regular, w/Sun Dried Tomato), Ranch, Raspberry Vinaigrette, Russian, Sesame Ginger, Sweet Onion, Thousand Island, Zesty Italian)

Wegmans Brand -
Basil Vinaigrette
Caramelized Onion & Bacon

S

Cracked Pepper Ranch Dressing
Creamy (Curry & Roasted Red Pepper, Italian, Ranch)
Fat Free (FYFGA Roasted Red Pepper, Parmesan Italian, Red Wine Vinegar)
Light (Garlic Italian, Golden Caesar, Parmesan Peppercorn Ranch, Ranch)
Organic FYFGA (Creamy Caesar, Italian, Raspberry Vinaigrette, Vinaigrette Balsamic)
Parmesan Italian
Roasted Sweet Red Pepper & Garlic
Thousand Island
Three Spice Garden French
Traditional Italian
Whipped Dressing

Wild Thymes -
Salad Refresher (Black Currant, Mango, Meyer Lemon, Morello Cherry, Passion Fruit, Pomegranate, Raspberry, Tangerine)
Vinaigrette (Mediterranean Balsamic, Parmesan Walnut Caesar, Raspberry Pear Balsamic, Tuscan Tomato Basil)

Winn & Lovett - Ranch

Winn Dixie - Balsamic Vinaigrette, Chunky Blue Cheese, Creamy (French, Ranch), Fat Free (Italian, Ranch, Thousand Island), Garden Ranch, Honey Mustard, House Italian, Italian (Fat Free, Regular, Zesty), Raspberry Vinagrette, Robust Italian, Thousand Island

Wish-Bone -
Balsamic Italian Vinaigrette
Blue Cheese (Chunky, Fat Free)
Deluxe French (Low Fat, Regular)
Italian (Fat Free, Light, Regular, Robusto)
Ranch (Light, Regular)
Raspberry Hazelnut Vinaigrette
Salad Spritzers Vinaigrette (Italian, Ranch)
Western

Salami...see Sausage and/or Deli Meat

Salmon...see also Fish

... *All Fresh Fish Is Gluten-Free (Non-Marinated, Unseasoned)

Beacon Light - Steam Series Lemon & Dill Atlantic Salmon

Bumble Bee - Blueback, Keta, Pink, Premium Pink Skinless & Boneless Pouch, Prime Fillet Atlantic, Prime Fillet Salmon Steaks Lemon & Dill, Red, Smoked Salmon Fillets In Oil

Chicken Of The Sea - All Salmon Products

Crown Prince - Natural (Alaskan (Alderwood Smoked Coho Salmon, Pink Salmon), Skinless & Boneless Pacific Pink Salmon)

Food Club Brand - Pink Canned

Great Value Brand (Wal-Mart) - Canned Alaskan Pink Salmon

Henry & Lisa's - 4 oz. Wild Alaskan, Battered Salmon Filets, Canned Wild Alaskan Pink

Hill Country Fare H-E-B - Pink

Hy-Vee - Frozen

Kirkland Signature -

Canned Wild Alaskan Sockeye

Fresh Smoked Salmon (Imported, Wild Alaskan Sockeye)

Frozen (Farmed Atlantic Salmon Skinless Boneless Portions, Sockeye Salmon Fillets)

Meijer Brand - Canned Salmon (Pink, Sock Eye Red)

Morey's -

Fish Creations Wild Pacific Salmon (Seasoned Grill, Wood Roasted)

Marinated Salmon (Garlic Cracked Pepper, Lemon Dill, Seasoned Grill)

Smoked (Nuggets, Whole Wild Keta, Wild Keta Chunks, Wild Keta Fillets (All Flavors), Wild Keta Party Packs (Cajun, Original, Peppered, Sun Dried Tomato), Wild Keta Portions, Wild Keta Sampler)

Pure Market Express ▲ - Vegan ●

St. Dalfour - Gourmet On The Go Wild Salmon w/Vegetables

Trader Joe's - Pink Salmon Skinless Boneless, Premium Salmon Patties **! !**, Salmon Burger, Smoked Salmon

Trident Seafood Corporation ▲ - All Canned Salmon Products, All Smoked Salmon Products, Salmon Burgers ●

S Salsa

    Amy's - Organic (Black Bean & Corn ★, Medium ★, Mild ★)

    Bone Suckin' Sauce - Hot, Regular

    Central Market H-E-B - All Natural Roja Hatch

    Chi-Chi's -

        Fiesta (Con Queso, Garden, Hot)

        Original Recipe (Medium, Mild)

        Thick & Chunky (Black Bean & Corn, Hot, Medium, Mild)

    Cookwell & Company - Escabeche Style, Roasted Corn & Black
        Bean Salsa, Tomatillo

    Dave's Gourmet - Insanity Salsa

    Dei Fratelli -

        Black Bean 'N Corn Medium

        Casera (Medium Hot, Mild)

        Chipotle Medium

        Original (Medium, Mild)

    Drew's - Organic (Black Bean Cilantro & Corn Medium, Chipotle
        Lime Medium, Double Fire Roasted Medium, Hot, Medium, Mild)

    Embasa - Hot Salsa Casera, Medium Salsa Mexicana

    Emeril's - Kicked Up Chunky, Original Recipe, Roasted Gaaahlic,
        Southwest Style

    Fischer & Wieser - Artichoke & Olive, Black Bean & Corn, Chipotle &
        Corn, Cilantro & Olive, Das Peach Haus, Hatch Chile & Pineapple,
        Havana Mojito, Hot Habanero, Salsa A La Charra, Salsa Verde
        Ranchera, Timpone's Salsa Muy Rica

    Food Club Brand - Hot, Medium, Mild, Thick & Chunky (Hot,
        Medium, Mild)

    Frontera - Gourmet Mexican Salsa (Chipotle, Corn & Poblano,
        Double Roasted Tomato, Guajillo, Jalapeno Cilantro, Mango Key
        Lime, Medium Chunky Tomato, Mild Chunky Tomato, Red Pepper
        & Garlic, Roasted Habanero, Roasted Tomato, Spanish Olive,
        Tomatillo)

    Gordon Food Service - Chunky

Green Mountain Gringo ▲ - All Varieties
H-E-B - Chipotle, Chunky (Hot Picante, Medium, Mild), Habanera, Restaurant Style, Salsa Con Queso, Salsa Dip (Medium, Mild)
Hannaford Brand -
　Mild
　Southwestern (Medium, Mild)
Herdez - Salsa Casera
Herr's - Chunky (Medium, Mild)
Hill Country Fare H-E-B - Salsa Con Queso
Hy-Vee - Medium, Mild, Salsa Con Queso Medium, Thick & Chunky (Hot, Medium, Mild)
La Victoria -
　Cilantro (Medium, Mild)
　Jalapena Extra Hot (Green, Red)
　Salsa Ranchera Hot
　Suprema (Medium, Mild)
　Thick 'N Chunky (Hot, Medium, Mild, Verde (Medium, Mild))
　Victoria Hot
Litehouse - Medium
Lowes Foods Brand -
　Salsa Con Queso
　Thick & Chunky (Medium, Mild)
Meijer Brand -
　Original (Hot, Medium, Mild)
　Restaurant Style (Hot, Medium, Mild)
　Santa Fe Style (Medium, Mild)
　Thick & Chunky (Hot, Medium, Mild)
Melissa's - Salsa Casera
Mezzetta ▲ - California Habanero
Miguel's - Black Bean & Corn, Chipotle, Medium, Mild, Roasted Garlic
Mixes From The Heartland ▲ - Mix (Corn & Tomato ●, Garden ●, Kick N Hot ●, Sun Dried Tomato ●, Tex Mex ●)
Mother's Mountain - New England Chili Salsa

S

Mrs. Renfro's - Black Bean, Chipotle Corn, Garlic, Ghost Pepper, Green, Habanero, Hot, Mango Habanero, Medium, Mild, Peach, Pineapple, Pomegranate, Raspberry Chipotle, Roasted, Tequila

My Essentials - Con Queso Medium, Medium

Nature's Basket - Organic (Black Bean & Corn, Medium, Mild, Pineapple)

Newman's Own -
All Natural (Hot, Medium, Mild)
Black Bean & Corn
Chunky (Peach, Pineapple, Roasted Garlic)
Farmer's Garden
Mango
Tequila Lime

O Organics - Chipotle, Chunky Bell Pepper, Fire Roasted Tomato, Mild

Old Dutch - Restaurante Style Salsa (Con Queso, Medium, Mild, Ocina Del Norta Roasted Jalapeno, Peach & Pineapple)

Old El Paso -
Cheese 'N Salsa (Medium, Mild)
Thick 'N Chunky (Hot, Medium, Mild)

On The Border - Hot, Medium, Mild

Organicville - Medium ●, Mild ●, Pineapple ●

Ortega -
Black Bean & Corn
Garden Vegetable (Medium, Mild)
Original (Medium, Mild)
Salsa Verde
Thick & Chunky (Medium, Mild)

Pace -
Chunky (Medium, Mild)
Pico De Gallo
Pineapple Mango Chipotle
Thick & Chunky (Extra Mild, Hot, Medium, Mild)
Verde

Pastor Chuck Orchards - Apple ●
Peppadew ▲ - Mango Peppadew
Publix - All Natural (Hot, Medium, Mild), Thick & Chunky (Hot, Medium, Mild)
Publix GreenWise Market - Organic (Medium, Mild)
Pure Market Express ▲ - Red Pepper Corn ●, Sassy ●
Que Pasa - All Flavors ★
Sabra - Salsa (Chunky Pico De Gallo, Classic, Homestyle, Southwestern Style)
Safeway Select -
    3 Bean Medium
    Chipotle Medium
    Chunky (Habanero, Mango Lime, Pico De Gallo, Roasted Corn)
    Chunky Classic (Medium, Mild)
    Garlic Lovers
    Peach Pineapple Medium
    Roasted Tomato Medium
    Southwest (Hot, Medium, Mild)
    Verde Medium
Salpica - Chipotle Garlic, Cilantro Green Olive, Fall Harvest, Grilled Pineapple Key Lime, Habanero Lime, Mango Peach, Roasted Corn & Bean, Rustic Tomato
Santa Barbara - Black Bean & Corn, Garden Style, Grilled Pineapple Chipotle, Habanero Lime, Hot, Mango & Peach, Medium, Mild, Pico De Gallo, Roasted (Chili, Garlic, Tomatillo), Taquera, Texas Style
Santitas - Restaurant Style **! !**
Sauza - Traditional
Signature Cafe - Caribbean Fruit Salsa, Fresca (Hot, Mild)
Simply Organic - Salsa Mix ●
Taco Bell -
    Salsa Con Queso (Medium, Mild)
    Thick 'N Chunky (Medium, Mild)

S

Taste Of Inspiration - Black Bean ❗, Corn & Chili ❗, Mango Lime ❗,
   Peach ❗, Raspberry Wine ❗

Tostitos -
   All Natural (Hot Chunky ❗❗, Medium Chunky ❗❗, Mild Chunky ❗❗,
   Pineapple & Peach Medium ❗❗)
   Restaurant Style ❗❗
   Salsa Con Queso ❗❗

Trader Joe's - Authentica ❗❗, Chunky, Corn & Chili Tomatoless❗❗,
   Double Roasted ❗❗, Fire Roasted Tomato ❗❗, Fresh (All
   Varieties❗❗), Garlic Chipotle ❗❗, Hot Chipotle, Pineapple ❗❗, Spicy
   Smoky Peach, Verde ❗❗

Walnut Acres - Organic (Fiesta Cilantro, Midnight Sun, Sweet
   Southwestern Peach)

Wegmans Brand -
   FYFGA
      Hot
      Medium
      Mild
      Organic (Hot, Mango, Medium, Mild)
      Roasted (Chipotle, Salsa Verde, Sweet Pepper, Tomato)
      Santa Fe Style

Wholly - Hot, Medium, Mild

Wildwood - Organic (Emerald Valley (Hot, Medium, Mild), Hot,
   Medium, Mild)

Winn Dixie - Hot, Medium, Mild, Salsa Con Queso

Wise - Medium, Mild

Salt

Badia - Garlic Salt ●

Gordon Food Service - Salt Packet

Great Value Brand (Wal-Mart) - Iodized, Plain

Hannaford Brand - Iodized, Regular

HimalaSalt - Himalaya Pink Sea Salt Grinder ●, Primordial Himalaya
   Sea Salt (Coarse Grain ●, Fine Grain Shaker ●)

La Baleine - Sea Salt

Lawry's - Seasoned Salt (25% Less Sodium **! !**, Regular **! !**)

Manischewitz

McCormick - Grinders (Garlic Sea Salt, Sea Salt), Mediterranean Spiced Sea Salt, Sicilian Sea Salt

Meijer Brand - Iodized, Plain

Morton - Coarse Kosher Salt, Iodized Table Salt, Lite Salt Mixture, Plain Table Salt, Salt Substitute, Sea Salt (Coarse, Fine)

No Salt - Salt Substitute

Nuts.com - Citric Acid ●

Odell's - Popcorn Salt

Publix

Safeway Brand - Iodized, Plain, Rock

Shiloh Farms - Himalayan Pink **! !**

Spartan Brand - Garlic, Iodized, Plain

The Vegetarian Express - All Purpose Veggie Salt **!**

Victoria Gourmet - Salt Australian Flake Salt, Sea Salt (Anglesey, Celtic, Trapani)

Wegmans Brand - Iodized, Plain, Sea Salt (Coarse Crystals, Fine Crystals, Fleur De Sel)

Sandwich Meat...see Deli Meat

Sardines

... *All Fresh Fish Is Gluten-Free (Non-Marinated, Unseasoned)

Bumble Bee - Sardines In (Hot Sauce, Mustard, Oil, Water)

Chicken Of The Sea - All Sardine Varieties

Crown Prince - Crosspacked Brisling In Olive Oil, In Water, One Layer Brisling (In Mustard, In Oil/No Salt Added, In Soybean Oil, In Tomato), Skinless & Boneless In Olive Oil, Two Layer Brisling (In Olive Oil, In Soybean Oil)

Ocean Prince -

Lightly Smoked (In Oil, w/Green Chilies)

Premium Skinless & Boneless In Oil

Sardines In (Louisiana Hot Sauce, Mustard, Tomato Sauce, Water)

Trader Joe's - Skinless Boneless Sardines In Olive Oil

S Sauces...(includes Marinara, Pasta, Tomato, Misc.)

    A Taste Of Thai - Garlic Chili Pepper, Pad Thai, Peanut Satay, Peanut Sauce Mix, Sweet Red Chili

    Allegro - Gold Buckle Brisket Sauce

    Amy's - Organic Family Marinara (Light In Sodium ★, Regular ★), Organic Tomato Basil (Light In Sodium ★, Regular ★)

    Badia - Chimichurri Sauce ●, Sour Orange ●

    Baxters - Mint Sauce

    Bertolli -

    Alfredo Sauce (Garlic, Mushroom, Regular)

    Pasta Sauce (Five Cheese, Four Cheese Rosa, Italian Sausage, Marinara w/Burgundy Wine, Tomato & Basil, Vidalia Onion w/Roasted Garlic, Vodka)

    Black Horse ▲ - Apricot, Chili Verde, Hot & Spicy, Marionberry Pepper Sauce, Raspberry Mustard Sauce, Savory

    Bove's Of Vermont -

    All Natural (Basil, Marinara, Mushroom & Wine, Roasted Garlic, Sweet Red Pepper, Vodka)

    Organic (Basil, Vodka)

    Capa Di Roma - Arrustica, Fresh Basil, Marinara, Roasted Garlic

    Central Market H-E-B - Organic Pasta Sauce (Garlic Lover's, Mushroom, Primavera, Tomato & Basil)

    Classico -

    Red Sauce

        Cabernet Marinara w/Herbs

        Caramelized Onion & Roasted Garlic

        Fire Roasted Tomato & Garlic

        Florentine Spinach & Cheese

        Four Cheese

        Italian Sausage w/Peppers & Onions

        Marinara w/Plum Tomatoes

        Mushroom & Ripe Olives

        Organic (Spinach & Garlic, Tomato Herbs & Spices)

        Portobello Crimini & Champignon Mushroom

        Roasted Garlic

    Spicy Red Pepper
    Spicy Tomato (& Basil, & Pesto)
    Sun Dried Tomato
    Tomato & Basil
    Traditional Sweet Basil
    Tuscan Olive & Garlic
    Vodka Sauce
  Traditional Pizza Sauce

Contadina - Sauce (Extra Thick & Zesty, Regular, w/Garlic & Onion, w/Italian Herbs)

Cookwell & Company -
  Dessert Sauce (Bananas Foster, Cherries Jubilee)
  Sweet Heat Sauce (Grilled Pineapple & Candied Jalapeño, Mango Green Apple & Habanero)
  Two Step Cacciatore Mix

Cuisine Sante ▲ - Brown Sauce Mix ●, White Roux Base For Soups & Sauces ●

Dave's Gourmet - Pasta Sauce (Butternut Squash, Organic (Red Heirloom, Roasted Garlic & Sweet Basil, Spicy Heirloom Marinara), Wild Mushroom)

Dei Fratelli -
  Canned Sauce (Italian, Spaghetti, Tomato)
  Pasta Sauce (Arrabbiata, Fire Roasted Vegetable, Homestyle, Marinara, Mushroom, Three Cheese, Tomato & Basil, Traditional)

Del Fuerte - Tomato Sauce

Del Monte - All Tomato Products *(Except Spaghetti Sauce Flavor)*

DelGrosso -
  Organic Pasta Sauce (Garden Medley, Roasted Garlic, Tomato Basil)
  Pasta Sauce (Extra Tomatoes Onions & Garlic, Garden Style, Meat Flavored, Meatless, Mushroom, Pepperoni Flavored, Three Cheese, Tomato Basil)
  Pizza Sauce (Deluxe, New York Style, Pepperoni)
  Ultra Premium La Famiglia Sauces (Aunt Cindy's Sun Dried Tomato Sonata, Aunt Linda's Arrabiata Memories, Aunt Mary Ann's

S

Sunday Marinara, Chef John's Tomato Basil Masterpiece, Uncle Bo's Roasted Red Pepper Tour, Uncle Fred's Fireworks, Uncle Jim's Late Night Puttanesca, Uncle Joe's Vodka Celebration)

Devya - Simmer Sauce (Butter Chicken, Channa Masala, Vegetable Curry)

Di Lusso - Sweet Onion Sauce

Dietz & Watson ▲ - Hoagie Dressing ●, Sweet Vidalia Onions In Sauce ●

Don Pepino - Marinara Sauce, Spaghetti Sauce

Dorothy Lane Market - Original Marinara

Eden Organic - Spaghetti Sauce (Organic, Organic No Salt Added)

Emeril's -

Pasta Sauce

Cacciatore Dinner

Eggplant & Gaaahlic

Homestyle Marinara

Italian Style Tomato & Basil

Kicked Up Tomato

Roasted (Gaahlic, Red Pepper)

Sicilian Gravy

Three Cheese

Vodka

Ethnic Gourmet - Simmer Sauce (Bombay Curry, Calcutta Masala, Delhi Korma, Punjab Saag Spinach)

Fischer & Wieser -

All Purpose Vegetable & Meat Marinade

Asian Wasabi Plum

Charred Pineapple Bourbon

Chipotle Sauce (Blueberry, Four Star Black Raspberry, Original Roasted Raspberry, Plum Chipotle Grilling Sauce, Pomegranate & Mango, Roasted Blackberry)

Currycot Indian Style Apricot Curry Sauce

Especial Pasilla Chile

Harvest Peach & Hatch Pepper

Mango Ginger Habanero

Mom's Organic Pasta Sauce (Sicilian Roasted Pepper, Tomato & Basil Traditional)

Mom's Pasta Sauce (Arrabbiata, Artichoke Heart & Asiago Cheese, Fresh Garlic & Basil Spaghetti, Fresh Olives & Capers Puttanesca, Martini, Special Marinara)

Papaya Lime Serrano

Sweet & Savory Onion Glaze

Sweet Sour & Smokey Mustard Sauce

Follow Your Heart - Organic Balsamic Vinaigrette (Low Fat **!**, Regular **!**)

Food Club Brand -

Pasta Sauce (Four Cheese, Garlic & Onion, Marinara, Mushroom & Olive)

Spaghetti Sauce (Garden Vegetable, Garlic & Cheese, Meat, Mushroom, Regular, Three Cheese, Traditional)

Frontera -

Cooking Sauce (Red Chile & Roasted Garlic, Roasted Garlic & Chipotle)

Grilling Sauce (Chipotle Honey Mustard, Red Pepper Sesame)

Skillet Sauce (Chipotle Garlic Taco, Key Lime Cilantro Taco, New Mexico Taco, Texas Original Taco)

Slow Cook Sauce (Garlicky Carnitas w/Lime & Chipotle, Red Chile Barbacoa)

Taco Sauce (Chipotle Garlic, Roasted Tomato)

Full Circle - Organic Pasta Sauce (Portabella Mushroom, Roasted Garlic, Tomato Basil), Organic Tomato Sauce

Full Flavor Foods ▲ - Sauce Mix (Alfredo ●, Cheese ●, Vegetarian Mushroom ●)

Gone Native - Pasta Sauce (Tomato & Basil, Tomato & Crimini Mushroom)

Gordon Food Service - California Tomato, Marinara Regular, Sweet & Savory

H-E-B - Pasta Sauce (Four Cheese, Garlic & Herb, Mushroom/Onion, Puttanesca, Spicy Red Pepper, Spinach & Cheese, Tomato Basil, Vegetable Primavera)

S

Hannaford Brand - Onion & Garlic, Pasta Sauce (Four Cheese, Mushroom & Olive, Roasted Garlic, Tomato & Basil), Sweet Pepper & Onion, Tomato

Hill Country Fare H-E-B -
Canned Pasta Sauce (Four Cheese, Meat, Mushroom, Traditional)
Carne Guisada
Pasta Sauce (Garden Medley, Meat, Mushroom, Parmesan & Romano, Sauteed Onion & Garlic, Tomato/Garlic/Onion, Traditional (Regular, w/Meat, w/Mushroom))

Hunt's - Roasted Garlic Sauce, Tomato Sauce (Basil Garlic & Oregano, No Salt Added, Regular)

Hy-Vee - Spaghetti Sauce (3 Cheese, Garden, Mushroom, Tomato Garlic & Onion, Traditional, w/Meat), Tomato Sauce

Jimi Mac's - Super Sauce (Medium, Mild, Original Spicy)

Kroger Brand - Pasta Sauce (Marinara, Six Cheese)

Kroger Value - Garlic Herb, Mushroom, Traditional

La Famiglia Delgrosso -
Aunt Cindy's Sun Dried Tomato Sonata
Aunt Linda's Arrabbiata Memories
Aunt Mary Ann's Sunday Marinara
Chef John's Tomato Basil Masterpiece
Uncle Bo's Roasted Red Pepper Tour
Uncle Fred's Fireworks Sauce
Uncle Jim's Late Night Puttanesca
Uncle Joe's Vodka Celebration

Le Veneziane - Pasta Sauce (Tomato Arrabiata, Tomato Basil)

Lee Kum Kee - Satay, Shrimp Sauce Finely Ground

Lowes Foods Brand -
Spaghetti Sauce (Traditional, w/Meat, w/Mushrooms)
Tomato Sauce

Lucini - Hearty Artichoke Tomato Sauce, Rustic Tomato Basil Sauce, Rustic Tomato Vodka Sauce, Sicilian Olive & Wild Caper Sauce, Spicy Tuscan Tomato Sauce, Tuscan Marinara & Roasted Garlic Sauce

Mayacamas -
  Gourmet Sauce Hollandaise ★
  Pasta Sauce Mix (Alfredo ★, Chicken Fettuccine ★, Creamy
    Clam ★, Creamy Pesto ★, Peppered Lemon ★, Pesto ★)
  Skillet Toss Mix (Black Olive Pesto ★, Dried Tomato ★, Garden
    Style Recipe ★, Green Olive Pesto ★, Mushroom Sauce ★,
    Seafood Pasta Recipe ★, Spicy Pasta Recipe ★)

Meijer Brand -
  Extra Chunky Spaghetti Sauce (3 Cheese, Garden Combo, Garlic
    & Cheese, Mushroom & Green Pepper)
  Pasta Sauce Select (Four Cheese, Marinara, Mushroom & Olive,
    Onion & Garlic)
  Regular Spaghetti Sauce (Plain, w/Meat, w/Mushroom)
  Tomato Sauce (Organic, Regular)

Mezzetta ▲ - Napa Valley Bistro Pasta Sauce (Arrabbiata, Artichoke
  Marinara, Artichoke Parmesan Marinara, Creamy Marinara,
  Creamy Vodka Style Marinara, Fire Roasted Marinara, Homemade
  Style Marinara, Porcini Mushroom, Puttanesca, Roasted Garlic,
  Tomato Basil)

Mr. Spice Organic - Sauce & Marinade (Garlic Steak ★, Ginger Stir
  Fry ★, Honey BBQ ★, Honey Mustard ★, Hot Wing ★, Indian
  Curry ★, Sweet & Sour ★, Thai Peanut ★)

My Essentials - Garlic w/Herb, Meat, Roasted Garlic

Nature's Basket - Marinara, Organic Vodka Cream, Roasted Garlic,
  Three Cheese, Tomato Basil

Newman's Own -
  Alfredo Sauce (Regular, Roasted Garlic)
  Cabernet Marinara
  Fire Roasted Tomato & Garlic
  Five Cheese
  Fra Diavolo
  Garden Peppers
  Italian Sausage & Peppers
  Marinara (Regular, w/Mushroom)
  Organic (Marinara, Tomato Basil, Traditional Herb)

S

Roasted Garlic (& Peppers, Regular)

Sockarooni

Sweet Onion & Roasted Garlic

Tomato Basil Bombolina

Vodka

Nomato - Nomato Sauce

O Organics - Marinara, Roasted Garlic, Tomato, Tomato Basil

Olde Cape Cod - Grilling Sauce (Chipotle, Honey Orange, Sweet & Bold)

Organicville - Organic Pasta Sauce (Italian Herb ●, Marinara ●, Portabella ●, Tomato Basil ●)

Panda Brand -

Lo Mein Oyster Flavored Sauce

Oyster Flavored Sauce *(Green Label Only)*

Patak's Original - Simmer Sauce (Butter Chicken, Jalfrezi Curry, Korma Curry, Mango Curry, Mild Curry, Rogan Josh Curry, Tikka Masala Curry)

Patsy's Pasta Sauce - Marinara, Pizzaiola, Tomato Basil

Prego -

Chunky Garden (Combo, Mushroom & Green Pepper, Mushroom Supreme w/Baby Portobello, Tomato Onion & Garlic)

Flavored w/Meat

Fresh Mushroom

Heart Smart (Mushroom, Ricotta Parmesan, Roasted Red Pepper & Garlic, Traditional)

Italian Sausage & Garlic

Marinara

Roasted (Garlic & Herb, Garlic Parmesan)

Three Cheese

Tomato Basil Garlic

Traditional

Publix -

Parmesan & Romano

Pasta Sauce (Chunky Mushroom, Garden Style, Marinara, Traditional, Traditional Meat)

Premium Pasta Sauce (Basil & Tomato, Creamy Vodka, Four
    Cheese, Sausage & Peppers)
Tomato & Garlic & Onion
Tomato Sauce (No Salt Added, Regular)

Pure Market Express ▲ - Pad Thai ●, Pasta Sauce (Creamy Garlic Dill ●,
    Garlic Alfredo ●, Spicy Peanut ●)

Ragu -
Cheesy (Classic Alfredo, Double Cheddar, Light Parmesan Alfredo,
    Roasted Garlic Parmesan)
Chunky (Garden Combination, Mama's Special Garden, Mushroom
    & Green Pepper, Roasted Red Pepper & Onion, Sundried Tomato
    & Sweet Basil, Super Chunky Mushroom, Super Vegetable
    Primavera, Tomato Garlic & Onion)
Light (No Sugar Added Tomato & Basil, Tomato & Basil)
Old World Style (Flavored w/Meat, Marinara, Mushroom, Sweet
    Tomato Basil, Tomato & Mozzarella, Traditional)
Organic (Garden Veggie, Traditional)
Robusto (7 Herb Tomato, Chopped Tomato Olive Oil & Garlic,
    Parmesan & Romano, Roasted Garlic, Sauteed Onion & Garlic,
    Sauteed Onion & Mushroom, Six Cheese, Sweet Italian Sausage &
    Cheese)

Rao's Specialty Foods -
Dinner To Go Italian Sausage & Mushrooms
Homemade (Arrabbiata, Cuore DiPomodoro, Marinara, Puttanesca,
    Roasted Eggplant, Sensitive Formula Marinara, Southern Italian
    Pepper & Mushroom, Tomato Basil, Vodka)

S&W - Homestyle Tomato Sauce

Safeway - Tomato

Safeway Select -
Gourmet Dipping Sauce Roasted Garlic
Pasta Sauce (Alfredo, Arrabiatta, Artichoke Pesto, Four Cheese,
    Garlic Basil, Marinara, Mushroom/Onion, Roasted Garlic Alfredo,
    Roasted Onion & Garlic, Spicy Red Bell Pepper, Sun Dried
    Tomatoes & Olives, Tomato Alfredo, Tomato Basil, Vodka)

S

Saffron Road - Simmer Sauce (Lemongrass Basil ●, Moroccan Tagine ●, Rogan Josh ●, Tikka Masala ●)

Salpica - Texas Picante

San-J - Gluten Free (Asian BBQ ●, Sweet & Tangy ●, Szechuan ●, Thai Peanut ●), Orange ●

Santa Barbara Olive Co. - Pasta Sauce (Roasted Garlic, Wine & Mushroom)

Sauces 'N Love ▲ -
Chimichurri (Cilantro, Traditional Parsley)
Cream Based Sauces (Creamy Lobster Sauce, Sugo Rosa)
Red Sauces (Absolutely Bolognese, Arrabbiata, Barely Bolognese, Fresh Marinara & Pizza, Pommodoro & Basilico, Puttanesca)

Scarpetta ▲ - Arrabbiata, Barely Bolognese, Bruschetta Toppings (Tomato & Artichoke, Tomato & Capers), Marinara, Puttanesca, Tomato & Arugula, Tuscan Vodka

Sclafani - Spaghetti Sauce

Seeds Of Change -
Indian Simmer Sauce (Jalfrezi **! !**, Korma **! !**, Madras **! !**, Tikka Masala**! !**)
Madras Sauce **! !**
Pasta Sauce (Arrabiatta Di Roma **! !**, Marinara Di Venezia **! !**, Romagna Three Cheese **! !**, Tomato Basil Genovese **! !**, Tuscan Tomato & Garlic **! !**, Vodka Americano **! !**)

Sharwood's - Balti, Bhuna, Bhut Jolokia Curry, Cantonese Curry, Goan Vindaloo, Jalfrezi, Korma, Madras, Pineapple & Coconut, Plum Sauce, Rogan Josh, Saag Masala, Spicy Tikka Masala, Sweet Chilli Sauce, Sweet Chilli Stir Fry, Tikka Masala, Two Step (Coconut & Curry Biryani, Mint & Coriander Biryani, Tomato & Cumin Biryani)

Simply Organic - Sauce Mix (Alfredo ●, Garden Vegetable Spaghetti ●, Italian Herb Spaghetti ●, Mole ●, Mushroom ●, Roasted Garlic Spaghetti ●, Tomato Basil Spaghetti ●)

Spartan Brand - Spaghetti Sauce (3 Cheese, Chunky Garden Combo, Mushroom & Onion, Tomato Basil Garlic, Traditional, w/Meat, w/Mushroom), Tomato Sauce

Spicy Nothings - Simmer Sauces (Classic Curry, Coconut Curry, Lentil Curry, Spicy & Tangy Curry, Spinach Curry)

Steel's - Agave Teriyaki (Regular ●, Wasabi ●), Hoisin ●, Mango Curry ●

Sweet Baby Ray's -
　　Dipping Sauce (Creamy Buffalo Wing !!, Honey Mustard !!, Ray's Signature !!)
　　Marinade & Sauce (Buffalo Wing Sauce !!, Steakhouse !!)

Taste of Inspiration -
　　Barbeque (Maple Chipotle !, Spicy Mango !, Wild Maine Blueberry !)
　　Grilling (Caribbean Mango !, Chipotle !, Sweet Apple !)
　　Pasta Sauce (Arrabiata !, Primavera !, Roasted Garlic w/Eggplant !, Tomato & Basil !)

Tasty Bite - Simmer (Good Korma !, Pad Thai !, Rogan Josh !, Satay Partay !, Tikka Masala !)

Texas Pete ▲ - Pepper

Thai Kitchen - 10 Minute Simmer Sauce (Green Curry, Panang Curry, Red Curry)

The Ginger People - Ginger Lemon Grass !, Ginger Wasabi !, Hot Ginger Jalapeno !, Sweet Ginger Chili !, Thai Green Curry !

Trader Joe's -
　　Organic (Chocolate Midnight Moo !!, Marinara Sauce (No Salt Added, Regular !!), Spaghetti Sauce !!, Tomato Basil Marinara !!, Vodka Sauce !!)
　　Regular (Arrabiata !!, Bruschetta, Chili Pepper !!, Curry Simmer !, Masala Simmer, Roasted Garlic Marinara, Rustico, Thai Curry (Red !!, Yellow !!), Three Cheese, Tomato Basil Marinara !!, Traditional Marinara !!, Tuscano Marinara Low Fat, Whole Peeled Tomatoes w/Basil)

Trenipoti - Gluten Free Pasta Sauces (Arrabbiata ●, Marinara (Classic ●, Tuscan Style ●), Marsala ●, Picatta ●, Pizza Sauce ●)

Walden Farms - Pasta (Garlic & Herb, Tomato & Basil)

Walnut Acres - Organic (Garlic Garlic, Marinara & Zinfandel, Marinara w/Herbs, Roasted Garlic, Sweet Pepper & Onion, Tomato & Basil (Low Sodium, Regular), Tomato & Mushroom, Zesty Basil)

S

Wan Ja Shan - Organic Wheat Free Ponzu

Wegmans Brand -
    Bruschetta Topping Artichoke Asiago
    FYFGA (Mushroom, Parmesan Romano, Sauce Flavored w/Meat, Smooth Marinara, Tomato Basil)
    Horseradish Cream
    Italian Classics (Alfredo, Bolognese, Diavolo Sauce, Grandma's Pomodoro, Lemon & Caper Sauce, Mushroom Marsala, Portobello Mushroom, Puttanesca, Vodka Sauce, White Clam Sauce)
    Organic Pasta Sauce (Marinara, Roasted Garlic, Tomato Basil)
    Pizza Sauce Chunky FYFGA
    Remoulade
    Tomato Regular

Wild Thymes - Dipping Sauce (Indian Vindaloo Curry, Moroccan Spicy Pepper, Thai Chili Roasted Garlic)

Wildwood - Aioli Zesty Garlic

Winn & Lovett - Classic Marinara, Four Cheese, Hot Arrabiata, Primavera, Tomato Basil, Vodka Creme

Winn Dixie - Classic Fra Diavolo, Garden Combination, Garlic & Onion, Meat, Mushroom, Parmesan & Romano, Tomato Sauce, Traditional

Woodstock Farms - Organic Tomato Sauce (No Salt, Original)

XO - XO Sauce

Sauerkraut

    B&G
    Boar's Head
    Cortland Valley Organic
    Dietz & Watson ▲ - Sauerkraut ●
    Eden Organic - Organic
    Flanagan - Krrrrisp Kraut (Bavarian, Regular)
    Food Club Brand
    Great Value Brand (Wal-Mart) - Canned
    Hannaford Brand
    Krrrrisp Kraut - All Varieties

Meijer Brand
S&W - All Canned Vegetables
Safeway Brand
Silver Floss
Spartan Brand
Wegmans Brand - FYFGA
Willie's
Woodstock Farms - Organic

Sausage
Abraham - Diced Prosciutto
Aidells -
    Apricot Ginger Breakfast Links
    Artichoke & Garlic
    Burmese Curry
    Cajun Style Andouille (Minis, Regular)
    Chicken & Apple Breakfast Links (Minis, Regular)
    Mango (Breakfast Links, Regular)
    Organic (Cajun Style Andouille, Chicken & Apple, Spinach & Feta, Sun Dried Tomato, Sweet Basil & Roasted Garlic)
    Pesto
    Portobello Mushroom
    Smoked Chorizo
    Sun Dried Tomato & Mozzarella
    Whiskey Fennel
Al Fresco -
    Chicken Sausage
        Breakfast Sausages (Apple Maple, Country Style, Wild Blueberry)
        Dinner Sausage Fully Cooked (Buffalo Style, Chipotle Chorizo, Roasted Garlic, Roasted Pepper & Asiago, Spicy Jalapeno, Spinach & Feta, Sundried Tomato, Sweet Apple, Sweet Italian Style)
        Fresh Dinner Sausages (Buffalo Style, Hot Italian, Roasted Garlic & Herb, Spicy Chipotle, Sweet Apple, Sweet Italian Style)
        Fully Cooked Uncured Chicken Franks

S   **Applegate -**
      Deli Counter (Pepperoni (Sliced **!**, Whole **!**), Salametti **!**, Salami
        (Genoa **!**, Herb **!**, Pepper **!**, Uncured Turkey **!**), Soppressata **!**),
      Deli Meat (Natural Turkey Salami **!**, Natural Soppressata (Hot **!**,
        Regular **!**))
      Genoa Salami (Natural **!**, Organic **!**)
      Natural Breakfast (Chicken & Apple **!**, Chicken & Maple **!**, Chicken
        & Sage **!**, Classic Pork **!**, Savory Turkey **!**)
      Natural Hot Dogs (Big Apple **!**, Uncured Chicken **!**)
      Natural Uncured Pepperoni **!**
      Organic Sausages (Andouille **!**, Chicken & Apple **!**, Fire Roasted
        Red Pepper **!**, Pork Kielbasa **!**, Smoked Pork Bratwurst **!**, Spinach
        & Feta **!**, Sweet Italian **!**)
      The Great Organic Uncured Hot Dog (Beef **!**, Chicken **!**, Stadium
        Beef **!**, Turkey **!**)
      The Greatest Little Organic Smokey Pork Cocktail Franks **!**
      The Super Natural Uncured Hot Dog (Beef **!**, Turkey **!**)
    Armour - 1877 (Hard Salami, Reduced Fat Hard Salami), Cotto Salami,
      Deli Sandwich Style Pepperoni, Hard Salami, Hickory Smoked
      Summer Sausage, Novara Hard Salami, Pepperoni Turkey
    Artisan Fresh - Chicken & Apple, Gourmet Spinach & Artichoke
      Chicken Sausage, Italian Style, Mozzarella & Roasted Garlic
    Boar's Head - All Varieties
    Busseto -
      Coppa (Dry, Hot Dry)
      Dry Salami (Black Pepper, Italian, Rosette De Lyon)
      Herbs De Provence
      Pepper Coated Salami
      Premium Genoa Salami
    Butterball -
      Breakfast (Fully Cooked Sausage Patties, Fully Cooked Turkey
        Sausage Links, Turkey Sausage Links)
      Premium Turkey Franks (Bun Size, Jumbo, Regular)

Turkey Sausage (Dinner (Polska Kielbasa, Smoked), Fresh
(Bratwurst, Hot Italian Style, Sweet Italian Style), Smoked,
Smoked Cheddar, Smoked Hot)

Canino's - Bratwurst ●, Breakfast Sausage ●, German Brand Sausage ●,
Hot Chorizo ●, Hot Italian Sausage ●, Mild Italian Sausage ●, Polish
Sausage ●, Spicy Cajun Style Sausage ●, Sweet Italian Sausage ●

Carolina Turkey - Turkey

Castle Wood Reserve - Deli Meat Hard Salami

Casual Gourmet - Chicken Sausage Roasted Red Pepper & Spinach

Coleman's Natural Foods -
All Natural Uncured (Beef Hot Dog, Beef Pork Franks)
Chicken Sausage (Mild Italian, Spicy Andouille, Spicy Chipotle,
Spicy Cilantro, Spicy Italian, Spinach & Feta Cheese, Sun Dried
Tomato & Basil)
Fully Cooked Bratwurst
Organic Chicken Sausage (Mild Italian, Spinach & Feta, Sun Dried
Tomato & Basil, Sweet Apple)
Polish Kielbasa

Columbus Salame -
Artisan Salame (Cacciatore, Crespone, Felino, Finocchiona Gigante,
Finocchiona Mini, Hot Sopressata, Secchi)
Classic Salame (Cajun, Calabrese, Chorizo, Genoa, Habanero,
Herb, Italian Dry, Pepper, Rosette De Lyon, Sopressata, Toscano)

Di Lusso -
Beef Summer
Deli Counter (Pepperoni, Salami (Genoa, Hard, Italian Dry,
Natural Casing Genoa, Sopressata))
Hickory Smoked Summer

Dietz & Watson ▲ -
Abruzzese (Hot ●, Sweet ●)
Baby Genoa (Pepper Salame ●, Salame ●)
Beef (Hot ●, Smoked (Hot ●, Mild ●))
Beef Cooked Salami ●

S

Beef Franks (New York Deli ● *(Except Fat Free And Gourmet Lite)*, Deli ●, Foot Long ●, Frankfurters ●, Gourmet Lite ●, Mini Cocktail ●, New York Brand ●, New York Griddle ●)

Beef Summer Sausage ●

Black Forest (Bratwurst ●, Wieners ●)

Black Forest Braunschweiger Liverwurst (Natural Casing ●, Regular ●)

Cacciatore ●

Cheese Franks w/Bacon ●

Chicken (Andouille ●, Bratwurst ●, Buffalo Style ●, Italian ●, Jerk ●, Pepper & Onion Sausage ●)

Classic Peppered Loaf ●

Deli Counter (Beerwurst ●, Blutwurst ●, Cooked Salami ●, Deluxe Loaf ●, Genoa Salami ●, Hard Salami ●, Honey Roll ●, Krakow ●, Lunch Roll ●, Mortadella ●, Olive Loaf ●, Pickle & Pimiento Loaf ●, Slicing Pepperoni ●)

Deli Counter Sopressata (Hot ●, Sweet ●)

Deli Franks ●

Genoa Salame Pepper Wrap ●

Gourmet Lite Franks ●

Grillers (Italian ●, Polska Kielbasa ●, Pork Roll Grillin' Links ●, South Philly Style Pepper & Onion ●)

Head Cheese ●

Hot Sopressata ●

Jalapeno Peppers Cheese Franks ●

Knockwurst ●

Landjaeger ●

Mini Chorizo ●

Mortadella (Deli Counter w/Pistachios ●, Pre Sliced ●)

Natural Casing (Black Forest (Bauernwurst ●, Cooked Fresh Liver Ring ●, Hungarian Brand Bratwurst ●, Wieners ●), Blood Kiska ●, Cheddarwurst ●, Knockwurst ●, New York Beef Franks ●, Polska Kielbasa (Classic ●, Regular ●))

P & P Loaf ●

Panino (Buffalo Cheese ●, Pizzaz ●, Prosciutto ●, Salame ●, Toasted Onion Cheese ●)

Pre Sliced (Braunschweiger Liverwurst ●, Capocolla (Hot ●,
    Sweet●), Cooked Salami ●, Genoa Salami ●, Sopressata ●)
Salame (Hard ●, Hot & Zesty ●, Milano Paper Wrap ●, Mini ●)
Salami Natural Casing Genoa ●
Smoked (Hot ●, Mild ●)
Souse Roll ●
Super Franks ●
Twin Stick Pepperoni ●

Eckrich -
Beef Franks (Jumbo, Regular)
Breakfast Smoky Links (Beef, Cheese, Lite, Maple, Original)
Bun Length (Bacon & Cheddar, Jalapeno & Cheddar, Smoked Beef)
Country Fresh Roll Sausage
Deli Meat (Hard Salami (Lo Fat, Regular), Pepperoni Regular, Regular
    Summer Sausage, Salami (Cotto, Genoa))
Franks (Bun Sized Beef, Jumbo Cheese, Regular Lite)
Grillers Smoked Sausage (Cheddar, Original)
Li'l Smokies
Lunch Meat (Pepperoni, Salami (Cotto, Hard))
Original Meat Franks (Bun Sized, Franks, Jumbo)
Polska Kielbasa
Rope Smoked (Beef (Mesquite, Regular, Skinless), Cheddar,
    Hardwood, Jalapeno & Cheddar, Polska Kielbasa (Hardwood,
    Hardwood Skinless, Old World), Skinless)
Smoked Pre Sliced (Original, Turkey)
Smoked Sausage (Angus Beef, Regular, Skinless Turkey, XL Skinless
    Angus Beef)

Empire Kosher - Chicken Franks, Turkey Franks

Farmer John -
Dinner Sausage (Beef Link (Hot, Regular), Classic Polish, Premium
    Rope (Beef, Classic, Mild Jalapeno Pepper), Premium Smoked
    (Hot Louisiana, Mild Jalapeno, Red Hots Extra Hot, w/Bacon))
Franks & Wieners (Beef Franks (Big Game, Classic 10 oz., Classic
    w/Sharp Cheddar Cheese, Jumbo, Regular 16 oz.), Dodger Dogs,
    Premium (Jumbo Meat Wieners, Meat Wieners))

S

Pork Roll Sausage (Mild, Spicy)
Pork Sausage Links (Chorizo Style, Classic, Old Fashioned Maple, Original Lower Fat)
Pork Sausage Patties (Mild, Original Lower Fat, Spicy)

Five Star Brand ▲ - Beef Franks Mild, Bratwurst, Cooked Salami, Garlic Knockwurst, German Franks (Hot, Mild), Head Cheese, Jumbo Beef Wieners, Natural Casing Less Salt Kielbasa, Pepperoni Sticks, Prasky, Skinless Beef Kielbasa, Slovenian Franks, Smoked Bratwurst, Synthetic Casing Wieners (Beef, Low Salt, Regular)

Fratelli Beretta - Big Sopressata, Bresaola, Cacciatorino, Coppa, Dry Sausage, Milano, Mortadella, Nostrano, Pancetta, Sopressata

Garrett County Farms -
Andouille ★
Beef Franks Hot Dogs (4XL Big ★, Old Fashioned ★, Premium ★)
Cheese Franks ★
Chorizo ★
Cocktail Franks ★
Frozen (Chicken Apple Sausage (Links ★, Patties ★), Sunrise Maple Sausage Links ★, Turkey (Burgers ★, Maple Sausage Links ★, Maple Sausage Patties ★))
Morning Maple Turkey Breakfast Links ★
Polska Kielbasa ★
Pork Sausage Linguica ★
Sliced Uncured Pepperoni ★
The Original Deli Franks ★
Turkey (Andouille Sausage ★, Kielbasa ★, Tom Toms (Hoy & Spicy ★, Original ★))

Giant Eagle Brand -
Breakfast Sausage (Fully Cooked Patties, Links (Maple, Original), Patties Original, Roll (Original, Savory, Zesty Hot))
Polska Kielbasa (Beef, Links, Pork & Beef)
Pork & Beef Smoked Sausage
Smoked Sausage Links (Cheese, Chili, Cheese & Onion, Jalapeno & Cheese)

Gordon Food Service -
> Franks (3 Meat (Classic, Cocktail), Beef (Angus, Mini, Regular), Beef & Pork Regular)
> Links (Buffet Regular, Cooked Skinless, Italian, Kielbasa, Maple Regular, Polish, Pork (Pure, Skinless), Smoked)
> Patties (Cooked, Regular)
> Smoked (Cocktail, Regular)

Great Value Brand (Wal-Mart) - Breakfast (Fully Cooked (Beef Breakfast Patties, Original Pork Patties, Pork Links, Turkey Breakfast Patties), Maple Pork Patties, Spicy Pork Patties), Canned Vienna Sausage

H-E-B -
> Chicken Sausage (Andouille, Fajita, Poblano & Cheddar)
> Hard Salami Tub
> Premium Sausage (Beef Ring, Cheese Smoked Ring, Jalapeno Cheddar Smoked, Jalapeno Smoked Ring, Link (Beef, Cheese, Jalapeno, Mesquite, Pork & Beef), Original Pork & Beef Value Pack, Pork & Beef Ring, Value Pack (Beef, Jalapeno))
> Sausage On A Stick
> Smoked Sausage (Garlic Ring, Lean)

Habbersett - Pork Sausage (Hearty Links, Links), Pork Sausage Roll, Quick 'N Easy (Sausage Links, Sausage Patties)

Hannaford Brand - Hot Dogs Weiners

Heaven Mills ▲ - Kishka Stuffing (Cholent ●, Vegetable ●)

Hebrew National -
> Deli Meat (Beef Salami, Lean Beef Salami)
> Franks (97% Fat Free, Beef, Bun Length All Beef, Jumbo Beef, Quarter Pound Beef, Reduced Fat Beef)
> Knockwurst
> Polish Sausage

Hertel's - All Original Fresh Sausages *(Except British Bangers)*

Hill Country Fare H-E-B -
> Fresh (Beef, Polish, Regular, w/Cheese)
> Red Hot Links (Bag, Box)

S

Smoked (Beef (Cocktail, Regular, Skinless), Cheese, Cocktail,
Mesquite, Polish (Regular, Skinless), Regular, Skinless)
Smokey Links
Vienna

Hillshire Farms -
Cheddar Wurst
Gourmet Creations (Beef & Bacon, Beef & Jalapeno, Chicken
Apple, Sweet Italian Style w/Peppers & Mozzarella Cheese)
Links (Beef Hot, Cheddar Wurst, Hot, Polska Kielbasa (Regular,
Turkey), Smoked (Beef, Bratwurst, Hot & Spicy Italian, Turkey
w/ Pepper Jack Cheese))
Lit'l Beef Franks
Lit'l Polskas
Lit'l Smokies (Applewood Smoked Chicken, Beef, Cheddar,
Regular, Turkey)
Lit'l Wieners
Polska Kielbasa (Beef, Lite, Regular, Turkey)
Smoked Bratwurst
Smoked Sausage (Beef, Hardwood Chicken, Hot, Italian Style, Lite,
Regular, Turkey)
Summer Sausage (Beef, Regular, Yard O Beef)

Homestead Creek - Gourmet Spinach & Artichoke Chicken
Sausage

Honeysuckle White -
Hardwood Smoked Turkey Franks
Hickory Smoked Cooked Turkey Salami
Turkey Sausage (Breakfast (Links, Patties), Chipotle Seasoned
Links, Fully Cooked Smoked (Original Links, Original Rope,
Polish Rope), Italian (Hot Links, Sweet Links), Mild Italian Roll,
Traditional Bratwurst)

Hormel -
Crumbled
Hard Salami
Homeland Hard Salami

Little Sizzlers (Hot & Spicy Links, Links, Patties)
Natural Choice (Deli Meat Hard Salami, Hard Salami, Pepperoni, Smoked Ring)
Pepperoni (Bite Sized, Diced, Hard Salami Stix, Hot & Spicy, Italian Dry Stix, Mild, Original Minis, Regular, Sandwich Style, Snac Pacs, Stick, Stix, Stix & Cheese, Thick Slice, Turkey, Turkey Minis)
Pizza Topping Beef Crumbles
Pizza Toppings Italian Sausage
Smokies
Wranglers Franks (Beef, Cheese, Smoked Original)

Hy-Vee - Beef Summer, Cooked Salami, Little Smokies (Beef, Regular), Pepperoni, Polish, Summer Sausage, Thin Sliced Pastrami

Ian's - Wheat Free Gluten Free Recipe Popcorn Turkey Corn

Isernio's - Chicken Apple Link ●, Chicken Apple ●, Chicken Basil & Sun Dried Tomato ●, Chicken Bratwurst Grillers ●, Chicken Breakfast ●, Chicken Spinach & Feta ●, Hot Italian Chicken ●, Hot Italian ●, Italian Chicken ●, Mild Italian ●, Pork Breakfast Link ●, Sausage Roll (Chicken Breakfast Sausage ●, Hot Italian Chicken Sausage ●, Italian Chicken Sausage ●, Spicy Chicken Breakfast Sausage ●)

Jennie-O Turkey Store -
Breakfast Lover's Turkey Sausage
Fresh (Breakfast Sausage (Maple Links, Mild Links, Mild Patties), Dinner Sausage (Hot Italian, Lean Turkey Bratwurst, Sweet Italian), Lean Turkey Patties)
Jumbo Turkey Franks

Jimmy Dean -
Fresh Sausage (Maple Links, Original Links, Original Patties)
Fully Cooked Hearty Crumbles (Hot, Original, Turkey)
Fully Cooked Links (Maple, Original, Turkey)
Fully Cooked Patties (Hot, Maple, Original, Turkey)
Heat 'N Serve (Sausage Links (Hot, Maple, Original), Sausage Patties Original)

S

Heat 'N Serve (Sausage Links Turkey, Sausage Patties Turkey)

Pork Roll Sausage (All Natural Regular, Country Mild, Hot, Italian, Maple, Reduced Fat, Regular, Sage)

Johnsonville -

Bratwurst (Beef, Cheddar, Hot 'N Spicy, Original, Patties, Smoked, Stadium)

Breakfast Sausage Links (Brown Sugar & Honey, Original, Vermont Maple Syrup, Wisconsin Cheddar Cheese)

Breakfast Sausage Patties (Original, Vermont Maple Syrup)

Chicken Sausage (3 Cheese Italian Style, Apple, Chipotle Monterey Jack Cheese)

Italian Ground Sausage (Hot, Mild, Sweet)

Italian Links (Four Cheese, Hot, Mild, Sweet)

Sausage (Chorizo, Irish O'Garlic, Polish Kielbasa)

Smoked Sausage (Beddar w/Cheddar, Beef Hot Links, Chili Cheese, Jalapeno & Cheddar, New Orleans, Turkey, Turkey w/Cheddar)

Summer Sausage (Beef, Deli Bites (Beef, Original, Salami), Garlic, Old World Recipe, Original)

Jones Dairy Farm -

All Natural (Pork Sausage (Original Roll ●, Patties ●), Pork Sausage Links (& Rice ●, Hearty ●, Little ●, Little Maple ●))

Golden Brown All Natural Fully Cooked (Sausage & Rice Links (Light ●, Regular ●), Sausage Links (Beef ●, Maple ●, Mild ●, Pork & Uncured Bacon ●, Spicy Pork ●, Turkey ●), Sausage Patties (Maple ●, Mild ●))

Kayem -

Bratwurst (Cheddar ‼, Original ‼)

Franks (Beef Fenway Style ‼, Beef Hot Dogs ‼, Beef Minis ‼, Fenway Style ‼, Hot Dogs ‼, Jumbo Beef Hot Dogs ‼, Jumbo Hot Dogs ‼, Lower Sodium Hot Dogs ‼, Minis ‼, Old Tyme (Natural Casing ‼, Natural Casing Beef ‼, Natural Casing Reds ‼), Skinnies ‼)

Kielbasa (Fresh ‼, Old World Style ‼, Polish ‼)

Natural (4 Pepper Hot Italian ‼, Sweet Italian ‼)

S

Kroger Brand - Polska Kielbasa, Smoked All Beef, Smoked Sausage
Lightlife - Tofu Pups
Lou's Famous - Chicken Sausage (Aged Provolone, Apple, Artichoke
& Calamata, Feta Cheese & Spinach, Peppers & Onion, Roasted
Red Pepper & Garlic, Spicy Italian, Sundried Tomato)
Mulay's -
Ground Sausage (Breakfast ●, Mild Italian ●, Original ●, Original
Italian ●)
Links (Breakfast ●, Killer Hot ●, Mild Italian ●, Original ●, Original
Italian ●)
Old Wisconsin -
Grilling Sausages (Bratwurst Festival Links, Cheddar Smoked
Sausage Links, Natural Casing Wiener Smoked Links, Polish
Sausage Smoked Links)
Summer Sausage (Beef, Garlic, Original)
Open Nature - Chicken (Italian, Smoked Andouille), Sun Dried
Tomato & Basil, Uncured Beef Franks
Organic Prairie -
Frozen Organic Retail (Brown & Serve Pork, Italian Chicken, Pork
Bratwurst, Pork Breakfast Chub, Pork Italian, Uncured Beef Hot
Dogs, Uncured Chicken Hot Dogs)
Organic (Breakfast Pork Sausage Roll, Brown & Serve Breakfast
Sausage, Pork Bratwurst, Pork Italian Sausage, Uncured Beef
Summer)
Uncured (Beef Hot Dogs, Pepperoni)
Oscar Mayer -
Beef Franks (Bun Length, Classic, Light, Premium)
Cheese Dogs
Cotto Salami (Beef, Oven Roasted & White Chicken, Regular)
Deli Fresh Beef Salami
Deli Meat (Braunschweiger Liver Sausage, Regular Cotto Salami,
Sliced Pepperoni, Sub Kit Ham & Beef Salami)
Franks (Selects Angus Bun Length, Selects Premium Beef,
Uncured Natural Smoke Beef, XXL Premium Beef)

S

Premium Franks (Beef & Cheddar, Jalapeno & Cheddar)

Summer Sausage Regular

Turkey Franks (Bun Length, Cheese Franks, Classic, Hardwood Smoked)

Wieners (98% Fat Free, Bun Length, Classic, Light, Selects)

Perdue - Deli Turkey (Bologna, Salami), Turkey Sausage Seasoned Fresh Lean Sweet Italian

Primo Naturale -

Chorizo (Sliced Dried, Stick Dried)

Chub Salami (Genoa, Original, w/Black Pepper, w/Herbs)

Pepperoni (Pillow Pack, Sliced Dried, Stick, Whole Large Diameter)

Sliced Salami (Hard, Original, Premium Genoa, w/Black Pepper, w/Herbs)

Sopressata (Sliced, Sticks, Whole)

Whole Chorizo

Whole Salami (Black Pepper, Genoa, Hard, Herb, Original)

Primo Taglio - Salami Genoa

Publix -

Deli Pre Pack Sliced Hard Salami Reduced Fat

Franks (Beef, Meat)

Fresh (Bratwurst, Italian (Hot, Mild), Turkey Italian (Hot, Mild))

Publix GreenWise Market - Chicken (Herb & Tomato, Hot Italian, Mild Italian)

Pure Market Express ▲ - Sausage ●

Rocky Jr. - Rocky Dogs Uncured Chicken Hot Dogs

Safeway Brand - Beef Franks, Hot Dogs, Smoked, Turkey Franks

Shelton's -

Franks (Smoked Chicken, Smoked Turkey, Uncured Chicken)

Turkey Sausage (Breakfast, Italian, Patties)

Turkey Sticks (Pepperoni, Regular)

Uncured Turkey

Smithfield - Breakfast Sausage Mild Pork Roll, Smoked Sausage Loops Natural Hickory Smoke Beef

The Original Brat Hans -
  Chicken Sausage (Mild Italian, Organic (Apple, Bratwurst,
     Breakfast Links, Spinach & Feta, Sweet Italian), Skinless
     Breakfast Links, Spicy Andouille, Spicy Chipotle, Spicy Cilantro,
     Spicy Italian, Spinach & Feta, Sun Dried Tomato & Basil, Sweet
     Apple)
  Knockwurst w/Garlic
  Original Bratwurst
  Uncured German Style Wiener
  Weisswurst w/ Parsley
Thumann's - All Varieties ●*(Except Franks For Deep Frying)*
Trader Joe's - All Sausage, Uncured All Beef Hot Dogs
Wegmans Brand -
  Beef Hot Dogs Skinless
  Cocktail Hot Dogs Skinless Frankfurters
  Pepperoni Italian Style (Regular, Sliced)
  Red Hot Dogs Skinless (Lite, Regular)
  Uncured Skinless (Beef Hot Dogs, Hot Dogs)
Wellshire Farms -
  Andouille ★
  Beef Franks Hot Dogs (4XL Big ★, Old Fashioned ★, Premium ★)
  Cheese Franks ★
  Chorizo ★
  Cocktail Franks ★
  Frozen (Chicken Apple Sausage (Links ★, Patties ★), Sunrise
     Maple Sausage Links ★, Turkey (Burgers ★, Maple Sausage
     Links ★, Maple Sausage Patties ★))
  Morning Maple Turkey Breakfast Link Sausage ★
  Polska Kielbasa ★
  Pork Sausage Linguica ★
  Sliced Uncured Pepperoni ★
  The Original Deli Franks ★
  Turkey (Andouille Sausage ★, Franks ★, Kielbasa ★, Tom
     Toms (Hot & Spicy ★, Original ★))

S

Winn Dixie -
Hot Dogs (Jumbo Beef, Meat Franks, w/Cheese & Chicken)
Pepperoni
Smoked (Hot, Original, Polish, Polish Kielbasa)

Scallops
... *All Fresh Seafood Is Gluten-Free (Non-Marinated, Unseasoned)
Kirkland Signature - Frozen Raw Sea
Whole Catch - Fresh Sea Scallops

Scones/Scone Mix
Breakaway Bakery ▲ - Scones (Apple Fig ●, Lemon Raisin ●, Orange Cranberry ●)
Cause You're Special ▲ - English Scone Mix
Choices Rice Bakery ▲ - Scones
Gluten Free Mama ▲ - Mama's Scone Mix ●
Gluten Free Pantry ▲ - Muffin & Scone Mix
Kneaded Specialties ▲ - Scones (Blueberry Lemon ●, Cranberry Orange ●, Double Chocolate Chip ●)
Silly Yak Bakery -
GF Scone Mix ●
GF Scones (Almond Joy ●, Apple Walnut ●, Apricot ●, Blackberry ●, Blueberry ●, Cherry Chocolate ●, Chocolate Raspberry ●, Coffee Chocolate Chip ●, Cranberry Orange ●, Lemon Blueberry ●, Lemon Cream ●, Lemon Poppy Seed ●, Maple Walnut ●, Mixed Berry●, Oatmeal Blueberry ●, Oatmeal Raisin ●, Orange Chocolate Chip●, Peach ●, Peanut Butter Chocolate ●, Pineapple Coconut ●, Pumpkin ●, Raspberry ●)
GFCF Scones (Blueberry ●, Chocolate Chip ●, Chocolate Raspberry ●, Poppy Seed ●Raspberry ●)
Simply Organic ▲ - Gluten Free Chai Spice Scone Mix ●
Whole Foods Market Gluten Free Bakehouse ▲ - Scones (Almond, Cranberry Orange)

Seafood Sauce...see also Cocktail Sauce
Lee Kum Kee - Shrimp Sauce Finely Ground
Mayacamas - Seafood Pasta Skillet Toss Mix ★
McCormick - Cajun, Lemon Butter Dill (Fat Free, Regular), Lemon Herb,

Mediterranean, Original Cocktail Sauce, Santa Fe Style, Scampi

Safeway Brand - Cocktail

Simply Delicious - Organic Seafood Sauce w/Lemon

Texas Pete ▲ - Seafood Cocktail

Trader Joe's - Seafood Cocktail Sauce **!!**

Walden Farms

Seasoning Packets...see Seasonings

Seasonings

Accent - Flavor Enhancer (All Varieties)

Adolph's - Original Tenderizer **!!**, Tenderizer Seasoned w/Spices **!!**

American Natural & Organic Spices ▲ - Adobo Seas Sf ●, All Purpose ●, Allspice Ground ●, Allspice Whole ●, Anise Ground ●, Anise Star Whole ●, Anise Whole ●, Annatto Ground ●, Annatto Seed ●, Apple Pie Spice ●, Arrowroot ●, Baharat Sf ●, Barbeque Sf ●, Basil ●, Beef Burger Sf ●, Bouquet Garni Sf ●, Cajun Seasoning ●, Caraway Seeds ●, Cardamom Decorticated ●, Cardamom Ground ●, Cardamom Pods Green ●, Cayenne Pepper ●, Celery Ground ●, Celery Salt ●, Celery Seeds ●, Chicken Kabob Sf ●, Chili Ancho Ground ●, Chili California Ground ●, Chili Chipotle Ground Chili Con Carne Sf ●, Chili Guajillo Ground ●, Chili Habanero Ground ●, Chili Jalapeno Ground ●, Chili New Mexico Ground ●, Chili Pepper Crushed ●, Chili Pepper Whole ●, Chili Powder ●, Chimichurri Sf ●, Chinese Five Spice Sf ●, Chives ●, Cilantro Flakes ●, Cinnamon Ground ●, Cinnamon Sticks ●, Cloves Ground ●, Cloves Whole ●, Coriander Ground ●, Coriander Seeds ●, Cream Of Tartar ●, Cumin Ground ●, Cumin Seed Whole ●, Curry Powder Hot ●, Curry Powder Salt Free ●, Curry Powder ●, Curry Thai Red Salt Free ●, Dill Seed ●, Dill Weed ●, Epazote ●, Fajita Seasoning Sf ●, Fennel Ground ●, Fennel Seeds ●, Fenugreek (Ground ●, Seeds ●), Fines Herbes Sf ●, Fish Grill & Broil Sf ●, Flaxseed ●, French Four Spice Sf ●, Galangal ●, Garam Masala ●, Garlic (Bread ●, Granulates ●, Herbs ●, Minced ●, Pepper ●, Sliced ●, Toasted ●), Ginger Ground ●, Greek Seasoning Sf ●, Gumbo File ●, Harissa Sf ●, Herbs De Provence ●, Horseradish Powder ●, Italian Seasoning ●, Jerk

S

Seasoning Sf ●, Juniper Berries ●, Lamb Seasoning Sf ●, Lavender ●, Lemon (Grass ●, Peel ●, Pepper ●), Mace Ground ●, Marjoram (Ground ●, Whole ●), Meatloaf Seasoning Sf ●, Mediterranean Seas Sf ●, Mexican Seasoning Sf ●, Mint (Peppermint ●, Spearmint ●), Mulling Spice Blend ●, Mustard (Ground ●, Seeds Brown ●, Seeds Yellow ●), Nigella Seed ●, Nutmeg (Ground ●, Whole ●), Onion Granulates ●, Orange Peel ●, Oregano (Ground ●, Mediterranean ●, Mexican ●), Organic (Allspice (Ground ●, Whole ●), Almond Extract ●, Anise Star Whole ●, Basil ●, Bay Leave Whole ●, Cajun Seasoning ●, Caraway Seeds ●, Cardamom (Green ●, Ground ●, Original ●), Cayenne Pepper ●, Celery Seeds ●, Chili (Ancho Ground ●, Chipotle Ground ●, Pepper Crush ●, Powder ●), Chinese Five Spice ●, Cinnamon (Ground ●, Sticks ●), Cloves (Ground ●, Whole ●), Coriander (Ground ●, Seeds ●), Cumin Ground ●, Cumin Seeds Whole ●, Curry (Powder ●, Thai Herb ●), Dill Weed ●, Fennel Seeds ●, Garam Masala ●, Garlic Granulates ●, Ginger Ground ●, Herbs De Provence ●, Italian Season ●, Juniper Berries ●, Lemon Extract ●, Marjoram Whole ●, Melange Pepper ●, Mexican Seasoning ●, Mustard (Ground ●, Seed Brown ●, Seed Yellow ●), Nutmeg (Ground ●, Whole ●), Onion Granulates ●, Orange Extract ●, Oregano Mediterranean ●, Panch Phoron Sf ●, Paprika (Regular ●, Smoked ●), Parsley ●, Pasta & Spaghetti Sf ●, Pepper Black Long ●, Pepper Ground (Black ●, White ●), Peppercorn (Black ●, Green ●, Melange ●, Melody ●, Pink ●, Szechuan ●, White ●), Pickling Seasoning ●, Pizza Spice Sf ●, Poppy Seeds ●, Pork Chop Sf ●, Poultry Seasoning ●, Pumpkin Pie Spice ●, Rosemary Whole ●, Saffron ●, Sage (Ground ●, Rubbed ●, Whole ●), Sesame (Seed Black ●, Seed White ●), Tarragon ●, Thyme ●, Turmeric ●, Vanilla Extract ●), Ras El Hanout Sf ●, Rib Eye Steak Sf ●, Rice Seasoning Sf ●, Rosemary (Ground ●, Whole ●), Safflower ●, Saffron ●, Sage (Ground ●, Rubbed ●, Whole ●), Sambal Ulek Sf ●, Savory Ground ●, Savory ●, Sesame Seed (Black ●, White ●), Shawarma Sf ●, Shish Kabob Sf ●, Shrimp/Crab Grill & Broil Sf ●, Sumac ●, Taco Seasoning Sf ●, Tandoori Masala Sf ●, Tarragon ●, Thai Spice Blend

S

Sf ●, Thyme Ground ●, Thyme ●, Tsatsiki Greek Yogurt ●, Turmeric ●, Vanilla (Bean ●, Extract ●), Vegetable Seas Sf ●, Vindaloo Seasoning Sf ●, Wasabi Powder Sf ●, Zatar Sf ●

Amore - Herb Paste

Arora Creations -

Organic Seasoning Packets (Bhindi Masala, Chicken Tikka Masala, Goan Shrimp Curry, Gobi, Punjabi Chhole, Rajmah, Tandoori Chicken)

Regular Seasoning Packets (Bhindi Masala, Chicken Tikka Masala, Goan Shrimp Curry, Gobi, Punjabi Chhole, Rajmah, Tandoori Chicken)

Badia -

All Single Ingredient Herbs & Spices ●

Blends (Adobo ●, Adobo w/Pepper ●, Barbecue Seasoning ●, Blackened Redfish Seasoning ●, Celery Salt ●, Complete Seasoning ●, Fajita Seasoning ●, Five Spices ●, Garam Masala ●, Garlic & Parsley ●, Garlic Minced In Oil ●, Garlic Salt ●, Herbes De Provence ●, Italian Seasoning ●, Poultry Seasoning ●, Steak Seasoning ●)

Bone Suckin' Sauce - Seasoning & Rub (Hot, Original)

Bragg - Sea Kelp Delight, Sprinkle Seasoning

Cali Fine Foods ▲ - Gourmet Seasoning Packets (Dill Delight ●, Garlic Gusto ●, Herb Medley ●, Spicy Fiesta ●, Sweet & Spicy BBQ ●)

Chef Paul Prudhommes Magic - All Magic Seasoning Blends *(Except Breading Magic & Gumbo Gravy Magic)*

Chi-Chi's - Fiesta Restaurante Seasoning Mix

Dave's Gourmet - Insanity Spice

Dorothy Lane Market - Grilling & Seasoning Rub

Durkee - All Food Coloring, All Liquid Flavorings, All Pepper Black/White, All Steak Seasonings, Allspice, Alum, Anise Seed, Apple Pie Spice, Arrowroot, Basil, Bay Leaves, Buttermilk Ranch Dressing, Caraway Seed, Cardamom, Cayenne Pepper, Celery Flakes, Celery Seed, Chicken & Rib Rub, Chicken Seasoning, Chili Powder, Chives, Cilantro, Cinnamon, Cloves, Coriander, Cream Of Tartar, Crushed

S

Red Pepper, Cumin, Curry Powder, Dill Seed/Weed, Fennel, Garlic Minced, Garlic Pepper, Garlic Powder, Garlic Salt, Ginger, Hickory Smoke Salt, Italian Seasoning, Jamaican Jerk Seasoning, Lemon & Herb, Lemon Peel, Lemon Pepper, Lime Pepper, Mace, Marjoram, Meat Tenderizer (Seasoned, Unseasoned), Mint Leaves, Mr. Pepper, MSG, Mustard, Nutmeg, Onion Minced, Onion Powder, Onion Salt, Orange Peel, Oregano, Oriental 5 Spice, Paprika, Parsley, Pepper Green Bell, Pickling Spice, Pizza Seasoning, Poppy Seed, Poultry Seasoning, Pumpkin Pie Spice, Rosemary, Rosemary Garlic Seasoning, Sage, Sesame Seed, Six Pepper Blend, Smokey Mesquite Seasoning, Spicy Spaghetti Seasoning, Tarragon, Thyme, Turmeric

Durkee California Style Blends - Garlic Powder, Garlic Salt, Onion Powder, Onion Salt

Earthbound Farm - Organic Herb Purées (Basil, Cilantro, Dill), Organic Purées (Chili Pepper, Garlic, Ginger)

Ellbee's - Rubs (All Flavors)

Emeril's -
Bam It Salad Seasoning,
Bamburger, Essence (Bayou Blast, Garlic Parmesan, Italian, Original, Southwest), Rub (Chicken, Fish, Rib, Steak, Turkey)

Food Club Brand - Chili Powder Regular, Cinnamon, Garlic (Powder, Salt), Minced Onion, Oregano Leaves, Paprika, Parsley Flakes, Pepper Black, Salt (Iodized, Plain), Seasoning Mix Spaghetti Mix, Taco Seasoning Mix

Gayelord Hauser -
All Varieties (Spice Garden Herbs & Spices) *(Except Seas'N Grill)*
Spike Magic (5 Herb, Garlic, Hot 'N Spicy, Onion, Original, Salt Free, Vegit)

Grandma Ferdon's ▲ - Chili Powder ●, Pure Spices (Basil ●, Caraway Seeds ●, Garlic Flakes ●, Ground (Allspice ●, Black Pepper ●, Cinnamon●, Cloves ●, Coriander ●, Ginger ●, Nutmeg ●), Italian Seasoning ●, Lemon Peel ●, Marjoram ●, Onion Flakes ●, Onion Powder●, Paprika ●), Taco Seasoning ●

seasonings

S

H-E-B - Blackened, Borracho, Brisket Rub, Cajun, Fajita Seasoning (Beef, Chicken), Seafood (Boil, Seasoning), Steak

Hannaford Brand - Basil Leaves, Bay Leaves, Celery Salt, Chili Powder, Crushed Red Pepper, Garlic Powder, Garlic Salt, Ground Black Pepper, Ground Cinnamon, Ground Ginger, Ground Mustard, Ground Nutmeg, Minced Onion, Oregano Leaves, Paprika

Hill Country Fare H-E-B - Chili Powder, Chopped Onions, Fajita Spice (Chicken, Regular), Garlic Powder, Garlic Salt, Ground Comino, Meat Tenderizer, Nutmeg, Onion (Powder, Salt), Parsley Flakes, Pepper (Ground Black, Lemon), Rubbed Sage, Seasoning Salt

HimalaSalt - Organic Peppercorn Grinder (Green ●, White ●), Peppercorn & Salt Gift Sets Organic Peppercorn Zen Cube Kit ●, Peppercorn & Salt Sets (HimalaSalt Grinder w/Green Peppercorn & Pink Peppercorn Grinders ●, Salt & Pepper Grinders ●)

Hol Grain ▲ - Seasoning Mix (Chili ●, Fajitas ●)

Hy-Vee - Basil Leaf, Bay Leaves, Black Pepper, Chicken Grill Seasoning, Chili Powder, Chopped Onion, Dill Weed, Garlic Powder, Garlic Salt, Grinders (Black Peppercorn, Peppercorn Melange, Sea Salt & Kosher), Ground Cinnamon, Ground Cloves, Ground Mustard, Iodized Salt, Italian Seasoning, Meat Tenderizer, Orange & Lemon Pepper, Oregano Leaf, Paprika, Parsley Flakes, Plain Salt, Red Crushed Pepper, Rosemary, Salt & Pepper Shaker, Seasoned Salt, Steak Grilling Seasoning, Thyme

Kernel Season's - Popcorn Seasoning (Apple Cinnamon ●, Barbecue ●, Butter ●, Cajun ●, Caramel ●, Chili Lime ●, Chocolate Marshmallow ●, Jalapeno ●, Kettle Corn ●, Milk Chocolate Caramel ●, Nacho Cheddar ●, Parmesan & Garlic ●, Pumpkin Spice ●, Ranch ●, Salt ●, Salt & Vinegar ●, Sour Cream & Onion ●, White Cheddar ●), Popcorn Spritzer ●

Kirkland Signature - Chopped Onion, Garlic Salt, Malabar Black Pepper, Sea Salt (Grinder, Pure), Tellicherry Pepper (Grinder, Whole Peppercorns)

S

Konriko ▲ - Chipotle Seasoning ●, Creole Seasoning ●, Dry Mojo Seasoning ●

Kootenay Kitchen - Traditional Gomashio

Kraft -
Parmesan Seasoning Blends (Cracked Black Pepper & Toasted Onion, Hearty Tuscan Herbs, Rosemary & Garlic)
Sizzling Salads (Southwest Chicken, Tuscan Chicken)

Lawry's -
Garlic (Pepper ‼, Powder ‼, Salt ‼)
Lemon Pepper ‼
Salt Free 17 ‼
Seasoned Pepper ‼
Seasoned Salt (25% Less Sodium ‼, Black Pepper ‼, Regular ‼)
Seasoning Mixes (Chicken Fajitas ‼, Chicken Taco ‼, Chimichurri Burrito Casserole ‼, Creamy Basil Chicken Tortellini ‼, Extra Thick & Rich Spaghetti Sauce ‼, Fajitas ‼, Lemon Butter Dill Tilapia ‼, Mediterranean Sundried Tomato & Garlic Chicken ‼, Original Style Spaghetti Sauce ‼, Sicilian Lasagna w/Basil & Oregano ‼, Sloppy Joes ‼, Southwest Chicken Skillet ‼, Tenderizing Beef Marinade ‼)

Litehouse - Dried (Basil, Chives, Cilantro, Dill, Garlic, Italian Herb Blend, Mushrooms, Oregano, Parsley, Poultry Herb Blend, Red Onion, Salad Herb Blend, Spring Onion)

Lowes Foods Brand - Black Pepper, Chili Powder, Cinnamon Ground, Garlic Powder, Paprika, Steak Seasoning

Lydia's Organics - Seasoning

Mayacamas - Chicken BBQ ★, Curry Blend ★, Salad Delight ★, Savory Salt ★

McCormick -
Bag 'N Season (Chicken, Herb Roasted Pork Tenderloin, Pork Chops, Swiss Steak)
California Style (Garlic (Crushed, Minced, Pepper, Powder w/ Parsley, Salt w/Parsley), Lemon Pepper, Onion (Minced, Powder))

Gourmet Collection

100% Organic (Basil Leaves, Cayenne Red Pepper, Celery Seed, Chinese Ginger, Coarse Grind Black Pepper, Crushed Red Pepper, Crushed Rosemary, Curry Powder, Dill Weed, Fennel Seed, Garlic Powder, Ground Cloves, Ground Coriander, Ground Cumin, Ground Mustard, Ground Nutmeg, Ground White Pepper, Herbes De Provence, Italian Seasoning, Marjoram Leaves, Oregano Leaves, Paprika, Parsley Flakes, Poppy Seed, Rosemary Leaves, Rubbed Sage, Saigon Cinnamon, Sesame Seed, Tellicherry Black Peppercorns, Thyme Leaves, Turkish Bay Leaves), Ancho Chili Powder, Anise Seed, Arrowroot, Black Peppercorns, Black Sesame Seed, Blends (Bon Appetite, Cajun Seasoning, Celery Salt, Chinese Five Spice, Cocoa Chili, Cuban Seasoning, Curry Powder, Garam Masala, Garlic Salt, Greek Seasoning, Herbes De Provence, Hot Madras Curry Powder, Jamaican Jerk, Lemon & Pepper, Mediterranean Spiced Sea Salt, Moroccan Ras El Hanout, Poultry Seasoning, Red Curry Powder, Southwest, Tuscan), California Lemon Peel, Caraway Seed, Cardamom Seed, Celery Seed, Chevril Leaves, Chili Powder, Chipotle Chili Pepper, Chopped Chives, Cilantro Leaves, Coarse Grind Black Pepper, Coriander Seed, Cracked Black Pepper, Cream Of Tartar, Crushed Red Pepper, Crushed Rosemary, Crystallized Ginger, Cumin Seed, Dalmation Sage Leaves, Diced Jalapeno Pepper, Dill Seed, Dill Weed, Fennel Seed, Garlic Powder, Green Peppercorns, Ground Cardamom, Ground Cayenne Red Pepper, Ground Cloves, Ground Coriander Seed, Ground Cumin, Ground Ginger, Ground Jamaican Allspice, Ground Mace, Ground Marjoram, Ground Mediterranean Oregano, Ground Mustard, Ground Nutmeg, Ground Savory, Ground Thyme, Ground Turmeric, Ground White Pepper, Italian Seasoning, Lemongrass, Madagascar Vanilla Beans, Marjoram Leaves, Mediterranean Basil Leaves, Mediterranean Oregano Leaves, Mexican Oregano Leaves, Mexican Style Chili Powder, Mint Flakes, Onion Powder, Orange Peel, Paprika, Parsley Flakes, Peppercorn Melange,

Poppy Seed, Roasted Ground Coriander, Roasted Ground Cumin, Roasted Ground Ginger, Roasted Saigon Cinnamon, Rosemary Leaves, Rubbed Dalmation Sage, Saigon Cinnamon, Sesame Seed, Sicilian Sea Salt, Smoked Paprika, Spanish Saffron, Stick Cinnamon, Tarragon Leaves, Thyme Leaves, Toasted Sesame Seed, Turkish Bay Leaves, Wasabi Powder, Whole Cloves, Whole Jamaican Allspice, Whole Nutmeg, Yellow Mustard Seed)

Grill Mates Marinade Packets (Brown Sugar Bourbon, Mexican Fiesta)

Grill Mates Dry Rub (Applewood, Chicken, Cowboy, Pork, Slow & Low (Memphis Pit BBQ, Smokin' Texas BBQ), Steak, Sweet & Smoky)

Grill Mates Grinders (Montreal Chicken, Montreal Steak)

Grill Mates Seasoning Blend (Fiery Five Pepper, Molasses Bacon, Steakhouse Onion Burger)

Grill Mates Seasoning Blends (25% Less Sodium Montreal Chicken, 25% Less Sodium Montreal Steak, Barbecue, Hamburger, Lemon Pepper w/Herbs, Mesquite, Montreal Chicken, Montreal Steak, Roasted Garlic & Herb, Smokehouse Maple, Spicy Montreal Steak)

Grinders (Black Peppercorn, Cinnamon Sugar, Garlic Pepper, Garlic Sea Salt, Italian Herb, Lemon & Pepper, Peppercorn Medley, Sea Salt)

Meat Tenderizer (Seasoned, Unseasoned)

Perfect Pinch (Lemon Herb, Mediterranean Herb, Original Chicken, Parmesan Herb, Roasted Garlic & Bell Pepper, Rotisserie Chicken, Salad Supreme, Salt Free (Garlic & Herb, Garlic Pepper))

Seafood Rubs (Herb w/Lemon, Sweet Citrus & Spice Salmon)

Seafood Steamers (Garlic Butter, Lemon Garlic, Shrimp & Crab Boil)

Seasoning Packets (Chicken Tinga, Chipotle Meatballs, Creamy Garlic Alfredo Sauce, Enchilada Sauce Mix, Fajitas, Guacamole, Hickory Barbeque Buffalo Wings, Italian Chicken & Pasta Bake, Italian Style Spaghetti, Mexican Rice, Pesto, Sloppy Joes, Southwest Chicken Quesadilla, Taco (30% Less Sodium, 30% Less Sodium Mild, Chicken, Hot, Mild, Original, Pork), Tex Mex Chili, Thick & Zesty Spaghetti Sauce)

Slow Cookers (Barbeque Pulled Pork, Chicken Noodle Soup, Chili, Italian Herb Chicken, Southern BBQ Ribs)

Spices (Alum, Anise Seed, Apple Pie Spice, Basil Leaves, Bay Leaves, Black Peppercorns, Caraway Seed, Celery Flakes, Celery Salt, Celery Seed, Chives, Chopped Onions, Cilantro Leaves, Cinnamon Sticks, Cinnamon Sugar, Coarse Ground Black Pepper, Cream Of Tartar, Crushed Red Pepper, Cumin Seed, Curry Powder, Dill Seed, Dill Weed, Fennel Seed, Garlic Powder, Garlic Salt, Ground Allspice, Ground Black Pepper, Ground Cinnamon, Ground Cloves, Ground Cumin, Ground Ginger, Ground Mace, Ground Marjoram, Ground Mustard, Ground Nutmeg, Ground Oregano, Ground Red Pepper, Ground Sage, Ground Thyme, Ground Turmeric, Ground White Pepper, Hot Mexican Style Chili Powder, Hot Shot Black & Red Pepper Blend, Marjoram Leaves, Minced Garlic, Minced Onions, Mixed Pickling Spice, Mustard Seed, Onion Powder, Onion Salt, Oregano Leaves, Paprika, Parsley Flakes, Perfect Pinch Italian Seasoning, Poppy Seed, Poultry Seasoning, Pumpkin Pie Spice, Rosemary Leaves, Rubbed Sage, Sesame Seed, Sliced Garlic, Smokehouse Ground Black Pepper, Tarragon Leaves, Thyme Leaves, Whole Allspice, Whole Cloves, Whole Mexican Oregano)

Meijer Brand - Black Pepper, Chili Powder, Cinnamon, Garlic Powder, Garlic Salt, Mild Taco Seasoning Packet, Minced Onion, Onion Salt, Oregano Leaves, Paprika, Parsley Flakes, Seasoned Salt, Spaghetti Mix, Taco Seasoning Packet

Melissa's - Garlic In Pure Olive Oil

Midwest Country Fare - Chili Powder, Chopped Onion, Cinnamon, Garlic Powder, Garlic Salt, Ground Black Pepper, Italian, Onion Powder, Parsley Flakes, Pure Ground Black Pepper, Season Salt

Miss Bev's - Rooster Rub

Morton - Canning & Pickling Salt, Garlic Salt, Hot Salt, Lite Salt Mixture, Nature's Seasons Seasoning Blend, Popcorn Salt, Salt & Pepper Shakers, Salt Stubstitute, Sausage & Meat Loaf Seasoning, Seasoned Salt, Smoke Flavored Sugar Cure, Sugar Cure, Tender Quick Mix

S

Nantucket Off-Shore - Garden !, Rub (Bayou !, Dragon !, Mt. Olympus !, Nantucket !, Prairie !, Pueblo !, Rasta !, Renaissance !), Shellfish Boil !, St. Remy !

Navitas Naturals ▲ - Mesquite Powder

Nielsen-Massey - Madagascar Bourbon Pure Vanilla Powder ●

NOH - Seasoning Packets (Chinese Lemon Chicken, Hawaiian Spicy Chicken, Hawaiian Style Curry, Korean Kim Chee, Portuguese Vinha D'Alhos)

Nueva Cocina - Latin Beef & Taco Seasoning, Seasoning & Veggie Mix (Chipotle Taco, Taco Fresco)

Nuts.com - Chamomile Flowers ●, Garam Masala ●, Ground Sumac ●, Hibiscus Flowers ●, Mahlab ●, Mixed Syrian Spices ●, Spearmint ●, Whole Licorice Root ●

O Organics - Basil Leaves, Bay Leaves, Cayenne Peppers, Chili Powder, Ground Cinnamon, Ground Cloves, Ground Cumin, Ground Nutmeg, Paprika

Old Bay - 30% Less Sodium, Blackened Seasoning, Garlic & Herb, Lemon & Herb, Original, Rub, Seafood Steamer

Old El Paso - Burrito Seasoning Mix

Ortega - Taco Seasoning Mix (40% Less Sodium, Chipotle, Hot & Spicy, Jalapeno & Onion, Original)

Polaner ▲ - Ready To Use Wet Spices (All Varieties)

Publix - Adobo Seasoning w/o Pepper, Adobo Seasoning w/Pepper, Black Pepper, Chili Powder, Cinnamon, Garlic Powder, Garlic Powder w/Parsley, Garlic Salt, Ground Ginger, Ground Red Pepper, Italian Seasonings, Lemon & Pepper, Minced Onion, Onion Powder, Paprika, Parsley Flakes, Salt, Seasoned Salt, Taco Seasoning Mix, Whole Basil Leaves, Whole Bay Leaves, Whole Black Pepper, Whole Oregano

Safeway Brand - All Spices & Seasonings, Fajita Seasoning Mix, Meat Marinade Mix

Safeway Select - All Rubs & Seasonings

Sharwood's - Curry Powder (Hot, Medium, Mild)

Simply Organic -
> Adjustable Grinders (BBQ Ground Up, Chophouse Seasoning, Citrus A'peel, Daily Grind, Get Crackin', Grind To A Salt)
> Grilling Seasons (Chicken ●, Citrus 'N Herb ●, Orange Ginger ●, Seafood ●, Spicy Steak ●, Steak ●, Vegetable ●)
> Mulling Spice Mix ●
> Seasoning Mix (Black Bean ●, Dirty Rice ●, Enchilada ●, Fajita ●, Fish Taco ●, Gumbo Base ●, Jambalaya ●, Mild Chili ●, Red Bean ●, Salsa Verde ●, Sloppy Joe ●, Southwest Taco ●, Spicy Chili ●, Spicy Taco ●, Vegetarian Chili ●)
> Spices & Seasonings (All Purpose Seasoning, All Seasons Salt, Basil, Bay Leaf, Black Pepper, Black Peppercorns, Black Sesame Seed, Cayenne, Celery Salt, Chili Powder, Chipotle Pepper, Cilantro, Cinnamon, Cinnamon Sticks, Coriander, Crushed Red Pepper, Cumin, Curry Powder, Dill Weed, Garam Masala, Garlic 'N Herb, Garlic Pepper, Garlic Powder, Garlic Salt, Ginger, Ground Cloves, Herbs De Provence, Italian Seasoning, Lemon Peel, Marjoram, Mexican Seasoning, Minced Onion, Mustard, Nutmeg, Oregano, Paprika, Parsley, Poppy Seed, Poultry Seasoning, Pumpkin Pie Spice, Rosemary, Sage, Sesame Seed, Tarragon, Thyme, Turmeric, Vanilla Beans)

Spartan Brand - Black Pepper, Chili Powder, Cinnamon, Garlic Powder, Garlic Salt, Ground Nutmeg, Iodized Salt, Minced Onion, Oregano Leaves, Paprika, Parsley Flakes, Salt

Spice Islands - 100% Organic (All Varieties), All Food Coloring, All Liquid Flavorings, All Steak Seasonings, Allspice (Ground, Whole), Alum, Ancho Chile Powder, Anise (Seed, Star), Apple Pie Spice, Arrowroot, Basil, Bay Leaves, Caraway Seed, Cardamom, Cayenne Pepper, Celery Flakes, Celery Seed, Chicken & Rib Rub, Chicken Seasoning, Chipotle Chili, Chives, Cilantro, Cinnamon (Ground Saigon, Sticks), Cloves (Ground, Whole), Coriander, Cream Of Tartar, Cumin (Ground, Whole), Curry Powder, Dill Weed, Fennel Seed, Garlic (Minced, Powder), Ginger (Crystallized, Ground), Gourmet Blends (All Varieties), Grinders (All Varieties), Hickory Smoke Salt, Italian Seasoning, Jamaican Jerk Seasoning,

S

Lemon Peel, Lemon Pepper, Lime Pepper, Mace, Marjoram, Meat Tenderizer (Seasoned, Unseasoned), Mint, Mr. Pepper, MSG, Mustard (Ground, Seed), Nutmeg (Ground, Whole), Onion (Minced, Powder), Onion Salt, Orange Peel, Oregano (Ground, Regular), Oriental 5 Spice, Paprika (Regular, Smoked), Parsilla Chile Powder, Parsley, Pepper Black (Cracked, Fine Grind, Medium Grind), Pepper Green Bell, Pickling Spice, Poppy Seed, Poultry Seasoning, Pumpkin Pie Spice, Red Pepper Crushed, Rosemary, Rosemary Garlic Seasoning, Saffron, Sage, Sea Salt, Sesame Seed (Black, Regular), Six Pepper Blend, Smokey Mesquite Seasoning, Spicy Spaghetti Seasoning, Tarragon, Thyme (Ground, Regular), Turmeric, Vanilla Bean, White Pepper, World Flavors (All Varieties)

Spice Islands Specialty - Beau Monde, Fine Herbs, Garlic Pepper Seasoning, Italian Herb Seasoning, Old Hickory Smoked Salt, Summer Savory

Spicely ▲ - All Varieties (100% Certified Organic Extracts ●, Natural Spices ●, Organic Spices ●, Seasoning Blends ●)

Stubb's - Spice Rub (Bar B Q ●, Burger ●, Chile Lime ●, Herbal Mustard ●, Rosemary Ginger ●)

The Spice Hunter - 100% Organic (Allspice, Basil, Bay Leaves, Black Pepper (Coarsely Ground, Whole), Cilantro, Cinnamon, Cloves, Coriander, Cumin, Dill Weed, Fennel, Garlic, Ginger, Marjoram, Nutmeg, Onion (Granulated, Minced), Oregano, Paprika, Parsley Flakes, Red Pepper, Rosemary, Sage, Tarragon, Thyme, Turmeric), Arrowroot, Basil Leaves, Bay Leaves Whole, Black Pepper (Coarse, Fine), Caraway Seeds, Cardamom, Celery Seeds, Chile Pepper (Chipotle Crushed, Crushed, New Mexico Ground), Chives, Cilantro, Cinnamon Ground, Cinnamon Sticks, Cloves (Madagascar Ground, Penang Whole), Coriander, Cream Of Tartar, Cumin, Cumin Seeds, Dill Weed, Fennel, Fresh At Hand (Basil, Chives, Dill, Garlic, Ginger, Italian Herbs, Onion Mix, Oregano, Rosemary, Thyme), Garlic (California, Roasted), Ginger (Australian Crystallized Chopped, Chinese Ground), Jamaican Allspice (Ground, Whole), Juniper Berries, Lemon Grass, Lemon Peel,

Mace, Marjoram, Mint, Nutmeg (Ground, Whole), Onion, Orange Peel, Oregano, Paprika (Smoked, Sweet), Parsley, Peppercorns (Black, Pink, Tellicherry, White), Pine Nuts, Poppy Seeds, Red Pepper, Rosemary Leaves, Saffron Strands, Sage, Sesame Seeds, Shallots, Star Anise, Tarragon, Thyme, Turmeric, Vanilla Bean, White Pepper, Yellow Mustard Ground

Tones - All Food Coloring, All Liquid Flavorings, All Steak Seasonings, Allspice, Alum, Anise Seed, Apple Pie Spice, Arrowroot, Basil, Bay Leaves, Buttermilk Ranch Dressing Mix, Caraway Seed, Cardamom, Cayenne Pepper, Celery Flakes, Celery Seed, Chicken & Rib Rub, Chicken Seasoning, Chili Powder, Chinese 5 Spice, Chives, Cilantro, Cinnamon, Cloves, Coriander, Cream Of Tartar, Crushed Red Pepper, Cumin, Curry Powder, Dill Seed/Weed, Fennel, Garlic Minced, Garlic Pepper, Garlic Powder, Garlic Salt, Ginger, Hickory Smoke Salt, Italian Seasoning, Jamaican Jerk Seasoning, Lemon & Herb, Lemon Peel, Lemon Pepper, Lime Pepper, Mace, Marjoram, Meat Tenderizer (Seasoned, Unseasoned), Mint Leaves, Mr. Pepper, MSG, Mustard, Nutmeg, Onion Minced, Onion Powder, Onion Salt, Orange Peel, Oregano, Paprika, Parsley, Pepper Green Bell, Pickling Spice, Pizza Seasoning, Poppy Seed, Poultry Seasoning, Pumpkin Pie Spice, Rosemary, Rosemary Garlic Seasoning, Sage, Sesame Seed, Six Pepper Blend, Smokey Mesquite Seasoning, Spicy Spaghetti Seasoning, Tarragon, Thyme, Turmeric

Trader Joe's - All Private Label Spices, Frozen Chopped Basil, Frozen Chopped Cilantro, Taco Seasoning

Victoria Gourmet - 7 Seed Crust, Brining Blend (Asian, Smoky, Spicy, Traditional), Cinnamon Chili Rub, Curry, Fire Roasted Tomatoes, Ginger Citrus, Herbes De Provence, Holiday, Jalapeno Pepper Flakes, Lemon Pepper (No Salt, Original), Mediterranean, Moroccan, Mulling Spices, New Orleans, Pepper (Chef's Grind Black, Cracked Black, Ground White, Mill Mix, Shaker Grind Black), Peppercorns (Organic Tellicherry, White), Pie Spices, Pizza, Red Bell Peppers, Red Pepper Flakes, Roasted Garlic Slices,

S

Seafood, Shallots, Sicilian, Smoky Paprika Chipotle, Texas Red, Toasted Onion Herb, Toasted Sesame Ginger, Tuscan

Watkins - Seasoning (Chicken, Poultry)

Weber Grill Creations -

Grinders (Chicago Steak, Kick 'N Chicken, Roasted Garlic & Herb, Six Pepper Fusion, Twisted Citrus Garlic)

Seasoning (Boston Bay, Burgundy Beef, Chicago Steak, Gourmet Burger, Kick 'N Chicken, Mango Lime Seafood, N'Orleans Cajun, Roasted Garlic & Herb, Seasoning Salt, Smokey Mesquite, Steak 'N Chop, Veggie Grill, Zesty Lemon Seasoning)

Wegmans Brand - Black Pepper, Salt (Iodized, Plain), Sea Salt (Coarse Crystals, Fine Crystals, Fleur De Sel)

Wright's - Liquid Smoke (Hickory Seasoning, Mesquite)

Seaweed

Annie Chun's - Seaweed Snacks (Sesame, Wasabi)

Eden Organic - Agar Agar Bars, Agar Agar Flakes

Nagai's - Sushi Nori Roasted Seaweed

Navitas Naturals ▲ - Nori Sheets

Yaki - Sushi Nori Roasted Seaweed

Yamamotoyama - Roasted Nori **!**, Temaki Party Toasted **!**

Seeds

Arrowhead Mills - Flax, Mechanically Hulled Sesame, Organic Golden Flax, Sunflower, Unhulled Sesame

David Seeds - All Flavors Are Gluten Free

Eden Organic - Organic Pumpkin (Dry Roasted & Salted, Spicy Dry Roasted w/Tamari)

El Peto ▲ - Whole Flax Seeds

Frito-Lay - Sunflower Seeds (Dill Pickle **!!**, Flamas **!!**, Kernels **!!**, Ranch **!!**, Regular **!!**)

Gerbs Pumpkin Seeds ▲ - Sunflower Seeds w/Sea Salt ●

Gopal's - Sprouties (Cheesy, Kefir, Original, Savory)

Go Raw ▲ - Seed Mix (Simple ●, Spicy ●), Seeds (Sprouted Pumpkin ●, Sprouted Sunflower ●), Sprouted Organic Flax Seeds ●

Hail Merry ▲ - Salt 'N Pepper Sunflower Seeds ●

Kaia Foods ▲ -
　　Sprouted Pumpkin Seeds (Orange & Spice ●, Party Mix ●, Sea Salt & Vinegar ●)
　　Sprouted Sunflower Seeds (Cocoa Mole ●, Garlic & Sea Salt ●, Sweet Curry ●, Teriyaki ●)

Lowes Foods Brand - Sunflower Seeds

Meijer Brand - Sunflower (Plain, Salted In Shell)

Navitas Naturals ▲ - Chia (Powder, Seed), Hemp (Powder, Seeds)

NoNuttin' Foods ▲ - Raw Sunflower ●

Nuchia - Original Chia

Nuts.com - Chia Seeds (Organic ●, Regular ●, White ●), Chocolate Covered Sunflower Seeds (Blue ●, Green ●, Pink ●, Purple ●, White ●, Yellow ●), Hemp ●, Hulled Sesame Seeds ●, Organic Raw No Shell Hemp ●, Pepitas (Organic Dry Roasted Salted No Shell Pumpkin Seeds ●, Organic No Shell Pumpkin Seeds ●, Raw No Shell Pumpkin Seeds ●, Roasted (Salted No Shell Pumpkin Seeds●, Unsalted No Shell Pumpkin Seeds ●)), Pumpkin Seeds (Organic Tamari Roasted No Shell ●, Raw In Shell ●, Sprouted ●), Roasted Squash Seeds Unsalted In Shell ●, Sunflower Seeds (Chocolate Covered ●, Israeli Unsalted In Shell ●, Organic (Raw No Shell ●, Roasted Salted No Shell ●, Tamari Roasted No Shell ●), Raw (In Shell ●, No Shell ●), Roasted (Salted In Shell ●, Salted No Shell ●, Unsalted In Shell ●, Unsalted No Shell ●)), Watermelon Seeds ●

Planters - Roasted Salted Pepitas, Sunflower (Go Nuts Kernels, Kernels Dry Roasted, Roasted & Salted)

Pure Market Express ▲ - Spicy Pepitos ●

Purely Chia ▲ - White Chia Seed (Micro Milled ●, Whole ●)

Running Food ▲ - Chia Seed (Milled ●, Whole ●)

Ruth's Hemp Power - Raw Goodness Chia Seed, SoftHemp Shelled

Shiloh Farms - Black Chia ‼, Organic (Alfalfa ‼, Black Sesame ‼, Chia ‼, Hulled Sesame ‼, Poppy ‼, Shelled Pumpkin ‼, Shelled Sunflower ‼, Unhulled Sesame ‼), Raw In Shell Sunflower ‼, White Chia ‼

S

Spitz - Seasoned Pumpkin **!!**, Sunflower (Chili Lime **!!**, Cracked Pepper**!!**, Dill Pickle **!!**, Salted **!!**, Seasoned **!!**, Smoky BBQ **!!**, Spicy**!!**)

Trader Joe's - Pumpkin Seeds & Pepitas, Sunflower

Tropical Traditions - Whole Golden Flax Seeds

Woodstock Farms -

    Natural Seeds (Pumpkin (Roasted & Salted, Shelled), Sunflower Hulled (Regular, Roasted No Salt))

    Organic Seeds (Flax, Hulled Sesame, Pumpkin Shelled, Sunflower (Hulled, Tamari), Tamari Pumpkin, White Quinoa)

Sesame Oil...see Oil

Sesame Seeds...see Seeds

Shakes

    Amazake - Almond, Amazing Mango, Banana Appeal, Chocolate (Almond, Chimp), Cool Coconut, Go Hazelnuts, Oh So Original, Rice Nog, Tiger Chai, Vanilla (Gorilla, Pecan Pie)

    Arbonne - Protein Shake Mix (Chocolate **!**, Vanilla **!**)

    Betty Lou's - Protein Shake (Chocolate **!** ●, Orange Cream **!** ●, Vanilla **!** ●)

    Garelick Farms - Chug (Chocolate Milkshake, Cookies 'N Cream Milkshake, Vanilla Milkshake)

    Glucerna - Classic Butter Pecan, Creamy Strawberry, Homemade Vanilla, Rich Chocolate

    Nesquik - Milk Shake

    Nuts.com -

        Organic Powder (Acai ●, Hemp Protein ●, Lucuma ●, Maca ●, Mesquite ●, Noni ●, Pomegranate ●, Raw (Strawberry ●, VitaCherry ●, Wild Blueberry ●), Red Maca ●, Yumberry ●),

        Powder (Apple Cider Vinegar ●, Camu Camu ●, Chamomile ●, Chlorella ●, Dandelion Root ●, Echinacea ●, Ginkgo Leaf ●, Goji Berry ●, Gotu Kola ●, Green Tea ●, Mangosteen ●, Pumpkin Seed ●, Spirulina ●, Stevia ●, Tomato ●)

    Safeway Brand - Nutritional Shake/Drink Including Plus (All Flavors), Weight Loss Shake (Chocolate Royale, Milk Chocolate, Vanilla)

    Worldwide Pure Protein - Banana Cream, Frosty Chocolate, Strawberry Cream, Vanilla Cream

S

Shortening

    Bakers & Chefs - 100% Pure Creamy Liquid Shortening

    Earth Balance - Natural Shortening

    Food Club Brand

    Hy-Vee - Vegetable (Butter Flavor Shortening, Oil Shortening)

    Lowes Foods Brand - Shortening

    Meijer Brand

    Midwest Country Fare - Pre Creamed Shortening

    Publix - Vegetable Shortening

    Spartan Brand - Butter Flavored Vegetable Shortening, Finest Vegetable

    Tropical Traditions - Organic Palm Shortening

    Wegmans Brand - Vegetable

    Winn Dixie

Shrimp

    ... *All Fresh Seafood Is Gluten-Free (Non-Marinated, Unseasoned)

    Bumble Bee - Deveined Shrimp (Large, Medium, Small), Large, Medium, Small, Tiny

    Chicken Of The Sea - All Shrimp Products

    Crown Prince - Broken, Tiny

    Great Value Brand (Wal-Mart) - Canned Tiny Shrimp

    Henry & Lisa's - Uncooked Natural

    Hy-Vee - Frozen Cooked, Platter

    Kirkland Signature - Frozen Tail On (Cooked, Raw)

    Sweet Bay - All Frozen

    Whole Catch - Cooked, Raw, Wild Key West Pink Shell On

Shrimp Sauce...see Cocktail Sauce

Sloppy Joe Sauce

    Dei Fratelli - Canned Sloppy Joe Sauce

    Food Club Brand

    H-E-B - Sloppy Joe Mix

    Hannaford Brand

    Heinz - Sloppy Joe Sauce

    Hormel - Not So Sloppy Joe

    Hy-Vee

S

Kroger Brand
Meijer Brand - Sloppy Joe Sauce
Safeway Brand
Simply Organic - Sloppy Joe Seasoning Mix ●
Spartan Brand - Mix, Sauce
Winn Dixie - Original

Smoke
Colgin - All Liquid Smoke Varieties
Wright's - Liquid Smoke (Hickory Seasoning, Mesquite)

Smoked Sausage...see Sausage
Smoked Turkey...see Turkey

Smoothies
Bolthouse Farms - Fruit Smoothie (Amazing Mango, Berry Boost, Blue Goodness, C Boost, Green Goodness, Strawberry Banana)
Earth's Best Organic Baby Food - Sesame Street Fruit Yogurt Smoothie (Apple Blueberry, Mixed Berry, Peach Banana, Pear Mango, Strawberry Banana)
Ella's Kitchen - Smoothie Fruits (The Green One, The Purple One, The Red One, The Yellow One)
Hansen's Smoothie Nectar - Energy Island Blast, Mango Pineapple, Peach Berry, Strawberry Banana
Jamba - Smoothie Kits (Caribbean Passion, Mango A Go Go, Orange Dream Machine, Razzmatazz, Strawberries Wild)
Jell-O - Smoothie Snacks (Mixed Berry, Strawberry Banana)
Lucerne - All Varieties
Mixl -
All Natural Lean Performance Shakes (All Flavors)
All Natural Protein Shakes (All Flavors)
Naked - Juice Smoothie (Berry Blast, Berry Veggie, Mighty Mango, Orange Carrot, Protein Zone (Double Berry, Mango, Regular), Reduced Calorie (Citrus Lemongrass, Lychee, Peach Guava, Tropical), Strawberry Banana)
Pure Market Express ▲ - Athena ●, Bold Tomato ●, Caribbean Blend ●, Chocolate Banana Milkshake ●, Classic Green ●, Cran Orange Splash●,

Creamy Strawberry ●, Fruit Fabulousity ●, Lime Berry ●, Orange Mango Creamsicle ●, Pandora's Peach ●, Pina Colada Song ●, Pom Party ●, Raspberry Smash ●, Razzle ●, Ruby Red Sunrise ●, Tahitian Treat ●, Thin Mint ●, Tropical Peach ●

Sambazon -
Acai w/(Blueberry & Pomegranate, Strawberry & Banana)
Energy Acai Berry Yerba Mate & Guarana
Protein Smoothies (Acai & Chocolate, Chocolate Almond Coconut Milk, Vanilla)

Tillamook - All Yogurt Smoothies **!**

WholeSoy & Co. - All Varieties **! !**

Snacks

Aimee's Livin' Magic - All Snacks

AllerEnergy ▲ - Soft Pretzels

Annie Chun's - Seaweed Snacks (Sesame, Wasabi)

Annie's -
Organic Bunny Fruit Snacks (Berry Patch **! !**, Pink Lemonade **! !**, Summer Strawberry **! !**, Sunny Citrus **! !**, Tropical Treat **! !**)
Organic Grapes Galore Fruit Snacks **! !**
Organic Orchard Real Fruit Bites (Apple **! !**, Cherry **! !**, Grape **! !**, Strawberry **! !**)

Baffles - Snack Clusters (Caramel Crunch, Cheddar Cheese, Chocolate, Cinnamon Crisp, Trail Mix)

Bajans - Bhuja Cracker Mix

Baked Cheetos - Crunchy 100 Calorie Mini Bites Cheese **! !**, Crunchy Cheese **! !**, Flamin' Hot Cheese **! !**

Baken-Ets - Pork Skins (Cracklins Hot 'N Spicy **! !**, Hot 'N Spicy **! !**, Tangy BBQ **! !**, Traditional **! !**)

Betty Lou's - Nut Butter Balls (Almond ●, Cashew Pecan ●, Coconut Macadamia ●, High Protein Almond ●, Peanut ●, Spirulina Ginseng ●)

Boulder Canyon Natural Foods - White Cheddar Multigrain Puffs ★

Calbee Snack Salad - Snapea Crisps **! !**

S

Caroline's Desserts - Krispette (Amaretto Bianco ●, Boo Boo Bar●, Caramel Apple ●, Cocoa Jayne ●, Egg Nog ●, Mint Everest ●, Myrtle's Turtles ●, Not So Plain Jayne ●, Oh Joy ●, Peanut Casanova ●, Peppermint Spark ●, Roca Crunch ●, Sonoma Sunshine ●, Sweet Cherrity ●, Sweet Joe ●, The Great Almondo ●, Tiki Bar ●, Triple Chocolate Nirvana ●)

CheeCha ▲ - Gluten Free Potato Puffs (Luscious Lime, Mediterranean Ginger, Original, Sea Salt & Spiced Pepper, Sea Salt & Vinegar)

Cheeky Monkey ▲ - Peanut Butter Puffs ●

Cheetos -
Baked (Crunchy Cheese !!, Flamin' Hot Cheese !!)
Flavored Snacks
  Crunchy (Cheddar Jalapeno !!, Cheese !!, Cheesy Cheddar BBQ !!, Fiery Fusion Sizzlin' Cayenne & Cheese !!, Flamin' Hot Cheese !!, Salsa Con Queso !!)
  Fantastix Flavored Baked Corn/Potato (Chili Cheese !!, Flamin Hot !!)
  Flamin' Hot (Cheese !!, Limon Cheese !!)
  Puffs (Cheese !!, Honey BBQ Cheese !!, Natural White Cheddar Cheese ★)
  Twisted Cheese !!

Chester's - Butter Flavored Puffcorn !!, Cheddar Cheese Flavored Popcorn !!, Cheese Flavored Puffcorn !!, Chili Cheese Flavored Fries !!, Flamin' Hot Flavored (Fries !!, Puffcorn !!)

Chi-Chi's - Nacho Cheese Snackers

Corn Nuts - Barbeque, Chile Picante, Nacho Cheese, Original, Ranch

Cracker Jack - Original Caramel Coated Popcorn & Peanuts !!

Crunchies -
All Natural Edamame
Freeze Dried (Blueberries, Cinnamon Apple, Corn Snack (BBQ, Regular, Spiced Ranch), Mango, Mixed Fruit, Organic (100% Bananas, 100% Peas, 100% Strawberries), Pears, Pineapple, Raspberries, Roasted Veggies, Strawberries, Tropical Fruit, Very Berry)
Seasoned Veggie Edamame (Grilled w/Wild Rice, Salted)

David Seeds - All Flavors

Deep River Snacks -

Baked Fries (Jalapeno & Cheddar ●, Mesquite BBQ ●)

Sharp White Cheddar Popcorn ●

Eat Smart - Naturals (Garden Veggie Crisps ●, Garden Veggie Stix, White Cheddar Cheese (Corn & Rice Puffs, Multi Grain Cheese Puffs ●))

Eden Organic - All Mixed Up (Regular, Too), Wild Berry Mix

Edward & Sons - Brown Rice Snaps (Black Sesame, Cheddar, Onion Garlic, Plain Unsalted, Sesame (Tamari, Unsalted), Tamari Seaweed, Toasted Onion, Vegetable)

El's Kitchen ▲ - Medleys (Cheddar, Original, Sour Cream & Onion), Snaps

Ener-G ▲ - Cinnamon Crackers Pieces

Food Club Brand - Potato Sticks

Funyuns - Onion Flavored Rings (Flamin' Hot !!, Regular !!)

Garden Of Eatin' - Baked (Cheddar Crunchitos, Cheddar Puffs)

Gerbs Pumpkin Seeds ▲ -

Baked Kernel Pumpkin Seeds (Roasted Red Pepper ●, Toasted Onion & Garlic ●, Touch of Sea Salt ●)

Whole Roasted Pumpkin Seeds (Light Sea Salt ●, Sea Salt 'N Cracked Pepper ●)

Gladcorn - A Maizing Corn Snack (Bar B Q ●, Gourmet Cheddar ●, Jalapeno ●, Original ●)

Glenny's - Brown Rice Marshmallow Treat (Chocolate ●, Creamy Vanilla ●, Peanut Caramel ●, Raspberry Jubilee ●)

Glutino ▲ - Bagel Chips (Original, Parmesan Garlic)

Gopal's - Power Wraps (Italian, Japanese, Masala, Mexican, Raw Curry, Texas BBQ, Vegan Curry)

Go Raw ▲ -

Flax Snax (Pizza ●, Simple ●, Spicy ●, Sunflower ●)

Granola (Apple Cinnamon ●, Live ●, Live Chocolate ●, Simple ●)

Seed Mix (Simple ●, Spicy ●)

S

Seeds (Sprouted Pumpkin ●, Sprouted Sunflower ●)
Sprouted Organic Flax Seeds ●
Super Chips (Pumpkin ●, Spirulina ●)

Herr's - Cheese Curls (Baked, Honey, Hot), Pork Rinds (BBQ Flavored, Original)

Hill Country Fare H-E-B - Cheese Puffs, Crunchy Cheese Snacks, Pork Rinds (BBQ, Hot & Spicy, Lemon Chile, Regular, Salt & Vinegar)

Hy-Vee - Cheese Balls, Fruit Snacks (Dinosaurs, Peanuts, Sharks, Snoopy, Variety Pack, Veggie Tales)

Johnsonville - Summer Sausage Deli Bites (Beef, Original, Salami)

Kay's Naturals - Protein Chips (Chili Nacho Cheese ●, Crispy Parmesan●, Lemon Herb ●, Sweet BBQ ●), White Cheddar Kruncheeze ●

Kroger Brand - Cheese Balls, Cheese Curls (Baked, Crunchy, Value), Popcorn (Butter, Cheese, Gourmet White Cheddar, Salted)

LesserEvil -
Kettle Corn (Black & White **!!**, Classic Kettle **!!**)
Krinkle Sticks (Original **!!**, Sour Cream & Onion **!!**, White Cheddar**!!**)

Lowes Foods Brand - Cheese Crunchy, Cheese Puffs, Pork Rinds (BBQ, Hot, Regular)

Majans ▲ -
Bhuja (Cracker Mix, Crunchy Seasoned Peas, Fruit Mix, Nut Mix, Original Mix, Seasoned Almonds, Seasoned Cashews, Seasoned Peanuts)
Monsoon Chips (Hot & Spicy, Vinegar & Salt)

Manischewitz - Viennese Crunch

Mareblu Naturals ▲ -
Crunch Bags (Almond ●, Cashew ●, Cashew Coconut ●, CranMango Cashew ●, Dark Chocolate Almond ●, Pecan Cinnamon ●, Pecan Cranberry Cinnamon ●)
Crunch Bars (Almond ●, Cashew ●)
Trail Mix Crunch Bags (Blueberry Pomegranate ●, Cranberry Pomegranate ●, Cranblueberry ●, Cranstrawberry ●, Pecan ●, Pistachio ●)

Trail Mix Crunch Bars (BlueCran Pomegranate ●, Mango
Pomegranate ●, Pistachio ●, Strawberry Pomegranate ●)

Mariani - Cranberry Crunch **! !**, Yogurt Raisins **! !**

Mary's Gone Crackers ▲ - Sticks And Twigs Pretzels (Chipotle
Tomato ●, Curry ●, Sea Salt ●)

Meijer Brand - Snacks (Caramel Corn, Cheese (Popcorn, Pops, Puffs),
Cheezy Treats, Chicago Style Popcorn, Potato Sticks, Purple Cow
Butter Popcorn, White Cheddar (Popcorn, Puffs), Xtreme Snack
Bars)

Michael Season's -

Baked Cheese Curls (Cheddar ★, Hot Chili Pepper ★)

Baked Cheese Puffs (Cheddar ★, Jalapeno ★)

Baked White Cheddar Pops ★

Ultimate (Cheddar Cheese Curls ★, Cheddar Cheese Puffs ★,
White Cheddar Cheese Puffs ★)

Mini Pops ▲ - Popped Sorghum (Baby White Cheddar ●, Cutie
Caramel Clusters ●, Hot 'N Chilly Chili ●, Itsy Bitsy Chili Cheese ●,
Itty Bitty Butter ●, Nano Pepper & Herb ●, Petite Plain ●, Subatomic
Sea Salt ●)

Mrs. Crimble's - Cheese Bites (Original Cheese, Sour Cream &
Onion, Tomato Olive & Oregano), Slightly Salted Corn Cakes

Mrs. May's Naturals -

Almond Rice Stix (Cinnamon Cranberry ●, Cran Blueberry ●,
Mango Strawberry ●, Roasted Seaweed ●)

Crunch (Almond ●, Black Sesame ●, Cashew ●, Coconut Almond●,
Cran Blueberry ●, Cran Tropical ●, Pomegranate Raspberry ●,
Pumpkin ●, Strawberry Pineapple ●, Sunflower ●, Ultimate ●,
Walnut ●, White Sesame ●)

Sesame Strips (Acai Strawberry ●, Black Sesame ●, Goji
Cranberry●, Pomegranate Blueberry ●, White Sesame ●)

Munchos - Regular Potato Crisps **! !**

Natural Nectar - Choco Dream Rice Sticks, Cracklesnax (Potato
Squares, Shoestring Potato Sticks, Veggie Squares)

Navitas Naturals ▲ - Dried Yacon Slices, Power Snack Cacao Goji
Superfruit, Power Snack Superfood (Blueberry Hemp, Citrus Chia)

S

Nutland - Crunch (Almond ●, Berries & Cherries ●, Cashew ●, Pecan ●, Pistachio ●, Trail Mix ●)

Nuts.com - Organic Pecan Date Rolls ●, Organic Walnut Date Rolls ●, Raw Organic Cacao Beans ●, Soy Beans (Dry Roasted Halves ●, Hickory Smoked ●, Spicy BBQ ●), Turkish Delight (Almond ●, Mixed Nut ●, Pistachio ●)

Old Dutch -
Bac'N Puffs
Baked (Cheese Stix, Crunchy Curls)
Puffcorn (Caramel, Original)

Orgran ▲ - Choc Pockets, Crimpers (Original, Salt & Vinegar), Toasted Corn Dippers

Original Tings - Crunchy Corn Sticks

Oskri Organics - Honey Crunch (Almond, Cashew w/Cranberries, Pecan w/Raisins)

Pajeda's - Crunchy Cheese !

Paskesz - Diddles (Barbeque, Onion & Garlic)

Pirate's Booty - Baked Rice & Corn Puffs (Aged White Cheddar, Barrrrrbeque, Chocolate, New York Pizza, Sour Cream & Onion, Veggie)

Planters -
CarbWell (Caramel Chocolate Crunch Nut Bar, Peanut Butter Crunch Nut Bar)
Go Nuts (Peanut Bar Original, Peanuts (Dry Roasted, Honey Roasted, Salted), Smoky Bacon, Sunflower Kernels)
Trail Mix (Appalachian Blend, Fruit & Nut, Nut & Chocolate *(1.7 oz. Size Only)*, Nuts Seeds & Raisins)

Popcorners - Popped Corn Chips (Butter, Caramel, Cheesy Jalapeno, Kettle, Sea Salt, White Cheddar)

Post - Cocoa Pebbles Snack Bar, Fruity Pebbles Snack Bar

Pro Bites - Protein On the Go (Chili Nacho ●, French Toast ●)

Publix - Crunchy Cheese Curls, Crunchy Cheese Puffs, Mini Rice Cakes (Caramel !, Cheddar !, Ranch)

Pure Market Express ▲ - Bacon Jalapeno Poppers ●, Pepperoni Bites ●, Spicy Pepitos ●

Ricepod - Chili Mix, Wasabi Mix

Roland - Feng Shui Roasted Chestnuts, Hot Wasabi Green Peas, Maki Rolls, Roasted & Salted Edamame

Russo's Gluten Free Gourmet ▲ - Mozzarella Sticks

Schar ▲ - Cheese Bites

Seapoint Farms - Roasted Edamame Blends (Berry **!**, Sunshine **!**)

Sensible Foods - Organic (Crunch Dried Soy Nuts, Crunch Dried Sweet Corn)

Sharkies ▲ -
Kids Omega 3 Smart Twists (Berry Surf, Tropical Wave)
Kids Organic Fruit Chews (Berry Bites, Fruit Splash)
Kids Sports Chews (Berry Blasters, Tropical Splash)
Organic Sports Chews (Berry Blast, Citrus Squeeze, Fruit Splash, Watermelon Scream)

Smart Puffs - Real Wisconsin Cheddar Baked Cheese Puffs

Smartfood -
Popcorn (Kettle Corn **!!**, Movie Theater Butter **!!**)
White Cheddar Cheese Flavored Popcorn (Reduced Fat **!!**, Regular **!!**)

Snackwell's - Popcorn (Cinnamon Creme Drizzle Caramel **!!**, White Fudge Drizzle Caramel **!!**)

Snikiddy -
All Natural Baked Fries (Barbeque, Bold Buffalo, Cheddar Cheese, Classic Ketchup, Original, Sea Salt, Southwest Cheddar)
Puffs (Grilled Cheese, Mac 'N Cheese)

Snyder's Of Hanover - Eat Smart Naturals White Cheddar Multigrain Cheese Puffs ●, Gluten Free Pretzel Sticks ●

Spartan Brand - Fruit Snacks (Curious George, Dinosaurs, Star Wars, Variety Pack)

Sunbelt - Fruit Jammers, Gummy Bears

The Good Bean - Roasted Chickpea Snacks (Cracked Pepper, Sea Salt, Smoky Chili & Lime, Sweet Cinnamon)

Tings - Original

S

Trader Joe's - Buccaneer Joes White Cheddar Corn Puffs, Crunchy Curls **! !**, Green Bean Snacks **! !**, Reduced Fat Cheese Crunchies **! !**, Sea Salt & Pepper Rice Crisps **! !**, White Corn Tortilla Strips **! !**

UTZ -
Cheese Balls (Baked, Hot Cheese)
Cheese Crunchies (Hot, Regular)
Cheese Curls (Baked, Hot Cheese, White Cheddar)
Cheese Twists
Popcorn (Butter, Caramel w/Peanuts, Cheese, White Cheddar)
Potato Stix
Puff 'N Corn (Caramel, Cheese, Original)
Rice Crisps (Garden Salsa, Sea Salt, Sweet Chili, Sweet Potato)

Wise -
Cheez Doodles (Cheez Balls, Crunchy, Puffed, White Cheddar Puffed)
Doodle O's
Hot Flavored Onion Rings
Nacho Twisters
Onion Flavored Rings
Popcorn (Hot Cheese, Original Butter Flavored, Reduced Fat Butter Flavored, Reduced Fat White Cheddar Flavored, White Cheddar Flavored, Wise $2 Price Cheese)

Woodstock Farms -
Organic Snack Mixes (Campfire Trail, Cranberry Walnut Cashew, Goji Berry Power, Trail Mix)
Snack Mixes (California Supreme, Cape Cod Cranberry, Cascade Trail Mix, Choco Cranberry Crunch, Chocolate Cherry Munch, Cranberrys Cove, Enchanted Trail, Gourmet Trail, In The Raw, Mocha Madness, On The Trail)

Yogavive ▲ - Apple Chips (Apple Cinnamon ●, Caramel ●, Original ●, Peach ●, Strawberry ●)

Soda Pop/Carbonated Beverages
7up - All Varieties
A & W - Root Beer

soda pop/carbonated beverages

Aquafina - FlavorSplash (Grape, Lemon, Peach Mango, Raspberry, Strawberry Kiwi, Wild Berry)

Barq's Root Beer - Caffeine Free, Diet, Diet French Vanilla Creme Soda, Diet Red Creme Soda, French Vanilla Creme Soda, Red Creme Soda, Regular

Blue Sky - All Soda Varieties **!**

Boylan Bottleworks - Birch Beer (Creamy Red, Diet, Original), Black Cherry, Creme, Diet (Black Cherry, Cane Cola, Creme, Root Beer), Ginger Ale, Grape, Natural (Black Cherry, Cane Cola, Creme Vanilla, Root Beer), Orange, Orange Creme, Root Beer, Seltzer (Lemon, Orange, Pure), Sugar Cane Cola

Canada Dry - Club Soda (All Varieties), Ginger Ale (Cranberry, Diet, Regular), Seltzer (All Varieties), Tonic Water (All Varieties)

Carver's - Ginger Ale

Cascal - Fermented Soda (Berry Cassis, Bright Citrus, Crisp White, Fresh Tropical, Ripe Rouge)

Clear American (Wal-Mart) - Sparkling Water (Black Cherry, Golden Peach, Key Lime, Lemon, Mandarin Orange, Pomegranate Blueberry Acai, Raspberry Apple, Strawberry, White Grape, Wild Cherry)

Coca-Cola -
  Cherry Coke (Diet, Regular, Zero)
  Classic Coke (Caffeine Free, Regular, w/Lime, Zero)
  Diet Coke (Caffeine Free, Regular, w/Lime, w/Splenda)
  Vanilla Coke (Diet, Regular, Zero)

Crush - Cherry, Grape, Orange, Strawberry

Diet Rite - All Varieties

Dr. Pepper - All Varieties

Dry - Soda (Juniper Berry, Kumquat, Lavendar, Lemongrass, Rhubarb, Vanilla Bean)

Fanta - Apple, Grape, Grapefruit, Orange (Regular, Zero), Peach, Pineapple, Strawberry

Fiesta Mirinda - Mango, Pina

Food Club Brand - Club Soda, Cola (Diet, Regular), Ginger Ale, Grape, Lemon Lime, Orange, Root Beer, Strawberry

S

Fresca - Black Cherry, Original, Peach

Great Value Brand (Wal-Mart) - Low Sodium Club Soda, Sodium Free
Seltzer, Tonic Water (Calorie Free, Regular)

Guayaki - All Sparkling Teas

Hannaford Brand - Seltzer Water

Hansen's - All Sodas

Hires - Root Beer

Hy-Vee -

Cherry Cola

Club Soda

Cola (Diet, Regular)

Cream Soda

Dr. Hy Vee (Diet, Regular)

Fruit Punch Regular

Gingerale

Grape

Hee Haw (Diet, Regular)

Lemon Lime

Orange (Diet, Regular)

Root Beer (Diet, Regular)

Seltzer Water

Sour

Strawberry

Tonic Water

Water Cooler (Black Cherry, Key Lime, Kiwi Strawberry, Mixed Berry,
Peach, Peach Melba, Raspberry, Strawberry, White Grape)

I.B.C. - Root Beer

Inca Kola - Diet, Regular

Kas Mas

Manzanita Sol

Meijer Brand -

Cola (Cherry, Diet, Diet Red, Original)

Cranberry (Diet, Lemonade, Soda)

Cream Soda (Diet, Organic (Lemon Lime, Orange, Original), Original)

Dr M (Cherry Vanilla, Cherry Vanilla Diet, Diet, Original)

S

Encore (Blue (Diet, Original), Cola (Cherry, Diet Cherry, Original), Diet Cherry, Red (Cherry, Diet, Diet Caffeine Free, Original, Zero))

Fruit Punch

Ginger Ale

Grape (Diet, Soda)

Grapefruit

Lemon Lime

Lemonade

Lemonade Lime Diet

Orange (Diet, Soda)

Red Pop

Rocky Mist (Diet, Original)

Root Beer (Diet, Organic, Original)

Mello Yello - Original

Mountain Dew -

Caffeine Free (Diet, Regular)

Code Red (Diet, Regular)

Diet (Regular, Supernova)

Game Fuel (Citrus Cherry, Tropical)

Live Wire

Regular

Throwback

Voltage

White Out

Mug -

Cream Soda (Diet, Regular)

Root Beer (Diet, Regular)

My Essentials - All Soda Flavors

Northern Neck - Ginger Ale (Diet, Regular)

Olde Brooklyn - All Flavors

Orangina - Sparkling Citrus Beverage

Patio - Gingerale, Quinine Tonic

S

Pepsi -
    Caffeine Free Pepsi (Diet, Regular)
    Cherry Vanilla
    Lime (Diet, Regular)
    Made In Mexico
    Max
    Natural
    Next
    One
    Pepsi (Diet, Regular)
    Throwback
    Vanilla Diet
    Wild Cherry (Diet, Regular)

Pibb - Xtra, Zero

Publix - Black Cherry Soda, Cherry Cola, Citrus Hit Soda, Club Soda, Cola Regular, Cream Soda, Diet (Cola, Ginger Ale, Tonic Water), Diet Orange, Dr. Publix, Fruit Punch, Ginger Ale, Grape Soda, Lemon Lime Seltzer, Lemon Lime Soda, Mountain Splash, Orange Soda, Raspberry Seltzer, Root Beer, Tonic Water

RC Cola - All Varieties

Red Flash - Original

Reed's - Ginger Brew (Cherry, Extra, Original, Premium, Raspberry, Spiced Apple Cider)

Refreshe -
    Black Cherry
    Clear Sparkling Water (Cranberry Raspberry, Key Lime, Raspberry Blackberry, Strawberry Kiwi, Strawberry Watermelon, Tangerine Grapefruit, Tangerine Lime, Wild Cherry)
    Club Soda
    Cola (Diet, Regular)
    Cream Soda
    Dr. Dynamite
    Ginger Ale
    Grape

Italian Soda (Blood Orange, Cranberry Acai, Mixed Berry, Pink Grapefruit, Pomegranate, Tropical Blend)

Mountain Breeze

Orange (Diet, Regular)

Punch

Root Beer (Diet, Regular)

Sodas Punch

Strawberry

Safeway Select - Sodas All Varieties *(Except Punch)*

Santa Cruz ▲ - Organic Sparkling Beverages (All Varieties)

Schweppes - All Varieties

Sierra Mist - Cranberry Splash (Diet, Regular), Diet, Regular, Ruby Splash (Diet, Regular)

Sioux City - Soda (Birch Beer, Cream, Orange Cream, Root Beer, Sarsaparilla)

Sprecher - Sodas (All Flavors)

Sprite - Green, Regular, Zero

Squirt - All Varieties

Steaz - Diet Black Cherry, Organic (Key Lime, Orange, Raspberry, Root Beer)

Stewarts - Cream Soda, Grape, Key Lime, Orange Cream (Diet, Regular), Root Beer (Diet, Regular)

Sun Drop - Caffeine Free, Caffeine Free Diet, Cherry Lemon, Diet, Regular

Sunkist - Cherry Limeade, Diet Orange, Fruit Punch, Grape, Lemonade (Diet Sparkling, Sparkling), Orange, Peach, Pineapple, Strawberry

Tab - Original

Trader Joe's -

French Market Sparkling Beverages

Organic Sparkling Beverages (Grapefruit, Lemon)

Refreshers (Blueberry, Pomegranate, Tangerine)

Sparkling Juice Beverages (Apple Cider, Blueberry, Cranberry, Pomegranate)

Sparkling Water (All Flavors)

S

Tropicana Twister Soda - Grape, Orange (Diet, Regular), Strawberry

Vernors - Diet, Regular

Virgil's - Zero (Black Cherry Cream Soda, Cream Soda, Real Cola, Root Beer)

Wegmans Brand -

Aqua Mineral Water (Italian, Lemon, Lemongrass, Lime)

Frizzante European Soda (Blood Orange, Blueberry Lemon, Sicilian Lemon, Sour Cherry Lemon)

FYFGA Sparkling Beverage Tangerine Lime w/Sweeteners

FYFGA Sparkling Water (Lemon, Lime, Mandarin Orange, Mixed Berry, Natural, Raspberry, Tangerine)

Soda (Cherry Black, Club Soda, Cola (Caffeine Free, Caffeine Free Diet, Cherry, Diet, Regular), Cream Soda, Diet (Grapefruit, Lemon, Lime), Diet Wedge (Cherry Grapefruit, Grapefruit), Dr. W Cola (Diet, Regular), Fountain Root Beer (Diet, Regular), Ginger Ale (Diet, Regular), Grape Soda, Green Apple Sparkling Soda (Diet, Regular), Lime, Tonic (Diet, Regular), W UP (Diet, Regular))

Sparkling Beverage (Black Cherry Regular, Cranberry Blend, Cranberry Raspberry Regular, Key Lime, Mineral Water, Peach Grapefruit (Diet, Regular))

Welch's ▲ - All Varieties

White Rock - All Flavors

Winn Dixie - Soda (All Varieties), Sparkling Water (All Varieties)

Zevia - All Natural Soda (Cola, Ginger Ale, Lemon Lime Twist, Orange)

Sorbet

Double Rainbow - Chocolate **!!**, Coconut **!!**, Lemon **!!**, Mango Tangerine **!!**

Haagen-Dazs - Blackberry Cabernet, Chocolate, Mango, Orchard Peach, Raspberry, Strawberry, Zesty Lemon

Jolly Llama - Sorbet Squeeze Ups (Banana Coconut, Blueberry, Mango, Peach, Raspberry, Strawberry)

Pure Market Express ▲ - Cherry ●, Mango ●, Peach ●, Strawberry ●

Sambazon - All Natural Acai Berry

Trader Joe's - All Varieties

Wegmans Brand - Green Apple, Lemon, Raspberry

Sorghum

    Eden Organic - Organic Sweet

Soup

    A Taste Of Thai - Coconut Ginger Soup Base

    Abundant Life Foods ▲ - Soup Mix (Butternut Squash, Corn
        Chowder, Cream Of (Asparagus, Broccoli, Chicken Vegetable,
        Mushroom), Potato Leek, Tomato Basil)

    Amy's -

        Indian Dal Golden Lentil ★

        Organic

            Black Bean Vegetable ★

            Chunky Tomato Bisque (Light In Sodium ★, Regular ★)

            Chunky Vegetable ★

            Cream Of Tomato (Light In Sodium ★, Regular ★)

            Curried ★

            Fire Roasted Southwestern Vegetable ★

            Hearty (French Country Vegetable ★, Rustic Italian Vegetable ★,
                Spanish Rice & Red Bean ★)

            Lentil (Light In Sodium ★, Regular ★)

            Lentil Vegetable (Light In Sodium ★, Regular ★)

            Split Pea (Light In Sodium ★, Regular ★)

            Summer Corn & Vegetable ★

            Tuscan Bean & Rice ★

        Thai Coconut **!**

    Andean Dream ▲ - Quinoa Noodle (Tomato, Vegetarian)

    Augason Farms ▲ - Gluten Free Creamy Potato Mix ●, Gluten Free
        Vegetable Stew Blend ●

    Baxters -

        Chunky (Chicken & Vegetable Casserole, Country Vegetable,
        Smoked Bacon & Three Bean)

S

Deli Inspired (Red Lentil Dahl & Beechwood Smoked Bacon, Roast Tomato & Parmesan w/Smoked Garlic)

Favourites (Chicken Broth, Cock A Leekie, French Onion, Lentil & Bacon, Pea & Ham, Potato & Leek, Scotch Vegetable w/Lamb)

Healthy (Chicken & Vegetable, Puy Lentil & Tomato, Spicy Tomato & Rice w/Sweetcorn, Tomato & Brown Lentil)

Luxury (Beef Consomme, Lobster Bisque)

Vegetarian (Carrot & Butterbean, Country Garden, Mediterranean Tomato, Tomato & Butterbean)

Boulder Soup Works ▲ - Carrot Ginger w/Coconut ●, Garden Minestrone ●, Green Pea w/Dill ●, Potato Leek ●, Red Lentil Dahl ●, Roasted Tomato Basil ●, White Bean w/Tomato ●

Cookwell & Company - Cheese Enchilada, Hatch Verde Tortilla, Red Pepper & Tomato, Tomato Basil, Tortilla Soup

Cuisine Sante ▲ - Soup Mix (Sweet Corn ●, Tomato ●), White Roux Base For Soups & Sauces ●

Dinty Moore - Beef Stew, Chicken Stew

Dr. McDougall's -

Black Bean

Black Bean & Lime

Chunky Tomato

Lentil (Light Sodium, Regular)

Pad Thai Noodle

Roasted Pepper Tomato

Split Pea

Spring Onion Noodle

Tamale w/Baked Chips

Tortilla w/Baked Chips

Vegetable (Light Sodium, Regular)

Edward & Sons - Miso Cup (Japanese Restaurant Style, Organic Traditional w/Tofu, Original Golden Vegetable, Reduced Sodium, Savory w/Seaweed)

El Peto ▲ - Soup Concentrate (Beef, Chicken, Onion, Tomato, Tomato Vegetable, Vegetable)

Fischer & Wieser - Mom's Limited Edition Tomato Basil
Food Club Brand - Beef Stew
Frontera - Black Bean Tomato, Classic Tortilla, Roasted Tomato, Roasted Vegetable
Frontier Soups -
  Corn Chowder Mix (Florida Sunshine Red Pepper ★, Illinois Prairie ★)
  Soup Mix
    Carolina Springtime Asparagus Almond ★
    Chicago Bistro French Onion ★
    Connecticut Cottage Chicken Noodle ★
    Holiday Gathering Cranberry Bean ★
    Hungarian Goulash ★
    Idaho Outpost Potato Leek ★
    Indiana Harvest Sausage Lentil ★
    Louisiana Red Bean Gumbo ★
    Minnesota Heartland II Bean ★
    Mississippi Delta Tomato Basil ★
    Mississippi Homestead Garden Gazpacho ★
    Nebraska Barnraising Split Pea ★
    New Mexico Mesa Spicy Fiesta ★
    New Orleans Jambalaya ★
    New York Corner Cafe Minestrone ★
    Oregon Lakes Wild Rice & Mushroom ★
    San Francisco Thai Golden Peanut ★
    South Of The Border Tortilla ★
    Texas Wrangler Black Bean ★
    Virginia Blue Ridge Broccoli Cheddar ★
    Wisconsin Lakeshore Wild Rice ★
  Stew Mix (Colorado Campfire Chicken Stew ★, New England Seaport Fisherman's ★)
Full Flavor Foods ▲ -
  Soup Mix Cream ●
  Soup Stock Mix (Beef ●, Chicken ●)

S

Fungus Among Us - Organic Soup Mix (Moroccan Porcini & Green Lentil, Smoked Oyster Mushroom Chowder, Spicy Shiitake & Vegetable)

Gluten Free Cafe - Black Bean ●, Chicken Noodle ●, Cream Of Mushroom ●, Veggie Noodle ●

Grandma Ferdon's ▲ - Soup Mix (Cream ●, Onion ●)

H-E-B - Cheesy Chicken Enchilada, Pouch (Creamy Mushroom, Fall Harvest, Loaded Baked Potato, Poblano Corn Chowder)

Hill Country Fare H-E-B - Chicken Rice, Condensed Chicken & Rice

Hormel - Microwave (Bean & Ham, Chicken w/ Vegetable & Rice)

Hy-Vee - Onion

Imagine -

Organic Creamy

Acorn Squash & Mango

Broccoli

Butternut Squash

Corn & Lemongrass

Light In Sodium (Garden Broccoli, Garden Tomato, Harvest Corn, Red Bliss Potato & Roasted Garlic, Sweet Potato)

Portobello Mushroom

Potato Leek

Sweet Pea

Sweet Potato

Tomato

Tomato Basil

Kettle Cuisine -

Chicken w/Rice Noodles ●

Chili (Angus Beef Steak w/Beans ●, Chicken w/White Beans ●, Three Bean ●)

New England Clam Chowder ●

Organic Mushroom & Potato ●

Roasted Vegetable ●

Southwestern Chicken & Corn Chowder ●

Thai Curry Chicken ●

Tomato w/Garden Vegetables ●

Kirkland Signature - Stock Pot (Chicken Tortilla Soup Especial, Loaded Baked Potato)

Lowes Foods Brand - Chicken & Wild Rice, New England Style Clam Chowder

Manischewitz - Borscht

Medifast - Chicken & Wild Rice ●, Maryland Crab ●

Meijer Brand - Condensed Chicken w/Rice, Homestyle Chicken w/ Rice

Mixes From The Heartland ▲ - Soup Mix (Beer Cheese ●, Broccoli & Cheese ●, Cajun Bean ●, Cajun Pastalaya ●, Cheeseburger Chowder ●, Chicken Veggie ●, Corn Chowder ●, Cowboy ●, Cream Of (Broccoli ●, Celery ●, Mushroom ●), Green Chili Hamburger ●, Green Chili Stew ●, Hamburger Pasta ●, Harvest Chicken & Rice ●, Italian Bean ●, Minestrone ●, Navy Bean ●, Pasta Veggie ●, Potato ●, Southwest Chicken Stew ●, Tex Mex Pasta ●, Texas Sausage & Bean ●, Tortilla Pasta ●, Wild Rice & Mushroom ●)

Nueva Cocina - Chipotle Black Bean, Cuban Style Black Bean, Latin Lentil, Red Bean, Spanish Style White Bean, Sweet Corn w/Green Chiles

O Organics - Butternut Squash, Lentil, Southwest Blackbean

Orgran ▲ - Tomato Soup Mix For Cup

Ortega - Soup Mix (Black Bean, Tortilla Soup)

Pacific Natural Foods -
> All Natural (Rosemary Potato Chowder, Thai Sweet Potato)
> All Natural Frozen Chipotle Sweet Potato
> Cashew Carrot Ginger
> Condensed Organic Cream Of (Celery, Chicken, Mushroom)
> Curried Red Lentil
> Organic (French Onion, Roasted Red Pepper & Tomato (Light Sodium, Regular))
> Organic Bisque (Butternut Squash, Cashew Carrot Ginger, Hearty Tomato, Roasted Red Pepper & Tomato)
> Organic Chicken (& Wild Rice, Santa Fe Style)

Organic Creamy (Butternut Squash, Light Sodium (Butternut Squash, Tomato), Tomato)

Soup Starter Organic (Beef Pho, Chicken Pho, Tom Yum, Tortilla, Vegetarian Pho)

Spicy Black Bean

Progresso -

High Fiber Chicken Tuscany

Reduced Sodium Garden Vegetable

Rich & Hearty (Chicken Corn Chowder Flavored w/Bacon, New England Clam Chowder)

Traditional (99% Fat Free New England Clam Chowder, Chicken Cheese Enchilada Flavor, Chicken Rice w/Vegetables, Manhattan Clam Chowder, New England Clam Chowder, Potato Broccoli & Cheese Chowder, Southwestern Style Chicken, Split Pea w/Ham)

Vegetable Classics (99% Fat Free Lentil, Creamy Mushroom, French Onion, Garden Vegetable, Hearty Black Bean Flavored w/Bacon, Lentil)

Pure Market Express ▲ - Corn Chowder ●, French Onion ●, Spicy Cilantro Soup ●, Tomato Herb ●, Tzatziki ●, Watermelon ●

Really Great Food Company ▲ - Black Bean, Golden Pea, Split Pea, Sweet Corn Chowder

Safeway Brand - Onion Soup Mix

Safeway Select - Signature Soups (Autumn Harvest Butternut Squash, Baked Potato Soup w/Bacon, Fiesta Chicken Tortilla, Rosemary Chicken & White Bean)

Sharwood's - Tarka Dahl

Signature Cafe - Coconut & Red Curry Chicken, Roasted Red Pepper & Crab Bisque

Simply Asia - Rice Noodle Soup Bowl (Garlic Sesame, Sesame Chicken, Spring Vegetable)

StoreHouse Foods - Chunky Corn Chowder, Creamy Broccoli Cheddar Cheese, Creamy Potato Cheddar Soup

Tabatchnick -
Frozen (Balsamic Tomato & Rice, Black Bean, Cabbage, Cream Of Broccoli, Cream Of Spinach, Creamed Spinach, New England Potato, Old Fashioned Potato, Southwest Bean, Split Pea, Split Pea Low Sodium, Thick & Creamy Corn Chowder, Tuscany Lentil, Wilderness Wild Rice, Yankee Bean)
Microwavable Bowl (Balsamic Tomato & Rice, Southwest Bean, Split Pea)
Shelf Stable (Cream Of Mushroom, Creamy Tomato, Roasted Red Pepper & Tomato, Wisconsin Cheddar Cheese)

Thai Kitchen -
Instant Rice Noodle Soup (Bangkok Curry, Garlic & Vegetable, Lemongrass & Chili, Spring Onion, Thai Ginger)
Rice Noodle Soup Bowl (Lemongrass & Chili, Roasted Garlic, Spring Onion, Thai Ginger)

Trader Joe's -
Organic (Black Bean !!, Butternut Squash !!, Creamy Corn & Roasted Red Pepper (Low Sodium, Regular !!), Creamy Tomato, Lentil Soup w/Vegetables !!, Split Pea !!, Sweet Potato Bisque, Tomato & Roasted Red Pepper !!, Tomato Bisque !!)
Regular (Carrot Ginger !!, Corn & Roasted Red Pepper !!, Instant Rice Noodle Soup (Mushroom, Roasted Garlic, Spring Onion), Latin Black Bean, Miso 4 Pack, Sweet Potato Bisque !!)

Wegmans Brand - FYFGA (Broccoli & Vermont White Cheddar, Caribean Black Bean, Moroccan Lentil w/Chick Pea, Spicy Red Lentil Chili), Gazpacho, Lobster Bisque

Westbrae - Instant White Miso

Wolfgang Puck - Organic (Black Bean, Free Range Chicken w/White & Wild Rice, Hearty Lentil Vegetable, Signature Butternut Squash, Signature Tortilla, Tomato Basil Bisque)

Sour Cream
Alouette - Creme Fraiche
Breakstone's - All Natural, Fat Free, Reduced Fat
Cabot - Light, No Fat, Regular

S

Cascade Fresh
Daisy Brand - All Varieties
Follow Your Heart - Vegan Gourmet !
Food Club Brand - Light, Non Fat, Regular
Friendship - All Varieties
Hannaford Brand - All Varieties
Hood - All Varieties
Horizon Organic - All Varieties
Hy-Vee - Light, Regular
Kemps - All Varieties
Knudsen - All Varieties
Lowes Foods Brand - Lite, Non Fat, Regular
Lucerne - Light, Non Fat, Regular
Nancy's - All Cultured Dairy & Soy Products
O Organics
Open Nature
Organic Valley - Low Fat, Regular
Prairie Farms - Fat Free, Light, Regular
Publix - Fat Free, Light, Regular
Pure Market Express ▲ - Vegan ●
Shamrock Farms - Light, Organic, Traditional
Spartan Brand - Low Fat, Regular
Tillamook - All Varieties !
Trader Joe's - All Varieties
Wayfare - We Can't Say It's Sour Cream Original ●
Wegmans Brand - Fat Free, FYFGA (Light, Regular)
Winn Dixie - Fat Free, Light, Regular

Soy Beverage/Soy Milk

8th Continent Soymilk - Complete Vanilla, Fat Free (Original, Vanilla), Light (Chocolate, Original, Vanilla), Original, Vanilla
Earth Balance - Soymilk (Chocolate, Original, Unsweetened, Vanilla)
Eden Organic - Eden Organic (Blend, Soy Unsweetened)
El Peto ▲ - Soya Milk Powder

Great Value Brand (Wal-Mart) - Light Vanilla, Original (Chocolate, Plain, Vanilla)

H-E-B - Light Soy Milk (Plain, Vanilla), Soy Milk (Chocolate, Plain, Vanilla)

Kirkland Signature - Organic (Plain, Vanilla)

Meijer Brand - Soymilk (Chocolate, Organic, Vanilla)

Nature's Place - Regular (Refrigerated, Shelf Stable)

O Organics - Soy Milk

Organic Valley - Chocolate, Original, Soy Creamer (French Vanilla, Original), Unsweetened, Vanilla

Pacific Natural Foods - All Varieties

Publix GreenWise Market - Light (Plain, Vanilla), Organic Soy Milk (Chocolate, Plain, Vanilla)

Silk Soymilk - All Varieties

Soy Dream -
  Refrigerated Non Dairy Soymilk
    Classic Original
    Enriched (Original, Vanilla)
  Shelf Stable Non Dairy Soymilk
    Classic Vanilla
    Enriched (Chocolate, Original, Vanilla)

Sunrise - Soya Beverage (Light Fortified Sweetened, Organic Unsweetened, Sweetened, Unsweetened)

Trader Joe's - All Soy Beverages **!!**

Vitasoy ▲ - Soymilk (Holly Nog, Peppermint Chocolate)

Wegmans Brand - Organic FYFGA (Original, Vanilla)

Westsoy -
  Organic Soy Milk Original
  Organic Unsweetened Soy Milk (Almond, Chocolate, Original, Vanilla)
  Soy Milk
    Lite (Plain, Vanilla)
    Low Fat (Plain, Vanilla)
    Non Fat (Plain, Vanilla)
    Plus (Plain, Vanilla)

S

Wildwood - Organic All Varieties

ZenSoy - All Varieties (Soy Milk, Soy On The Go)

Soy Burgers...see Burgers

Soy Lecithin

Bob's Red Mill ▲ - Granules ★

Soy Sauce

Eden Organic - Organic Tamari Soy Sauce (Naturally Brewed,
Traditionally Brewed)

Food Club Brand

Hannaford Brand - Light, Regular

Hy-Vee - Light, Regular

Kari-Out Company - Panda Brand Low Sodium Soy Sauce Packets

King Soba - Tamari

Lowes Foods Brand - Light, Regular

San-J -

Organic (Reduced Sodium Tamari Gluten Free Soy Sauce ●,
Tamari Gluten Free Soy Sauce ●)

Tamari Gluten Free Soy Sauce (Original ●, Reduced Sodium ●)

Spartan Brand - Less Sodium, Original

Wan Ja Shan - Organic Gluten Free Tamari (Less Sodium, Regular)

Soy Yogurt...see Yogurt

Soymilk...see Soy Beverage/Soy Milk

Spaghetti... see Pasta

Spaghetti Sauce...see Sauces

Spices...see Seasonings

Spinach

... *All Fresh Fruits & Vegetables Are Gluten-Free*

Birds Eye - All Plain Frozen Vegetables

C & W - All Plain Frozen Vegetables !!

Del Monte - Leaf/Chopped

Dr. Praeger's - Spinach Littles !

Food Club Brand - Canned, Frozen (Leaf, Spinach (Chopped, Cut Leaf))

Freshlike - Frozen Plain Spinach

Great Value Brand (Wal-Mart) - Canned Whole Leaf Spinach

Green Giant - Frozen Creamed Spinach w/Artificial Cream Flavor

Hannaford Brand - Whole Leaf

Hy-Vee - Canned, Frozen (Chopped, Leaf)

Lowes Foods Brand - Frozen (Chopped, Leaf)

Meijer Brand -
Canned (Cut Leaf, No Salt, Regular)
Frozen (Chopped, Chopped Organic, Cut Leaf, Leaf, Regular)

Nuts.com - Simply Spinach Freeze Dried Vegetables ●

O Organics - Chopped Frozen

Pictsweet - All Plain Frozen Vegetables

Publix - Canned, Frozen (Chopped, Cut Leaf, Leaf)

Publix GreenWise Market - Organic (Baby Spinach Salad, Spinach)

S&W - All Canned Vegetables

Safeway Brand - Canned Leaf, Frozen Chopped

Signature Cafe - Side Dish Savory Asiago Creamed Spinach

Spartan Brand - Canned Cut Leaf, Frozen (Chopped, Cut, Leaf)

Tabatchnick - Frozen Creamed Spinach

Tasty Bite - Kashmir Spinach !, Spinach Dal !

Trader Joe's - Frozen Organic Chopped

Wegmans Brand - Frozen (FYFGA (Chopped, Cut Leaf), In Cream Sauce, Whole Leaf)

Winn Dixie - Canned (No Salt Added, Regular), Frozen (Chopped, Cut Leaf)

Woodstock Farms - Organic Frozen (Chopped, Cut)

Sports Drinks

Gatorade -
G Series Perform 02
G Powder (Fruit Punch, Grape, Lemon Lime, Orange)
G2 Lo Cal (Blueberry Pomegranate, Fruit Punch, Glacier Freeze, Grape, Lemon Lime, Orange)
G2 Powder Packets (Fruit Punch, Grape)
Original G (Berry, Cool Blue, Frost Glacier Freeze, Frost Riptide Rush, Fruit Punch, Grape, Lemon Lime, Lemonade, Orange, Raspberry Melon, Strawberry Watermelon, Tropical Blend)

S

    G Series Prime 01 (Berry, Fruit Punch, Orange)

    G Series PRO (01 Prime, 02 Perform, 03 Recover)

    G Series Recover 03 (Lemon Lime Orange, Mixed Berry)

    G2 Natural (Berry, Orange Citrus)

    Recover 03 (All Flavors)

Meijer Brand - Drink Thirst Quencher (Fruit Punch, Lemon Lime, Orange)

Powerade -

    Ion 4 (Fruit Punch, Grape, Lemon Lime, Mountain Berry Blast, Orange, Sour Melon, Strawberry Lemonade, White Cherry)

    Zero (Fruit Punch, Grape, Lemon Lime, Mixed Berry, Orange, Strawberry)

Wegmans Brand - MVP Sport Drink (Blue Freeze, Fruit Punch, Grape, Lemon Lime, Raspberry Lemonade)

Spread

Alouette - Soft Spreadable Cheese (Garlic & Herbs, Light (Garlic & Herbs, Spinach Artichoke), Pepper Medley, Savory Vegetable, Spinach Artichoke, Sundried Tomato & Basil)

Benecol - Light, Regular

Bett's - Cheese Spread (Blue Cheese'N Herbs, Cheddar & Horseradish Spread, Chesapeake Crab, Herbs'N Spices, Hot 'N Tangy Buffalo Style, Smoked Salmon & Chives)

Blue Bonnet - All Spreads

Canoleo - 100% Canola Margarine

Cantare - Olive Tapenade (Traditional, w/Crumbled Goat Cheese Feta)

Copper Cowbell - Asiago Cheese

Country Crock - All Spreads

Dietz & Watson ▲ - Jalapeno ●, Muffuletta Mix ●, Sandwich Spread ●

Dorothy Lane Market - Asiago Roasted Garlic, BLT, Cheddar Pimento, Danish Gouda & Nut, Emerald Pub, Scallion Cream Cheese, Smoked Salmon, Sun Dried Tomato, Three Italian Cheese

Earth Balance -

    Natural Buttery Spread (Olive Oil, Original, Soy Free, Soy Garden)

    Natural Shortening

    Organic Buttery Spread Original Whipped

    Vegan Buttery Sticks

Eden Organic - Butter (Apple, Apple Cherry, Cherry)

Food Club Brand - Margarine Spread

Gordon Food Service - Margarine Whipped

Great Value Brand (Wal-Mart) - Buttery Spread, Margarine (Buttery Spread, Cardio Choice, I Totally Thought It Was Butter, Regular)

H-E-B - Feta Spread (Herb & Onion, Spicy Tomato)

Hy-Vee - 100% Corn Oil Margarine, Best Thing Since Butter, Soft Margarine (Regular, Rich & Creamy), Soft Spread, Vegetable Margarine Quarters

I Can't Believe It's Not Butter - All Varieties

Jet-Puffed - Marshmallow Creme

Kraft - Cheez Whiz Original

Kroger Brand - Churngold Spread, Value Spread

Land-O-Lakes -
  Butter w/Olive Oil
  Fresh Buttery Taste
  Garlic Butter
  Honey Butter
  Margarine
  Salted Butter
  Spreadable Butter w/Canola Oil
  Unsalted Butter
  Whipped (Salted Butter, Unsalted Butter)

Lawry's - Garlic Spread **!!**

Lowes Foods Brand - Margarine (Patties, Quarters, Soft 1 lb., Spread, Squeeze)

Manischewitz - Apple Butter Spread

Marmite - Flavored Yeast Extract

Meijer Brand -
  Margarine Corn Oil Quarters
  Margarine Soft (Sleeve, Tub)
  Spread (48% Crock, 70% Quarters, No Ifs Ands Or Butter, Tub)

Mezzetta ▲ - Sandwich Spread (Chimichurri, Jalapeno, Jalapeno w/Mexican Style Cheese, Kalamata Olive, Mediterranean Olive,

S

Peperoncini & Feta, Roasted Red Bell Pepper & Chipotle, Sun Dried Tomato)

Move Over Butter - All Spreads

Odell's - Clarified Butter

Olivio - Butter Spread (Light, Original), Spreadable (Coconut Spread, Light, Regular)

Organic Farming - Nocciolata

Parkay - All Flavors

Peloponnese - Baba Ganoush, Eggplant Meze, Eggplant Spread, Kalamata Olive Spread, Sweet Pepper Spread

Polaner ▲ - All Varieties

Publix - Homestyle Spread 48% Vegetable Oil, Original Spread Quarters 70% Vegetable Oil

Sabra - Classic Tahini Spread

Smart Balance -

Buttery Spread

Extra Virgin Olive Oil

Light (Extra Virgin Olive Oil, Heart Right, Omega 3, Original, Original w/Flax)

Omega 3

Organic Certified

Original (Regular, w/Flax)

w/Calcium

Whipped Low Sodium Lightly Salted

Spartan Brand - 48% Spread, 70% Quarters Spread, Butter, Is It Butter 70% Spread, Margarine Soft Tub, Unsalted

Tartex -

Champignon

Chardonnay Cote D'Or

Cremisso (Horseradish Apple, Peppers Chili, Tomato Basil, Zucchini Curry)

Delicacy

Exquisite

Green Pepper

Herbs
Hungarian
Mediterrana
Mexicana
Olivera
Organic Pate In Tubes (Chilli, Classic, Green Olive, Herb, Herb & Garlic, Mushroom, Roasted Onion & Pink Peppercorn, Sundried Tomato)
Pate (Chanterelle Mushroom, Grilled Aubergine, Porcini Mushrooms & Cranberry)
Pate Creme (Rocket & Mustard, Sundried Tomato & Vandouvan)
Pesto
Pomodoro D'Italia
Provence Herbs
Ratatouille
Shiitake
Truffle Champagne
The Ginger People - Ginger Spread **!**
Trader Joe's - Artichoke Red Pepper Tapenade **!!**, Eggplant Garlic Spread, Lemon Curd, Olive Green Tapenade **!!**, Red Pepper Spread w/Garlic & Eggplant
Underwood - Deviled Ham Spread
Walden Farms - Spreads (Apple Butter, Apricot, Blueberry, Grape, Orange, Raspberry, Strawberry)
Wegmans Brand - Vegetable Oil Margarine Spread
Wildwood - Aioli Zesty Garlic
Willow Run - Soybean Margarine
Sprinkles...see Baking Decorations & Frostings
Squash
... *All Fresh Fruits & Vegetables Are Gluten-Free*
C & W - All Plain Frozen Vegetables **!!**
Meijer Brand - Frozen Squash Cooked (Regular, Winter)
Pictsweet - All Plain Frozen Vegetables, Cracked Pepper Seasoned Okra & Squash

S

Publix - Frozen (Cooked Squash, Yellow Sliced)

Winn Dixie - Frozen Yellow

Starch

AgVantage Naturals ▲ - Tapioca ●

Argo - Corn

Augason Farms ▲ - Gluten Free (Potato Starch ●, Tapioca Flour ●),
    Gluten Free Ultimate Gel ●

Bob's Red Mill ▲ - Arrowroot ★, Corn ★, Potato ★

Cause You're Special ▲ - Corn Starch, Potato Starch, Tapioca

Clabber Girl - Corn !

El Peto ▲ - Arrowroot, Corn, Potato

Ener-G ▲ - Potato

Expandex ▲ - Modified Tapioca Starch ●

Gifts Of Nature ▲ - Expandex Modified Tapioca Starch ●, Potato ●

Gillian's Foods ▲ - Potato ●

Grandma Ferdon's ▲ - Corn Starch ●, Potato ●, Tapioca ●

Hannaford Brand - Corn

Hearth Club - Corn

Hill Country Fare H-E-B - Corn

Hol Grain ▲ - 100% Rice Starch ●

Hy-Vee - Corn

Kingsford - Corn

Let's Do...Organic - Organic (Cornstarch, Tapioca)

Manischewitz - Potato

Meijer Brand - Corn

Nuts.com - Gluten Free Corn Starch ●, Potato Starch ●

Really Great Food Company ▲ - Potato, Tapioca

Red Leaf - Potato

Rumford - Corn !

Safeway Brand - Corn

Spartan Brand - Corn

Tate & Lyle - Corn, Tapioca

Steak...see Beef

   ... *All Fresh Cut Meat Is Gluten-Free (Non-Marinated, Unseasoned)*

Steak Sauce

    A.l. - Bold & Spicy w/Tabasco, Carb Well, Cracked Peppercorn, Regular Steak Sauce, Smoky Mesquite, Supreme Garlic, Sweet Hickory, Teriyaki, Thick & Hearty

    Fischer & Wieser - Traditional Steak & Grilling Sauce

    Food Club Brand - Regular

    Hannaford Brand

    Heinz - Traditional

    Hy-Vee - Classic, Vidalia Onion

    Jack Daniel's - Original, Smokey

    Jim Beam - Original Steak Sauce

    Kurtz - Original

    Lea & Perrins - Traditional

    Lowes Foods Brand - Regular

    Meijer Brand

    Mr. Spice Organic - Garlic Steak ★

    Safeway Brand - Bold, Original

    Spartan Brand - Original

Stew

    Dinty Moore - Beef, Chicken, Compleats Microwave Meals Beef

Stir Fry Sauce

    Mr. Spice Organic - Ginger Stir Fry Sauce & Marinade ★

Stir Fry Vegetables

    Amy's - Asian Noodle Stir Fry ★, Thai Stir Fry ★

    C & W - The Ultimate Asian Blend ‼, The Ultimate Early Harvest Blend ‼, The Ultimate Southwest Blend ‼, The Ultimate Stir Fry‼

    Lowes Foods Brand - Peking Stir Fry

    Meijer Brand - Frozen Vegetable Stir Fry

    Wegmans Brand - FYFGA (Asian, Far East, Hong Kong)

Stock

    Cuisine Sante ▲ - Beef Flavored ●, Chicken Flavored ●, Low Sodium (Beef Flavored ●, Chicken Flavored ●), Vegetable ●

    Emeril's - Beef, Chicken, Organic Vegetable

S

Full Flavor Foods ▲ - Soup Stock Mix (Beef ●, Chicken ●)

Imagine - Organic Cooking Stock (Beef, Chicken, Low Sodium Beef, Vegetable)

Kirkland Signature - Chicken (Organic, Regular)

Kitchen Basics ▲ -
Original (Beef, Chicken, Clam, Ham, Pork, Seafood, Turkey, Veal)
Unsalted (Beef, Chicken, Vegetable)

Massel -
Perfect Stock Powder (Beef Style, Chicken Style, Vegetable Style)
Stock Powder (Beef Style, Chicken Style, Vegetable Style)

Swanson - Beef Carton, Chicken Carton

Wegmans Brand - FYFGA Culinary Stock (Beef Flavored, Chicken, Thai, Vegetable)

Wolfgang Puck - All Natural Chicken

Strawberries

*... *All Fresh Fruits & Vegetables Are Gluten-Free*

Annie's - Organic Orchard Real Fruit Bites Strawberry !!

Augason Farms ▲ - Gluten Free Freeze Dried Whole ●

C & W - All Plain Frozen Fruits !!

Food Club Brand - Frozen (Sliced, Whole)

Full Circle - Organic Whole Strawberries

Great Value Brand (Wal-Mart) - Frozen (Sliced w/Sugar, Whole)

Hill Country Fare H-E-B - Frozen Strawberries (In Syrup, w/Cream)

Hy-Vee - Frozen (Sliced, w/Sugar, Whole)

KatySweet ▲ - Chocolate Dipped ●

Kirkland Signature - Frozen Whole

Lowes Foods Brand - Frozen (Sliced (Lite, w/Sugar), Whole)

Mariani - Dried !!

Meijer Brand - Frozen (Organic, Sliced), Whole Individually Quick Frozen

Nuts.com - Dried ●, Natural Dried Juice Infused ●, Organic Simply ●, Organic ●, Simply Whole ●, Simply ●

O Organics - Whole

Oskri Organics - Dried Strawberries

Publix - Frozen (Sliced, Sweetened, Whole)
Safeway Brand - Frozen (Sliced w/Sugar, Sliced w/Sweetener, Whole)
Spartan Brand - Frozen (Sliced In Sugar, Whole)
Trader Joe's - Frozen (Grade A Fancy, Organic)
Wegmans Brand - Frozen (Sliced (Light, w/Sugar), Whole)
Winn Dixie - Frozen (Sugar Whole, Sweetener, Whole)
Woodstock Farms - Organic Frozen Whole Strawberries

Strudel
Celiac Specialties ▲ - Apple, Blueberry, Cherry

Stuffing
Aleia's ▲ - Plain ●, Savory ●
Andrea's Gluten Free ▲ - Herb Stuffing Bread
Apple's Bakery ▲ - Gluten Free Stuffing Cubes
Celiac Specialties ▲ - Stuffing Mix
Deerfields Gluten Free Bakery ▲ - Stuffing Cubes
El Peto ▲ - Stuffing
Gillian's Foods ▲ - Gluten Free Stuffing ●
Grandma Ferdon's ▲ - Sage Dressing ●
Mixes From The Heartland ▲ - Cornbread Stuffing Mix ●
Mrs. Crimble's - Stuffing Mix
Sweet Christine's Bakery - Gluten Free Bread Cubes ●
Three Bakers ▲ - Herb Seasoned Whole Grain Cubed Stuffing
West Meadow Farm Bakery - Stuffing Mix ●
Whole Foods Market Gluten Free Bakehouse ▲ - Stuffing Cubes

Sugar
Augason Farms ▲ - White Granulated ● *(45 lb./6 Gallon Pail Only)*
Bakers & Chefs - Old Fashioned Flavor Light Brown, Ultra Fine
   Powdered
Billington's - Natural Sugar (Demerara, Light Brown Muscovado)
Crystal Sugar ▲ - All Sugar Products
Dixie Crystals - All Varieties
Domino - Agave Nectar (Amber, Light), Brown, Brownulated,
   Confectioners, Cubes, Demerara Washed Raw Cane, Granulated,
   Lite Sugar & Stevia Blend, Organic, Sticks, Sugar 'N Cinnamon,
   Superfine, Tablets

S

El Peto ▲ - Icing Sugar

Food Club Brand - Granulated, Light Brown, Powdered

Great Value Brand (Wal-Mart) - Confectioners Powdered, Light Brown, Pure Cane

Hain Pure Foods - Organic (Light Brown, Powdered, Regular), Turbinado

Hannaford Brand - Dark Brown, Granulated, Light Brown, Powdered

Heavenly Sugar - Premium Organic Sugar

Hy-Vee - Confectioners Powdered, Dark Brown, Light Brown, Pure Cane

Imperial Sugar ▲ - All Varieties

Lowes Foods Brand - Granulated, Light Brown, Powdered

Meijer Brand - Confectioners, Dark Brown, Granulated, Light Brown

Midwest Country Fare - Granulated, Light Browned, Powdered

Navitas Naturals ▲ - Palm Sugar

Nielsen-Massey - Madagascar Bourbon Pure Vanilla Sugar ●

Nuts.com - Organic Evaporated Cane Juice ●, Organic Palm Sugar ●

O Organics - Evaporated Cane Juice, Light Brown, Powdered, Turbinado

Organic Nectars - Superfine Coconut Sugar

Phildesco - Coconut

Publix - Dark Brown, Granulated, Light Brown, Powdered

Purely Elizabeth - Organic Coconut Palm Sugar

Rapunzel - Organic Whole Cane, Powdered

Rodelle - Cinnamon Sugar, Vanilla Sugar

Safeway Brand - Brown (Dark, Light), Granulated, Powdered

Sauza - Agave Nectar

Shiloh Farms - Organic (Date !!, Maple !!)

Spartan Brand - Confectioners Powdered, Dark Brown, Granulated, Light Brown

Trader Joe's - All Varieties

Velvet Sugar - Powdered

Wegmans Brand - Dark Brown, Granulated White, Light Brown Pure Cane

Wholesome Sweeteners - All Varieties

Winn Dixie - Granulated, Light Brown, Powdered

S

Woodstock Farms - Organic (Brown, Powdered, Pure Cane, Turbinado)

Sugar Substitute/Sweetener

Equal - Flavor For Water (Black Cherry, Lemon Lime, Mandarin Orange), Lemon, Packets, Peach, Spoonful, Sugar Lite, Tablets, Vanilla

Fifty50 - Granulated Fructose

Food Club Brand - Aspartame, Sugar Substitute

Great Value Brand (Wal-Mart) - No Calorie Sweetener, No Calorie Sweetener w/Aspartame

Hannaford Brand - Sweetener (Aspartame, Sweet Choice)

Hy-Vee - Aspartame Sweetener, Delecta Sugar Substitute

Kirkland Signature - No Calorie Sweetener Made w/Sucralose

Krisda - Premium Stevia Extract

Lowes Foods Brand - Sucralose Sweetener

Madhava - Agave Nectar (All Varieties)

Navitas Naturals ▲ - Lucuma Powder

NutraSweet

Sauza - Agave Nectar

Spartan Brand - Granulated Sugar Substitute

Splenda -
  Brown Sugar Blend
  Flavors For Coffee (French Vanilla, Hazelnut, Mocha)
  Minis
  No Calorie Sweetener (Granulated, Packets, w/Fiber)
  Sugar Blend

SugarTwin - Granulated (Brown, White), Original Packets

Sweet And Low

Sweet Fiber - All Natural Sweetener ●

Wegmans Brand - Sugar Substitute w/Saccharin, Sweetener w/Aspartame

Wholesome Sweeteners - All Varieties

Winn Dixie - Sugar Sweetener Substitute

Sunflower Seeds...see Seeds

S Sweet & Sour Sauce
   Ah So - Sweet & Sour
   Contadina
   Mr. Spice Organic - Sweet & Sour Sauce & Marinade ★
   Safeway Select - Sweet & Sour Gourmet Dipping Sauce
   San-J - Gluten Free Sweet & Tangy ●
   Steel's - Sweet & Sour Sauce ●
   Wegmans Brand - Sweet & Sour
Sweet Potatoes
   *... *All Fresh Fruits & Vegetables Are Gluten-Free*
   Dr. Praeger's - Sweet Potato Littles !, Sweet Potato Pancake !
   Meijer Brand - Cut Light Syrup
Sweetener...see Sugar Substitute/Sweetener
Swiss Chard
   *... *All Fresh Fruits & Vegetables Are Gluten-Free*
Swordfish...see also Fish
   *... *All Fresh Fish Is Gluten-Free (Non-Marinated, Unseasoned)*
   Whole Catch - Fresh Fillet
Syrup
   Beehive - Corn Syrup
   Black Horse ▲ - Marionberry, Raspberry
   Brer Rabbit - Syrup (Full, Light)
   Central Market H-E-B - Maple (Dark, Medium)
   ChocAlive ▲ - Dark Chocolate Sauce
   Crown - Corn Syrup (Golden, Lily White)
   Dagoba ▲ - Chocolate Syrup ★
   Food Club Brand - Butter Flavored, Chocolate Syrup, Lite Corn, Maple 100% Dark Amber
   Full Circle - Organic Maple
   Gordon Food Service - Pancake Maple
   Great Northern - Organic Maple (Agave Syrup Blend, Blueberry, Cranberry, Dark Amber Grade A, Dark Amber Grade B)
   Hannaford Brand - Chocolate, Pancake (100% Pure Maple, Butter Flavored, Lite, Regular, Sugar Free), Strawberry
   Hershey's - Chocolate (Lite, Regular, Special Dark)

S

Hill Country Fare H-E-B - Butter (Lite, Rich), Corn (Dark, Light), Lite, Original, Pancake/Waffle (Butter, Lite, Regular), Sugar Free

Hy-Vee - Butter Flavor, Chocolate, Lite, Low Calorie Sugar Free, Pancake & Waffle, Strawberry

Jelly Belly - Breakfast Syrup (Tutti Fruitti, Very Cherry)

Jim Beam - Original Pancake Syrup

Karo ▲ - All Varieties

Log Cabin - Butter Flavored, Country Kitchen, Lite, Original

Lowes Foods Brand - 2% Maple (Lite, Original), Butter Flavored, Chocolate, Light Corn Syrup *(Only Red Label)*

Lundberg ▲ - Sweet Dreams Brown Rice Syrup (Eco Farmed, Organic)

Maple Grove Farms Of Vermont - Flavored Syrups (Apricot, Blueberry, Boysenberry, Raspberry, Strawberry), Organic, Pure, Sugar Free (Butter Flavor, Cozy Cottage, Maple Grove, Vermont)

Maple Ridge - Buttery, White Corn

Maple Valley - 100% Pure Organic Maple Syrup

Meijer Brand - Butter, Chocolate, Lite, Lite Butter, Lite Corn, Regular

Midwest Country Fare - Chocolate, Pancake & Waffle (Butter, Original)

Mrs. Renfro's - Cane, Country

Navitas Naturals ▲ - Yacon Syrup

Nesquik - All Flavors

Nestle - Nesquik Syrup (All Flavors)

O Organics - 100% Pure Maple

Old Tyme - All Varieties

Organic Nectars - Agave Syrup (All Varieties), Dessert Syrup (All Flavors)

Oskri Organics - Date

Publix - Pancake (Butter Flavor, Lite Butter Flavor, Original, Sugar Free)

Safeway Brand - Butter, Butter Light, Chocolate, Light, Original

Safeway Select - Pure Maple

Santa Cruz ▲ - Dessert Toppings All Varieties

Smucker's ▲ - All Fruit Syrup, Pure Maple Syrup, Sugar Free Breakfast Syrup

Spartan Brand - 2% Real Maple, Artificial Butter, Light Corn Syrup, Reduced Calorie (Artificial Butter Flavor, Lite)

S   **The Ginger People** - Organic Ginger Syrup **!**

Torani -

Flavored Coffee Syrup (Almond (Regular, Roca), Amaretto, Apple (Green, Regular), Bananas Foster, Blackberry, Blood Orange, Blueberry, Butter (Pecan, Rum), Butterscotch, Cane Sugar Sweetener, Caramel (Regular *(NOT Classic Caramel Or Sugar Free Classic Caramel)*, Salted), Chai Tea Spice, Cheesecake, Cherry (Lime, Regular), Chocolate (Bianco, Chip Cookie Dough, Macadamia Nut, Milano, Mint), Cinnamon (Brown Sugar, Regular), Classic Root Beer, Coconut, Coffee, Cranberry Bay Leaf, Creme (Caramel, De Banana, De Cacao, De Menthe), Cupcake, English Toffee, Ginger, Gingerbread, Grape, Guava, Hazelnut (Classic, Regular), Hibiscus, Huckleberry, Irish Cream, Italian Eggnog, Kiwi, Lemon, Lime, Macadamia Nut, Mango, Maple, Orange & Spice, Passion Fruit, Peach, Peanut Butter, Peppermint, Pineapple, Pink Grapefruit, Pomegranate, Pumpkin (Pie, Spice), Raspberry (Blue, Red, Regular), Ruby Red Grapefruit, Shortbread, Strawberry, Tangerine, Tiramisu, Vanilla (Bean, Cinnamon, French *(NOT Sugar Free French Vanilla)*, Honey, Regular))

Sugar Free Flavored Coffee Syrup (Almond (Regular, Roca), Black Cherry, Brown Sugar Cinnamon, Caramel (Regular *(NOT Classic Caramel Or Sugar Free Classic Caramel)*, Salted), Chocolate (Chip Cookie Dough, Macadamia Nut, Regular, White), Coconut, Coffee, Hazelnut (Classic, Regular), Irish Cream, Lemon, Lime, Mango, Orange, Peach, Peanut Butter, Peppermint, Pumpkin Pie, Raspberry, Strawberry, Sweetener, Vanilla (Bean, Regular), Watermelon)

Trader Joe's - All Maple Syrup

Tropical Traditions - Brown Rice Syrup

Vermont Maid - Butter Lite, Regular, Sugar Free

Walden Farms - Fruit Syrups (Blueberry, Strawberry), Single Serve Packets (Chocolate, Pancake), Syrup (Caramel, Chocolate, Pancake)

Wegmans Brand - Dessert Sauce (Creamy Caramel, Milk Chocolate, Raspberry Chocolate, Triple Chocolate), Flavored (Chocolate, Maraschino Cherry), Organic FYFGA Maple Syrup, Regular (Pancake Light, Pure Maple Dark Amber)

Winn & Lovett - Organic Maple (All Varieties)

Winn Dixie - Butter Flavor, Chocolate, Lite, Regular, Strawberry

T

Taco Meat
Pure Market Express ▲ - Taco Meat ●

Taco Sauce
Food Club Brand - Mild
Hannaford Brand - Medium, Mild
Hy-Vee - Medium, Mild
La Victoria - Chipotle Medium, Green (Medium, Mild), Red (Medium, Mild)
Lowes Foods Brand - Mild
Old El Paso - Hot, Medium, Mild
Ortega - Green Mild, Original (Hot, Medium, Mild)
Pace - Medium, Mild
Spartan Brand - Fat Free (Medium, Mild)
Taco Bell - Medium, Mild, Restaurant Sauce (Hot, Mild)

Taco Seasoning...see also Seasonings
Chi-Chi's - Fiesta Restaurante Seasoning Mix
Hy-Vee - Regular
Meijer Brand - Taco Seasoning
Nueva Cocina - Latin Beef & Taco Seasoning, Seasoning & Veggie Mix (Chipotle Taco, Taco Fresco)
Old El Paso - Taco Seasoning Mix (25% Less Sodium, Hot & Spicy, Mild, Original)
Ortega - Chipotle Mix, Hot & Spicy Mix, Jalapeno & Onion Mix, Taco Seasoning Mix
Simply Organic - Seasoning Mix (Fish Taco ●, Southwest Taco ●, Spicy Taco ●)
Trader Joe's - Taco Seasoning

T Taco Shells
    Food Club Brand - Taco Shells
    Garden of Eatin' - Corn Taco Shells (Blue, Yellow)
    Hy-Vee - Taco Shells
    Lowes Foods Brand - Taco Shells
    Meijer Brand - Taco Shells
    Mission - Corn Taco Shells (Jumbo !, Regular !)
    Old El Paso - Stand 'N Stuff Yellow Corn Taco Shells, Taco Shells (Super Stuffer, White Corn, Yellow Corn)
    Ortega - Hard Shells (White Corn, Whole Grain Corn, Yellow Corn)
    Safeway Brand - Jumbo Corn
    Taco Bell - Taco Shells (12 ct., 18 ct.)
Tahini
    Arrowhead Mills - Organic Sesame Tahini
    Krinos - Tahini
    Lee Kum Kee - Sesame Seed Paste
    MaraNatha - Natural w/Salt (Creamy Raw, Creamy Roasted)
    Nuts.com - Organic Sesame Tahini ●
    Oskri Organics - Tahini, Tahini & Honey, Tahini & Molasses
    Peloponnese - Tahini Paste
    Sabra - Classic Tahini Spread
    Woodstock Farms - Unsalted Sesame Tahini (All Natural, Organic)
Tamales
    Amy's - Roasted Vegetables ★, Verde Black Bean ★, Verde Cheese ★
    Delimex - Beef
    Hormel - Beef
    Trader Joe's - Handcrafted (Beef, Cheese & Green Chilies, Chicken & Cheese)
Tangerines
    ... *All Fresh Fruits & Vegetables Are Gluten-Free*
Tapioca
    Let's Do...Organic - Organic (Granules, Pearls, Starch)
Taquitos
    Delimex - Corn (Beef, Chicken, Three Cheese)

Starlite Cuisine - Crispy Soy (Beef Style, Chicken Style, Chorizo & Black Bean Style)

Trader Joe's - Black Bean & Cheese, Frozen Chicken Taquitos

Tartar Sauce

Best Foods - Regular

Big Y

Cains - Regular

Follow Your Heart - Tartar Sauce!

Food Club Brand - Squeeze Bottle

Hannaford Brand

Heinz - Regular

Hellmann's - Regular

Ken's Steak House - Refrigerated, Shelf Stable

Legal - Regular

Lowes Foods Brand - Regular

McCormick - Fat Free, Original

Old Bay

Royal Food Products - Garden Fresh, Royal Deluxe

Simply Delicious - Organic Tartar Sauce

Spartan Brand

Wegmans Brand - Regular

Tarts

Choices Rice Bakery ▲ - Butter, Pecan Squares, Vegetarian Mince

Crave Bakery ▲ - Apple Frangipane, Apricot Frangipane, Lemon, Pumpkin

El Peto ▲ - Butter, Lemon, Pecan, Raspberry, Tart Shells (Sweetened, Unsweetened)

Foods By George ▲ - Pecan Tarts

Hail Merry ▲ - Merry's Miracle Tarts (Chocolate ●, Chocolate Mint ●, Chocolate Raw Almond Butter ●, Meyer Lemon ●, Persian Lime ●)

Heaven Mills ▲ - Hamantaschen (Apricot ●, Chocolate ●)

Pure Knead ▲ - Tarts (Blueberry ●, Lemon ●, Strawberry Balsamic ●, Tomato Onion & Basil ●)

Pure Market Express ▲ - Lemon ●

West Meadow Farm Bakery - Gluten Free Pecan Tassies ●

T Tater Tots...see Potatoes

Tea

    Aimee's Livin' Magic - All Teas

    Arizona - All Varieties

    Badia - All Flavors ●

    Bay Estate - Green w/Citrus

    Bigelow Tea -

        All Novus Varieties

        All Organic Varieties

        American Classic (Loose Tea Green, Pyramid Bags (Charleston Blended, Charleston Breakfast, Island Green, Island Green Mint, Plantation Peach, Rockville Raspberry), Regular)

        Arizona Green (Honey Ginseng, Mandarine Orange, Pomegranate Acai)

        Coconut Water w/Green Tea Mix (Mango, Pomegranate Acai, Regular)

        Dajeerling

        Decaffeinated (Constant Comment, Earl Grey, English Teatime, French Vanilla, Green Tea, Green Tea w/Lemon, Lemon Lift, Spiced Chai)

        Easy Mix Iced (Green w/Pomegranate, Red Raspberry)

        English Breakfast

        English Teatime

        Flavored Tea (Cinnamon Stick, Constant Comment, Earl Grey, Eggnogg'n, French Vanilla, Lemon Lift, Plantation Mint, Pumpkin Spice, Raspberry Royale, Spiced Chai, Vanilla (Caramel, Chai))

        Green Tea (Blueberry, Chai Green, Constant Comment Green, Earl Grey Green, Jasmine Green, Regular)

        Green Tea w/(Lemon, Mango, Mint, Peach, Pomegranate)

        Gretzky's Green (Decaf, Regular, w/Pomegranate)

        Herbal Tea (Apple Cider, Chamomile Mango, Chamomile Mint, Chinese Oolong, Cinnamon Apple, Cozy Chamomile, Cranberry Apple, Cranberry Ginseng, Fruit & Almond, Ginger Snappish, Hibiscus & Rose Hips, Lemon Ginger, Mint Medley,

Orange & Spice, Peppermint, Pomegranate Blueberry,
Pomegranate Pizzazz, Red Raspberry, Sweet Dreams,
Sweetheart Cinnamon, Wild Blueberry Acai)

Iced Tea Perfect Peach

K Cups (Cozy Chamomile, Green (Chai, Regular, w/
Pomegranate), Mint Medley)

Loose Tea (Constant Comment, Earl Grey, English Breakfast,
Governor Grey)

Pods (Cozy Chamomile, Green Tea)

Brisk - Iced Tea (Lemon, Peach, Raspberry, Strawberry Melon, Sweet)

Caribou - All Flavors

Celestial Seasonings -

Bottled Tea Kombucha (Antioxidant Superfruit, Digestion Meyer
Lemon Ginger, Energy Pomelo Citrus, Metabolism Berry Guava,
Super Green Tropical Blend)

Chai (Decaf Sweet Coconut Thai, Honey Vanilla White Tea, India
Spice (Decaf, Regular))

Cool Brew Iced Tea (Blueberry Ice, Peach Ice, Raspberry Ice,
Tropical Fruit)

Green Tea (Antioxidant, Blueberry Breeze, Decaf (Green,
Mandarin Orchard, Mint, Sleepytime Lemon Jasmine), Gen Mai
Cha, Honey Lemon Ginseng, Peach Blossom, Pomegranate,
Raspberry Gardens)

Herbal Tea (Acai Mango Zinger, Bengal Spice, Black Cherry Berry,
Caffeine Free, Chamomile, Cinnamon Apple Spice, Country
Peach Passion, Cranberry Apple Zinger, Fruit Tea Sampler,
Herb Tea Sampler, Honey Vanilla Chamomile, Lemon Zinger,
Mandarin Orange Spice, Mint Magic, Morning Thunder,
Peppermint, Raspberry Zinger, Red Zinger, Sleepytime,
Sleepytime Vanilla, Sweet Apple Chamomile, Tangerine
Orange Zinger, Tension Tamer, Tropic of Strawberry, True
Blueberry, Wild Berry Zinger)

Holiday Tea (Candy Cane Lane, Nutcracker Sweet)

Rooibos Tea (African Orange Mango, Madagascar Vanilla, Moroccan Pomegranate Red, Safari Spice)

Sweet Zinger Iced Tea (Acai Mango, Raspberry, Tangerine Orange, Wild Berry)

Wellness Tea (All Natural Herbal (Echinacea Complete Care, Sleepytime Extra, Sleepytime Sinus Soother, Sleepytime Throat Tamer), Antioxidant Max (Blackberry Pomegranate, Blood Orange Star Fruit, Dragon Fruit Melon), LaxaTea, Metabo Balance, Tummy Mint)

White Tea (Decaf, Imperial White Peach, Perfectly Pear)

Choice Organic Teas - All Varieties

Food Club Brand - Tea Bags (Family Size (Regular, Tagless), Regular, Tagless)

Full Circle - Organic Tea (Chai, Cranberry, Green w/Blueberry, White w/Pomegranate)

Fuze - Black & Green Tea Acai Berry, Green Tea Honey & Ginseng

Gloria Jean's - All Varieties

Gold Peak - Black Tea Raspberry, Green Tea (Lemonade, Regular), Iced Tea (Diet, Lemon, Sweet, Unsweetened)

Great Value Brand (Wal-Mart) - Refrigerated (Green, Sugar Free Sweet Tea, Sweet Tea), Tea 100% Natural Green (Decaf, Regular)

Guayaki - All Sparkling Teas, Bottled Yerba Mate (All Flavors), Organic Yerba Mate All Tea Bags & Loose Tea

Hampstead - Organic (Darjeeling, English Breakfast, Fennel Liquorice, Ginger Green, Green, Lemon Ginger, Lemon Valerian, Rosehip Hibiscus)

Hansen's - All Varieties

Higgins & Burke - All Varieties

Honest - Assam Black, Black Forest Berry, Classic Green, Community Green, Green Dragon, Half & Half, Heavenly Lemon Tulsi, Honey Green, Jasmine Green Energy, Just Black, Just Green, Lemon Black, Lori's Lemon, Mango Acai White, Moroccan Mint Green, Peach Oo La Long, Peach White, Perfect White, Pomegranate Red w/Goji Berry, Zero Calorie Passion Fruit Green Tea

Hy-Vee - Bottled (Diet Green Tea w/Citrus, Green Tea w/Citrus, Green Tea w/Mixed Berry), Chai Black, Chamomile Herbal, Cinnamon Apple Herbal, Decaf (Green, Tea Bags), Dream Easy Herbal, Earl Grey Black, English Breakfast Black, Family Size Tea Bags, Green Tea Bags, Honey Lemon Ginseng, Jasmine Green, Orange & Spice Specialty, Peppermint Herbal, Rooibos Red Herbal, Strawberry Herbal Tea Bags, White Tea w/Pomegranate

Inko's White Tea - Apricot, Blueberry, Cherry Vanilla, Energy, Honeydew, Lemon, Lychee, Original, Unsweetened Hint O'Mint, Unsweetened Honeysuckle, Unsweetened Original, White Peach

Ito En Tea - Bottled (Green Jasmine, Green White, Pure Green, Sweetened (Apple, Peach))

Lipton -

Black Tea Bags (Cold Brew, Decaf, Decaf Cold Brew, Decaf Pitcher Sized, Hint Of Peach, Hint Of Raspberry, Pitcher Sized, Regular)

Bottled Iced Tea (Diet (Green w/Citrus, Green w/Mixed Berry, Sparkling Green w/Strawberry Kiwi, White w/Raspberry), Diet Green w/Watermelon, Green w/Citrus, Green w/Passionfruit Mango, Half & Half Tea Lemonade, Iced Tea w/Lemon, Pure Leaf (Extra Sweet, Green w/Honey, Iced w/Lemon, Iced w/Peach, Iced w/Raspberry, Sweetened, Unsweetened), Sweet Iced, w/Pomegranate Blueberry, White w/Raspberry)

Diet Iced Tea Mix (Lemon (Decaf, Green Tea Honey &, Regular), Peach, Raspberry, Unsweetened)

Flavored Tea Bags (French Vanilla, Orange & Spice, Spiced Chai)

Green Tea Bags (100% Natural, 100% Natural Decaf, Acai Dragonfruit & Melon, Black Currant & Vanilla, Cranberry Pomegranate, Decaf Blackberry & Pomegranate Superfruit, Decaf Honey Lemon, Honey, Lemon Ginseng, Mint, Mixed Berry, Orange Passionfruit & Jasmine, Passionfruit & Coconut, Purple Acai & Blueberry, Red Goji & Raspberry, w/Citrus, White Mangosteen & Peach)

Herbal Tea Bags (Cinnamon Apple, Ginger Twist, Lemon, Orange, Peppermint, Quietly Chamomile)

T

Iced Tea Mix (Decaf Unsweetened, Green Tea Blackberry & Pomegranate, Lemon (Decaf, Regular), Mango, Summer Peach, Unsweetened, Wild Raspberry)

Iced Tea To Go (Energize Green w/Blueberry & Pomegranate, Green w/Citrus, Green w/Honey & Lemon, Green w/Mandarin & Mango, Regular w/Natural Lemon, White w/Raspberry)

Pyramid Tea Bags (Bavarian Wild Berry, Bedtime Story Herbal, Black Pearl, Green w/Mandarin Orange, Red w/Harvest Strawberry & Passionfruit, Tuscan Lemon, Vanilla Caramel Truffle, White w/Blueberry & Pomegranate, White w/Island Mango & Peach)

Lowes Foods Brand - Green (Decaf, Regular), Tea Bags (Decaf, Regular)

Medifast - Chai Latte ●, Iced Tea (Peach ●, Raspberry ●)

Meijer Brand -

Bottled Tea (Green w/Citrus (Diet, Regular), White w/Raspberry (Diet, Regular))

Iced Tea Mix

Instant

Tea Bags (Chai, Decaf, Earl Grey (Decaf, Regular), English Breakfast, Green (Berry, Decaf, Honey Lemon Ginseng, Jasmine, Regular), Herbal (Chamomile, Chamomile Mint, Cinnamon Apple, Peppermint), Orange Spice Black, Organic (Chai, Chamomile, Earl Grey, English Breakfast, Green, Peppermint), Regular)

Midwest Country Fare - Tea Bags 100 ct.

Minute Maid - Lemonade Iced Tea, Pomegranate Tea

Mother Parkers - All Tea (Black, Flavored, Green, Herbal)

My Essentials - All (Bags, Instant)

Nestea -

Brews (Berry Oolong, Classic, Mango)

Diet White Tea Berry Honey

Green Tea Citrus (Diet, Regular)

Half & Half

Iced Tea (Lemon (Diet, Sweetened), Raspberry)

Instant Tea Mix (All Varieties)

Red Tea

Tropical Mango

Unsweetened

Newman's Own - Lemon Aided Iced Tea

NOH - Instant Hawaiian Iced Tea

Numi - All Varieties

O Organics - Bags (Earl Grey, Green, Mint Herbal), Refrigerated Bottled All Flavors

Oregon Chai - All Chai Tea Latte Liquid Concentrates, All Tea Bag Varieties, Chai Tea Latte Powdered Mix (Original, Slightly Sweet)

Organic India - Tulsi Tea (Chai Masala, Green, India Breakfast, Lemon Ginger, Red Mango)

Prairie Farms - Iced Tea (Sugar Free, Sweetened, Unsweetened)

Publix - Deli Iced Tea (Sweetened, Unsweetened), Tea Bags (All Varieties)

Pura Vida - All Varieties

Red Rose - All Varieties

Republic of Tea - Be Well Red (Get A Grip ●, Get Wellness ●), Black (All Day Breakfast ●, Assam Breakfast ●, Big Bold ●, Bing Cherry Vanilla ●, Black Vanilla Bean Almond ●, Blackberry Sage ●, British Breakfast ●, Calorie Free Naturally Sweet ●, Cinnamon Plum ●, Comfort & Joy ●, Cranberry Blood Orange ●, Darjeeling First Flush, Decaf (Apricot ●, Blackberry Sage ●, British Breakfast ●, Earl Greyer ●, Ginger Peach ●, Mango Ceylon ●, Strawberry Cherry ●, Vanilla Almond ●), Earl Greyer ●, Eat Pray Love Blood Orange Cinnamon ●, Ginger Peach ●, Golden Yunnan ●, Imperial Republic Lychee ●, Imperial Republic Pu Erh ●, Jerry Cherry ●, Lapsang Souchon ●, Lucky Irish Breakfast ●, Mango Ceylon ●, Organic Ceylon Breakfast ●, PassionFruit Papaya ●, Phoobsering Rare Darjeeling ●, Raspberry Quince ●, Republic Chai ●, Republic Darjeeling ●, Rohini Rare Pearl ●, Rose Petal ●, Tea Of Good Tidings ●, Vanilla Almond ●, Vanilla Pear ●, Watermelon Blackberry ●, Wild Blueberry ●, Winter Cinnamon ●), Fair Trade (Apricot Decaf ●, Cranberry Blood Orange ●, Wild Blueberry ●), Green (Acai ●, Acerola Cherry ●, Apple Blossom ●, Big Hojicha ●, Black Raspberry ●, Blood

T

Orange ●, Blueberry Lemon ●, Blueberry ●, Decaf (Honey Ginseng ●, Kiwi Pear ●, Pomegranate ●, The People's Green ●, Wild Berry Plum ●), Double Matcha ●, Dragon Well ●, Flower of Prosperity ●, Flowering (Dancing Blossom ●, Lychee Blossom ●), Ginger Peach ●, Goji Raspberry ●, Gua Pian Leaf ●, Holiday Plum Spice ●, Honey Ginseng ●, Jasmine Jazz ●, Jasmine Pearls Leaf ●, Kiwi Pear ●, Moroccan Mint ●, Orange Spice ●, Organic (Dancing Leaves ●, Earl Greyer ●, Lemon w/Honey ●, Turmeric Ginger ●), Pineapple Ginger ●, Pink Grapefruit ●, Pink Lady Apple ●, Pink Lemonade ●, Pomegranate ●, Republic Chai ●, Sea Buckthorn Apple Rooibos ●, Sky Between The Branches ●, Spring Cherry ●, Tea of Inquiry ●, The People's Green ●, Wild Berry Plum ●), Herbal (Be Well Red (Get Charged ●, Get Clean ●, Get Gorgeous ●, Get Happy ●, Get Heart ●, Get It Going ●, Get Lost ●, Get Maternal ●, Get Passionate ●, Get Relaxed ●, Get Relief ●, Get Smart ●, Get Some Zzz's ●), Cardamon Cinnamon ●, Chamomile Lemon ●, Desert Sage ●, Double Dark Chocolate Mate ●, Ginseng Peppermint ●, Hot Apple Cider ●, Hot Apple Cider ●, Imperial Republic Snow Rose ●, Lemon Wintergreen ●, Orange Ginger Mint ●, Organic (Cedarburg Red ●, Double Red Rooibos ●, Flowering Fruit ●, Mint Fields ●, Temple Of Health ●), PassionFruit Mango ●, Rainforest ●, Red (Cherry Apple ●, Cinnamon Orange ●, Dream By The Fire ●, Earl Greyer ●, Ginger Peach ●, Good Hope Vanilla ●, PassionFruit Mango ●, Pomegranate Vanilla ●, Republic Chai ●, Safari Sunset ●, Strawberry Chocolate ●, Strawberry Vanilla ●, Tangerine ●), Tangerine Hibiscus ●, Yerba Mate Latte ●), Hibiscus Superflower (Blueberry ●, Key Lime ●, Natural ●, Pineapple Lychee ●, Vanilla Apple ●), Iced (Tart Cherry ●, Watermelon Mint ●), Oolong (Dragon ●, Imperial Republic Monkey Picked ●, Imperial Republic Orchid ●, Old Bush Shui Xian Rare ●, Osmanthus Rare Estate ●, Peach Blossom ●, Ti Kuan Yin ●, Wuyi ●), Organic Matcha Powder ●, Raw Green Bush Tea (Black Currant Cardamon ●, Mango Chili ●, Plantain Coconut ●), Red (Apricot Honey ●, Caramel Apple ●, Year of The Tiger ●), White (Asian Jasmine ●, Decaf Kiwi Pear ●, Emperor's ●, Ginger Peach ●, Honeydew Melon ●, Honeysuckle ●,

Orange Blossom ●, Persimmon ●, Pineapple Guava ●, Red Cherry ●, Silver Rain ●, Vanilla Coconut ●)

Rishi Tea ▲ - All Varieties *(Except Chocolate Chai & Red Ginseng Recharge)*

Safeway Brand - Black, Tea Bags (Decaffeinated (Black, Green), Green)

Salada Tea - Decaffeinated & Regular (Black, Fruit, Green, White)

Santa Cruz ▲ - Bottled Tea All Varieties

Snapple -
    Can (Lemon Iced, Peach Green, Refreshing Green, Southern Sweet)
    Diet (Green, Half N Half, Lemon, Papaya Mango, Peach, Peach
        Green, Plum A Granate, Raspberry, Trop A Rocka)
    Green
    Half N Half
    Lemon
    Nectarine White
    Papaya Mango
    Peach
    Pomegranate Raspberry Red
    Raspberry
    Sweet
    Tea Will Be Loved

SoBe - Lean Diet Honey Green

Sokenbicha - Defend, Revive

Spartan Brand - Orange Pekoe Tea Bags (Decaf, Regular)

St. Dalfour - All Flavors

Stash Tea - All Varieties

Sweet Leaf - Bottled (Citrus Green, Half & Half Lemonade Tea, Lemon, Lemon & Lime Unsweet, Mint & Honey, Peach, Raspberry, Sweet Tea), Diet Bottled (Citrus Green, Original Sweet, Peach)

Swiss Premium - Diet Iced Tea w/Lemon Flavor, Natural Tea Cooler, Sweetened Green Tea, Sweetened Iced Tea w/Lemon Flavor

Tazo Tea - Brambleberry, Giant Peach, Organic (Iced Black, Iced Green)

Twinings Tea - All Varieties (Teas, Fruit and Herbal Infusions)

T

V8 - V Fusion + Tea (Pineapple Mango Green Tea, Pomegranate Green Tea, Raspberry Green Tea)

Wegmans Brand - Black Tea, Decaf (Black Tea, Green Tea), Earl Grey (Black, Black Decaf, Green), English Breakfast Black, Green Tea, Ice Tea Mix (Regular, w/Natural Lemon Flavor & Sugar (Decaf, Regular)), Iced Tea (Diet, Regular), Regular Bags

Winn Dixie - Regular & Family (Decaffeinated, Tea Bags)

Teff

Bob's Red Mill ▲ - Flour ★, Whole Grain ★

La Tortilla Factory - Ivory Gluten Free Teff Wraps ●

Shiloh Farms - Brown ‼, Ivory ‼

Tempeh

Lightlife - Flax, Garden Veggie, Organic Soy, Wild Rice

Tequila

... *All Distilled Alcohol Is Gluten-Free*

Teriyaki Sauce

Organicville - Island Teriyaki ●, Sesame Teriyaki ●

Premier Japan - Wheat Free

San-J - Gluten Free Teriyaki Stir Fry & Marinade ●

Tikka

Amy's - Indian Paneer ★

Sharwood's - Sauce (Spicy Tikka Masala, Tikka Masala)

Trader Joe's - Chicken Tikka Masala, Paneer Tikka ‼

Tilapia...see Fish

... *All Fresh Fish Is Gluten-Free (Non-Marinated, Unseasoned)*

Tofu

Amy's - Indian Mattar ★

Lightlife - Tofu Pups

Marigold - Braised ★

Melissa's - Extra Firm, Firm, Soft

Mori-Nu - All Silken Tofu ★

Nasoya ▲ - Cubed, Extra Firm, Firm, Lite Firm, Lite Silken, Silken, Soft, Sprouted (Extra Firm Vac Pack, Super Firm), Tofu Plus (Extra Firm, Firm)

Sunrise - Chinese Puff, Extra Firm, Firm, Fried, Homemade Style Fried, Medium Firm, Premium (Extra Soft, Medium Firm, Soft), Pressed, Silken Tube, Soft, Tofu Desserts (Almond, Banana, Coconut, Custard Flavor, Maple Caramel, Original, Peach Mango), Tofu Puff

Trader Joe's - Organic (Extra Firm, Firm)

Wegmans Brand - Extra Firm, Organic (Extra Firm, Firm)

Wildwood - Organic (SprouTofu Super Firm (Cubed, Regular), Water Pack (Extra Firm, Firm, Medium Soft, Super Firm)), Taco Crumbles

Woodstock Farms - Organic Tofu (Extra Firm, Firm)

Tomatillos

*... *All Fresh Fruits & Vegetables Are Gluten-Free*

Embasa - Whole Tomatillos

Las Palmas - Crushed Tomatillos

Tomato Paste

Amore - Tomato Paste

Bionaturae ▲ - Organic

Contadina - Regular, w/Roasted Garlic, w/Tomato Pesto

Del Monte - All Tomato Products *(Except Spaghetti Sauce Flavor)*

Full Circle - Organic

Gordon Food Service - California

Hannaford Brand

Hunt's - All Flavors

Lowes Foods Brand - Tomato

Meijer Brand - Domestic, Organic

Nature's Basket - Organic Tomato Paste

O Organics

Publix - Regular

Publix GreenWise Market - Organic

S&W - All Canned Vegetables

Safeway

Spartan Brand

Wegmans Brand - Organic FYFGA, Regular

Winn Dixie - Regular

Woodstock Farms

T Tomato Puree

    Contadina - Regular

    Dei Fratelli - Regular

    Meijer Brand - Regular

    S&W - All Canned Vegetables

    Sclafani - Tomato Puree

    Wegmans Brand - FYFGA Regular

    Winn Dixie - Regular

Tomato Sauce...see Sauces

Tomatoes

    ... *All Fresh Fruits & Vegetables Are Gluten-Free

    Amore - Sun Dried Tomato Paste

    Bionaturae ▲ - Organic (Strained, Whole Peeled & Diced, Whole Peeled Diced & Crushed)

    Cara Mia - Sun Dried

    Contadina -

        All Crushed

        All Stewed

        Diced (Petite Cut, Regular, w/Burgundy Wine & Olive Oil, w/Italian Herbs, w/Roasted Garlic, w/Roasted Red Pepper, w/Zucchini Bell Pepper & Carrots)

    Dei Fratelli -

        Chili Ready Diced

        Chopped (Italian, Mexican Tomatoes & Jalapenos, w/Onions & Garlic)

        Crushed (Regular, w/Basil & Herbs)

        Diced (In Hearty Sauce, Low Sodium, Seasoned)

        No Salt Whole

        Petite Diced (Regular, w/Onion & Celery & Pepper)

        Stewed

        Whole (In Puree, Regular)

    Del Monte - All Tomato Products *(Except Spaghetti Sauce Flavor)*

    Eden Organic -

        Crushed (Regular, w/Basil, w/Onion & Garlic)

        Diced (Regular, w/Basil, w/Green Chilies, w/Roasted Onion)

        Whole Tomatoes (Regular, w/Basil)

Food Club Brand -
    Crushed (In Puree, Regular)
    Diced (& Green Chiles, In Juice, In Juice No Salt, Italian, Mexican,
        Regular, w/Garlic & Onion)
    Diced Chili Ready (Regular, w/Onions)
    Diced Petite (Peeled w/Green Chilies, Regular, Smoked Chipotle,
        Southwestern, w/Sweet Onion)
    Petite Diced
    Puree
    Stewed (Italian Style, Mexican Style, Regular)
    Whole Peeled (No Salt, Regular)
Full Circle - Organic Crushed Tomatoes w/Basil
Gone Native - Crushed, Whole
Gordon Food Service -
    Crushed
    Diced (California, Petite, w/Juice)
    Puree (California, Regular)
    Stewed Sliced
    Whole Peeled
Great Value Brand (Wal-Mart) - Fire Roasted (Diced, Tex Mex Style)
Hunt's - All Flavors ★
Hy-Vee -
    Diced (Regular, w/Chilies, w/Garlic & Onion)
    Italian Style (Diced, Stewed)
    Original Diced & Green Chilies
    Petite Diced (Regular, w/Garlic & Olive Oil, w/Sweet Onion)
    Tomato Paste
    Whole Peeled No Salt
Jovial - Crushed, Diced, Whole Peeled
Lowes Foods Brand - Canned (Crushed In Puree, Diced (No Salt,
    Petite, Regular, w/Green Chilies), Italian, Paste, Sauce, Stewed,
    Stewed, Whole)
Lucini - Tuscan Harvest Plum Tomatoes (Diced Peeled, Whole
    Peeled)
Mariani - Sun Dried (Halves **!!**, Julienne **!!**)

T

Meijer Brand -
    Crushed In Puree
    Diced (Chili Ready, In Italian, In Juice, Organic, Petite, Regular,
        w/Green Chilies)
    Stewed (Italian, Mexican, Regular)
    Whole (Peeled, Peeled No Salt, Peeled Organic, w/Basil Organic)
Melissa's - Sun Dried **!**
Mezzetta ▲ - Sun Ripened Dried (In Olive Oil, Julienne Cut In Olive
    Oil, Regular)
Midwest Country Fare - Diced, Stewed, Whole Peeled
My Essentials -
    Diced (Crushed, Italian, No Salt Added, Regular, w/Green Chilies,
        w/Roasted Garlic & Onion)
    Kitchen Ready Crushed In Heavy Puree
    Puree
    Stewed (Italian, Mexican, No Salt Added, Regular)
    Whole Peeled
Nature's Basket - Organic (Diced, Whole Peeled)
Nature's Place - Canned
Nuts.com - Dried Tomatoes (Julienne ●, Organic Sun Dried ●, Sun
    Dried ●, Sun Dried w/Olive Oil ●)
O Organics - Diced (No Salt Added, Regular, w/Basil Garlic &
    Oregano), Whole Peeled
Pictsweet - All Plain Frozen Vegetables
Publix - Crushed, Diced (Italian Style, No Salt Added, Petite, Regular
    Summer Sausage, w/Green Chilies, w/Roasted Garlic & Onion),
    Paste, Peeled Whole, Sauce, Sliced & Stewed
Publix GreenWise Market - Organic (Crushed, Diced, Diced
    w/Basil Garlic & Oregano, Paste, Sauce)
Ro-Tel - All Flavors *(Except Sauces)*
S&W - All Canned Vegetables
Safeway Brand - Crushed, Diced (Fire Roasted, Peeled, Peeled No
    Salt, Petite), Italian Style Stewed, Mexican Style Stewed, Whole
    Peeled
Sclafani - Crushed Tomatoes, Tomato Puree

Spartan Brand - Crushed, Diced (Chili Ready, Italian Style, Mexican, No Salt Added, Regular, w/Garlic & Onion, w/Green Chilies), Italian Stewed, Sliced Stewed, Whole Peeled

Trader Joe's - All Sun Dried Tomatoes, Whole Peeled Tomatoes w/Basil

Wegmans Brand -
Crushed
Diced (Petite, Regular)
FYFGA (Diced (Chili Style, w/Garlic & Onion), Tomato Puree)
Italian Classics (Course Ground, Crushed w/Italian Style Herb, Kitchen Cut Roma Tomatoes w/Basil, Sun Dried Tomatoes w/Capers, Whole Roma w/Garlic & Basil)
Italian Style (Diced Tomatoes, Stewed, Whole w/Basil)
Peeled Whole (No Salt Added, Regular)
Stewed

Winn Dixie - Canned (Crushed, Diced, Diced w/Chilies, Italian Style (Diced, Stewed), Paste, Petite Diced, Petite Diced w/Onion Celery Green Peppers, Puree, Sauce, Stewed, Whole Peeled)

Woodstock Farms -
Organic
Crushed w/Basil
Diced (Basil & Garlic, Italian Herbs, No Salt, Original)
Sauce (No Salt Added, Original)
Whole Peeled (In Juice, w/Basil)

Tonic...see Soda Pop/Carbonated Beverages

Tortilla Chips...see Chips

Tortillas
Chi-Chi's - Gluten Free Corn
Don Pancho - Gluten Free Flour Tortillas
Food For Life - Wheat & Gluten Free Brown Rice
French Meadow Bakery - Gluten Free Tortillas ●
Guerrero - Tortillas De Maiz (Blanco, Estilo Ranchero, Taqueras)
La Tortilla Factory - Ivory Gluten Free Teff Wraps ●
Manny's - Corn Tortillas
Maria & Ricardo's - Gluten Free Tortillas ●

T

    Mission - Corn Tortillas (Estilo Casero White **!**, Super Size White **!**,
      Super Size Yellow **!**, White **!**, Yellow **!**)

    Que Pasa - Corn Tortillas **!**

    Rudi's Gluten-Free Bakery - Gluten Free (Fiesta ●, Plain ●, Spinach ●)

    Toovaloo - Gluten Free Amaranth Flax

    Trader Joe's - Corn Tortillas (Handmade **! !**, Original **! !**)

Tostadas

    Guerrero - Caseras Amarillas, Caseras Doraditas, Norteñas Classicas

    Mission - Amarillas **!**, Nortenas Rojas **!**

    Old El Paso - Tostada Shells

    Ortega - Tostada Shells

Trail Mix...see also Nuts

    Back To Nature - Harvest Blend, Nantucket Blend, Sonoma Blend

    Eden Organic - All Mixed Up, All Mixed Up Too

    Enjoy Life ▲ - Not Nuts Seed & Fruit Mix (Beach Bash ●, Mountain
      Mambo ●)

    Lydia's Organics - Savory Trail Mix

    Mareblu Naturals ▲ -

      Crunch Bags (Almond ●, Cashew ●, Cashew Coconut ●,
        CranMango Cashew ●, Dark Chocolate Almond ●, Pecan
        Cinnamon ●, Pecan Cranberry Cinnamon ●)

      Trail Mix Crunch Bags (Blueberry Pomegranate ●, Cranberry
        Pomegranate ●, Cranblueberry ●, Cranstrawberry ●, Pecan ●,
        Pistachio ●)

    Mauk Family Farms - Raw Trail Mix ●

    Navitas Naturals ▲ - All Flavors

    NoNuttin' Foods ▲ - Trail Mix (Berry Delight ●, Energy Explosion ●,
      Fruit Explosion ●)

    Nuts.com - Mango Goji Fire Sprouted ●, Wild Berry Sprouted ●

    Oskri Organics - Honey Crunch (Almond, Cashew w/Cranberries,
      Pecan w/Raisins)

    Pure Market Express ▲ - The Goji Trail ●

    Sweet Perry Orchards - Fruit & Nut Mix (Baja Blend **! !**, Ginger Zip **! !**,
      Trek Trio **! !**)

Trader Joe's - Go Raw Trek Mix **!**, Nutty American Trek Mix, Pumpkin Seeds & Pepitas, Rainbows End Trail Mix **!**, Simply Almonds Cashews & Cranberries Trek Mix, Simply The Best Trek Mix **!**, Sweet Savory & Tart Trek Mix **!**, Tempting Trail Mix **!**

Woodstock Farms - Cascade, Choco Cranberry Crunch, Chocolate Cherry Munch, Cranberry's Cove, Enchanted, Gourmet, In The Raw, Mocha Madness, On The Trail, Organic

Trek Mix...see Trail Mix

Tuna...see also Fish

... *All Fresh Fish Is Gluten-Free (Non-Marinated, Unseasoned)*

Blue Horizon - Albacore Tuna Bites

Bumble Bee -

Chunk White Albacore (In Oil, In Water)

Light (Chunk In Oil, Chunk In Water, Premium In Water Pouch)

Premium Albacore Tuna In Water Pouch

Premium Fillet Tonno In Olive Oil

Prime Fillet (Solid White Albacore In Water, Solid White Albacore Very Low Sodium In Water)

Prime Fillet Albacore Steak Entrees (Lemon & Cracked Pepper, Mesquite Grilled)

Sensations Seasoned Tuna Medley (Lemon & Cracked Pepper, Sundried Tomato & Basil)

Solid White Albacore (In Oil, In Water)

Chicken Of The Sea - All Products *(Except Tuna Salad Kit)*

Coral - Chunk Light Tuna (In Oil, In Water)

Crown Prince - Natural Albacore (Solid White, Solid White No Salt Added)

Great Value Brand (Wal-Mart) - Pouch w/Water, Premium Chunk Light Tuna In Water, Solid White Albacore Tuna In Water

H-E-B -

Albacore (In Water, Pouch)

Chunk Light (In Spring Water, In Water, Pouch)

Henry & Lisa's - Canned Solid White Albacore

Hill Country Fare H-E-B - In Spring Water Solid White, In Water (Chunk Light Tuna, Solid White Albacore)

T

Hy-Vee - Chunk Light Tuna In (Oil, Water)

Kirkland Signature - Canned Solid White Albacore, Fresh Ahi

Lowes Foods Brand - Chunk Lite

Member's Mark - Highest Quality Solid White Albacore Tuna In Water

Midwest Country Fare - Chunk Light Tuna Packed In Water

Safeway Brand - Chunk Light

Spartan Brand - Chunk Light, Solid White Albacore

Starkist -

    Creations (Hickory Smoked, Sweet & Spicy, Zesty Lemon Pepper)

    Pouch (Albacore White (Low Sodium, Regular), Chunk Light (In Sunflower Oil, Low Sodium))

    Tuna Selects (Albacore Tuna Fillet, Low Sodium, Solid Light Tuna Fillet In Olive Oil, Solid Light Tuna Fillet In Water, Very Low Sodium, Yellowfin Marinated Tuna Fillet w/Roasted Garlic)

    Yellowfin Tuna In Extra Virgin Olive Oil Pouch

Trader Joe's - All Canned Tuna, Marinated Ahi Tuna Steaks

Wegmans Brand - Albacore In Water, FYFGA Light Yellowfin Tuna In Water

Winn Dixie - Albacore, Chunk Light

Turkey...see also Deli Meat

*... *All Fresh Poultry Is Gluten-Free (Non-Marinated, Unseasoned)*

Al Fresco - Deli Antibiotic Free Turkey Breast (Hickory Smoked, Oven Roasted)

Always Tender - Fresh Flavored Turkey Honey Mustard

Applegate -

    Deli Counter (Herb !, Honey Maple !, No Salt !, Oven Roasted Breast !, Oven Roasted Breast Layout !, Peppered !, Smoked !, Southwestern !, Turkey Pastrami !)

    Deli Meat

        Natural (Herb Turkey Breast !, Honey & Maple Turkey Breast !, Roasted Turkey Breast !, Smoked Turkey Breast !, Turkey Bologna !, Turkey Salami !)

        Organic (Herb Turkey Breast !, Roasted Breast !, Smoked Turkey Breast !)

Natural Uncured Turkey Hot Dogs **!**

Organic Turkey Burgers **!**

Organic Uncured Turkey Hot Dogs **!**

Armour - Deli (Oven Roasted, Oven Roasted w/Broth, Smoked)

Boar's Head - All Varieties

Bowman & Landes - All Raw Turkey Products

Buddig -

Deli Cuts (Honey Roasted Turkey, Oven Roasted Turkey, Smoked Turkey)

Fix Quix Turkey Breast Cubes

Original (Honey Roasted Turkey, Mesquite Turkey, Oven Roasted Turkey, Turkey Deli Meat)

Butterball -

All Natural Turkey (Cutlets, Filets, Strips, Tenders)

Burgers (Fresh (All Natural, Seasoned), Frozen Seasoned)

Fresh Fully Cooked Turkey (Oven Baked, Smoked)

Fresh Turkey (Li'l Butterball, Whole)

Frozen Boneless Roast (Breast (Cajun Style, Savory Herb), Turkey, Turkey Breast)

Frozen Fully Cooked Turkey (Li'l Butterball Oven Baked, Oven Baked, Smoked)

Frozen Ready To Roast Boneless Skinless Turkey Breast (Classic Oven Style, Smoked Flavor)

Frozen Turkey (Li'l Butterball, Whole *(Except Stuffed Turkeys)*)

Fully Cooked Turkey Breast Roast (Deep Fried, Oven Roasted)

Ground Turkey (Italian Style, Regular, Seasoned, Turkey Breast, White)

Ground Turkey Chub (All Natural (85/15, 93/7), Seasoned)

Lunch Meat

Extra Thin Sliced Deep Fried Turkey Breast (Buttery Herb, Cajun Style, Original, Thanksgiving Style)

Extra Thin Sliced Turkey Breast (Honey Roasted, Oven Roasted, Rotisserie Seasoned, Smoked)

T

      Lean Family Size (Honey Roasted Turkey Breast, Oven Roasted Turkey Breast, Smoked Turkey Breast, Turkey Bologna, Turkey Ham)

      Thick Sliced (Honey Roasted, Oven Roasted, Smoked)

      Thick Sliced Deep Fried Turkey Breast (Cajun Style, Original, Thanksgiving Style)

      Thin Sliced (Honey Roasted, Oven Roasted, Rotisserie Seasoned, Smoked)

Oven Roasted Turkey Breast Strips

Tenderloins (Herb Roasted, Lemon Pepper)

Turkey Bacon (Lower Sodium, Regular, Thin & Crispy)

Turkey Breast (Fully Cooked Whole (Baked, Smoked), Ready To Roast (Classic Oven Style, Smoked Flavor))

Turkey Breasts (Fresh Whole, Frozen Whole)

Turkey Drumsticks

Turkey Mignons

Turkey Sausage (Fresh Bratwurst, Fresh Breakfast Links, Fresh Hot Italian Style, Fresh Sweet Italian Style, Polska Kielbasa Dinner, Smoked, Smoked Cheddar, Smoked Dinner, Smoked Hot)

Turkey Thighs

Turkey Wings

Carolina Turkey - Ground, Sausage

Castle Wood Reserve - Deli Meat (Herb Roasted Turkey Breast, Hickory Smoked Turkey, Oven Roasted Turkey, Turkey Pastrami)

Di Lusso - Deli Counter (Cajun Style, Cracked Pepper, Golden Brown, Honey, Honey Mesquite, Reduced Sodium, Smoked, Sun Dried Tomato)

Dietz & Watson ▲ - Applewood Smoked ●, Bacon Lover's Turkey●, Black Forest Chef Carved Smoked ●, Black Forest Turkey ●, Black Pepper ●, Butter Basted ●, Cajun Style ●, Carving Ready●, Chef Carved ●, Chipotle Pepper ●, Fire Roasted Breast Of Turkey●, Glazed Honey Cured Breast ●, Gourmet Gold'N Brown ●, Gourmet Lite No Salt ●, Gourmet Lite ●, Herb Lemon Butter ●, Herb Roasted ●, Honey Mustard ●, Italian Style ●, London Broil●,

Maple & Honey ●, Mesquite Smoked ●, Oven Classic ●, Oven Roasted ●, Pepper & Garlic ●, Pre Sliced (Black Forest Smoked●, Honey Cured ●), Roasted ●, Santa Fe Brand ●, Slow Roasted●, Smoked Breast Fillets ●, Smoked Julienne Strips ●, Smoked Peppercorn ●, Turkey Ham ●

Eating Right - Deli Sliced (Oven Roasted, Smoked)

Eckrich - Deli Meat (Fried Skinless, Mesquite Smoked, Oven Roasted, Smoked)

Empire Kosher -
All Natural (Breast, Breast w/Skin)
Drumsticks
Frozen (Ground, Whole, Whole Breast)
Fully Cooked BBQ
Ground Turkey (Fresh, Frozen, White)
Half Turkey Breast
Skinless Oven Breast
Slices (Smoked Turkey Breast, Turkey Bologna, Turkey Pastrami, Turkey Salami)
Smoked Breast (Honey, Skinless)
Tenders
Thighs
Turkey Franks
Turkey Pastrami Whole
Whole

Garrett County Farms - Andouille Sausage ★, Franks ★, Kielbasa ★, Morning Maple Turkey Breakfast Links ★, Sliced (Oven Roasted Turkey Breast ★, Smoked Turkey Breast ★, Turkey Bologna ★), Turkey Ham (Ham Steak ★, Sliced Nuggets ★, Uncured ★), Turkey Tom Toms (Hot & Spicy ★, Original ★), Uncured Turkey Ham ★

Gordon Food Service - Cook In Bag (Breasts, Thigh), Cooked Breast, Deli Meat (Sliced Breast, Smoked Sliced Breast)

H-E-B - Fried Breast Of Turkey, Turkey Breast (Cajun, Fajita, Honey Smoked, Maple, Mesquite Smoked (Pre Sliced, Regular), Oven

T

Roasted, Peppercorn, Salsa, Sun Dried Tomato), Turkey Tub
(Honey, Mesquite Smoked, Oven Roasted, Peppered, Refill
(Mesquite Smoked, Oven Roasted))

Hill Country Fare H-E-B - Turkey (Peppered, White Meat)

Hillshire Farms -

Deli Select

Hearty Slices Oven Roasted Turkey Breast

Thin Sliced Turkey Breast (Honey Roasted, Oven Roasted,
Smoked)

Ultra Thin Turkey Breast (Cracked Black Pepper, Lower Sodium
(Honey Roasted, Oven Roasted), Mesquite Smoked, Oven
Roasted)

Honeysuckle White -

Estate Recipe Turkey Deli Meat (Buffalo Style, Canadian Brand
Maple, Dry Roasted, Hickory Smoked (Honey Pepper, Original,
Sun Dried Tomato), Honey Smoked, Mesquite Smoked)

Fresh (Bone In Turkey Breast, Breast (Boneless Skinless, Cutlets,
Roast, Tenderloins, Thin Cut Slices Scallopini & Milanesa),
Drumsticks, Neck Pieces, Split Breast, Thighs, Wing (Drumettes,
Portions), Wings)

Frozen (Bone In Turkey Breast, Boneless Turkey, Boneless Turkey
Breast w/Gravy Packet)

Fully Cooked Hickory Smoked Bone In Turkey Breast

Fully Cooked Smoked Sausage (Chipotle Links, Original Links)

Ground Turkey (85/15, 93/7, 97% Fat Free, 99% Fat Free, Fresh
Patties, Roll (93/7, 99% Fat Free), Rolls)

Hardwood Smoked (Bacon, Franks)

Hickory Smoked Deli Meat (Cooked Turkey Salami, Turkey Ham,
Turkey Pastrami)

Lunch Meat Deli Sliced (Hickory Smoked Honey Turkey Breast,
Hickory Smoked Turkey Breast, Oven Roasted Turkey Breast,
Turkey Pastrami)

Hickory Smoked Turkey Ham

Marinated Turkey Selections (Bacon Ranch Turkey Breast Tenderloins, Cracked Pepper Turkey Breast Tenderloins, Creamy Dijon Mustard Breast Tenderloins, Homestyle Breast Tenderloins, Lemon Garlic Breast Tenderloins, Rotisserie Turkey Breast Tenderloins, Zesty Italian Herb Breast Tenderloins)

Ready To Roast Turkey Breast

Sausage (Breakfast (Patties, Roll), Links (Breakfast, Hot Italian, Sweet Italian, Traditional Bratwurst), Roll (Breakfast, Mild Italian))

Turkey Bologna

Turkey Breast Deli Meats (Cajun Style Hickory Smoked, Golden Roasted, Hickory Smoked (Peppered, Regular), Honey Mesquite Smoked, Oil Browned, Original Rotisserie, Oven Prepared)

Whole Young Turkey (Fresh, Fresh All Natural, Frozen, Frozen All Natural, Fully Cooked (Hickory Smoked, Oven Roasted))

Hormel -
Chunk Meats Turkey

Deli Meat Natural Choice (Honey, Oven Roasted, Smoked)

Julienne

Natural Choice Deli Meat (Honey Deli, Mesquite, Oven Roasted, Oven Roasted Deli)

Refrigerated Entrees Turkey Breast Roast

Turkey Pepperoni

Hy-Vee - All Natural (Fresh, Frozen), Cubed, Deli Thin Slices Turkey Breast (Honey Roasted, Oven Roasted), Thin Sliced (Honey Turkey, Turkey)

Isaly's - All Deli Meat

Jennie-O Turkey Store -
Breakfast Lover's Turkey Sausage

Deli Meat Grand Champion Turkey Breast (Hickory Smoked, Honey Cured, Oven Roasted)

Flavored Tenderloins (Applewood Smoked, Lemon Garlic, Savory Roast)

T

Fresh (Breakfast Sausage (Lean Links, Lean Patties, Maple Links), Dinner Sausage (Hot Italian, Lean Turkey Bratwurst, Sweet Italian), Ground Turkey (Extra Lean, Lean), Tray (Breast Slices, Breast Tenderloins))

Frozen (Ground Turkey Regular, Turkey Burgers (All Natural, Savory Seasoned))

Jumbo Turkey Franks

Pan Roasts w/Gravy (White, White/Dark Combo)

Jones Dairy Farm - Golden Brown All Natural Fully Cooked Sausage Links Turkey ●

Kayem - Deli Meat (Buffalo Style Breast ! !, Homestyle ! !)

Kirkland Signature - Deli Meat Sliced Turkey Breast (Honey Roasted, Oven Roasted Browned In Vegetable Oil)

Meijer Brand -

Deli Meat Turkey Breast (Hickory Smoked, Honey Roasted)

Frozen (Breast Tenders, Duckling, Split Breast, Turkey Breast, Turkey Breast Young)

Gold Turkey (Hen, Tom)

Hen Turkey

Lunch Meat (Sliced Chipped Meat, Turkey Breast 97% Fat Free)

Regular Turkey Breast

Tom Turkey

Turkey Basted w/Timer

Turkey Breast (Fresh, Fresh Natural)

Member's Mark - Premium Chunk Turkey Breast In Water

Open Nature - Deli Meat (Oven Roasted, Smoked)

Organic Prairie - Frozen Organic Retail (Ground Chub, Whole Young w/Giblets), Organic (Ground Turkey, Whole Young Turkey), Pre Sliced Deli Meat (Roast Slices, Smoked Slices)

Oscar Mayer -

Carving Board Deli Meat Oven Roasted Turkey

Deli Fresh (Cracked Black Peppered Turkey Breast, Honey Smoked Turkey Breast, Mesquite Turkey Breast, Oven Roasted, Oven Roasted Turkey Breast, Smoked Turkey Breast)

Deli Meat (Breast & White Honey Smoked, Mesquite Smoked White, Natural Oven Roasted Breast, Oven Roasted, Oven Roasted Turkey & Cheese, Oven Roasted w/Cheese, Oven Roasted White Turkey, Premium Smoked, Smoked, Smoked White Turkey, Sub Kit Ham & Turkey Breast, Turkey Ham, Turkey Ham w/Smoke Flavor, Variety Pack)

Perdue -
Carving Classics Pan Roasted Turkey Breast (Cracked Pepper, Honey Smoked, Original)
Carving Turkey (Ham Honey Smoked, Whole)
Carving Turkey Breast (Hickory Smoked, Honey Smoked, Mesquite Smoked, Oven Roasted)
Deli Dark Turkey Pastrami Hickory Smoked
Deli Pick Ups Sliced Turkey (Golden Browned, Ham Honey Smoked, Honey Smoked, Mesquite Smoked, Oven Roasted, Smoked)
Ground Turkey (Burgers, Fresh Breast, Fresh Lean)
Healthsense Turkey Breast Oven Roasted Fat Free & Reduced Sodium
Short Cuts Carved Turkey Breast Oven Roasted
Turkey Sausage Seasoned Fresh Lean Sweet Italian
Whole Turkey Seasoned w/Broth

Primo Taglio - Turkey Breast (Natural Hickory Smoked, Natural Hickory Smoked Peppered, Oven Roast)

Private Selection - Deli Meat Turkey (Honey Smoked, Oven Roasted)

Publix -
Deli Pre Pack Lunch Meats (Extra Thin Sliced Oven Roasted Turkey Breast, Extra Thin Sliced Smoked Turkey Breast, Smoked Turkey, Turkey Breast)
Ground Turkey (Breast, Regular)

Safeway - Deli Meat (All Thin Sliced & Regular)

Sara Lee - Deli Meat Slices (Cracked Pepper Turkey Breast, Hardwood Smoked Turkey Breast, Honey Roasted Turkey Breast, Oven Roasted Turkey Breast)

Shelton's -
> Free Range Ground Turkey (1 lb. Chub Pack, 3 lb. Chub Pack)
> Free Range Ground White Turkey 1 lb. Chub Pack
> Free Range Whole Turkey (16-26 lbs., 8-15 lbs.)
> Organic (Large, Whole Small)
> Turkey Burgers

SPAM - Oven Roasted Turkey

Thumann's - All Varieties ●

Trader Joe's - Deli Meat (Oven Roasted Turkey Breast, Smoked Turkey Breast Sliced), Fresh All Natural

Tropical Traditions - Pastured Whole Turkey

Valley Fresh - All Varieties

Wegmans Brand - Thin Sliced (Oven Roasted, Smoked Breast, Smoked Honey Breast)

Wellshire Farms -
> Morning Maple Turkey Breakfast Links ★
> Sliced (Oven Roasted Turkey Breast ★, Smoked Turkey Breast ★, Turkey Bologna ★)
> Turkey (Andouille Sausage ★, Franks ★, Kielbasa ★)
> Turkey Ham (Ham Steak ★, Nuggets ★, Uncured ★)
> Turkey Tom Toms (Hot & Spicy ★, Original ★)
> Uncured Turkey Ham
> Wellshire Organic Turkey Bacon

Turkey Bacon...see Bacon

Turkey Burgers...see Burgers and/or Turkey

Turkey Ham...see Ham and/or Turkey

Turkey Jerky...see Jerky/Beef Sticks

Turkey Lunch Meat...see Deli Meat

Turnips
> ... *All Fresh Fruits & Vegetables Are Gluten-Free*
> **Lowes Foods Brand -** Turnip Greens w/Diced Turnips
> **Pictsweet -** All Plain Frozen Vegetables
> **Safeway Brand -** Frozen Chopped
> **Winn Dixie -** Frozen (Chopped, Regular)

U

V

Vanilla Extract...see Extract

Vanilla Powder
    Gifts Of Nature ▲ - Cooks Vanilla Powder ●
    Mixes From The Heartland ▲ - Powdered Vanilla ●
    Really Great Food Company ▲

Vegetable Juice...see Drinks/Juice

Vegetable Oil...see Oil

Vinegar
    Bakers & Chefs - White Distilled
    Bionaturae ▲ - Organic Balsamic
    Bragg - Apple Cider
    Central Market H-E-B - Organic Balsamic
    Dave's Gourmet - Precocious Pepper Vinegar
    Eden Organic - Organic (Apple Cider, Brown Rice, Red Wine, Ume Plum)
    Filippo Berio ▲ - Red Wine
    Food Club Brand - Balsamic, Cider, Italian (Red Wine, White Wine), White
    Great Value Brand (Wal-Mart) - Apple Cider, Balsamic, Distilled White, Premium (Garlic Flavored Red Wine, Red Wine)
    Hannaford Brand - Apple Cider, Balsamic, Red Wine, White
    Heinz - Apple Cider, Distilled White, Garlic Wine, Red Wine
    Holland House - All Vinegars *(Except Malt Vinegar)*
    Hy-Vee - Apple Cider Flavored Distilled, White Distilled
    Kirkland Signature - Balsamic Vinegar Of Modena
    Lowes Foods Brand - Cider, White
    Lucini - Balsamic Vinegar Of Modena, Balsamico Artisan Vinegar (Charmavi, Dark Cherry, Savory Fig), Italian Wine Vinegar (Pinot Grigio, Pinot Noir)
    Meijer Brand - Balsamic, Balsamic Aged (12 Yr., 4 Yr.), Cider, Red Wine, Regular, White, White Distilled, White Wine

V

W

Musselman's - Apple Cider, White Distilled
Newman's Own Organics - Balsamic **!!**
O Organics - Balsamic
Publix - Apple Cider, Balsamic, Red Wine, White Distilled
Publix GreenWise Market - Balsamic, Red Wine
Regina - All Varieties
Safeway Brand - Apple Cider, Distilled
Safeway Select - Balsamic, Red Wine, Rice, White Wine
Santa Barbara Olive Co. - Basil, Garlic & Pepper, Oregano, Tarragon
Spartan Brand - Apple Cider, White
Spectrum - Balsamic, Organic (Apple Cider (Filtered, Unfiltered),
    Balsamic, Brown Rice (Seasoned, Unseasoned), Distilled White,
    Golden Balsamic, Red Wine, White Wine (Pear, Pomegranate,
    Regular))
Star - Balsamic, Garlic Wine, Golden Balsamic, Italian Kitchen
    (Garlic Wine, Red Wine, White Wine), Natural Rice, Red Raspberry,
    Seasoned Rice
Trader Joe's - Orange Muscat Champagne
Tropical Traditions - Coconut Water Vinegar
Wegmans Brand - Apple Cider, Italian Classics (Chianti Red Wine,
    Four Leaf Balsamic, Three Leaf Balsamic, Tuscan White Wine, Two
    Leaf Balsamic Spray), Red Wine, White Distilled
Winn Dixie - Apple Cider, White
Vitamins...see Gluten-Free OTC Pharmacy Section
Vodka
    *... *All Distilled Alcohol Is Gluten-Free*

W

Wafers...see Cookies
Waffles/Waffle Mix
Arrowhead Mills - Gluten Free Pancake & Waffle Mix
Bloomfield Farms ▲ - Gluten Free Pancake & Waffle Mix ●
Cause You're Special ▲ - Hearty Pancake & Waffle Mix
Choices Rice Bakery ▲ - Waffles

El Peto ▲ - Waffles (Belgium, Belgium Milk Free Corn Free)

Food-Tek Fast & Fresh - Waffle Mix ★

Gifts Of Nature ▲ - Pancake & Waffle Mix ●

Gluten Free Sensations ▲ - Pancake & Waffle Mix

Grandma Ferdon's ▲ - Pancake/Waffle Mix ●, Waffles ●

Hodgson Mill ▲ - Gluten Free Pancake & Waffle Mix w/Flaxseed

Hol Grain ▲ - Pancake & Waffle Mix ●

Kinnikinnick ▲ - Homestyle Waffles (Cinnamon & Brown Sugar, Original), Pancake & Waffle Mix

Laurel's Sweet Treats ▲ - Pancake & Waffle Mix

Namaste Foods ▲ - Waffle & Pancake Mix

Nature's Path - Frozen Organic Waffles (Buckwheat Wildberry ●, Homestyle Gluten Free ●, Mesa Sunrise Omega 3 ●)

Simply Organic ▲ - Gluten Free Pancake & Waffle Mix ●

Sylvan Border Farm - Pancake & Waffle Mix

The Grain Exchange - Belgium Waffles

Trader Joe's - Gluten Free Pancake & Waffle Mix, Wheat Free Toaster Waffles ‼

Van's Natural Foods - Wheat & Gluten Free Waffles (Apple Cinnamon ★, Blueberry ★, Buckwheat w/Berries ★, Flax ★, Totally Natural (Minis ★, Regular ★)

Walnuts...see Nuts

Wasabi

Eden Organic - Wasabi Powder

Hime - Powdered Sushi Wasabi

McCormick - Wasabi Powder

S & B - Prepared Wasabi In Tube

Spectrum - Organic Wasabi Mayonnaise

Sushi Sonic - Real Wasabi

Water

Acqua Panna - Natural Spring

Aquafina -

Flavor Splash (Grape, Lemon, Peach Mango, Raspberry, Strawberry Kiwi, Wild Berry)

W

Purified Drinking Water
Sparkling Water (Berry Burst, Citrus Twist)
Aquarius Spring - Natural Spring Water
Arrowhead - Mountain Spring
Calistoga - Sparkling Mineral Water (All Flavors)
Dasani - Grape, Lemon, Purified, Raspberry, Strawberry
Deer Park - Natural Spring
Deja Blue - Purified Drinking Water
Evian - Natural Spring Water
Fiji - Natural Artesian
Food Club Brand - Distilled, Spring Natural
Fruit2O ▲ - All Varieties
Gordon Food Service - Lemon (Honey, Nectar)
Hannaford Brand - Natural Spring, Seltzer Water
Hansen's - Junior Water
Hy-Vee - Coolers (All Flavors), Natural Spring, Premium Distilled, Purified, Refreshers (All Flavors), Spring, Tonic
Ice Mountain - Spring Water
Kirkland Signature - Spring Water
Lowes Foods Brand - Drinking, Spring
Meijer Brand -
  Calcium
  Distilled
  Flavored (Crystal Quencher (Black Cherry, Key Lime, Kiwi Strawberry, Mandarin Orange, Mango Passion Fruit, Pink Grapefruit, Pomegranate Cherry, Raspberry, Tangerine Lime, Tropical Island, White Grape), Fit 20 (Berry, Black Cherry, Grape, Kiwi Strawberry, Lemon), Lemon, Orange, Rainbow Pack, Raspberry, Strawberry)
  Gold (Artesian, Regular)
  Natural Calcium
  Purified
  Regular
  Sparkling
  Spring

494

My Essentials - Sparkling (Black Cherry, Key Lime, Kiwi Strawberry, Peach, Raspberry, Tropical Punch, White Grape)

Nestle Pure Life - Purified

Ozarka - Natural Spring

Perrier - Carbonated Natural Spring

Poland Spring - Natural Spring

Publix - Spring Water

Refreshe - Drinking, Nutrient Enhanced Water (All Flavors), Purified Drinking, Seltzer, Spring, Tonic Water

San Pellegrino - Sparkling Mineral

Smart Water (Glaceau)

Snapple - Spring Water

SoBe -

Lifewater (Agave Lemonade, Blackberry Grape, Orange Tangerine, Pomegranate Cherry, Strawberry Kiwi, w/Purevia (Acai Fruit Punch, B Energy Black Cherry Dragonfruit, B Energy Strawberry Apricot, Black & Blue Berry, Cherimoya Punch, Fuji Apple Pear, Mango Melon, Strawberry Dragonfruit, Yumberry Pomegranate)

Lifewater With Coconut Water (Mango Mandarin, Pacific Coconut, Pomegranate Nectarine)

Spartan Brand - Water (Distilled, Drinking, Natural Spring)

Sweet Bay - Distilled, Drinking Water w/Minerals, Natural Spring Water Sodium Free

Trader Joe's - All Sparkling

Vitaminwater (Glaceau) - All Varieties

Wegmans Brand -

Aqua Mineral Water (Italian, Lemon, Lemongrass, Lime, Mixed Berry)

FYFGA Sparkling Water (Lemon, Lime, Mandarin Orange, Mineral, Mixed Berry, Natural, Raspberry, Tangerine Lime)

Spring Water (FYFGA Regular, w/Fluoride)

Vitamin Infused (Acai Blueberry Pomegranate, Dragon Fruit, Fruit Punch, Lemonade, Raspberry Apple)

W **Winn Dixie** - Distilled, Drinking, Purified, Sparkling Water (All Flavors), Spring Water

Zephyrhills - All Varieties (Sparkling Natural Spring), Natural Spring

Water Chestnuts

Ka-Me - Sliced/Peeled **!**, Whole/Peeled **!**

Reese - Diced, Sliced, Whole

Spartan Brand - Canned (Sliced, Whole)

Watermelon

*... *All Fresh Fruits & Vegetables Are Gluten-Free*

Whipping Cream

Cabot - Whipped Cream Aerosol

Cool Whip - Topping (Extra Creamy, Free, Lite, Original, Season's Delight (French Vanilla, Sweet Cinnamon), Sugar Free)

Dream Whip - Whipped Topping Mix

Food Club Brand -

Aerosol Whipped Topping (Extra Creamy, Original)

Frozen Whipped Topping (Extra Creamy, Fat Free, Light, Original)

Garelick Farms - Ultra Pasteurized Whipping Cream

Giant Eagle Brand - Light Whipping Cream

Gordon Food Service - Heavy (36%, 40%), Light Real Aerosol

Great Value Brand (Wal-Mart) -

Heavy Whipping Cream

Sweetened Whipped Cream Ultra Pasteurized Aerosol (Extra Creamy, Regular)

Hannaford Brand - All Frozen

Hood - Instant Whipped Cream (Light, Original), Sugar Free Light

Horizon Organic - All Varieties

Hy-Vee - Aerosol (Extra Creamy, Light), Frozen Lite Whipped, Frozen Whipped Topping (Extra Creamy, Fat Free, Regular), Real Whipped Cream (Lite, Regular)

Lowes Foods Brand - Frozen Whipped Topping (Fat Free, Lite, Regular), Whipping Cream (Heavy, Light, Regular)

Lucerne - Aerosol Whipping Cream (Extra Creamy, Light), Heavy Whipping Cream

W

Meijer Brand -
   Frozen Whipped Topping (Extra Creamy, Fat Free, Lite, Original)
   Ultra Pasteurized (Heavy Whipping Cream, Whipped Cream
      Aerosol (Non Dairy, Regular))
MimicCreme - Almond & Cashew Cream (Sugar Free Sweetened,
   Sweetened, Unsweetened), Healthy Top Cream
My Essentials - All Aerosol
Organic Valley - Heavy Whipping Cream
Prairie Farms - Half & Half (Fat Free, Heavy Whipping, Regular, Ultra
   Pasteurized), Ultra Pasteurized Heavy Whipping Cream
Publix - Aerosol Whipped Cream (Heavy, Light), Aerosol Whipped
   Topping Fat Free, Heavy Whipping Cream, Whipping Cream
Reddi-Wip - All Flavors
Safeway Brand - Light, Regular
Shamrock Farms - Fresh Whipping, Heavy Cream
Soyatoo - Rice Whip, Soy Whip (Whippable Soy Topping, Whipped
   Topping)
Spartan Brand - Frozen Whipped Topping (Light, Regular)
Wegmans Brand - Extra Creamy Whipped Heavy Cream, Light, Regular,
   Whipped Topping (Extra Creamy, Fat Free, Lite, Regular)
Winn Dixie - Aerosol (Extra Creamy, Original), Frozen

Whiskey
   ... *All Distilled Alcohol Is Gluten-Free*
Wine
   ... *All Wine Made In The USA Is Gluten-Free*
Wing Sauce
   Di Lusso - Buffalo Wing Sauce
   Frank's RedHot - Buffalo (Hot, Regular)
   Jim Beam - Original Wing Sauce
   Ken's Steak House - Buffalo Wing Sauce
   Moore's Marinade - Buffalo Wing ★, Honey BBQ Wing ★
   Mr. Spice Organic - Salt Free Hot Wing Sauce & Marinade ★
   Texas Pete ▲ - Buffalo Wing, Extra Mild Buffalo, Fiery Sweet
   Wing-Time - Buffalo Wing Sauce (Garlic, Hot, Medium, Mild, Super Hot)

W Wings
X ... *All Fresh Poultry Is Gluten-Free (Non-Marinated, Unseasoned)*
   Great Value Brand (Wal-Mart) - Frozen Wing Sections
   Honeysuckle White - Chicken (Barbecue Glazed, Buffalo Style, Oven Roasted)
   Trader Joe's - Chicken Wings
   Wegmans Brand - Jumbo Buffalo Style Chicken

Worcestershire Sauce
   Food Club Brand
   French's
   Great Value Brand (Wal-Mart) - Worcestershire Sauce
   Hannaford Brand
   Heinz
   Hill Country Fare H-E-B - Regular
   Hy-Vee - Light, Regular
   Lea & Perrins - Low Sodium, Original, Thick Classic
   Lowes Foods Brand
   Meijer Brand
   Safeway Brand
   Spartan Brand
   The Wizard's - Organic Gluten Free Vegan Worcestershire
   Wan Ja Shan - Organic Gluten Free

Wraps
   Amy's - Indian Aloo Mattar ★, Teriyaki ★, Tofu Scramble Breakfast ★

X

Xanthan Gum
   Augason Farms ▲ - Xanthan Gum ●
   Bob's Red Mill ▲ - Xanthan Gum ★
   Cause You're Special ▲
   El Peto ▲
   Ener-G ▲
   Gifts Of Nature ▲ - Xanthan Gum ●
   Hodgson Mill ▲
   Ingredient Solutions

Mixes From The Heartland ▲ - Xanthan Gum ●
Nuts.com - Xanthan Gum ●
Really Great Food Company ▲

Yams
... *All Fresh Fruits & Vegetables Are Gluten-Free
Food Club Brand - Canned Sweet Cut
Kroger Brand - Canned Candied
S&W - All Canned Vegetables
Spartan Brand - Yams Cut

Yeast
Bakipan - Active Dry, Bread Machine, Fast Rising Instant
Bob's Red Mill ▲ - Active Dry ★, Nutritional Food ★
Bragg - Nutritional Yeast
El Peto ▲
Fleischmann's - All Varieties
Gayelord Hauser - Flake Form 100% Natural Brewer's Yeast
Marmite - Flavored Yeast Extract
Nuts.com - Gluten Free (Nutritional Yeast ●, Yeast ●)
Really Great Food Company ▲ - Yeast
Red Star - Active Dry, Bread Machine, Fresh, Quick Rise
SAF - Bread Machine, Gold Instant, Gourmet Perfect Rise, Red Instant, Traditional Active Dry

Yogurt
Amande - Cultured Almond Milk Yogurt (Blueberry, Cherry, Coconut, Peach, Plain, Raspberry, Strawberry, Vanilla)
Brown Cow Yogurt -
    Cream Top (Apricot Mango ●, Blueberry ●, Cherry Vanilla ●, Chocolate ●, Coffee ●, Maple ●, Peach ●, Plain ●, Raspberry ●, Strawberry ●, Vanilla ●)
    Greek (Blueberry ●, Plain ●, Strawberry ●, Vanilla ●)
    Low Fat (Black Cherry ●, Blueberry ●, Boysenberry ●, Lemon Twist ●, Peach ●, Plain ●, Strawberry ●, Vanilla ●, Vanilla Bean ●)
    Non Fat (Blueberry ●, Lemon ●, Plain ●, Strawberry ●, Vanilla ●)

Y Cabot - Greek Style (Lowfat Blueberry, Lowfat Plain, Lowfat
Strawberry, Lowfat Vanilla Bean, Plain), Nonfat Plain
Cascade Fresh - All Varieties
Chobani -
Champions (Honeynana ●, Orange Vanilla ●, Vanilla Chocolate
Chunk ●, Verryberry ●)
Low Fat (Mango ●, Passion Fruit ●, Pineapple ●, Plain ●, Strawberry
Banana ●)
Multiserve (Plain (Low Fat ●, Non Fat ●), Strawberry ●, Vanilla ●)
Non Fat (Apple Cinnamon ●, Black Cherry ●, Blood Orange ●,
Blueberry ●, Honey ●, Lemon ●, Peach ●, Plain ●, Pomegranate ●,
Raspberry ●, Strawberry ●, Vanilla ●)
Dannon - Plain (Activia 24 oz. Container, Low Fat, Natural, Non Fat)
Earth's Best Organic Baby Food - Baby Yogurt (Apple ★, Banana
Mango ★, Peach Pear ★, Vanilla Prune ★)
Fage - All Flavors ●
Giant Eagle Brand -
32 oz. (Lowfat Plain, Non Fat Plain)
Blended (Blackberry, Blueberry, Mixed Berry, Peach, Raspberry,
Strawberry, Strawberry Banana, Vanilla)
Light (Banana Creme, Blackberry, Blueberry, Key Lime, Lemon
Chiffon, Mixed Berry, Orange Creme, Peach, Raspberry,
Raspberry Lemonade, Strawberry, Strawberry Banana, Vanilla)
Great Value Brand (Wal-Mart) - Light Yogurt (Banana Cream Pie,
Blueberry, Cherry, Key Lime Pie, Orange Cream Pie, Peach,
Raspberry, Strawberry, Strawberry Banana, Vanilla)
Horizon Organic - All Varieties
Hy-Vee -
Fat Free Plain
Hy Active (Blueberry, Peach, Strawberry, Vanilla)
Light (Banana Cream, Blueberry, Cherry, Lemon Chiffon, Peach,
Raspberry, Strawberry, Strawberry Banana, Vanilla)
Low Fat (Black Cherry, Blueberry, Cherry Vanilla, Lemon, Mixed
Berry, Plain, Raspberry, Strawberry, Strawberry Banana)

Kemps - All Varieties
Lactaid - Lactose Free Non Fat (Blueberry, Peach, Strawberry, Vanilla)
Lifeway ▲ - Lassi Yogurt Drink (All Varieties)
Lowes Foods Brand -
　Drinkable Yogurts (Mixed Berry, Strawberry, Strawberry Banana)
　Lite (Black Cherry, Blueberry, Key Lime, Lemon Chiffon, Peach,
　　Raspberry, Strawberry, Vanilla)
　Low Fat Vanilla
　Non Fat Plain
　Regular (Black Cherry, Blueberry, Mixed Berry, Peach, Strawberry,
　　Strawberry Banana)
Lucerne - Fat Free (All Varieties)
Meijer Brand -
　Blended (Boysenberry, Strawberry, Strawberry Banana, Tropical Fruit)
　Fruit On The Bottom (Blueberry, Peach, Raspberry, Strawberry)
　Lite (Banana Creme, Black Cherry, Blueberry, Cherry Vanilla,
　　Coconut Cream, Lemon Chiffon, Mint Chocolate, Peach,
　　Raspberry, Strawberry, Strawberry Banana, Vanilla)
　Low Fat Blended (Blueberry, Cherry, Mixed Berry, Peach, Pina Colada,
　　Raspberry)
　Low Fat Vanilla
　Tube Yo Lar (Strawberry Banana, Strawberry Blueberry, Tropical
　　Punch Raspberry)
My Essentials - All Flavors
Nancy's - All Cultured Dairy & Soy Varieties
Nature's Basket -
　Organic
　　Blueberry *(6 oz. Only)*
　　Peach *(6 oz. Only)*
　　Raspberry Low Fat *(6 oz. Only)*
　　Strawberry *(6 oz. Only)*
　　Vanilla *(6 oz. Only)*
Nogurt - Organic (Blueberry ●, Chocolate ●, Orange ●, Pomegranate ●)
O Organics - All Flavors

Y

Oikos - Organic Greek (Blueberry ●, Caramel ●, Chocolate ●, Honey ●, Plain ●, Strawberry ●, Vanilla ●)

Organic Valley - Berry, Plain, Vanilla

Prairie Farms -

Fat Free (Banana Creme Pie, Black Cherry, Blueberry, Cherry Vanilla, Keylime Pie, Mixed Berry, Orange Creme, Peach, Raspberry, Strawberry, Vanilla)

Low Fat (Apricot, Black Cherry, Blackberry, Blueberry, Cherry Vanilla, Peach, Pineapple, Raspberry)

Publix -

Creamy Blends (Black Cherry, Blueberry, Original, Peach, Strawberry, Vanilla)

Fat Free Plain

Fat Free Light (Apple Pie, Banana Creme Pie, Blueberry, Cappuccino, Caramel Creme, Cherry, Cherry Vanilla, Coconut Creme Pie, Honey Almond, Key Lime Pie, Lemon Chiffon, Mandarin Orange, Peach, Raspberry, Strawberry, Strawberry Banana, Vanilla, Wild Berry Crumb Cake)

Fruit On The Bottom (Banana, Black Cherry, Blackberry, Blueberry, Cherry, Guava, Mango, Mixed Berry, Peach, Pineapple, Raspberry, Strawberry, Strawberry Banana, Tropical Blend)

Just 4 Kidz (Blue Raspberry & Cotton Candy, Grape Bubblegum & Watermelon, Strawberry & Blueberry, Strawberry Banana & Cherry)

Multi Packs Creamy Blends (Black Cherry & Mixed Berry, Blueberry & Strawberry Banana, Peach & Strawberry)

No Sugar Added (Blueberry, Cranberry Raspberry, Peach, Strawberry, Vanilla)

Redwood Hill Farm - Goat Milk Yogurt (Apricot Mango, Blueberry, Cranberry Orange, Plain, Strawberry, Vanilla, Wildflower Honey)

Siggi's ▲ -

Icelandic Style Skyr (Acai & Mixed Berry ●, Blueberry ●, Grapefruit ●, Orange & Ginger ●, Peach ●, Plain ●, Pomegranate & Passion Fruit ●, Strawberry ●, Vanilla ●)

Probiotic Drinkable Non Fat Yogurt (Blueberry ●, Plain ●, Strawberry ●)

Silk Live - All Varieties

So Delicious - Coconut Milk Yogurt (Blueberry ●, Chocolate ●, Greek Style (Blueberry ●, Chocolate ●, Plain ●, Raspberry ●, Strawberry ●, Vanilla ●), Passionate Mango ●, Pina Colada ●, Plain ●, Raspberry ●, Strawberry Banana ●, Strawberry ●, Vanilla ●)

Spartan Brand - Black Cherry, Blueberry, Cherry Vanilla, Light Banana, Mango, Mixed Berry, Peach, Raspberry, Strawberry, Strawberry Banana, Vanilla

Stonyfield Organic -
All Frozen Yogurts ● *(Except Cookies & Cream)*
All Smoothies ●
All Soy Yogurts ●
All YoBaby ●
All YoKids ●
All YoToddler *(Except YoToddler Plus Fruit & Cereal)*

Tillamook - Yogurt & Yogurt Smoothies **!**

Trader Joe's - All Varieties (Regular, Soy)

Wegmans Brand -
Blended Low Fat (Blueberry, Cherry, Coffee, Key Lime, Lemon, Mixed Berry, Orange Cream, Peach, Raspberry, Strawberry, Strawberry Banana, Vanilla)
Fruit On The Bottom (Fat Free (Black Cherry, Blueberry, Lemon, Mixed Berry, Peach, Raspberry, Strawberry, Strawberry Banana), Low Fat (Apricot Mango, Blueberry, Cherry, Cherry Vanilla, Lemon, Mixed Berry, Peach, Pina Colada, Pineapple, Raspberry, Strawberry, Strawberry Banana, Strawberry Kiwi))
Light Blended Non Fat (Blueberry, Key Lime, Mixed Berry, Orange Cream, Peach, Raspberry, Strawberry, Strawberry Banana, Vanilla)
Low Fat Vanilla
Organic FYFGA Super Yogurt Blended Lowfat (Blueberry, Peach, Plain, Raspberry, Strawberry, Vanilla)
Plain (Low Fat, Nonfat)

Y

Weight Watchers - Apple Pie A La Mode, Black Cherry, Blueberry Pie, Caramel Spice Cake, Cherry Cheesecake, Coconut Cream Pie

WholeSoy & Co. - All Products (Frozen Yogurts **!!**, Smoothies **!!**, Yogurts **!!**)

Winn Dixie - All Varieties

Yo-J - All Varieties

Yoplait -

All Natural Plain Fat Free (16 oz., 32 oz.)

Delights Parfait (Cherry Cheesecake, Chocolate Eclair, Chocolate Raspberry, Creme Caramel, Grasshopper Pie, Lemon Torte, Triple Berry Creme)

Fiber One (Blueberry, Key Lime Pie, Peach, Strawberry, Vanilla)

Go Gurt (Banana Split/Strawberry Milkshake, Cool Cotton Candy/Burstin' Melon Berry, Perry Berry/Summer Punch, Strawberry Banana Burst/Watermelon Meltdown, Strawberry Kiwi Kick/Chill Out Cherry, Strawberry Riptide/Bikini Bottom Berry, Strawberry Splash/Berry Blue Blast)

Greek (Blueberry, Honey Vanilla, Key Lime, Peach, Plain, Strawberry)

Kids (Strawberry, Strawberry Banana, Vroom Vroom Vanilla)

Lactose Free (Cherry, French Vanilla, Peach, Strawberry)

Large Size (Creamy Vanilla, Light Fat Free (Creamy Strawberry, Creamy Vanilla), Original (Creamy Harvest Peach, Creamy Strawberry, Creamy Strawberry Banana))

Light (Apple Turnover, Apricot Mango, Banana Cream Pie, Black Forest Cake, Blackberry, Blueberry Patch, Boston Cream Pie, Harvest Peach, Key Lime Pie, Lemon Cream Pie, Orange Creme, Pineapple Upside Down Cake, Raspberry Cheesecake, Raspberry Lemonade, Red Raspberry, Red Velvet Cake, Strawberries 'N Bananas, Strawberry, Strawberry Orange Sunrise, Strawberry Shortcake, Triple Berry Torte, Vanilla Cherry, Very Cherry, Very Vanilla, White Chocolate Strawberry)

Light Thick & Creamy (Blueberry Pie, Cherry Cobbler, Cinnamon Roll, French Vanilla, Key Lime Pie, Lemon Meringue, Strawberry)

Original (Blackberry Harvest, Blackberry Pomegranate, Blueberry

Acai, Boston Cream Pie, Boysenberry, Cherry Orchard, Cherry Pomegranate, French Vanilla, Harvest Peach, Key Lime Pie, Lemon Burst, Mango, Mixed Berry, Mountain Blueberry, Orange Creme, Pear, Pina Colada, Pineapple, Red Raspberry, Strawberry, Strawberry Banana, Strawberry Cheesecake, Strawberry Kiwi, Strawberry Lemonade, Strawberry Mango)

Splitz (Birthday Cake, Rainbow Sherbet, Strawberry Banana Split, Strawberry Sundae)

Thick & Creamy (Blackberry Harvest, Key Lime Pie, Peaches 'N Cream, Royal Raspberry, Strawberry, Strawberry Banana, Vanilla)

Trix Yogurt (Cotton Candy, Raspberry Rainbow, Strawberry Banana, Strawberry Punch, Triple Cherry)

Whips (Cherry Cheesecake, Chocolate, Chocolate Raspberry, Key Lime Pie, Lemon Burst, Orange Creme, Peaches 'N Cream, Raspberry Mousse, Strawberry Mist, Vanilla Creme)

Yoplus (Blackberry Pomegranate, Strawberry, Vanilla)

Z

Zucchini

... *All Fresh Fruits & Vegetables Are Gluten-Free

C & W - All Plain Frozen Vegetables **! !**

Del Monte - Zucchini w/Italian Style Tomato Sauce

Trader Joe's - Frozen Misto Alla Grigio **! !**

Gluten-Free
Over The Counter (OTC)
Pharmacy Guide

Rx Allergy/Sinus/Cold/Flu Relief

Actifed - Tablets

Afrin - Nasal Spray

Airborne -
  Chewable Tablets (Berry, Citrus)
  Effervescence (Lemon Lime, Pink Grapefruit, Very Berry,
    Zesty Orange)
  On The Go (Lemon Lime, Very Berry)

Benadryl - All Products

Children's Motrin - Cold Suspension Berry

Children's Sudafed - Nasal Decongestant Grape Liquid, PE Liquid
  (Cough & Cold Grape, Nasal Decongestant Raspberry)

Children's Tylenol -
  Plus Cold (& Allergy, & Cough Dye Free Grape, & Stuffy Nose, &
    Stuffy Nose Dye Free Grape, Grape)
  Plus Cough (& Runny Nose, & Sore Throat)
  Plus Flu Bubble Gum
  Plus Multi Symptom Cold Grape (Dye Free, Regular)

Children's Zyrtec - Allergy Syrup (Bubble Gum, Grape)

Claritin - Children's (Grape Chews, Grape Syrup), D, Liquid Gels,
  Original Tablets

Cold-Eeze - Cold Remedy Lozenges (All Flavors)

Dayquil - All Varieties

Halls -
  Cough Drops Regular (Cherry, Honey Lemon, Ice Blue, Mentho
    Lyptus, Spearmint, Strawberry, Tropical Fruit)
  Cough Drops Sugar Free (Black Cherry, Cherry, Citrus Blend,
    Fresh Mint, Honey Berry, Honey Lemon, Mountain Menthol,
    Peppermint, Spearmint)
  Halls Breezers (Cool Berry, Cool Creamy Strawberry, Sugar Free
    Cool Berry, Tropical Chill)
  Halls Defense (Assorted Citrus, Harvest Cherry, Strawberry,
    Sugar Free, Watermelon)

Rx

Halls Naturals (Honey Lemon Chamomile, Mountain Berry w/Soothing Honey Center)

Halls Plus (Cherry, Honey Lemon, Icy Lemon, Icy Strawberry)

Halls Refresh (Juicy Strawberry, Lemon Raspberry, Refreshing Mint, Tropical Wave)

Kirkland Signature - Children's Pain Relief Plus Multisymptom Cold

Little Remedies - All Varieties (Little Colds, Little Fevers, Little Noses)

Meijer -
  Cold Child Suspension Grape
  Cough Cold (Child Suspension Cherry, Infant Drops Cherry)
  Daytime 6hr (Liquid, Liquid Gels)
  Dibromm (DM Grape Elixir, Grape Elixir)
  Diphedryl (Capsules, Cherry Elixir, Tablets)
  Effervescent Cold Tablets
  Ibuprofen Sinus Brown Caplets
  Loratadine (D 24hr Tablets, QD Tablets)
  Naproxen Sodium Sinus Cold Caplets
  Nasal Spray (Extra Moist Liquid, Liquid, Multi Symptom Liquid, No Drip Pump Liquid)
  Nitetime 6hr (Cherry Liquid, Liquid Gels, Original Liquid)
  Nitetime Cough 6hr Cherry Liquid
  PE Allergy Sinus Caplets
  PE Cold Flu Day Cool Caplets
  PE Severe Congestion Caplets
  Pedia Cough Decongestion Drops
  Tri Acting Nitetime Grape Liquid
  Tussin (CF Liquid, Cough Cold Softgels, CS Liquid, DM Clear Liquid, DM Liquid, Pedia Cough Cold Liquid)

Nyquil - All Varieties

Olbas - Aromatherapy Massage Oil & Inhalant, Cough Syrup, Inhaler

PediaCare -
  24 Hour Allergy Cherry
  Allergy & Cold Grape
  Children's Plus w/Acetaminophen

Rx   Children's w/o Acetaminophen
Cough & Congestion
Fever Reducer Pain Reliever (Cherry, Cherry & Grape, Dye Free)
Long Lasting Multi Symptom & Cold
Primatene - Mist
Scot-Tussin - For Diabetics (Cough, Cough Suppressant & Cold Relief,
Multi Action Cold & Allergy)
St. Claire's Organics ▲ - Cough Calming Syrup, Decongest Inhaler,
Herbal Throat Spray, Infection Formula, Throat Soothers
Sudafed - 12 Hour (Pressure & Pain, Sinus), 24 Hour
Tylenol - Cold & Flu Severe, Cold Severe Congestion Caplets, Cold Sore
Throat, Sinus Severe Congestion
Vicks - All Products *(Except VapoDrops)*
Walgreens -
Allergy Multi Symptom (Day Caplets, Day Quick Gels, Day/Night
Caplet Combo Pack, Night Caplets)
Allergy Sinus Decongestant Daytime Caplets
Apap Junior Strength Rapid Tab (Bubble Gum, Grape)
Chest Congestion Caplets
Children's (Multi Symptom, Plus Cold, Plus Flu Bubble Gum)
Cold (Decongestant Multi Symptom (Day, Night), Head Congestion
(Day, Day Severe, Night), Liquid Caplet (Day, Night), Liquid Caplet
Sinus (Day, Night), Multi Symptom (Day Quick Gel, Day Severe
Caplets, Day Severe Capsules, Day/Night Caplet Combo, Nite
Cool Caplets), Tablets)
Cold & Flu Nighttime Relief Liquicaps
Cough & Sore Throat Cherry
Extended Cough Relief Adult Grape
Flu Relief Maximum Strength Tablets
Mucus Relief Tablets (DM Expectorant, PE Expectorant, Regular)
Runny Rhino Cold Relief Pops
Severe Allergy Caplets
Sinex Long Acting Spray
Sinus Congestion & Pain (Day (Caplets, Gelcaps, Quick Gels,
Severe Caplets), Day Night Caplet Combo)

Rx

Sinus D Daytime Caplets
Throat Lozenge Cherry
Wal-Act Tablets
Wal-Born Effervescent Tablets (Grape, Lemon Lime, Orange)
Wal-Dryl (Capsules, D Allergy Sinus, Dye Free Liquigels, Minitabs,
  Severe Allergy & Sinus)
Wal-Finate (Allergy Tablets, D Tablets)
Wal-Flu Warming Relief Severe Cold (Daytime Cherry,
  Nighttime Cherry)
Walgreens Child Plus Cough Nose Cherry
Walgreens Comfort Gel Supreme Cherry
Walgreens Soothe (Cherry, Original)
Wal-Mucil Smooth Sugar Berry
Wal-Phed (Cold Cough Caplets, D Tablets, PE (Nighttime Cold,
  Non Drying Sinus, Severe Cold, Sinus Headache, Tablets),
  Sinus & Allergy)
Wal-Tap DM Children's Cold Cough Elixir Red Grape
Wal-Tussin Cough (Long Acting Orange, Softgels)
Zyrtec - Allergy (Liquid Gels, Tablets, Zyrtec-D Tablets)

Antacids

Digestive Advantage - Crohn's & Colitis, Irritable Bowel Syndrome,
  Lactose Intolerance
Lactaid - Dietary Supplement (Fast Act Caplets, Fast Act Chewables,
  Original Strength Caplets)
Meijer -
  Antacid Calcium (Peppermint Chewables, Ultra Fruit Chewables,
    XS Berry Chewables, XS Chewables, XS Fruit Chewables, XS
    Tropical Chewables, XS Wintergreen Chewables)
  Antacid Fast Acting Liquid (Maximum Strength Cherry, Maximum
    Strength Original, Regular Strength Original)
  Cimetidine Tablets
  Dairy Digestive (Regular Strength, Ultra Caplets)

Rx   Effervescent Antacid Pain Tablets

Milk Of Magnesia (Cherry Liquid, Mint Liquid, Original Liquid)

Pink Bismuth (Chewables, Maximum Strength Liquid, Regular
    Strength Liquid)

Ranitidine

Mylanta -

Maximum Strength (Cherry, Mint, Original)

Regular Strength (Mint, Original)

Supreme (Cherry)

Ultimate Strength (Cherry)

Pepcid AC - Maximum Strength AC EZ Chews, Tablets

Pepto Bismol - All Varieties

St. Claire's Organics ▲ - Tummy Soothers

Tagamet HB

Tums - All Flavors *(Except Smoothies)*

Walgreens -

Antacid Chewable Tablets (Assorted, Maximum Strength
    Lemon, Original Mint, Peppermint, Ultra Tabs (Berry, Fruit, Mint),
    Wintergreen)

Lactose Relief

Anti-Aging Products

100% Pure - All Serums

Arbonne -

FC5 (Exfoliating New Cell Scrub, Hydrating Eye Crème,
    Moisturizing Night Crème, Nurturing Day Lotion w/SPF 20, Oil
    Absorbing Day Lotion w/SPF 20, Purifying Cleanser & Toner, Skin
    Conditioning Oil, Ultra Hydrating Hand Crème)

NutriMinC RE9 Retaliate Wrinkle Filler

RE9 Advanced (Age Defying Neck Cream, Cellular Renewal
    Masque, Firming Body Cream, Instant Lift Gel, Night Repair
    Creme, Nourishing Body Wash, Restorative Day Creme SPF 20)

RE9 Advanced For Men Exfoliating Wash

anti-aging products

Rx

Revalage (Age Spot Brightening (Day Cream w/SPF 30, Hand
   Therapy w/SPF 30), Concentrated Age Spot Minimizer,
   Intensive Pro Brightening Night Serum)

Desert Essence Organics - Age Reversal Pomegranate (Eye Serum,
   Face Serum, Facial Cleansing Gel)

Juice Beauty -
   Exfoliating Cleanser
   Green Apple Nutrient Eye Cream
   Moisturizer Stem Cellular Repair
   Organic (Facial Rejuvenating Mask, Treatment Oil)
   Serum (Green Apple Age Defy, Stem Cellular Repair Booster)
   Smoothing Eye Concentrate
   Stem Cellular Repair Eye Treatment

Kiss My Face - C The Change Ester C Serum, Intensive Repair Night
   Creme, Under Age Ultra Hydrating Moisturizer

Logona Naturkosmetik -
   Age Protection (Clarifying Toner, Cleansing Foam, Day Cream,
      Eye Gel, Facial Steam Bath, Hydro Active Ampule Therapy,
      Hydro Lipid Balance, Moisture Treatment, Night Cream, Skin
      Firming Gel, Wrinkle Therapy Fluid)
   Age Protection Anti Cellulite Massage Oil

Oil Of Olay - Regenerist Fragrance Free Regenerating Serum, Total
   Effects Fragrance Free

Roc -
   Brilliance
      Eye & Lash Anti Aging Primer
      Moisturizer (Day Rejuvenating, Night Recharging)
   Multi Correxion (4 Zone Daily Moisturizer, Eye Treatment, Lift Anti
      Gravity (Day Moisturizer, Eye Cream, Night Cream), Night
      Treatment, Nourish Stress Repair (Eye Cream, Night Cream),
      Skin Renewing Serum)
   Retinol Correxion
      Deep Wrinkle (Daily Moisturizer SPF 30, Filler, Night Cream)
      Eye Cream

Rx   Instant Facial Smoother
            Resurfacing (Daily Disks, Max Wrinkle System)
            Sensitive (Eye Cream, Night Cream)
Simple - Vital Vitamin Night Cream
Sophyto -
    Anti Aging Antioxidant Serum ●
    Marine Peptide Brightening Treatment ●
    Multivitamin Facial Serum ●
    PH Optimizing Restorative Toner ●
    Tocotrienol Super Skin Concentrate ●

Antibiotic/Analgesic Ointment & Spray

Band-Aid - Hurt Free Antiseptic Wash
Cortaid - Intensive Therapy, Maximum Strength
Desitin - Baby Ointment (Maximum Strength Original Paste, Multi
    Purpose Ointment, Rapid Relief Cream)
Desert Essence Organics - Don't Be Rash Diaper Cream, Relief
    Spray, Tea Tree Oil (Eco Harvest, Kinder To Skin Australian,
    Organic, Pure Australian)
Dr. Bronner's - Organic Lavender Hand Sanitizing Spray
EO - Hand Sanitizer (Gel ●, Spray ●, Wipes ●)
Hy-Vee Health Market - Allergy Creme 2%, Calamine Lotion,
    Hydrocortisone Cream 1%, Triple Antibiotic Ointment Plus
Little Remedies - Little Ouchies Pain Relieving Spray
Olbas - Analgesic Salve
Walgreens - Hydrogen Peroxide

Anti-Diarrhea

Children's Imodium - A D Liquid
Digestive Advantage - Crohn's & Colitis, Irritable Bowel Syndrome,
    Lactose Intolerance

Rx

Imodium - A D EZ Chews, AD Caplets, Advanced Chewable Tablets, Multi Symptom Relief (Caplets, Chewable Tablets)

Lactaid - Dietary Supplement (Fast Act Caplets, Fast Act Chewables, Original Strength)

Meijer - Loperamide (Caplets, Liquid), Pink Bismuth (Chewables, Maximum Strength Liquid, Regular Strength Liquid)

Mylanta - Maximum Strength (Cherry, Mint, Original), Regular Strength (Mint, Original), Supreme, Ultimate Strength Liquid

Pepto Bismol - All Varieties

St. Claire's Organics ▲ - Tummy Soothers

Walgreens - Anti Diarrheal Caplets, Lactose Relief

Anti-Fungal

AZO - AZO Yeast Tablets

Hy-Vee Health Market - Anti-Fungal Foot Care Creme

Lotrimin - All Varieties

Meijer -
Miconazole 2% Spray Liquid
Miconazole Cream (3 Day Disapp. Combo, 3 Day Preapp. Combo, 7 Day Disapp., 7 Day Reapp.)
Tioconazole I Day Ointment Disapp.
Tolnaftate 1% Spray (Liquid, Powder)

Tinactin - All Varieties

Walgreens - Tioconazole I Day Ointment Disapp.

Anti-Gas

Digestive Advantage - Crohn's & Colitis, Irritable Bowel Syndrome, Lactose Intolerance

Infant's Mylicon - Drops Non Staining

Lactaid - Dietary Supplement (Fast Act Caplets, Fast Act Chewables, Original Strength)

Little Remedies - Little Tummys (All Varieties)

Rx **Meijer** - Gas Relief Ultra Softgels, Simethicone Nonstaining Drops
Mylanta -
Gas Maximum Strength Chewables (Cherry, Mint)
Maximum Strength (Cherry, Mint, Original)
Regular Strength (Mint, Original)
Supreme
Ultimate Strength Liquid
Mylicon - Drops
Phazyme
St. Claire's Organics ▲ - Tummy Soothers
Walgreens - Cherry Gas Relief Tablets, Lactose Relief

Baby Care

Arbonne - ABC Baby Care (Body Oil, Hair & Body Wash, Herbal
Diaper Rash Cream, Lotion, Sunscreen SPF 30)
California Baby -
Aromatherapy Massage Oil (Calming, Eucalyptus Ease, I Love You,
Overtired & Cranky, Super Sensitive)
Aromatherapy Spritzer (Calming, Colds & Flu, I Love You,
Overtired & Cranky)
Bath Drops (Calming, Eucalyptus Ease, Overtired & Cranky,
Super Booster)
Bathroom Freshener Diffuser Oil
Bubble Bath (Calendula, Calming, Chamomile & Herbs,
Eucalyptus Ease, I Love You, Light & Happy, Overtired & Cranky,
Party, Super Sensitive)
Calming Non Talc Powder
Cream (Aloe Vera, Calendula, Calming)
Diaper Area Wash (Calming, Calming & Non Burning)
Diaper Rash Cream
Everyday Lotion (Calendula, Calming, Overtired & Cranky,
Summer Blend, Super Sensitive)
French Lavender Oil

baby care

Rx

Hair Conditioner (Calendula, Calming, Overtired & Cranky, Super Sensitive, Swimmer's Defense, Tea Tree & Lavender)

Hair Detangler Calming

Hand Wash (First Aid Moisturizing, Natural Antibacterial Blend, No Fragrance)

Jelly Mousse Natural Hair Gel (Calming, Overtired & Cranky)

Natural Bug Blend Bug Repellent

Natural Pregnancy Nourishing (Cream, Emulsion)

Shampoo & Body Wash (Calendula, Calming, Calming, Overtired & Cranky, Super Sensitive, Swimmer's Defense, Tea Tree & Lavender)

Soothing & Healing Spray For Sunburn & Dry Skin

Sunscreen

    SPF 18 (Everyday/Year Round, Super Sensitive)

    SPF 30+ (Everyday/Year Round, No Fragrance, Summer Blend, Super Sensitive)

    SPF 30+ Sunblock Stick (Everyday/Year Round, No Fragrance, Super Sensitive)

Tea Tree Oil

Dakota Free ▲ - Baby Your Skin Balm, No Lavender Baby Balm

Desert Essence Organics - Baby Cuddle Bun Soothing Body & Massage Oil, Don't Be Rash Diaper Cream, My Sweetie Pie Lotion, Oh So Clean 2 In 1 Gentle Foaming Hair & Body Cleaner

Desitin - Baby Ointment (Maximum Strength Original Paste, Multi Purpose Ointment, Rapid Relief Cream)

Hugo Naturals - Baby Hugo (Chamomile & Vanilla Baby Oil, Chamomile & Vanilla Foaming Milk Bath, Chamomile & Vanilla Handcrafted Soap, Unscented Baby Powder, Unscented Diaper Cream)

Johnson's Baby -

    3 In 1 Shampoo Condition Body Wash

    Baby Bar

    Baby Lotion (Aloe Vera & Vitamin E, Honey Apple, Natural, Original, Shea & Cocoa Butter)

    Baby Oil (Gel, w/Shea & Cocoa Butter)

Rx   Baby Powder (Medicated Zinc Oxide Skin Protectant, Pure
            Cornstarch w/Magnolia Petals, w/Aloe Vera & Vitamin E)
        Baby Shampoo
        Baby Wash (Bedtime Bath, Bedtime Bubble Bath, Bubble Bath,
            Head To Toe (Natural Foaming, Regular), Moisture Care,
            Moisture Honey Apple, Soothing Vapor)
        Daily Face & Body Lotion w/SPF 40
        Hand & Face Wipes
        Shampoo w/Natural Lavender

Little Remedies - Cradle Cap Lotion For Baby's Scalp
Logona Naturkosmetik - Baby (Calendula Baby Oil, Calendula
    Body Lotion, Cream)
Method - All Baby & Kids Products
Nature's Baby Organics - Ah Choo Chest Rub, Diaper Ointment,
    Face & Body Moisturizer, Organic Baby Oil, Organic Soothing
    Stick, Silky Dusting Powder Fragrance Free
Shea Moisture - Baby Head To Toe (Ointment, Wash & Shampoo),
    Baby Healing Lotion

Bath Salts/Bubble Bath

Arbonne -
    Aromassentials (Awaken Sea Salt Scrub 16oz, Unwind Bath Salts)
    SeaSource Detox Spa (Foaming Sea Salt Scrub, Purifying Sea Soak)
    Unwind (Bath Salts, Sea Salt Scrub)
California Baby -
    Bath Drops (Calming, Eucalyptus Ease, Overtired & Cranky,
        Super Booster)
    Bubble Bath (Calendula, Calming, Chamomile & Herbs,
        Eucalyptus Ease, I Love You, Light & Happy, Overtired & Cranky,
        Party, Super Sensitive)
Dakota Free ▲ -
    Bath Set (Geranium, Lavender, Rosemary, Tea Tree)
    Fragrance Free Bath Crystals

Rx

Prairie Mint Food Scrub & Soak
Sweet Body Scrub
EO - Bubble Bath (Coconut & Vanilla w/Tangerine ●, Eucalyptus
& Arnica ●, French Lavender ●, Hinoki & Ginger ●, Rose &
Chamomile ●)
HimalaSalt - Healing Rituals Organic Bath Salt (Gift Set ●, Lavender
●, Rose ●)
Hugo Naturals - All Varieties (Bath Salt, Fizzy Bath Bomb)
Johnson's Baby - Bedtime Bath, Bedtime Bubble Bath, Bubble Bath
Kiss My Face - Early To Bed Shower Gel & Foaming Bath Wash
Logona Naturkosmetik - Kids Bubble Bath
Nature's Baby Organics - Bubble Bath (Lovely Lavender, Tangy
Tangerine)
Olbas - Herbal Bath

Cosmetics

100% Pure - All Cosmetics
Afterglow Cosmetics ▲ - All Products
Arbonne -
Blush
Bronzer
Cream Concealer
Eye (Liner, Makeup Remover, Shadow)
Eyebrow Gel
Lash Enhancer
Lip Liner
Lipstick
Liquid Eyeliner
Loose Translucent Powder
Makeup Primer
Natural Radiance Mineral Powder Foundation SPF 15
Perfecting Liquid Foundation w/SPF 15
Sheer Finish Tinted Moisturizer w/SPF 15

Rx

Sheer Glow Highlighter
Sheer Pressed Powder
Triple Action Mascara

Bonne Bell -

Blushing Gels
Cosmic Cheeks
Cream Concealer
Dazzle Dust
Eye Pencils & Definers
Face & Body Sparkle
Gel Bronze
Get Glowin Eyes & Face
Glimmer Bronze
Ice Creamies Sponge On
Kiss Of Color
Mascara (All Varieties)
Nail Lacquers
Pressed Powders
Sponge On Sparklers

Desert Essence Organics - Blemish Touch Stick

Earth's Beauty - All Varieties (Eye/Brow Liner Pencils, Lip Cosmetics, Powdered Cosmetics), Mascara

Juice Beauty - Blemish Clearing Powder, Correcting Concealer, Glowing Cheek Color, Illuminating Eye Color, Perfecting Foundation, Refining Finishing Powder

Larenim - All Cosmetics

Logona Naturkosmetik -

Blush Powder (Apricot 01, Mauve 03, Peach 02)
Cover Stick (Camoflauge 02, Natural 01)
Cream Concealer
Eyeshadow Duo (Pastell & Azure 01, Pastell & Emerald 02)
Highlighter (Gold 2, Silver 01)
Lip Liner Pencils (Burgundy 01, Mauve 02, Nutmeg 03)

Lipstick (Mahogany 07, Orchid 03, Pink 02, Pure Red 05, Rose 01, **Rx**
  Scarlet Red 04)
Lipstick Pencils (Apricot 05, Aubergine 08, Coral 03, Ruby
  Red 04, Terracotta 06)
Liquid (Eyeliner Anthracite 02, Foundation Make-Up Fluid
  Light Beige 01)
Make Up Powders (Golden Bronze 02, Sunny Gold 03)
Mascara (Anthracite 03, Brown 02)
Red Apple Lipstick - Lip Products (All Varieties)
Simple - Eye Make Up Remover, Soothing Eye Balm
Warm Earth - All Cosmetics
Wet N Wild -
  Body (Mega Shimmer Shimmer Dust, Mega Sparkle Confetti)
  Cheeks (Color Icon Blusher, Color Icon Bronzer, Mega Glow
    Illuminating Powder, Ultimate Minerals Bronzer)
  Concealer Cover (Coverstick, Liquid Concealer Wand)
  Eyebrows Ultimate Brow Kit
  Eyeliner (Color Icon (Brow & Eye Liner, Shimmer Pencil), H2O
    Proof Liquid Eyeliner, Mega Eyes Creme Eyeliner, Mega Eyes
    Defining Marker, Mega Last Retractable Eyeliner, Mega Liner
    Liquid Eyeliner, Perfect Pair Eye Wand, Twin Eye/Brow Pencil)
  Eyeshadow (Color Icon (Eyeshadow Collection, Eyeshadow Single,
    Eyeshadow Trio, Shimmer Single), Idol Eyes Creme Shadow,
    Perfect Pair Eye Wand)
  Foundation (Foundation Primer, Intuitive Blend Shade Adjusting,
    Ultimate Match Foundation SPF 15, Ultimate Sheer Tinted
    Moisturizer SPF 15)
  Mascara (Mega Lash Clinical Mascara, Mega Lash Clinical Serum,
    Mega Length, Mega Length Water Proof, Mega Plump, Mega
    Plump Waterproof, Mega Volume, Mega Wink)
  Nails (Fast Dry Nail Color, Mega Last Nail Color, Wild Shine Nail
    Color)

Rx   Cough Drops/Sore Throat Spray/Lozenges

Chloraseptic - All Varieties (Liquids, Sprays) *(Except Lozenges)*
Cold-Eeze - Cold Remedy Lozenges (All Flavors)
Halls -
    Cough Drops Regular (Cherry, Honey Lemon, Ice Blue,
        Mentholyptus, Spearmint, Strawberry, Tropical Fruit)
    Cough Drops Sugar Free (Cherry, Citrus Blend, Fresh Mint, Honey
        Berry, Honey Lemon, Mountain Menthol, Peppermint,
        Spearmint)
    Halls Breezers (Cool Berry, Cool Creamy Strawberry, Sugar Free
        Cool Berry, Tropical Chill)
    Halls Defense (Assorted Citrus, Harvest Cherry, Strawberry, Sugar
        Free, Watermelon)
    Halls Naturals (Honey Lemon Chamomile, Mountain Berry
        w/Soothing Honey Center)
    Halls Plus (Cherry, Honey Lemon, Icy Lemon, Icy Strawberry)
    Halls Refresh (Juicy Strawberry, Lemon Raspberry, Refreshing
        Mint, Tropical Wave)
Hy-Vee Health Market - Cough Drops (Cherry Eucalyptus, Honey
    Lemon, Menthol)
Little Remedies - Little Colds (All Varieties)
Luden's - Cough Drops (All Varieties)
Meijer - Cherry Sore Throat Spray
Olbas - Lozenges, Pastilles
Organix - All Products
Vicks - Formula 44 Sore Throat Spray
Walgreens -
    Cold Syrup
    Comfort Gel Supreme Cherry
    Cough & Sore Throat Cherry
    Soothe (Cherry, Original)
    Throat Lozenges Cherry

Deodorant

Rx

Crystal - All Varieties (Crystal Essence, Deodorants)
Dakota Free ▲ - Solid Stick Deodorant, Triple Duty Mint
Desert Essence Organics - Dry By Nature, Natural Roll On, Tea Tree
   Oil w/Lavender
Dove -
  Men's Deodorant
     Anti Perspirant & Deodorant (Aqua Impact, Clean Comfort,
       Clean Comfort Clinical Protection)
     Deodorant (Clean Comfort, Extra Fresh)
  Women's
     Aerosol Powder
     Clinical Protection (Cool Essentials, Original Clean,
       Visibly Smooth Wild Rose)
     Clinical Protection Anti Perspirant & Deodorant (Rebalance,
       Revive, Skin Renew Cleartone, Soothing Chamomile)
     Go Fresh (Burst, Energizing, Essentials, Rebalance, Revive)
     Go Sleeveless (Beauty Finish, Nourished Beauty)
     Invisible Solid (Fresh, Original Clean, Sensitive Skin)
     Roll On Powder
     Visibly Smooth Wild Rose
Green Beaver - All Products
Hugo Naturals - Deodorant (All Varieties)
Kiss My Face -
  Active Life Stick (Lavender, Peaceful Patchouli)
  Liquid Rock Roll On (Cucumber Green Tea, Fragrance Free,
    Lavender, Patchouli, Sport)
Logona Naturkosmetik -
  Deodorant Spray (Asia Series, Logona Mann, Mediterran Series,
    Nordic Series, Pur Free Fragrance/Hypo Allergenic)
  Roll On Deodorant (Oriental Series, Tropic Series)
Naturally Fresh Deodorant Crystal - All Products
Nature's Baby Organics - PU Natural All Purpose Deodorizer
  (Lavender Chamomile, Vanilla Tangerine)

Rx Tom's Of Maine -
    Crystal Confidence Roll On Deodorant (Citrus Zest,
      Fragrance Free, Wild Garden)
    Natural Deodorant Stick (Long Lasting, Sensitive Care)

Detox

Arbonne - 7 Day Body Cleanse, Herbal Colon Cleanse
Dr. Price's - All Detox Products (Stage 1●, Stage 2●, Stage 3●, Stage 4●,
    Stage 5●),
Renew Life - Cleansing (Candi Gone, Cleanse More, Cleanse Smart, Daily
    Multi Detox, Diet Start Cleanse, First Cleanse, Heavy Metal Cleanse,
    Liver Detox, ParaGone For Kids, Power Cleanse, Total Kidney Detox)

Diabetic Products

Enterex - All Products
Glucerna - All Varieties (Shakes, Snack Shakes)
Glucoburst - Gel, Glucose Tablets, Vanilla Drink
Scot-Tussin -
    Cough,
    Cough Suppressant & Cold Relief
    Multi Action Cold & Allergy
Walgreens -
    Glucose Tablets (Assorted, Grape, Orange, Raspberry, Sour Apple)
    Glucoshot (Lemon Lime, Mixed Berry)

Eye Care

Clear Eyes - All Products
Simple - Revitalizing Eye Roll On
Visine - All Eye Drops, Total Eye Soothing Wipes

Facial Wash/Acne Treatment

Rx

100% Pure - All Varieties (Cleansers, Scrubs & Masks, Toners)

Arbonne -

Awaken Sea Salt Scrub

Balancing Cream (PhytoProlief, Prolief)

Clear Advantage (Acne Lotion, Clarifying Toner, Clarifying Wash, Skin Support Supplement, Spot Treatment)

FC5 (Deep Cleansing Mask, Exfoliating New Cell Scrub, Hydrating Cleanser & Freshener, Mattifying Powder, Purifying Cleanser & Toner)

SeaSource Detox Spa (Detoxifying Rescue Wash, Sea Mud Face & Body Mask)

Bonne Bell - All 10 0 6 Lotions

Clean & Clear -

Acne Medication

Advantage Treatment (Mark A.M., Spot A.M.)

Persa Gel 10

Advantage (3 In 1 Exfoliating Cleanser, 3 In 1 Foaming Acne Wash)

Cleanser

Acne Continuous Control

Blackhead Eraser Cleansing Mask

Daily Pore

Deep Action (Cream, Sensitive)

Finishes (Even Tone, Pore Perfecting)

Foaming Facial (Oil Free, Sensitive Skin)

Make Up Dissolving Facial Cleansing Wipes

Morning Burst

Detoxifying

Facial

Fruit Infusions (Hydrating, Purifying, Reviving)

Shine Control Facial

Skin Brightening Facial

Rx Cleansing Devices
    Advantage (Acne Control Kit, Blackhead Eraser)
    Morning Burst Surge Energizing Power Cleanser
Deep Cleaning Astringent (Regular, Sensitive)
Moisturizer
    Advantage Acne Control
    Dual Action
    Finishes Pore
    Perfecting
    Morning Glow
Oil Absorbing Sheets
Scrub
    Blackhead Eraser
    Deep Action Exfoliating
    Morning Burst
        Detoxifying
        Facial
        In Shower Facial
        Shine Control Facial
        Skin Brightening Facial

Dakota Free ▲ - Countenance Facial Cleansing Powder, Facial
Cleanser Scrub & Mask

Desert Essence Organics - Cleansing Towelettes, Gentle Nourishing
Organic Cleanser, Tea Tree Oil Facial Cleansing Pads, Thoroughly
Clean Face Wash

Dove -
Men's Body & Face Wash
    Clean (Comfort, Defense)
    Deep Clean
    Extra Fresh
    Fresh Awake
    Sensitive Clean

Hugo Naturals - All Varieties (Scrubs & Polishes)
Johnson's Baby - Hand & Face Wipes

Rx

Juice Beauty -
Blemish (Be Gone, Clearing Cleanser)
Green Apple Cleansing Gel
Organic Facial Wash
Peel (Deluxe Green Apple Sensitive, Green Apple Full Strength,
Green Apple Sensitive)
Serum (Antioxidant, Blemish Clearing, Soothing)
Kiss My Face -
Break Out Botanical Acne Gel
Face Wash (Balancing Act Facial Toner, Brightening Day Creme,
Clean For A Day Creamy Face Cleanser, Pore Shrink Deep Pore
Cleansing Mask, So Refined Jojoba & Mint Facial Scrub, Start Up
Exfoliating Face Wash)
Oil Of Olay - Cleansing Cloths Sensitive
Simple - Cleansing Facial Wipes, Exfoliating Facial Wipes,
Moisturizing Facial Wash, Refreshing Facial Wash Gel, Smoothing
Facial Scrub, Soothing Facial Toner
Sophyto - Dual Action Exfoliating Treatment ●, Natural Glycolic
Foaming Cleanser ●, Purifying Silken Cleanser ●

Hair Styling Products

California Baby - Hair Detangler Calming, Jelly Mousse Natural Hair
Gel (Calming, Overtired & Cranky)
Dakota Free ▲ - EO Paint, Fragrance Free Moisturizer, Wild Rose
Moisturizer
Desert Essence Organics - Coconut Styling Products (Defrizzer &
Heat Protector, Shine & Refine Hair Lotion, Soft Curls Hair Cream)
Dove -
Hair Therapy Nourishing Oil *(Except Daily Treatment)*
Nourishing Oil Care Hair Treatment
Anti Frizz Serum
Leave In Smoothing Cream

Rx Style + Care
Frizz Free Shine Crème Serum
Nourishing Amplifier Mousse
Nourishing Curls (Defining Gel, Whipped Cream Mousse)
Nourishing Dry Ends Serum
Replenishment Spray
Strength & Shine Hairspray (Extra Hold, Flexible Hold)

Dr. Bronner's - Lavender Hair Conditioner & Style Cream

EO -
French Lavender Detangler Spray ●
Smooth Conditioning Serum Wild Rose & Coconut ●
Styling Products (Nourishing Cream Lavender & Coconut ●,
Tame Curl Control Gel Coconut & Vanilla ●)
Wild Rose & Coconut Conditioning Serum ●

Gluten-Free Savonnerie ▲ - All Products

Hugo Naturals - Styling Gel

Johnson's Baby - No More Tangles (Buddies Detangler, Kids
Detangling Spray Strawberry Sensation)

Keys ▲ - All Products

Kiss My Face - Styling Products Upper Management Styling Gel

Logona Naturkosmetik -
Color Plus Preparation Coloring Aid
Herbal Hair Color Cream (Copper Blonde, Indian Summer,
Nougat Brown, Teak, Tizian)
Logona Mann (Hair Gel, Hair Lotion)
Mineral Hair Cleansers Cleansing Gel (Lotus Flower White
Lavender, Patchouli Lavender)
Styling Aid (Bamboo Blow Dry Styler, Coconut Oil, Conditioner
Spray, Jojoba Hair Repair, Silk Protein Hair Spray, Style & Shine
Hair Gel)

Organix -
Awapuhi Ginger (Dry Styling Oil, Instant Recovery Mask)
Brazilian Keratin (30 Day Treatment, Anti Breakage Serum, Flat
Iron Spray, Keratin Therapy Jar, Shimmering Oil)
Coconut Milk Split End Mender

Rx

Hair Treatments (All Varieties)
Macadamia Oil Intense Moisture Mask
Moroccan Argan Oil (Intense Moisturizing Treatment, Penetrating For Extra Dry Hair)
Styling Products (All Varieties)
Shea Moisture - Curly Hair (Curl & Style Milk, Curl Enhancing Smoothie, Curling Souffle, Hold & Shine Moisture Mist), Deep Treatment Masque
Surface - All Hair Products
Surya Brasil - Color Products

Hand & Body Soap

100% Pure - All Varieties (Baths & Soaps, Washes & Scrubs)
Arbonne - FC5 (Exfoliating Body Scrub, Invigorating Body Cleanser), Unwind Bath & Shower Gel
Better Life - Natural Hand & Body Soap (Cool Yule, Go Forth & Conquer, No Regrets)
Bonne Bell - Shower 2000 Gels
California Baby -
   Hand Wash (First Aid Moisturizing, Natural Antibacterial Blend, No Fragrance)
   Shampoo & Body Wash (Calendula, Calming, Swimmer's Defense, Tea Tree & Lavender)
Clean & Clear - Morning Burst Body Wash (Boost, Charge, Splash)
Dakota Free ▲ - Bars (Babassu, Organic Sunflower, Pure Prairie Soap w/Shea Butter), Sophie Soap
Desert Essence Organics -
   Body Wash (Bulgarian Lavender, Coconut, Fragrance Free, Green Apple & Ginger, Italian Red Grape, Red Raspberry, Sweet Almond, Vanilla Chai)
   Castile Liquid Soap
   Hand Wash (Coconut, Grapefruit, Lavender, Vanilla Chai)
   Oh So Clean 2 In 1 Gentle Foaming Hair & Body Cleaner

Rx Dove -

    Beauty Bar
        Gentle Exfoliating
        Go Fresh (Burst, Cool Moisture, Revive)
        Nourishing Care Shea Butter
        Pink
        Sensitive Skin Unscented
        Summer Care
        White
        Winter Care
    Body Wash
        Cream Oil (Regular, Ultra Rich Velvet)
        Deep Moisture Nourishing
        Gentle Exfoliating
        Go Fresh (Burst, Cool Moisture, Rebalance, Revive)
        Sensitive Skin
        Shea Butter Cream Oil
        Visiblecare (Renewing Crème, Softening Crème, Toning)
        Winter Care
    Men's Bars
        Deep Clean Purifying Grains
        Extra Fresh Invigorating Formula
    Men's Body & Face Wash
        Clean (Comfort, Defense)
        Deep Clean
        Extra Fresh
        Fresh Awake
        Sensitive Clean

Dr. Bronner's - All Scents (Body Balm, Castille Bar Soap, Hand & Body Soaps, Liquid Castille Soap)

Ecover - Heavy Duty Hand Cleaner, Lavender & Aloe Hand Soap

EO -

    Everyday Bar
        Lavender w/Aloe ●

hand & body soap

Rx

    Rose & Chamomile w/Shea Butter ●
    Wild Rose w/Shea Butter ●
Foaming Hand & Body Soap Coconut Vanilla & Organic ●
Liquid Hand Soap
    Chocolate & Mint ●
    French Lavender ●
    Lemon & Eucalyptus ●
    Peppermint & Tea Tree ●
    Rose Geranium & Citrus ●
    Rosemary & Mint ●
    Unscented w/Coconut Milk ●
  Shower Gel
    Chocolate & Peppermint ●
    Grapefruit & Mint ●
    Lavender ●
    Orange Fusion ●
    Rose & Chamomile ●
Fleurish Beauty - Aloe & Shea Body Wash
Full Circle - All Shower Gels
Gillette - Mens Body Wash (All Varieties)
Gluten-Free Savonnerie ▲ - All Products
Gojo -
  Hand Cleaner (Cherry Gel Pumice, Green Certified Foam)
  Handwash (El Foam, Luxury Foam, Premium Foam
    w/Skin Conditioners)
  Skin Cleanser (All Purpose, Lotion)
Green Beaver - All Soap & Body Wash
Hugo Naturals -
  Hand Sanitizer (All Varieties)
  Handcrafted Soap (All Varieties *(Except Shea Butter & Oatmeal*
    Mint Artisan Bulk Soap))
  Foaming Hand Soap (All Varieties)
  Liquid Hand Soaps (All Varieties)
  Shower Gel (All Varieties)

Rx Johnson's - Body Wash (24 Hour (Deep Hydrating, Nourishing
Green Tea), 2 In 1 Shower & Shave)

Johnson's Baby -

Baby Bar

Baby Wash

Head To Toe (Natural Foaming, Regular)

Moisture (Care, Honey Apple)

Soothing Vapor

Hand & Face Wipes

Juice Beauty - Cleansing Milk, Green Apple Mousse Hand & Body
Cleanser

Keys ▲ - All Products

Kiss My Face -

Bath & Shower Gel

Active Athletic Birch & Eucalyptus

Anti Stress Wood Pine & Ginseng

Cardamom & Mint

Early To Bed Clove & Ylang Ylang

Early To Rise Wild Mint & Citrus

Mandarin Ginger Lily

Peaceful Patchouli

Silky Soft Lavender & Lily

Kids Orange U Smart (Bubble Wash, Self Foaming Hand Wash,
Whale Soap)

Moisture Hand Soap

Anjou Pear

Fragrance Free

GermAside Tea Tree

Mandarin Orange

Peaceful Patchouli

Sonora Almond

Natural Pure Olive Oil Soap

Fragrance Free

Olive & (Aloe, Chamomile, Green Tea, Honey, Lavender)

Rx

Peace Soap

    100% Natural All Purpose Castille Soap (Grassy Mint, Lavender Mandarine, Lemongrass Clary Sage, Pomegranate Acai)

    100% Natural Foaming Castille Soap (Grassy Mint, Lavender Mandarin, Lemongrass Clary Sage, Pomegranate Acai)

    Sudz C Weed Shower Gel

Logona Naturkosmetik -

    Asia Series (Body Gel, Body Wash)

    Logona Mann Shampoo & Shower Gel

    Meditearranean Series Body Wash

    Pur Free Fragrance/Hypo Allergenic (Cleansing Milk, Glycerine Soap, Moisture Cream, Shampoo & Shower Gel)

    Shampoo & Shower Gel

Method - All Products

Provon - Foaming Handwash w/Advanced Moisturizers, Hand Cleaner (Green Certified, w/Moisturizers)

Pure Provence - Certified Organic Triple Milled Soap (Acai Cranberry ●, Cactus Pear ●, Grapefruit ●, Lavender ●, Moroccan Mint ●, Pomegranate Passion Fruit ●)

Purell - SF607 Instant Hand Sanitizing Foam

Sappo Hill Soapworks - Almond, Aloe Vera, Cucumber, Desert Sage, Jasmine, Lavender, Natural Fragrance Free, Sandalwood

Surya Brasil - All Products

Tom's Of Maine - Bars (Daily Moisture, Deodorant, Exfoliating, Relaxing, Sensitive)

Household Cleaning Products

Better Life -

    Cleansing Scrubber Even The Kitchen Sink

    Dish Liquid Dish It Out

    Floor Cleaner Simply Floored

    Glass Cleaner I Can See Clearly Wow

    Nursery Cleaner 2am Miracle

Rx
    Stainless Steel Cleaner Einshine
    Stone & Countertop Cleaner Take It For Granite
    What Ever All Purpose Cleaner (Clary Sage & Citrus, Scent Free)
    Wood Cleaner Oak Y Dokey

Biokleen -
    All Dishwashing Liquids
    Bac Out (Drain Care, Fresh Fabric Freshener, Septic Care)
    Oxygen Bleach Plus
    Produce Wash

Comet - Bathroom Spray & Powder

Dakota Free ▲ -
    Dishwashing (Free Liquid, Oxy Dish)
    Laundry (Allergy Free Detergent, Oxy Boost Stain Remover,
       Safe 'N Soft Fabric Softener, Stain Free Pre Treater)
    PureGreen24 Hard Surface Sanitizer

Desert Essence Organics - Sweet Dreams (Natural All Surface
    Cleaner, Natural Odor Absorbing Air Freshener)

Dr. Bronner's - Sal Suds All Surface Cleaner

Ecover -
    Automatic Dishwasher (Powder, Powder ZERO, Tablets,
       Tablets ZERO)
    Cleaner (All Purpose, Bathroom, Floor Soap, Glass & Surface,
       Limescale Remover)
    Dishwashing Liquid (Grapefruit & Green Tea, Herbal)
    Laundry Cream Scrub
    Rinse Aid

Jade & Pearl - Natural Hand & Surface Sanitizer

Method - All Varieties (Cleaners, Dishwashing Products, Laundry
    Products)

Spic And Span - All Varities (Liquids & Powders)

Laundry Detergent & Softener

Biokleen - All Varieties (Laundry Powders & Liquids)

Dakota Free ▲ - Laundry (Allergy Free Detergent, Oxy Boost Stain **Rx**
Remover, Safe 'N Soft Fabric Softener, Stain Free Pre Treater)

Ecover -

Fabric Softener (Morning Fresh, Sunny Day)

Laundry

Delicate Wash

Laundry Powder

Liquid Concentrate (Sunny Day, ZERO)

Non Chlorine Bleach (Liquid, Powder)

Powder ZERO

Stain Remover, Wash

Method - Laundry Products (All Varieties)

Publix - Free & Clear Fabric Softener Sheets

Laxatives/Hemorrhoidal Relief

Citrucel - All Products

Ensure - All Shakes

Fiber Choice -

Assorted Berry Plus Calcium

Orange Prebiotic Fiber

Sugar Free (Assorted, Orange)

Sugar Free Prebiotic Fiber (Plus Antioxidants Berry Pomegranate,
Plus Calcium & D Assorted Berry, Weight Management)

Fleet - Adult Suppositories, Fiber Gummies, Soflax Stool Softener

Konsyl - Psyllium Fiber (All Powders, Packets, & Caps), Senna Prompt

Meijer -

Fiber Therapy Caplets

Hemorrhoidal (Cream, Ointment, Suppository)

Laxative Tablet (Natural MS, Senna, Womens)

NVP (Capsules, Original Orange Powder, Original Regular Powder,
Smooth Orange Powder, Sugar Free Smooth Orange Powder)

Metamucil - All Capsules, All Powders

Pedia-Lax - Chewables, Fiber Gummies, Liquid Stool Softener,
Suppositories

Rx **Tucks** - Hemorrhoidal Ointment, Hydrocortisone Anti Itch Ointment, Medicated Pads, Take Alongs Medicated Towelettes
Vitafusion - Fiber Well (Gummies, Weight Management Gummies)
Walgreens -
Castor Oil
Fiber
Berry Chewable Tablets
Caplets (Laxative, Plus Calcium, Regular)
Soluble Powder
Laxative Tablets (Maximum Strength, Regular Strength)
Women's Laxative

Lip Care

Arbonne - Before Sun Lip Saver SPF 30, Lip Polish
Blistex -
Cold & Allergy Lip Soother
Complete Moisture
DCT SPF 20
Deep Renewal
Five Star Lip Protection
Fruit Smoothies (Berry Explosion, Melon Melody, Triple Tropical)
Herbal Answer
Lip (Infusion Moisture Splash, Massage, Medex)
Medicated Lip (Balm (Berry, Mint, Regular), Ointment)
Natural Cooling Comfort
Raspberry Lemonade Blast
Revive & Restore
RPM For Men
Silk & Shine
Simple Essentials
Bonne Bell - Lip (Burst, D Votions, Definer, Frosting, Glam, Kiss This Gloss, Lites Sponge On)
Carlson - E Gem Lip Care

lip care

Rx

Dakota Free ▲ - Honey Lipz, Identity Lip Support
Desert Essence Organics -
    Lip Rescue (Moisturizing, Therapeutic, Ultra Hydrating)
    Lip Tints (Coconut, Italian Red Grape, Red Raspberry,
        Vanilla Chai)
Dr. Bronner's - Lip Balm (All Flavors)
Earth's Beauty - Lip Cosmetics (All Varieties)
EO - Organic Lip Balm (Lavender ●, Peppermint ●)
EOS -
    Lip Balm Smooth Sphere (Honeysuckle Honeydew, Lemon Drop,
        Medicated Tangerine, Strawberry Sorbet, Summer Fruit,
        Sweet Mint)
    Lip Balm Smooth Stick (Pomegranate Raspberry, Sweet Mint,
        Vanilla Bean)
Hugo Naturals - All Lip Balm Varieties
Juice Beauty - Conditioning Lip Color, Moisturizer (Organic Lip, SPF
    8 Lip, SPF 8 Lip - Naturally Clear), Reflecting Gloss
Kiss My Face - Lip Balm (Coconut Pineapple, Cranberry Orange,
    Ginger Mango, Sliced Peach, Sport SPF 30, Strawberry, Treat Mint,
    Vanilla Honey)
Lip Smackers - Lip Jello Balms, Lip Rolly Smackers, Liquid, Squeezy
    Smackers (Clears, Shimmers), Skittles Liquid Lip
Logona Naturkosmetik - Age Protection Lip Contour Cream
Vitamin Water - Lip Balms (All Varieties)
Wet N Wild -
    Lip Balm (Juicy Lip Balm SPF 15, Natural Blend Lip Shimmer)
    Lip Color (Mega Last, Mega Shield Lip Color SPF 15, Mega Slicks
        Lip Color Pencil, Perfect Pair Lip Wand, Silk Finish Lipstick, Wild
        Shine Lip Lacquer)
    Lip Gloss (Diamond Brilliance Moisturizing Lip Sheen, Glassy
        Gloss Lip Gel, Mega Brilliance, Mega Slicks)
    Lipliner (Color Icon Lipliner, Perfect Pair Lip Wand)

Rx   Lotions & Body Oils

100% Pure - All Butters & Creams, All Eye Creams, All Moisturizers
Arbonne -
    Awaken Body Lotion
    FC5 (Conditioning Body Moisture, Cooling Foot Creme)
    SeaSource Detox Spa (5 In 1 Essential Massage Oil, Remineralizing
        Body Lotion 24 Hr., Renewing Body Gelee)
    Shea Butter Hand & Body Lotion
    Unwind (Body Lotion, Massage Oil)
Better Life - Natural Hand & Body Lotion (Cool Calm Collected,
    Work It Own It)
California Baby -
    Aromatherapy Massage Oil (Calming, Eucalyptus Ease, I Love You,
        Super Sensitive)
    Cream (Calendula, Calming)
    Everyday Lotion (Calendula, Calming, Overtired & Cranky,
        Summer Blend, Super Sensitive)
    French Lavender Oil
    Natural Pregnancy Nourishing (Cream, Emulsion)
    Tea Tree Oil
Carlson - ADE (Cream, Ointment), E Gem (Cream, Oil Drops),
    Key E (Cream, Ointment)
Cloverine - Salve
Curel - All Lotions (Daily Moisture Original, Fragrance Free, Hand
    & Cuticle Treatment, Itch Defense, Sensitive Skin Remedy, Skin
    Nourishing), Foot Therapy
Dakota Free ▲ -
    Day's End Intense Moisturizer
    Fragrance Free Moisturizer
    Lavender Relief
    Massage & Bath Oil (Fragrance Free, Lavender, Lavender Lite)
    Super Tea Tree
    Tea Tree Gel
    Wild Rose Moisturizer

lotions & body oils

Rx

Desert Essence Organics -
- Baby Care (Cuddle Bun Soothing Body & Massage Oil, My Sweetie Pie Lotion)
- Daily Essential (Moisturizer, Defense Lotion SPF 15)
- Gentle Nourishing (Day Cream SPF 15, Day Cream SPF 15, Night Cream)
- Hand & Body Lotion (Bulgarian Lavender, Coconut, Coconut Lime, Fragrance Free, Spicy Citrus, Sweet Almond, Tropical Coconut, Vanilla Chai)
- Oil
    - Jojoba (100% Pure, Organic)
    - Nourishing Body (Cactus Flower, Regular)
    - Organic Lavender Tea Tree Oil
- Pistachio Foot Repair Cream
- Pumpkin Hand Repair Cream
- Thoroughly Clean Oil Control Lotion

Dove - Cream Oil Body Lotion (Intensive, Pro Age, Sensitive Skin, Shea Butter)

Dr. Bronner's - Lotion All Scents

EO - Body Lotion (Coconut & Vanilla w/Tangerine ●, French Lavender●, Geranium & Citrus ●, Grapefruit & Mint ●, Lemon Verbena ●, Rose & Chamomile ●, Unscented ●)

Fleurish Beauty - Luxe Lotion

Full Circle - All Lotions

Gluten-Free Savonnerie ▲ - All Products

Green Beaver - All Products

Hugo Naturals - Baby Hugo Oh So Soft Chamomile & Vanilla Lotion, Body Butters (All Varieties), Massage & Body Oils (All Varieties), Over Lotions (All Varieties)

Hy-Vee Health Market - Oil Of Beauty Lotion

Johnson's -
- Body Lotion
    - Deep Hydrating Lotion
    - Melt Away Stress (Body Lotion, Massaging Moisturizer)
    - Nourishing Green Tea
    - Body Wash 24 Hour (Long Lasting Softness, Melt Away Stress)

Rx **Johnson's Baby** -
 Baby Lotion (Aloe Vera & Vitamin E, Daily Face & Body Lotion
  w/SPF 40, Deep Hydrating Hand Cream, Honey Apple, Natural,
  Original, Shea & Cocoa Butter)
 Baby Oil (Gel, w/Shea & Cocoa Butter)
Juice Beauty -
 Moisturizer
  Green Apple (Age Defy, Firming Body, SPF 15)
  Nutrient
  Oil Free
  SPF 30 (Mineral Sheer, Tinted Mineral (Sand, Tan))
Keys ▲ - All Products
Kiss My Face - Hand Creme (Grapefruit & Bergamot, Hand Alert
 Rosemary & Mint)
Little Remedies - Little Remedies Intensive Moisture Therapy
Logona Naturkosmetik -
 Age Protection Hand Cream
 Aloe Day Cream
 Daily Care Bio Aloe & Lime Body Oil
 Kids Body Milk
 Logona Mann (Face & Body Lotion, Moisture Fluid)
 Mediterranean Series (Body Lotion, Body Oil)
 Oriental Series Body Butter
 Pur Free Fragrance/Hypo Allergenic (Body Lotion, Cleansing Milk)
 Tropic Series (Body Butter, Body Wash)
Lubriderm -
 Advanced Therapy (Original Lotion, w/SPF 30)
 Daily Moisture Lotion (Fragrance Free, Original, Sensitive Skin,
  w/Shea & Cocoa Butter, w/SPF 15)
 Intense Skin Repair (Body Lotion, Ointment)
 Men's 3 In 1 Lotion Fragrance Free
 Soothing Relief Lotion

Oil Of Olay - Moisturizing Lotion Sensitive Skin **Rx**
Simple - Hydrating Light Moisturizer, Replenshing Rich Moisturizer, Vital Vitamin Day Cream
Sophyto - Balancing Daily Moisturizer ●, Omega Daily Moisturizer ●
St. Claire's Organics ▲ - Athletic Recovery Oil
Surya Brasil - All Products

Misc. Products

Arbonne - 7 Day Body Cleanse, Awaken Rejuvenating Body Mist, Herbal Colon Cleanse, Unwind Rejuvenating Body Mist
Band-Aid - All Band Aids, Friction Block Stick, Water Block Plus Band Aids
Bonne Bell - All Colognes
California Baby - Natural Bug Blend Bug Repellent
Compound W - Wart Remover (All Varieties)
Crayola - All Products *(Except Play Dough)*
Dakota Free ▲ - Cuticle & Nail Treatment Oil, Insect Repellant (Outdoor Gel, Outdoor Spray)
Don't Bite Me - Insect Repellant Patch
Dr. Willard's - Willard Water ●
Elmer's - All Products *(Except Finger Paint)*
Freezone - Corn & Callus Remover
Jade & Pearl - All Natural Insect Repellent
Kiss My Face - Foot Scrub Peppermint
Logona Naturkosmetik - Natural Nails (Cuticle Fluid, Nail Repair Therapy), Natural Nails Hand Care Concentrate
New-Skin - Liquid Bandage
Surya Brasil - Henna & Tattoo Products
Walgreens - Callus Reducing Ointment, Callus Remover (Extra Thick, Regular)

Rx ## Motion Sickness

Dramamine - Original
Meijer - Anti Nausea Liquid
Wal-Dram - Tablets (Less Drowsy, Motion Sickness, Motion Sickness Chewable, Travel Sickness)

Oral Hygiene

Aquafresh - Advanced, Cavity Protection, Extra Fresh, Extreme Clean, IsoActive, Kids (All Varieties), Sensitive Maximum Strength, Tartar Control Whitening, Ultimate White, White & Shine
Biotene - All Products
Colgate - Cavity Protection Great Regular Flavor Toothpaste
Crest - All Products
Dakota Free ▲ - EO Paint
Dentsply Caulk - All Dental Materials *(at the dentist)*
Desert Essence Organics - Natural Tea Tree Oil Toothpaste (& Neem Wintergreen, Fennel, Ginger, Mint), Tea Tree Oil Mouthwash
Efferdent - Denture Cleanser
Effergrip - Denture Adhesive Cream
Enamel Pro -
   Fluoride Topical Gel
     Bubblegum *(at the dentist)*
     Cherry *(at the dentist)*
     Orange *(at the dentist)*
     Strawberry *(at the dentist)*
   Fluoride Varnish Strawberries N' Cream *(at the dentist)*
   Fluoride Varnish Bubblegum *(at the dentist)*
   Prophy Paste (All Flavors) *(at the dentist)*
Glide - Floss
Glitter - Prophy Paste (All Flavors) *(at the dentist)*
Green Beaver - All Products

oral hygiene

Rx

Hy-Vee Health Market -
  Dental Floss
    Unwaxed
    Waxed (Mint, Unflavored)
  Denture Mint Cleanser
  Mouthwash
    Antiseptic (Blue Mint, Mint, Peppermint, Spring Mint)
    Rinse (Anti Cavity Mint Fluoride, Anti Plaque, Anti Plaque Mint, Pre Brush)
Jason - All Toothpaste Varieties *(Must Say 'No Gluten' On Box)*
Kiss My Face -
  Kids Berry Smart Toothpaste (Fluoride Free, w/Fluoride)
  Mouthwash Spearmint Breath Blast Regular
  Spearmint Breath Blast Anticavity w/Fluoride
  Toothpaste Whitening Aloe Vera Gel
Kolorz - Prophy Paste (All Flavors) *(at the dentist)*
Listerine -
  Agent Cool Blue Tinting Rinse
  Antiseptic Mouthwash (All Varieties)
  Pocket Paks Oral Care Strips (All Varieties)
  Smart Rinse
  Totalcare Anticavity Mouthwash (All Varieties)
  Whitening (Pen, Pre Brush Treatment Rinse, Vibrant White Rinse)
  ZERO Mouthwash
Logona Naturkosmetik -
  Herbal Dental Gel (Peppermint, Rosemary & Sage)
  Kids (Spearmint, Strawberry)
  Toothpaste (Mineral, Sensitive)
Nupro - Fluoride *(at the dentist)*, Prophy Paste *(at the dentist)*
Oasis - Moisturizing (Mouth Spray, Mouthwash)
Polident - Denture Cleanser
Publix - Dental Floss (All Flavors)
Scope - All Mouthwash
Sensodyne - All Pronamel Products

Rx   **Sparkle** - Prophy Paste (All Flavors) *(at the dentist)*
       Sparkle Free - Prophy Paste (All Flavors) *(at the dentist)*
       St. Claire's Organics ▲ - Icy Mint Herbal Mouthwash
       Tom's Of Maine -
           Children's Natural (Anticavity Fluoride Toothpaste, Fluoride Free
             Toothpaste)
           Floss Antiplaque Flat Original
           Maximum Strength Sensitive Fluoride Toothpaste
           Natural
              Antiplaque Fluoride Free Toothpaste w/Propolis & Myrrh
              Antiplaque Plus Whitening Gel Fluoride Free
              Cleansing Mouthwash
              Sensitive Toothpaste Fluoride
              Whole Care Toothpaste Gel
           Simply White Toothpaste (Clean & Gentle w/Fluoride, Clean Mint,
             Sweet Mint Gel)
           Wicked Fresh Mouthwash
       Walgreens -
           Antiseptic Mouthwash (Amber, Blue Mint, Spring Mint)
           Denture Cream (Mint, Original)
           Toothpaste (Herbal Mint, Minty Fresh, Sensitive (Mint, Whitening
             Paste))
           Total
       Zap - Fluoride Gel (All Flavors) *(at the dentist)*, Foam Fluoride (All
           Flavors) *(at the dentist)*
       Ziroxide - Prophy Paste *(at the dentist)*

Pain Relief

AZO - PMS, Relief From UTI Symptoms (Maximum Strength,
    Standard)
Children's Motrin - Suspension (Berry, Bubblegum, Dye Free, Grape)
Children's Tylenol -
    Meltaways (Bubblegum Burst, Cherry Blast, Grape Punch)

Rx

Oral Suspension Liquid (Cherry Burst, Grape)
Plus Cold (& Allergy, & Cough Dye Free Grape, & Stuffy Nose Dye Free Grape, Grape)
Plus Cough (& Runny Nose, & Sore Throat)
Plus Flu Bubble Gum
Plus Multi Symptom Cold Grape (Dye Free, Regular)
Dakota Free ▲ - Lavender Relief
Dermoplast - All Pain Relieving Spray Varieties
Infant's Motrin - Drops (Dye Free, Regular)
Infant's Tylenol - Drops (Cherry, Grape), Oral Suspension Liquid
Junior Motrin - Caplets, Chewable Grape, Chewable Orange
Junior Tylenol - Meltaways (Bubblegum Burst, Grape Punch)
Kirkland Signature - Children's Pain Relief Plus Multisymptom Cold, Ibuprofen IB
Little Remedies - All Little Fevers Varieties, Little Ouchies Pain Relieving Spray, Little Teethers Gel
Meijer -
Apap (Caplet, Cool Caplet, ER Caplet Red, ER Caplet White, ETS Tablet, Gelcap, Geltab, Tablet)
Apap Child Suspension (Bubblegum, Cherry, Grape)
Apap Infant Cherry Suspension
Aspirin (Adult Orange Chewables, Child Orange Chewables, Coated Tablets, Coated Yellow Tablets)
Aspirin Enteric Coated (Tablet, Yellow Tablet)
Headache Tablets
Ibuprofen (Caplets Brown, Caplets Orange, Child Suspension Bubblegum, Junior Caplets, Junior Chewables Orange, Tablets Brown, Tablets Orange)
Migraine Caplets
Naproxen Sodium (Caplets, NCRC Caplets, Tablets)
Momentum - Backache Relief
Motrin - IB (Caplets, Tablets)
Outgro - Pain Relieving Liquid For Feet
Percogesic - Original & Extra Strength

Rx St. Joseph ▲ - All Products

Tylenol - 8Hr Muscle Aches & Pains, Arthritis Pain Caplets, Extra Strength (Caplets, EZ Tabs, Rapid Blast Liquid, Rapid Release Gelcaps), Regular Strength Tablets

Walgreens -

Adult Low Strength Aspirin (Chewable, Enteric)

Aspirin Tablets

    Bottle

    Box

    Chewable Low Dose (Cherry, Orange)

    Tri Buffered

    Yellow Label

Bachache Relief Caplets

Extra Strong Headache Relief Tablets

Extra Strong Pain Reliever Caplets

    Easy Open

    Quick Gels (PM, Regular)

    Regular

    Twin

Extra Strong Women's Menstrual Caplets

Headache Relief PM Tablets

Ibuprofen Tablets

    Brown (Caplets, Tablets)

    Dye & Color Free

    Dye Free

    Orange (Caplets, Tablets)

Knee Pain Relief Ortho (For Men, For Women)

Menstrual Relief (Caplets, Gelcaps)

Urinary Pain Relief

Pet Food

Acana - Grain Free For Cats (Grasslands, Pacifica, Wild Prairie), Grain Free For Dogs (Grasslands, Pacifica, Ranchlands, Wild Prairie)

pet food

Rx

Green Dog Naturals - Healthy Motion (Chewable, Powder), Immuno Build

IAMS -

Canine Savory Sauce
    Adult (Active Maturity Roasted Beef, Country Style Chicken, Pot Roast, Sizzlin Bacon)
    Puppy Roasted Beef
Canine Sporting 29/18
Healthy Naturals Dry Cat Food Adult Weight Control
Premium Protection Dry Cat Food (Adult Cat, Kitten, Mature Adult, Senior Plus)
Premium Protection Dry Dog Food Puppy
ProActive Health Canned Cat Food (Adult Filets w/Chicken In Gravy, Adult Filets w/Salmon In Sauce, Adult Filets w/Skipjack Tuna In Sauce, Adult Pate w/Chicken & Liver, Adult Pate w/Pacific Salmon, Adult Pate w/Seafood Sampler, Adult Premium w/ (Country Style Turkey & Giblets, Gourmet Chicken, Lamb & Rice, Select Oceanfish, Tender Beef), Kitten Premium Pate w/Gourmet Chicken)
ProActive Health Canned Dog Food (Adult Ground Dinner w/ (Beef & Rice, Chicken & Rice, Lamb & Rice, Turkey & Rice), Adult Ground Mixed Grill w/Chicken & Beef)
ProActive Health Dry Cat Food (Adult Active Maturity Hairball Care, Adult Digestive Care, Adult Hairball Care, Adult Indoor Weight & Hairball Care, Adult Multi Cat w/Chicken, Adult Original Chicken, Adult Original Ocean Fish w/Rice, Adult Original w/Lamb & Rice, Adult Original w/Tuna, Adult Weight Control, Kitten, Mature Adult, Multi Cat w/Chicken & Salmon, Senior Plus)
ProActive Health Dry Dog Food (Adult Chunks, Adult Mini Chunks, Mature Adult Small & Toy Breed, Smart Puppy Large Breed, Smart Puppy Original, Smart Puppy Small & Toy Breeds)
Puppy Ground Dinner with Chicken & Rice

Rx Veterinary Formula

    Canned Cat Food (Intestinal Low Residue Feline, Maximum Calorie Canine & Feline, Renal Plus, Urinary O Plus Moderate pH/O, Urinary S Low Ph/S Feline, Weight Loss Restricted Calorie Feline)

    Canned Dog Food (Canine Formula (Intestinal Low Residue, Skin & Coat Response FP), Maximum Calorie Plus)

    Dry Cat Food (Glucose & Weight Control Plus Optimum Weight Control, Intestinal Low Residue, Renal Plus, Urinary O Plus Moderate pH/O, Urinary S Plus Low pH/S, Weight Loss/Mobility Plus Restricted Calorie)

    Dry Dog Food (Intestinal Low Residue (Canine, Puppy), Prostora Max Canine, Renal Plus, Skin & Coat Plus Response FP)

Nutro -

    Natural Choice Adult Dog Dry Food (High Energy **!!**, Large Breed Lamb Meal & Rice **!!**, Lite **!!**)

    Natural Choice Grain Free Dog Dry Food (Adult Natural Lamb Meal & Potato Formula, Adult Natural Turkey Meal & Potato Formula, Adult Natural Venison Meal & Potato Formula, Large Breed Adult Lamb Meal & Rice Formula)

    Natural Choice Puppy Dry Food (Lamb Meal & Rice Formula **!!**, Large Breed Lamb Meal & Rice Formula **!!**)

Purina One - Adult Cat (Hairball & Healthy Weight Formula, Salmon & Tuna Flavor)

Rainbow Light -

    Green Dog Naturals

        Healthy Motion (Chewable, Powder)

        Immuno Build

Royal Canin -

    Veterinary Diets Canine (Hypoallergenic, Potato & Duck, Potato & Rabbit, Potato & Venison, Potato & Whitefish)

    Veterinary Diets Feline (Green Peas & Duck, Green Peas & Lamb, Green Peas & Rabbit, Green Peas & Venison, Hypoallergenic)

Rx

Science Diet -

Dry Food

Adult Cat (Hairball Control, Hairball Control Light, Indoor, Oral Care, Sensitive Skin)

Adult Cat Optimal Care (Oceanfish & Rice, Original)

Adult Dog (Active, High Energy, Large Breed, Oral Care, Sensitive Skin)

Adult Dog Light (Large Breed, Regular, Small & Toy Breed, Small Bites)

Kitten Indoor

Kitten Healthy Development (Oceanfish & Rice, Original)

Mature Adult Cat (Active Longevity Original, Hairball Control, Indoor)

Mature Adult Dog (Active Longevity, Large Breed, Small Bites)

Puppy (Healthy Development Original, Large Breed, Small & Toy Breed, Small Bites)

Play Dough

Aroma Dough - All Natural Playing Dough

Crayola - Air Dry Clay, Model Magic, Model Magic Fusion, Modeling Clay *(Crayola Play Dough is NOT Gluten Free)*

Mama K's - Play Clay (Bergamot, Cardamom, Chamomile, Geranium, Lavender, Lemongrass, Sweet Orange)

Max's Mud -

Sculpting Dough

91% Organic Natural Red ●

92% Organic Natural Purple ●

93% Organic Natural Orange ●

94% Organic Natural Yellow ●

Natural Mud (Natural Blue ●, Natural Green ●)

Organic Mud (Natural Brown ●, Natural White ●)

Rx   Shampoo & Conditioner

100% Pure - All Conditioners, All Shampoos

Arbonne -
     ABC Baby Care Hair & Body Wash
     FC5 (Nourishing Daily Conditioner, Nourishing Daily Shampoo)
     Intelligence (Daily Self Adjusting Shampoo w/Tea Tree Oil,
         Rejuvenating Cream, Thermal Fusion Hair & Scalp Revitalizer)
     Sea Source Detox Spa Fortifying Hair Mask

California Baby -
     Conditioner (Swimmer's Defense, Tea Tree & Lavender)
     Hair Conditioner (Calendula, Calming, Overtired & Cranky,
         Super Sensitive)
     Shampoo & Body Wash (Calendula, Calming, Overtired & Cranky,
         Super Sensitive, Swimmer's Defense, Tea Tree & Lavender)

Desert Essence Organics -
     Conditioner (Coconut, Fragrance Free, Green Apple & Ginger,
         Italian Red Grape, Lemon Tea Tree, Red Raspberry)
     Oh So Clean 2 In 1 Gentle Foaming Hair & Body Cleaner
     Shampoo (Coconut, Fragrance Free, Green Apple & Ginger, Italian
         Red Grape, Lemon Tea Tree, Red Raspberry)

Dove -
     Damage Therapy Conditioner (Color Repair, Cool Moisture, Daily
         Moisture Treatment, Energize, Intensive Repair Daily Treatment,
         Revival, Volume Boost)
     Damage Therapy Shampoo (Color Repair, Cool Moisture, Daily
         Moisture, Energize, Intensive Repair, Revival, Volume Boost)
     Hair Therapy Nourishing Oil Care Shampoo
     Refresh & Care Dry Shampoo

Dr. Bronner's - Citrus Conditioning Hair Rinse, Lavender Hair
     Conditioner & Style Creme

EO -
     Conditioner (Chamomile & Honey ●, Coconut & Hibiscus ●,
         Deep Conditioner Wild Lime & Ginger ●, French Lavender ●,
         Rose Geranium & Citrus ●, Rosemary & Mint ●)

shampoo & conditioner

Rx

Rosemary & Cedarwood Pre Shampoo Treatment ●
Shampoo (Chamomile & Honey ●, Coconut & Hibiscus ●, French
Lavender ●, Rose & Chamomile ●, Rosemary & Mint ●,
Sweet Orange ●)
Wild Lime & Ginger Hair Repair ●
Fleurish Beauty - Premium Conditioner, Premium Shampoo
Full Circle - All Varieties (Conditioners, Shampoos)
Gluten-Free Savonnerie ▲ - All Products
Green Beaver - All Products
Head & Shoulders -
Citrus Breeze (2 In 1 Shampoo & Conditioner, Shampoo)
Classic Clean (2 In 1 Shampoo & Conditioner, Conditioner,
Shampoo)
Clinical Strength (All Varieties)
Dry Scalp Care (2 In 1 Shampoo & Conditioner, Conditioner,
Shampoo)
Extra Volume Shampoo
Green Apple (2 In 1 Shampoo & Conditioner, Conditioner,
Shampoo)
Hair Endurance (All Varieties)
Itchy Scalp Care (Conditioner, Shampoo)
Ocean Lift (2 In 1 Shampoo & Conditioner, Shampoo)
Refresh Shampoo
Sensitive Care (All Varieties)
Smooth & Silky (2 In 1 Shampoo & Conditioner, Conditioner,
Shampoo)
Hugo Naturals - All Varieties (Conditioner, Shampoo), Baby Hugo
Chamomile & Vanilla Shampoo & Baby Wash
Hy-Vee Health Market - Shampoo Every Day Basic 2 In 1 Dandruff
Johnson's Baby - 3 In 1 Shampoo Condition Body Wash, Baby
Shampoo, No More Tangles (Detangling Spray, Extra Conditioning
Shampoo, Leave In Conditioner, Shampoo), Shampoo (Natural,
w/Natural Lavender)

Rx Keys ▲ - All Products

Logona Naturkosmetik - Bamboo Cream Shampoo, Calendula Baby Shampoo, Logona Mann Shampoo & Shower Gel, Pur Free Fragrance/Hypo Allergenic Shampoo & Shower Gel, Shampoo & Shower Gel

Meijer - Minoxidil 5% Liquid (30 Day, 90 Day)

Organix - All Shampoos & Conditioners

Shea Moisture - Baby Head To Toe Wash & Shampoo, Moisture Retention Shampoo, Restorative Conditioner

Surface - All Hair Products

Surya Brasil - All Products

Shaving Products

Arbonne - RE9 Advanced For Men Post Shave Balm, RE9 Advanced For Men Shave Gel

Dr. Bronner's - Shaving Gel (All Scents)

Gillette -
Fusion (Clear Pro Glide Shave Gel, Hydragel Cooling, Irritation Defense Gel, Moisturizing, Pure & Sensitive)
LubriStrips
Pre Shave Formulas
Sensitive Shave Foam
Shave Gel (Extra Comfort, Moisturizing)

Kiss My Face - Moisture Shave (Green Tea & Bamboo, Key Lime, Lavender & Shea, Patchouli)

Logona Naturkosmetik - Logona Mann (Aftershave Balm, Aftershave Lotion, Shaving Cream)

Pure Silk - Moisturizing Shave Cream (Cherry Blossom, Dry Skin, Melon Splash, Plumeria, Raspberry Mist, Sensitive Skin)

Surya Brasil - All Products

Sleep Aids

Meijer - Sleep Aid Nitetime (Caplets, Tablets)

Motrin - PM

Rx

Natrol - Melatonin 5mg
Simply Sleep - Caplets
Sominex - Maximum Strength, Original
Tylenol - PM Caplets
Walgreens - Nighttime Sleep Aid

Stay Awake

Arbonne - Energy Fizz Tabs (Citrus, Pomegranate)
Meijer - Stay Awake Tablets
Vivarin - Tablets
Walgreens - Awake Caffeine Caplets

Sunblock/Sun Tanning Products

Arbonne - Before Sun (Damage Control Water Resistant Sunscreen
SPF 30, Glow With It After Sun Lotion, Made In The Shade Self
Tanner Sunscreen SPF 15)
California Baby -
Soothing & Healing Spray For Sunburn & Dry Skin
Sunscreen
SPF 18 (Everyday/Year Round, Super Sensitive)
SPF 30 + Sunblock Stick Everday/Year Round
SPF 30+ (Everyday/Year Round, No Fragrance, Summer Blend,
Super Sensitive)
SPF 30+ Sunblock Stick (No Fragrance, Super Sensitive)
Coppertone - All Varieties (Oil Free, Pure & Simple, Sensitive, Sport,
Ultra Guard, Water Babies)
Desert Essence Organics - Age Reversal SPF 30 Mineral Sunscreen,
Daily Essential Defense Lotion SPF15
Johnson's Baby - Daily Face & Body Lotion w/SPF 40

Rx Kiss My Face -
  Cell Mate Facial Creme & Sunscreen
  Face Factor (SPF 30, SPF 50)
  Hot Spots SPF 30
  Kids Sun Stick SPF 30 (Blue, Pink, White)
  Sport Spray SPF 50
  Sun Spray (Lotion SPF 30, Oil SPF 30)

Supplements

Accuflora - Probiotic Acidophilus
Arbonne -
  Antioxidant & Immunity Booster
  Daily Fiber Boost
  Daily Power Packs (For Men, For Women)
  Digestion Plus
  Fit Chews
  Going Going Gone
  Herbal Detox Tea
  Joint Support
  NutriMinC RE9 Resist Essential Fatty Acid Dietary
  Omega 3 Plus
  Protein Shake Mix (Chocolate, Vanilla)
  Protein Shake Ready To Drink (Chocolate, Vanilla)
  RE9 Advanced Collagen Support Dietary Supplement
  Super Chews For Kids & Teens
  Women's Balancing Menopause Support
AZO - Cranberry
Biochem -
  & Whey Powder (100% Acai ●, 100% Berries ●, 100% Hemp ●,
    100% Raw Foods ●)
  100% Egg Protein ●
  100% Greens & Whey Vanilla (Regular ●, Single Serve Packets ●)
  100% Vegan Protein Powder (Vanilla ●, Chocolate ●)
  100% Whey Protein Powder Chocolate ●

supplements

Rx

BioPure ●

Carb Phaser 1000 ●

L Glutamine Muscle Support 1000 ●

Lean Results ●

Omega Burn ●

Tri Protein Plus Powder Vanilla ●

Ultimate (Creatine Monohydrate ●, Fat Metabolizer ●, Protein System Chocolate ●)

Bio-K+ - Fresh Probiotic (Calcium ●, Dairy Free ●, Organic ●, Original ●, Strawberry ●)

Carlson -

Able Eyes

Aces (+ZN, Gold, Regular)

Aler Key

Alfalfa Complete

Aloe Vera Gel

Alpha Lipoic

Amino Acids (5 HTP Healthy Mood, Acetyl L Carnitine, Amino Blend, DLPA, L Arginine, L Carnitine, L Glutamine, L Lysine, L Methionine, L Proline, L Tyrosine, NAC)

Blood Nutrients

Brewers Yeast

Cardi Rite

CoQ10

Cranberry Concentrate

Easy Soy

Eye Rite

Fish Oils (Cod Liver (All Varieties), EPA Gems, Fish Oil Q, For Kids Cod Liver Oil, Kids Chewable DHA, Kids Very Finest Fish Oil, Multi, Salmon Oil (& GLA, Regular), Super (DHA, Omega 3 Fish Oils), Very Finest Fish Oil (Chewable, Regular)

Food Enzymes (HCL & Pepsin, D.A. #34)

Gene Right

GLA

Glucosamine Sulfate

Rx   Glutathione Booster
Golden Primrose
Grape Seed Extract
Grapefruit Pectin
Heart Energy
Heartbeat Elite
Herbals (Garlic, Ginko Biloba Plus, Golden Aloe)
Hi Fiber Powder
Homocysteine Guard Elite
Kelp
Leci Key Granules
Lecithin
Liquid Cal 600
Lutein (Regular, w/Kale)
Lycopene
Moisture Eyes
Nutra Support (Bone, Immune, Joint, Memory, Prostate)
Organs & Glands (Vital #1 Adrenal, Vital #27 Thymus)
Phosphatidyl (Choline, Serine)
Prenatal
Pro Rite
Psyllium
Rhythm Right
Right For (Cholesterol, Menopause)
Sytrinol
CeliAct - Fish Oil
Coromega - Omega 3 Pudding (Chocolate Orange, Orange)
Country Life -
Digestive Enzymes (Maxi Zyme ●, Super Strength Pancreatin ●)
5 HTP ●
7 Keto Trim ●
Acetyl L Carnitine ●
Activated Charcoal 260mg ●
Aller Max ●

supplements

Rx

Bee Propolis 500mg ●
Bio Active Hyaluronic Acid ●
Bone Density Factors ●
Bone Solid ●
Celadrin ●
Chromium Picolinate 200mcg ●
Circu Pressure ●
Circulation Factors ●
CLA Tonalin 1000mg ●
Cod Liver Oil ●
CoQ10
   100mg ●
   30mg ●
   60mg ●
   Maxi Sorb (30mg ●, Mega 60mg ●, Ultra 100mg ●)
Cran Complete UT Formula ●
Daily (Dophilus ●, Fiber X ●, Immune ●)
DHEA
   10mg ●
   25mg ●
   Complex For (Men ●, Women ●)
Digestive Enzymes (Betaine Hydrochloride ●, Dairy Zyme Caps ●,
   Gluten Zyme ●, Triple Strength Bromelain 500mg ●, Tropical
   Papaya ●)
DLPA Caps 1000mg ●
DMAE Coenzymed ●
Estro G Balance ●
Evening Primrose Oil 500mg ●
For Men & Women (Go Less ●, VaricoVein ●)
Gaba Relaxer ●
GenaSlim ●
Glucosamine Chrondroitin Formula ●
Glycemic Factors ●
Glycine ●
Green Tea Extract ●

Rx Herbal (Ginseng Supreme Complex ●, Milk Thistle Extract ●, Saw Palmetto & Pygeum (Caps ●, Extract ●), Tea Tree Oil ●, Yohimbe Power ●)

Homocysteine Shield ●

L Arginine (& L Ornithine ●, Caps 500mg ●)

L Carnitine Caps (250mg ●, 500mg ●)

L Glutamine Caps (1000mg ●, 500mg ●)

L Lysine (1000mg ●, 500mg (Caps ●, Regular ●))

L Methionine 500mg ●

L Phenylalanine ●

L Theanine 200mg ●

L Tyrosine Caps ●

Lecithin (1200mg ●, Granules ●)

Liga Tend ●

Lipoic Acid (100mg ●, 200mg ●, Active ●)

Liquid (Fiber ●, Goji & Acai ●)

Liver Support Factors ●

Malic Relief Formula ●

Max Amino Caps ●

Maxi Baby Dophilus ●

Melatonin (1 mg ●, 3mg ●)

Menapause Support ●

NAC N Acetyl Cysteine 750mg ●

Natural Acidophilus w/Pectin ●

Nature's Garlic ●

Norwegian Kelp 225mcg ●

Nutra Chol Less ●

Olive Leaf Extract ●

Omega (Cardio Factors ●, Postpartum Mom ●, Prenatal Mom ●, Relief ●, Surge (High DHA ●, High EPA ●, Regular ●), Ultra (Concentrated ●, DHA/EPA ●))

Omega 3 (1000mg ●, Mood ●, Super ●)

Phosphatidyl Choline Complex 1200mg ●

Phosphatidylserine Complex ●

supplements

Rx

    Power Dophilus ●
    Pregnenolone (10mg ●, 30mg ●)
    Prosta Max For Men ●
    Pycnogenol (50mg ●, 50mg ●)
    R-Lipoic Acid ●
    RNA/DNA ●
    Shark Cartilage Caps 800mg ●
    Sharp Thought ●
    Stress Shield ●
    Super Fiber Psyllium Seed Husk Powder ●
    Superior B12 3000mg ●
    Taurine ●
    Thyro Max Support ●
    Ultra Oils ●
    Well Max w/NAC ●
    Zinc Picolinate ●

Culturelle - Probiotics
Dr. Price's - All Energy & Metabolism Products ●
Dr. Willard's - Willard Water ●
EleCare - For Infants ★
EleCare Jr. - For Children ★
Ensure - All Shakes
Flex A Min - Double Strength, Super Glucosamine 2000 Plus, Triple Strength Bone Shield, Triple Strength Joint Flex
Freeda - All Supplements ●
Giant Eagle Brand -
    ABC Senior Tablet
    Calcium (600 w/Vitamin D, Hi Cal, Magnesium)
    Calcium/Magnesium/Zinc
    Chondroitin Complex
    Co Q10 (150mg, 200 mg)
    Cod Liver Oil
    Cranberry
    Echinacea 400mg

Rx Echinacea/Goldenseal
Fish Oil 1000mg
Garlic Deodorized
Garlic/Parsley
Ginseng (250mg, Plus)
Glucosamine Chondroitin
Glucose Orange Tablets
Green Tea Extract
Maximum Strength Glucosamine/Chondroitin
Milk Thistle
Multi Day (Calcium Iron & Zinc, Vitamin)
Omega 3 Fish Oil 1200mg
Saw Palmetto
Selenium
St. John's Wort
Triple Strength Glucosamine/Chondroitin

Ginkoba - Memory
Ginsana - Energy
GlutaSolve - Powdered Glutamine Supplement Packets
Good 'N Natural - 5 HTP Capsules, Acetyl L Carnitine Capsules,
Caprylic Acid Tablets, Charcoal Capsules, Pycnogenol Capsules
Hy-Vee Health Market -
Acail Berry Softgels
Acidophilus
Acidophilus Probiotic Blend Caplets
Alpha Lipoic Acid Tablets
Beauty Gelatin Caplet
Biotin (800mcg, Maximum Strength 5000mcg Capsules)
Cider Vinegar Tablets
Cranberry Extract Caplets
Enteric Coated Fish Oil 1000mg Omega 3
Enteric Coated Triple Omega Complex 3 6 9
Evening Primrose Oil 500mg

supplements

Rx

Fish Oil (1000mg Omega 3, 1200mg Softgels)
Flaxseed Oil Softgels
Folic Acid (400mcg Tablets, 800mcg Tablets)
Glucosamine
   1000mg Tablets (Maximum Strength, Regular Strength)
   500mg Caplets
Glucosamine & Chondroitin
   Caplets (Original Strength, Regular)
   Tablets (Plus, Triple Strength)
Herbal Energizer Caplets
Iron (27mg Tablets, 65mg Tablets)
L Lysine 600mg Tablets
Lutein (10mg Tablets, 20mg Softgels)
Magnesium 250mg Tablets
Melatonin 5mg Tablets
MgO 400mg Tablets
MSM 1000mg Tablets
Norwegian Cod Liver Oil
Nutritional Drink (Chocolate, Chocolate Plus, Strawberry,
   Strawberry Plus, Vanilla, Vanilla Plus)
Papaya Enzymes Chewables
Stress B Tablets (Plus Iron, Regular, w/Zinc)
Therapeutic M Tablets
Iceland Health -
   Advanced Memory Formula w/Omega 3
   Bone Health
   Co Q10 Softgels
   Glucose Control Formula
   Joint Health Formula
   Maximum Strength Omega 3 Softgels
   Multivitamin
   Omega 3 Regular Strength + Vitamin D3
   Omega Ultimate Shield
Iron Tek - 100% Protein ●, CLA 1140 Higher Potency ●, Creatine
   Monohydrate ●, Glutamine Powder ●, Liquid Amino Complex ●,

Rx   Micell Edge ●, Pure Tonalin CLA Complex ●

Kirkland Signature - Glucosamine HCI 1500mg w/Chondroitin 1200m, Omega 3 Fish Oil

Kirkman -

Acetyl L Carnitine

Acidophilus Powder

Alpha (Ketoglutaric Acid, Lipoic Acid)

Amino Support (Hypoallergenic Capsules, Powder)

Beta Glucan

Bifido Complex (Advanced Formula, Regular)

Biofilm Defense

Buffered Magnesium

   Glycinate (Capsules, Powder)

   Glycinate Bio Max Series Powder

   Oxide

Carb Digest w/Isogest

CD (Biotic, Herbal)

Chromium

Cod Liver Oil (Lemon Lime Liquid, Regular Liquid, w/Vitamins A & D)

Coenzyme Q10 (Capsules, Chewable Tablets, Tablets w/ Sucralose, w/Idebenone)

Colostrum Gold (Flavored, Unflavored)

Creatine Hypoallergenic 500mg Capsules

D Biotin Capsules

Detox Aid (Advanced Formula, Diet & Complexing)

DMAE (Capsules, Chewable Wafers)

DMG (Capsules, Capsules w/Folic Acid & B12, Capsules w/Folinic Acid & B12, Liquid, Maximum Strength Capsules, w/B12 & Folinic Acid Liquid, w/Folinic Acid & Methyl B12)

DPP IV Forte

DRN

   Detoxification Booster Capsules, Lithium, Vitamin/Mineral Based Supplement (Capsules, Powder)

Rx

EFA Powder
EnZym Complete Chewable w/Isogest
EnZym Complete DPP IV (Capsules, II Capsules, Max Spectrum w/Isogest)
EnZymAid Multi Enzyme Complex
Everyday Multi Vitamin (Regular, w/o Vitamins A & D)
Folic Acid (Chewable Tablets, w/B12 Capsules)
Folinic Acid (Capsules, w/B12 Capsules)
GABA (Plain, w/Niacinamide & Inositol)
Gastro Support
Gastromune AI Support
Ginkgo Biloba
Glucosamine Sulfate
Glycine
Grape Extract
Grapefruit Seed Extract
Idebenone
Immuno Aid (Advanced Formula, Regular)
Inositol Pure Soluble Powder
Iron Bio Max Series (Capsules, Liquid)
L Carnosine
L Glutamine
L Taurine
Lactobacillus (Acidophilus, Duo)
Magnesium (Citrate Soluble Powder, Glycinate Bio Max Series, Malate, Sulfate Cream)
Max Spectrum EnZym Complete/DPP IV Fruit Free w/Isogest
Maximum Spectrum Enzyme Complete/DPP IV Fruit Free
Melatonin (Chewables, Plus Magnesium, Slo Release Tablets)
Methylcobalamin Concentrated Powder
Milk Thistle
Mito Cell Support
Molybdenum
Multi Flora Spectrum

Rx
N Acetyl Cysteine

Nordic Naturals ProEFA Junior

Nu Thera (Everyday Companion, EveryDay Companion Powder, w/o Vitamins A & D, w/P5P)

P5P (Regular, w/Magnesium Glycinate)

Phenol Assist (Companion, Regular)

Pre Biotic Fiber Powder

Pro Bio (Chewable Wafers, Defense, Gold, Inulin Free, Super Bio Max)

Pro Culture Gold

Reduced L Glatathione (Capsules, Lotion)

Saccharomyces Boulardii

Spectrum Complete (Capsules, Powder Flavored, Powder Regular)

Super Cranberry Extract (Capsules, Chewables)

Super Nu Thera (Caplets, Capsules, Powder, Raspberry Flavored Concentrate, Raspberry Liquid, Tropical Fruit Liquid, w/o Vitamin A & D Capsules, w/o Vitamins A & D (P5P Cherry Liquid, Powder), w/P5P Caplets, w/P5P Green Apple Flavored Concentrate, w/P5P New Improved Powder)

Super Pro Bio Bio Max Series

Thera Response

TMG (Capsules, Capsules w/Folic Acid & B12, Liquid, Powder w/ Folic Acid & B12, w/Folic Acid & B12, w/Folic Acid & Methyl B12, w/Folinic Acid & B12, w/Folinic Acid & Methyl B12)

Yeast Aid (Capsules, Powder)

Zinc Sulfate Topical Cream

L'il Critters - Fruit & Veggie Gummy Bears, Omega 3 DHA

Meijer -

Acidophilus Bifido RS

Antioxidant (Natural Caplets, Regular, w/Zinc Tablets)

Astraxanthin

Beta Carotene Natural Softgels

Biocosinol

supplements

Rx

Chromium Picolinate
Cinnamon Capsules
CLA Conjugated Linolenic Acid
Co Q10 (Capsules, Softgels)
Cod Liver Oil
Cranberry Caplets
Cranmax
DHA
Echinacea Caplets
EPA Eicosapentaenoic Acid
Estroplus Extra Strength
Evening Primrose Oil Softgels
Ferrous Gluconate Tablets
Fish Oil (Concentrate, Enteric Coated, Enteric Softgels, Extra
    Strength, Extra Strength Enteric Coated, Hi Potency Softgels,
    Softgels, w/Co Q10)
Flax Seed Oil Softgels
Focus Smart
Folic Natural Tablets
Garlic Hi Potency Odorless Tablets
Ginkgo Biloba Caplets
Ginseng Softgels
GLA Gamma Linolenic Acid
Glucosamine & Collagen & HA
Glucosamine Chondroitin (3X, All Day Double Strength Tablets,
    Extra Strength, Plus MSM, Regular Strength Caplets, SOD Free
    Caplets, w/HA Tablets, w/MSM Double Strength Caplets, w/
    MSM HLA Caplets)
Glucosamine (Complex Caplets, Sulfate Caplets)
Green Tea
Hair Skin Nail
Lecithin Softgels
Lutein (Capsules, Softgels)
Lycopene Capsules

Rx
    Memory & Mood Supplement
Menopause Complex AM PM
Odor Free Garlic
Omega Super Softgels
Panax Ginseng
Papaya Enzyme Natural
Phytosterol Esters
Policosanol Capsules
Potassium Natural Caplets
Saw Palmetto Softgels
Soy Isoflavones
St. John's Wort Caplets
Super Omega
Vision Formula w/Lutein
Vitamin Mineral Herb Menopause Supplement

Member's Mark - Cinnamon 500 mg, CoQ 10 (200mg, 400mg), Cranberry, Fish Oil (1200mg, All Natural Enteric 1400 mg), Garlic 1000mg, Ginkgo Biloba, Glucosamine 1500mg + MSM 1500mg, Omega 3 6 9, Red Yeast Rice 600mg

Natrol - CoQ10 100mg, Fish Oil & Vitamin D 3, Ginkgo Biloba, Immune Boost, L Carnitine 500mg, Omega 3 Fish Oil 1200mg

Nature's Basket -
    Acidophilus Bifidus
Advanced Antioxidant Complex Veg Caps
Alpha Lipoic Acid
Amino Acid Complex Tabs
Beta Carotene 25000 IU
Biotin (500mg, 5mg Veg Caps)
Brain Formula
Cardio Formula
Chelated Cal Mag
Chewable (Calcium, Peppermint Enzyme)
Cholesterol Complex
Chromium Picolinate

supplements

Rx

Co Q 10 (100mg, 30mg, 60mg)
Cod Liver Oil
Complete Omega Complex
Concentrated Omega 3
Echinacea 400mg
Enzyme Complex w/Herbs
EPA & DHA Softgels
Evening Primrose Oil
Eye Formula
Fiber Complex
Flax Seed Oil 1000mg
Folic Acid 800
Garlic 500mg
Ginkgo Biloba 80mg
Glucosamine (Chondroitin, Chondroitin MSM Tabs, Sulfate)
Green Tea Extract 250mg
Joint Formula Softgels
Kidfit Tigers
L Glutamine 500mg
Lecithin 1200mg
Liver Detox Complex
Maximum One
Mega Magnesium
Melatonin 3mg
Mens (45+, Multi Food Rich)
Milk Thistle 175mg
Niacin 100mg
Nomax Selenium
Non GMO Soy Protein Powder
Ocu Complete
One Daily Multiple 60
Potassium 99mg
Prenatal Complete
Prostate Formula

Rx   Psyllium Husk
Whey Protein Powder (Chocolate, Original)

Nordic Naturals - Arctic Cod Liver Oil Lquid (Peach, Regular),
Balanced Omega Combination, Cod Liver Oil Soft Gels, DHA
Junior Strawberry, Omega 3 Gummies Tangerine, ProDHA, ProEFA
Soft Gels, ProEPA, ProOmega Soft Gels

Novasource - Renal Formula

Nutrition Now - All Varieties

Os-Cal - Calcium Supplement (Calcium + D3, Chewable, Extra D3
Caplet, Ultra)

Pedia-Lax - Probiotic Yums

Pioneer - All Supplements ★

Prebiotin - Dietary Supplement (Bone Health, Prebiotic Fiber)

Publix -

Antioxidant w/Zinc Tablets

Balanced Nutritional Drink (Chocolate, Chocolate Plus,
Strawberry, Strawberry Plus, Vanilla, Vanilla Plus)

Calcium (Citrate Caplets, Magnesium Zinc Caplets, Oyster Shell
w/Vitamin D Tablets, Tablets, w/Soy Tablets, w/Vitamin D
Caplets)

Co Q10 Softgels

Cranberry Caplets

Echinacea Caplets

Evening Primrose Oil Softgels

Fish Oil Softgels

Flax Seed Oil Softgels

Folic 400mcg Natural Tablets

Garlic (High Potency Odorless Tablets, Oil Softgels)

Gelatin Synthetic Caplets

Ginkgo Biloba Caplets

Ginseng Softgels

Glucosamine Chondroitin (Double Strength Caplets,
Sodium Free Caplets)

L Lysine Natural Tablets

supplements

Rx

Magnesium Natural Tablets

Niacin (Tablets, Time Release Tablets)

Panax Ginseng Caplets

Potassium Natural (Caplets, Tablets)

Saw Palmetto Softgels

Selenium Tablets

Vitamin Mineral Herbs Menopausal Supplement Caplet

Zinc Natural Caplets

Rainbow Light -

Arthx Relief

Herbal Prescriptives (3 Way Stress Management, Black Cohosh Meno Relief, Candida Cleanse, Counter Attack, Deep Defense, Get Well Soon, Gingko Bacopa Quick Thinking, Milk Thistle Plus, Nail Hair & Skin Connection, Pain Eze, PMS Relief, Theramend Cox 2 Flex)

Just Once (DHA 250 Smart Essentials, Everyone's Omega Fish & Flax Oil)

Omega (Brain Performance, Cardio Performance, Skin & Mood)

Osteo Build Food Based Formula

Plant Source Enzymes (Complete Menopause, Women's Answer)

Thinberry Diet

Renew Life - Enzymes (Candi Zyme, Constipation Stop, Digest More, Digest More Ultra, Gas Stop, Heartburn Prevention, Indigestion Stop, Lactose STOP, Paragone), Probiotics Ultimate Flora (Adult Formula, Critical Care, Senior Formula, Vaginal Support)

Schiff - Move Free (Advanced !, Advanced Plus MSM Tablets !), Probiotics Acidophilus Tablets

Simplexity Health - Acidophilus, Alpha Sun (Capsules, Tablets), Bifidus, ImmuSun, Omega Sun (Capsules, Tablets), OsteoSun, Simply SBGA, StemPlex, Super Q10, Super Sun Smoothie

Simply Right - Cinnamon Plus Chromium, Ginkgo Biloba, Lutein, Omega 3 6 9, Red Yeast Rice

ThreeLac - Probiotic

Vitafusion - Gummy Vitamins (CoQ 10, Daily Vision)

Rx Walgreens -
3 In 1 (Mens, Womens)
5HTP Fast Acting Capsules Maximum Strength
Acetyl L Carnitine
Acidophilus (Bifidus Regularis Beads, Capsules, Chewable,
Chewable Wafers w/Bifidus, Gold Capsules, Ultimate Probiotic)
Apple Cider Vinegar Tablets
Bilberry Softgels Extra Strength
Biotin Super Strength Tablets
Black Cohosh Root
Breast Solutions Complex Tablet
Cholesterol Health Caplets
Cinnamon (Capsules, Plus Chromium Capsules)
Citrate Of Magnesium (Low Sodium Cherry, Regular)
Co Q10 Softges
Cod Liver Oil Softgels
Collagen w/Vitamin C Tablets
Cranberry
Extract Tablets, Triple Strength Softgels (Regular, w/C&E)
Echinacea
Estronatural Caplets
Evening Primrose Oil
Finest Naturals
  Coenzyme Q10 Chewable Tablets
  Cranberry Tablets
  DHA Omega 3 Softgels
  Echinacea (Tablets, w/Vitamin C Capsules)
  Estronatural Caplets (Extra Strength, Regular)
  Fish Oil Enteric Softgels
  Flaxseed Oil Softgels
  Ginkgo (Capsules, Tablets)
  Ginseng Capsules
  Grapeseed Tablets
  Green Tea Capsules

supplements

Rx

Iron
L Carnitine Capsule
Milk Thistle Capsules
Natural DHA Complete
Pomegranate Capsules
Primrose Oil Softgels
Resveratrol Capsules
Saw Palmetto Softgels
Soy Isoflavonoid Capsules
St. John's Wort Tablets
Fish Oil Softgels
  Cholesterol Free
  EPA Bonus
  High Potency
  Highly Concentrated Omega 3
  Odorless (Double Strength, Regular)
  Regular
  w/Co Q10
Flax Seed Oil (Fish Borage, Liquid, Softgels)
Flush Free Niacin
Garlic (High Potency Odorless, Odorless, Regular)
Ginger Root Capsules
Ginkgo Biloba
Ginsana
Ginseng (Complex Plus Royal Jelly, Softgels)
Glucosamine & Condroitin
  DS Caplets
  MSM Advanced
  Triple Strength
  Sulfate
Grapeseed Extract Tablets
Green Tea Extract w/EGCG
Gripe Water
Horny Goat Weed

Rx   L Arginine Tablets
L Carnitine Caplets
Lecithin Softgels
Lutein (Plus Billberry, Softgels)
Magnesium Tablets (Natural, Oxide, Regular)
Melatonin Tablets
Milk Thistle Softgels
Natural Woman Menopause Supplement
Omega Super Softgels (Cholesterol Health, Regular)
Papaya Enzyme Natural Tablet
Pomegranate
Red Yeast Rice
Resveratrol
Saw Palmetto (Capsules, Softgels)
Sea Thin
Shark Cartilage Caplets
Skin Hair & Nails Formula
St. John's Wort (Extract, Tablets)
Super Goat Weed
Super Strength Enzyme Formula Tablets
Tea Tree Oil Liquid
Turmeric Curcumin Capsules
Valerian Root (Extra Strength, Plus Calming Blend)
Zinc Natural Caplets
Zrii - The Original Amalaki ●

Vitamins & Minerals

Arbonne - Calcium Plus
Carlson -
   Chelated (Cal Mag, Calcium, Calcium, Chromium, Copper, Iron,
      Magnesium, Manganese, Zinc)
   Chew Iron
   Complexed (Phosphorus, Potassium)

vitamins & minerals

Rx

Herbals Vitamin C w/Echinacea
Iodine
Liquid (Cal Mag, Calcium, Magnesium, Mulitiple Minerals)
Magnesium
Moly B
Multivitamins & Minerals (For Kids Chewable, Mini Multi,
    Multi Gel, Super 1 Daily, Super 2 Daily & Fish Oil, Super 75)
Potassium
Selenium (Capsules, Tablets)
Sulfur MSM (Capsules, Powder)
Vitamin A (Caro Plete, Natural, Palmitate, Super Beta Carotene,
    w/Pectin, Water Soluble)
Vitamin B
    B 50 Gel
    B Complete (100, 50, Regular)
    B1 All Strengths
    B12 (SL, Time Release)
    B2 All Strengths
    B6 (All Strengths, Liquid)
    Biotin
    Folic Acid
    Niacin Products
    Pantethine Time Release
    Pantothenic Acid (Liquid, Time Release)
    Time Release B
    Tri B Homocysteine
Vitamin C
    Bioflavonoids
    C Gel
    Crystals
    For Kids Chewable
    Mild C (Capsules, Chewable, Crystals, Time Release)
    One Gram C
    Rose Hip C

Rx

Rutin
Super C Complex
Time Release C (Bio, Regular)
Vitamin D
Vitamin E
   Aqua Gem E
   D Alpha Gems
   E Gems (Elite, Gamma, Plus, Regular, Veg, w/C)
   E Sel
   Key E (Kaps, Powder, Regular)
   Tocotrienols
Vitamin K
Zinc (Ease, Regular)
CeliAct - Multivitamin
Country Life -
   Action Max For Men(Regular ●, XXXtreme For Men ●)
   Arthro Joint & Muscle Support Factors ●
   Beta Carotene ●
   Biotin (500mcg ●, Hi Potency 1000mcg ●, High Potency 5mg ●)
   Cal Mag Citrate w/Vitamin D ●
   Cal Snack ●
   Calcium Caps ●
   Calcium Citrate w/Vitamin D ●
   Calcium Magnesium (& Potassium ●, Caps ●, Complex
      1000mg/500mg ●, Mini Tabs 500mg/250mg ●, w/Vitamin D
      Complex ●, w/Vitamin D Complex ●)
   Calcium Magnesium Zinc (Regular ●, w/L Glutamic Acid ●)
   Carotenoid ●
   Chelated Molybdenum ●
   Chewable Adult Multi ●
   Choline (650mg ●, Inositol Complex ●)
   Chromium Complex 200mcg ●
   Citrus Bioflavanoids (1000mg ●, 500mg ●)
   Daily Multi Sorb ●

Rx

Dolphins Pals Multivitamin (DHA Gummies For Kids ●,
     Multivitamin & Mineral ●)
Easy Iron 25mg ●
Folic Acid 800mcg ●
Grape Seed Extract (100mg ●, 200mg ●, 50mg ●,
     Grape Complete ●)
Inositol Powder ●
Iron Aid ●
Liquid (Dolphin Pals ●, Multi Vitamin & Mineral Complex ●,
     Target Mins Calcium/Magnesium ●)
Lutein 20mg ●
Magnesium (300mg ●, Chelated 250mg ●, Citrate ●)
Max For Men Multivitamin & Mineral (Iron Free ●, w/Iron ●)
Max Sorb
     Multivitamin & Mineral (Beyond Food ●, Superior Mulitiple ●)
          Seniority Multivitamin ●)
Maxi (Hair ●, Pre Natal ●, Sorb QM 1 ●)
Maxine
     Daily Multiple For Women (Iron Free ●, Regular ●)
     Menopause Formula ●
     Multivitamin & Mineral (Regular ●, w/Iron ●)
MSM (1000mg ●, 500mg ●)
Multivitamin
     Daily Total One (Regular ●, w/Max Sorb ●)
     Essential Life Capsules ●
     Maxi Baby Care ●
     Multi 100 ●
     Tall Tree Children's Chewable ●
Natural Vitamin A & D 10000 IU/400IU ●
Nerve & Osteo Support ●
Niacin (100mg ●, 500mg ●, Flush Free 400mg ●)
Niacinimide ●
P5P Pyridoxal Phosphate 50mg ●
PABA 1000 mg ●

Rx

Pantothenic Acid (1000mg ●, 250mg ●, 500mg ●)

Potassium 99mg Amino Acid Chelated Complex
w/Potassium Citrate ●

Rutin (500mg ●, Bio Complex ●)

Selenium (100mcg ●, 200mcg ●)

Super 10 Antioxidant ●

Target Mins Potassium 99mg ●

Total Mins
Iron Free (25mg ●, w/Boron ●),
w/Iron ●

Vitamin A (10000 IU ●, Dry 10000 IU ●)

Vitamin B
Action B Caps (100 ●, 50 ●)
Active B6 Caps 50mg ●
B1 100mg ●
B12 (1000mcg ●, 500mcg ●)
B2 100mg ●
B6 (100mg ●, 200mg ●, 50mg ●)
Basic B Caps ●
Coenzyme B Complex Caps ●, Maxi B Caps (w/Folic Acid ●,
w/Taurine 100mg ●)
Stress "M" ●
Sublingual B12 500mcg ●
Super Potency Hi B100 ●

Vitamin C
1000mg Time Release ●
500mg ●
Buffer C pH Controlled (1000mg ●, 500mg ●)
Buffered (1000mg ●, 500mg ●)
C Crystals ●
Cap C 500 ●
Chewable (Acerola 500mg ●, Orange Juice 250mg ●,
Orange Juice 500mg ●)
Complex 500mg ●

Rx

      Maxi Baby C Liquid ●
      Maxi C (Caps 1000mg ●, Complex 1000mg ●)
      Superior ●
   Vitamin D (Dry 1000 IU ●, Natural 400 IU ●)
   Vitamin D3 (1000 IU ●, 2500 IU ●, 5000 IU ●)
   Vitamin E
      Natural (100 IU ●, 1000 IU ●, 200 IU ●, 400 IU ●, Dry 400 IU ●)
      Natural Complex (1000 IU ●, 400 IU ●)
   Vitamin K1 100mcg ●
   Water Factors ●
   Zinc (50mg ●, Chelated ●, Lozenges w/Vitamin C ●)
Dr. Price's - All B Complexes ●, All Daily Multivitamins ●, All Minerals ●
Freeda - All Vitamins ●
Giant Eagle Brand -
   Childs (Extra C, Iron, Vitamin)
   Multi Day (+ Iron, Minerals)
   Vitamin ABC Plus Tablets
   Vitamin B 12
   Vitamin B 6 100 mg
   Vitamin C (250mg, 500mg)
   Vitamin C & E Softgels
   Vitamin D 400
   Vitamin E (1000 IU, 400 IU, 400 IU Natural, 400 Water
      Dispersible)
Hy-Vee Health Market -
   Animal Shapes (Children's Chewables, Plus Vitamin C
      Chewables)
   B 12 (1000mcg Prolonged Release Tablets, 5000mcg Tablets,
      500mcg Tablets)
   B 12 Sublingual Tablets (2500mcg, 5000mcg)
   B 6 100mcg
   Balanced B
   Calcium
      Caplets (600mg, Plus)

Rx
Magnesium & Zinc Plus D
Oyster Shell (500mg Plus D Tablets, 500mg Tablets)
Calcium Citrate (Caplets, w/D Caplets)
Calcium w/Vitamin D (1000mg, 600mg)
Chewables (Children's Complete, Children's w/Iron,
    Vitamin C 250mg)
Mega Multiple (Men's Tablets, Women's Tablets)
Niacin (500mg Flush Free Caplets, Tablets)
One Daily Tablets (Essential, Maximum, Men's, Women's)
Potassium 99mg Tablets
Prenatal Tablets
Sentry Performance Tablets
Vitamin C (1000mg, 1000mg Prolonged Release, 1000mg w/
    Rosehips, 500mg, 500mg Time Released, 500mg w/Rosehips)
Vitamin D Tablets
    (1000IU, 400IU, 5000IU, Maximum Strength 2000IU)
Vitamin E (1000, 1000IU Di Alpha Softgels, 200, 400)
Zinc (Chelated Tablets, Chewables w/Vitamin C & B6,
    Gluconate 50mg Tablets)
Kirkland Signature - Calcium 600mg Plus D3, Calcium Citrate
    w/500mg Calcium, Daily Multi, Mature Multi, Premium
    Performance Multi, Vitamin B 100, Vitamin C 1000mg, Vitamin D 3
    2000 IU, Vitamin E 400 IU
Kirkman -
    Advanced Adult Multi Vitamin
    Advanced Mineral Support
    B Complex w/CoEnzymes Pro Support (Capsules, Powder)
    Buffered Vitamin C Powder
    Calcium Bio Max Series
    Calcium Magnesium Liquid
    Calcium w/o Vitamin D Bio Max Series
    Calcium w/Vitamin D (Chewable Tablets, Powder Unflavored)
    Children's Chewable Multi Vitamin/Mineral (Capsules, Wafers,
        Wafers w/Zylitol)

vitamins & minerals

Rx

D Biotin

IP 5 w/Calcium & Magnesium Flavored Powder

IP 6 w/Calcium & Magnesium Flavored Powder

Multi Mineral Complex Pro Support

Mycellized Vitamin A Liquid

Selenium

Vanadium

Vitamin B6 (Capsules, Magnesium Vitamin/Mineral
Chewable Wafers)

Vitamin C (Bio Max Series Buffered Powder Flavored, Bio Max
Series Buffered Powder Unflavored, Capsules, Chewable Tablets
w/Stevia, Chewables)

Vitamin D

Vitamin D3 Capsules

Vitamin E

Zinc (Bio Max Series, Liquid, Liquid w/Sucralose, Liquid w/
Sucralose, Picolinate, w/Vitamin C & Slippery Elm Lozenges)

L'il Critters - Gummy Bears (Calcium, Vitamin D), Gummy Vites
Complete, Immune C Plus Zinc & Echinacea

Little Remedies - Little Tummys Yummy Fiber Supplements

Meijer -

50 Plus w/Ester C

A Shaped (Gummy Chewables, w/Iron Chewables)

Advanced Formula w/Ester C

Calcium (All Day w/Vitamin D, Citrate Chewable, Citrate w/
Vitamin D Caplets, Coral, Magnesium Zinc Caplets, Natural
Oyster Shell Tablets, Phosphorus Plus D, Tablets, w/D
Chewables, w/D Mineral Tablets, w/Soy Tablets)

Central Vitamin Select

Daily Energy Multi Caplets

Ester C

Ferrous Sulfate (Green Tablets, TR Tablets)

Multivitamin (Bone Health, Cardio Caplets, Century Advantage,
Century Mature Tablets, Century Tablets, Hi Potency Men, Hi

Rx   Potency Women, Inov., Inov. Complete, Inov. Prenatal, Prenatal
Tablets, RDI Cholesterol Caplets, RDI Diet Tablets, RDI Men
Tablets, RDI Tablets, SNR Tablets, Super Kid Chewables,
Thera M Caplets)

Niacin Tablets

One Daily Plus (Mens Tablets, Womens Tablets)

Slow Release Iron

Teen Multi Caplets

Vitamin A

Vitamin B (Natural Tablets, Synthetic Tablets, Time Release
Tablets)

Vitamin B12 Tablets

Vitamin C (Caplets, Fruit Chewables, Natural w/Rosehips Caplets,
Synthetic Orange Chewables, Synthetic Tablets)

Vitamin E (Blended Softgels, Natural Softgels, Oil, Regular,
Synthetic Softgels, w/Fish Oil, w/Vitamin C)

Zinc Natural Caplets

Member's Mark - Calcium Liquigels 600mg, Mature Multi,
Potassium, Slow Release Iron, Sublingual Vitamin B12 2500 mg,
Super B Complex w/ C, Vitamin B12, Vitamin D3 5000 IU

Natrol - Easy C Regenerating Complex 500mg, My Favorite Multiple
(For Women, Liquid Formula, Take One), Vitamin B 12 5000mcg
Fast Dissolve, Women's Menopause Formula

Nature's Basket -
All Day C 500mg
B 12 Lozenges
B Complex (100mg, 50mg)
Cal Mag (Regular, Zinc)
Chewable Calcium
Ester C Complete
Softgels Multi
Supreme Stress B Cap
Vegetarian Multi
Vitamin C (1000mg, 500mg, 500mg w/RH, Chewable 500mg)

Rx

    Vitamin D Oil
    Vitamin E (200IU, 400IU)
    Womens (45, Multi Food Rich)
    Zinc (50mg, Lozenges Cool LMN)

Nordic Naturals - Berries Multivitamin Gummies

Nutrition Now - All Varieties

Perry - Prenatal

Pioneer - All Vitamins ★

Publix -

    Animal Shapes Chewables (Children's Complete, Regular, w/Iron, w/Vitamin C)

    Ferrous Sulfate Tablets

    Multi Vitamin
        Century (Advantage Tablets, Senior Tablets, Tablets)
        Men Tablets
        Prenatal Tablets
        Senior Tablets
        Stress w/Zinc Tablets
        Tablets
        w/Calcium Iron Tablets
        w/Iron Tablets

    Vitamin A 8000IU Natural Softgels

    Vitamin B (50 Natural, 6, Complex w/Vitamin C, Natural Complex w/Vitamin C)

    Vitamin C
        Chewables (Fruit, Organic)
        Tablets
        Time Release Tablets

    Vitamin C Natural w/Rose Hips (Caplets 500mg, Tablets (1000mg, 250mg, 500mg)

    Vitamin E (1000IU, 200IU, 400IU)

Rainbow Light -
    Berry D Licious 2500 IU Vitamin D3
    Food Based Formula

Rx   Calcium Citrate Chocolate Chewable
Complete B Complex
Complete Iron Mini Tabs
Energy B Complex
Everyday Calcium
Super C 1000 Mg
Food Based Multivitamin
50+ Mini Tab Age Defense Formula
Active Senior
Active Teen Health
Advanced Nutritional System Iron Free
Complete Nutritional System (Iron Free, Multivitamin)
Complete Prenatal System
Energizer One
Just Once
Magnesium Calcium+
Menopause One
Men's One
Performance Energy For Men
Prenatal (One, Petite)
Rejuvenage 40+
Women's One
Schiff - Niacin Flush Free Tablets
Simply Right - Calcium w/Vitamin D3, Children's Mulitvitamin Gummies, Complete Multi, Mature Multi, Niacin, Vitamin C w/ Natural Rose Hips
Slice of Life - Gummy Vitamins For Adults (All Varieties)
Viactiv - Calcium Soft Chews
Vitafusion - Gummy Vitamins (B Complex, Calcium, Daily Immune, Defense E, Energy B12, Men's Daily Mulitvitamin Formula, MultiVites, Omega 3, Platinum 50+, Power C, Prenatal Vitamins, Vitamin D, Women's Daily Multivitamin Formula)
Walgreens -
Alpha Lipoic Acid Capsules

Rx

B 12
    Oral
    Sublingual (Liquid, Tablet)
B Complex + C T/R Tablets
Biotin Tablets
Calcium Chewable (Caramel, Chocolate)
Creamies (Fruit, Neapolitan, Softgels, w/Vitamin D Chews)
Disney Princess Gummies Multivitamin
Finest Naturals Vitamin D 3 Softgels
Multi Vitamin
    50 Plus
    Century Advantage Tablets
    High Potency Men's
    Mature Tablets
    Prenatal
    RDI Tablet
    RDI w/Iron
Niacin (EP Plain, SLO, Softgels)
Potassium Natural Tablets
Prenatal Complete Plus DHA (Softgels, Tablet)
Super B Maxi Complex Caplets
Vitamin C (Regular, w/Rose Hips)
Vitamin D
Vitamin E 400 Natural D Alpha Softgels
Vitamin E Oil
Yummi Bears - Gummy Vitamins For Children (All Varieties (Organic, Original))

Weight Loss

Alli
CLA Tonalin - Softgels
Natrol - Carb Intercept Phase 2 + Chromium, Pure CitriMax, Slenderite, Tonalin CLA
Vitafusion - Fiber Well Weight Management Gummies

Index

index

index

index

U

Y

Z

Gluten-Free OTC Pharmacy

index

Gluten-Free Sponsors

NOTES

NOTES

NOTES

NOTES

NOTES

Making Gluten-Free Living Easy!

Cecelia's Marketplace
Kalamazoo, Michigan

www.CeceliasMarketplace.com

Mail In Order Form

💻 Online Orders: www.CeceliasMarketplace.com

✉ Mail Orders: Kal-Haven Publishing
P.O. Box 20383
Kalamazoo, MI 49019
U.S.A.

Title	Quantity	Price	Total
Gluten-Free Grocery Shopping Guide	_____	(x $24.95) =	_____
Gluten/Casein Free Grocery Shopping Guide	_____	(x $24.95) =	_____
Gluten/Casein/Soy Free Grocery Shopping Guide	_____	(x $24.95) =	_____
Easy 30 Day Gluten-Free Diet Diet Book	_____	(x $19.95) =	_____
Gluten-Free Mexican Cookbook	_____	(x $14.95) =	_____

Sales Tax: Michigan residents please add 6% sales tax ⎯⎯⎯⎯

Sub Total: ⎯⎯⎯⎯

Shipping: (quantities 1-2 add $5.95)
(quantities 3-6 add $11.95) ⎯⎯⎯⎯

Total: ⎯⎯⎯⎯

* Please make check or money order payable to **Kal-Haven Publishing**

Name: _____

Address: _____

City: _____ State: _____ Zip: _____

Email address: _____

Making Gluten-Free Living Easy!

Cecelia's Marketplace
Kalamazoo, Michigan

www.CeceliasMarketplace.com

Mail In Order Form

💻 Online Orders: www.CeceliasMarketplace.com

✉ Mail Orders: Kal-Haven Publishing
P.O. Box 20383
Kalamazoo, MI 49019
U.S.A.

Title	Quantity	Price	Total
Gluten-Free Grocery Shopping Guide	_____	(x $24.95) =	_____
Gluten/Casein Free Grocery Shopping Guide	_____	(x $24.95) =	_____
Gluten/Casein/Soy Free Grocery Shopping Guide	_____	(x $24.95) =	_____
Easy 30 Day Gluten-Free Diet Diet Book	_____	(x $19.95) =	_____
Gluten-Free Mexican Cookbook	_____	(x $14.95) =	_____

Sales Tax: Michigan residents please add 6% sales tax _____

Sub Total: _____

Shipping: (quantities 1-2 add $5.95)
(quantities 3-6 add $11.95) _____

Total: _____

* Please make check or money order payable to **Kal-Haven Publishing**

Name: _____

Address: _____

City: _____ State: _____ Zip: _____

Email address: _____

Making Gluten-Free Living Easy!

Cecelia's Marketplace
Kalamazoo, Michigan

www.CeceliasMarketplace.com

Mail In Order Form

💻 Online Orders: www.CeceliasMarketplace.com

✉ Mail Orders: Kal-Haven Publishing
   P.O. Box 20383
   Kalamazoo, MI 49019
   U.S.A.

Title	Quantity	Price	Total
Gluten-Free Grocery Shopping Guide	_____	(x $24.95) =	_____
Gluten/Casein Free Grocery Shopping Guide	_____	(x $24.95) =	_____
Gluten/Casein/Soy Free Grocery Shopping Guide	_____	(x $24.95) =	_____
Easy 30 Day Gluten-Free Diet Diet Book	_____	(x $19.95) =	_____
Gluten-Free Mexican Cookbook	_____	(x $14.95) =	_____

Sales Tax: Michigan residents please add 6% sales tax _____

Sub Total: _____
Shipping: (quantities 1-2 add $5.95)
           (quantities 3-6 add $11.95) _____

Total: _____

* Please make check or money order payable to **Kal-Haven Publishing**

Name: _____

Address: _____

City: _____ State: _____ Zip: _____

Email address: _____

Making Gluten-Free Living Easy!

Cecelia's Marketplace
Kalamazoo, Michigan

www.CeceliasMarketplace.com

Mail In Order Form

💻 Online Orders: www.CeceliasMarketplace.com

✉ Mail Orders: Kal-Haven Publishing
P.O. Box 20383
Kalamazoo, MI 49019
U.S.A.

Title	Quantity	Price	Total
Gluten-Free Grocery Shopping Guide	_____	(x $24.95) =	_____
Gluten/Casein Free Grocery Shopping Guide	_____	(x $24.95) =	_____
Gluten/Casein/Soy Free Grocery Shopping Guide	_____	(x $24.95) =	_____
Easy 30 Day Gluten-Free Diet Diet Book	_____	(x $19.95) =	_____
Gluten-Free Mexican Cookbook	_____	(x $14.95) =	_____

Sales Tax: Michigan residents please add 6% sales tax _____

Sub Total: _____

Shipping: (quantities 1-2 add $5.95)

(quantities 3-6 add $11.95) _____

Total: _____

* Please make check or money order payable to **Kal-Haven Publishing**

Name: _____

Address: _____

City: _____ State: _____ Zip: _____

Email address: _____